Lecture Notes in Computer Science 8004

Commenced Publication in 1973
Founding and Former Series Editors:
Gerhard Goos, Juris Hartmanis, and Jan van Leeuwen

Masaaki Kurosu (Ed.)

Human-Computer Interaction

Human-Centred Design Approaches, Methods, Tools, and Environments

15th International Conference, HCI International 2013
Las Vegas, NV, USA, July 21-26, 2013
Proceedings, Part I

Volume Editor

Masaaki Kurosu
The Open University of Japan
2-11 Wakaba, Mihama-ku, Chiba-shi 261-8586, Japan
E-mail: masaakikurosu@spa.nifty.com

ISSN 0302-9743 e-ISSN 1611-3349
ISBN 978-3-642-39231-3 e-ISBN 978-3-642-39232-0
DOI 10.1007/978-3-642-39232-0
Springer Heidelberg Dordrecht London New York

Library of Congress Control Number: 2013941394

CR Subject Classification (1998): H.5, K.3, H.3, D.2, I.2.9-11

LNCS Sublibrary: SL 3 – Information Systems and Application, incl. Internet/Web and HCI

Typesetting: Camera-ready by author, data conversion by Scientific Publishing Services, Chennai, India

Printed on acid-free paper

Springer is part of Springer Science+Business Media (www.springer.com)

Foreword

The 15th International Conference on Human–Computer Interaction, HCI International 2013, was held in Las Vegas, Nevada, USA, 21–26 July 2013, incorporating 12 conferences / thematic areas:

Thematic areas:

- Human–Computer Interaction
- Human Interface and the Management of Information

Affiliated conferences:

- 10th International Conference on Engineering Psychology and Cognitive Ergonomics
- 7th International Conference on Universal Access in Human–Computer Interaction
- 5th International Conference on Virtual, Augmented and Mixed Reality
- 5th International Conference on Cross-Cultural Design
- 5th International Conference on Online Communities and Social Computing
- 7th International Conference on Augmented Cognition
- 4th International Conference on Digital Human Modeling and Applications in Health, Safety, Ergonomics and Risk Management
- 2nd International Conference on Design, User Experience and Usability
- 1st International Conference on Distributed, Ambient and Pervasive Interactions
- 1st International Conference on Human Aspects of Information Security, Privacy and Trust

A total of 5210 individuals from academia, research institutes, industry and governmental agencies from 70 countries submitted contributions, and 1666 papers and 303 posters were included in the program. These papers address the latest research and development efforts and highlight the human aspects of design and use of computing systems. The papers accepted for presentation thoroughly cover the entire field of Human–Computer Interaction, addressing major advances in knowledge and effective use of computers in a variety of application areas.

This volume, edited by Masaaki Kurosu, contains papers focusing on the thematic area of Human–Computer Interaction, and addressing the following major topics:

- HCI and Human Centred Design
- Evaluation Methods and Techniques
- User Interface Design and Development Methods and Environments
- Aesthetics and Kansei in HCI

The remaining volumes of the HCI International 2013 proceedings are:

- Volume 2, LNCS 8005, Human–Computer Interaction: Applications and Services (Part II), edited by Masaaki Kurosu
- Volume 3, LNCS 8006, Human–Computer Interaction: Users and Contexts of Use (Part III), edited by Masaaki Kurosu
- Volume 4, LNCS 8007, Human–Computer Interaction: Interaction Modalities and Techniques (Part IV), edited by Masaaki Kurosu
- Volume 5, LNCS 8008, Human–Computer Interaction: Towards Intelligent and Implicit Interaction (Part V), edited by Masaaki Kurosu
- Volume 6, LNCS 8009, Universal Access in Human–Computer Interaction: Design Methods, Tools and Interaction Techniques for eInclusion (Part I), edited by Constantine Stephanidis and Margherita Antona
- Volume 7, LNCS 8010, Universal Access in Human–Computer Interaction: User and Context Diversity (Part II), edited by Constantine Stephanidis and Margherita Antona
- Volume 8, LNCS 8011, Universal Access in Human–Computer Interaction: Applications and Services for Quality of Life (Part III), edited by Constantine Stephanidis and Margherita Antona
- Volume 9, LNCS 8012, Design, User Experience, and Usability: Design Philosophy, Methods and Tools (Part I), edited by Aaron Marcus
- Volume 10, LNCS 8013, Design, User Experience, and Usability: Health, Learning, Playing, Cultural, and Cross-Cultural User Experience (Part II), edited by Aaron Marcus
- Volume 11, LNCS 8014, Design, User Experience, and Usability: User Experience in Novel Technological Environments (Part III), edited by Aaron Marcus
- Volume 12, LNCS 8015, Design, User Experience, and Usability: Web, Mobile and Product Design (Part IV), edited by Aaron Marcus
- Volume 13, LNCS 8016, Human Interface and the Management of Information: Information and Interaction Design (Part I), edited by Sakae Yamamoto
- Volume 14, LNCS 8017, Human Interface and the Management of Information: Information and Interaction for Health, Safety, Mobility and Complex Environments (Part II), edited by Sakae Yamamoto
- Volume 15, LNCS 8018, Human Interface and the Management of Information: Information and Interaction for Learning, Culture, Collaboration and Business (Part III), edited by Sakae Yamamoto
- Volume 16, LNAI 8019, Engineering Psychology and Cognitive Ergonomics: Understanding Human Cognition (Part I), edited by Don Harris
- Volume 17, LNAI 8020, Engineering Psychology and Cognitive Ergonomics: Applications and Services (Part II), edited by Don Harris
- Volume 18, LNCS 8021, Virtual, Augmented and Mixed Reality: Designing and Developing Augmented and Virtual Environments (Part I), edited by Randall Shumaker
- Volume 19, LNCS 8022, Virtual, Augmented and Mixed Reality: Systems and Applications (Part II), edited by Randall Shumaker

- Volume 20, LNCS 8023, Cross-Cultural Design: Methods, Practice and Case Studies (Part I), edited by P.L. Patrick Rau
- Volume 21, LNCS 8024, Cross-Cultural Design: Cultural Differences in Everyday Life (Part II), edited by P.L. Patrick Rau
- Volume 22, LNCS 8025, Digital Human Modeling and Applications in Health, Safety, Ergonomics and Risk Management: Healthcare and Safety of the Environment and Transport (Part I), edited by Vincent G. Duffy
- Volume 23, LNCS 8026, Digital Human Modeling and Applications in Health, Safety, Ergonomics and Risk Management: Human Body Modeling and Ergonomics (Part II), edited by Vincent G. Duffy
- Volume 24, LNAI 8027, Foundations of Augmented Cognition, edited by Dylan D. Schmorrow and Cali M. Fidopiastis
- Volume 25, LNCS 8028, Distributed, Ambient and Pervasive Interactions, edited by Norbert Streitz and Constantine Stephanidis
- Volume 26, LNCS 8029, Online Communities and Social Computing, edited by A. Ant Ozok and Panayiotis Zaphiris
- Volume 27, LNCS 8030, Human Aspects of Information Security, Privacy and Trust, edited by Louis Marinos and Ioannis Askoxylakis
- Volume 28, CCIS 373, HCI International 2013 Posters Proceedings (Part I), edited by Constantine Stephanidis
- Volume 29, CCIS 374, HCI International 2013 Posters Proceedings (Part II), edited by Constantine Stephanidis

I would like to thank the Program Chairs and the members of the Program Boards of all affiliated conferences and thematic areas, listed below, for their contribution to the highest scientific quality and the overall success of the HCI International 2013 conference.

This conference could not have been possible without the continuous support and advice of the Founding Chair and Conference Scientific Advisor, Prof. Gavriel Salvendy, as well as the dedicated work and outstanding efforts of the Communications Chair and Editor of HCI International News, Abbas Moallem.

I would also like to thank for their contribution towards the smooth organization of the HCI International 2013 Conference the members of the Human–Computer Interaction Laboratory of ICS-FORTH, and in particular George Paparoulis, Maria Pitsoulaki, Stavroula Ntoa, Maria Bouhli and George Kapnas.

May 2013

Constantine Stephanidis
General Chair, HCI International 2013

Organization

Human–Computer Interaction

Program Chair: Masaaki Kurosu, Japan

Jose Abdelnour-Nocera, UK
Sebastiano Bagnara, Italy
Simone Barbosa, Brazil
Tomas Berns, Sweden
Nigel Bevan, UK
Simone Borsci, UK
Apala Lahiri Chavan, India
Sherry Chen, Taiwan
Kevin Clark, USA
Torkil Clemmensen, Denmark
Xiaowen Fang, USA
Shin'ichi Fukuzumi, Japan
Vicki Hanson, UK
Ayako Hashizume, Japan
Anzai Hiroyuki, Italy
Sheue-Ling Hwang, Taiwan
Wonil Hwang, South Korea
Minna Isomursu, Finland
Yong Gu Ji, South Korea
Esther Jun, USA
Mitsuhiko Karashima, Japan
Kyungdoh Kim, South Korea
Heidi Krömker, Germany
Chen Ling, USA
Yan Liu, USA
Zhengjie Liu, P.R. China
Loïc Martínez Normand, Spain
Chang S. Nam, USA
Naoko Okuizumi, Japan
Noriko Osaka, Japan
Philippe Palanque, France
Hans Persson, Sweden
Ling Rothrock, USA
Naoki Sakakibara, Japan
Dominique Scapin, France
Guangfeng Song, USA
Sanjay Tripathi, India
Chui Yin Wong, Malaysia
Toshiki Yamaoka, Japan
Kazuhiko Yamazaki, Japan
Ryoji Yoshitake, Japan
Silvia Zimmermann, Switzerland

Human Interface and the Management of Information

Program Chair: Sakae Yamamoto, Japan

Hans-Jorg Bullinger, Germany
Alan Chan, Hong Kong
Gilsoo Cho, South Korea
Jon R. Gunderson, USA
Shin'ichi Fukuzumi, Japan
Michitaka Hirose, Japan
Jhilmil Jain, USA
Yasufumi Kume, Japan
Mark Lehto, USA
Hiroyuki Miki, Japan
Hirohiko Mori, Japan
Fiona Fui-Hoon Nah, USA
Shogo Nishida, Japan
Robert Proctor, USA
Youngho Rhee, South Korea
Katsunori Shimohara, Japan

Michale Smith, USA
Tsutomu Tabe, Japan
Hiroshi Tsuji, Japan
Kim-Phuong Vu, USA
Tomio Watanabe, Japan
Hidekazu Yoshikawa, Japan

Engineering Psychology and Cognitive Ergonomics

Program Chair: Don Harris, UK

Guy Andre Boy, USA
Joakim Dahlman, Sweden
Trevor Dobbins, UK
Mike Feary, USA
Shan Fu, P.R. China
Michaela Heese, Austria
Hung-Sying Jing, Taiwan
Wen-Chin Li, Taiwan
Mark A. Neerincx, The Netherlands
Jan M. Noyes, UK
Taezoon Park, Singapore
Paul Salmon, Australia
Axel Schulte, Germany
Siraj Shaikh, UK
Sarah C. Sharples, UK
Anthony Smoker, UK
Neville A. Stanton, UK
Alex Stedmon, UK
Xianghong Sun, P.R. China
Andrew Thatcher, South Africa
Matthew J.W. Thomas, Australia
Rolf Zon, The Netherlands

Universal Access in Human–Computer Interaction

Program Chairs: Constantine Stephanidis, Greece, and Margherita Antona, Greece

Julio Abascal, Spain
Ray Adams, UK
Gisela Susanne Bahr, USA
Margit Betke, USA
Christian Bühler, Germany
Stefan Carmien, Spain
Jerzy Charytonowicz, Poland
Carlos Duarte, Portugal
Pier Luigi Emiliani, Italy
Qin Gao, P.R. China
Andrina Granić, Croatia
Andreas Holzinger, Austria
Josette Jones, USA
Simeon Keates, UK
Georgios Kouroupetroglou, Greece
Patrick Langdon, UK
Seongil Lee, Korea
Ana Isabel B.B. Paraguay, Brazil
Helen Petrie, UK
Michael Pieper, Germany
Enrico Pontelli, USA
Jaime Sanchez, Chile
Anthony Savidis, Greece
Christian Stary, Austria
Hirotada Ueda, Japan
Gerhard Weber, Germany
Harald Weber, Germany

Virtual, Augmented and Mixed Reality

Program Chair: Randall Shumaker, USA

Waymon Armstrong, USA
Juan Cendan, USA
Rudy Darken, USA
Cali M. Fidopiastis, USA
Charles Hughes, USA
David Kaber, USA
Hirokazu Kato, Japan
Denis Laurendeau, Canada
Fotis Liarokapis, UK
Mark Livingston, USA
Michael Macedonia, USA
Gordon Mair, UK
Jose San Martin, Spain
Jacquelyn Morie, USA
Albert "Skip" Rizzo, USA
Kay Stanney, USA
Christopher Stapleton, USA
Gregory Welch, USA

Cross-Cultural Design

Program Chair: P.L. Patrick Rau, P.R. China

Pilsung Choe, P.R. China
Henry Been-Lirn Duh, Singapore
Vanessa Evers, The Netherlands
Paul Fu, USA
Zhiyong Fu, P.R. China
Fu Guo, P.R. China
Sung H. Han, Korea
Toshikazu Kato, Japan
Dyi-Yih Michael Lin, Taiwan
Rungtai Lin, Taiwan
Sheau-Farn Max Liang, Taiwan
Liang Ma, P.R. China
Alexander Mädche, Germany
Katsuhiko Ogawa, Japan
Tom Plocher, USA
Kerstin Röse, Germany
Supriya Singh, Australia
Hsiu-Ping Yueh, Taiwan
Liang (Leon) Zeng, USA
Chen Zhao, USA

Online Communities and Social Computing

Program Chairs: A. Ant Ozok, USA, and Panayiotis Zaphiris, Cyprus

Areej Al-Wabil, Saudi Arabia
Leonelo Almeida, Brazil
Bjørn Andersen, Norway
Chee Siang Ang, UK
Aneesha Bakharia, Australia
Ania Bobrowicz, UK
Paul Cairns, UK
Farzin Deravi, UK
Andri Ioannou, Cyprus
Slava Kisilevich, Germany
Niki Lambropoulos, Greece
Effie Law, Switzerland
Soo Ling Lim, UK
Fernando Loizides, Cyprus
Gabriele Meiselwitz, USA
Anthony Norcio, USA
Elaine Raybourn, USA
Panote Siriaraya, UK
David Stuart, UK
June Wei, USA

Augmented Cognition

Program Chairs: Dylan D. Schmorrow, USA, and Cali M. Fidopiastis, USA

Robert Arrabito, Canada
Richard Backs, USA
Chris Berka, USA
Joseph Cohn, USA
Martha E. Crosby, USA
Julie Drexler, USA
Ivy Estabrooke, USA
Chris Forsythe, USA
Wai Tat Fu, USA
Rodolphe Gentili, USA
Marc Grootjen, The Netherlands
Jefferson Grubb, USA
Ming Hou, Canada
Santosh Mathan, USA
Rob Matthews, Australia
Dennis McBride, USA
Jeff Morrison, USA
Mark A. Neerincx, The Netherlands
Denise Nicholson, USA
Banu Onaral, USA
Lee Sciarini, USA
Kay Stanney, USA
Roy Stripling, USA
Rob Taylor, UK
Karl van Orden, USA

Digital Human Modeling and Applications in Health, Safety, Ergonomics and Risk Management

Program Chair: Vincent G. Duffy, USA and Russia

Karim Abdel-Malek, USA
Giuseppe Andreoni, Italy
Daniel Carruth, USA
Eliza Yingzi Du, USA
Enda Fallon, Ireland
Afzal Godil, USA
Ravindra Goonetilleke, Hong Kong
Bo Hoege, Germany
Waldemar Karwowski, USA
Zhizhong Li, P.R. China
Kang Li, USA
Tim Marler, USA
Michelle Robertson, USA
Matthias Rötting, Germany
Peter Vink, The Netherlands
Mao-Jiun Wang, Taiwan
Xuguang Wang, France
Jingzhou (James) Yang, USA
Xiugan Yuan, P.R. China
Gülcin Yücel Hoge, Germany

Design, User Experience, and Usability

Program Chair: Aaron Marcus, USA

Sisira Adikari, Australia
Ronald Baecker, Canada
Arne Berger, Germany
Jamie Blustein, Canada
Ana Boa-Ventura, USA
Jan Brejcha, Czech Republic
Lorenzo Cantoni, Switzerland
Maximilian Eibl, Germany

Anthony Faiola, USA
Emilie Gould, USA
Zelda Harrison, USA
Rüdiger Heimgärtner, Germany
Brigitte Herrmann, Germany
Steffen Hess, Germany
Kaleem Khan, Canada
Jennifer McGinn, USA
Francisco Rebelo, Portugal
Michael Renner, Switzerland
Kerem Rızvanoğlu, Turkey
Marcelo Soares, Brazil
Christian Sturm, Germany
Michele Visciola, Italy

Distributed, Ambient and Pervasive Interactions

Program Chairs: Norbert Streitz, Germany, and Constantine Stephanidis, Greece

Emile Aarts, The Netherlands
Adnan Abu-Dayya, Qatar
Juan Carlos Augusto, UK
Boris de Ruyter, The Netherlands
Anind Dey, USA
Dimitris Grammenos, Greece
Nuno M. Guimaraes, Portugal
Shin'ichi Konomi, Japan
Carsten Magerkurth, Switzerland
Christian Müller-Tomfelde, Australia
Fabio Paternó, Italy
Gilles Privat, France
Harald Reiterer, Germany
Carsten Röcker, Germany
Reiner Wichert, Germany
Woontack Woo, South Korea
Xenophon Zabulis, Greece

Human Aspects of Information Security, Privacy and Trust

Program Chairs: Louis Marinos, ENISA EU, and Ioannis Askoxylakis, Greece

Claudio Agostino Ardagna, Italy
Zinaida Benenson, Germany
Daniele Catteddu, Italy
Raoul Chiesa, Italy
Bryan Cline, USA
Sadie Creese, UK
Jorge Cuellar, Germany
Marc Dacier, USA
Dieter Gollmann, Germany
Kirstie Hawkey, Canada
Jaap-Henk Hoepman, The Netherlands
Cagatay Karabat, Turkey
Angelos Keromytis, USA
Ayako Komatsu, Japan
Ronald Leenes, The Netherlands
Javier Lopez, Spain
Steve Marsh, Canada
Gregorio Martinez, Spain
Emilio Mordini, Italy
Yuko Murayama, Japan
Masakatsu Nishigaki, Japan
Aljosa Pasic, Spain
Milan Petković, The Netherlands
Joachim Posegga, Germany
Jean-Jacques Quisquater, Belgium
Damien Sauveron, France
George Spanoudakis, UK
Kerry-Lynn Thomson, South Africa

Julien Touzeau, France
Theo Tryfonas, UK
João Vilela, Portugal
Claire Vishik, UK
Melanie Volkamer, Germany

External Reviewers

Maysoon Abulkhair, Saudi Arabia
Ilia Adami, Greece
Vishal Barot, UK
Stephan Böhm, Germany
Vassilis Charissis, UK
Francisco Cipolla-Ficarra, Spain
Maria De Marsico, Italy
Marc Fabri, UK
David Fonseca, Spain
Linda Harley, USA
Yasushi Ikei, Japan
Wei Ji, USA
Nouf Khashman, Canada
John Killilea, USA
Iosif Klironomos, Greece
Ute Klotz, Switzerland
Maria Korozi, Greece
Kentaro Kotani, Japan
Vassilis Kouroumalis, Greece
Stephanie Lackey, USA
Janelle LaMarche, USA
Asterios Leonidis, Greece
Nickolas Macchiarella, USA
George Margetis, Greece
Matthew Marraffino, USA
Joseph Mercado, USA
Claudia Mont'Alvão, Brazil
Yoichi Motomura, Japan
Karsten Nebe, Germany
Stavroula Ntoa, Greece
Martin Osen, Austria
Stephen Prior, UK
Farid Shirazi, Canada
Jan Stelovsky, USA
Sarah Swierenga, USA

HCI International 2014

The 16th International Conference on Human–Computer Interaction, HCI International 2014, will be held jointly with the affiliated conferences in the summer of 2014. It will cover a broad spectrum of themes related to Human–Computer Interaction, including theoretical issues, methods, tools, processes and case studies in HCI design, as well as novel interaction techniques, interfaces and applications. The proceedings will be published by Springer. More information about the topics, as well as the venue and dates of the conference, will be announced through the HCI International Conference series website: http://www.hci-international.org/

General Chair
Professor Constantine Stephanidis
University of Crete and ICS-FORTH
Heraklion, Crete, Greece
Email: cs@ics.forth.gr

Table of Contents – Part I

HCI and Human Centred Design

Evaluation Methods and Techniques

User Interface Design and Development Methods and Environments

Aesthetics and Kansei in HCI

Part I
HCI and Human Centred Design

HCI Education in Brazil: Challenges and Opportunities

Clodis Boscarioli[1], Sílvia Amélia Bim[2], Milene S. Silveira[3], Raquel Oliveira Prates[4], and Simone Diniz Junqueira Barbosa[5]

[1] Departamento de Ciência da Computação, UNIOESTE, Cascavel, PR, Brazil
clodis.boscarioli@unioeste.br

[2] Departamento de Informática, UTFPR, Curitiba, PR, Brazil
sabim@utfpr.edu.br

[3] Faculdade de Informática, PUCRS, Porto Alegre, RS, Brazil
milene.silveira@pucrs.br

[4] Departamento de Ciência da Computação, UFMG, Belo Horizonte, MG, Brazil
rprates@dcc.ufmg.br

[5] Departamento de Informática, PUC-Rio, Rio de Janeiro, RJ, Brazil
simone@inf.puc-rio.br

Abstract. HCI Education in Brazil has come a long way. Since 1999, the Brazilian Computer Society (SBC) included HCI in its reference curriculum for its Computing courses. Since then, the community has discussed the perspective of the area in our country. From 2010 to this day, we have held a series of workshops on HCI Education, called WEIHC, as a permanent discussion forum within the Brazilian HCI conference, IHC. We report here the results of the WEIHC discussions and of two surveys, conducted in 2009 and in 2012, to help us assess the status of HCI Education in Brazil. Despite the advances of the Brazilian HCI community, our surveys show that we still face some important challenges. We should curate existing teaching material to further enhance collaboration among professors, to increase the quality of our courses, and to broaden HCI awareness across all related departments.

Keywords: HCI Education, Brazilian HCI community.

1 Introduction

HCI Education in Brazil has come a long way. In 1999, the Brazilian Computer Society (SBC)[1] included HCI as a recommended course in its reference curricula for three of its Computing courses: Information Systems, Computer Science and Computer Engineering. This inclusion brought the necessity to deepen the discussion about what was being taught in the related courses. Thus, in 2002, a first discussion on the topic was organized in a workshop during the Brazilian Symposium on Human Factors in Computing Systems (IHC) in which professors exchanged their experiences in teaching HCI. In IHC 2006, a working group on HCI Education in Brazil was organized. In 2010, the working group became a permanent workshop to take

[1] http://www.sbc.org.br/en/

M. Kurosu (Ed.): Human-Computer Interaction, Part I, HCII 2013, LNCS 8004, pp. 3–12, 2013.

place annually during IHC, entitled Workshop on HCI Education (WEIHC). Besides the discussions fostered by the workshop, the community felt the need to have a better understanding of how HCI was being taught in Brazil, that is, which universities offered the course, was it a mandatory or optional course, was it offered at the undergraduate or graduate level, among other questions. In order to generate this view, two surveys were independently applied – one in 2009 and another in 2012. In the article, we present a summary of the discussions and the results of the surveys.

2 HCI Education Discussions in Brazil

The inclusion by SBC of HCI as a recommended course in the reference curricula for Information Systems, Computer Science and Computer Engineering degrees was a huge advance for the HCI area in Brazil. Courses all around the country began to include HCI as a course or as part of other courses, and the absence of a reference syllabus for teaching HCI was a great challenge to these courses' professors, who had to define which contents were essential and how they would be better taught.

In this context, in 2002, we organized a workshop on HCI education in Brazil, and professors exchanged their experiences. However, the discussions were not recorded. As the inclusion of HCI courses increased in universities, in 2006 we decided to hold, a working group on HCI Education alongside IHC. The main goal of the working group was to discuss an HCI syllabus that could be used as basis to the various HCI courses available in our universities, from undergraduate to graduate courses.

Through a process that included the submission of the syllabus of their HCI courses and direct invitation to Brazilian professors with recognized experience in the area, 15 participants were selected to participate in the working group. They represented three of our five regions in Brazil (3 from the Northeast, 3 from the South, and 9 from the Southeast) and had diverse experience in teaching HCI in undergraduate and graduate courses. From these 15 participants, 10 participated in the discussion during the conference, and the other 5 sent their contributions before then, so that everyone involved in the workshop could analyze them. The participants were divided into 2 groups to discuss the topics considered most important to be taught in the courses: one group responsible for undergraduate and other for graduate syllabus.

Considering the syllabus available for analysis and the experience of the participants, each group developed an initial recommended syllabus. The group responsible for the undergraduate course elaborated a syllabus for an introductory (and mandatory, if possible) HCI course and its related literature. As the graduate programs in the country have HCI courses with distinct focus and depth, instead of a syllabus, the participants proposed the goals of an HCI course in this context and their main topics of discussion. For graduate courses, there was no recommendation of related literature. Instead, the participants recommended a set of materials and practices to be held during the course.

From the two recommendations that resulted from the workshop [7], several refereed papers at the next HCI Education workshop held during IHC have presented studies on HCI Education in Brazil, which explored ways to implement the proposals suggested by the 2006 working group and going even beyond what was first recommended. In the following IHC, in 2008, we did not have a specific education working group, but this topic emerged naturally during the panel "HCI in Brazil – Lessons Learned and New Perspectives" [5]. In this panel, the participants highlighted the contribution of the consolidation of the Brazilian HCI community to education, explicitly mentioning the aforementioned recommended HCI syllabus and the large number of universities offering mandatory or optional HCI courses. The participants also depicted some challenges for the future, and education was mentioned again, highlighting the need for more HCI educational material in Portuguese; for discussing the main theories and research areas of HCI with the undergraduate students; and, mainly, for discussing with them the importance of multidisciplinary dialogs. Our goal should be to prepare students to take into consideration the broad diversity of users we have in Brazil and to understand the social responsibility we have as producers of technology giving all citizens equal opportunity and access to information and services [5].

In 2010, as an answer to the HCI community's yearnings expressed in the 2008 panel, the I WEIHC – Workshop about HCI Education was organized [1]. And, since 2010, we have held this workshop as a permanent discussion forum within our IHC conference. Every year WEIHC brings together 20 to 30 participants, representing several of the Brazilian states. In 2011 and 2012, the workshop crossed the Brazilian borders and brought professors from other Latin American countries (mostly from Chile and Colombia) to share lessons learned and to discuss common challenges and opportunities. The success of the WEIHC workshop series led the Executive Committee of the SBC Special Commission in HCI (CEIHC) at SBC to include in its executive committee an advisory position responsible for advancing HCI Education.

The main objective of WEIHC is to discuss HCI Education under two perspectives. The first one regards the syllabus being taught, and tries to identify the need for different HCI courses and their syllabi, which could be taught according to the resources and goals of the courses' curricula. The second one is about the pedagogical practices, and aims at investigating how the contents are presented, how the students' knowledge is evaluated and what the difficulties that students and teachers have in the Education process are. In the last three editions of WEIHC, the target audience was professors of HCI courses or of courses that included an HCI module, both in undergraduate and graduate programs, and master and doctoral HCI students who intend to become professors in this area.

Each workshop edition lasted eight hours with different activities scheduled. In 2010 the workshop started with a round table for the presentation of all participants. Then the organizers made a brief introduction on the Brazilian and international scenario on teaching IHC. Next, the eight papers selected were presented and the authors had the opportunity to answer questions from other participants on topics such as: (i) teaching strategies, (ii) the relationship of HCI and other disciplines, and (iii) and HCI in the industry. The workshop continued with discussions focused on issues selected by the participants, such as: HCI in the classroom, education support, dissemination, and evolution of the area in the country. These discussions generated a list of actions and suggestions for solving the problems identified [2].

In the following year, 2011, the eight selected articles were grouped into three thematic sessions: HCI integration with other disciplines, HCI integration with extension projects, and experiences and discussions about teaching HCI. After the paper presentations, two representatives of the Usability Professionals' Association (UPA) in São Paulo were invited to share with the participants the results of a survey on the User Experience professional profile in Brazil. Once the presentations were finished, there was a discussion to define the topics of interest to be discussed by the participants, who were divided into groups. Each group had half an hour to discuss the issues and then presented their main suggestions which, in turn, were discussed by all participants as a single, larger group [3].

In the third edition, in 2012, the event schedule featured three invited lectures on the experience in teaching HCI and the relationship between industry and academia, discussing opportunities and prospects. In addition, six papers were selected, all of them presented reports of teaching experience or research of new teaching methods. Of the six papers, one reported a Chilean experience, whereas the other five were from Brazilian authors. The selected papers were about the adherence of the HCI courses to the reference syllabus elaborated by SBC, the teaching similarities across universities located in different states, and the process of teaching and learning, discussing how students appropriate the theoretical concepts of HCI when building software artifacts [4].

We observed that HCI has been taught in different semesters in Brazilian universities. In general, we can say that, in courses taught in the early semesters, the goal is to teach the students about the main interface concepts, making them aware of the importance of the interaction layer between the user and the computer system and its impacts in people's lives, and providing them with notions of best practices in user interface design and evaluation. Conversely, courses offered in the final semesters also encourage or require students to develop practical projects applying the learned HCI concepts.

The 2012 event ended with three working groups, with members of different profiles discussing the challenges of the area and, mainly, what the community could do to improve the teaching and the dissemination of the HCI area in Brazilian computing (and related) courses.

3 HCI Education Surveys

We report in this section the results of two surveys that aimed at assessing the status of HCI Education in Brazil. The first one was conducted in 2009 and its goal was to collect data about how HCI courses were being taught in the country [6]. The second one was conducted in 2012 and intended to identify the opportunities and challenges in teaching HCI as perceived by the HCI community, including professors, students and professionals. It used a questionnaire produced by SIGCHI that would allow for a comparison of how HCI education was perceived in different countries.

3.1 2009 Survey on HCI Teaching in Brazil

The recommendation to include HCI in computing courses caused many universities to include an HCI course in their curricula. Informally, we noticed that many new courses were being offered in many different universities. In order to collect data regarding HCI teaching in Brazil we prepared a survey. To the best of our knowledge this was the first survey regarding HCI education applied in Brazil [6].

The survey collected data about the University and the department in which the course was being taught, the professors' background, the course level (undergraduate or graduate) and the syllabi of the courses being taught. The survey was conducted through the distribution of an electronic questionnaire made available for about 3 weeks, from end of November to mid December 2009. Professors who taught HCI were invited to participate through an electronic message sent to SBC's and CEIHC's electronic discussion lists. Additionally, HCI researchers from other areas (i.e., Design and Communication) were individually contacted and invited to participate, as well as to forward the invitation to other potential participants and interest lists. The majority of the participants of the survey had a computing-based background. However, this is most probably a result of the survey's distribution strategy than of how HCI courses are distributed throughout different fields. In order to have indicators in that direction, in January 2010 we analyzed the top 100 CVs in the Brazilian Lattes System[2] that came up in a search for the word "usability". Although the data in the CVs about the courses is usually not complete and the analysis cannot be considered conclusive, it indicated that besides the computer degrees, courses in production engineering and design also included many HCI courses.

The survey was completed by 89 professors from sixty-three 63 different universities (some were from different campi or institutes within a same university). Most of the participants (89%) were affiliated to a Computing-related department (such as Computer Science or Informatics). The universities were spread among 18 different states (out of 27) and all 5 regions of Brazil – 56% from the Southeast of Brazil; 21% from the South; 10% from the Northeast, 9% from the Middlewest and 4% from the North.

Regarding their background, 83% of the participants had their background in a computing-based course, whereas the other 17% were scattered throughout a number of different areas ranging from Communication to Engineering, including areas such as Graphic Design, Architecture and even Oceanography. Participants' degree levels also varied: 55% were PhDs, whereas 38% had a master´s course, around one third of them were PhD students, and 7% were master students or had completed some other graduate course. When asked about their research fields, 67.4% listed HCI as one of their main research areas, 40% listed Software Engineering, 38.2% listed computers and education and 18% listed collaborative systems. Other fields of research scattered in many areas, varying from Information Science, to Cognitive Neuropsycholinguistics and Computer Networks.

[2] The Brazilian Lattes System (http://lattes.cnpq.br/) is a system in which widely used by data repository for CV system funding agencies and universities in Brazil, and most professors and graduate students in the country have their CV registered in the system.

Participants were asked to list all the courses they taught and to inform for each one of them whether it was an undergraduate or graduate course and its syllabus. In total 141 courses were described. Most professors (59%) entered one course into the survey, but a few (7%) listed four different courses. Of the 141 courses, 57% were for undergraduate degrees, 23% for graduate degrees, 18% were offered both to undergraduate and graduate programs and 2% did not answer.

The professors entered the syllabus in different levels of detail. In order to analyze them we classified them in three distinct levels, according to the topics they covered. Each course was classified as:

- HCI module: Includes an HCI module in a course in a related area;
- Introductory: Introduces basic HCI concepts and gives a general overview of HCI field;
- Advanced: Focuses in a specific HCI topic;

Most courses (81 out of 141 or 57%) were classified as introductory courses. Most of the courses partially covered the syllabus proposed by the HCI community, and only a few (around 5) covered the whole syllabus. Some of them directed the course to a focus, such as usability, ergonomics or a specific technology. Finally, a few adopted the first syllabus proposed in the SBC reference curriculum. Out of the 141 courses, 39 (or 28%) were considered Advanced. They covered a varied range of HCI topics, such as 3D interaction, Interfaces for Games or Semiotic Engineering Theory of HCI, among others. The remaining courses (21 out of 141 or 15%) were HCI modules and were taught mainly in Software Engineering, Computer Graphics or Distance Education courses.

The survey provided a good initial view of HCI teaching in Brazil, at least in computer-based degrees. However, the results are not meant to be statistically representative, since we did not have a known universe of the HCI professors in Brazil.

3.2 2012 Survey on HCI Education: Challenges and Opportunities

The SIGCHI/ACM HCI Education working group conducted an exploratory investigation on HCI Education [8], which led them to prepare an online survey. This survey was lent to us from the Brazilian HCI community to translate and apply to our HCI students, researchers, and professionals.

In addition to demographic data, the survey contained five sections: disciplines related to HCI, exploring the multidisciplinary nature of the area; topics and application areas, both traditional and emerging; design and empirical research methods; challenges to HCI education; and resources for HCI education, in the form of books, conference (and their proceedings), and journals.

Participants were invited via mailing lists and social networks, and they were also asked to propagate the invitation to anyone who might be interested. The survey was completed by 109 people, mostly with a Computer Science background (see Table 1): 49 professors and researchers, 45 students, and 10 practitioners, from a wide range of age groups and from the five geographic regions in the country, with a few respondents from abroad.[3]

Table 1. Respondents' ages and geographic regions

background	respondents	age	respondents	region	respondents
Computing	57 (52.3%)	20 or less	3 (3%)	CO	3 (3%)
HCI	29 (26.6%)	21 a 30	40 (37%)	N	3 (3%)
Design	9 (8.3%)	31 a 40	40 (37%)	NE	14 (13%)
Psychology	3 (2.8%)	41 a 50	20 (19%)	S	18 (17%)
Other	10 (9.2%)	51 a 40	4 (4%)	SE	68 (62%)
		61 or more	1 (1%)	abroad	3 (3%)

Because the HCI area has first matured in the Southeast (SE), we had more respondents from that region, followed by the South (S) and the Northeast (NE).

Teaching Resources. The survey included a few open questions regarding teaching resources. Most of the books with a high mention count (7 or higher) were either written by Brazilian authors or had a Portuguese translation (Figure 1). This result is in line with discussions held during our HCI Education workshops, regarding the need for high-quality teaching material in Portuguese.

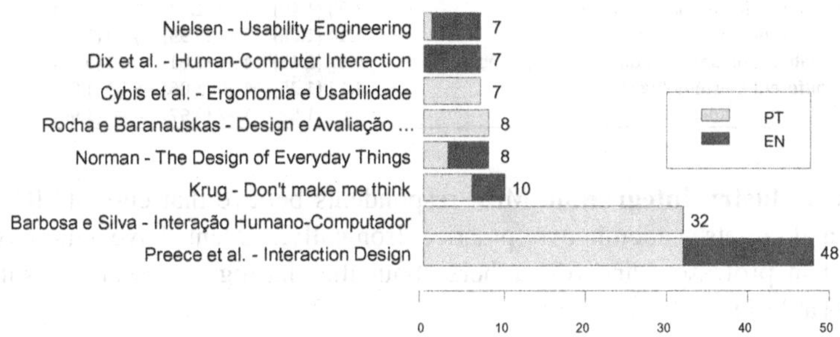

Fig. 1. Recommended books that received three or more mentions. PT = in Portuguese, EN = in English.

Challenges Related to HCI Education. The survey contained four questions related to HCI education, with answers ranging from 1 (very easy to address) to 5 (very significant challenge), in addition to 0 (I don't agree this is a challenge). Table 2 presents a summary the results, together with an indication of the significant differences (resulting from a Wilcoxon test) between respondents with different profiles.

[3] As with the previous survey, the population of HCI professors, researchers, students and practitioners is unknown, and as such we cannot claim to have reached a representative sample.

Table 2. Differences in opinion regarding HCI education challenges from respondents with different profiles (A = professors and researchers, S = students, and P = practitioners)

	A	S	P	Wilcoxon		
1. Integration of HCI Education and Practice	**X̄ (SD)**	**X̄ (SD)**	**X̄ (SD)**	**AxS**	**AxP**	**SxP**
a. adopting a common curriculum	3 71 (1.72)	4.04 (1.31)	4.30 (1.83)			
b. advocating the importance of HCI to computer scientists	4.18 (0.93)	4.44 (0.84)	4.50 (1.35)			
c. advocating the importance of HCI to the general public	4.00 (1.17)	4.33 (0.85)	5.00 (0.67)		*	*
d. applying practical activities + conceptual approaches	3.78 (1.21)	4.22 (1.13)	5.00 (0.82)		*	*
e. forming a unified theoretical perspective	3.24 (2.03)	4.18 (1.47)	4.40 (1.84)	*		
	A	S	P	Wilcoxon		
2. HCI Education as an Interdisciplinary Area	**X̄ (SD)**	**X̄ (SD)**	**X̄ (SD)**	**DxE**	**DxP**	**ExP**
a. how to approach HCI as a complex interdisciplinary field	3.92 (1.26)	4.29 (0.94)	4.60 (0.52)			
b. representing breadth and interdisciplinarity in HCI	3.82 (1.17)	4.36 (1.13)	4.80 (0.79)	*	*	
c. representing depth in HCI	3.98 (1.09)	4.56 (0.81)	4.40 (0.97)	*		
d. sufficient practice in HCI	4.18 (0.88)	4.49 (0.89)	4.60 (1.43)			
e. sufficient theory in HCI	3.94 (1.11)	4.29 (1.04)	4.00 (1.56)			
f. building on previous education to reach mastery	3.73 (1.34)	4.24 (1.42)	4.40 (1.58)			
	A	S	P	Wilcoxon		
3. HCI Education with a Range of Perspectives and Goals	**X̄ (SD)**	**X̄ (SD)**	**X̄ (SD)**	**DxE**	**DxP**	**ExP**
a. supporting different or parallel curricula to reflect unique student needs	3.57 (1.83)	3.89 (1.68)	4.90 (0.88)		*	*
b. supporting a flexible curriculum to reflect unique student needs	3.82 (1.42)	4.42 (1.14)	4.30 (1.06)	*		
c. teaching students with a range of perspectives and goals	3.96 (1.21)	4.53 (1.08)	4.20 (1.40)	*		
d. including a common introductory course in HCI curricula	3.51 (1.32)	4.09 (1.26)	3.50 (1.78)	*		
e. offering similar courses targeting different audiences	3.16 (1.75)	4.07 (1.29)	3.30 (1.89)	*		
	A	S	P	Wilcoxon		
4. HCI Education in Academia	**X̄ (SD)**	**X̄ (SD)**	**X̄ (SD)**	**DxE**	**DxP**	**ExP**
a. advocating the importance of HCI in different departments	4.02 (1.20)	4.36 (0.98)	5.00 (0.82)		*	
b. finding a home for HCI in smaller institutions	3.98 (1.49)	4.13 (1.34)	4.70 (1.77)		*	
c. encouraging interdisciplinary collaboration	4.14 (1.06)	4.44 (0.99)	4.90 (1.10)		*	
d. fostering collaboration between different programs	4.27 (1.13)	4.44 (0.81)	4.90 (0.99)			
e. respecting different epistemologies	4.12 (1.25)	4.20 (1.06)	5.00 (1.05)		*	*
f. situating HCI within academia	3.65 (1.52)	4.42 (0.97)	4.40 (1.96)	*	*	

Academy–Industry Integration. Most respondents believe that current HCI education in Brazil targets academia over practice. Ironically, students have a more optimistic view than professors and researchers about the sharing of research results with industry (Table 3).

Table 3. How do you see the relation between academia and industry in HCI education?

	A	S	P	Wilcoxon
	X̄ (SD)	**X̄ (SD)**	**X̄ (SD)**	**AxS**
▪ HCI education prepares students more to academia than to industry.	3.78 (1.16)	3.78 (1.06)	4.40 (1.35)	
▪ HCI education prepares students more to industry than to academia.	2.47 (1.31)	2.53 (1.24)	2.90 (2.08)	
▪ Not enough research is shared between academia and industry.	4.51 (0.79)	4.11 (1.05)	4.40 (1.17)	*
▪ There are divides between academia and industry.	4.53 (0.94)	4.36 (0.93)	4.60 (1.07)	

These results point to the need to address the challenges the community finds relevant, but also to investigate more deeply the root causes for the differences in respondents' opinions so we can better satisfy the needs and expectations of all parties interested in HCI.

4 Discussion: Challenges and Opportunities

The workshops in HCI education have created a forum for the HCI community to exchange experiences regarding HCI education, discuss the challenges involved and work on plans of actions to deal with them. The 2009 survey collected a first set of data regarding HCI teaching throughout Brazil. In some departments, HCI is a mandatory course, in others it is an elective course or not yet offered. Some departments offer one or two additional elective disciplines, which usually explore HCI evaluation, design methods and techniques in depth.

The analysis indicated that, although many professors used the HCI syllabus proposed by the community in 2006, it may include a broad range of topics that cannot usually be covered in one course. One the one hand, this broad coverage has allowed professors to tailor their courses to their teaching context, on the other it has not been able to create a more structured proposal that could be followed by professors. In the 2012 survey adopting a common curriculum was also perceived as a challenge, mainly by practitioners. These results justify the effort in WEIHC to define specific syllabi more appropriate to different contexts.

Because Brazil is a Portuguese-speaking country, most professors tend to recommend in their courses material written in this language, creating an increasing demand for updated resources. The Brazilian HCI community has faced this demand by producing at least five high-quality HCI textbooks in the past ten years. From the top ten books recommended in our 2012 survey, three were written in Portuguese, five were translated from English to Portuguese, and two were in English.

As the community has matured, ties between academia and industry have also been fostered, so much so that CEIHC has also established an advisory position for an industry representative, who has worked with CEIHC to find ways to increase practitioners' participation in our national event. While industry participation in IHC may still be viewed as timid, once a company has sent one or more representatives to an edition of our conference, it has kept sending them to its next editions. Their participation has had at least three positive effects:

- it has made us increasingly aware of their goals and needs regarding the education of HCI professionals;
- it has clearly demonstrated to students the importance of HCI research and practice; and
- it has resulted in fruitful collaboration projects.

Some efforts have been made to increase students' awareness and interest in HCI. In that direction, in the past three editions of IHC we have held a student evaluation competition, which has attracted submissions from all over the country, often resulting from an articulation of the proposed competition challenge with class projects.

5 Conclusions and Future Work

Despite the advances of HCI Education in Brazil, our surveys show that we still face some important challenges. First, we need to further strengthen our ties with industry, to ensure our students will find a good HCI position after they graduate, and with university departments (both CS and otherwise), to form professionals that are comfortable with the interdisciplinary work required of HCI. Second, we should promote continuous education programs to keep our professors up-to-date on the latest developments in HCI Education. Finally, we should curate existing teaching material to further enhance collaboration among professors, to increase the quality of our courses, and to broaden HCI awareness across all related departments. To do so, our first step is to continue collecting data on HCI education. Thus, a new version of the 2009 survey to collect information about courses and how they are being taught is being prepared to provide updated information and insights on how HCI teaching has evolved. Other initiative is to advance HCI in the other regions. In 2012, IHC was held in the Middlewestern (CO) region, and in 2013 it will be held in the Northern (N) region. With this purposeful movement, we intend to have critical mass throughout the country in the near future.

Acknowledgements. The authors thank all survey respondents for the invaluable information provided. Simone Diniz Junqueira Barbosa thanks CNPq (processes #313031/2009-6 and #308490/2012-6) for the support to her research work. Clodis Boscarioli thanks Fundação Araucária for the support to his research work.

References

1. Bim, S.A., Winckler, M., Prates, R.O., Silveira, M.S.: Workshop sobre o Ensino de IHC (WEIHC). In: Anais Estendidos do IX Simpósio de Fatores Humanos em Sistemas Computacionais (IHC 2010), vol. II, pp. 275–276. SBC, Porto Alegre (2010)
2. Bim, S.A., Prates, R.O., Silveira, M.S., Winckler, M.A.: Ensino de IHC - Atualizando as Discussões sobre a Experiência Brasileira. In: Anais do XIX Workshop sobre Educação em Computação (WEI). SBC, Porto Alegre (2011)
3. Bim, S.A., Prates, R.O., Silveira, M.S.: Ensino de IHC - Compartilhando as Experiências Docentes no Contexto Brasileiro. In: Anais do Simpósio de Fatores Humanos em Sistemas Computacionais (IHC 2012), pp. 195–198. SBC, Porto Alegre (2012)
4. Boscarioli, C., Bim, S.A.: Anais do Workshop sobre o Ensino de IHC – WEIHC 2012. CEUR-WS.org, Cuibá (2012), http://ceur-ws.org/Vol-967/
5. de Souza, C.S., Baranauskas, M.C., Prates, R.O., Pimenta, M.S.: HCI in Brazil: lessons learned and new perspectives. In: Proceedings of the VIII Brazilian Symposium on Human Factors in Computing Systems, pp. 358–359. SBC, Porto Alegre (2008)
6. Prates, R.O., Filgueiras, L.: Usability in Brazil. In: Douglas, I., Zhengjie, L. (eds.) Global Usability, 1st edn., vol. 1, pp. 91–110. Springer, London (2011)
7. Silveira, M.S., Prates, R.O.: Uma Proposta da Comunidade para o Ensino de IHC no Brasil. In: Anais do XV Workshop sobre Educação em Computação (WEI), pp. 76–84. SBC, Porto Alegre (2007)
8. SIGCHI Education, http://www.sigchi.org/resources/education

Semiotics of Interaction: Towards a UI Alphabet

Jan Brejcha[1] and Aaron Marcus[2]

[1] Information Science and Librarianship, Charles University, Prague, Czech Republic
jan@brejcha.name
[2] Aaron Marcus and Associates, Inc., Berkeley (CA), U.S.A.
aaron.marcus@amanda.com

Abstract. In our thinking and acting, natural language plays a central part. This language defines a structure even before we form something, and it can be regarded as the architecture of design. To be able to grasp the expression of these structures in HCI, we chose the perspective of linguistics and semiotics. The semiotics perspective in the context of HCI is increasingly popular in presenting a different approach to UX. In our paper, we take this perspective to build a set of semiotic heuristics which we then used to evaluate a complex UI example. We present a semiotic evaluation method and report the results of our in-depth investigation.

Keywords: Analysis and design methods, Evaluation methods and techniques, Interaction design, Qualitative and Quantitative Measurement and Evaluation, Semiotics.

1 Introduction

In our thinking and acting, natural language plays a central part. This language defines a structure even before we form something and can be regarded as the architecture of design. Our consciousness is the result of language informing design. Grammar allows for many combinations of objects and actions, but ideology establishes the privileged connection of the two of what is correct and possible. In order to set forth the privileged connection, ideology employs different forms of persuasion. To grasp the expression of these structures in HCI, we chose the perspective of linguistics and semiotics.

By semiotics we mean a theory of signs. We combine the Anglo-American semiotics (semeiotics) perspective with the French semiology ("sémiologie") approach. [3] According to Peirce, a sign is "something that stands for someone or something in some respect or capacity." [4][page 99] Four dimensions form the sign: lexical [5], syntactics, semantics, and pragmatics. [10]

The semiotics perspective in the context of HCI is increasingly popular in presenting a different approach to UX planning, researching, analyzing, designing, implementing, evaluating, documenting, training, and maintaining. [7] The classical linguistic and semiotic foundations of HCI were previously set down by, *e.g.*, Nadin [11], Andersen [2], and De Souza [13]. In our paper, we take their contribution to

M. Kurosu (Ed.): Human-Computer Interaction, Part I, HCII 2013, LNCS 8004, pp. 13–21, 2013.

build a set of semiotic heuristics that we then used to evaluate a complex UI example. We present a semiotic evaluation method and report the results of our in-depth investigation.

2 Semiotic Foundation

Our view is based on the assumption that HCI takes place between different actors (users, systems, designers) in a setting or paradigm. The semiotics of interaction is closely related to language as a system of signs. The semiotics of interaction is by definition time-based and the same holds true for language. Because of this, we may find some interesting parallels. The UI designer establishes grammar rules (syntax) for the combination of its elements. UIs are built from different components (metaphors, mental models, navigation, interaction, appearance) [8]. The manner in which UIs are built is governed by a set of rules given by the designer, e.g., every UI produced can follow a different intrinsic language grammar. The choice of elements is then subject to the goal (pragmatics) of the entire UI. Therefore, we should structure the UI language according to the actors and audience we want to address.

Interaction is subject to the languages present in any UI: a language both of display and actions. [14] We define the former as a visible language which is a systematic language of expression conveying specific information that can be translated from one kind of language to another. The latter is based on user input which makes it an interaction language. Based on our decision to act (or refrain from acting) on an object, we start an interaction. The visible and interaction language is expressed through UI components.

Looking at the UI components from the language perspective, we can structure them organically to create a UI grammar. UI grammar is composed of basic elements: interaction sentence, interaction games, rhetorical tropes, interaction phases, and patterns. The grammar elements concern both the noun and verb phrase of a sentence. Discrete elements are the smallest elements to have a meaning. The interaction sentence is a meaningful unit describing a task in a user's interaction. A set of interaction sentences with the same goal form an interaction game. The narrative in UI is made both by the designer's meta-communication and the temporal aspect of perceiving UI elements. Rhetorical tropes are devices of persuasion and emphasis, often presented as metaphors. Patterns are typical configurations of UI language components in different settings. From the defined semiotic and UI language principles, we extracted a set of heuristics which could be used as an UI glossary both for evaluation and design.

2.1 Semiotic Heuristics

Actors, Audience and Paradigm. Defining who the UI users are, who the intended audience of the UI is and what the leading interaction paradigm is. Communication from the UI to the actors should be concise, clear, and unambiguous. The audience can be revealed, *e.g.*, by contrasting two or more UIs with in similar semantic spaces (*e.g.*, functions).

Symbols. Different kinds of symbols connote different semantic spaces, cultural backgrounds and address different audiences. The symbols should be intelligible for the audience and should not carry a pejorative or contrary meaning. Symbols should be chosen to support the rhetorical tropes and can be formed by signs or their attributes.

Syntax. Signs should be used in any given context only once and should not be in conflict with its context. Similar signs should be placed in similar places. The signs should be divisible into identifiable elements and allow for building meaningful chains. The signs should be internally (within a UI) and externally consistent (across multiple UIs). The system processes are revealed by UI language components.

Rhetorical Tropes. The most common rhetorical tropes in the UI are devices of substitution: metaphor, metonymy, prosopopoeia, and synecdoche. The rhetorical tropes used should be both intelligible for the audience and minimal. The general metaphor of the UI should help users build correct expectations of future interaction through consistent mental models.

Interaction Phases. The interaction should form meaningful temporal units. The beginning of the interaction should be consistent with both middle and end. All the parts of the interaction should follow user's expectations and should pertain clearly to the current interaction game. The user should not be forced to perform a different action than intended. The signs present on a UI should lead the user in a sequence towards the goal of the interaction game through a controlled narration.

Patterns. UI language components form different kinds of patterns. The number of the expected interaction sentences should be as low as possible, possibly not exceeding the 7±2 limit [9]. The interaction sentence should have as little number of words as possible. The results of similar functions should be returned in a similar time frame.

3 Research Method

We developed a semiotic analysis method that takes as input the interaction sentence transcript with figures of the UI. Because it is an evaluation method carried by experts, we wanted to compare it with a well-known method to see whether the results would differ and how. To compare the methods of expert evaluation we chose heuristic evaluation (HE) and semiotic analysis (SA). For HE heuristics, we chose those used by Aaron Marcus and Associates, Inc. [7]. Our criteria for the methods were: fast and easy to do, results accessible to non-experts and comparable to previous data. The goal was to validate the SA against a non-semiotic method.

As input for this comparison, we chose a UI corpus [3] consisting of similar portions of two complex graphic design applications: Adobe® Photoshop® and the GNU Image Manipulation Program, or GIMP. Traditionally, these methods have been employed for goal-oriented work applications. However, they can be also applied to a range of different applications, including entertainment applications, where the goal is not always clearly defined, both in a static or mobile setting. In order to better compare and analyze the corpus, we aligned the semantic spaces (e.g., the features, tools, functions) of the application by their title from the products' marketing publications and user manuals. [12] The following list of actions constitute the semantics of the selected UIs: Barrel distortion, Clone objects in perspective, Customize the UI, Eliminate an object, Reduce red-eye.

4 Results

We present our analysis results from the SA and HE of both of the compared UIs following the extracted UI corpus.

4.1 UI Annotation

We annotated the UIs using a transcript of interaction sentences from actions. As an example of the action we chose, *Clone objects in perspective.* Table 1 contains the interaction sentences that were extracted from both applications.

Table 1. Interaction sentence comparison of Adobe Photoshop and the GIMP

	Adobe Photoshop	**GIMP**
0	Open the picture to adjust.	Open the picture to adjust.
1	Find the proper function in the menu or tool palette.	Find the proper function in the menu or tool palette.
	(a) The sub-task involved was to look at the toolbox for a button resembling the intended action. Nothing like that was found.	(a) The sub-task involved was to look through the menu items (especially in what seemed as most related: Image -> Adjustments, Filters, and Tools -> Transform Tools) for a relative command (it was found under Tools -> Paint Tools -> Perspective Clone).
	(b) Alternatively to look through the menu items (especially in what seemed as most related: Image -> Adjustments, and Filter) for a relative command (it was found under Filter -> Vanishing point…). (A window called "Vanishing Point" appears. The window sports a live preview, "Create Plane Tool", and "Clone Tool", among others.)	(b) Alternatively to look at the toolbox for a button resembling the intended action. It was found as Perspective Clone. (Boxes on each corner of the image appeared, the pointer changed to crosshair with the tool attribute and the toolbox expanded to show the "Modify Perspective" selected and the "Perspective Clone" radio button.)

Table 1. *(continued)*

2	Click the four corners according to the information line provided ("Click the four corners of a perspective plane or object in the image to create an editing plane. Tear off perpendicular planes from the stretch nodes of existing…)".	Drag the four corner boxes to define the perspective plane to clone.
3	Select the "Clone tool".	Click on the "Perspective Clone" radio button to change the tool.
4	Option-click in the plane to set the source ("Opt+click in a plane, to set a source point for the clone. Once the source point is set, click+drag to paint or clone. Shift+click to extend the stroke to last click.").	Control-click the source in the defined plane.
5	Click-drag (to paint) several times to clone in the perspective. See the proposed results in the preview.	Click-drag (to paint) several times to clone in the perspective.
6	Click "OK" to apply the changes.	Save changes to the file.
7	Save changes to the file.	

4.2 Semiotic Analysis

Adobe Photoshop SA Analysis

Actors, Audience and Paradigm. All of the objects involved in the interaction pertain to the leading paradigm of "Window, icon, menu, pointing device" (WIMP). The paradigm is constituted by the menu bar, tool bars, main window containing the image, dialog windows, icons and pointer. The paradigm is bound to the GUI metaphor. Adobe Photoshop is meant for professionals. This distinction of audience is manifested implicitly by the channel of distribution (commercial software) and explicitly in the marketing documentation (Adobe Photoshop's slogan reads: "The professional standard in desktop digital imaging" [1]. The menu paradigm is constructed by combining noun-verb or verb-noun items which seems deliberate (only one model should be chosen.) A more specific audience for this function is photographers and advertising designers.

Symbols. The users are addressed by symbols pertaining to the user domain. In this case, the application icon and splash screen of Adobe Photoshop features a colorful feather. The connotations are elegance, simplicity and naturalness which one would expect from a professional tool. What might break the expectation, however, is the historical usage of the image that symbolizes a writing pen. The other screens (and toolbars) are very compact and grey. The menus are only text-based, whereas the toolbar has only icons (with a textual label). The icons in the toolbar are related to their object in different ways but are connected to the prevailing metaphor and follow the application genre conventions.

Syntax. The system processes are constituted by UI language components, as described earlier. In the interaction transcript, we can find all the elements mentioned. There are basic lexemes ("click", "option-click"), interaction sentences ("Open the picture to adjust."), rhetorical tropes (*e.g.*, metaphors, such as "Vanishing Point", or "Clone Tool"), interaction games (these are the complete functions enabling us to accomplish our goal, *e.g.* "Clone an object in perspective"). The designer's narration element is found in the tool-tip help reinforcing the icon meaning, in the status bar of the window or a dialog window for which help is given by instructions regarding use of the tool and in other dialog windows which presents the user with different choices. Finally, in the Help menu, the text comprehensively describes the program functions. In the "Vanishing Point" window, the designer's narration gives detailed instructions for all the steps involved.

Rhetorical Tropes. The most prominent of the rhetorical tropes in this context is the metaphor. The program metaphor builds upon the concepts of a painter's canvas or photographer's studio. The product tries to transfer the environment into the present paradigm. For that reason, the image is placed on a "canvas", the pointer changes to different "brushes", the user can further apply different optical "filters", or use a choice of retouching "tools". By applying this approach, a number of inconsistencies emerge which force users to alter or update their interpretation of the metaphor. The canvas, for example, is in fact infinite and can be resized in different ways at any time. The picture "lying" on the canvas may consist of multiple layers. Almost any tool can be customized using the "brush" metaphor: one can modify the thickness, shape, or profile of the brush. A filter can be used afterwards, applied as a part of retouching. More fundamentally, time can also be manipulated through the "undo" function that cycles back through the history of actions.

Interaction Phases. On the level of interaction sentence, the interaction changes to reflect the constant evaluation of results on the user's part. The interaction sentence is then modified or repeated accordingly. Considering the example from the transcripts, the action is modified after the system's feedback (when clicking on the plane to clone with the clone tool, the user is instructed to option-click on the source plane first), the action is repeated (drag the brush several times to paint the object in the new perspective), or the action is needed only once (when applying the changes by pressing the "OK" button). The middle of the interaction game differs from the beginning and end because a new window is shown keeping the user accordingly away from the picture he or she opened.

GIMP SA Analysis

Actors, Audience and Paradigm. All of the objects involved in the interaction pertain to the leading paradigm of "Window, icon, menu, pointing device" (WIMP). The paradigm is constituted by the menu bar, tool bars, main window containing the image, dialog windows, icons and a pointer. The paradigm is bound to the GUI metaphor. GIMP is intended for amateur/semi-professionals and programmers. This distinction is manifested implicitly by the channel of distribution (open-source) and explicitly in the marketing documentation (in GIMP it is by stating, that "[i]n the free software world, there is generally no distinction between users and developers." [6]. The menu paradigm is constructed by combining noun-verb or verb-noun items which seems deliberate (only one model should be chosen). GIMP shares the same user group as Adobe Photoshop (photographers and advertising designers).

Symbols. The users are addressed by symbols related to the user domain. In this case, Gimp's icon of a stylized dog head connotes playfulness, fun and also ease of use. The icon is not used on the splash screen, however, in favor of a planet picture. The toolbars and other screens show larger and more colorful button icons and larger dialog windows which are easily reached by the pointer. The icon symbols used in the menus, *e.g.*, in the "Tools" menu, makes no distinction between nouns (*e.g.*, Pencil, Eraser, Text) and verbs *(e.g.*, Zoom, Measure, Heal) which could be helpful. Also, the symbols are created by different methods (*e.g.*, the Pencil tool has an iconic representation of a pen but the Zoom tool icon is created by metonymy with its action and uses a zooming lens; other are connected only loosely, as in the case of Swap Colors).

Syntax. The system processes are constituted by the same UI language components analyzed above for Adobe Photoshop. In GIMP, there is only a difference in the tool metaphor used ("Perspective Clone Tool").

Rhetorical Tropes. Perhaps the most prominent of the rhetorical tropes in this context is the metaphor. As is the case of syntax, the same set of metaphors is shared with Adobe Photoshop.

Interaction Phases. The interaction phases are similar to those mentioned above in the Adobe Photoshop analysis. Also, the interaction sentence level is similar. However, the middle phase (where the user works on the picture) seems to be more consistent with beginning and end. This is because the user keeps working in the image window and is not distracted by other windows or palettes.

4.3 Heuristic Analysis

Adobe Photoshop HE Analysis

Direct Manipulation/See and Point; Error Prevention. Although the user can use the tool directly on the image, they are reminded every time to select a source region first. Instead of forcing the user to go "backwards", the program should allow the user to select the region afterwards. Such change in the perceived interaction timeline also violates the principle of Error prevention.

Modelessness. By selecting the vanishing point function, the user is presented with a new window (named "Vanishing Point") containing the image to manipulate and a reduced set of controls (buttons, check-boxes, and drop-down menus). After the adjustments, the user has to click “OK” to transfer the changes to the image in the main window underneath. A better solution seems to be using standard controls and not introducing a different working environment. By doing so, we would also eliminate the extra step of applying the changes.

Recognition Rather Than Recall. All of the needed actions are visible and the system provides inline help. However, the toolbar on the top-left does not show which tools are necessary for the operation and in which sequence they should be applied.

Visible Interfaces/WYSIWYG. The vanishing point function was not present on the toolbar and was only accessible through the menu bar. Since it is one of the advertised features, it should be as readily accessible as possible.

GIMP HE Analysis

Direct Manipulation/See and Point; Error Prevention. Although the user can use the tool directly on the image, he or she is reminded every time to select a source region first. Instead of forcing the user to go “backwards“, the program should allow the user to select the region afterwards. Such change in the perceived interaction timeline also violates the principle of Error prevention.

Recognition Rather Than Recall. All of the needed actions are visible and the system provides inline help. However, the toolbar on the top-left does not show which tools are necessary for the operation and in which sequence they should be applied (“Modify Perspective” or “Perspective Clone”?).

Match between System and Real World. The Perspective Clone tool is located under Paint Tools and thus supports the metaphor of painting on the picture. However, in the virtual environment this could be problematic as the clone tool is connected with image transformation and/or filtering.

5 Discussion

By comparing the output from the HE and SA analysis, HE proved to be more concise. However, of the 16 heuristics used, only a small number could be applied on each occasion. The application of the 6 elements of SA tended to be more verbose, but, on the other hand, the elements could be applied every time. Whereas SA could seem repetitive in some instances, it provided a solid context of analysis. Both the methods (HE and SA) could be used not only on the interaction sentence level but also as for a general appreciation of the entire UI. During the general analysis only portions of the UI are selected and suggestions made to other similar parts of the UI.

In summary, our study demonstrated the depth of investigation and breadth of insight that SA can achieve in HCI and how this could enhance the current practice. Both methods could be merged to provide a best-of-both solution.

Acknowledgements. The author recognizes the assistance of the AM+A library and document archive for providing information and examples for this text.

References

1. Adobe, Inc.: What's New in Adobe® Photoshop® CS2 (2005), `http://www.adobe.com/aboutadobe/pressroom/pressmaterials/creativesuite2/pdfs/ps/PSCS2-WN.pdf` (last accessed February 18, 2013)
2. Andersen, P.B.: A theory of computer semiotics: semiotic approaches to construction and assessment of computer systems. Cambridge University Press (1997)
3. Barthes, R.: Elements of Semiology. Hill and Wang (April 1977)
4. Buchler, J.: Philosophical writings of Peirce. Dover (1955)
5. Eco, U.: A Theory of Semiotics. Advances in Semiotics. Indiana University Press (February 1979)
6. The GIMP Team. GIMP - Development (2009), `http://gimp.org/develop/` (last accessed September 19, 2009)
7. Marcus, A., et al.: Heuristic Evaluation Guidelines. Aaron Marcus and Associates, Inc. (2003) (Internal document)
8. Marcus, A.: Dare we define user-interface design? Interactions 9(5), 19–24 (2002)
9. Miller, A.G.: The magical number seven, plus or minus two: some limits on our capacity for processing information. Psychological Review 101(2), 343–352 (1956)
10. Morris, C.W.: Foundations of the Theory of Signs. The University of Chicago Press (1970)
11. Nadin, M.: Interface design: A semiotic paradigm. Semiotica 69(3), 269–302 (1988)
12. De Souza, C.S., et al.: The semiotic inspection method. In: Proceedings of VII Brazilian Symposium on Human Factors in Computing Systems (2006)
13. De Souza, C.S.: The Semiotic Engineering of Human-Computer Interaction (Acting with Technology). The MIT Press (2005)
14. Sutherland: On-line graphical specification of computer procedures. PhD Thesis (1966), `http://oai.dtic.mil`

Engagingdesign – Methods for Collective Creativity

Paul Chamberlain and Claire Craig

Lab4Living, Art & Design Research Centre, Sheffield Hallam University,
Cantor Building, 153 Arundel Street, Sheffield S1 2NU, UK
{p.m.chamberlain,claire c.craig}@shu.ac.uk

Abstract. Research often problematises issues older people face and the development of technologies for older users is regularly driven by this agenda. This paper describes a research programme that positions older people as active participants rather than passive respondents focusing on their preferences and aspirations rather than their impairments. 'Engagingdesign' is a transnational research platform developed by the authors that facilitates creative methods for engaging older people and provides a scaffold for collective creativity. Data collected through interviews and focus groups is transformed through critical artefacts that provide a forum or theatre for conversation through exhibition that in turn becomes the medium and method for further data collection.

Keywords: User–centred design methods, older users, design, co-creation, participatory design.

1 Introduction

'I tell you what is the worst thing that I come across and it still annoys me now is some people not all people but some people treat you like your brain dead. And they are so patronising as if because you're retired your brains gone. You know they took it out, when you left work they took it out and gave it to somebody else. It really annoys me when they do that'............older participant – engagingdesign

As the number of people aged 65 and over is set to rise by 2 billion by 2050, efforts to understand the needs of older people have become a priority for research and policy. Much research problematises issues older people face and the development of technologies for older users are often driven by this agenda. Older people are generally still viewed through the 'medical model' that focuses on impairment and from a position that reflects the idea that individuals need to be monitored or need help and assistance. Older people have therefore tended to be viewed with pity as passive recipients, rather than active participants in research. It is less common to find research that focuses on the broader aspirations in relation to their lives. Research has revealed [1] 'how people aged over 70 are persistently seen as incapable and pitiable when compared with other groups and there is unthinking disregard for older people's preferences and aspirations'. The 'old' are not a homogenous group but demonstrate considerable diversity in age, lifestyle, culture, physical and emotional wellbeing and

M. Kurosu (Ed.): Human-Computer Interaction, Part I, HCII 2013, LNCS 8004, pp. 22–31, 2013.

it is important to recognise individuality in shaping what people want and value. Katz et el [2] suggest 'Little is known about what these (older) people want and value, while negative assumptions are sometimes made about their ability to comment on and participate in decision-making and collective action'. Research in HCI, according to Microsoft [3], typically positions older people as recipients of care whereas the social sciences literature shows instead that older people are often providers of care, even to their adult children, and that placing them in the role of 'receiver' may have negative ramifications for self-esteem. Katz et el [2] advocate the promotion of equality between people of different ages, addressing the future needs of an ageing and diverse population, and eliminating discrimination against older people. 'We need to be alive to trends which appear to exacerbate age segregation, and seek initiatives which can bring different generations together around issues of shared interest and importance'. Links between older people and young people are invaluable, helping to break down prejudice on both sides and fostering understanding [1]. Significantly our research acknowledges the changing aspirations of new generations of older people.

2 Building Partnerships

According to Sanders [4] through advances in technology and the evolution of human-centered design practices we are witnessing a shift in focus from individual to 'collective creativity' that can provide a new role for designers as creators of scaffolds or infrastructures upon which non-designers can express their creativity. Bohm [5] suggests everyone is creative but non-designers are generally not in the habit of expressing their creativity that is likely to be latent. Interaction design has provided a new design space that has emerged in response to new communication technologies. It is a space where the focus has shifted from form to information. Designing 'experiences' has emerged as a theme for design practitioners but Sanders believes this is a myopic perspective. 'Experience is a subjective phenomenon. You can't design experience. Experience is in people'. She believes; 'Collective creativity and user participation are a much-needed antidote to interaction design's preoccupation with "Experience Design." If you think of products, interfaces and spaces as being scaffolds on which ordinary people can create their own experiences, the design challenge changes'. Sanders suggests the new role of designers will be to learn how to access and understand the dreams of ordinary people to create scaffolds that help people realize their dreams. 'Designers will transform from being designers of "stuff" to being the builders of scaffolds for experiencing. And ordinary people will begin to use and express their latent creativity'.

3 Engagingdesign

Engagingdesign is a transnational research platform created by the authors (Chamberlain is a Designer, Craig an Occupational therapist) that provides the scaffold described by Sanders for collective creativity with a focus on older people but embracing a broad demographic. The philosophical drive for our multi-method approach to engagement is researching 'with' rather than 'on' older people who are active participants rather than passive respondents. There are many user-centred research methods for collecting data such as questionnaires, interviews, video observation etc. Whilst each method has to be carefully selected and implemented appropriate to the research enquiry significant challenges are presented when the data has to be meaningfully translated. Kolko [6] claims the process of translating data and research into knowledge is the most critical part of the design process. He states research in itself does not produce new ideas and highlights the importance of incubation and translation and states, 'we rarely engage in conversation about making meaning out of data'. Chamberlain [7] has described how the concept of the exhibition is embedded within the culture of art and design and has a long history as a form of gathering employed to prompt academic discourse. The period (17th century) in which salons dominated has been labeled the 'age of conversation' and salons themselves 'theatres of conversation', [8]. Key to our research is the role of objects, critical artefacts, that do not necessarily present solutions but considered questions informed by data to create 'exhibitions' as prompts and a theatre for conversation.

Our research is based on the premise that older people offer a valued resource and asset to families, communities and society and we have actively sought ways to tap into these strengths. We developed and utilised a range of novel and innovative research methodologies to engage with older people across two continents. The initial phase of research 'engagingaging', funded by the British Council aimed to understand the needs of the aging population in order to inform the design of products and systems to support independence and well-being in later life. The research compared the experiences of older people living in Taiwan with those of older people in the UK. Chamberlain and Craig in collaboration with academic researchers at Chang Gung University's Product Design Research Lab conducted a series of workshops and home visits with older people in the respective countries. Taiwan was selected for study as it has a comparable land mass with the UK (small island), and it has a fast developing high-tech industry with one of the world's highest concentration of internet access. Its traditional culture, where older children look after elderly parents, is changing, with many moving to work overseas. Like many countries, it is experiencing a significant demographic shift as a result of an ageing population. Initial data was captured using semi structured interviews but with a focused discussion around objects. Invited participants were asked to bring two objects (or photographs) to the sessions, one being their favorite, and one they hated but couldn't live without. Participants from the UK were recruited from local care homes and community groups e.g. Sheffield Elders, Sheffield 50+ and the University of the Third Age. Participants from Taiwan were recruited from the Chang Gung Health and Cultural village a vast purpose built community (4,500 residents) for older people. This was complimented by home visits in the UK and Taiwan to engage with people living independently. Using a practice-based research methodology we developed the equivalent of a grounded theory approach, transforming data collected through interviews into 'critical artefacts' which were then exhibited in a number of highly prestigious galleries including the Museum of Contemporary Art, Taipei, the Building Centre, London, The Taipei Cultural Centre and the SIA gallery Sheffield. Included in the exhibitions for example was a collection of furniture 'Stigmas' (fig. 1) designed by Chamberlain to embody the findings of interview data gained from older people in relation to the physical and attitudinal challenges they face in everyday life. Rather than acting as solutions, the furniture formed a series of 'critical artefacts' to pose questions and promote discussion to gain rich, in-depth data used to further our understanding of the needs of an ageing population.

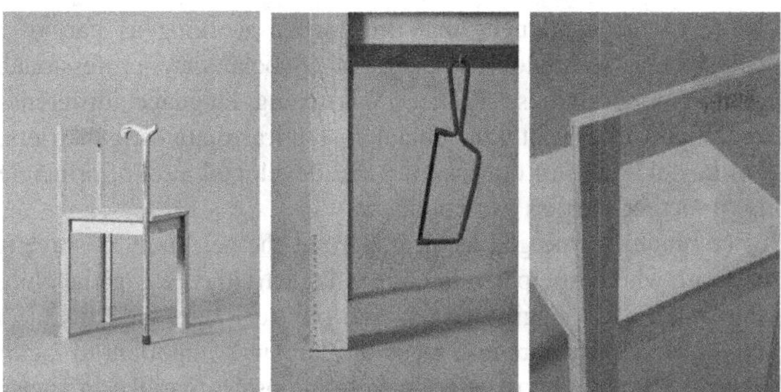

Fig. 1. STIGMAS – Critical artefacts posing questions not answers

The exhibitions, engagingdesign, (Fig. 2) provided the theatre for conversation and became the medium and method for further data collection. Linked to each of the exhibitions was a series of workshops that included, older people, families, design students, health students, medical professionals and the Chinese Community (Sheffield, UK).

Fig. 2. Engaging people in the UK and Taiwan

3.1 Responses to the Exhibitions

'The artifacts in the exhibition stimulate deep thought related to older people for participants and visitors. It announces and informs the awareness of issues we all might face in the future'. Curator of Museum of Contemporary Art, Taipei, Taiwan.

'engagingaging was a fresh approach and broke the rules on what we normally expect from an exhibition. It dealt with some difficult and controversial issues in a friendly and accessible way'. Curator of the Taipei Cultural Centre.

'Elders could learn from this exhibition and understand not everything is negative when getting older. Meanwhile this is a nice exhibition to help younger generations understand elders lifestyles and make them more aware of older people'. Epoch Times, December 2010

'I am so glad someone is thinking about us and the exhibition is a great opportunity for us to share our experiences with younger people'. Visitor to exhibition, Taiwan

We turned some of the challenges that arise when working as part of an interdisciplinary (designers, technologists, health and social care professionals) trans-cultural team into opportunities. Rather than seeing language, different research paradigms, and contrasting health and social care infrastructures as barriers, we embraced these as key elements of our learning and developed a set of principles for the transferability of methods across two continents.

A sense of community emerged as an important theme. Many positive responses emerged from those who participated in communal activities (e.g. game clubs, Bridge (UK) and Mah-Jong (TW), singing groups and physical activity, Tai Chi (TW) and walking groups (UK). A structure and sense of place was important to facilitate such activities, however the ability for individuals to choose to partake in such activities was crucial.

The importance for older people to maintain cultural and intellectual life, through music, cooking, art and craft. We must acknowledge the need for older people to keep learning but also recognise they can act as teachers passing on their valuable experiences. The importance of continuing to make a contribution to society and feeling valued is significant and many participants engaged in volunteer work.

Generally younger participants collectively took the position that older people struggle with all types of new technology and specifically design students felt it was their role to make products easier to use for older people. However the workshops revealed many adept older users of technology and a variety of reasons why older users might not extensively interact with technology. Often it was not the case they couldn't but they either didn't see a need to or couldn't be bothered.

'I realise that one frustrating thing about getting older is the way you become invisible. Yes, you sort of fade into non-existence'. Older participant - engagingdesign

4 Exhibition in a Box

Developing the notion of the exhibition as a research tool and inspired by Duchamp's 'Boite en valise' (Box in a suitcase) the exhibition is distilled into a 'suitcase' and aims to compare the experiences of older people to inform design in supporting and empowering independence and quality of life in later life. Rather than the onus being placed on older people to physically access traditional exhibition space, 'exhibition in box' seeks to bring the exhibition to the older person and to transform the home into the research arena providing individuals a tangible prompt to scaffold conversation. Exhibition in a box captures the essence of the larger gallery exhibitions but is an exhibition in its own right.

The American Painter Washington Allston first used the term "objective correlative" about 1840, but T. S. Eliot made it famous and revived it in an influential essay on Hamlet in the year 1919. Eliot wrote;

The only way of expressing emotion in the form of art is by finding an 'objective correlative'; in other words, a set of objects, a situation, a chain of events which shall be the formula of that particular emotion. (9)

If writers or poets or playwrights want to create an emotional reaction in the audience, they must find a combination of images, objects, or description evoking the appropriate emotion. The source of the emotional reaction isn't in one particular object, one particular image, or one particular word. Instead, the emotion originates in the combination of these phenomena when they appear together. Objective correlatives can therefore be described as exercises in economy allowing writers to communicate universal concepts tastefully and subtlety. The idea is to turn an object, event or character in the story into a translating mechanism that poses some greater question that's not directly on the page. The objects selected for our exhibition in a box are in essence object correlatives that facilitate narratives and ways of expressing emotion around ageing.

A set of principles has been developed and employed that primarily positions the older participants as the 'expert' and encourages choice and decision-making. The box comprises of everyday objects, photographs, textual material and 'critical artefacts' defined through the user-workshops undertaken in conjunction with the earlier large-scale exhibition. The 'exhibits' (in the box) are prompts that enable engagement with users in a range of contextual environments the components of which become part of the exhibition. Each 'exhibition', as Duchamp's, is unique through the iterative and evolving contribution from the participants.

Observation forms an important part of user-centred design research. Spradley (10) suggests nine dimensions of any social situation that provide a map for action–based data collection; Space, Actors, Activities, Objects, Acts, Events, Time, Goals and Feelings. According to Robson (11) these dimensions describe the setting, people and the events that are taking place. Descriptions of these settings are as follows.

Table 1. Exhibition in a box provides a physical map of Spradley's theory

Dimension - Spradley	Description - Robson	Exhibition in a box
Space	Layout of the physical space	The space within the box and the location of the workshop, defined as 'the exhibition'
Actors	The people involved	The researchers and the participants
Activities	Activities of the actors	Facilitated by the researchers (or guidelines) and prompted by the artefacts.
Objects	Physical elements	Objects contained within the box and the environment the workshop takes place
Acts	Individual Actions	Individual and collective acts prompted by the objects
Events	Particular occasions	The workshop/exhibition

Table 1. *(continued)*

Time	Sequence of events	Each workshop event is semi-structured and time limited.
Goals	What the actors are attempting to accomplish	Contents of the box prompt tasks both individual and collective. Our goal is to understand aspirations and preferences and develop insight into value and meaning.
Feelings	Emotion in particular contexts	Prompted by the objects in the box and captured through writings, drawings, audio/video recordings and transcripted for analyses.

Exhibition in a box (fig. 3) contains physical objects and photographs of artefacts (created by the research team including photographs of the Stigma collection), found objects and selected stories gathered and developed through the iterative research to date. Objects have been carefully selected to code, represent and prompt further discussion on themes that have emerged from the earlier research. Key themes include mobility, hygiene, relationships, identity, communication, technology, food, art, money, recreation, safety and work and are represented through the set of found objects that include, keys, dice, soap, pencil, watch, stone, glove, post-card, spoon. The objects can combine to create objective correlatives prompting and enabling participants to express emotional responses. E.g. pencil and post card may prompt discussion around travel, communication or technology (analogue vs. digital).

'I don't know why I hold on to mine (keys), because a stranger lives there now.....I feel a lot of comfort in them jangling in my pocket. They remind me of the old days. Being able to lock your own front door is one of the things that I miss most. It's the loss of privacy and control'..........Participant, engagingdesign

The research data gathered through the series of engagingdesign events has informed the creation of numerous 'critical artefacts' that prompt further discourse through 'what if?' scenarios. Some selected examples contained within the exhibition in the box that focus on our interaction with technology include the following.

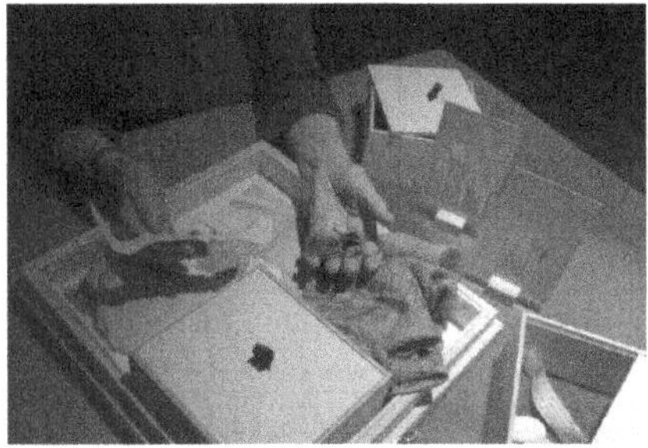

Fig. 3. 'Exhibition in a box'

Fig. 4. Biscuit Buddy

'It's not that I am not able to learn to use new technology, at my age I just can't be bothered to learn to use yet another thing'. Biscuit buddy (Chamberlain, Bowen) (Fig. 4) embeds communication technology in an everyday object, a biscuit tin, and ritual, tea-time. The idea is that removing the lid alerts a friend with a similar device and automatically opens up a channel for communication without the need for another product, learning another interface and adopting a new routine. Should we develop new devices that have specific functions or embed technology in everyday objects and rituals?

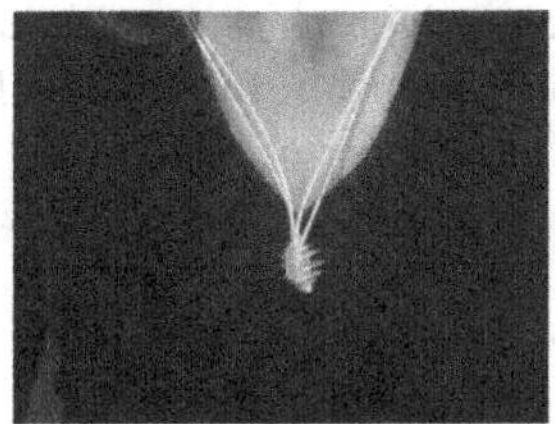

Fig. 5. 'Love links' – monitoring wellbeing

Fig. 6. Home hospital – family x-rays

'My daughter bought me this mobile phone in case of emergency, but I just keep it in the drawer.' Safety alarms, such as fall alarms, stigmatise users and establish communication with family and loved ones only in times of crisis that set up a situations of anxiety. Objects to cherish could provide a positive continuous 'link' and reminder by monitoring loved ones wellbeing. 'Love links' (Chamberlain, Bowen) (Fig. 5) monitors wellbeing by creating a permanent visual communication link between loved ones in the form of a precious gift e.g. jewelry (rather than device). An alert (lack of activity or fall) breaks the communication link causing change in the object activity (e.g. change of colour). Can we change the negative connotations of monitoring devices?

'I think when you're getting older when you're house bound, I think it, it makes you wonder where you are. You forget what day it is, they tell you what day it is on television or whatever. Your days go all into one'. Home hospital (Chamberlain) (Fig.6) Interrupt your TV viewing and check out the state of your health. Converging technologies present many potential benefits but should we retain boundaries between work, health and play?

Health technologies have in themselves been largely responsible for extended life and will play a critical role in the future but we must not underestimate the value and role of recreation in our lives. Extended life should not just be concerned with survival but with the quality of life. According to Johnson (12) people of all ages need to enjoy themselves, although what gives pleasure to individuals is highly personal and may change with time and circumstances. Age UK (1) acknowledge that humour is an important way of retaining control and personal identity in the face of loss and change. Hubbard et el (13) describe jokes being used to make light of ageing bodies, to manage concerns about accidents, and also to engage those with communication difficulties through practical jokes. While adopting a rigorous protocol in use exhibition in a box deliberately has a sense of game play to incite 'fun' and to help overcome what is often imbalance and inequalities of researcher of participant. Katz et el (2) conclude, *'All of us, regardless of age, need opportunities to show others who we are and to feel good about ourselves.'*

'Because when you get older you do say some outrageous things! Yeah. You're allowed to when you're older'. engagingdesign participant.

Exhibition in a box has identified to date ten partner organisations (research centres and health professionals) across Europe who have made a commitment to utilising exhibition in a box to help continue our study. Ongoing research will focus on gathering further insights from participants but also evaluate the exhibition in a box as a research tool that can provide the scaffold for ordinary people to present their latent creativity. Initial feedback from the workshops to date in the UK and the Netherlands suggests the exhibition in a box does facilitate empowerment for older people providing them with a voice and opportunity for choice and decision-making. Woman participants have tended to focus more on the emotional aspects of their lives while men on practicality and function. The objects have allowed different ways for participants to express their personal identity and in many cases their creativity prompting them to describe things they have made previously in their life and suggest new ways of doing things. The findings to date also challenge negative assumptions about older people and their willingness to participate in activities which could enhance their own lives or those of others.

5 Conclusion

Technological developments present exciting opportunities for designers and offer enormous potential to positively impact and support our ageing society. Too often research problematises issues older people face who become passive recipients of technological interventions. Engagingdesign importantly positions older people as active participants, as experts and as individuals enabling them to comment, participate in decision-making and collective action. We must not view the 'old' as a homogenous group but as individuals and address the future needs of an ageing and diverse population, seeking initiatives which can bring different generations together around issues of shared interest and importance. Our research recognizes and responds to the European Union's (14) mission for solidarity between generations in providing a shared forum and methods for engaging individuals, families and communities of all ages. The research team's objective is to utilise the new knowledge that emerges from our studies to inform creative design responses. However the research programme has highlighted the value in the process itself not just for design, the research academic community and industry but also for older people themselves. Participants have not just been utilised as a resource from which to collect data but importantly become empowered valued citizens by providing them opportunity for involvement, autonomy and control. Increasingly we experience a saturation of data and as Kolko (6) highlights it is crucial we engage in conversation to make meaning out of this data. The research team have provided through 'exhibition' in its varied formats a theatre for this conversation in an attempt to establish meaning of this data. Crucially engagingdesign provides the scaffold upon which non-designers can express their latent creativity and engage in collective creation with designers to realise their dreams by defining and shaping what people need and value.

References

1. Delivering dignity improving later life. Independent Commission on Dignity for Care a Collaboration established by the NHS Confederation, the Local Government Association and Age UK, `http://www.nhsconfed.org/Documents/dignity.pdf`
2. Katz, J., Holland, C., Peace, S., Taylor, E.: A better life: what older people with high support needs value. Open University (2011) ISBN 978-1-85935-861-0
3. Microsoft Research, Designing for Older People, `http://research.microsoft.com/en-us/projects/seniors/`
4. Sanders, L.: Collective Creativity. AIGA Journal of Interaction Design Education (7) (June 2003)
5. Bohm, D.: On Creativity. Routledge, London (1998) ISBN 10: 0-415-33640-4 and ISBN 13: 978-0-415-33640-6
6. Kolko, J.: Exposing the Magic of Design, A practical guide to the methods and theory of synthesis. Human Technology Interaction. Oxford University Press (2011) ISBN 978-0-19-974433-6
7. Chamberlain, P., Yoxall, A.: Of Mice and Men. The Role of Interactive Exhibitions as Research Tools for Inclusive Design, vol. 15(1), pp. 57–78. Ashgate Publications (2012)
8. Benedetta, C.: The Age of Conversation. New York Review Books, New York (2005) ISBN 978590172148
9. Cuddon's, J.A.: Dictionary of Literary Terms. Wiley-Blackwell (2013) ISBN 978-1-4443-3327-5
10. Spradley, J.P.: Participant Observation. Holt, Reinhart and Wilson, New York (1980)
11. Robson, C.: Real World Research – a resource for social scientists and practitioner-researchers. John Wiley & Sons Ltd. (2002) ISBN 978-1-4051-8241-6 and 978—1-4051-82409
12. Johnson, J., Rolph, S., Smith, R.: Residential Care Transformed: Revisiting 'The Last Refuge'. Palgrave Macmillan, Basingstoke (2010)
13. Hubbard, G., Tester, S., Downs, M.G.: Meaningful social interactions between older people in institutional care settings. Ageing & Society 23(1), 99–114 (2003)
14. Age Platform Europe. Towards an age friendly EU

Toward a New Design Philosophy of HCI: Knowledge of Collaborative Action of "We" Human-and-Technology

HyunKyoung Cho[1] and Joonsung Yoon[2]

[1] GIST, Cultural Technology Institute, Korea
hkcho@gist.ac.kr
[2] Global School of Media, Soongsil University, Korea
dryoon@maat.kr

Abstract. This research examines a new design philosophy of HCI in the collaborative action-based context interdependent perspective. To frame a new perspective of design philosophy of interactive technologies, the study proposes "We" human-and-technology as a response for alternative perspectives of reference in inter-active systems design and alternative ways of understanding the relationships and collaborative actions between humans and new digital technologies. It argues the problem of knowledge provoked by the collaborative action of "We" human-and-technology, through three keys: reflecting, performing, and invaginating. Its aim is to reveal that HCI design practices establish a new knowledge beyond the logic of opposition reinforcing the mutual degradation between technology and human, thought and action, subject and object.

Keywords: "We" human-and-technology, collaborative action, knowledge, reflecting, performing, invaginating, HCI design.

1 Introduction

The only action corresponds to the human condition; the human existence and its condition. The way in which we humans produce our means of life articulates itself in the mode of performing our life beyond the material and physical one. The human condition is a whole from the perspective of the idea of social relations embodied in the real movement of life. It designates the knowledge as the intertwinement of reason and experience in the actual life-process.

Max Horkheimer and Theodor W. Adorno define the human condition as a paradox of knowledge embracing both enlightenment and myth. It has the twofold character of enlightenment traversing the universal movement of mind and a nihilistic, life-denying power [1].[1] On the one hand, we humans create our own condition, and on the other, everything we create turns immediately into a condition. This implies that the human existence and its condition supplement each other, so long as the supplementation assumes that the human condition can be transformed by the performing of action. Here the problematic is that like human-human communication,

[1] Max Horkheimer and Theodor W. Adorno, *Dialectic of Enlightenment* (California, Standford: Standford University Press, 2002), p. 36.

M. Kurosu (Ed.): Human-Computer Interaction, Part I, HCII 2013, LNCS 8004, pp. 32–40, 2013.

technology and humans act and react. In particular, computational technology is endowed with highly intelligent and perceptive qualities; has its own laws; and the system itself evolves. With the ability of autonomy and emergence, technology performs the autonomous and emergent action beyond human control. It becomes 'a performer (a collaborator)' collaborating with humans [2].[2]

Technology as performer (collaborator) transforms the human condition. The transformation, the expanded human condition by the collaborative action of we humans and technology can be called as "We" human-and-technology. The word of "We" human-and-technology indicates that identity of we humans is organized by collaborative actions between we humans and technology in HCI design. "We" human-and-technology is a response to the need for alternative frames of reference in inter-active systems design and alternative ways of understanding the relationships and collaborative actions between humans and new digital technologies. It is to point to a growing interest in the design philosophy of interactive technologies.

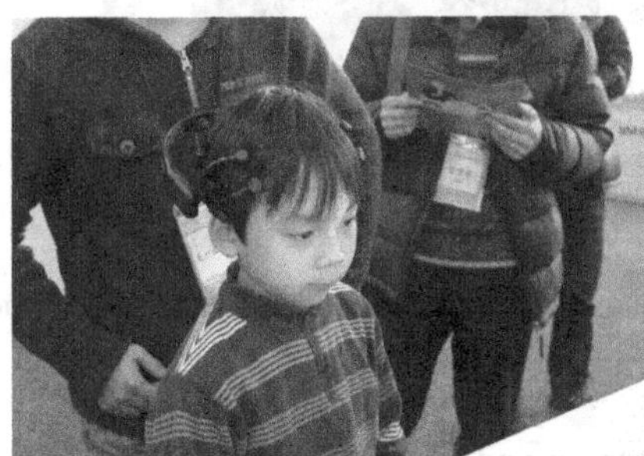

Fig. 1. HCI Design with BCI, Brain-Computer Collaborative Action: *Racing Car Game* designed by Bio-Computing Laboratory at GIST, Korea. EPOC and Carrera Slot Car.[3]

HCI design techniques evolve beyond conscious or direct inputs. Especially, HCI design with Brain-Computer Interface (BCI) shows that the collaborative action of "We" human-and-technology involves both conscious and non-conscious inputs. It expands the collaborative action into a kind of biofeedback. It suggests the brain-signal processing as a new way for collaborative action of "We" human-and-technology.

For example, Racing Car Game (Fig.1) as an ongoing research-led practice about the design of HCI with BCI is constituted by the concentration between human and computer as collaborators. The brain-computer collaborative action changes the car's velocity; it can improve the attention state; when the collaboration between human and computer gets stronger, the concentration level goes higher. In Racing Car Game, brainwave is the key measure. It represents the concentration as the degree of

---

[2] The concept of collaborative action was first presented in HyunKyoung Cho and Joonsung Yoon, "Performative Art: The Politics of Doubleness," *Leonardo*, 42:3 (New York: The MIT Press, 2009), pp. 282—283.

[3] EPOC is as a 14-channel wireless EEG system developed by Emotiv Systems.

collaborative action of "We" human-and-technology. Car's velocity shows the concentration level using electroencephalography (EEG). Racing Car Game's system is implemented under BCI2000 platform (general purpose software in BCI research). Graphical software visualizes concentration index, and hardware module controls the velocity of a racing car.

Fig. 2. Brain Game of "We" human-and-technology: Communication without physical and visible movement[4]

As a new way of HCI design for "We" human-and-technology, the collaborative action through brain activities allows us a communication without physical and visible movement between human and computer (Fig.2). Brain signals create a new philosophical and aesthetic dimension of HCI design constituted by the collaborative action of "We" human-and-technology. In HCI design practices, the collaborative action of "We" human-and-technology becomes an imagination itself; in terms of communications without physical and visible movement and interface. Brain-Computer Interactive design considers the collaborative action of "We" human-and-technology as both knowledge of practical arts and practical arts themselves. It presents that HCI design constituted by collaborative action of "We" human-and-technology stimulates a network of conceptual relations rather than merely perceptions of the visible aspects of singles works.

2 Reflecting

The collaborative action of "We" human-and-technology reflects the knowledge concealing the live relations between technology and human. The human subject-centered

[4] *Racing Car Game* Exhibition. The design of HCI with BCI is a part of my ongoing research project, "Arts in Laboratory: the aesthetic reconstruction of technological experiments."

dichotomy assumes that human controls actions at his own will, while technology is a simple technological tool. It fosters the instrumental understanding on the relationship of technology and human. It defines the collaboration of technology and human as the represented relation that *expresses* the subjective experience through the representation of object. In the knowledge excluding technology as an equal partner, both the technology and humans are subordinated into the instrumental, and the interaction between them remains an impure one, a means to represent the knowledge itself (the knowledge system).

As a new philosophy of HCI design, knowledge of collaborative action of "We" human-and-technology rejects the instrumental rationality, the idea that underlines the collaborative action of "We" human-and-technology as a tool to express the represented knowledge. It might be a solution to overcoming human-subject centered instrumental knowledge. HCI design of "We" human-and-technology proposes a collaborative perspective; 'the collaborative being-with-the technology in the world' [3].[5] It restores the significance of action as what happens in the realm of the performing, and saves the real, lived, and free relation between technology and humans. It ultimately cultivates 'the spirit of humanity' that allows us to be critical, the examined and liberal life from the bondage of habit and custom [4].[6]

In HCI design practices, the collaborative action of "We" human-and-technology reflects the history of action that has been degraded into the instrument to represent thinking. It embraces both the history of ideas (the analysis of systems of representations) and the history of mentalities (the analysis of attitudes and type of action). The reflecting knowledge of HCI design of "We" human-and-technology presents that action is an apex of human activities, insofar as it testifies the multiplicity as the essence of life. In digital environments, the newness is that technology plays a role as a performer (a collaborator) like a human, and the process of technology-human interaction follows the logic of human communication; technology and humans directly acts and reacts as a human-human communication. This reflection of HCI design constituted by the collaborative action of "We" human-and-technology changes what the human is doing; how humans act. It insists that the definition of human action should be reconsidered in the collaborative relationship with technology.

A new philosophy of HCI design stresses that technology and humans reciprocally share the action's process and its result. This sharing weaves a hybrid network constituted by performers (collaborators) in an equitable manner. Thus HCI design performed by collaborative action of "We" human-and-technology leads us to a radical shift of knowledge/power on two points: from the human subject-centered dichotomy to the inter-subjective networking, from knowledge qua thinking to that qua acting. The shifts retain the knowledge, its great intelligence, which does reflect the new human identity constituted by the collaborative action of "We" human-and-technology.

---

[5] Martin Heidegger, *Being and Time* (London: Blackwell Publishing, 1962).

[6] Martha C. Nussbaum, *Cultivating Humanity: A Classical Defense of Reform in Liberal Education* (Cambridge: Harvard University Press, 2003).

3 Performing

The collaborative action of "We" human-and-technology is amplified by design practices of HCI. One of significance quietness of HCI design is that the collaborative action of "We" human-and-technology becomes work itself. As equal collaborators, human and technology communicate using actions, and there is nothing without theirs equal collaboration. The collaborative action of "We" human-and-technology has a structure of reciprocal conversation. In HCI design practices, the process of when the collaborative action of "We" human-and-technology is performed involves with the performative [5].[7]

In this linguistic concept, HCI design of "We" human- and-technology can be considered as a kind of utterance, and the performative action is characterized by the fact that the performativity articulates what happens, embracing action itself as well as consequences and effects of action beyond the propositional content. At this point, HCI design performed by the collaborative action of "We" human-and-technology becomes actually an open work against the fixed meaning and authority.

Within the performing knowledge of HCI design, actions cause epistemological troubles. As a point where we humans meet technology, the performative of HCI design of "We" human-and-technology critiques essentially a fundamental failure of instrumental knowledge based on the logic of opposition. It reveals that the binary frame hides itself from the ways that instrumental knowledge necessarily depends on and requires exclusion. The binary frame is based on homonymous heteronomy. The problem is that the instrumental produces an empty equality because it identifies parts as the part which is separated from the sum of the parts. Although parts identify as a whole, as an entity of equal parts, they are not a whole of equals inasmuch as the instrumental distinguishes between ruler and ruled, inferior and superiors. Instead of an empty idea, HCI design performed by the collaborative action of human and technology notes the network of equals. It means that as a new way introduced by technology, a new notion of the relation of we humans and technology is a network constituted by equality of parts that have no part. It justifies that there is a contesting collaboration between equal parts.

When HCI design is performed by "We" human-and-technology, the relation of we humans and technology is in the 'doing.' The 'doing' related to the placing of 'does' is a curious act especially in a context that would avoid the representational

[7] As J.L Austin's linguistic observations of speech act, performativity is defined as "to say something is to do something." It indicates that the issuing of an utterance is performing not description or representation of actions, but actions. It is identified with the illocutionary and perlocutionary act depending on the extent of consequences and effects arising from the speech act: according to speech act theory, illocutionary acts have certain consequences beyond the propositional content, and perlocutionary acts are utterances that generate a chain of effects. J. L. Austin, *How to Do Things with Words* (Cambridge, MA: Harvard University Press, 1975).

knowledge in which we humans and technology are tied to the instrumental rationality. The regime of representation assumes that 'to do' is to represent. However, knowledge of HCI design performed by collaborative action of "We" human-and-technology insist that 'to do' is to present: 'to do' is what happens in the regime of presentation. 'To do' denies that one of them, humans or technology, determines what is significant and what is not. 'To do' asks questions why must the relation of "We" human-and-technology be placed within one of them?

As the doing of a network of equal parts, HCI design of "We" human-and-technology presents a new definition of the relation of we humans and technology as a way that we perform. We have to perform to know who we are (the characteristics of "We" human-and-technology). The relation between we humans and technology is a mobilization, and thus it misses its own movement. Although "We" human-and-technology is a relation as such, it is not there because it is in the process of happening: it can be addressed as an utterance: a system beyond two systems of thought and action. The visibility of relation that is not there is embodied as a performative way of linking meaning and action, of framing the relation between the sayable and the visible.

In other words, HCI design of "We" human-and-technology happens as 'to do' as it makes visible the system of meaning in real time. It is not a question of meaning being represented by an action. Instead, meaning is understood as action, something that does. And, in that process of 'to do', it attains the performative as the visible. With this performing knowledge of HCI design, the relation of we humans and technology occurs. This occurrence critiques the instrumentalization of technology: the historical and critical ease with which technology is confined to the instrumental. On the other hand, it challenges the idealization of action: an account of action as a form of representation.

As a result, HCI design performed by collaborative action of "We" human-and-technology becomes the non-representational link between two systems of meaning and action. It attains the position of a collaborative relation without characterizing it in either positive or negative terms. It pushes the realm of representational politics to a negative extreme. At the same time, it embraces the significance of its desired social critique and the politics that such a desire assumes. The relation of we humans and technology therefore is in the double determination of commonality and exclusivity. It establishes at one and the same time something common that is both shared and exclusive parts. This double determination structures a network so that everything possessing visibility is assigned a part. The network recalls the "actant-network" in Bruno Latour's insight to embrace both "actors" (who act) and "systems" (which behave) [6].[8] In the performing of HCI design, the relation of we humans and technology is a contested collaboration between actants (equal parts). Here, to become visible is that the relation takes place in equality: in order for mobilization to become visible, the relation must take place in equality. In other words, the equality between actants in network marks a collaboration that arises as soon as actants contest their invisibility

[8] Bruno Latour, *We Have Never Been Modern* (Cambridge: Harvard University Press, 1993).

by the performative. This contesting collaboration is the rational occasion of "We" human-and-technology. As a result, equality cannot be recognized as the object or issue of relation between we humans and technology.

The performativity of contesting collaboration between actants in network is a source for HCI design practices. Through the performing of knowledge, HCI design of "We" human-and-technology enable us to examine further and better identify the notion of individual and social freedom. It provides the key for self-criticism (self-awareness) to decipher our reality. It recalls that "Man's condition, his protects and collaboration with others on tasks that strengthen man's totality, are new issues which require genuine inspiration [7]."[9]

4 Invaginating

Knowledge of HCI design constituted by collaborative action of "We" human-and-technology is invaginatory [8][9].[10] It works in the terrain of the confrontation between the question and its answer. Instead of drawing a line of demarcation between question and answer, it invaginates the two into a solution. Here the invaginating is a 'seeking' to necessity of asking of an answering in a questioning (inquiry). It is an active 'investigating' for an entity both with regard to the fact that the problem of collaborative action is, and with regard to its reading as it is. It is guided beforehand by what is sought. Insofar as seeking something incorporates that which is asked about, knowledge is somehow an investigative questioning of something. In addition to what is asked about, there is a seeking of that which is interrogated.

In this case, HCI design of "We" human-and-technology is a seeking questioning of a movement of critical analysis in which one tries to read how the different questions and answers to the problem have been constructed; but also how theses different questions and answers result from its problem. It appears that any new solutions that might be added to the others would arise from the current problem of knowledge. At this point, we could say that knowledge of HCI design performed by of collaborative action of "We" human-and-technology repeats one another. The essential point is that it is not a mere folding but an immanent and synthetic repetition. It produces the reiterating differences of self-reference in the self-reflexivity.

Especially, HCI design intervenes in power and knowledge relations. It questions the problem of knowledge itself, and poses its answer within its problem. The

---

[9] Frantz Fanon, *The Wretched of The Earth* (New York: Grove Press, 2004), p. 236.

[10] In this study, the concept of invagination refers to Jacques Derrida and Rosaline Krauss's notion. In the discourse of the narrative, Derrida describes it as "the folding of one story within another through the invention of a character who exactly repeats the opening of the first story, thereby setting it off on its narrative course once more." Krauss applies Derrida's notion into the modernist reflexivity of post-medium supported by technology. Derrida, "The Law of Genre," *Glyph 7* (Baltimore: Johns Hopkins University Press, 1980), pp.202-232. Rosaline Krauss, "Two Moments from the Post-Medium Condition," *OCTOBER,* Vol.116, No.1, Spring (New York: The MIT Press, 2006), pp.55-62.

re-conception of knowledge within knowledge reveals an essential lack of the knowledge based on the dichotomy, the binary frame. This lack can be explained with the understanding of supplementation. Philosophy as a knowledge defines the word 'supplement' as something that completes or makes an addition to complete. It means that the supplement supports both completeness and un-completeness, and thus its understanding can be invested in the indeterminacy. However, the supplementary structure has been considered in one perspective that defines the supplement as 'an inessential extra, added to something complete it in itself' [10][11].[11]

The supplement serves to enhance the presence of something that is already complete and self-sufficient. This idea reinforces the dichotomy based on the logic of opposition; this perspective presupposes that the action is a supplement of thought; the object is a supplement of subject; technology is a supplement of humans. When knowledge is rooted from the supplementary structure supporting the logic of opposition, the so-called desire for the neutral such as performed knowledge is degraded as the immoral, ugly, and even dangerous. For example, in a dichotomy, the idea of a university is an attitude (experience) of human subject that represents knowledge of the object for the thinking practice. Judgment depends on the laws of morality and reason based on the logic of opposition of moral and immoral, good and evil; wherein what is universal is parallel to what is moral and good.

As an intervention on the knowledge/power system based on the logic of opposition, HCI design of "We" human-and-technology admits the supplementary structure's incompleteness as the surplus derived from its essential lack [12].[12] Insofar as the supplement is defined as *an unessential extra addition* to completeness itself, it is exactly what was supposed to be complete in itself. It grants that there is a hole originated from the incompleteness of the supplementary structure itself.

The invaginating knowledge of HCI design explains that the supplement does not enhance the completeness's presence, but rather underscores its absence. When the absence, the hole should be filled by something, it is an essential lack. The lack evolves with a desire organized in the relation to action to object. The failure of action

[11] The logic of supplement was taken from Jean Jacques Rousseau. He used the term in order to explain the relationship between speech and writing. Derrida revisited Rousseau's logic of speech supplement. Rousseau notes that writing may become a 'dangerous supplement,' if it is used as a substitute for speech. Whereas, Derrida states that writing can be the supplement of speech. Even if writing is viewed as a supplement to speech, writing may still add meaning to speech, and it may still provide a kind of presence. Here, Derrida's emphasis is that there is an original lack of the supplementary structure rooted in Western thinking. In order to avoid the supplement between writing and speech, Derrida invokes the term invagination. Derrida, *Of Grammatology* (Baltimore: Johns Hopkins University Press, 1998), and "Signature Event Context," *Limited Inc* (Evanston, IL: Northwestern University Press, 1988) pp.1-24.

[12] The word 'lack' was used in Jacque Lacan's view. See, Lacan's "On Freud's "Trieb" and the Psychoanalysis's Desire," *Ecrits* (New York: W.W. Norton & Company, 2005),pp.721-725. Derrida also used the term 'lack' in the discussion of structure. He insists that the supplement is to fill the original lack of Western thinking.

towards the impossible and untouchable object is what we call knowledge as reality constituted by the Real [13].[13]

Acknowledgments. This research is supported by Ministry of Culture, Sports and Tourism (MCST) and Korea Creative Content Agency (KOCCA) in the Culture Technology (CT) Research & Development Program 2012.

References

1. Horkheimer, M., Adorno, T.W.: Dialectic of Enlightenment. Stanford University Press, California (2002)
2. Cho, H.K., Yoon, J.S.: Performative Art: The Politics of Doubleness. Leonardo 42(3), 282–283 (2009)
3. Heidegger, M.: Being and Time. Blackwell Publishing, London (1962)
4. Nussbaum, M.C.: Cultivating Humanity: A Classical Defense of Reform in Liberal Education. Harvard University Press, Cambridge (2003)
5. Austin, J.L.: How to Do Things with Words. Harvard University Press, Cambridge (1975)
6. Latour, B.: We Have Never Been Modern. Harvard University Press, Cambridge (1993)
7. Fanon, F.: The Wretched of the Earth. Grove Press, New York (2004)
8. Derrida, J.: The Law of Genre. In: Glyph 7. Johns Hopkins University Press, Baltimore (1980)
9. Krauss, R.: Two Moments from the Post-Medium Condition. October 116(1) (Spring 2006)
10. Derrida, J.: Of Grammatology. Johns Hopkins University Press, Baltimore (1998)
11. Derrida, J.: Signature Event Context. In: Limited Inc. Northwestern University Press, Evanston (1988)
12. Lacan, J.: Ecrits. W.W. Norton &Company, New York (2005)
13. Marx, K., Engles, F.: The German Ideology. International Publishers Co., New York (1970)

---

[13] Lacanian notion of reality and the Real cannot be explained in the ideology that emphasizes the completeness of the supplementary structure. Lacan defines the reality as an image projected by the Real. This means that the reality is constitutive of the Real. Here, it should be mentioned that the relationship of reality and the Real does not to the completeness as the One, insofar as the reality is constituted by the Real. In the case, the Real is no less than the impossible, uncomplete. At this point, there is a parallel between Lacan and Marx's insight. Marx emphasizes that the real and lived relation (the human condition) is constituted by the actual life-process, not the consciousness. When Marx denies the reality constituted by its consciousness, Marx's 'the actual life-process' corresponds to Lacan's the Real. What both Marx and Lacan want to read is ultimately the problem of knowledge that reinforces the completeness what is supposed to be complete in itself. For the further study of Marx's insight, see Karl Marx and Friedrich Engles, *The German Ideology* (New York: International Publishers Co., 1970).

The Link between Inclusive Design and Innovation: Some Key Elements

Kristin Skeide Fuglerud[1] and David Sloan[2]

[1] Norsk Regnesentral, Gaustadalléen 23, P.O. Box 114, Blindern, NO-0314 Oslo, Norway
kristin.skeide.fuglerud@nr.no
[2] School of Computing, University of Dundee, Scotland, UK
DSloan@computing.dundee.ac.uk

Abstract. It is often said that universal design and similar approaches can be a source of innovation. In this paper key elements in inclusive design are identified, and examples of innovations related to inclusive design are presented. Then, some core elements of the inclusive design process that will help spur innovation are identified. Based on this the link between inclusive design and innovation is discussed. Finally, some recommendations for an inclusive and innovative design process are presented.

Keywords: inclusive design, accessibility, universal design, user-centered design, user diversity, user involvement, innovation.

1 Introduction

The concept of Inclusive design in ICT is being embraced by politicians as a means to include everybody in the information society. An important driver for the push to develop inclusive technology is demographic change. In particular, populations across the Western world are ageing, and there is a need for more efficient ways of taking care of the ageing population, while enabling older people to use ICTs with independence and success. Inclusive ICT products and services are seen as vital tools in meeting these challenges. It is expected that such tools can empower people, and help them to live more independent, active and interconnected lives. Another important driver for inclusive design is developments within the human rights and disability movement. Because ICT is an integrated part of the society, it is recognized that being able to take part in the information society is a prerequisite to fully be able to take part in the society, and thus inclusive ICT is needed.

While policy makers and human rights advocates have embraced the ideas of inclusive design, it seems necessary with more conviction in order to make the industry, service owners, and buyers embrace these ideas. Common arguments for why industry should do inclusive design are ethics - it is the right thing to do, demographics and customer satisfaction - a growing component of the customer base, in number and in economic power, is older people, commercial - increasing the potential customer base, and legislative and regulatory concerns - more and more countries includes

M. Kurosu (Ed.): Human-Computer Interaction, Part I, HCII 2013, LNCS 8004, pp. 41–50, 2013.

clauses about accessibility in their legislation. Another important driver for inclusive design is that it can lead to innovative designs [1-3].

While the overall motivation, principles and design objectives of inclusive design are quite easy to grasp, it is less clear when it comes to details in how to do this in practice [4]. The main objective in this paper is to take a closer look at what elements are considered important in an inclusive design process; and to link this with experiences of what have been important aspects of research and development resulting in inclusive innovations. Finally some concrete suggestions for key features of an innovative and inclusive design process are given.

2 Key Elements of Inclusive Design

There are several design approaches that encompass the goal of producing ICT products and services that can be used by broad and diverse populations, including disabled, elderly people and people with poor ICT skills, people with reading and writing difficulties, the poor or otherwise disadvantaged users, etc. Examples of such design approaches are "Universal Design" [5], "Universal Usability"[3], "Universal Access" [6], "User Sensitive Inclusive Design" [7], "Inclusive Design [8], "Design for all" [9], and Ability Based Design [10]. In this paper, these design directions are labelled inclusive design approaches (IDA).

While many think of IDA as design for disabled people, the general intention of these approaches is to design mainstream ICT such that it can be used by as many people as possible, including elderly and disabled people. In the following we discuss some elements that can be regarded as key elements of these approaches. Adherence to standards and guidelines is a frequently mentioned approach in IDA. Guidelines from the W3C's Web Accessibility Initiative (WAI) are commonly referred to. Examples of international standards are ISO/IEC 40500:2012 Information Technology - W3C Web Content Accessibility Guidelines (WCAG) 2.0 [11] and ISO 9241:2008, Ergonomics of human-system interaction – Part 20 Accessibility guidelines for information/communication technology (ICT) [12] and Part 171: Guidance on software accessibility [13]. While there is broad consensus that following accessibility standards and guidelines is usually a precondition for accessible design, a number of authors have noted that this this is not enough to achieve genuine inclusive experiences. A solution that conforms to accessibility guidelines may be technically or theoretically accessible, but at the same it may be so difficult to use for certain user groups that it is hard or even impossible to use in practice [14]. Guidelines and standards are helpful to remove many accessibility barriers, but far from all.

Results from empirical research have suggested that conformance to WCAG 2.0 will only solve about half of the problems encountered by visually impaired users [15]. It is necessary to complement with other methods such as evaluations with disabled users [15, 16]. Therefore, many researchers have arrived at the conclusion that in addition to conformance with accessibility guidelines, IDA needs to be based on principles of user-centered design (UCD) [16-18]. A central standard for UCD is ISO 9241-210:2010 Ergonomics of human-system interaction. Part 210: Human-centred design for interactive systems. In this standard the term "human" is used instead of "user" in order to emphasize that it addresses a number of stakeholders, not just those typically considered as direct users of a system. According to this standard, a human-centred approach includes the following principles: The design is based upon an explicit understanding of users, tasks and environments; users are involved throughout design and development; the design is driven and refined by user-centered evaluation; the process is iterative; the design addresses the whole user experience; and the design team includes multidisciplinary skills and perspectives. Thus, the key elements of inclusive design processes can be summarized as:

- Include multidisciplinary skills and perspectives,
- adapt and apply accessibility guidelines and standards,
- iterative development,
- focus on users with diverse accessibility needs and their usage contexts early and throughout the development process,
- evaluate designs with elderly and people with disabilities, and
- focus on the whole user experience.

3 Examples of Innovations Related to Inclusive Design

It is interesting to observe that many efforts at developing technology to assist people with some kind of disability has resulted in innovations which later have laid the foundation for a broad range of mainstream technology [19]. An example is the work of Alexander Graham Bell who was concerned with aiding deaf people to communicate. In 1875, he came up with a simple receiver that could turn electricity into sound. This research has later inspired the invention of the microphone, speaker, telephone, speech recognition, speech synthesis, stereophonic recording and the transistor [19].

Other examples include text-messaging over land lines for deaf people, which later developed into mobile telephone text messaging, early remote control systems which was first developed for motor-impaired people and predictive text systems also first developed for motor-impaired people used, later picked up and developed into T9 word prediction systems in mobile phones [2]. Likewise, assistive technology for blind people has inspired the development of a browser which translates content from Web pages into speech. This technology can provide web access to anyone in eyes busy-environments in [19].

In the book "Innovating with people: The business of inclusive design", a number of successful cases from different design disciplines are presented, among them travel information systems, a telecommunication product – the Two Tone Phone, and the Norwegian governments website `www.gowernment.no` [20].

During the last decade several design challenge events have been conducted to encourage industry to engage in inclusive design. This has for example been done at the European Business Conference (EBC); The Vodafone Smart Accessibility award scheme for mobile phone apps [21] and the SS12 Code for a Cause competition [22] are other examples. The basic idea of such events is to let designers – who may be professionals, or students - work with disabled people to solve a real-world design challenge. Several such design challenge projects have been widely praised and even resulted in new business opportunities [21, 23]. Companies involved in such events have stated that inclusive design can be especially valuable as a source of innovation and differentiation [24].

The final example is taken from a semester long design class where students were given the task of designing something for a grandparent [25]. The undergraduate teams included students from product design, interaction design and art programmes. The student assignment was to design networked objects for a grandparent. While the students would learn about elderly people as a group, they would at the same time deliberately design for an individual and not a whole population. The results in this particular class stood out from other similar design classes. The panellists from industry, chosen to give expert critique after the student presentations, were impressed by the originality and creativity of the student projects [25].

4 Experiences from Design of Inclusive Innovations

In reflecting on why the student project referred to above made such an impact, the authors highlight several aspects [25]. Among them is the importance of designing for one particular person in contrast to a group or a whole population. It is pointed out that the details, far from being mere details, actually are what constitutes the design [25]. Designing for a grandparent meant that the students could develop deep knowledge and an empathic relationship with the user. It is also pointed out that the student teams were multi-disciplinary. Similarly, one of the winners of the Vodafone Smart Accessibility award originally made the app for his five year-old autistic son. It had more than 4000 users two years after its first release [24]. Although one cannot generalise from one disabled individual to all people with similar impairments, these examples demonstrate that an in-depth exploration of a single case can spur new and creative ideas. When interviewing participants in the EBC inclusive design challenge mentioned in the previous section, it was found that designers considered the opportunity to interact with disabled people as particularly useful and valuable [26]. The interaction with disabled people during the design informed them about latent problems that they would not have predicted otherwise [23].

In the book "Design and the Digital Divide – Insights from 40 years in computer support for older and disable people", Alan F. Newell reflects on the development of assistive technologies that later made the way into mainstream products. When considering the development of the predecessor technology for TV subtitles he says; "The most important aspects of this research were the multi-disciplinary approach of detailed research into the requirements of deaf viewers and the analysis of the captioning process" [2]. In other words, the research team acquired a deep knowledge of the user group in question, i.e. the deaf people, and of the application area in question, i.e. the captioning process. The importance of examining the use of any system in real contexts is also emphasised [2]. In a report conducted by the National Council of Disability in the US it was found that that leadership, more than any other single factor, accounted for the various agencies embrace of accessibility and for success in achieving it [27, 28]. The leadership had taken different forms in the different agencies. However, in all the cases a person's leadership and engagement seemed to have sprung out of some kind of life experience or personal commitment, and this had evolved into sustained efforts in the workplace. Thus, it is not unlikely that such commitment has sprung out of a deep understanding and knowledge about the situation of disabled people, either because of own disability or disability of a person whom which they had a close relationship to.

A number of successful cases from different design disciplines are presented [20]. In all the cases, various people-centered research techniques were used, and the selected approaches in each case are described. They vary from being low contact methods, such as questionnaires, to medium contact methods, such as interviews, to high contact methods, such as workshops with users. The people-centered research in the cases are characterized by being based on real life first hand observation, or direct information through dialogue, mostly performed in context and involving older or disabled users and other users that challenges the design.

In general, there is a growing recognition among researchers of the crucial role of users in innovation. Empirical research from world-class best practices innovation companies has found that market orientation, and customer knowledge is one of the key factors that drive innovation. Getting close to the customer is a top priority in industrial innovation [29], and users are found to be important in radical and especially in discontinuous innovation [30]. In order to suggest fruitful changes to a situation, it is necessary to understand the situation as it is. A deep understanding of particular users and their context can provide excellent conditions for creativity that matters [31]. The deep knowledge acquired are valuable when the development teams need to evaluate and prioritize ideas based on how well they may fit into or enhance a particular situation for particular users [31]. Although acquiring such deep knowledge may take some time in the beginning, it can also improve design efficiency because it can help to limit the exploration of dead ends. The benefits of user involvement to software design have been shown in several studies, and lack of user involvement has repeatedly been associated with failed software projects [32].

Also newer forms of user involvement seem to be promising. In one study it was found that crowdsourcing among users can actually outperform professional idea generation, particularly when it comes to ideas to solve their own needs, and providing that the users had some knowledge about existing solutions [33].

5 Inclusive Design Practise in Industry

Studies of inclusive design practices in the ICT industry reveal that there is a gap between theory and practice, i.e., design practices in industry does not include all the key elements of inclusive design. While automated accessibly tools have a strong attraction in terms of efficiency, manual evaluations and evaluations with users are less frequently performed [16]. Tight delivery deadlines may be an important obstacle [23]. It is found that the concept of iterative development is not always fully understood, and that it can be difficult to incorporate it in a development organization because it does not fit well with the organization's project management methods or the business plans [34]. Another major obstacle is that design teams may have difficulty gaining access to representative users, and particularly users with disabilities [23]. It is also found that designers worry that they may inadvertently offend people with disabilities because of lack of experience in interacting with them [23].

Encouragingly, ethnographic approaches which are used to gain deep insight and knowledge about human domains, have become increasingly popular. Such approaches are not only used in academia, but also by successful design teams in industry, such as at Xerox Palto Alto Research Center [24], IDEO and Microsoft [31].

6 Discussion

There is a pressure on industry to make inclusive products and services. The emphasis is on conformance to accessibility standards and guidelines. Surveys of industry practices indicate that important principles of inclusive design, such as user involvement and iterative design are not followed, although there are exceptions. From the examples presented in this paper, it seems that deep knowledge of older and disabled users and their context has been important in many successful inclusive design stories. The role of interdisciplinary teams and close engagement with users are frequently mentioned. It must be emphasized that the examples in this paper are not drawn from an exhaustive study of inclusive innovations and all the circumstances surrounding them. Therefore, there may be other common characteristics of these cases, other than those mentioned above, which has also been important for the development of the aforementioned innovations. Drawing of conclusions must therefore be made with caution. Nevertheless, the examples, experiences and research referred to above suggest that acquiring a deep and detailed knowledge of disabled people and their needs in relation to a context, such as a particular situation or application area, has been important in inclusive design innovations. Moreover, several such innovations have sprung out of work based on few users, or even one single user. Pullin [35] illustrate this point by a quote by Dunne; "Populations can validate a design, but individuals can inspire new thinking". While usability and accessibility testing is valuable in order to uncover usability and accessibility problems, evaluation by itself is not particularly effective for soliciting constructive suggestions from users about how to improve a design. It is mainly a means to identify problems, not to provide solutions [36]. In order to inspire suggestions high contact methods, such as participatory design may be more suitable [37]. Moreover, it seems that genuine innovation and effective inclusive design stems from involving disabled people early and throughout the design cycle, rather than as subjects of accessibility testing of more or less finished designs. However, in order to let disabled participants contribute, the methods used need to be inclusive. Examples of some interesting approaches to modifying existing methods to enable people with specific accessibility needs to take part design activities is described in [38].

An important reason that technology developed for people with disabilities has resulted in mainstream innovations, is that there is often an overlap between the needs of people who have a particular disability and the needs users without disabilities in particular contexts or situations. Careful design for disabled people can result in technology that can be useful in situations or contexts where one or more senses or abilities are constrained [39, 40]. Disabled people can contribute with very creative ideas by suggesting unusual ways of doing things, or even by describing how they use existing technology and solutions in new or alternative ways. Because people with disabilities have had to cope with specific needs in various situations during their life, they have lots of experience with ways to cope. They have developed practices that are effective in accommodating their particular needs in particular situations. In that way, people with disabilities have a much broader base of experience related to certain design challenges, such as designs for situations where a capability are constrained, than people without disabilities do. This base of experience can be a rich source of ideas and creativity. For example, a blind person may have a lot of experience in of how to manage and operate technology without vision, which can be valuable when developing technology for situations where eyes are busy or for technology without a screen, etc. Some of the main obstacles to the uptake of inclusive design in the ICT -industry are related to perception, technical barriers and organizational barriers [1]. The perception barrier may be related to the seemingly elusive goal of designing for everybody. The goal of designing for everybody may easily give an impression of something that is totally utopian and impossible to do. The question is, where to start if we wish to complement the guidelines based approach, how shall we go about it, what type of users should we look for and how many users is enough?

Are there some useful strategies for selecting and involving users? Pullin et al [35] suggest focusing on "outriders", or so-called "extra-ordinary" users. These extra-ordinary users are older users with multiple minor disabilities and users with some severe disabilities, but otherwise in the target population of the solution in question. Another similar approach may be to select "edge-cases", i.e. disabled people who are on the borderline of being able to use a product, but who would commonly be expected to be able to use it [41]. In [20] "lead users" are users that places greater demands on a product or system and therefore challenges it in ways beyond that of the average mainstream user. The lead users can be older people, people with disabilities, children or people with diverse cultural backgrounds. The selected users should be included in the design process from the beginning to inspire innovation. If selected carefully, involving between six to twelve people in such a process can be enough [20]. In order to ensure inclusivity however, the design should also be evaluated with broader samples of users [41].

Parallel design is another approach to broaden the design space and not to narrow into one idea too soon. Research suggests that when designers create multiple alternatives in parallel, they produce higher quality, more diverse work and experience a greater increase in self-efficacy [37]. A suggestion is to create parallel design for users with reductions in different types of capabilities (e.g. vision, hearing, mobility and cognition), and then work to integrate these ideas into one solution [42]. This allow for insight into each case and a period of concentration on coming up with god design ideas for each case. By doing it in parallel, it can be done without increasing the overall design period. A less resource-intensive approach could be to consider seeking out alternative and existing products working for various user groups as inspiration in the first parallel design phase. These solutions should have some similarities with the design task at hand, or at least have related or interesting parts. The search for such products should include assistive technology. After the initial exploration some of the best ideas are combined into one solution. There may be conflicts between user groups, and therefore, the deep knowledge of each of the cases is essential in order to be able to identify impossible solutions and to prioritize design ideas that may not work for certain user groups. This knowledge can also be used to decide whether particular features or functionality should be common for all users, or whether personalisation or adaption based on user profiles might be appropriate.

7 Conclusion

There is evidence that some of the key principles for inclusive design, namely engagement with users with disabilities, as well as iterative design are rarely followed in industry, although there are some noticeable exceptions. Thus, there is currently a gap between theory of inclusive design and practices in industry. At the same time there is a political and legislative pressure for industry to develop inclusive ICT-solutions. However, the legislative requirements tend to put a too one-sided focus on accessibility standards which do not emphasize the development process. By reducing inclusive design to a matter of compliance to accessibility standards, one do not only risk designing solutions that are in practice not particularly inclusive, but one also risk missing out on one major potential gain of inclusive design, namely the potential for innovation. Finally, some suggestions for inclusive design processes that may spur innovation are provided.

Acknowledgements. The work with this paper has been partly financed by the Norwegian research council through the e-Me project. Special thanks to Abertay University Dundee, UK, which hosted the first author during autumn 2012, and colleagues at Dundee University, UK, whose work within inclusive design has been a rich source of inspiration.

References

1. Dong, H., Keates, S., Clarkson, P.J.: Inclusive Design in Industry: Barriers, Drivers and the Business Case. In: Stary, C., Stephanidis, C. (eds.) UI4ALL 2004. LNCS, vol. 3196, pp. 305–319. Springer, Heidelberg (2004)
2. Newell, A.F.: Design and the Digital Divide: Insights from 40 years in Computer Support for Older and Disabled People. Morgan & Claypool Publishers (2011)
3. Shneiderman, B., Hochheiser, H.: Universal usability as a stimulus to advanced interface design. Behaviour & Information Technology 20, 367–376 (2001)
4. Keates, S., Clarkson, P.J.: Countering design exclusion: bridging the gap between usability and accessibility. Universal Access in the Information Society 2, 215–225 (2003)
5. Center for Universal Design, NC State University, http://www.ncsu.edu/project/design-projects/udi/center-for-universal-design/the-principles-of-universal-design/

6. Stephanidis, C., Savidis, A.: Universal Access in the Information Society: Methods, Tools, and Interaction Technologies. Universal Access in the Information Society 1, 40–55 (2001)
7. Gregor, P., Newell, A.F., Zajicek, M.: Designing for dynamic diversity: interfaces for older people. In: Proceedings of the Fifth International ACM Conference on Assistive Technologies, pp. 151–156. ACM (2002)
8. Clarkson, J.P., Coleman, R., Keates, S., Lebbon, C. (eds.): Inclusive design: Design for the whole population. Springer, London (2003)
9. European Design for All e-Accessibility Network, `http://www.edean.org`
10. Wobbrock, J.O., Kane, S.K., Gajos, K.Z., Haradam, S., Froehlich, J.: Ability-Based Design: Concept, Principles and Examples. ACM Trans. Access. Comput. 3, 1–27 (2011)
11. ISO/IEC 40500:2012: Information Technology – W3C Web Content Accessibility Guidelines (WCAG) 2.0 (2012)
12. ISO 9241-20:2008: Ergonomics of human-system interaction - Part 20: Accessibility guidelines for information/communication technology (ICT) equipment and services. ISO (2008)
13. ISO 9241-171:2008: Ergonomics of human-system interaction - Part 171: Guidance on software accessibility, p. 88. ISO (2008)
14. Theofanos, M.F., Redish, J.: Bridging the gap: between accessibility and usability. Interactions 10, 36–51 (2003)
15. Power, C., Freire, A.P., Petrie, H., Swallow, D.: Guidelines are only half of the story: accessibility problems encountered by blind users on the web. In: Proceedings of the SIGCHI Conference on Human Factors in Computing Systems, Austin, Texas, USA, pp. 433–442. ACM (2012)
16. Arrue, M., Vigo, M., Abascal, J.: Automatic Evaluation of Mobile Web Accessibility. In: Stephanidis, C., Pieper, M. (eds.) ERCIM Ws UI4ALL 2006. LNCS, vol. 4397, pp. 244–260. Springer, Heidelberg (2007)
17. Kelly, B., Sloan, D., Brown, S., Seale, J., Lauke, P., Ball, S., Smith, S.: Accessibility 2.0: Next steps for web accessibility. Journal of Access Services 6, 265–294 (2009)
18. Paddison, C., Englefield, P.: Applying heuristics to perform a rigorous accessibility inspection in a commercial context. In: Proceedings of the 2003 Conference on Universal Usability, Vancouver, British Columbia, Canada. ACM (2003)
19. Jacobs, S.: Fueling the Creation of New Electronic Curbcuts, vol. 2012. The Center for an accessible society (1999), `http://www.accessiblesociety.org/topics/technology/eleccurbcut.htm`
20. Eikhaug, O., Gherawo, R., Plumbe, C., Berg, M.S., Kunur, M. (eds.): Innovating with people. The business of inclusive design. The Norwegian Design Council (2010)
21. Dredge, S.: Android apps scoop prizes in 2012 Smart Accessibility Awards contest (2012), `http://www.guardian.co.uk/technology/appsblog/2012/dec/17/2012-smart-accessibility-apps-awards`
22. Project: Possibility, `http://ss12.info/`
23. Dong, H., Keates, S., Clarkson, P.J., Cassim, J.: Implementing Inclusive Design: The Discrepancy between Theory and Practice. In: Carbonell, N., Stephanidis, C. (eds.) UI4ALL 2002. LNCS, vol. 2615, pp. 106–117. Springer, Heidelberg (2003)
24. Dong, H., Cassim, J., Coleman, R.: Addressing the Challenges of Inclusive Design: A Case Study Approach. In: Stephanidis, C., Pieper, M. (eds.) ERCIM Ws UI4ALL 2006. LNCS, vol. 4397, pp. 273–286. Springer, Heidelberg (2007)
25. Pullin, G., Rogers, J., Banks, R., Regan, T., Napier, A., Duplock, P.: Social Digital Objects for Grandparents. In: Include 2011 Conference on Inclusive and People-centred Design. Royal College of Art, London (2011)

26. Dong, H., Keates, S., Clarkson, J.: Inclusive design in industry: motivations and barriers. SIGCAPH Comput. Phys. Handicap., 9–10 (2003)
27. NCD: The accessible future. National Council on Disability (2001)
28. Kline, J.: Strategic IT Accessibility: Enabling the Organization. Live Oak Book Company (2011)
29. Shum, P., Lin, G.: A world class new product development best practices model. International Journal of Production Research 45, 1609–1629 (2007)
30. Kyng, M.: Bridging the Gap Between Politics and Techniques: On the next practices of participatory design. Scandinavian Journal of Information Systems 22, Article 5 (2010)
31. Blomberg, J., Burrell, M., Guest, G.: An ethnographic approach to design. In: Julie, A.J., Andrew, S. (eds.) The Human-Computer Interaction Handbook: Fundamentals, Evolving Technologies and Emerging Applications, pp. 964–986. L. Erlbaum Associates Inc. (2003)
32. Kujala, S.: Effective user involvement in product development by improving the analysis of user needs. Behaviour & Information Technology 27, 457–473 (2008)
33. Poetz, M.K., Schreier, M.: The Value of Crowdsourcing: Can Users Really Compete with Professionals in Generating New Product Ideas? Journal of Product Innovation Management 29, 245–256 (2012)
34. Cajander, Å.: Usability - Who Cares? The introduction of User-Centered Systems Design in Organisations. Faculty of Science and Technology, PhD, p. 122. Uppsala University (2011)
35. Pullin, G., Newell, A.F.: Focussing on Extra-Ordinary Users. In: Stephanidis, C. (ed.) HCI 2007, Part I. LNCS, vol. 4554, pp. 253–262. Springer, Heidelberg (2007)
36. Tohidi, M., Buxton, W., Baecker, R., Sellen, A.: Getting the right design and the design right. In: Proceedings of the SIGCHI Conference on Human Factors in Computing Systems, Monteal, Quebec, Canada, pp. 1243–1252. ACM (2006)
37. Dow, S.P., Glassco, A., Kass, J., Schwarz, M., Schwartz, D.L., Klemmer, S.R.: Parallel prototyping leads to better design results, more divergence, and increased self-efficacy. ACM Trans. Comput.-Hum. Interact. 17, 1–24 (2010)
38. Prior, S., Waller, A., Kroll, T.: Focus groups as a requirements gathering method with adults with severe speech and physical impairments. Behaviour & Information Technology, 1–10 (2011)
39. Vanderheiden, G.: Fundamental principles and priority setting for universal usability. In: Proceedings on the 2000 Conference on Universal Usability, Arlington, Virginia, United States. ACM Press (2000)
40. Fuglerud, K.S.: Universal design in ICT services. In: Vavik, T. (ed.) Inclusive Buildings, Products & Services: Challenges in Universal Design, Trondheim, Norway, pp. 244–267 (2009)
41. Keates, S.: Designing for Accessibility: A Business Guide to Countering Design Exclusion. Lawrence Erlbaum Associates, Inc., Publishers, Mahwah (2007)
42. Savidis, A., Stephanidis, C.: Unified user interface design: designing universally accessible interactions. Interacting with Computers 16, 243–270 (2004)

Tuning an HCI Curriculum for Master Students to Address Interactive Critical Systems Aspects

Michel Galindo[1], Célia Martinie[1], Philippe Palanque[1], Marco Winckler[1], and Peter Forbrig[2]

[1] IRIT, Université Paul Sabatier
118, route de Narbonne
31062 Toulouse Cedex 9, France
{galindo,martinie,palanque,winckler}@irit.fr
[2] Universität Rostock, Institut für Informatik,
Albert-Einstein-Straße 22, 18051 Rostock,
Germany
peter.forbrig@uni-rostock.de

Abstract. This paper presents the need for specific curricula in order to address the training of specialists in the area of Interactive Critical Systems. Indeed, while curricula are usually built in order to produce specialists in one discipline (e.g. computer science) dealing with systems or products requires training in multiple disciplines. The area of Interactive Critical Systems requires deep knowledge in computer science, dependability, Human-Computer Interaction and safety engineering. We report in this paper how these various disciplines have been integrated in a master program at Université Toulouse III, France and highlight the carrier paths followed by the graduated students and how these carriers are oriented towards aeronautics and space application domains.

1 Introduction

Since the advent of personal computing, the average expertise of users in terms of computers science is constantly dropping. Accordingly, user interface usability (efficiency, effectiveness and satisfaction) has become increasingly important in software development in particularly because this aspect can determine the adoption or rejection of the entire software [1]. Nowadays, the user interface takes a very important share of design and development tasks in modern software development [4]. Aware of the fact that designers and developers need appropriate training to cope with users' needs and expectations about the user interface of interactive systems, the Association for Computing Machinery[1] (ACM) and the International Federation for Information processing (IFIP) hold permanent working groups for promoting the education on Human-Computer Interaction (HCI).

[1] ACM Special Interest Group on Computer Human Interaction : http://www.sigchi.org/

M. Kurosu (Ed.): Human-Computer Interaction, Part I, HCII 2013, LNCS 8004, pp. 51–60, 2013.

The occurrence of HCI courses in undergraduate programs is essential to present concepts (e.g. usability, accessibility, User Experience [2]) and techniques (e.g. prototyping [7], user interface evaluation) necessary for designing user-centered interactive systems. In the last years there were increasing numbers of undergraduate programs in Computer Science that propose courses of Introduction to Human-Computer Interaction (HCI) in their curriculum. However, these courses rarely exceed 40 hours (in front of student), which is by far not enough to prepare students to work as usability professionals. However, this kind of course makes it possible for them to understand the underlying development process of User Centered approaches [5], to cooperate with specialists in that domain and to understand the costs and benefits of such approaches [2]. In order to cover this gap, specialized master 2 programs have been created in the last decade around the world (see the list of HCI programs provided by Gary Perlman [6]).

It goes without saying that the success of graduating programs in HCI is related to an increasing demand for professionals with a strong understanding of usability and user experience. The interests of the industry can easily be measured in terms of internship and job offers. However, there is a paradox: whilst some companies look for professionals with very specific skills (e.g. usability evaluation methods, development of multimodal interaction techniques, etc.) to fill a position in development teams, others companies have limited competencies in HCI in-house so that they recruit professionals to initiate a usability culture inside their organization. Moreover, graduate programs should cope with companies' expectations in terms of required technological background (e.g. mobile, Web, multimodal interfaces, etc.) and knowledge on the idiosyncrasy of the application domains (e.g. gaming, workspace applications, safety-critical systems, airspace, e-government, healthcare etc.).

2 The Basics of a Curriculum in HCI

Fig. 1 presents the map of HCI as it appears in the curriculum of HCI[2] proposed by ACM Special Interest Group on Computer Human Interaction. As stated in this curriculum, the area of HCI can be split in 4 main groups of content: (U) the use and context of computers, (H) human characteristics, (C) computer system and interface architecture, and (D) the development process.

As this curriculum has been developed in the early 90s it clearly represent an "old-fashioned" view of the domain of HCI but it is important to note that it is far away from obsolete as new development in the field can very easily positioned within this framework. One underlying assumption from this map is that there is one user interacting in a static way with a single computer with an input device being a mouse and one output device being a screen. The development process (section D) clearly exhibit's the iterative nature of development in order to address evolutions of user needs and improve usability through evaluations.

[2] `http://old.sigchi.org/cdg/cdg2.html` retrieved March 1st, 2013.

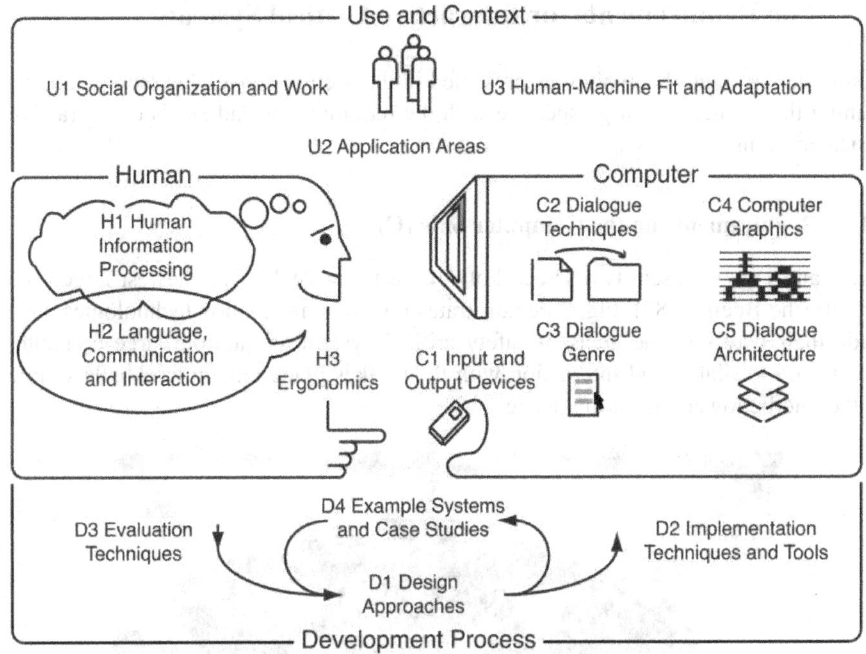

Fig. 1. Representation of the content of Human-Computer Interaction[1]

Current development in the area of HCI would propose evolutions to this map adding at least:

- For the computer side (C): the interaction with multiple combined input devices going beyond the mouse including multimodal input [12] (e.g. touch and multi-touch interactions) and multimedia output. Evolutions should also gather new technologies such as interaction on the move with mobile devices.
- For the Human side (H): interactions now take place mainly in a multi-user perspective including collaborative activities and social computing [13]. These capabilities have strong impacts on the computer aspects bringing in the perspectives of distributive systems together with privacy and security aspects [10] which usually conflict with usability [8] and user experience [15].
- For the development side (D): iterative processes have made their way in the area of software engineering with the trends of agile processes and extreme programming [14] however inclusion of usability aspects within them remains a challenge only addressed by researchers in the area of HCI [9].
- For the use and context (U): new interactions have spread in many contexts, environments and organizations due to the simultaneous distribution of computing devices at home and in the workplace.

3 The Requirements for Interactive Critical Systems

Taking into account the evolutions presented in the section above, this section aims at refining them when put in perspective with the requirements and needs of interactive critical systems.

3.1 Requirements on the Computer Side (C)

Fig. 2 and Fig. 3 present two screenshots of the flight deck of the newest large civil aircraft (the Boeing 787). Fig. 2 demonstrates how new interaction technologies have made their way into the areas of safety critical system as multiple large computer screens are available and interaction with them takes place though trackballs visible on the middle lower part of the image.

Fig. 2. The Interactive Cockpit of new Civil Aircrafts (here Boeing 787[3])

Fig. 3 is an image of the head-up display providing contextual information to the pilots. This information has to be used by the pilot crew simultaneously with the ones provided on the large displays.

Fig. 3. Close-up view of the Boeing 787 head up display

[3] Image from `http://www.aviationnews.eu/`

Future aircraft cockpits are likely to embed touch interactions which fits perfectly with the long lasting trend of embedding new interaction technologies in the area of critical systems when they reach the adequate level of maturity. We can even see that the speed of take up of interaction technologies is correlated to the level of criticality of the domain. In Air Traffic Management voice and tactile interactions were considered many years ago [16] and more recently for satellite ground segments [17].

3.2 Requirements on the Human Side (H)

Safety, privacy and security [18] have to be handled in a coherent way identifying potential conflicts early enough and ensuring their adequate treatment. Regulatory authorities in the various areas of critical systems add constraints to deal with issues related to argumentation and traceability of choices (see next section on development process). Addressing cooperation mechanisms for action and decision [20], human error [22], impact of automation [21] on human behavior are key elements of the overall resilience of the interactive critical system [19].

3.3 Requirements on the Development Process Side (D)

While HCI and discount software engineering approaches promote iterative processes producing rapidly modifiable artifacts, interactive critical systems call for systematic verifiable methods, processes and tools to provide means of assessing the resilience of the systems. New phases within the development process appear with prominent places such as traceability (as required in standards such as DO178B [24] and ESARR 6 [23]), training [25], barrier identifications and incident/accident analysis [19] and support for certification [24]. Some recent contributions have proposed complex processes trying to bridge this, at first glance, unbridgeable gaps [26].

3.4 Requirements on the Context and Use Side (U)

As for most of the interactive applications, interactive critical systems have to address different requirements depending on the application domain under consideration. For instance, certification is only required for systems with high risks to the citizen (such as nuclear power plants or large civil aircrafts) and is not present for military systems or satellite ground segments. However, some invariants remain including training of operators (as the systems are usually complex), means for addressing scalability and deep knowledge of the underlying engineering principles of these systems.

4 HCI Curriculum of the M2IHM Master Program

Previous section has in fact highlighted the needs for extensions of standard curriculum in HCI to encompass requirements from the safety critical area. We will show how such requirements have been deployed in a 2 years master on HCI programme at Université Toulouse III – Paul Sabatier.

The M2IHM[4] is a Master 2 program on Human-Computer Interaction that is jointly held by the University Paul Sabatier (UPS) and the National School of Civil Aviation (*Ecole Nationale d'Aviation Civile* - ENAC) in Toulouse, France. It is basically an option for the final year (i.e. 5th) of studies in Computer Science. The M2IHM, based in Toulouse, France, was created in September 2000 and it is the pioneer in HCI Education in France.

Students should apply for one of the 25 positions available, and, despite it is not officially an international master program, >15% of the students come from abroad (e.g. Germany, Spain, China, Tunisia). The main goal of the M2IHM is to teach HCI to students that follow a prior education on Computer Sciences. After following the M2IHM courses, students should also develop skills in HCI such as be able to: i) carry on projects using a user-centered design approach; ii) understand, chose and apply ergonomic recommendations whenever it is appropriate; iii) assess the qualities and defects of a user interface.

4.1 Organization and Content

The M2IHM program is deployed in two semesters (see Table 1). The first semesters is dedicated to courses whilst the second semesters is devoted to a group project called *"chef d'œuvre"* and an internship. The *"chef d'œuvre"* is an exploratory study during which the students can identify and assess different design option for a given interactive system, mainly proposed by industrial partners. This project is carried out by a group of 3-4 students and should cover all phases of the development process of an interactive system. It also must include a bibliographical survey. The internship occurs between 18-26 weeks and should be performed in an industrial context or with a research lab. The subject requires a prior approval from the pedagogical team.

Table 1. Teaching units of the M2IHM for 2011-2012

Semester 1 (total 457 hours)	
Teaching units	**Lessons / Contents**
UE 1 : Human factors	• Cognitive models of human processing • Software ergonomics • Task analysis and task modeling • Usability evaluation methods • Inquiry methods for HCI • Statistics applied to HCI • Accessibility and universal design • Requirement analysis for interactive systems
UE 2 : Methodologies for research in HCI	• Engineering interactive systems • Principles of empirical HCI research
UE 3 : Information visualization	• Information representation and display • 2D visualization and interaction
UE 4 : Design and development of user interfaces	• Development process of interactive systems • Prototyping and Agile methods

[4] *Master 2 Interaction Homme-Machine*: `http://www.masterihm.fr`

Table 1. *(continued)*

UE 5 : Interaction techniques and application domains	• Multimodal interaction techniques • Interaction techniques for the Web • Collaborative Systems • Mobile applications • 3D visualization and interaction • Multimedia systems
UE 6 : Programming techniques for interactive systems	• Component-based software for interactive systems (COM and Net-Beans) • Participatory design • Web technologies • UML for HCI • Advanced programming for HCI
UE 7 : English and Project Management	• English (training for TOEIC/TOFFEL) • Project management

Semester 2	
Teaching units	**Lessons / Contents**
"Chef d'œuvre"	• Exploratory project
Internship	• Internship in the industry or research lab

4.2 Application Domains of Internships

The internships performed by the M2IHM student can be classified in five main application domains: aeronautics and aerospace, automotive, desktop applications, multimedia & Web, and new interaction techniques. As show by Fig. 4, 41% of internships performed from 2001 to 2010 occurred in the domain of aeronautics and aerospace which can be easily explained by the strong presence of companies like EADS/Airbus, Thales Avionics, Eurocopter, *Centre National d'Etudes Spatiales* (CNES). Desktop and office applications, which includes the development of collaborative systems, graphical editors and improvement of the ergonomic of existing applications, comes in second with 26% of internships.

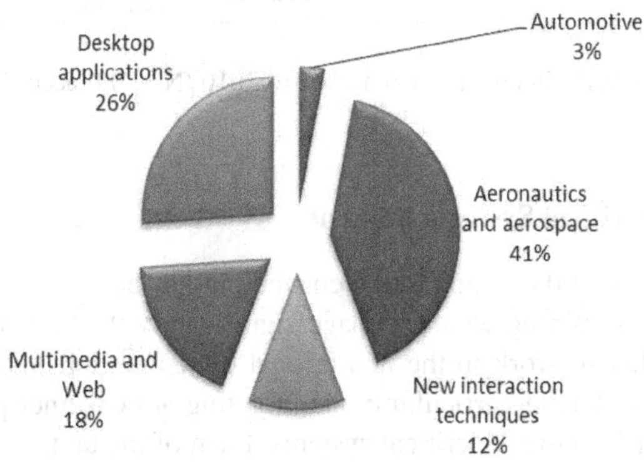

Fig. 4. Distribution of M2IHM internships from 2001 to 2010 (N = 209) accordingly to the application domain

Multimedia and Web applications sum up 18%. The category new interaction techniques encompass a large set of applications such as for the interactive TV, games, mobile systems, 3D and virtual reality, touchscreen, voice recognition... The automotive sector concerned 3% of internships.

Fig.5 presents the evolution of the internships over the years. It is interesting to notice that this evolution can be paralleled by changes in the market. For example, the automotive was responsible for 7 internships from 2002 to 2007 which correspond to the transfer of the R&D department of Siemens from Toulouse in 2008. The majority of internships occurs in the Toulouse area (>60%). In 15% of the cases, internships are performed abroad (ex. Australia, Austria, Canadá, Chile, Espanha, Japão, UK. The increasing number of internship offers in the aeronautics domain can also be paralleled to the expansion of recent programs such as the A380, A400M and A350 at Airbus (see Fig.5).

There is a large set of offers for internship concerning desktop applications but these are often seen as the last choice by students who often prefer new interaction techniques. Nonetheless, offers for internships with new interaction techniques are not so frequent. For instance, in 2010 the number of offers represented 28% (N=7, where 3 involving *multitouch*, 1 ambient systems/demotic, 2 games, 1 mobile applications), but looking back to previous years, the number of internships in this category was lower and it concerned different application domains (an iTV applications in 2009 and 3 virtual reality in 2008). A trend in this sector is thus difficult to assess.

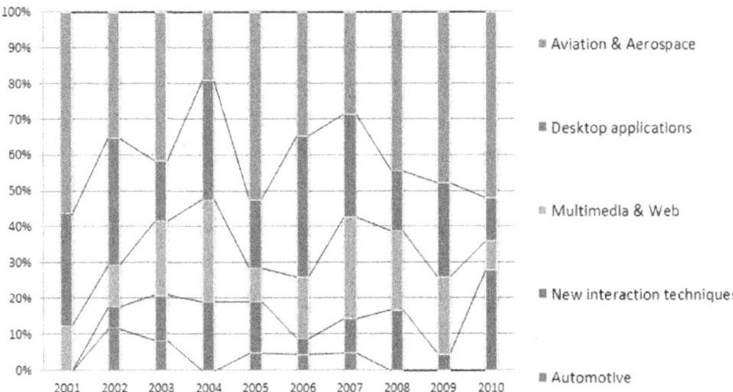

Fig. 5. Evolution of M2IHM internships from 2001 to 2010 (N= 209) according to the application domain

4.3 Interactive Critical Systems Content

The design driver around the tuning of the curriculum has been related to the fact that reducing current HCI training would damage significantly the knowledge of the students and their ability to work in the non-critical domains. For this reason we have decided to produce a double curriculum: one targeting at consumer products and the other one targeting at interactive critical systems. Each of the units presented above is thus split into 3 parts:

- A basic part containing the main principles and root knowledge of that area which is taught to all the students
- A part dedicated to the critical systems requirements addressing issues related to training, certification, human error, development standards, …
- A part dedicated to the consumer product market focusing on hedonic properties of user experience, design, large scale usability testing, ….

5 Conclusion and Future Work

This paper has presented the rationale for deep tuning of HCI curriculum when specific application domains are considered. We have tried to demonstrate that interactive critical systems require specific attentions and specific qualification in order to be designed and implemented in conformance with regulatory authorities that sometimes conflict and are incompatible with mainstream HCI knowledge and practice.

Acknowledgements. This work is partly funded by Fly Higher EU project (http://www.flyhigher.eu/), Airbus under the contract CIFRE PBO D08028747-788/2008 and R&T CNES (National Space Studies Center) Tortuga R-S08/BS-0003-029. Special thanks to Yannick Jestin for his support in the management of the Master on HCI in Toulouse.

References

1. Bastide, R., Sy, O., Palanque, P., Navarre, D.: Formal specification of CORBA services: experience and lessons learned. In: ACM Conference on Object-Oriented Programming, Systems, Languages, and Applications (OOPSLA 2000), Minneapolis, Minnesota USA, pp. 105–117. ACM Press (2000)
2. Bias, E.G., Mayhew, D.J. (eds.): 1994 Cost-Justifying Usability, 334 Pages. Morgan Kaufmann (May 16, 1994)
3. Law, E.: The measurability and predictability of user experience. In: Proceedings of the 3rd ACM SIGCHI Symposium on Engineering Interactive Computing Systems (EICS 2011), pp. 1–10. ACM, New York (2011)
4. Myers, B.A., Rosson, M.B.: Survey on user interface programming. In: Proceedings of the SIGCHI Conference on Human Factors in Computing Systems (CHI 1992), pp. 195–202. ACM, New York (1992)
5. Norman, D., Drapper, S.: User Centred System Design. L. Erlbaum, U.S. (1986)
6. Perlman, G.: Education in HCI, `http://www.hcibib.org/education/` (last visit on February 02, 2012)
7. Rettig, M.: Prototyping for tiny fingers. Commun. ACM 37(4), 21–27 (1994)
8. Masip, L., Martinie, C., Winckler, M., Palanque, P., Granollers, T., Oliva, M.: A design process for exhibiting design choices and trade-offs in (Potentially) conflicting user interface guidelines. In: Winckler, M., Forbrig, P., Bernhaupt, R. (eds.) HCSE 2012. LNCS, vol. 7623, pp. 53–71. Springer, Heidelberg (2012)

9. Haikara, J.: Usability in agile software development: Extending the interaction design process with personas approach. In: Concas, G., Damiani, E., Scotto, M., Succi, G. (eds.) XP 2007. LNCS, vol. 4536, pp. 153–156. Springer, Heidelberg (2007)
10. Brodie, C., Karat, C.-M., Karat, J., Feng, J.: Usable security and privacy: a case study of developing privacy management tools. In: Proceedings of the 2005 Symposium on Usable Privacy and Security (SOUPS 2005), pp. 35–43. ACM, New York (2005)
11. Avizienis, A., Laprie, J.-C., Randell, B., Landwehr, C.: Basic Concepts and Taxonomy of Dependable and Secure Computing. IEEE Trans. Dependable Secur. Comput. 1(1), 11–33 (2004)
12. Lalanne, D., Nigay, L., Palanque, P., Robinson, P., Vanderdonckt, J., Ladry, J.-F.: Fusion engines for multimodal input: a survey. In: Proceedings of the 2009 International Conference on Multimodal Interfaces (ICMI-MLMI 2009), pp. 153–160. ACM, New York (2009)
13. Louchheim, S., Price, S.: On Adoption of Social Computing in the Engineering Community. In: Proceedings of the 2010 IEEE Second International Conference on Social Computing (SOCIALCOM 2010), pp. 379–384. IEEE Computer Society, Washington, DC (2010)
14. Beck, K., Andres, C.: Extreme Programming Explained: Embrace Change, 2nd edn. Addison-Wesley Professional (2004)
15. Law, E.L.-C., Roto, V., Hassenzahl, M., Vermeeren, A.P.O.S., Kort, J.: Understanding, scoping and defining user experience: a survey approach. In: Proceedings (CHI 2009), pp. 719–728. ACM, New York (2009)
16. Chatty, S., Lecoanet, P.: Pen computing for air traffic control. In: Tauber, M.J. (ed.) Proceedings of the SIGCHI Conference on Human Factors in Computing Systems (CHI 1996), pp. 87–94. ACM, New York (1996)
17. Ould, M., Bastide, R., Navarre, D., Palanque, P., Rubio, F., Schyn, A.: Multimodal and 3D Graphic Man-Machine Interfaces to Improve Operations. In: Eighth International Conference on Space Operations, Montréal, Canada, May 17-21 (2004)
18. Brostoff, S., Angela Sasse, M.: Safe and sound: a safety-critical approach to security. In: Proceedings of the 2001 Workshop on New Security Paradigms (NSPW 2001), pp. 41–50. ACM, New York (2001)
19. Hollnagel, E.: Barriers and accident prevention. Ashgate, Aldershot (2004)
20. Cummings, M.L., Bruni, S.: Collaborative Human-Automation Decision Making. Springer Handbook of Automation, pp. 437–447 (2009)
21. Sarter, N.D., Woods, D.: How in the World Did I Ever Get Into That Mode? Mode Error and Awareness in Supervisory Control. Human Factors 37(1) (1995)
22. Reason, J.: Human Error. Cambridge University Press (1990)
23. ESARR 6. EUROCONTROL Safety Regulatory Requirement. Software in ATM Systems. Edition 1.0 (2003), `http://www.eurocontrol.int/src/public/standard_page/esarr6.html`
24. European Organisation for Civil Aviation Equipment. DO-178B, Software Consideration in Airborne Systems and Equipment Certification. EUROCAE (1992)
25. Salas, E., Cannon-Bower, J.: The Science of Training: A Decade of Progress. Ann. Review of Psychology, 471–499 (2001)
26. Martinie, C., Palanque, P., Navarre, D., Barboni, E.: A development process for usable large scale interactive critical systems: Application to satellite ground segments. In: Winckler, M., Forbrig, P., Bernhaupt, R. (eds.) HCSE 2012. LNCS, vol. 7623, pp. 72–93. Springer, Heidelberg (2012)

Ageing and Innovation

Matthias Göbel

Department of Human Kinetics and Ergonomics
Rhodes University, Grahamstown South Africa
m.goebel@ru.ac.za

1 The Classic Innovation Paradigm

Innovation is mostly associated with young people being open to new things and enthusiastic to try out something different. Even though an innovation might not be advantageous , most young persons are prepared to spend time to find out, and they are not disappointed if it does not work out as expected. This experience is considered as learning about different options and getting inspired, thus the innovation is rather an exploration tool to spark creativity.

In contrast to this, with increasing age people are becoming more cautious about spending their time efficiently. Thus, experiencing something at the risk of failure is seen critical. Further, elderly persons consider failing to use a new product as a negative experience. This explains a rather negative attitude of elderly persons with respect to be confronted with innovations. As a consequence innovation has a mostly negative connotation for elderly persons.

2 The Demand of Innovation Paradox

Innovations offering new features and new functions that are mostly focused on young users (see previous section), such as social media. This is likely motivated by the enthusiasm that can be achieved from young people. So in terms of testing the acceptance of new products young people appear to be much more attracted, and thus attractive for developers. However, the need of serious innovations is mostly for elderly persons. This refers to advances in user interface design as well as to new supportive functions. Innovations are essential for the elderly in order to benefit for their daily life. This is particularly true for functions enabling to participate to professional and social activities, which would not be possible or very much restricted without having that support. So, innovations for elderly persons go far beyond the 'nice feature' aspect often prioritized by younger users. So young people are much more open for innovations, but elderly people are in need of innovation.

3 The Economic Paradox

Similarly the budgets for affording innovations are mostly available for elderly. Young persons often have a very limited budget, particularly for fancy items. So

M. Kurosu (Ed.): Human-Computer Interaction, Part I, HCII 2013, LNCS 8004, pp. 61–67, 2013.

spending for one item is often corresponding to cuttings for other items. Further, prestigious aspects do count quite a lot for young users. This is true for elderly users as well, but here aspects of practicability do play an important role as well. As innovations are most expensive in the initial stages (due to the need for writing-off the investments for development), the practical value becomes an important justification.

In contrast to young people, many elderly persons do have spare budgets, and the essential value of innovative items and functions for elderly does justify corresponding investments. So from an economic perspective, elderly have much more potential to fund innovations than younger persons. However, the willingness to spend depends on the expected benefit.

4 Innovations for Elderly

For a long time, innovations for the elderly in the field of HCI have been focused on the user interface. On the physical side this is mostly related to the size of interaction elements (display and buttons), contrasting the general trend towards small and mobile equipment. On the software level easy usability was (and still is) considered a key feature to allow computer-illiterate users access to modern technologies. This is mostly to compensate physiological, cognitive and habituation deficits of elderly users. Basically those challenges are met to a large extent. However, the increasing complexity and mobility of modern devices put new challenges.

Some challenges for usability are still to be resolved by future technologies, such as displays with integrated lenses that make reading glasses redundant.

Another area of innovation is the provision of supportive functions for the elderly, helping to overcome barriers occurring due to the ageing process. Typical examples are remote and supervision controls that help to cope with physical immobility and a decreased cognitive reliability (Helander & Ming 2005).

Those technologies mostly result from the attempt to overcome typical bottlenecks of ageing. As a matter of fact, such an approach will create distinct features for elderly, contrasting the needs of younger users. This often results in stigmatizing product features, that are considered being not attractive, as specially made for elderly. Despite objective needs, elderly persons are keen to have products that are fancy and attractive for young users as well. So, innovations must at the same time consider usability benefits for elderly and and attractive appearance for younger users.

Today, most acute bottlenecks of elderly in standard products are met. This raises the question how to create further innovations for elderly that go beyond acute handling problems or age-specific deficits.

5 Elderly in the Innovation Process

Most innovation processes do stem from empathy, as deductive approaches are normally successful only for pure technological progress. Empathy might origin from developers and from users, ideally from both. However, innovation for the elderly faces two challenges with respect to the origin of empathy:

1. Professionals involved into the innovation process are mostly rather young, thus developing empathy for elderly is lacking the life experience. Hence it becomes difficult, if possible, to step into the toes of an elderly person for anything beyond the obvious restrictions of ageing. This is a particular challenge for the mental and emotional stages of ageing, an experience that is mostly excluded for empathy of younger persons (Darses & Wolff, 2006).
2. Elderly who could provide the requested empathy from a life experience point of view often lack the technological experience and awareness of current and upcoming technologies. So they face difficulties to look beyond their current life. This is particularly the case for real innovations, in other words: future applications and technologies that are not a continuation of current state-of-the-art.

The both aspects mentioned before are the essential for innovation. Even using random or brut force creativity methods requires appropriate filtering of upcoming ideas, and at this point the both above-mentioned factors become relevant.

A rather simple and common approach of meeting the need to bridge the gap between the both points of view addressed above is building a work team consisting of members of both groups. This rises however another conflict (apart from the practical challenge of time requirements to enable constructive communication), as one creative party normally faces a critical party that needs to be convinced. This constellation rather induces compromising than a real innovative working atmosphere.

In addition to the need of both groups to participate to this process, a systematic creative process would be required. Considering the specific needs of elderly a step by step approach was developed by Göbel (2012) that is based on identifying potentials for support by innovative technologies.

A three-dimensional matrix is created that specifies lacking or scarce resources (requested functions and services of a product which disable or at least impede the fulfillment of a task) against available resources. This is performed separately for the different tasks to be considered for the designed product. Those resource categories entail personal resources, the social environment and the technical environment, thus aiming for a holistic approach even if not all types of resources need to be considered in any case.

For the different fields built in this matrix a creative process is then performed with design professionals striving for ideas or concepts that link available resources to lacking resources. Not all matrix fields have to be filled, one field per column is sufficient. By far not all ideas will be innovative by nature. A second filtering process is then required in order to forward those ideas that are considered productive in terms of creating new products and services economically successful.

The basic concept behind this approach is to translate the user's perspective to an engineering design scheme. However, this is still a creativity tool.

This concept was basically intended to generate product ideas helping elderly persons to sustain an independent lifestyle while making use of available capacities as much as possible.

Empirical testing against the application of brainstorming as a universal creativity methods showed that the created innovations are more specific and more rational than the ideas created by brainstorming.

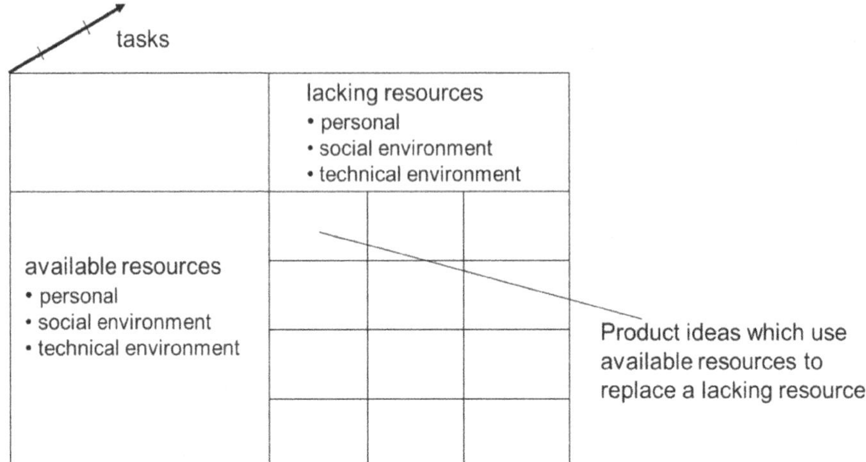

Fig. 1. The basic matrix of the Resource Transformation Approach (from Göbel 2011)

6 Modeling of Complex Human-Environment Systems

The aforementioned approaches relate very much to creativity, powered by empathy. A more engineering type of approach to create innovation is the identification of bottlenecks in a functional structure. This is not necessarily qualitative in nature, as creative methods mostly are. System modeling often raises quantitative bottlenecks in terms of lack of time, lack of competency, incompatibilities etc. Thus, less revolutionary innovations might be expected from system modeling, but rather optimizations. This is equally important for product quality, even if those aspects are not striking selling points.

Figure 2 shows the basic model of a human environment system as suggested by Emery (1959), Luczak (1997) and Carayon (2006).

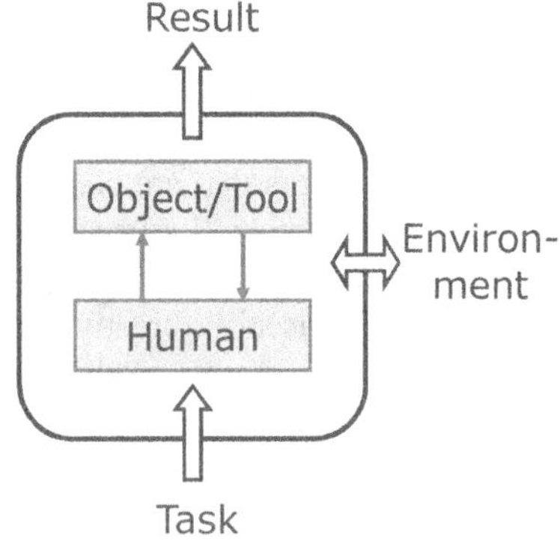

Fig. 2. Basic structure of a human-environment system

The identification of innovation potentials from a system model will however require a system model that allows outlining deficits in a functional structure. Hence, such a model is required to represent all relevant detail aspects. This is a trivial requirement, and such a strategy is commonly applied for technological systems. However, human-environment systems are complex in nature. Apart from the sheer number of elements required for detailed modeling, the following aspects of human-environment systems are not easily addressed by standard Systems Engineering (such as described by Pahl et al. 2007):

- Non-monotonous characteristics of humans: Technical systems normally have monotonous or even proportional characteristics, such as the relation between forces and masses of a machine. This is however not the case for the human factor, who is often described via a U-like or an inverted U characteristic. Often this is caused by complex substructures, balancing between different optimization aspects.
- Memory effect: Any conscious human response is linked to an individual learning process in a way that a response is necessarily based on previous learning. Complementary, any voluntary reaction affects the individual's experience on an endogenous and an exogenous level. Those constituents of personality validate the complexity attribute of any system that involves actively performing humans.
- Real and virtual representation: Human system elements have a physical (or biological) representation on the cell, bone, muscles etc. level. Many human system elements have a virtual representation at the same time, storing and conducting information. This is true for all brain and central nervous functions. The both types of representation interact as any virtual representation is based on a physical representation. This is for example relevant for human fatigue.

As a consequence a system structure is not directly accessible (despite a valid system structure might be developed). Meister (2000) identifies the invisibility of the relationship between the human and the environment being a central obstacle for ergonomic design. Physiologists can extract cells and study their contribution to the function of the human body, engineers may compute the relationships between the different components of a machine, but ergonomists will never be able to see or feel the human-environment relationship. They can only measure its effects and try to deduce the nature of the relationship from its effects.

Göbel and Zschernack (2012) suggested some formal extensions to the Systems Engineering approach in order to accommodate the required aspects of a functional human- environment system. Those encompass:

1. A basic description of a human-environment system on the base of five dimensions:
   - (a) *Elements* (objects, resources),
   - (b) *Interactions* (activities, operations, processes),
   - (c) *State* (effect, objective, outcome),
   - (d) *Sequence* (order, time), and
   - (e) *Localisation* (position, direction).

2. An open and hierarchical system structure, ranging from a basic cellular level up to social system. This requires a formal compatibility and consistency of all levels.
3. State variation of system elements: System element do not only store energy or information (like in imaginary system elements), but also change their state on a higher level (e.g. due to fatigue). This again feds back on the system characteristics.
4. Three different behavior characteristics of system elements. System elements may act
   (a) Schematically (with a uniform type of reaction), or
   (b) Algorithmically (with a flexible but reliable reaction), or
   (c) As a problem solver (creating new types of responses).
5. Flexible order and sequences of actions: Depending on action strategy the performed order of actions may be:
   (a) Necessary to perform a task correctly, or
   (b) Pragmatically chosen (e.g. to obtain maximum efficiency), or
   (c) Random (is the order in fact is irrelevant).
6. Synthesis of different objectives: For the development of action strategies not only task-related objectives require consideration, but resource-related and individual objectives as well. All three types of objectives have to be balanced.

The afore-mentioned components of an extended systems model do not make use of fundamentally new theories or concepts, but, in this form, allow integration of the most important factors of work systems modeling and work systems design in a formally consistent frame.

One might argue that such theoretical considerations have little practical value because they are too abstract to apply and do not provide quantitative output as pure engineering models would do. However, although there are numerous limitations to consider, such a type of modeling might be helpful to integrate and to structure different relevant human factors approaches.

7 Conclusions

Creating innovations for the elderly is somewhat different to other technological innovations, as the user group is rather skeptical, but in need for innovations and having a strong purchase power. Creating innovations for the elderly faces challenges for not stigmatizing. Thus, such innovations most be attractive for young users as well.

The innovation process needs to links the creative power of young people with the empathy of elderly. In order make such a complementary team successful a systematic creative process is suggested.

An alternative way is creating innovation is suggested by modeling the human-environment system and concluding deficits from this perspective. Despite the engineering effort such a consideration may outline handling deficits and potentials in the abstract phases of a product development process and, hence, save a lot of investments for product development and prototype engineering.

References

1. Caryon, P.: Human factors in complex sociotechnical systems. Applied Ergonomics 37(4), 525–535 (2006)
2. Darses, F., Wolff, M.: How do designers represent to themselves the users' needs. Applied Ergonomics 37(1), 757–764 (2006)
3. Emery, F.: Characteristics of Socio-Technical Systems. In: Emery, F. (ed.) The Emergence of a New Paradigm of Work. Centre for continuing. The Australian National University (1959, 1978)
4. Göbel, M.: Empathy meets Engineering - Implanting the user's perspective into a systematic design process. In: Karwowski, W., Soares, M., Stanton, N.A. (eds.) Human Factors and Ergonomics in Consumer Product Design, pp. 161–176. Taylor and Francis Publ. (2011)
5. Göbel, M., Zschernack, S.: A systems concept for modelling the ergonomics design process within the product conceptualisation and development frame. Theoretical Issues in Ergonomics Science 13(2), 169–186 (2012)
6. Helander, M.G., Ming, K.Y.: Identifying the needs of elderly for technological innovations in the smart home. In: Proceedings of the Human Factors and Ergonomics Society Annual Meeting, vol. 49(2), pp. 158–162 (September 2005)
7. Luczak, H.: Task Analysis. In: Salvendy, G. (ed.) Handbook of Human Factors and Ergonomics, 2nd edn., pp. 340–416. John Wiley and Sons, London (1997)
8. Pahl, G., Beitz, W., Feldhusen, J., Grote, K.-H., Wallace, K., Blessing, L.: Engineering Design - A Systematic Approach, 3rd edn. Springer, London (2007)

Understanding User Experience and Artifact Development through Qualitative Investigation: Ethnographic Approach for Human-Centered Design

Ayako Hashizume[1] and Masaaki Kurosu[2]

[1] Faculty of System Design, Tokyo Metropolitan University, Japan
hashiaya@sd.tmu.ac.jp
[2] The Open University of Japan, Japan
masaakikurosu@spa.nifty.com

Abstract. In this paper, we introduce a method for utilizing qualitative investigation in the development of artifacts. In particular, we discuss ethnography principles that developers and designers need to learn in order to improve artifact quality and user experience in accordance with the principles of human-centered design (HCD). The objective of ethnographic interview in the development of artifacts is to understand users in their real environment and to build personas and scenarios based on this understanding. This objective applies to the first two steps in the HCD process, which are "Understand and specify the context of use" and "Specify the user requirements." Furthermore, the investigative process of ethnographic research for development is outlined. While it is difficult to understand users through objective observation alone, and the fact that the knowledge that comes from interaction is also vital, the application of contextual inquiry through ethnography is a valuable tool for efficient understanding of the user in a short timeframe and with a limited number of observations.

Keywords: user experience, contextual inquiry, human-centered design, ethnographic interview, context of use.

1 Introduction

Recently, user experience (UX) has been regarded as an important aspect of the development of artifacts such as products, systems, or services. Previously, only practical qualities, such as performance and functionality, were sought after while using an artifact. However, recently perceptive user qualities, such as satisfaction, impression (wow factor) and joy, have been emphasized. Diller and his colleagues have stated that, as society matures, artifacts would increasingly be used to satisfy a user's sense of fulfillment or aesthetic interest. Thus, the individual association each user makes with an artifact has become important [1]. When using an artifact, users would comprehensively judge the importance that the artifact has in terms of what type of emotions it evokes, such as curiosity and the feeling of fulfillment. Therefore, it is necessary to collect UX information through user-centered qualitative

M. Kurosu (Ed.): Human-Computer Interaction, Part I, HCII 2013, LNCS 8004, pp. 68–76, 2013.

investigations and then develop the artifact taking its relationship with users into account. In this paper, we introduce a method for utilizing qualitative investigation in the development of an artifact. In particular, we discuss the principles of ethnography that developers and designers should learn in order to improve artifact quality and UX in accordance with the principles of human-centered design (HCD).

2 HCD Process

Perceptive quality has become an increasingly important parameter, and the focus of artifact development has shifted toward UX. The importance of understanding UX was included among the changes when ISO 13407:1999 was modified; part 210 of ISO 9241-210:2010 focused on HCD for interactive systems. In the modified ISO 9241-210, UX is defined as the user's perception and response during the use of an artifact, and "To achieve a good UX" is the goal of this HCD approach [2] [3]. By this definition, UX should include physical and psychological reactions and attitudes on the basis of the user's perceptions, emotions, and tastes before/during/after use. It is thought that UX will be also affected by the user's physical and psychological state and capability, which is related to the artifact's brand image, design, function, operability, effectiveness, or usage support, and UX.

Figure 1 shows the configuration of HCD's activity process as determined by ISO 9241-210, which explains the artifact design process. In this HCD process, "Plan a HCD process" is the starting point and "Designed solution meets user requirements" is the destination. The four steps between the starting point and the destination are crucial for the entire HCD process. The initial step, "Understand and specify the context of use," involves clarifying each user's characteristics, usage environment, and usage status through user investigations. The user investigation conducted in this stage includes questionnaires, group interviews, and onsite interviews or observations. Table 1 summarizes the various characteristics of these investigation methods. The purpose of the next step, "Specify the user requirements," is to establish an artifact design process that is in accordance with the user requirements determined by the investigation results conducted in the previous step. The "Persona Method" and "Scenario Method" are often used in this step. In the next step, "Produce design solutions to meet user requirements," the device or system is specifically designed using the "Rapid-prototyping Method" or "Paper-prototyping Method." In the last step, "Evaluate the designs against requirements," usability testing, and heuristic evaluation are conducted. Depending on the feedback from the "evaluation," each step could be iterated.

The most important HCD process step to improve UX with the artifact is "Understand and specify the context of use," in which each user's lifestyle and work situation must be captured. For this step, it would be appropriate to conduct a qualitative investigation through contextual inquiry [4], in which users are observed and, if necessary, thoroughly questioned about their everyday situations and behaviors. We will cover the details of this method in the section that discusses ethnographic research.

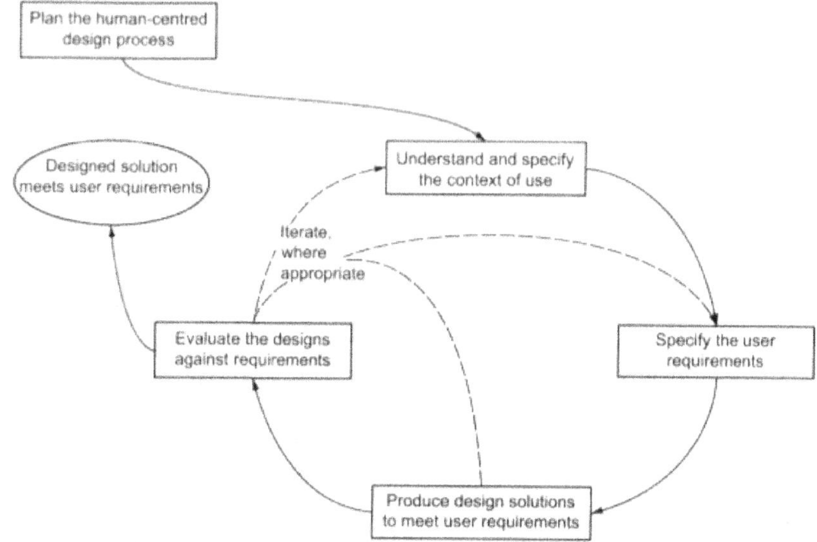

Fig. 1. HCD process (ISO 9241-210)

Table 1. Investigation methods and characteristics

Investigation method and characteristics	Interview		Observation		Paper questionnaire
	Unstructured interview	Structured interview	Unsystematic observation	Systematic observation	
Type of data	Linguistic data	Linguistic data	Visual data	Visual data	Linguistic data
Contents of data	Subjective	Subjective	Objective	Objective	Subjective
Linguistic skill required for targets	Capable of conversation	Capable of conversation	N/A	N/A	Capable of reading
Sample size	Small	Large	Small	Small	Large
Method to extract samples	Intentional sampling	Random selection	Intentional sampling	Random selection	Random selection
Necessity of mutual communication	Yes	Yes	Yes	No	No
Impact by investigators (answers, skills)	Large	Large	Large	Large	Small
Time required	Relatively long	Relatively long	Long	Long	Short
Privacy protection for targets	Privacy measures Required	Privacy measures required	Privacy measures required	Privacy measures required	Privacy can be easily be protected

3 Qualitative and Quantitative Investigation

User investigation is divided into quantitative and qualitative methods. The quantitative method is represented by experimental design, which seeks to elucidate universal characteristics or trends by focusing on a specific aspect on the basis of numerous case studies. The qualitative method, represented by interviews or case studies, aims to gather a comprehensive understanding of an individual user from multiple aspects on the basis of a limited number of case studies. Each of the investigative methods has a different purpose. The purpose of the quantitative method is to construct a generic principle that explains a phenomenon in a certain situation in order to extrapolate the possible consequences of several different situations. On the other hand, the purpose of the qualitative method is to grasp how each individual is trying to comprehend the reality of a certain situation and to interact with it from a subjective standpoint. Historically, there is antagonism between these investigation methods. Where quantitative investigation is the norm, qualitative investigation is often not accepted, and its validity and reliability has frequently been questioned.

The validity of qualitative investigation can be divided into internal and external validity. External validity is often questioned. Internal validity evaluates whether the relationship between the two variables defined in a hypothesis is being appropriately measured. Thus, internal validity corresponds to the credibility of the qualitative investigation. In other words, the focal point of internal validity is not only to discover the truth but also to determine whether the target of study is correctly reflected in the investigation results. External validity means determining whether the components of a hypothesis can be applied to other situations. In qualitative investigation, external validity corresponds to transferability. However, because the purpose of a qualitative investigation is not to conduct a hypothetical evaluation but to understand the target of the study and produce a hypothesis, it cannot be generalized in the same way as a quantitative investigation. Ohtani argues, "With the qualitative investigation, there is no formulated proceeding for data analysis, which is as comprehensive and generic as the statistical method for the quantitative investigation" [5]. In quantitative investigation, the targets of study are randomly chosen, and statistical analysis is used to evaluate the hypothesis. However, in qualitative investigation, it does not make sense to use statistical analysis because intentional sampling is adopted. Furthermore, the Grounded Theory Approach (GTA) emphasizes the necessity of grasping external validity through triangulation and improving the validity of the study using the triangulation method based on multiple people data [6].

Furthermore, reliability corresponds to stability, consistency, predictability, and accuracy of the quantitative investigation, which in turn corresponds to the dependability of the qualitative investigation. However, this dependability can be lost over time and is also vulnerable to the fatigue or stress of the participants and researchers. With quantitative investigation, reliability can be damaged by changes in investigation or study methods during the study. However, with a qualitative investigation, such changes are natural, and are even considered helpful in improving the accuracy of the investigation.

Table 2. Investigation methods and characteristics

Investigation Method	Pros	Cons
Quantitative Investigation	• Many samples can be handled due to ease of quantification. • Easy to analyze the data due to ease of numeric conversion. • Enables statistical assumption. • Replication study is possible due to its repeatability.	• Its standardization feature makes it hard to capture details. • Complicated interrelationship is hard to be understood. • Hard to understand the entire aspect. • Only static phenomena at a certain point can be handled.
Qualitative Investigation	• Enables a comprehensive understanding. • Investigation can be deeply pursued on each item. • Situation variance can be captured.	• Hard to generalize. • Re-examination is not possible.

The argument over quantitative and qualitative investigation methods intensified during the 1990s but settled considerably by the end of the 1990s. The theory behind this resolution was that, because each method had pros and cons, both should be used in a single study. This combined quantitative and qualitative investigation is called "Mixed Method Research." Using Mixed Method, it is possible to systematically combine the advantages of both methods. In other words, it becomes possible to depict the study targets more realistically. When Mixed Methods Research is conducted, it is important to specify a study design that explains how to combine both methods. By specifying the study design, a shot-in-the-dark type of "inappropriate study report" can be avoided [7]. Furthermore, when the processes of data collection and analysis are taken into consideration, the basics of both methods must be accommodated. For example, when a paper questionnaire is conducted with the same set of individuals after a participant observation study, a parametric evaluation method cannot be used to analyze the questionnaire results unless those questioned were randomly chosen from the participants of the observation study. In general, in a qualitative investigation, the study targets are often intentionally selected for observation. When a quantitative investigation is then conducted with the same targets, it is important to remember that only a nonparametric evaluation method can be used to analyze the results.

As mentioned above, when an artifact is being used or developed, its practical qualities tend to be the central focus. In contrast to the qualitative method, the quantitative investigation method involves user investigations or usability tests to count the number of errors during use or to measure the time required to achieve a goal, because the focus is on practical improvements by generalizing user requirements for the usage of artifacts. However, once the HCD process was generalized, investigators began to understand that examination of the actual usage environment would be more useful. In addition, as the demand for improved perceptive qualities and UX increased, qualitative investigation was deemed to be more appropriate, and consequently there has been increased interest in an ethnographic method. Understanding users' goals and requirements in their real living environments and developing artifacts taking these various realities into consideration contributes to the improvement of quality and UX of an artifact. However, from the perspective of a cultural anthropologist, Kimura made the following suggestion [8]:

"The expectation for ethnography from the industrial world seems to be a never satisfied desire. It is because ethnography is grasped as if it was a magical panacea capable of providing new resolutions against the dissatisfaction with the quantitative investigation, which only targets the limited variables mostly based on snapshot data. However, ethnography can never be a panacea. Moreover, since 2000's, the assumption that the methodology of combining qualitative investigation and quantitative investigation might be the key to develop social science and human science has been increasingly predominant."

4 Ethnographic Research for Development

Since the early 20th century, ethnography became a focus of attention in the fields of cultural anthropology and sociology, particularly at the Chicago School. Ethnography has been extensively used and is now receiving attention not only in research fields, such as psychology and education, but also in practical areas, such as business and administration. However, there is a significant overlap between ethnography and fieldwork. Ethnography presents a methodology for understanding a "site," whereas fieldwork is positioned as a step within the research process in which the actual site is visited and investigations are conducted. While ethnography is one of the methodologies included within the field of qualitative research, it is unique within that field because it has a low level of standardization and a high degree of freedom in detailing specific phenomena and their context, and in combining individual cases with theoretical considerations.

Now, we would like to introduce a contextual inquiry through ethnographic approach for HCD, which you might have recently heard of quite often. Ethnography is defined as a description or a report (monograph) of a particular culture. Ethnography is characterized by a long-term relationship in a natural setting, where the researchers actually live in a society and write a report based on their onsite observations and investigations. The essential condition for observing and describing a culture is that the target individuals must be in their "natural situation," and a long-term relationship is required for accurate observation.

Ethnographic research for HCD is completely different from ethnography as it is applied to cultural anthropology. The word "ethnography" gave rise to the expectation of a "magical panacea," as Kimura put it. The contextual inquiry through ethnographic interview might sound like a new investigative method; however, in most cases it is an onsite investigation through contextual inquiry, in which users' actual living situations and behaviors are observed and questioned. While it is difficult to understand users through objective observation alone, and the knowledge that comes from interaction is also vital, the application of contextual inquiry through ethnographic interview is a valuable tool to acquire an effective understanding of users in a short time with a limited number of observations.

The objective of ethnographic research in the development of artifacts is to understand users in their real environments and to build personas and scenarios based on this understanding. This objective applies to the first two steps in the HCD process

(Fig. 1), which are "Understand and specify the context of use" and "Specify the user requirements." The investigative process of contextual inquiry through ethnographic research is discussed in the following sections.

4.1 Selection of Investigation Targets

Investigators select the targets for a group interview after conducting a quantitative study, such as an online questionnaire, or a mail questionnaire. Target individuals for onsite investigations are determined by group interviews. Conducting both questionnaires and group interviews help select the investigation targets best suited for the effectiveness and objective of the subsequent investigations.

4.2 Onsite Investigation

Individuals involved in the artifact development would visit each target's home, office, or shop, and observe their field artifact usage or purchase activity artifact. In addition to onsite observations, investigators would also interview the target individuals and their family members, if needed, to collect information that could not be obtained from observation alone. The investigator group should comprise a primary interviewer and one or more secondary interviewers. In addition to asking supplementary questions, the secondary interviewers must also take notes, pictures, or record videos during the interview. The investigator group should conduct a briefing

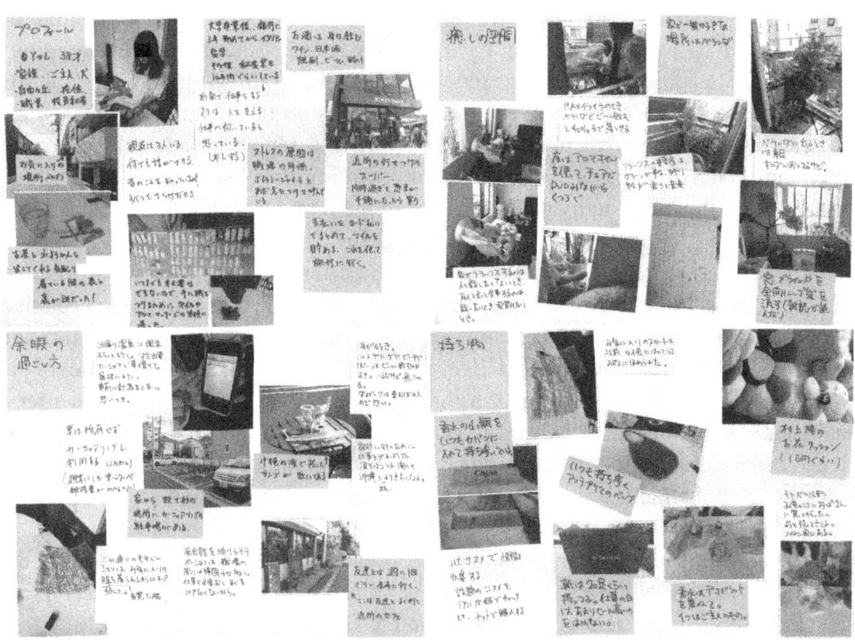

Fig. 2. Examples of Photo Panels

and debriefing before and after each home visit in order to establish mutual knowledge and understanding. During the debriefing, investigators should create photo panels using notes, pictures, or videos taken during the investigation of each target. The photo panel should include basic information for each target as well as the pictures and brief explanations of memorable scenes or characteristics that accord with the objectives of the investigation.

4.3 Downloading

Onsite investigators share the information obtained from observations and the onsite interview with development colleagues who did not accompany them. When sharing this information, the investigators explain their experience while using the environment by means of storytelling and photo panels.

4.4 Extract Scenes and Insights

After sharing the results of the onsite investigation, there is a general discussion about what the investigation targets said and what happened onsite. From that discussion, the investigators extract usage scenes and insights, and create a visual summary, such as a plan proposal, persona, or scenario.

5 Conclusion

Following this process of conducting onsite ethnographic interview investigations and using the investigation results for the development of an artifact shall lead to an improvement in artifacts and UX. However, if the investigators conduct an onsite investigation and do not have the specialized skills necessary for effective qualitative investigation, the collected data cannot be deemed as completely objective, and this would be problematic. The practical specialized skills necessary to conduct an effective qualitative investigation cannot be obtained solely from academic studies. Therefore, new investigators should necessarily accompany an expert for several onsite investigations to acquire these skills through practical experience.

References

1. Diller, S., Shedroff, N., Rhea, D.: Making Meaning: How Successful Businesses Deliver Meaningful Customer Experiences. New Riders, Berkeley (2006)
2. ISO13407: Ergonomics-Human-Centred Design Processes for Interactive Systems (1999)
3. ISO9241-210: Ergonomics of Human-System Interaction-Part 210: Human-Centred Design for Interactive Systems (2010)
4. Beyer, H., Holtzblatt, K.: Contextual design: defining customer-centered systems. Morgan Kaufmann Publishers Inc. (1997)

5. Ohtani, T.: SCAT: Steps for Coding and Theorization – Qualitative data analysis method suited for explicit process and small-scale data. Perceptive Engineering, Japan Society of Kansei Engineering 10(3) (2011)
6. Glaser, B.G., Strauss, A.L.: The discovery of grounded theory: Strategies for qualitative research. Aldine Publishing Company (1967)
7. Sato, I.: What is triangulation? International Nursing Review 28(2), 30–36 (2005)
8. Kimura, T.: Digital Network and Cultural Anthropology. Kokusai University (August 20, 2012), http://www.glocom.ac.jp/profile/2009/12/post_22.html

User Research for Experience Vision

Seiji Hayakawa[1], Yoshihiro Ueda[2], Kentaro Go[3], Katsumi Takahashi[4], Koji Yanagida[5], and Kazuhiko Yamazaki[6]

[1] Ricoh Company, Ltd., Ebina, 243-0460, Japan
Seiji.hayakawa@nts.ricoh.co.jp
[2] Fujitsu Design, Ltd., Kawasaki, 211-8588, Japan
y.ueda@jp.fujitsu.com
[3] University of Yamanashi, Kofu, 400-8511, Japan
go@yamanashi.ac.jp
[4] Holon Create Inc., Yokohama, 222-0033, Japan
takahasi@hol-on.co.jp
[5] Kurashiki University of Science and the Arts, Kurashiki, 712-8505, Japan
yanagida@arts.kusa.ac.jp
[6] Chiba Institute of Technology, Narashino, 275-0016, Japan
designkaz@gmail.com

Abstract. In the "Experience Vision: Vision Proposal Design Method," the first step is to set a project target and to conduct a qualitative survey. Next, users' essential needs are identified and an idea is developed to propose a vision. On the basis of a scenario from the perspective of users' essential needs, the proposal is formed, given shape and made precise. Finally, the proposal is evaluated, and then evolves into the development of products, systems, and services. This paper presents the interview method, the photo diary method, the photo essay method, and the superior-subordinate relationship analysis method laddering) in order to gain profound insight into users and to identify their essential needs, rather than their manifest needs. In addition, on the basis of users' essential needs, it explains the method of setting a user with persona and cast to embody the target user, as a viewpoint from which to describe a value scenario, an activity scenario, and an interaction scenario. [1]

Keywords: experience vision, service design, user's needs, persona.

1 What Are Intrinsic User Values?

Compared with the problem-solving design method frequently used to deal with manifest user needs, accurate grasp of intrinsic user values is required in the vision-centered design method that offers unprecedented products, systems, and services of higher customer satisfaction to meet user values that are more latent and intrinsic.

Intrinsic user values are not ones at specific levels of demand, such as the desire to have or do something. Intrinsic user values exist at a psychologically deeper level, wherein a person wants to feel something specific or has a deep desire to do something.

M. Kurosu (Ed.): Human-Computer Interaction, Part I, HCII 2013, LNCS 8004, pp. 77–84, 2013.

Needless to say, the levels of intrinsic user values differ from one project to another, just as intrinsic user values differ in the development of new scheduling software or in a customer service that offers a moment of greater enjoyment during a trip.

Discovered intrinsic user values are reflected in user evaluation items and the evaluation for scenario visualization (prototyping) that are developed in value scenarios, activity scenarios, and interaction scenarios.

2 Understanding Target Users and Methods Used

User understanding is the first step toward finding intrinsic user values. There are various ways for understanding users but generally put, there are external and internal understanding.

External understanding methods understand users externally by observing them from the outside and asking them direct questions. The questionnaire method, structured interviews for obtaining answers for predetermined items, the observation method and task analysis for observing user behaviors, and the photo diary method for making records by theme and time (explained below) represent external understanding methods.

Internal understanding methods are methods that ask users to look deep into themselves and express their feelings and thoughts. Representative internal understanding methods include the photo essay method for asking users to write an essay based on one or several photos chosen to match a theme (explained below), semi-structured interviews for changing questions and topics flexibly according to user reactions, in-depth interviews for obtaining deep answers by continually asking why, and the diary method involving recording the results of daily product or service usage.

The results of external user understanding are often compiled in the quantitative analysis method and tabulation method. Meanwhile, the results of internal understanding are presented in the method of assigning higher ranks to behaviors and feelings (laddering) in many cases. In the vision-centered design method, internal user understanding and the analysis of its results are prioritized over external user understanding and quantitative analysis of its results to reach intrinsic user values.

<table>
<tr><th></th><th>Manifest needs</th><th>Potential needs</th></tr>
<tr><td rowspan="2">External understanding</td><td>- Questionnaire Method
- Structured interviews
- Task analysis</td><td>- Behavioral observations</td></tr>
<tr><td colspan="2">Photo diaries</td></tr>
<tr><td rowspan="2">Internal understanding</td><td>- Diary Method</td><td>- Photo essays
- In-depth interviews</td></tr>
<tr><td colspan="2">Semi-structured interviews</td></tr>
</table>

Fig. 1. External and Internal User Understanding and Analysis Methods

Additionally, information collected for the purpose of understanding users becomes basic information for assuming and setting target users (user personas and user models).

3 Finding Intrinsic User Values Based on User Understanding in the Vision-Centered Design Method

In many cases where the vision-centered design method is adopted, a semi-structured interview or photo diary is produced as a means for internal user understanding. User needs are ranked higher based on such data and intrinsic user values are found for reaching user values that are more essential. A photo essay is also used to reinforce intrinsic user values in such cases. The visual flow of steps needed for finding intrinsic user values is shown below. There can be two or more intrinsic user values.

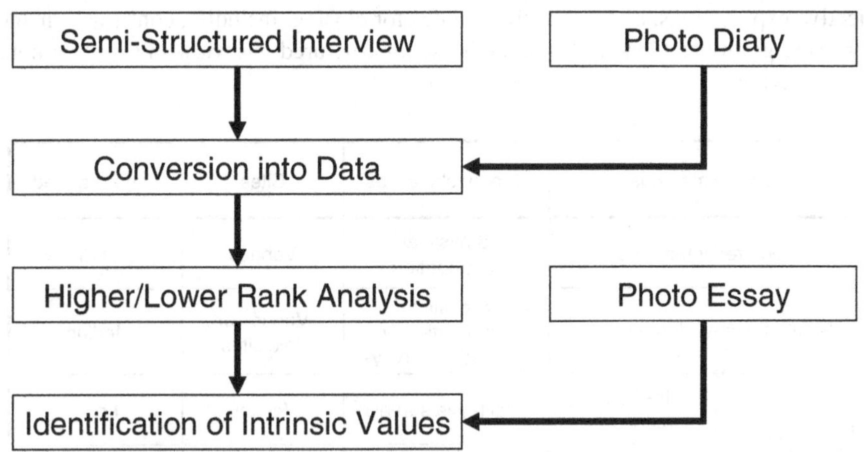

Fig. 2. Major Flow of Steps for Finding Intrinsic User Values

4 Semi-structured Interviews

Semi-structured interviews are also known as contextual interviews. Interview scenarios are produced for these interviews. Semi-structured interviews are an interview method for eliciting answers close to users' real intentions by flexibly changing questions and topics according to user reactions as needed. This interview method requires certain skills, such as those needed for flexibly changing the order of questions. Those skills can be obtained by accumulating a certain amount of practical experiences.

The most important point in the planning stage of a semi-structured interview is to clarify the objective, in other words, deciding what answer to elicit from an interviewee will make the interview successful. Preparations become more sufficient and more appropriate questions may be set when the interview objective becomes more specific. The efficiency of analysis also improves.

A scenario must be produced in the planning stage of a semi-structured interview. Essential points in the planning stage include anticipating the flow of the interview, arranging topics in order and eliminating omissions and oversights in question items.

Listening techniques can be cited as skills required in the implementation stage. An interviewer must develop conditions that make an interviewee feel comfortable, to speak with the attitude of paying consideration to the interviewee and lending an ear to what the interviewee has to say. An interviewer must not speak too much, but needs to share personal experiences and opinions with an interviewee. An interviewer also needs to summarize what an interviewee said on the spot for confirmation and sound out the interviewee's true feelings with open questions asking why and closed questions confirming the answer using "yes" or "no" in order to clarify the interviewee's opinions and views. Additional points an interviewer must be mindful of include time allocation for preventing topic omissions and changing question styles in accordance with the characteristics of each interviewee. For the interview periods, approximately five minutes should be reserved for introduction, including interview objective explanations, and five to 10 minutes for closing, including confirmation and expressing gratitude. Concluding an entire semi-structured interview in about an hour is one criterion.

<table>
<tr><th colspan="2">Interview methods</th><th>Survey objectives</th><th>Sites</th><th>Time required</th></tr>
<tr><td colspan="2">Structured interviews</td><td>Statistical aggregation</td><td>Venues</td><td>Short</td></tr>
<tr><td colspan="2">Semi-structured interviews</td><td>Statistical aggregation or qualitative surveys</td><td>Venues or field sites</td><td>Medium</td></tr>
<tr><td rowspan="2">Unstructured interviews</td><td>In-depth interviews</td><td>Qualitative surveys</td><td>Venues</td><td>Long</td></tr>
<tr><td>Ethnographic interviews</td><td>Qualitative surveys</td><td>Field sites</td><td>Long</td></tr>
<tr><td colspan="2">Group interviews</td><td>Statistical aggregation or qualitative surveys</td><td>Venues</td><td>Medium</td></tr>
</table>

Fig. 3. List of Interview Methods [2]

5 Photo Diary Method

The photo diary method is for understanding user needs and the state of product and service usage by taking the photos of user behaviors according to fixed periods and themes, and supplying the captured scenes with simple explanations and comments. Many of the scenes cut out from everyday life offer new discoveries.

Specifically, the photo diary method asks users to take photos of events in their immediate environment using fixed time units, such as one shot every 30 minutes.

Alternatively, the method requests that users photograph scenes related to specific themes, such as schedule management, and supply each photo with a simple comment and brief explanation. Users are asked to explain a scene in each of these photos. Previously unnoticed values are discovered through this procedure. The photo diary method also permits in-depth analysis of the state of usage when a specific product is chosen as a theme. Discoveries from a photo diary can be used as information for setting target users (user personas), as well as data for finding intrinsic user values.

Fig. 4. Photo Diary Example

6 Higher and Lower Rank Analysis Method

The higher and lower rank analysis method is a method for analyzing group interview data. Nobuyoshi Umezawa developed this method in 1993. Originally, higher and lower rank analysis was a method for classifying consumer needs identified in group interviews into three hierarchical groups (demands to have, demands to do, and demands to be) and finding intrinsic values from their relationships. In the vision-centered design method, the higher and lower rank analysis method is used for finding users' intrinsic values and potential needs by assigning higher ranks to users' behavioral targets (major reasons for behaviors), based on factual data and discoveries from interview data (remarks about values and events), photo diaries, and behavioral observations. In the vision-centered design method, intrinsic user values are found primarily through the assignment of higher ranks. The assignment of lower ranks, carried out for finding specific actions for higher rank assignment, can be used for creation of ideas.

In actual practice, data transcribed to cards are first grouped for finding if they belong to higher or lower ranks. Targets needs in higher ranks are then labeled and the levels of needs are adjusted. After these steps, values in higher ranks are deduced from among the related groups of needs, by answering the question asking the main reasons for finding values in it. Values in the highest rank tend to be something like, "I want to become happy," but there is no need to assign the top rank to this level. Hierarchies number three in principle, but there could be more. There is no need to adopt only one value as an intrinsic value either.

There is also a method called laddering for finding hierarchical structures. This method is similar to the higher and lower rank analysis method. Laddering is an interview method that structures concepts by developing hierarchical structures known as attributes, results, and values. Values found through the process of laddering are close to intrinsic user values identified in the vision-centered design method.

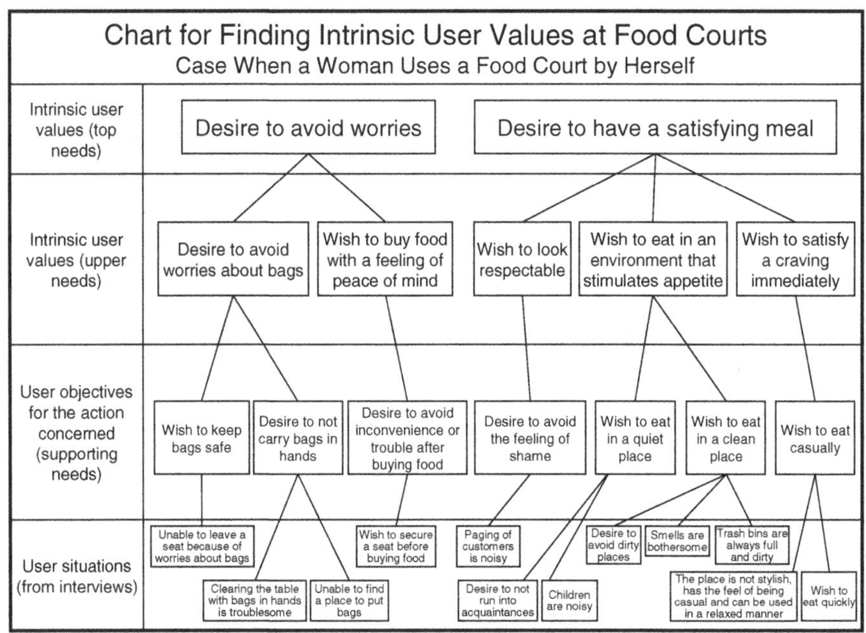

Fig. 5. Higher and Lower Rank Analysis (Laddering) Example [3]

7 Photo Essay Method

Photo essays are a method through which other people find users' intrinsic values or potential needs from an essay written by a user that is associated with a single photo taken by the user.

A user looks deep into himself or herself based on a theme, and expresses his or her thoughts through one or several photos combined with accompanying essays. The combined photos and essays express the user's reason for the thought and the meaning the user tries to communicate. Other people can use them as clues for finding intrinsic user values and materials for creating ideas from a user perspective.

In the vision-centered design method, discoveries from photo essays may be used for reinforcing intrinsic values found through higher and lower rank analysis, explained earlier. The discoveries can also be added to as new intrinsic values.

Shoe selection troubles me when I prepare for a trip.

Choosing clothing and other travel goods does not take that long because I have packaged them to a certain extent for my relatively frequent business trips. But selecting the right shoes is still sometimes difficult for me.

My personal wish is to travel with just one pair of shoes. But I must consider possibilities such as rain being forecast in areas I visit and long distances I am supposed to walk. I have also had problems in the past by having only one pair of leather shoes for business. Shoe selection always comes last when I prepare for a trip.

I currently handle the need to travel with an extra pair of shoes by using a suitcase that has shoe storage space. But the second pair in the suitcase has been keeping me from making my baggage more compact. Travelling lightly with two pairs of shoes has been a nagging issue for me.

Fig. 6. Photo Essay Example (Theme: Travel)

References

1. Yamazaki, K., et al.: Experience Vision. Maruzen Publishing, Japan (2012) ISBN 978-4-621-08565-1
2. Yamazaki, K., et al.: Information Design Classroom, p. 52. Maruzen Publishing, Japan (2010) ISBN 978-4-621-08272-0
3. Hirose, Y., et al.: Potential problem-solving design method applying the vision-centered approach – a food court redesign case. In: Ergo-Design Subcommittee Meeting for Presenting Conceptual Cases, pp. 29–34. Japan Ergonomics Society (2009)

Analyzing Varying Environmental Contexts in Public Transport

Stephan Hörold, Cindy Mayas, and Heidi Krömker

Ilmenau University of Technology,
Ilmenau, Germany
{stephan.hoerold,cindy.mayas,heidi.kroemker}@tu-ilmenau.de

Abstract. The basis for user-centered design is the knowledge of users and tasks. Developing systems, e.g. mobile applications, which are used at varying locations, requires knowledge of the environmental context as well. This paper describes an approach for the analysis of varying environmental contexts in public transport. The results are presented as context templates to derive information needs of users in public transport dependent on influencing context factors and can serve as a communication tool for interdisciplinary groups.

Keywords: context analysis, public transport, passenger information.

1 Introduction

Technology and systems can adapt themselves to people if relevant factors of the environmental context are known and systems have the necessary means, e.g. sensors, to identify the actual context.

Public transport can use new developments in communication interfaces, sensors and technology to develop new passenger information systems more in respect to the users. Passenger information can not only be static, stationary and collective but dynamic, mobile and individual [1]. These new developments and public transport itself present developers with several challenges [2] for the development of passenger information systems. Understanding the heterogeneous users [3], identifying the information needs [4] and analyzing the influences of the environment for task completion and information needs are some of these challenges.

The development of systems for varying contexts such as mobile passenger information systems differs from developing systems for fixed contexts, e.g. offices [5]. Several factors, e.g. noises, light, and other people, as well as tasks are dynamic and can change from one location to another.

This paper describes how a greatly varying environmental context can be analyzed and described, and how information needs can be derived in order to support the task completion.

M. Kurosu (Ed.): Human-Computer Interaction, Part I, HCII 2013, LNCS 8004, pp. 85–94, 2013.

2 Context in Public Transport

The environmental context in public transport is shaped by the travel chain. The travel chain [6] is a common tool for the description of the passengers' journey which functions independently from a special country or public transport system. It describes eight stages from planning the journey, e.g. at home, to the desired destination as seen in figure 1.

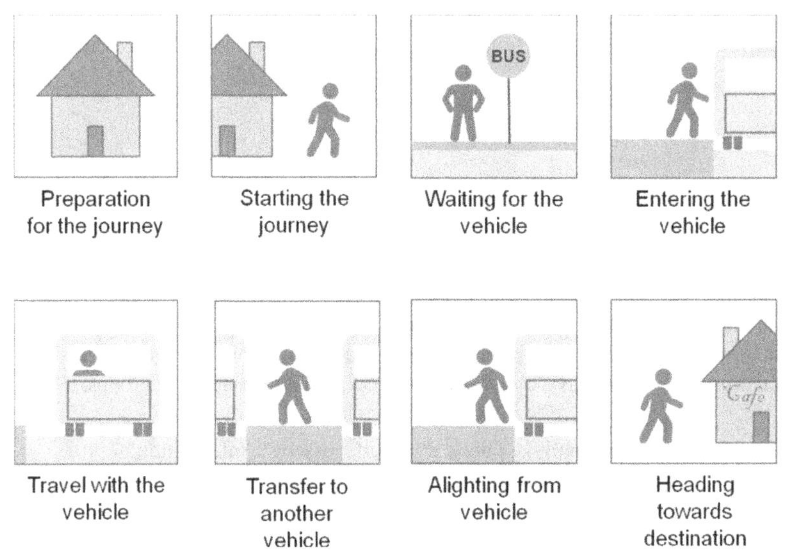

Fig. 1. Travel chain in public transport

The travel chain covers the stages in general but not the exact description of locations, as the characteristics of these locations are varying greatly [2]. For instance a stop point can be a sign or a main train station. A vehicle can be crowded or empty depending on date and time. In addition, the transport system can be based on one or a combination of several different means of transportation, e.g. bus, train or subway, which themselves shape the environment and the need for information.

Along the travel chain and for different kinds of locations passenger information systems are already implemented to support the use of public transport systems. Online platforms provide information for planning the journey and booking e.g. at home or at work, dynamic passenger information systems at train stations display real-time arrival and departure as well as disturbance information. In some cases these systems are already developed for a special environmental context along the travel chain, e.g. for a special type of station or mean of transport. In addition, these systems themselves are part of the environmental context.

To fulfill the requirements of the heterogeneous users of public transport within the development process of new dynamic and mobile passenger information systems as well as the improvement of existing ones, a clear understanding of factors which shape the environmental context of use is needed.

3 Method

The development of passenger information systems for different environmental contexts requires a clear understanding of influencing factors and typical context patterns. As development teams of passenger information systems often consist of experts from different areas, e.g. informatics, public transport, telematics, the description of these context templates have to be interdisciplinary understandable. Starting with the identification of relevant context factors, the following approach shows how these factors can be analyzed based on a context questionnaire and how the results can be used to identify typical context templates.

3.1 Identification of Context Factors

A first step to an analysis and description of the environmental context at the eight stages is the identification of factors which influence the user's task completion in mobile contexts. The factors for the mobile context of use by Krannich are a set of factors which can be used for this step [7]. In respect to the physical and social environment, these factors are:

- Location
- Light
- Noises
- Objects
- People
- Traffic density
- Social situation

The context of public transport is shaped by additional factors. A study with 30 participants conducted as part of a usability evaluation shows that the planning and decision making process as well as the need for information at different stages of the travel chain is influenced by:

- Weather conditions
- Shopping and public facilities
- Means of transportation available
- Type of stop point
- Type of vehicle

In addition, Krannich [7] defines time as a factor which influences e.g. light, weather and traffic density.

3.2 Context Analysis for Public Transport

In a second step these factors need to be differentiated for the field of public transport. Within public transport the factor traffic density for example includes public and individual means of transportation as well as travelers and other people. Table 1 shows this differentiation.

Table 1. Context factors for public transport

Context factor	Differentiation for public transport
Location	Stage of the travel chain Classification by population
Light	Light situation Brightness and Intensity
Noises	Source of noise Noise level
Objects	Technical information systems Non-technical information Vehicle or stop point equipment
People	Number of travelers and other people
Traffic density	Transportation infrastructure Density of individual and public means of transport Distance to other people
Social situation	Interaction with other people Chance of disturbances by others
Weather conditions	Temperature Actual weather
Facilities	Shopping facilities Public facilities
Means of transport available	Individual means of transportation Public means of transportation
Type of stop point	Kind of shelter
Type of vehicle	Vehicle parameters
Time	Date Time of day

Subsequently, the differentiated factors for mobile context of use in public transport need to be analyzed at each stage of the travel chain and with varying characteristics, e.g. in rural and urban areas. For this purpose, the factors were transferred into a context questionnaire. This context questionnaire provides an easy way for experts and laymen to analyze different locations.

3.3 Development of Context Templates

The last step is the description of typical context templates based on the results of the analysis at each stage of the travel chain. A context template should fulfill the following functions within the development of passenger information systems:

- Supporting the identification of information needs at different locations and for different kind of users and tasks along the travel chain
- Communication tool for interdisciplinary groups to understand, visualize and support a user oriented point of view
- Display the diversity of contexts along the travel chain when used as a set of context templates

To fulfill these functions, a context template for public transport is divided into six sections. The first section, consisting of the context templates name and stage of the travel chain, gives brief information about the template. The name should reflect in a few words what the template is about, e.g. rural bus stop in the evening, including a short description of the location and an indicator about the specialty of the template. The second section shows the context factors which describe the environment. The context factors which describe the public transport profile are summarized in the next section. Combined with the challenges section, these three sections give a detailed insight into the environmental context. A graphic representation in form of a photo or illustration gives an impression of the context described in the template and visualizes the most important features of the context. As last section, a description of the context including challenges and critical situations for the use of public transport and the development of passenger information systems, recorded during the analysis, concludes the context template.

3.4 Identifying Information Needs

The identification of information needs requires knowledge of the users' workflow, the performed tasks, available information and the passengers [8]. Which tasks are performed and which information is available often depends on the location of the user and the accessibility of information systems.

The developed context templates are an addition to the framework for identifying information needs [4]. For every task, which is performed by a user along the travel chain, the influences of the context can be analyzed. Based on the results of the original framework additional or redundant information needs can be identified.

Furthermore, the context templates in combination with persona descriptions [9] for public transport [3] can be used to communicate the information needs to the development team and to evaluate whether the information needs of users at different contexts along the travel chain are already satisfied by present passenger information systems or not.

4 Case Study

In a case study within German public transport, the described approach was used in the field to identify context templates and information needs of users in German public transport. In the following the analysis of stop points as important part of the travel chain is shown as an example.

4.1 Setup

The case study was conducted within different areas of Germany, reaching from rural to urban areas and covering a variety of different kinds of stops and means of public transportation. The analyzed 168 stop points were located in 21 different public transport companies and eight linked transport systems consisting of small, medium and large transportation networks.

For the implementation of the analysis the context questionnaire was transferred into an online survey system which allowed the use of tablets for entering the data directly at the stage of the travel chain. In addition pictures of the analyzed stop points were taken for later analysis.

4.2 Analysis of Results

A cluster analysis of the collected data shows that the analyzed stop points can be divided into five basic templates. The clustering was done in a two-step-cluster analysis with a good rating based on the work of Kaufman and Rousseeuw [10]. The Log-Likelihood Distance was used to handle the categorical variables. Main influencing factors for the clustering are the kind of shelter, means of public transport available and the kind of passenger information whether it is providing dynamic or static data. The five identified basic templates are:

Basic Template 1: Bus Stop with Shelter. This template describes a typical German bus stop with shelter and static passenger information. In most cases there are no technical passenger information systems installed at the stop point and no other public means of transportation close by.

Basic Template 2: Bus Stop without Shelter. A bus stop found in different areas which provides only the basic set of static information and no shelter. In some cases these stops are combined with the basic template 1 "Bus stop with shelter" so that one shelter for both directions is available.

Basic Template 3: Bus Stop with Dynamic Passenger Information. This stop point is shaped by technical dynamic information systems. The bus is the main mean of transport but additional means of transport are available in the area. In most cases a shelter is provided.

Basic Template 4: Streetcar Station with Shelter and Dynamic Information. Similar to template 3 this template is shaped by dynamic information systems. The streetcar is the main mean of transport and a shelter is provided in most cases. The template differs from template 3 mainly through other available means of transport as the distance to other means of transport is greater.

Basic Template 5: Main Railroad Station with Station Building. This station is a hub for different means of transportation which are varying due to the public transport system of the location. A station building provides shelter and different dynamic passenger information systems are placed inside and outside the building. In addition, public and commercial facilities can be found.

For planning and development of passenger information systems it is important to have a clear understanding of where these templates can be found within the public transport network and within cities of different size. The analysis revealed within the context factor location that the basic templates are spread through different city types in a similar way. In metropolises for example basic template 5, 4 and 3 can be found from the city center to suburbs starting with basic template 5 the main railroad station. Figure 2 shows the distribution for the five basic context templates in three of the six evaluated areas.

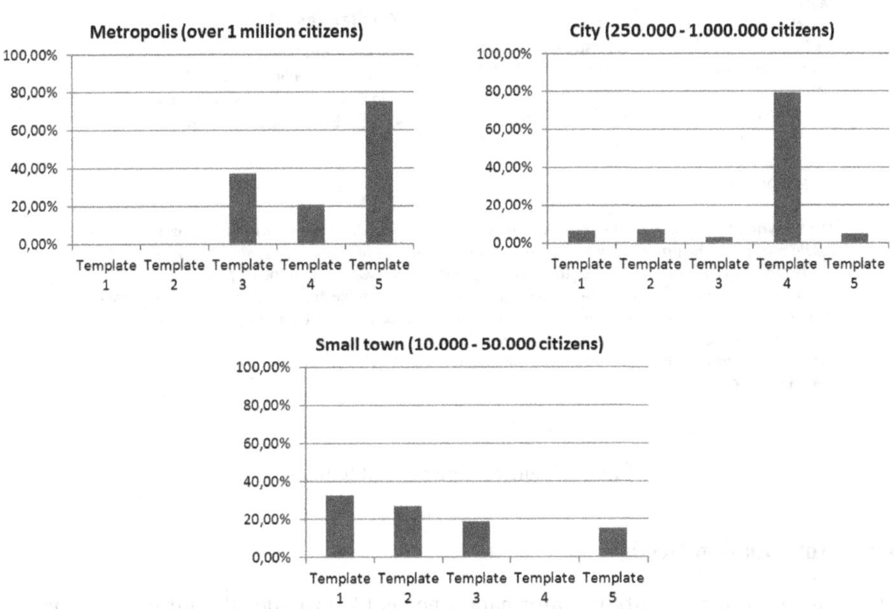

Fig. 2. Distribution of basic templates in different types of cities

4.3 Context Templates

The identified basic templates provide the basis for the development of context templates. As the characteristics of each location are varying in detail, the identification of information needs is challenging and needs additional information. This information can be derived from the context factors, e.g. time, equipment, weather conditions and social situation. Figure 3 shows a context template for the crowded rural bus stop with shelter.

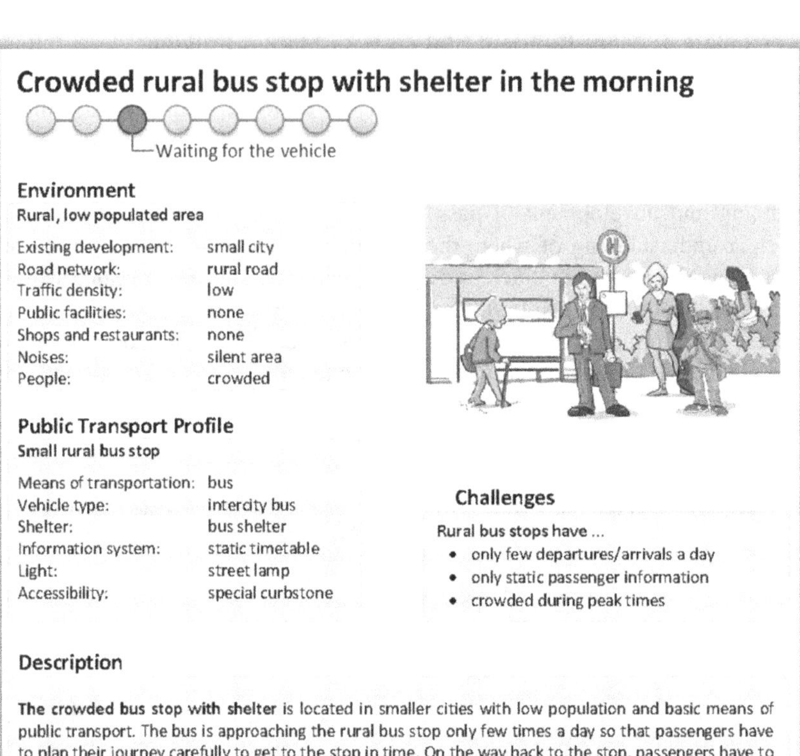

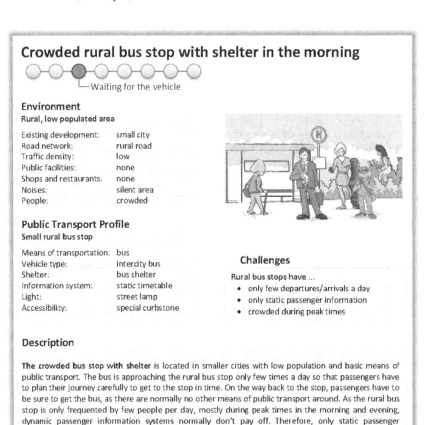

Fig. 3. Example for a context template

4.4 Information Needs

The framework for identifying information needs [4] provides the information needs of different users in public transport. It combines tasks along the travel chain with an information classification and can be combined with user descriptions, e.g. personas, so that the information needs for different users can be identified.

Without context templates, the result of the framework for the typical stop point task "checking remaining waiting time" contains the information needs:

- Time
- planned arrival and departure times
- real-time information about arrivals and departures
- disturbance information.

The described crowded rural bus stop only provides the information "planned arrival and departure times" to fulfill the information needs. In addition, the lack of other means of transport close by raises the need for information about alternatives in case of disturbances, e.g. telephone number to call a cab.

For the development of mobile passenger information systems the gap between provided information and information needs shows which information is missing and should be provided. Available information can be provided but consistency should be given a high priority. The absence of dynamic real-time information systems at the crowded rural bus stop in return drops consistency challenges regarding dynamic data.

5 Discussion

The identification of influencing context factors and context templates shown in the described approach allow a better understanding of different contexts and information needs of passengers along the travel chain. In addition, the results show where the identified basic templates can be found within different kind of cities and areas.

The context templates can serve as an addition to user and task descriptions and extend the framework for identifying the information needs in public transport. The combination of context templates and personas during the requirements analysis should be analyzed in further studies.

For other areas of application the context factors can be differentiated so that special characteristics can be addressed. This differentiation and the transfer into a questionnaire is a key success factor for this method and should be evaluated in a pre test before large scale studies are conducted.

Acknowledgements. Part of this work was funded by the German Federal Ministry of Economy and Technology (BMWi) grant number 19P10003L within the IP-KOM-ÖV project. The project develops an interface standard for passenger information in German public transport with focus on the connection between personal mobile devices, vehicle systems and public transport background computer systems.

References

1. Norbey, M., Krömker, H., Hörold, S., Mayas, C.: 2022: Reisezeit – schöne Zeit! In: Kempter, G. (ed.) Technik für Menschen im nächsten Jahrzehnt: Beiträge zum Usability Day X, pp. 22–41. Pabst Science Publ., Lengerich (2012)
2. Kolski, C., Uster, G., Robert, J.-M., Oliveira, K., David, B.: Interaction in Mobility: The Evaluation of Interactive Systems Used by Travellers in Transportation Contexts. In: Jacko, J.A. (ed.) Human-Computer Interaction, Part III, HCII 2011. LNCS, vol. 6763, pp. 301–310. Springer, Heidelberg (2011)
3. Mayas, C., Hörold, S., Krömker, H.: Meeting the Challenges of Individual Passenger Information with Personas. In: Stanton, N. (ed.) Advances in Human Aspects of Road and Rail Transportation, pp. 822–831. CRC Press, Boca Raton (2012)

4. Hörold, S., Mayas, C., Krömker, H.: Identifying the information needs of users in public transport. In: Stanton, N. (ed.) Advances in Human Aspects of Road and Rail Transportation, pp. 331–340. CRC Press, Boca Raton (2012)
5. Tamminen, S., Oulasvirta, A., Toiskallio, K., Kankainen, A.: Understanding mobile contexts. Personal and Ubiquitous Computing 8(2), 135–143 (2004)
6. Verband Deutscher Verkehrsunternehmen (VDV): Telematics in Public Transport in Germany. Alba Fachverlag, Düsseldorf (2001)
7. Krannich, D.: Mobile System Design – Herausforderungen, Anforderungen und Lösungsansätze für Design, Implementierung und Usability-Testing Mobiler Systeme. Books on Demand GmbH, Norderstedt (2010)
8. Heimonen, T.: Information needs and practices of active mobile Internet users. In: Proceedings of the 6th International Conference on Mobile Technology, Application & Systems (Mobility 2009). ACM, New York (2009)
9. Cooper, A., Reimann, R., Cronin, D.: About face 3: the essentials of interaction design. Wiley Publishing, Indianapolis (2007)
10. Kaufman, L., Rousseeuw, P.J.: Finding Groups in Data: An Introduction to Cluster Analysis. John Wiley & Sons, New York (1990)

The Conceptual Model of Experience Engineering (XE)

Masaaki Kurosu

The Open University of Japan
masaakikurosu@spa.nifty.com

Abstract. The conceptual model of XE (experience Engineering) was proposed to cover both of the products and services. It was also proposed to take "U" out from "UX" so that more adequate description of the people can be possible.

Keywords: experience engineering, XE, usability, UX, service, marketing.

1 Introduction

The term UX (User Experience) was first proposed by Norman as the concept that "*deals with all aspects of the user's interactions with the product: how it is perceived, learned, and used. It includes ease of use and, most important of all, the needs that the product fulfills.* (Norman, 1998, p.47)". He first used the term in 1993 at the meeting in Apple and he changed his job title from "User Interface Architect" to "User Experience Architect" (Wirtanen, 2012). Later, he wrote that "*I invented the term because I thought human interface and usability were too narrow. I wanted to cover all aspects of the person's experience with the system including industrial design, graphics, the interface, the physical interaction, and the manual.*" (Norman, 1998).

But he also wrote that "*Since then the term has spread widely, so much so that it is starting to lose its meaning*" and complained as "*User experience, human centered design, usability; all those things, even affordances. They just sort of entered the vocabulary and no longer have any special meaning. People use them often without having any idea why, what the word means, its origin, history, or what it's about.* (Merholz and Norman, 2007, p.1)"

Indeed, there are so many definitions to the term of the UX as are listed in http://www.allaboutux.org/. It was 2010 when the ISO standard adopted the term and gave the definition as "*the person's perceptions and responses resulting from the use and/or anticipated use of a product, system or service*" (ISO9241-210:2011, p.3). Unfortunately, this definition has not yet become popular, perhaps because this standard was too late to appear and neglected many of the past discussion on the concept (Law, et al. 2006, 2007, 2008, Kindsmuller and Mahite 2007, Loujus 2010) and the UX White Paper (Roto et al. 2011).

Besides, ISO9241-210 added the "service" to the system and the product as the target of HCD (Human-Centered Design) without careful deliberation on differences in terms of the design process, sub-concepts, etc.

This paper proposes a conceptual model for the HCD that can be applied to the service as well as the product and the system from the viewpoint of the experience (X).

M. Kurosu (Ed.): Human-Computer Interaction, Part I, HCII 2013, LNCS 8004, pp. 95–102, 2013.

2 HCD Process Model in ISO9241-210

ISO9241-210 proposed a process model for the HCD as shown in Fig. 1. The model is fundamentally the same with the one proposed in its previous version ISO13407:1999.

The process starts from "Plan the Human-Centered Activities", then proceed to "Understand and Specify the Context of Use", "Specify the User Requirements", "Produce Design Solutions" and "Evaluate". From "Evaluate" there are three feedback loops to previous three activities to form the iterative loops. And if the result of the "Evaluate" is acceptable, the process goes to "Design Solution Satisfies Requirements" to finalize the design process.

Although there are three iterative loops described in the figure and the whole design process seems to be iterative, it is seldom that the process goes back to "Understand and Specify the Context of Use" and "Specify the User Requirements". What frequently occurs and makes the process as a human-centered is the iteration between the "Evaluate" and "Produce Design Solutions". Then the whole cyclic process model will become a kind of the waterfall that has a local iteration.

Anyways, activities in the whole process especially "Understand and Specify the Context of Use" and "Evaluate" are human-centered because much user involvement is required for those stages. At this point, it is acceptable that the concept of HCD can be applied to the service as well as the product and the system.

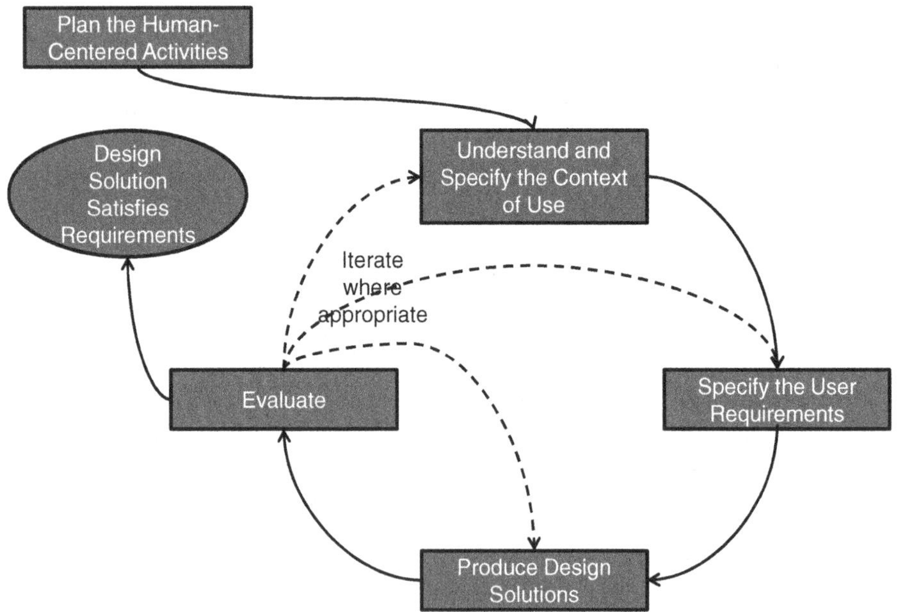

Fig. 1. The HCD Process Model in ISO9241-210 (1999)

3 UX Process Model in the UX White Paper

While the process model of ISO9241-210 was drawn from the viewpoint of the manufacturer, the UX process model in the UX White Paper was drawn from that of the user as in Fig. 2

The model starts "Before usage" where "Anticipated UX" is formed by "imagining the experience". Next is "During usage" where "Momentary UX" is formed by "experiencing". Then "After usage", "Episodic UX" is formed by "reflecting on an experience". Finally "Over time", "Cumulative UX" is formed by "recollecting multiple periods of use".

This model basically corresponds to the definition of UX in ISO9241-210 that referred to *"the use and/or anticipated use"* but is more thoughtful for referring to the experience afterwards.

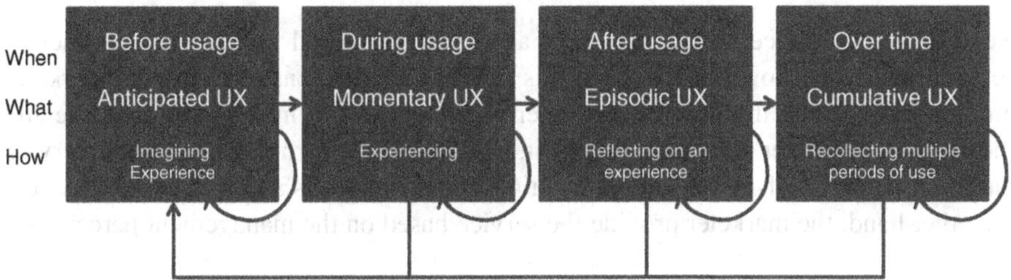

Fig. 2. The Process Model of UX in the UX White Paper (2011)

4 UX and Service

In ISO9241-210, the HCD claims to be relevant to the service in addition to the product and the system. The service is also referred in the UX White Paper as "'*System' is used to denote products, services, and artifacts – separately or combined in one form or another – that a person can interact with through a user interface* (p.6)". But the question arises whether the word "use" or "user" can be adequate for the service.

Clark (1940) was the first to differentiate the industry into three categories as "*Primary industries are defined as agriculture, forestry and fishing; secondary industries as manufacturing, mining and building; the tertiary industries include commerce, transport, services and other economic activities* (p.7)" He further wrote as "*Economics is defined as the study of the production, distribution and exchange of all those goods and services which are usually exchangeable, or are actually exchanged, for money* (p.1)".

In his idea, that "goods" and "services" are two different output of the industry, i.e. the former is the output of the secondary industries that include manufacturing and the latter the output of the tertiary industries that include the service. And, of course, "goods" are to be used. But how about the "services"? Is it simply "to use"? Are we 'using' doctors and nurses at hospitals to be cured? Are we 'using' teachers at schools to learn something? It's possible, but is not completely adequate. "Customer" is more appropriate in the situation of the service than the "user" and "to receive" or "to have" will be more appropriate than "to use" (though this issue is largely dependent on the language).

In this sense, the term "UX" is not adequate for the service and the better solution is just to use X (experience) in its broader sense. Fig. 1 was initially used for describing the process of the UE (usability engineering) in ISO13407. But when the standard was revised to be ISO9241-210 and the target of the standard was reconsidered to include the service, it should be called as the process of UXE (UX engineering), though nobody has ever called it as such. Because UXE is not adequate for the service, I would propose the name "XE" (experience engineering) for covering both of the goods and the services.

5 Service Quality Model

Regarding the service, Parasuraman et al. (1985) proposed a conceptual model of service quality as shown in Fig. 3. In this figure, both the consumer and the marketer are described where the flow of consumer is going down to meet the dashed line and the flow of marketer is coming up to it. The customer forms the expected service based on the word-of-mouth communications, personal needs and past experience. On the other hand, the marketer provide the service based on the management perceptions

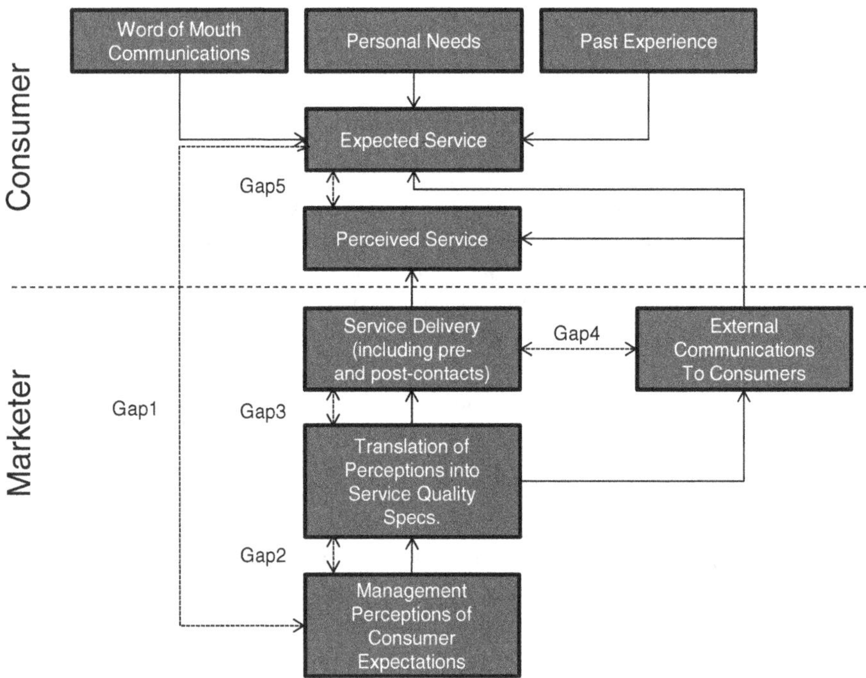

Fig. 3. Conceptual Model of Service Quality by Parasuraman et al. (1985)

of consumer expectations, then the translation of perceptions into service quality specifications will use the external communications to consumers. Finally, the marketer delivers the service including pre-/post-contacts. Finally, the matching will occur between the expected service and the perceived service, and the service quality will be perceived.

Fig. 1 was described from the viewpoint of the manufacturer and Fig. 2 was described from that of the user, but this figure includes both of the consumer and the marketer.

6 Proposed Model of XE

The author (2011, 2012) once proposed a model of UX and here will present a revised model for both of the goods and the services including the process on the side of the industry and the market as Fig. 4 and 5.

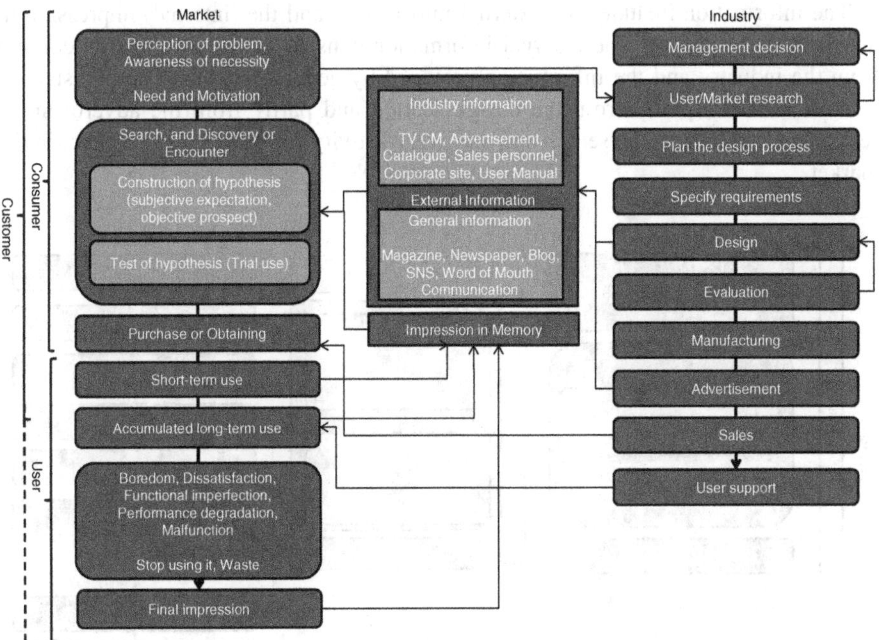

Fig. 4. Model of XE for goods

In either model, the market is drawn on the left and the industry on the right and the information relevant to the market (people) is positioned in between and the time course is drawn downwards.

The market side process will be triggered by the perception of problem or the awareness of necessity. Then the need and the motivation will arise. People start to search and discover/encounter some artifact and will construct the hypothesis including the subjective expectation and the objective prospect. If they may have a chance, they will test the hypothesis by the trial use. If the hypothesis is positive, people will purchase or obtain that artifact and start using it. After the short-term use, they usually continue to use it and the impression of long-term use will be accumulated in memory. But boredom, dissatisfaction, functional imperfection, performance degradation, and malfunction will let them cease to use it or waste it. Although the artifact is gone out of sight, the final impression will reside in memory.

The industry side process will be triggered by the decision of the manager, then the user/market research will be conducted. Based on the information obtained from the research, the design process will be planned and the design process as is depicted in ISO9241-210 will start including the specification of requirements, design and the evaluation. When the design is completed, the manufacturing will start and the advertisement will give the information to the market. The sales activity follows and the user support will be conducted for the user. In this process, there is one iteration between the user/market research and the management decision, and there is another iteration between the evaluation and the re-design.

The information includes the external information and the (internal) impression in the memory of people. The external information consists of the information coming from the industry and the information provided by general sources. The industry information comes partly from the design section and partly from the advertisement section and will affect the search and discovery activity for the adequate artifact in the market.

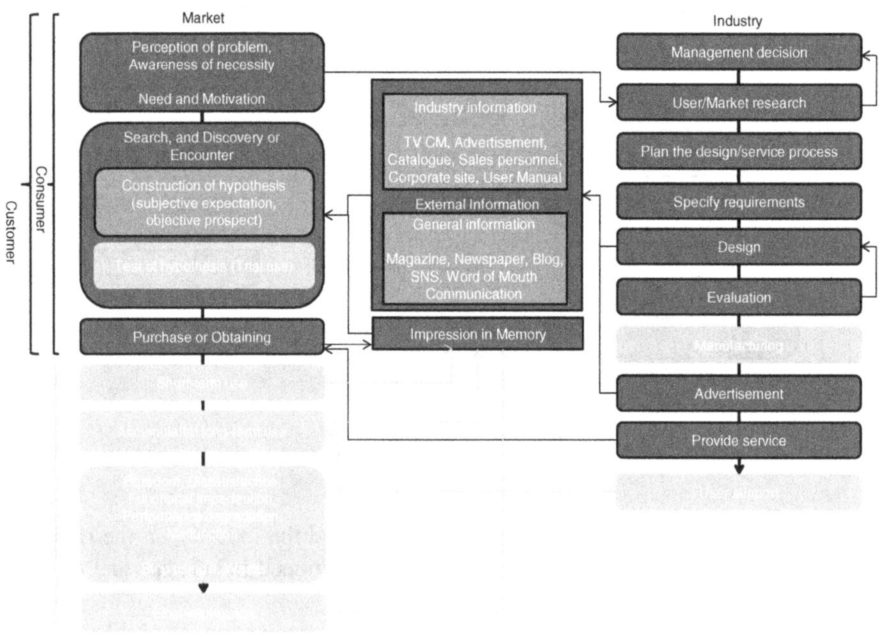

Fig. 5. Model of XE for services

Fig. 5 is fundamentally the same with Fig. 4 except irrelevant stages are greyed out. As shown in the figure, the user process are all greyed out because of the inseparability of production and consumption and the perishability of the service as was described as two of the major characteristics of service by Zeithaml et al. (1985). Other two characteristics of service also proposed by them, the intangibility and the heterogeneity, are not described in this figure.

7 Conclusion: XE as an Engineering

In this paper, the conceptual model of XE was proposed to cover both of the products and services. It was also proposed to take “U” out from “UX” so that more adequate description of the people can be possible.

For the XE to be legitimately in the engineering domain, it is still necessary to propose a new list of determinants of service quality similar to what Parasuraman et al. proposed in terms of the service and ISO9241-11 did in terms of the usability. Besides, adequate methods should be categorized (or developed) regarding the whole lifecycle process of the products and the services.

But, anyways, this is an initial proposal for the XE as a new domain of engineering.

References

Clark, C.: The Conditions of Economic Progress. Macmillan and Co. (1940)

ISO/IEC 13407:1999. Human-Centred Design Processes for Interactive Systems (1999)

ISO 9241-11:1998. Ergonomic Requirements for Office Work with Visual Display Terminals (VDTs) – Part 11: Guidance on Usability (1998)

ISO 9241-210:2010. Ergonomics of Human-System Interaction - Human-Centred Design for Interactive Systems (2010)

Kindsmuller, M.C., Mahlke, S.: MMI-Interaktiv Nr. 13 (2007), http://useworld.net/mmijij/ue

Kurosu, M.: UX in HCD. Seminar of HCD-Net (2011) (in Japanese)

Kurosu, M.: Describing Experiences in Different Mode of Behavior – GOB, POB, and SOB. In: KEER 2012 Conference (2012)

Law, E.L.-C., Bevan, N., Christou, G., Springett, M., Larusdottir, M. (eds.): Proceedings of the International Workshop on Meaningful Measures: Valid Useful User Experience Measurement (VUUM). COST (2008)

Law, E.L.-C., Hvannberg, E.T., Hassenzahl, M.: User eXperience – Towards a Unified View. In: The 2nd COST294-MAUSE International Open Workshop at NordiCHI 2006 (2006)

Law, E.L.-C., Vermeeren, A., Hassenzahl, M., Blythe, M. (eds.): Towards a UX Manifesto – COST294-MAUSE Affiliated Workshop. COST (2007), http://www.cost.esf.org/

Luojus, S.: From a Momentary Experience to a Lasting One. University of Oulu (2010)

Merholz, P., Norman, D.A.: Peter in Conversation with Don Norman About UX & Innovation (2007), http://www.adaptivepath.com/ideas/e000862

Norman, D.A.: The Invisible Computer – Why Good Products Can Fail, the Personal Computer is So Complex, and Information Appliances are the Solution. The MIT Press (1998)

Parasuraman, A., Zeithaml, V.A., Berry, L.L.: A Conceptual Model of Service Quality and Its Implications for Future Research. J. of Marketing 49, 41–50 (1985)

Roto, V., Law, E.L.-C., Vermeeren, A., Hoonhout, J. (eds.): User Experience White Paper – Bringing Clarity to the Concept of User Experience (2011), http://www.allaboutux.org/uxwhitepaper/

Wirtanen, A.: When did UX start being called UX (2012), http://ux.stackexchange.com/questions/27810/when-did-ux-start-being-called-ux

Zeithaml, V.A., Parasuraman, A., Berry, L.L.: Problems and Strategies in Services Marketing. Journal of Marketing 49, 33–46 (1985)

User Centered Inclusive Design Process: A 'Situationally-Induced Impairments and Disabilities' Perspective

Hyung Jun Oh, Hyo Chang Kim, Hwan Hwangbo, and Yong Gu Ji

Department of Information and Industrial Engineering, Yonsei University, Seoul, South Korea
hjuni1109@yonsei.ac.kr

Abstract. Mobile phones provide many functions to improve people's daily lives. However, there are some difficulties to apply the specialty of the mobile device on existing simple schematics of drawings and the approaches. Moreover, regarding handicapped people as special users is causing the stigma effect. Therefore, this research suggests an inclusive design process that by considering the idea of situationally-induced impairments and disabilities (SIID) for developing the product, its design is not only considered for the handicapped people, but also normal people can experience the handicapped situations.

Keywords: Inclusive Design, Accessibility, Smart Device, Mobile Application.

1 Introduction

Mobile phones provide many functions to improve people's daily lives, including call, video call, e-mail and Instant Message (IM), global positioning system (GPS) route displays, and multimedia messaging services (MMS). These functions enable communication, announcements, entertainment, or even mobile-electronic commerce (m-commerce). The portability of mobile phones enables these functions to be employed conveniently. Hence, mobile phones have become an integral part of people's daily lives [1]. However, disabilities experience difficulties using existing functions on mobile devices.

In 1990's, each government, civilian, academia, and industrial circle tries to reduce the level of information gap by increasing web accessibility through many kinds of devices. Actually, because of this effort, the reinforcement of equipment and information education was successfully happened [2]. However, today's incredibility of development of smart devices and Web 2.0 paradigm for mobile computing causes another increase of the information gap and the existing accessibility policy could not be supplemented properly [3].

Moreover, the common drawing and accessibility for handicapped people is existed, but since they decided handicapped people as static beings, the idea of SIID is not included.

M. Kurosu (Ed.): Human-Computer Interaction, Part I, HCII 2013, LNCS 8004, pp. 103–108, 2013.

Therefore, this research practically uses the idea of SIID to experience not only disabled user see as their problem, but also normal people can experience as the extensity of the handicapped situation to try to solve the problems together as the final goal.

2 Related Work

The discussion for the disable people is still on-going process and many different kinds of approaches are existed. In 2000, the unification of the approaches is accomplished and summary is shown in Table 1. For the distribution of the models, the point of disability's view is overly exaggerated, but effectively described about many different kinds of handicapped situations and people's differentiable reactions [4]. In the last social model, it describes the disability is not the defection of the body but look as the part of the society and gives the "Activity" and "Participation" as important parts that mobile device's flexibility of usage environment is going to be increasing case by case.

Table 1. Characteristics of disability model

Model	Perspective on Disabilities	Needs	Domain
Medical	Patients	Treatment, Cure	Medical
Rehabilitation	Clients	Assistance, AT	Engineering
Special Education	Children with disabilities	Education	Education
Legal	Citizens	Act, Laws	Politic
Social	Part of the Diversity of Life	Activity, Participation	Sociology

The concept of Situationally-induced impairment and disabilities (SIID) is introduced in the research from Sears [5]. In SIID, the idea of disability does not limit in bodily or mentally handicapped people, but also normal people also could experience the disability by external situation and environment. For example, in the shaking bus, we try to hold on the strap to stay in balance our body. In this case, a hand is used for balance the body that cannot execute the other task, and it is also applied for the normal people when they try to execute the task in the same disabled situation. In this disabled situation, it is called situationally-induced impairments and disabilities (SIID) and it extends the meaning of the disability that not only handicapped people's meaning, but also the normal people are applied in the meaning.

Through the idea of SIID, the application of SIID forms the many different kinds of images that are used in variety of researches especially to provide on countless mobile device research. Since the existent evaluation does not consider the side effect that are caused by various changes of situations, the device that provides the configuration does not match to the real environment's usability [11]. Moreover, the difficulty on performance side is occurred especially "when a person is moving" because of decreasing of motor ability that is on the configuration which mobile device provides [12]. The development of mobile device is increasing for its portability that it is getting smaller, and putting many different kinds of functions and utilities providing for users. Increasing portability naturally guides users into variable usage configurations that users are using mobile devices in many different situations of environments. However, various functionality and miniaturization technologies provided by mobile devices require more cognitive load, therefore non-disabled experience difficulties of using. Whether the user has disability or not under the limited circumstances of cognitive ability that one user can be seen as disabled. It is very important to ensure that this situational disability to be solved for user safety and securing the convenience.

Users with disabilities, using Assistive Technology to assist their disability feel that social 'stigma' is stamped to their disability. Because of this, they have negative attitude towards appropriate assistive technology as well as fears about soft look or the disabled [7]. Similarly, in the study of Hemmingsson [8], he founds that students are reluctant to use technologies making them look as 'deviants'. Through these reasons, the handicapped users want to cover or to be replaced something else "Assistive Technology" for not to be found [6], [9], [10]. The previous studies mention that people with disabilities might have their sense of alienation or social separation when we access disabled people as special users who require extra technologies. Through studies done in the past, designs concerning every disability circumstances are required in the product design rather than considering people with disabilities as special users who needs additional technologies.

Therefore this study suggests that concept of SIID should be considered in the product development process so that inclusive design process including the failure condition by considering existing design for people with disabilities as well as the general user experience.

3 Methods

This research is flowing In-depth Interview & Requirement analysis, Ideation & Concept generation, low-fidelity prototyping & Evaluation and Hi-fidelity prototyping & Evaluation. For satisfying the handicapped users' special needs, we derived paradigm of participatory design that at least two more handicapped users were included.

3.1 In-depth Interview and Requirement Analysis

In the requirement analysis phase, we recruited people with disabilities and conducted in-depth interview. We could contact and recruited 8 people thanks to the researchers in Pennsylvenia State University. Specifically, we were interested in people who had problems in use of mobile devices. Participants had a various type of disabilities and wide variety of backgrounds and occupations. There ages were 20 to 70. Three participants identified as female, five identified as male. The participants used a wide range of accessibility features, including assistive technology and accessibility related applications in mobile phone.

We met with each participant for a single 2 hour semi-structured interview focused on exploring their experiences with daily activity, mobile devices usage, and feelings about accessibility problems. During the interview, the participant and the interviewer talk about assistive devices that are used by each participant. Adding to that, each interview includes 10-minute idea creation session (Assume a phone with needed functions and advertise it to hypothetical customers) to explore the actual needs of people with disabilities.

Issues that arise in using mobile devices to people with disabilities that are discovered through the course of interview are re-interpretated as situationally-induced impairments and disabilities (SIID) which can happen to non-disabled in the circumstances of regular use.

For reinterpretation, each problem found through impaired users were classified to environmental 'context' causing SIID and 'activity' required by the user.

Concept of context means surrounding environment, user behavior, and device context which can cause SIID through the user's state in addition to the physical disability. Concept of activity refer to proactive behavior of the user through user call, text input, pointing behavior using smart devices on which you want to perform.

Through this process, as well as the requirements of users with disabilities and general user experience in the use of the device in the failure situations that require users to behave accordingly are analyzed.

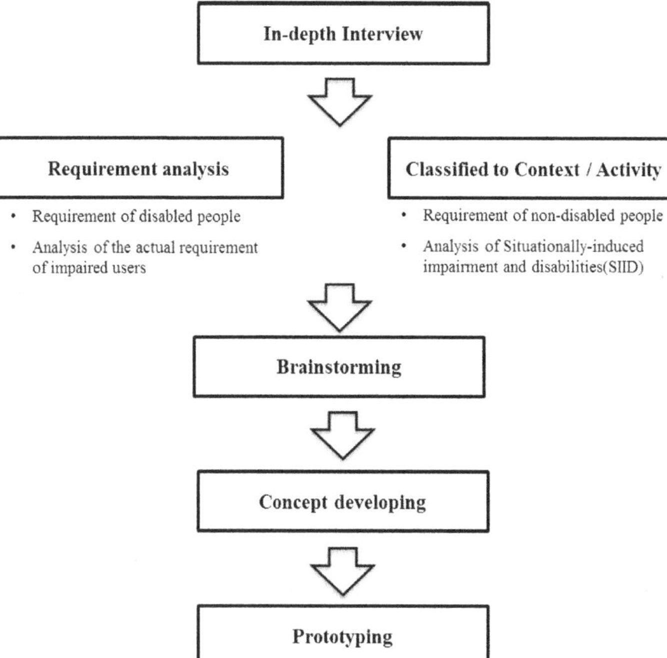

Fig. 1. Design process by considering for situational disabilities

4 Concept Development

In the stages of concept development include ideation phase and conceptualization phase. In the ideation stage, we used brainstorming and bodystorming as ideation methods. Through the conceptualization stages, we finished applying and organizing all the ideas of handicapped people's opinions and executed filtering to eliminate the useless ideas. Secondly, remaining ideas are classified within types and characters of handicapped people. Each group has certain criteria that are formed as unification, expansion, and abstraction. These three criteria are named within our segment. Finally, we designed UI flow and scenario for each conception.

4.1 Prototyping and Evaluation

In these conceptions, we selected one possible conception and concrete target user to build the paper prototype of the conception of UI. Paper prototype is proceeded to carry out the usable task and interview the handicapped people who use the smart devices. After the interview, there are several problems of paper prototype to compensate and we materialize completed UI. Through the previous interviews, we made experimental task. The task is used in comparative usability evaluations in between existing system and the completed UI that we materialized.

4.2 Results

Through the In-depth interview and Contextual mining, we can find out handicapped users' characteristics of using smart device. In the stage of Ideation, we can draw total numbers of 132 ideas, and in the stage of Conceptualization, we filtered out to useful 20 concepts.

In these 20 concepts, 5 concepts are proceeded with prototyping and evaluation that we confirmed the usage of our research's design process of effectiveness.

5 Discussion and Conclusion

Tools used by human can be divided into 'ready-to-hand' and 'present-at-hand'. 'Ready-to-hand' tools are the ones we use not consciously recognizing their operations, and 'present-at-hand' need our conscious efforts to operate [13]. To make technology more familiar to humans, the 'present-at-hand' should be transferred into 'ready-to-hand' by designs that suits human mental models. Design and outcomes that do not consider the cognitive limitations of users will not be actively utilized in various use contexts. To people with disabilities, these limitations are perceived more seriously. In our study, we do not distinguish between people with disabilities and people who are not, but only focus on the universal cognitive limitations that they both have. By doing so, we can suggest that various context that can cause cognitive limitations are integrated in designing digital devices. Moreover, we emphasize the methodological side of systems to integrate both supportive technologies and everyday technology to create more universal and applicable design solutions.

In this research, we make all types of handicapped people participated from the beginning of collecting of user requirement to evaluation of Ideation, Concept Development, and Prototyping. In the presently existent participatory design approach process, the handicapped users are special class to participate. Since the handicapped users are involved, the results that were produced can be possibly happened 'the rejection of acceptance' syndrome by handicapped people. Therefore, this research contains the steps of requirement analysis that not only the actual handicapped people involve, but also normal people's usage of the devices is considered that any kind of accidental happening is considered and prevented. Moreover, not only the approach for the handicapped people is improved, but also normal users' experiences of situational disabilities are prevented. By using the device, certain things such as deviant, stigma are also resolved. In this approach, the focus is not only for the handicapped people who need to have special needs but more likely to be pioneers to find out the new approaches of the usage of the devices and will provide designers new insights.

References

1. Leysia, P.: Mobile telephony in a connected life. Communications of the ACM 45, 78–82 (2002)
2. Reisenwitz, T., Iyer, R., Kuhlmeier, D.B., Eastman, J.K.: The elderly's internet usage: an updated look. Journal of Consumer Marketing 24(7), 406–418 (2007)
3. Schradie, J.: The digital production gap: The digital divide and web 2.0 collide. Poetics 39, 145–168 (2012)
4. Oishi, M.M.K., et al. (eds.): Design and Use of Assistive Technology: Social, 25 Technical, Ethical, and Economic Challenges. Springer Science+Business Media (2010)
5. Sears, A., Young, A.: Physical disabilities and computing technology: An analysis of impairments. In: The Human-Computer Interaction Handbook: Fundamentals, Evolving Technologies and Emerging Applications, pp. 482–503. Lawrence Erlbaum, USA (2003)
6. Lindsay, S., Brittain, K., Jackson, D., Ladha, C., Ladha, K., Olivier, P.: Empathy, participatory design and people with dementia. In: Proceedings of the 2012 ACM Annual Conference on Human Factors in Computing Systems, pp. 521–530. ACM (2012)
7. Parette, P., Scherer, M.: Assistive technology use and stigma. Education and Training in Developmental Disabilities 39, 217–226 (2004)
8. Hemmingsson, H., Lidstorm, H., Nygard, L.: Use of assistive technology devices in mainstream schools: students' perspective. AJOT: American Journal of Occupational Therapy 63(4), 463–472 (2009)
9. McNaney, R., Lindsay, S., Ladha, K., Ladha, C., Schofield, G., Plötz, T., Hammerla, N., Jackson, D., Walker, R., Miller, N., et al.: Cueing Swallowing in Parkinson's Disease. In: Proc. CHI 2011, pp. 619–622 (2011)
10. Shinohara, K., Wobbrock, J.O.: In the Shadow of Misperception: Assistive Technology Use and Social Interactions. In: CHI 2011, pp. 705–714 (2011)
11. Barnard, L., Yi, J., Jacko, J.A., Sears, A.: Capturing the effects of context on human performance in mobile computing systems (2004) (submitted for publication)
12. Kane, S.K., Wobbrock, J.O., Smith, I.E.: Getting off the treadmill: evaluating walking user interfaces for mobile devices in public spaces. In: MobileHCI 2008: Proceedings of the 10th International Conference on Human Computer Interaction (2008)
13. Chalmers, M.: A Historical View of Context. Computer Supported Cooperative Work 13(3), 223–247 (2004)

Applying Contextual Design to Multiple Teams in Emergency Management

Tania Randall[1], Jacquelyn Crebolder[1], Gerard Torenvliet[2], and Jeremy Leal[2]

[1] Defence R&D Canada – Atlantic, Dartmouth, Nova Scotia, B2Y 3Z7
{Tania.Randall,Jacqui.Crebolder}@drdc-rddc.gc.ca
[2] Esterline CMC Electronics, Ottawa, Ontario, K2K 2B2
Gerard@Torenvliet.ca, Jeremy.Daniel.Leal@gmail.com

Abstract. This paper describes a process of identifying a consolidated set of requirements for technology to support unclassified collaboration amongst emergency managers from distinct organizations, each with a role in domestic response. It describes the application and adaption of the inquiry and consolidation processes defined by the Contextual Design (CD) methodology [1] in order to generate a set of requirements that reflect the collaboration needs of the response community as a whole. This application of CD is unique in the sense that the inquiry and requirements analysis focus on a general process (collaboration) that requires flexibility in its usage, rather than a prescriptive, well-defined process or activity.

Keywords: contextual design, emergency management, work-flow models, collaboration tools.

1 Introduction

Emergency managers work in fast-paced, high-stress environments where having the right information at the right time is critical. Large-scale incidents invoke action from numerous organizations, each with a different mandate and role in the response, yet all with an overall goal to keep their citizens safe. For this team of teams to be effective, they must be able to share information and coordinate efforts. Much of this is currently achieved through phone and e-mail, and more recently through formal Situational Awareness tools [2]. Some members of our local emergency management community were looking for additional technology that would enable unstructured, unclassified, conversation-like, information exchange during a domestic response. At their request, we undertook the process of assessing their collective requirements for such computer-supported collaboration. To this end, semi-structured interviews with seven local organizations (including municipal, provincial and federal government organizations and a non-government organization in Canada) with roles in domestic response were conducted. The interview team's objectives for each interview included understanding the agency's role with respect to domestic response, its requirements to engage with other organizations, the current interfaces supporting such interactions, and the challenges they face with respect to inter-agency collaboration. Consolidation

M. Kurosu (Ed.): Human-Computer Interaction, Part I, HCII 2013, LNCS 8004, pp. 109–118, 2013.

of the lessons learned from each interview led us to the production of a list of hard and soft requirements for a collaboration tool that would meet the needs of the broad community.

Our methodology is rooted in "Contextual Design" (CD) [1], with modest adaptations, additions and omissions as needed to suit our use case. The CD methodology was chosen since it easily supported the creation of user requirements at an appropriate level of detail. We were aiming to understand which collaboration tool features or capabilities would best support *unstructured* (i.e., free form versus form-based) inter-agency collaboration, and needed only to understand the general types and formats of information exchange that would need to be supported, rather than the specific details of the exchange that might be better discovered through alternative processes such as task or cognitive work analyses. Beyer & Holtzblatt [1] note that CD can be used successfully as the scaffolding of a design project, a description that fits well with our usage. The discussion in this paper focuses primarily on the contextual inquiry and consolidation phases of CD, and describes our data collection and analysis process and resulting requirements in detail. It also touches on the development of a prototype solution that requires further investigation and community feedback.

2 Methodology

This section will describe the process used to uncover the requirements for software to support unclassified inter-agency collaboration.

2.1 Contextual Design

Contextual Design is a client-centered design process that is based upon a design team's in-depth understanding of how the client currently works and their ideas to improve that work in some way [1]. It begins with *contextual inquiry* which involves interviewing the client in their workplace while they work. *Team interpretation sessions* are then used to review interview sessions with other team members in order to create a shared view of the needs of each client. *Work modeling* is used to organize the interview data in diagrammatic formats that are easily interpreted and compared across clients; there are five types of models – workflow, sequence, culture, artifact, and physical. *Consolidation* is the process of extracting the information from individual diagrams into an overall picture of the client population and requirements. This is achieved, in part, through the creation of an *affinity diagram* which organizes all of the individual points from the interviews into hierarchical groupings with common themes. The CD process also includes many other components and stages (not applied in the paper), which carry the user through to the development of a final product.

2.2 Interviews

Requirements analysis interviews were conducted with seven different organizations involved in incident response, with representatives from municipal, provincial and federal government departments as well as a non-government organization.

True contextual interviews are meant to take place while people work, but this was not practical for our study – even if an emergency occurred within our timeframe, it is unlikely that we could ask questions during the response period. Instead, to maintain some context and to gain an understanding of the client's work environment, we opted for semi-structured interviews when the client was not actively dealing with an emergency. During the interview, we asked them to think back to significant incidents and walk us through their role, an idea borrowed from the Critical Incident Technique described by Klein [3] and which is consistent with retrospective inquiry described by Beyer & Holtzblatt [1].

Interview Administration: A group of four to five researchers participated in each interview, with one person acting as the lead interviewer in all interviews to maintain consistency and the others taking notes. While contextual inquiry is traditionally performed in a 1-1 setting, we were not at risk of getting in the way of work activities given our focus on retrospective accounts and this process produced an efficient way for everyone to gain an understanding of all client groups. At the beginning of each interview we stressed that we were there to learn from the interviewee, and ultimately to help their community; we were not there to judge their way of business.

Interview Protocol: We developed a flexible interview protocol designed to elicit information about: the organization's role in domestic response (to help put things in context); who they interact during an emergency, how (e.g., phone, e-mail, software tools) and why (e.g., to give/get a particular piece of information); the challenges they face with respect to inter-agency collaboration, and when these challenges are most pronounced, as well as their thoughts on how those challenges could be improved upon. Interview durations ranged from one to two hours.

Often in contextual inquiry, interviewers are not looking for something specific (e.g., [4]). They are simply observing a work process and may uncover a range of issues that are not necessarily related to each other. In our case, we were focused specifically on challenges in inter-agency collaboration so this allowed us to spend more time discussing the specific issue we were interested in.

Retrospective Accounts: Throughout each line of questioning, subjects were asked for concrete examples from past events involving multiple agencies. During these retrospective accounts, the lead interviewer would listen to what was said about collaboration and also what was not explicitly stated (e.g., how did you contact that organization, how frequently do you check that system, etc.) – follow-up questions could then be asked to fill in the blanks (Klein [3] discusses using this method to learn about decision points during retrospective accounts). Klein also suggests asking people to talk about the 'big events' because these are their best stories and people are enthusiastic about telling them. This is consistent with our experience during these interviews. In fact, discussion of the big events was especially useful since these events typically required involvement from many of the organizations we interviewed, and as such, different organizations often provided their perspective on the same event, allowing us to better understand how the various organizations fit together.

Post-interview Debriefs

Post-interview debriefs, held within the same day of the interview, were used to create a shared understanding of what we heard. To guide our debrief, we used four questions proposed by Sharon [5]: (1) What did participants say or do that surprised us? (2) What mattered most to the participants? (3) What themes emerged from the session? (4) What were the similarities and differences in what we have learned from these participants in contrast to previous interviews or prior knowledge? Working through these questions while the interview was still fresh in our minds helped us identify the most important points from the session.

Within one week of interview completion, researchers transcribed and amplified their handwritten notes and combined them into a single consolidated document that contained a single complete set of notes for each organization.

2.3 Work-Flow Models

In Contextual Design, work flow models are used to illustrate the collaboration and coordination necessary to do the work. The other models in CD offer detail that was not pertinent to our study.

To develop our work flow models for each organization, we extracted the following information from the consolidated interview data:

- The organization's mandate;
- The location where the organization works;
- The agencies and groups of agencies that collaborate with the organization (i.e., *collaboration partners*);
- The artefacts (documents, email, or other information objects) passed back and forth between the organization and its collaboration partners, as well as the mechanism for transfer;
- The conversations and conversation topics between an organization and its collaboration partners; and,
- Communication or coordination problems between the organization and any of its collaboration partners; these are referred to as *breakdowns* in CD, however, we refer to them as *collaboration challenges*.

With this information we developed two diagrams for each organization, one capturing the information flow amongst collaboration partners, and the other capturing collaboration challenges.

We then undertook a final review of the interview data to see if there was anything pertinent that was not captured in the diagrams; we integrated it where possible, and noted it separately otherwise (e.g., software must be usable). Figure 1 provides an example of both types of work flow models that were created for each organization.

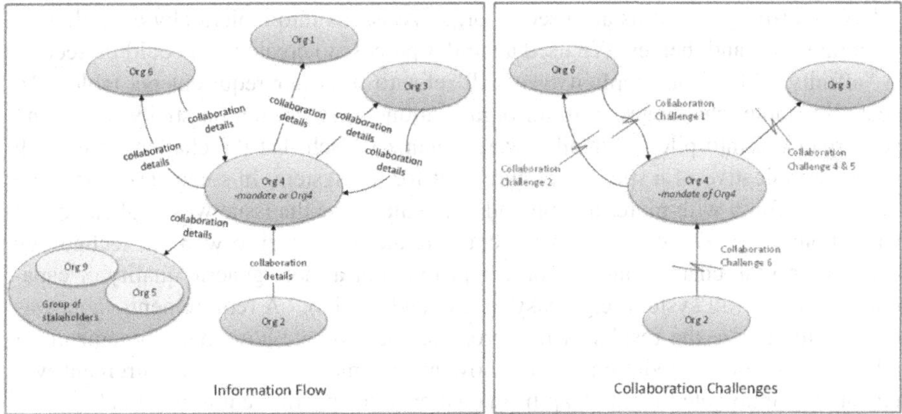

Fig. 1. Work flow models

"Collaboration details" could indicate artefacts being shared (e.g., incident reports) or conversations taking place through a particular means. Not shown here, the flow models also captured the location of the organization, definitions required to understand the collaboration details, and color-coding of "collaboration details" lines to indicate a common theme (e.g., building maritime military picture) within the data or conversation.

Group Review of Models

After creating work flow models for each organization, we brought our participants together as a group to review them collectively to ensure correctness, completeness, and validity from the perspective of all organizations. We worked through each model as a group, which inspired inputs from other organizations that also interacted with the organization under review; this often provided more insight into the breakdowns that had been previously identified. These breakdowns were often not seen as bi-directional (e.g., if org A cannot get information from org B, org B does not necessarily see this as a problem) and were not always realized by the offending organization(s). In addition to refining our work flow models, this integrated meeting with all stakeholders provides a useful venue to discuss the breakdowns in communication that do occur and generate some ideas on how to deal with them. While this collective review of models is not formally a part of contextual design, we found it to be very fruitful.

2.4 Consolidation of Challenges into a Requirements Table

With a solid understanding of the issues encountered by each organization, we had to consolidate this information into a picture of the whole population and develop an understanding of the implied system requirements.

In CD, affinity diagrams are used to organize issues into a hierarchy according to common issues and themes. We used a similar process to create what could be seen as an "affinity table"; for simplicity we will refer to it as our requirements table. To create this table, challenges from all organizations were written on sticky notes, and then organized into piles. Our piles were organized such that the challenges in each pile were indicative of a specific requirement for the system. In some cases, an issue shared an affinity with more than one pile, in which case the issue was duplicated and put in both piles. These requirements could relate to a specific web 2.0 technology (e.g., web portal, chat, social networking profiles) or a more generic quality or capability of the overall system (e.g., easy to use, audit trails). A requirements table was used to summarize the results of this process, and indicate how many organizations indicated a particular requirement and how many times overall the requirement was indicated. We do note that the leap from challenge to specific requirement is based on our experience and expertise with respect to collaboration tools; other researchers might have interpreted the potential solutions differently.

Figure 2 illustrates this process in a generic sense: challenges from all organizations are organized by a common theme (requirement), each grouping is named (according to the indicated requirement), and the results are summarized in tabular format.

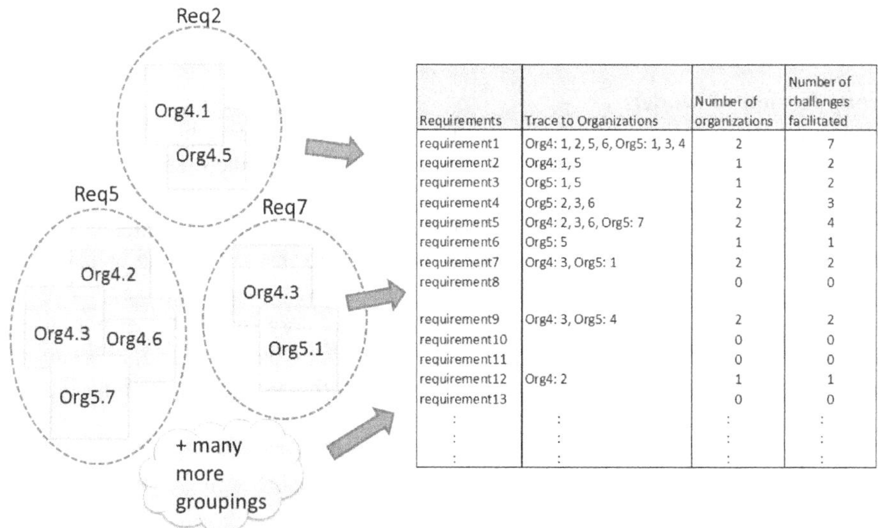

Requirements	Trace to Organizations	Number of organizations	Number of challenges facilitated
requirement1	Org4: 1, 2, 5, 6, Org5: 1, 3, 4	2	7
requirement2	Org4: 1, 5	1	2
requirement3	Org5: 1, 5	1	2
requirement4	Org5: 2, 3, 6	2	3
requirement5	Org4: 2, 3, 6, Org5: 7	2	4
requirement6	Org5: 5	1	1
requirement7	Org4: 3, Org5: 1	2	2
requirement8		0	0
requirement9	Org4: 3, Org5: 4	2	2
requirement10		0	0
requirement11		0	0
requirement12	Org4: 2	1	1
requirement13		0	0
:	:	:	:

Fig. 2. Illustration of the requirements analysis process

In addition to the identification of these requirements, we developed a set of general themes from the consolidated interview data that must be given consideration when building or selecting a new tool for this community.

3 Results

3.1 Collaboration Tool Requirements

The requirements analysis performed (as discussed in the previous section) led to the recommendation of a number of technology-related capabilities that would best support the community. Some of these are listed here (with the total number of times the requirement was indicated by the seven organizations in brackets):

- *a web publishing/portal (13):* by allowing each organization to publish up-to-date incident information on the web, the volume of e-mails sent and received can be reduced and the particular information needed can be identified and pulled more readily, on an as-needed basis;
- *a chat capability (12):* the use of chat is becoming increasingly common within many organizations (including the military) and has the known benefit of quick (and recordable) back-and-forth conversations between two or more users. Extending such generic capability to all government departments, as well as some external partners, would produce obvious benefits to the community with no/minimal training required;
- *ability to broadcast status / requests (8):* this would allow individuals to publish their individual status (e.g., "heading to the incident site" or "awaiting instructions on how to proceed with…"), quick notes (e.g., "click here for CNN update on the storm:…"), or broad requests (e.g., "Red Cross in need of 100 extra cots. Can anyone help?"). This is a Twitter[1]-like concept, but with a more controlled audience;
- *map sharing (7):* by supporting collaboration with common/consistent maps, all collaborators have the same visual perception of the events; such maps should support annotations (e.g., 'push pins', text, free-hand drawing), overlays (e.g., provincial district lines), GPS-based positions of responders, geo-tagged photos and videos of the incident, and printable views;
- *audit trails (5):* any information entered into the system should be logged and time-stamped for potential post-review or reconstruction of events; and,
- *a social networking capability (3):* including personnel profiles, contact information and areas of expertise.

The analysis also suggests that any tool should respect the various levels of information that might be shared (e.g. caveated or politically-sensitive information), support sharing with subsets of users/organizations in addition to community-wide sharing (i.e., need-to-know sharing), be broadly accessible through the public internet to appropriate government employees (i.e., not blocked by firewalls) and external partners, and be subjected to usability testing as a part of the procurement or development effort. Note that by the nature of the semi-structure interviews used, we may not have covered all issues in the same amount of depth in each interview. As such, the prioritization suggested by the number of times a requirement was indicated by all

[1] Twitter is an online micro-blogging service that allows sharing of text-based messages (limited to 140 characters) with other Twitter users from the general public.

organizations must be used with some caution. If not all features are to be included in a collaboration suite for the community, further investigation into the appropriate feature trade-offs may be warranted.

3.2 Collaborative Themes

Seven collaborative themes arose from the consolidated interview data which did not fit nicely into the workflow models:

- *organizations collaborate selfishly* - all parties must perceive a personal benefit from the tool if they are going to use it;
- *key collaborative challenges are not unique to this community* - differences in context, terminology, and information relevance must be managed any time different organizations collaborate, thus it is worth examining common tools that have been successful in other domains;
- *everyone is busy* - new tools must integrate well into existing workflows and have an overall positive impact on each organization's efficiency and effectiveness;
- *personnel are diverse*; new tools must be easy to use and ideally have applicability to user's other tasks outside of inter-agency collaboration so that familiarity and proficiency can be gained;
- *collaboration naturally occurs using the 'lowest common denominator' tools* - most interviewees referred to e-mail, BlackBerry/mobile devices, and phone as the most common mechanisms for communication during an emergency. This most likely follows from the fact that almost everyone has them and is accustomed to using them in other facets of their jobs/lives. Ideally, the government should raise the bar of common, government-wide tools by providing capabilities such as chat and web conferencing;
- *specialized tools are a double-edged sword* - while specialized (typically commercial) incident management tools can be quite effective when used within an organization, they are naturally complex and require training and practice to develop and maintain acceptable levels of proficiency. For broad inter-agency collaboration, where users range from full-time emergency management personnel to volunteers with minimal exposure to tools until response-day usage, the community may be better served by more generic, simplistic, collaboration capabilities; and ,
- *information is not free* - it is important to recognize that even when tools are in place to enable collaboration, there is no assurance that collaboration will occur. Information sharing will remain limited by organizational rules and boundaries, desire for a holistic team effort, and perception of personal gain.

4 Towards a Solution

Based on our requirements analyses, we believe that usage of a restricted-membership, private social networking tool would satisfy many of the requirements outlined through our investigation (web portal, chat, status updates). In addition to enabling new methods of inter-agency collaboration, we hypothesize that a community-based social networking tool will nurture and build inter-agency relationships, further enhancing overall team effectiveness [6].

Social networking and related collaboration tools are currently utilized by many organizations, both internally and externally, and in the daily lives of the general public. Common, freely-available tools such as MSN Messenger, Facebook, Twitter, Google Maps, and Google Docs offer much of the desired functionality, yet without the privacy or accessibility required by Canadian government entities for inter-agency collaboration. Comparable commercially available tools may mitigate the privacy and accessibility issues, but raise additional concerns about licensing costs (particularly for smaller communities with restricted budgets) and long-term product availability or vendor stability. With these issues in mind, we have begun investigating open source, self-hosted collaboration tool suites which may prove suitable in this environment.

For instance, Elgg [7] is a flexible, configurable and extendable, social networking suite. Initial efforts to take advantage of its configurability, however, have highlighted the requirement to obtain more input from the user community. For example, an appropriate organization of the various features has not yet been specified (e.g., placement of a chat window within a larger display), nor is it clear how one emergency should be separated from another within the system (e.g., should a new discussion group be created for each emergency?). The interviews conducted thus far were designed to focus on the underlying need and therefore did not delve into technology specifics. Thus, further community feedback will be required with respect to an appropriate presentation of capabilities. As well, user input will be required to develop a 'concept of use' for the final tool - users will need to know when it is appropriate to use the tool and which tool components are best-suited to which types of information sharing or requests (e.g., chat versus a discussion area).

5 Conclusions

Using the inquiry and analysis processes defined by the Contextual Design methodology to guide our research led us to the definition of requirements at an appropriate level. The usage of retrospective inquiry worked well, especially since many of the interviewees spoke about the same historical events. Our focus on discovering the requirements for a general capability (collaboration) rather than a specific, step-by-step process was handled well by the CD methodology. Following development of work flow models for each organization, all interviewees were brought together for a final integrated meeting (which is not standard CD procedure) to review the complete set of workflow models; this additional step proved very worthwhile in refining the individual models. Finally, through this process we created a consolidated view of requirements for a broad user community, supported by inputs from multiple distinct organizations; there is indeed a benefit to be gained by new technology, and this research effort has defined what capabilities that technology should include. Further community inputs are now required to determine the appropriate organization of and concept of use for these capabilities.

References

1. Beyer, H., Holtzblatt, K.: Contextual design: defining customer-centered systems. Morgan Kaufmann Publishers, San Francisco (1998) ISBN 1-55860-411-1
2. Pagotto, J., O'Donnell, D.: Canada's Multi-Agency Situational Awareness System – keeping it simple. In: Proceedings of the 9th International ISCRAM Conference, Vancouver, Canada (2012)
3. Klein, G.: Sources of Power: How People Make Decisions. Massachusetts Institute of Technology, Cambridge (1998) ISBN 0-262-61146-5
4. Gellatly, A., et al.: Journey: General Motors' Move to Incorporate Contextual Design Into Its Next Generation of Automotive HMI Designs. In: Proceedings of the Second International Conference on Automotive User Interfaces and Interactive Vehicular Applications 2010, Pittsburgh, Pennsylvania (2010)
5. Sharon, T.: It's our research: Getting stakeholder buy-in for user experience research projects. Morgan Kaufmann, Burlington (2012) ISBN-10: 0123851300
6. Crebolder, J., Randall, T.: Team development and virtual social networking. In: Proceedings of the 15th ICCRTS, Santa Monica, California (2010)
7. Costello, C.: Elgg 1.8 social networking. Packt Publishing Ltd., Birmingham (2010) ISBN-10: 1849511306

Visualization and Evaluation for Experience Vision

Katsumi Takahashi[1], Kazuhiko Yamazaki[2], Seiji Hayakawa[3], Koji Yanagida[4], Kentaro Go[5], and Yoshihiro Ueda[6]

[1] HOLON CREATE Inc., Yokohama, 222-0033, Japan
takahasi@holon-on.co.jp
[2] Chiba Institute of Technology, Narashino, 275-0016, Japan
designkaz@gmail.com
[3] Ricoh Company, Ltd., Yokohama, 222-8530, Japan
hayakawa@rdc.ricoh.co.jp
[4] Kurashiki University of Science and the Arts, Kurashiki, 712-8505, Japan
yanagida@arts.kusa.ac.jp
[5] University of Yamanashi, Kofu, 400-8511, Japan
go@yamanashi.ac.jp
[6] Fujitsu Design, Ltd., Kawasaki, 211-8588, Japan
y.ueda@jp.fujitsu.com

Abstract. The "Experience Vision: Vision Centered Design Method" is a comprehensive method which makes it possible to propose new and innovative products, systems and services that are currently unavailable, as well as proposing advances for those that currently exist. It encompasses the entire HCD (Human Centered Design) process, and presents a new vision with experiential value for both user and business from an HCD viewpoint.

In this paper I describe visualization and evaluation of structured scenario for we will implement Scenario based vision proposal design method. Only scenario will introduce visualization techniques to supplement the difficult part of the shared content. Then, the evaluation provides an example to advance to the next phase structured scenarios that are visualized.

Keywords: Experience Vision, vision centered design method, Structured Scenario-Based Design Method (SSBDM), value scenario, activity scenario, interaction scenario, scenario visualization, scenario evaluation.

1 Introduction

In the process for developing Experience Vision, as visualization and evaluation process is responsible for connecting to the next phase structured scenario.

- Visualization that corresponds to a structured scenario. There is a business aspects and the user aspects to this.
- The user aspects describe prototyping.
- The business model describes the business aspects.

M. Kurosu (Ed.): Human-Computer Interaction, Part I, HCII 2013, LNCS 8004, pp. 119–127, 2013.

- There is the timing and content of the evaluation is in the summary corresponding to the structured scenario.
- There is a point of view of users and business evaluation.

We will introduce them as a specific approach.

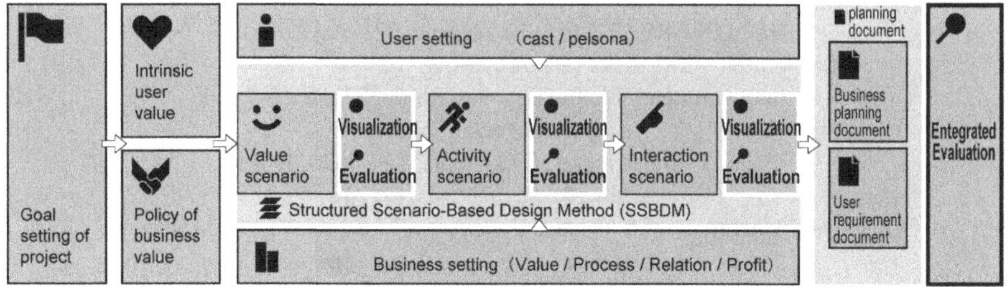

Fig. 1. Framework for Vision Centered Design Method and visualization, evaluation

2 Visualization for Experience Vision

The Vision centered design method, three scenarios were created by Structured Scenario-Based Design Method (SSBDM) is written in the text. If you do not know there is a just sentence description of the scenario. By the more visual information, such as sketches and prototypes scenarios written in the text, I will be able to evaluate the project's members share a concrete image of the target design. The Vision centered design method, taking into account both sides of the "business side visualization" and "visualization of user side." By accurately visualized two sides, the understanding of the scenario is promoted, leading to an appropriate evaluation.

2.1 Visualization Aspects of User (Prototyping)

Only text representation of Structured Scenario, it is difficult to imagine the user experience specifically for us. You can visualize the scenario appropriate to Interaction scenario and Activity scenario and Value scenario is desired.

Be divided into two stages "available" and "visible" way to visualize the user side. Start from the use of such storyboard sketches and in order to "visible" in the phase of Activity scenario and Value scenario. I want to be seen by a simple prototype using the hardware and software to be designed. Then, the production of the video image and use acting out is desirable to make it easier to understand the content of the experience.

Take advantage of, "available" prototype in order to verify the operation of the function and usability in the phase of Interaction scenario. Required as visualization may want to check the work for each task the Rapid Prototyping of GUI, or check on the reaction of feeling manipulated in Rapid Hotmock. In Vision centered design method is referred to as "prototyping" collectively, a method to visualize the scenario from the user side.

In traditional development, many design stage that has progressed to some extent, in order to evaluate the performance of creating a "prototype highly finished." This prototype will require time and money. Moreover, there is a case to be forced to compromise by modification by the major changes is difficult specification, development schedule is limited.

The Vision centered design method, as a method to produce a prototype of the original to create a "prototype simple." Its purpose is to verify from the viewpoint of various styles and designs. And it is to get early feedback from users by making the form visible features and ideas. In addition, to reduce the risk and cost of the project by incorporating in the early stages of the development process, the "prototype simple."

As a concrete method of "prototype simple", in Vision centered design method, take advantage of the following methods.

Table 1. Visualization technique aspects of user

Phase of the SSBDM	Visualization of user side
Value scenario Activity scenario	Story Board
	Paper Prototyping
	Acting Out (Roll Playing)
Interaction scenario	Rapid Prototyping
	GUI Rapid Prototyping
	Hotmock Rapid Prototyping

Technique Is Set to "Visible" and the Activity Scenario Value Scenario

Storyboard

Storyboard is what using sketches and photos, we visualize the experience of deployment scenarios. The scene of the scenario is visualized by the storyboard, easy to understand that everyone specific contexts.

Paper Prototyping

Paper prototyping is a method to create prototype ideas using paper products and interactions in systems and services, study design, presentation, and user evaluation.

Run in interface prototype that was created in the real issues paper prototyping is assumed.

Acting Out (Roll Playing)

By playing the cast along with Structured Scenario, configure the / system / products and services, Acting out is a technique used to study design, proposal and evaluation.

Technique Is Set to "Available" to Interaction Scenario

Rapid Prototyping

It is important from the viewpoint of the Human centered design, will be verified by presenting the user repeatedly prototype. Moreover, this process can be carried out upstream in the process of iterative development is found to be more highly effective. Rapid prototyping is called that due to recent advances in technology, and ideas at the planning stage of the development of the upstream process, carried out at a high speed by utilizing a simple prototyping techniques and tools.

Rapid Prototyping for Graphical User Interface (GUI)

As a way anyone can be performed quickly and easily prototyping of Graphical User Interface, how to use the PDF link or hyper link of the Power Point (Microsoft) is so widely used. In which they are referred to as Rapid Prototyping of GUI.

In this approach, the evaluation of the prototype can be fast by taking the log data of operation and the transition time and errors, using the graph hierarchy analysis method that can graphical analysis.

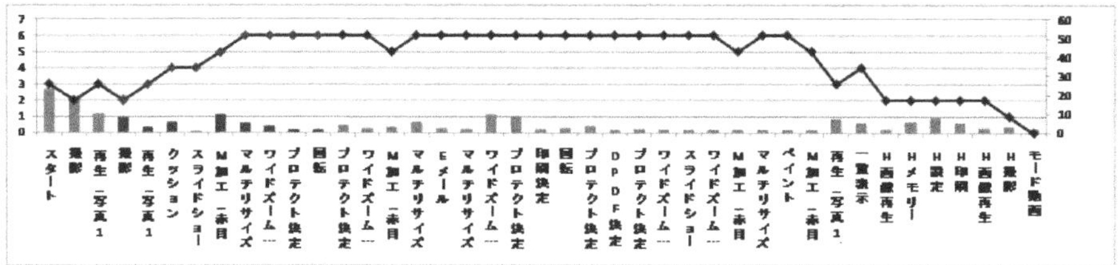

Fig. 2. The graph hierarchy analysis method

Rapid Prototyping by Hotmock

In order to check the color and shape of the product design, we've created a mock-up from the past. However, the verification of embedded devices as a prototype is not to complete just its color and shape. So, Hot Mockup meaning mockup to work, "Hotmock" as the abbreviation is used.

To produce Hotmock is simple prototyping of the development and testing of usability experience. Hotmock is produced as a working model that depends on the personal computer. In addition, you can quickly create a working model close to the product shape using Hotmock, was produced in the 3D printer I can evaluate more practical.

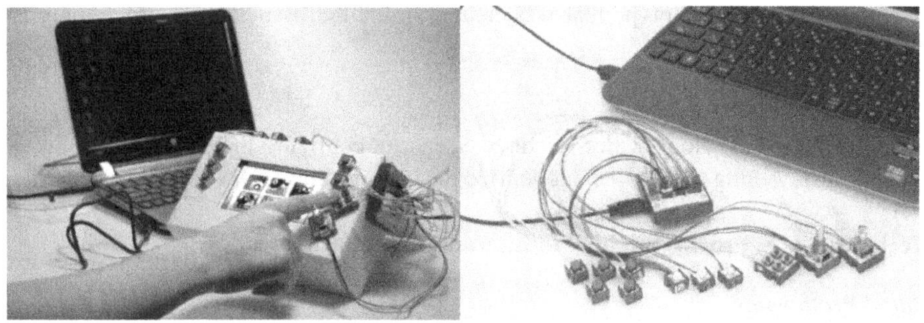

Fig. 3. Rapid prototyping by Hotmock

As a way to visualize the scenario from the side of the business, drawing business model is very effective. Business of network services using intelligent & communication technology, rather than business solely by the product description visual business model is very useful. Consider the activity scenario is basically to create a business model. Be evaluated at the business model diagram that visualizes the value scenario to meet the policy of business value and intrinsic user value is easy. Furthermore, in order to be able to overview the whole of the business written in Structured Scenario, business model diagram is different from the other evaluation are made.

2.2 Type of Business Model Diagram in Vision Centered Design Method

To visualize the Structured Scenario from the side of the business can be drawn with comprehensive business model diagram. Depending on the contents of the business activity, select how to draw that match the theme and the policy of business is efficient. There are the following four figures how to draw.

- *If you would draw a diagram of the value of the business.*

Performing modeling value based on the contents written in the Activity scenario, the user should receive whatever value written in Value scenario. To draw simple diagram is available for anyone in any act, how the user will receive the value.

- *If you would draw a diagram of the business process.*

Modeling of the process performed in line with the flow of the Activity scenario. Draw a path that will provide value to configure the business side. Draw in time series using the task in the Interaction scenario steps to provide value to the user.

- *If you would draw a diagram of the relationship between the businesses.*

The relation modeling taking into account the resources required to achieve the Value scenario. While to clarify the role of companies and organizations and all parties involved in the business, draw a correlation diagram positioned as the relationship with the user.

- *If you would draw a diagram of business profitability.*

The profit modeling of what was written in the Interaction scenario and Activity scenario. Draw describes a process for the collection of revenue in the contact value of the consideration to be provided to the user. It is also important to add the initial investment expenses, the expenses of running costs that need on an ongoing basis.

It is necessary to composite all of the parts and the individual characteristics of the diagram, and finally to draw the overall business model diagram. Use the Information Graphics, it can draw from the business model diagram Structured Scenario, visualization of the business side of Experience Vision is possible.

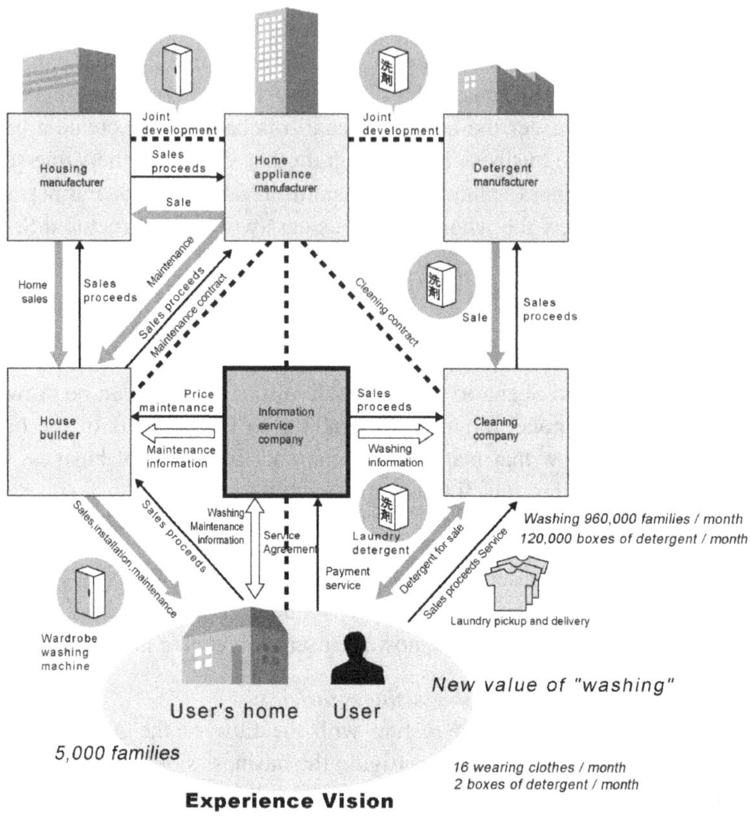

Fig. 4. Example of a business model diagram with information graphics

3 Overview of Structured Scenario Evaluation

3.1 Timing and Content of the Evaluation

In the Vision centered design method, is provided a process of "evaluation" and "visualization" to each phase of the Structured Scenario. We are configured to be able to find "The road to victory (Kachisuji)" of early phase process, proposed to efficiently together. Therefore, the evaluation done in each phase of the Structured Scenario is focused on a scenario should be selected to proceed to the next phase of the scenario from which to create more than one proposal. It also sets the evaluation process even after the full extent of the Structured Scenario was determined. Evaluation process does the evaluation of prototypes and business mode diagram guided into the overall scenario. It is necessary that the value that is put on the business model and the prototype is sufficiently effective to the user, which is the high degree of satisfaction. It has become something beneficial for the business of the company. It is important to evaluate the value of the proposals in these respects.

3.2 Concept of Evaluation in Vision Centered Design Method

The request to another specialist organization in general, we have evaluated in the past. However, today there is a need for efficiency and speed of development severely competitive business, it turned to speed up process of the evaluation and the design, development and systems products and services with high satisfaction for users in a short period of time is desirable . Recently agile development process has been expanding in the field of development software. In the evaluation of the usability is also developing techniques such as guerilla usability research. It just in time, easily, evaluated without applying too much cost has been emphasized. In this Vision centered design method, are organizing a project to put a member of the evaluation experts from the beginning. I think to be able to easily and timely evaluation in each phase of the Structured Scenario.

In addition, for the evaluation of the user viewpoint, and to clarify the purpose of the user for each phase of the Structured Scenario, we are focused on evaluation of the scenario. More specifically, the goal that the user wants to achieve in the target value scenario phase changes that the user wants to achieve in the interaction scenario phase. It is also important to assess whether the user is enabled to achieve the objectives of each phase of the scenario. These ideas in turn speed up the evaluation and development of Experience vision, it is an important part in order to realize the value in the user efficiently.

3.3 Evaluation of User Aspect and the Business Aspect

Specific assessment sets the evaluation item of "business aspects" and "user aspects" as well as the processes described so far, according to the evaluation method used them. Structured Scenario evaluation is carried out in each phase. And evaluate any business model and prototyping, which is created by integrating the scenario.

Evaluation of User Aspects. As a point of view from the aspect the user evaluation, this method sets the four "new", "attractive", "efficiency", "effective", so as to conform to the definition of the usability of the ISO9241-11 (5) are. "In particular usage, when the particular user, a product is used to achieve the specified objectives. Degree of user satisfaction, and effective and efficiency" In ISO as the usability is defined.

In addition, the "satisfaction" is the central issue in the development vision that the proposed method is aiming for. Considering this, among the factors that form the "satisfaction", evaluated with an emphasis on "attractive" and "new" in particular.

In the evaluation of the Structured Scenario is, we have set the point of view that emphasizes evaluation, depending on the phase of the scenario. it is important to "satisfaction" in terms of the evaluation value scenario. Therefore, perform an evaluation of "new" and about the "attractive" target for the user to focus on in its phase. Activity scenario get value provided in the action scenes "valid" is an important evaluation point of view. Evaluation point of view which is the focus of interaction scenario is "efficiency" of the interaction is at the center. In addition, prototyping and evaluation of the business model that's been developed through a comprehensive process, evaluated in terms of the user aspect of the previous four.

Evaluation of Business Aspect. Evaluation of aspects of the business is done on the set at the time of the start of the project "Management resources (channel, knowhow, information, money, etc.)","Policy of business value", "User setting", "Intrinsic user value", evaluated to be a relationship, such as the proposed prototype produce a profit. The following items are specific evaluation point of view.

1. *Evaluation of the "strategy" of business.*
   - Does the policy along the corporate and business domains?
   - Do you fit the brand vision?
   - Do you have the right product strategy, service strategy?
2. *Evaluation of the "potential" of business.*
   - Whether they meet the current business environment?
   - Does the company have adapted to the management resources?
3. *Evaluation of the "marketability" of business.*
   - Is there sufficient market size to enter?
   - Is the expected growth and profitability of the market to enter?
   - Do you be accepted in a market?
4. *Evaluation of the "feasibility" of business.*
   - Do you have the technology and know-how required to develop, or possible to acquisition?
   - Do you accept distribution channels and sales companies and dealers?
   - Can you achieve that goal in the development period?
5. *Evaluation of the "sociality" of business.*
   - Do you have along the compliance?
   - Is the CSR along (including the environment)?
   - Are you environmentally conscious?
   - Do you have to consider universal design?
   - Do you have to consider safety and security?

4 Summary and Future Work

Experience Vision development by Vision centered design method is advanced by the expansion of a structured scenario. In addition, it is important that I in order for the project members to share this approach, carried out efficiently, promote a combination of rapid visualization and evaluation a quick. Visualization is required to incorporate the latest methods. Then, it is necessary to quickly evaluate the various professional members. Promise to efficiently find Experience vision of the "road to victory (Kachisuji)" value in the visualization and evaluation technique due to the Vision centered design method.

That we will experience a number of cases, more quickly, accurate and up to now, I want to continue the study aims to develop techniques Experience Vision simple.

References

1. Takahashi, K., Yamazaki, K., Ueda, Y., Go, K., Hayakawa, S., Yanagida, K.: Experience Vision. Maruzen Publishing Co., Ltd., Japan (2012) ISBN 978-4-621-08565-3 C 3050
2. Yanagida, K., Ueda, Y., Go, K., Takahashi, K., Hayakawa, S., Yamazaki, K.: Vision-proposal Design Method. In: Kurosu, M. (ed.) HCD 2011. LNCS, vol. 6776, pp. 166–174. Springer, Heidelberg (2011)
3. Yanagida, K., Ueda, Y., Go, K., Takahashi, K., Hayakawa, S., Yamazaki, K.: Structured Scenario-based Design Method. In: Kurosu, M. (ed.) HCD 2009. LNCS, vol. 5619, pp. 374–380. Springer, Heidelberg (2009)

Confabulation in the Time of Transdisciplinarity: Reflection on HCI Education and a Call for Conversation

Nicholas True, Jeroen Peeters, and Daniel Fallman

Interactive Institute, Department of Informatics, Umeå University,
Östra Strandgatan 26A, 90333, Umeå, Sweden
{nic,jeroen,daniel.fallman}@tii.se

Abstract. As HCI becomes ever-increasingly more transdisciplinary it encounters increasingly complex problems practical, methodological, and pedagogical in natures. This paper is an introductory exploration of the influence HCI education has in bridging academia and industry as students become practitioners. We examined how design pedagogy materializes and takes shape in both work and student process/attitudes as they become professionals, suggesting there is an area of importance to the community that is overlooked. Education shapes designers, designers shape the world, which prompts the need for a dialogue on how education pedagogy shapes practitioners that embody methods, values, skills, goals, and practices. As practitioners embody their knowledge into designs there arises a discussion that ought to be had.

Keywords: Design, HCI, Education, Pedagogy, Practice.

1 Introduction

Recently HCI scholars have explored the inter/multi/transdisciplinary nature of the discourse. [e.g. 1, 2, 6] HCI is steadily incorporating elements from fields previously outside its scope. This is generally considered a move toward a more complete and holistic scholarly discourse. It brings up the question of how this impacts the students who study at HCI, Interaction Design, or User Experience Design programs and move on to professional practice. The inner workings of such educational programs are rarely discussed in venues outside of the institutions themselves.

It is logical that the education of professionals in the academy has significant and lasting impact on the design process they practice when they move into the industry.

These design practitioners carry with them the knowledge they acquired in school and it impacts how they practice design. In this paper we examine the educational process at two programs aimed at preparing people to practice design professionally. These programs are the Human Computer Interaction Design program at Indiana University in Bloomington, Indiana (Indiana) in the United States and the Industrial Design program at Eindhoven University of Technology in Eindhoven, the Netherlands (TU/e).

Nelson and Stolterman in "The Design Way" state: "In the struggle to understand and interact in an ever more complex and dynamic reality...the current traditions of

M. Kurosu (Ed.): Human-Computer Interaction, Part I, HCII 2013, LNCS 8004, pp. 128–136, 2013.

inquiry and action prevalent in our society do not give us the support we need... to meet the emergent challenges that now confront us and will continue to confront us in the future." [14] Our contribution is to explore and discuss two programs aiming to prepare people to use design for tackling the increasingly complex world. Furthermore, we call for an expansion of this discussion from institutions educating designers.

2 Background

Although the programs at Indiana and TU/e come from different roots, both educate designers. Nelson and Stolterman state: "Different epistemologies lead to radically different environments that may be more or less suitable for supporting design learning. Unfortunately there are very few educational... environments today built on a design epistemology that reflects design in an adequate way." [14] We aim to respond to this claim through a comparative analysis of two programs cultivating an education centered around design epistemologies. What follows is a brief description of both programs to frame the later comparative analysis.

2.1 Indiana University

The Human Computer Interaction Design program at Indiana University is a two-year professional Master's of Science program within the Department of Informatics. The primary goal of the program is to teach students to think like designers. The program combines theory, practice, literature, and methods into a highly structured curriculum to prepare students for a professional career. [12]

The program employs significant group-based project work much of which is created in collaboration with people from industry. High value is placed on diversity students come from a wide range of backgrounds and countries. During the process students develop and refine a design philosophy with particular focus on social responsibility and build life-long connections with their cohort. The culmination of the degree work is a semester-long capstone project to showcase the knowledge and skills they have acquired. [12]

2.2 TU/e

The Industrial Design program at the Eindhoven University of Technology distinguishes itself from other industrial design programs with both its focus and its approach. The aim of the program is to "educate designers of intelligent systems, related products and services, for social/societal information". [7] The program builds on the phenomenology of perception and ecological psychology. [9, 13]

The educational system follows a unique competency-centered learning model: students themselves are responsible for their own development and the formation of their own identity, skills and vision as designers. A large emphasis is placed on making, students learn through experience by reflection-on-action loops. [10, 11]

3 Objective

It is our aim to respond to Nelson and Stolterman, and contribute to the knowledge base of design culture. In this paper we will show how design culture and epistemology are being cultivated in practice, and other ways through design pedagogy. We believe that a core value to design is the desire to transform the world for the better. The students educated in design programs more-often-than-not become designers that engage in transformative practices. The way designers learn how to design undoubtedly impacts how they practice, we assert that through examination and discussion of these practices it may be possible to encourage discussion amongst those that teach design. We believe that open discussion among educators will help enable the cultivation of richer and more meaningful design culture within design education.

4 Methodology

To examine the design driven and reflective educational pedagogies of the respective institutions we employed the following methodological approaches. We began with a literature review to situate this paper within the discourse. Examining scholarship integral to the pedagogical, epistemological, and philosophical mission of the schools, lastly sample writings of faculty for grounding. [professors] Appropriating the ethnographic gaze, we conducted interviews and diary studies with current students, as well as guided reflections with past and present students. Close reading of student projects were used for grounded comparison of respective design processes. Heavily qualitative approaches are often met with consternation from the HCI community for lacking rigor. Our intent here is not to prove, rather to explain the rich context of both schools and show the actualization of theory in the form of practice.

5 Diary Studies

As a method of discerning how the pedagogical and educational missions of the respective programs correlate with student experience we conducted diary studies with current students. The goal of the diary studies was to encourage students to reflect about their education while it was happening. Students of both years, of both programs participated. The only prompt the students were given was that they should write about their academic experience for one week. We believe that by leaving the prompt open ended would result with a better overall "snapshot" than a more focused study. As both institutions employ reflection as a tool for learning we were also interested as to how reflective the diary studies would be. Once collected we performed a close reading of the studies noting how they aligned with the official stated goals of the programs. As two authors of this paper are graduates of Indiana and TU/e respectively their experience was used as a lens for evaluation.

5.1 Indiana

The diary studies from Indiana were conducted during early January 2013 with students from both the first and second year of the program. This is of note because the second year students were in the initial stages of developing their capstone projects. Also of note is that some participants traveled to attend the IxDA Interaction 13 conference in Toronto Canada. While students are encouraged to attend academic and professional conferences at Indiana, this is voluntary and accounts for some deviation from normal in the diary writings.

When evaluating the diary studies we compared them to the stated goals of the program, the educational methods employed, and looked for emotional responses within. The main question is best summarized as "is the impact of the program noticeable in the students thoughts?"

At Indiana the overarching goal, as stated above, is to teach students to think like designers. Simply stated; close reading of the students diary entries affirms that the educational process does in fact train students in the ways of design thinking and practice. There are a number of design methods explicitly mentioned, including but not limited to: affinity diagrams, contextual inquiry, ethnographic observations, case studies, workshops, critique, wireframing, sketching, design process, field notes, etc. Every student mentioned design literature, both required and elective. The PRInCiPleS framework [20] was mentioned with high frequency and students discuss how they use it to articulate what they accomplish through their process.

Outside of methods and literature there were some other interesting commonalities. Social consciousness was pervasive in the diary entries. One student recounts a discussion with peers about "design activism". Others mention the social value aspect of their designs and how this is a vital part of the process. One student discusses an ethical dilemma that they encountered while working on a design.

Of further note is the mention of involvement in research groups. A handful of students articulated working with professors of the program on academic research. While this is strictly on a volunteer basis, the students mention how they appreciate the experience and how it might help prepare them for their post-graduation endeavors. One student mentioned how this opportunity might increase their chances of being accepted to a Ph.D. program. Another common theme was the focus on applying for internships for first year students, or jobs for second year students. Core to both types of applications is the development of an online portfolio which is mandatory, reinforcing the status as a professional program intending to enable students to procure gainful employment after graduation. This is not to say that the program is exclusionary of academic pursuits, although they seem to be the exception rather than the rule.

5.2 TU/e

Due to the highly self-directed and varied nature of learning activities undertaken at TU/e at any one time, the diary studies of Master students are not representative of their whole educational experience. However, the salient aspects of what we observed upon close reading of the diary studies, clearly reflect the core-values of the program.

All of the students report on their graduation project, either by reflecting on their progress and experience of the project (as part of an internship or purely self-directed), or by reflecting upon preparations they are making before starting the project (e.g. contacting potential industry partners). These reflections are of a highly personal nature, in which students approach their projects from their own interests and value structures, implementing their vision and identity as a designer. This reflects the highly individualized and self-aware nature of the curriculum.

Each student also reflects to some extent on the act of making as an integral part of their design process. These reflections range from reflections on a process level (e.g. prototyping and modeling as a tool in materializing thoughts and gain insights into possible directions for an upcoming project), to more specific reflections on the process of building and testing a complex electronically based prototype of a new system. There is a clear focus on the physicalization and materialization of thinking, through a variety of media, as a generator of knowledge and method of gaining insights, clearly reflecting the Reflective Transformative Design Process [10] that is taught at the department.

Students also reflected on their future as professionals. Two students reflected on presently working at the design department of a global electronics company, and their process of positioning themselves within the company for possible future employment. One other student reflects on her perception of skills and attitudes required for a career as an independent designer and entrepreneur.

While this is a very high-level analysis of the diary study, the focus of our intervention is to see if aspects of the educational and pedagogical goals of the programs are evident in the student reflections. The answer is resoundingly affirmative.

6 Graduation Projects

Both degree programs culminate in a final project where students are tasked with actualizing the skills they have learned during their education. At Indiana the project is one semester, at TU/e it spans the entire second year. The projects selected received the highest marks at their respective institutions and as such, serve as exemplars. They were examined closely to see if traces of the educational goals and design pedagogy are observable.

6.1 Indiana

From Indiana we selected the Capstone of Jeremy White from 2012 titled: "From Food Allergies to Foodies: A 30 Year User Experience Vision" completed under the supervision of advisors Jeffrey Bardzell and Eli Blevis. [19] The project deliverable is in the form of a 151 page .PDF document created using the standard template created by Eli Blevis. [21]

The project is exemplary of the Indiana program in many ways. The most noticeable aspect is the utilization of the PRInCiPleS framework which is a staple of the program. [20] This is the framework students use to articulate design explanations. This framework consists of six parts to any design explanation which are: predispositions, research, insights, concepts, prototypes, and strategies. (For a more detailed explanation see [20]) Social value is also prominently featured as people with food allergies must pay close attention to what they consume for fear of allergic reaction causing physical consequences. Furthermore, considering the role food plays in sociality they may also experience emotional distress.

When comparing the mission, vision, and goal of the Indiana HCI/d program this project aligns itself quite well. He utilized many of the methods he learned such as: interviews, surveys, literature review, sketching, information visualization, concepting, concept systems, ideation, and iteration among others. He also clearly outlines, discussed, and articulates how he completed the personal design process he developed during his studies.

6.2 TU/e

From TU/e, we selected the Master graduation project of Jelle Stienstra, entitled "Augmented Speed-Skate Experience – Applied Movement Sonification". The project was completed in 2009 under the supervision of Kees Overbeeke, Stephan Wensveen and René Ahn. A 48 page thesis, one of the project deliverables, and one academic paper that resulted from the project, were examined. [16, 17, 18]

In this research-through-design project, Jelle aimed to empower professional speed-skating athletes to improve their technique by sonification of their movements. The project builds on existing theories on sonification as a method to add a new sense modality and support muscle learning. It is a personal project, in which the interests and vision of the designer are embodied, aiming to empower athletes to improve their performance. The project concluded with experiments in which hypotheses concerning the effects of sonification were tested using a working prototype.

When comparing the project to the vision and educational system of TU/e, we clearly see how this design project embodies the program's values. Making was an integral part of the design process, involving the design and building of a working prototype, embedded with a set of speed-skates, that wirelessly communicated with a server and provided the athlete with real-time sonification of her technique.

7 Discussion

The exploratory research above was centered around a single goal, to discover if and preliminarily how students actuate the knowledge and teaching they acquire at Indiana and TU/e in their personal design process. Through the studies we found that while the students develop their design process in a deeply personal way, the implications of their education are clearly visible both in their words and in their work.

Much of the educational process is resultant from academic scholarship, however that scholarship is often discussed in the context of the academy. Rarely is the real world impact of the educational process discussed as is pertains to how people transition from students to professionals, with regard to how and what they take with them into industry. We believe this to be an important, but overlooked aspect of design practice.

Responding to the call of Nelson and Stolterman we attempted to articulate that design culture is alive and well within the context of design education. Further, that the examination of the gap between pedagogy and design practice seems to be widening. The design world examines design work, the academy examines scholarship, we have made an initial attempt to examine how pedagogy is acted with or upon by students when they become practitioners. We believe that design as a discipline seeks to mold and shape the world, and that pedagogy as education molds and shapes people who will practice design. Lastly, we believe that this is an interesting area for future education deserving of discussion.

8 Conclusion

We found through our initial exploration that education shapes designers and those designers shape the world. We believe that as design seeks to "better" the world that there is a need for a cohesive and inclusive discussion around how education is acted upon by designers in design. Furthermore, we believe that we have shown that there is a distinct connection between how designers learn to design and how they do design. While this may seem intuitive we assert that there is an increasing need for these types of discussions as design becomes ever-increasingly transdisciplinary. As noted in this paper, the two programs we compared both produce designers, however, they do so in drastically different ways, with different methods, values, and goals, skills, and practices.

In summary, we believe this study, liminal as it may be, has exposed an interesting area of discussion currently lacking. The diversity of educational methods can strengthen the community, but it might also just as easily fracture. We believe we have merely scratched the surface with this study and encourage others to share perspectives with the hope of starting a constructive conversation within the field.

Finally, what we have attempted here is not just to look at the design work and/or results that are being produced, or just at the design pedagogy and educational values that guide these students as they gain competence and transition into professional careers. Rather, we have examined the bridge between these; in what way do these two viewpoints correlate and in what ways do they influence each other? We believe this discussion to be of value because these processes heavily influence the burgeoning field of interaction design, when these students become practicing designers they carry with them the aforementioned methods, values, goals, skills, and practices and embody them into their designs.

References

1. Bannon, L.: Reimagining HCI: toward a more human-centered perspective. Interactions 18(4), 50–57 (2011)
2. Bardzell, J.: Interaction criticism and aesthetics. In: Proceedings of the 27th International Conference on Human Factors in Computing Systems (CHI 2009), pp. 2357–2366. ACM, New York (2009)
3. Bardzell, S., Bardzell, J.: Towards a feminist HCI methodology: social science, feminism, and HCI. In: Proceedings of the SIGCHI Conference on Human Factors in Computing Systems (CHI 2011), pp. 675–684. ACM, New York (2011)
4. Blevis, E.: Sustainable interaction design: invention & disposal, renewal & reuse. In: Proceedings of the SIGCHI Conference on Human Factors in Computing Systems (CHI 2007), pp. 503–512. ACM, New York (2007)
5. Blevis, E., Stolterman, E.: FEATURE: Transcending disciplinary boundaries in interaction design. Interactions 16(5), 48–51 (2009)
6. Blythe, M.A., Overbeeke, C.J., Monk, A.F., Wright, P.C.: Funology: from usability to enjoyment. Kluwer Academic, Amsterdam (2003)
7. Department of Industrial Design, Eindhoven University of Technology website: `http://w3.id.tue.nl/nl/education/foundation/` (accessed February 25, 2013)
8. Fallman, D., Stolterman, E.: Establishing criteria of rigor and relevance in interaction design research. In: Mival, O., Bonner, J., Smyth, M., O'Neill, S. (eds.) Proceedings of the 2010 International Conference on the Interaction Design (Create 2010), pp. 58–63. British Computer Society, Swinton (2010)
9. Gibson, J.J.: The ecological approach to visual perception. Lawrence Erlbaum, London (1979) (reprinted in 1986)
10. Hummels, C., Frens, J.: The reflective transformative design process. In: Conference Proceedings of CHI 2009, Boston, Massachusetts, USA, April 4-9, pp. 2655–2658 (2009)
11. Hummels, C., Vinke, D.: Eindhoven designs: Developing the competence of designing intelligent systems, vol. 2. Eindhoven University of Technology, The Netherlands (2009)
12. Indiana University School of Informatics and Computing web-site: `http://www.soic.indiana.edu/graduate/programs/hcid/` (accessed January 11, 2012)
13. Merleau-Ponty, M.: Phenomenology of Perception. Humanities Press, New York (1962); Colin Smith (trans.)
14. Nelson, H., Stoltermam, E.: The Design Way: Intentional Change in an Unpredictable World. The MIT Press (2012)
15. Overbeeke, C.J., Djajadiningrat, J.P., Hummels, C.C.M., Wensveen, S.A.G.: Beauty in usability: forget about ease of use! In: Green, W.S., Jordan, P.W. (eds.) Pleasure with Products: Beyond Usability, pp. 9–16. Taylor & Francis (2002)
16. Stienstra, J.T.: Augmented Speed-Skate Experience, Applied Movement Sonification. Eindhoven University of Technology, Eindhoven (2009)
17. Stienstra, J.T., Bruns, M., Wensveen, S.A.G., Kuenen, C.D.: How to design for transformation of behavior through interactive materiality. In: Proceedings of the 7th Nordic Conference on Human-Computer Interaction (NordiCHI 2012), October 14-17. ACM, Copenhagen (2012)

18. Stienstra, J.T., Overbeeke, C.J., Wensveen, S.A.G.: Embodying Complexity through Movement Sonification: Case Study on Empowering the Speed-skater. In: Proc. CHItaly 2011, pp. 39–44. ACM, New York (2011)
19. White, J.: From Food Allergies to Foodies: A 30 Year User Experience Vision, http://delightfulsimplicity.net/portfolio/images/portfolio/FoodieAllergy/FoodieAllergy_Document_JeremyWhite.pdf
20. Blevis, E.: The PRInCiPleS Design Framework. In: Carroll, J. (ed.) Human Computer Interaction Series 1. Creativity and Rationale, vol. 20, pp. 143–169. Springer (2012)
21. Blevis, E.: Capstone Template, http://eli.informatics.indiana.edu/I694-Template-V1.1c.indd

Proposal for Experience Vision

Kazuhiko Yamazaki[1], Kentaro Go[2], Katsumi Takahashi[3], Seiji Hayakawa[4], Yoshihiro Ueda[5], and Koji Yanagida[6]

[1] Fujitsu Design Ltd., Kawasaki, 211-8588, Japan
y.ueda@jp.fujitsu.com
[5] Chiba Institute of Technology, Narashino, 275-0016, Japan
designkaz@gmail.com
[2] University of Yamanashi, Kofu, 400-8511, Japan
go@yamanashi.ac.jp
[3] Holon Create Inc., Yokohama, 222-0033, Japan
takahasi@hol-on.co.jp
[4] Ricoh Company, Ltd., Yokohama, 222-8530, Japan
hayakawa@rdc.ricoh.co.jp
[5] Fujitsu Design Ltd., Kawasaki, 211-8588, Japan
y.ueda@jp.fujitsu.com
[6] Kurashiki University of Science and the Arts, Kurashiki, 712-8505, Japan
yanagida@arts.kusa.ac.jp

Abstract. Recently, it was known the problem-solving design approach has limitation to create new business or design. And service design is focused to create new business. Based on these background, we propose vision centered design approach named "Experience Vision". Purpose of this research is to propose design approach and method to create new service design or new product design based on vision centered design approach. Experience Vision is a comprehensive design method to envision innovative services, systems and products which reflect upon potential stakeholders' experiences and company mission and vision. Core of Experience Vision is vision centered design approach based on human centered design process with business perspective. For this purpose, we developed "Frame work for vision centered design method "and "Structured Scenario-Based Design Method (SSBDM)". "Frame work for vision centered design method " is based on SSBDM and user centered design approach which is focused user and business. This frame is including "Goal setting of project", intrinsic user value, policy of business value, value scenario, activity scenario, interaction scenario, scenario visualization, scenario evaluation, planning documentation, and specification.

Keywords: experience vision, service design, scenario, scenario-based design.

1 Introduction

In this paper, we introduce vision centered design method named "Experience vision". It contains summary of vision centered design method, approach to vision centered

M. Kurosu (Ed.): Human-Computer Interaction, Part I, HCII 2013, LNCS 8004, pp. 137–145, 2013.

design method, comparison with problem-solving method and framework for vision-centered method. Following is four background of Experience Vision.

"Limitation of problem solving design method" is the first background. Recently, it is important to propose new service, new product and new services. Design method is expected to propose new vision including service based on human centered design approach.

"Importance of service design method" is another background. Recently, service business and service based system/ product are growing rapidly.

"Expected designing method for experience" is third background. Recently, value can experience becomes more important than product value. However, the design meth for experience is not established. Design method that takes into account the overall user experience is expected.

"Expected evolution based on latest IT technology" is fourth background. In recent years, the latest IT technology has evolved dramatically; to propose a new vision method that corresponds to this IT technology is desired.

"Expected designing method to create new vision based on HCD" is fifth background.

Based on these background, we propose vision centered design approach named "Experience Vision". Purpose of this research is to propose design approach and method to create new service design or new product design based on vision centered design approach.

Experience Vision is a comprehensive design method to envision innovative services, systems and products which reflect upon potential stakeholders' experiences and company mission and vision. Core of Experience Vision is vision centered design approach based on human centered design process with business perspective. For this purpose, we developed "Frame work for vision centered design method "and "Structured Scenario-Based Design Method (SSBDM)".

2 Summary of Vision Centered Design

Based on 5 background, Experience vision is a comprehensive design method to envision innovative services, systems and products which reflect upon potential stakeholders' experiences and company mission and vision.

There are two case for vision centered design method to adapt. One is "When it needs to create a new value to existing products and services," and another is "When it needs to produce new product or service if ever."

As expected effect of this method is an effective in the following five cases;

1. To develop an easy-to-use products and services than ever before.
2. To find out customer value as the source of the next generation of competition.
3. To reduce costs and speed up development by starting from vision.
4. To develop services and products that satisfy customers.
5. To contribute to the management of the company to clarify the vector for the next generation of business.

3 Concept of Vision Centered Design Approach

Following is 5 concept of vision centered design approach;

1. Starting from intrinsic user value

Most design method will start from problem-solving. Problem-solving method will focus visible user problem by user research or other research. By Problem-solving method, it is not easy to propose new system and product because focusing visible user interactions or activities.

User research and user observation method is often used for finding problems. New approach is needed to propose new system and product by starting from intrinsic user value.

2. Create idea from value level or service level

Problem solving is often the idea from a lower level and vision centered design approach will be starting from higher level to create idea. And a higher level means the intrinsic value of the users, business and service level.

3. Consistently through to system specifications from the user research

Often even if it has been found intrinsic user value by user research, it is not easy to reflect the final product and systems. It is considered one factor there was no description of intrinsic user value. In vision centered design method, scenario is utilized as the common description of intrinsic user value.

4. Consider to collaborate experts from different fields

"Collaboration of experts in different fields," is one of the principles of human-centered design. In case of vision centered design methods, "The experts from different fields, including expert user (designer) and business professionals in particular is important collaboration. In order to facilitate this collaboration, easy-to-understand visualization is the key to everyone.

5. Involve user from the beginning of design process

One of the principles of human-centered design approach is "Listening to the user at all times". In case of vision centered design approach, one of concept is "ask the user always from a higher level".

4 Vision Centered Design Approach vs. Problem-Solving Approach

Fig.1 can be represented as in compares the problem-solving approach to vision centered design approach by diagram of the basic design process. In this figure, the process will be described by the vertical axis for the classification of activities and is the horizontal axis is time of design process. The horizontal axis has 4 layer such as value, activity, interaction and fact.

The black lines represent the traditional problem-solving approach and orange lines represent vision centered design approach on Fig.1.

In case of problem-solving approach, design process is starting from setting the goals of the project, conduct user research and quantitative to understand the problems and needs of users from there, identify the problem, creating idea to solve the problem, evaluation the idea, led to the development of products and systems to the final.

In case of vision centered design approach, design process is starting from setting the goal of the project to propose vision, conduct user research qualitative to discover the intrinsic value of the user from there, creative jump by idea development, value scenario, activity scenario, and interaction scenarios, evaluate the proposal, to the development of products and systems to the final.

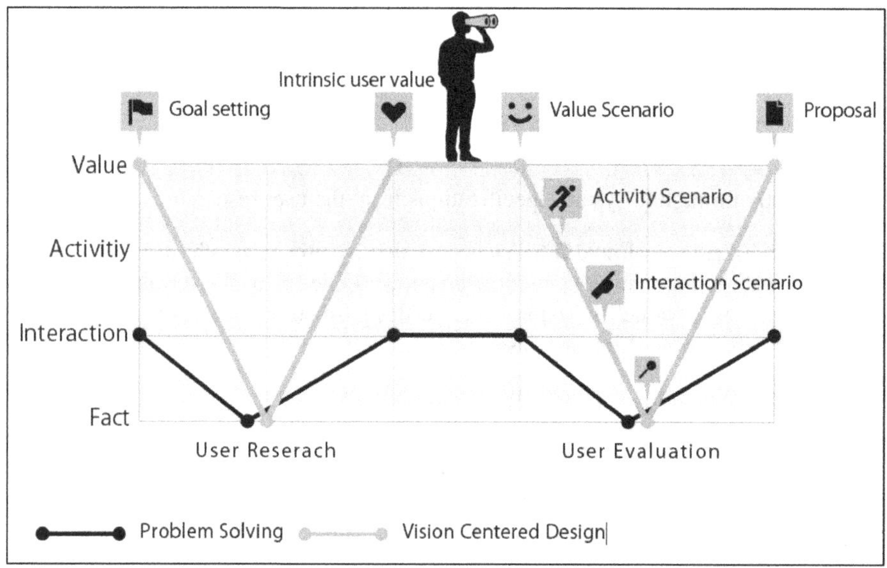

Fig. 1. Vision Centered Design Approach vs. Problem-solving Approach

5 Framework for Vision Centered Design Method

Core of Experience vision is vision centered design approach based on human centered design process with business perspective. For this purpose, we developed "Frame work for vision centered design method "and "Structured Scenario-Based Design Method (SSBDM)".

In the vision centered design method, scenarios (which are described from the user's perspective) will be introduced as a tool to describe and convey a vision of the future. Using scenarios for the design of services, systems and products has been a commonly addressed issue in the field of Human-Centered Design (HCD). SSBDM contains three layers of scenarios: value scenario, activity scenario, and interaction scenario.

As shown in Fig.2-Fig.5, "Frame work for vision centered design method " is based on SSBDM and user centered design approach which is focused user and business. This framework is including "Goal setting of project", intrinsic user value, policy of business value, user setting, business setting, value scenario, activity scenario, interaction scenario, scenario visualization, scenario evaluation, planning documentation, and specification.

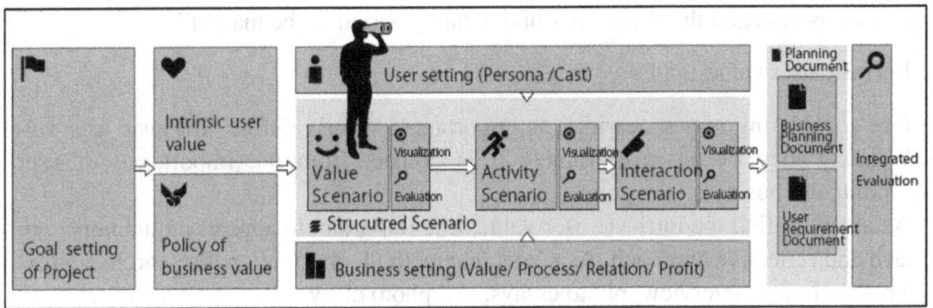

Fig. 2. Framework for Vision Centered Design Method

The following is the element of framework for vision centered design methods.

1. Goal setting of the project
2. Intrinsic user value
3. Policy of business value
4. User setting (Persona/ Cast)
5. Business setting (Value/ Process/ Relation/ Profit)
6. Structured scenario including Value, Activity and Interaction scenario
7. Visualization
8. Evaluation
9. Planning Document

Followings is each description for the element of framework for vision centered design methods.

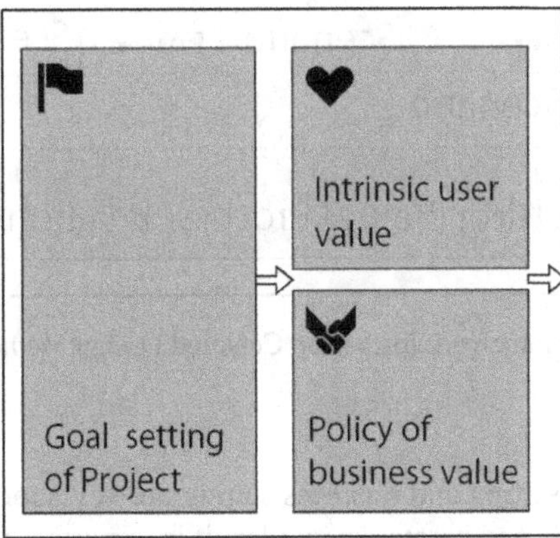

Fig. 3. Framework for Vision Centered Design Method-1

1. Goal setting of the project

As shown in Fig.3, the beginning of this method is to set project goal. For vision centered design approach, it is important to define project objectives to propose a vision as a first step. A setting for the target at each stage will consider user's viewpoint and business viewpoint. The goal from user viewpoint is including "When, where, who, or what kind experience". The goal of the business viewpoint is including "target position as a business and the company's brand, and position in the market".

2. Intrinsic user value

Before considering user scenario, it is important to clearly define "Intrinsic user value" and "Policy of business value". It is comers from the importance of user viewpoint and business viewpoint.

As a way to find the intrinsic user value, it is important to approach qualitative approach and reflective approach. As a concrete method, observational research, contextual research, user interview, photo essays, and photo diary.

3. Policy of business value

To clearly define policy of business value, it is important to reconfirm the corporate domain, such as division policy, and corporate policies. And then, we need to define policy of business value for each project.

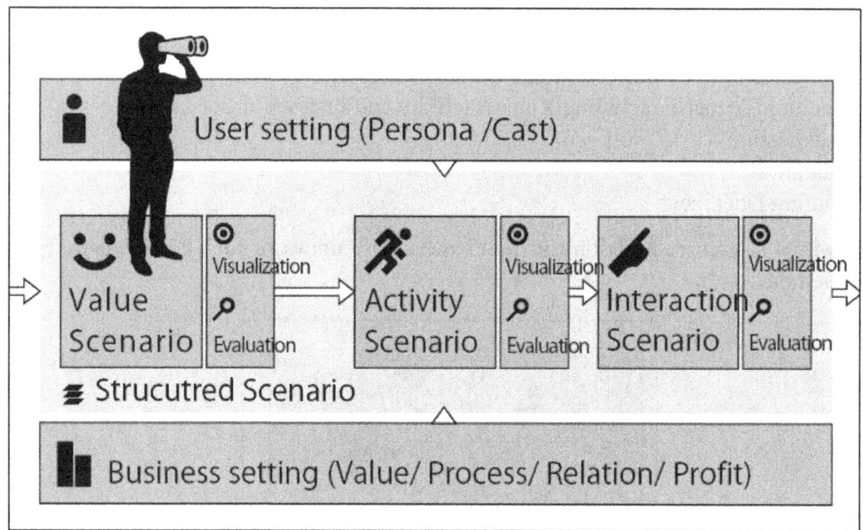

Fig. 4. Framework for Vision Centered Design Method-2

4. User setting

As shown in Fig.4, user setting and business setting are key approach for this method. In order to spread the idea and create a new idea, it is important to take steps to clarify the target users in stages.

The process for user setting is describing the approximate target user in setting the goals of the project, complete setting "user list, "temporary cast", "cast" and "persona. In addition, we need to link each scenario and each set of the target user.

5. Business setting

Vision centered design method is an approach to be considered from the early stages of both the business and the target user. Take steps to clarify in stages, and specification information about the business.

The process for business setting is describing the approximate business information in setting the goals of the project, defining policy of business value, draft business setting and detailed business setting. In addition, linking each scenario and business-related information, respectively.

6. Structured scenario

In the vision centered design approach, however, a scenario is used to describe a vision. That is, a scenario is created to explain the future goal resulting from the development. In this case, the scenario will function as a development goal. Unlike the problem-solving design approach, the act of designing will not always begin based on a scenario which describes the problematic situation, and the action can begin according to the designer's free, original idea and technology seeds. As a result of the design, visualization is required to share and assess the effect on users.

Scenario method structure, to create ideas for improving the "user satisfaction" and "efficiency of the system to develop" a, "the effectiveness of the services provided" by a scenario for each layer that are structured , finally is a method for describing the specifications of the product IT systems and truly usable.

With the vision centered design method, the scenario will be classified according to the hierarchy and then structured. Classifying the function of a services, systems and products with the focus on its components will make it easier to understand. It can be classified into three hierarchies here: value, activity, and interaction.

7. Visualization

Only scenario structure by text, it is difficult to imagine a concrete image. Utilize a technique called prototype, the user perspective to visualize the use of a technique called business model is a business perspective. By visualization of user and business, project member can be a member of the project evaluation and ideas to imagine a concrete image.

8. Evaluation

In the vision centered design method, is provided a process of "evaluation" and "visualization" to each phase of the Structured Scenario. After proposal and visualization, the evaluation done in each phase of the Structured Scenario is focused on a scenario should be selected to proceed to the next phase of the scenario from which to create more than one proposal. It also sets the evaluation process even after the full extent of the Structured Scenario was determined.

Evaluation process does the evaluation of prototypes and business mode diagram guided into the overall scenario. It is necessary that the value that is put on the business model and the proto-type is sufficiently effective to the user, which is the high degree of satisfaction. It has become something beneficial for the business of the company. It is important to evaluate the value of the proposals in these respects.

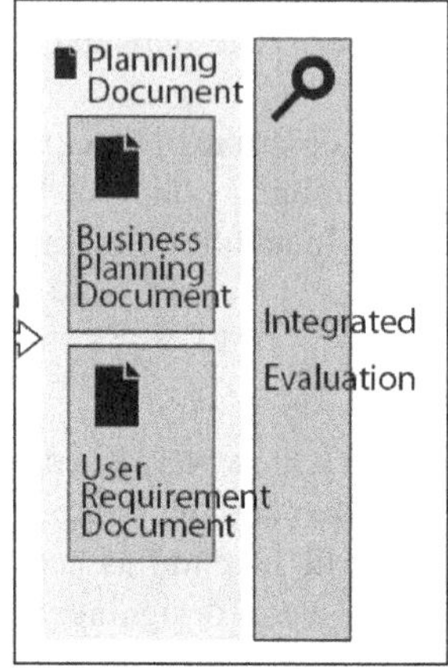

Fig. 5. Framework for Vision Centered Design Method-3

9. Planning document

As shown in Fig.5, final goal is planning document for this method. In the vision centered design method, after utilized structured scenario, it can be described "user requirements documentation" and "business planning documentation" as a part of planning document.

6 Conclusion

In this paper, we have described summary of vision centered, concept of vision centered design approach and framework of vision centered design method.

As a result of this study, we confirmed that framework of vision centered design method has possible is possible to propose new system and product.

We believe that *Experience Vision* (Vision Centered Design method), as a structured scenario method, is an effective way to efficiently produce sophisticated ideas.

References

1. Takahashi, K., Yamazaki, K., Ueda, Y., Go, K., Hayakawa, S., Yanagida, K.: Experience Vision. Maruzen Publishing Ltd., Japan (2012) ISBN 978-4-621-08565-3 C 3050
2. Go, K.: What Properties Make Scenarios Useful in Design for Usability. In: Kurosu, M. (ed.) HCD 2009. LNCS, vol. 5619, pp. 193–201. Springer, Heidelberg (2009)

3. Edited by Japan Industrial Designers' Association: Product Design, Works Corporation, pp. 116–117 (2009)
4. Yanagida, K., Ueda, Y., Go, K., Takahashi, K., Hayakawa, S., Yamazaki, K.: Vision-proposal Design Method. In: Kurosu, M. (ed.) HCD 2011. LNCS, vol. 6776, pp. 166–174. Springer, Heidelberg (2011)
5. Yanagida, K., Ueda, Y., Go, K., Takahashi, K., Hayakawa, S., Yamazaki, K.: Structured Scenario-based Design Method. In: Kurosu, M. (ed.) HCD 2009. LNCS, vol. 5619, pp. 374–380. Springer, Heidelberg (2009)

Collaborative User Experience Design Methods for Enterprise System

Hiroko Yasu[1], Naoko Iwata[2], and Izumi Kohno[1]

[1] NEC Corporation
h-yasu@ax.jp.nec.com, kohno@ay.jp.nec.com
[2] NEC Design & Promotion, Ltd., Japan
n-iwata@necdp.nec.co.jp

Abstract. The importance of user experience (UX) design has increased in enterprise field. In traditional product and service development, a division of labor between UX designers and engineers was necessary. It is, however, difficult to pursue the same development style in the enterprise field. Therefore, in this study, collaborative UX design Methods for Enterprise System between UX designers and engineers were proposed. These Methods were designed to allow UX designers and engineers to supplement each other's knowledge and experience. The first Method was UX Observation Tour, a behavioral observation method used to understand the psychological and/or physical characteristics as well as behavior patterns of target users. In this Method, UX designers and engineers shared user research experience through field work. The second Method was UX Idea Mapping. This was a method for establishing associations between the needs of target users and unique ideas that UX designers and engineers, who achieved a detailed understanding of the target users, developed together based on their expertise in systems. In this study, these two methods were applied to internal projects, and as a result, both Methods effectively promoted collaborative development of UX designs by the UX designers and engineers.

Keywords: User Experience, UX design, UX Method and UCD.

1 Introduction

UX design is effective in improving the value of the user experience, and its effectiveness has been proven in development of mobiles phones, computers, computer applications, and consumer products and services such as SNS and EC sites where the attractiveness of products directly influences their sales or market valuation.

In recent years, UX design has been used for developing consumer products and services. Its importance has also been increasing in the enterprise field.

In order to introduce UX designs into consumer product and service development, UX designers and engineers usually divide tasks. The division of tasks in each

M. Kurosu (Ed.): Human-Computer Interaction, Part I, HCII 2013, LNCS 8004, pp. 146–155, 2013.

development process allows the designers and engineers to take advantage of their expertise and effectively develop the target product or service (here, UX designers refers to those who have expertise in UX such as information architects, interaction designers, human researchers, and UX consultants, and engineers refers to those who have knowledge of technical and business in the enterprise systems fields such as product planners and developers.

As the importance of incorporating UX design into enterprise systems increases, it is important to establish an UX design methods for system development. However, in the enterprise field development, the nature of products and services as well as the knowledge required of engineers may differ from what would be required in consumer product and service development. In this case, UX development methods used in consumer product and service development cannot be applied to enterprise system development as they are. We have therefore proposed UX design methods that could be applied to enterprise system development.

In this paper, Chapter 2 describes the issues involved in applying traditional development styles to enterprise system development, Chapter 3 describes UX Observation Tour and UX Idea Mapping, which are the two proposed collaborative UX design Methods in enterprise system development, and Chapter 4 describes the results and effects of applying these Methods.

2 Issues

2.1 Traditional UX Design

A UX design is generally implemented through the flow of: '1.user research', '2.idea generation' and then '3.product or service design and development' (Fig.1).

The objective of user research is to obtain basic information for product or service ideas that would improve user experience. For this, it is necessary to collect user comments and behavioral data as objectively as possible in order to analyze and evaluate the psychology, environment, habits, and value concepts that exist in the backgrounds of these comments and behavior.

The objective of idea generation is to create ideas that would improve user experience and incorporate them in product and service development. The ideas must be created based on a good and detailed understanding of the psychological and/or physical characteristics, behavior, and environment of target users obtained through the analysis and evaluation phase of user research.

In the field of consumer product and service development, UX designers conduct the user research, and either UX designers or engineers are in charge of idea generation. An appropriate division of the company is appointed to carry out each process to adopt UX design methods efficiently and successfully.

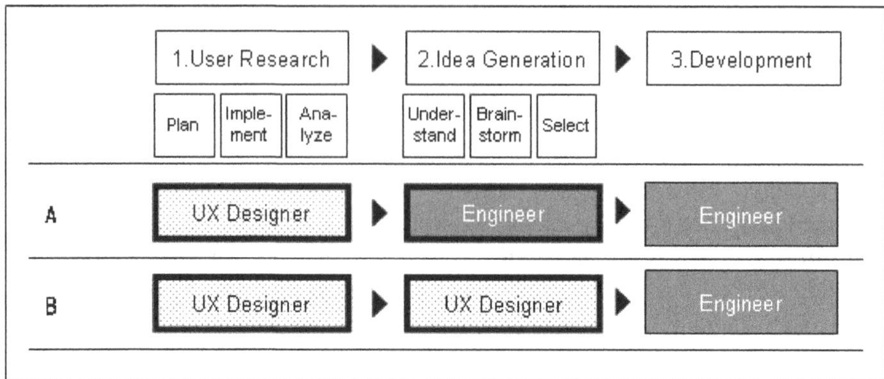

Fig. 1. UX design flow

2.2 Issues of Traditional UX Design in Field of Enterprise System

Although the traditional user research and idea generation methods described above have been proven successful in the field of consumer product development, they lead to the following 3 issues in the field of enterprise system development:

1. Unlike in the case of consumer product development, UX designers alone cannot implement user research in the field of enterprise system development. In a user research, it is necessary to create a research scenario. In the field of enterprise system development, which user types, tasks, or conditions are selected for the research depends on business tasks such as monitoring, and data input or making settings relies on skills. Therefore, selection of types of behavior and tasks depends on the tasks and skills required in a certain specialized field. Therefore, it is impossible for UX designers to fully understand the tasks and skills required to establish a research plan. In the implementation phase, it is necessary to collect user comments and information on their behavior by means of interviews, observation, and facilitation. However, UX experts, or UX designers, have limited understanding of user behavior expected by engineers. Therefore, they cannot observe users or obtain their comments completely. This means that UX experts alone cannot implement user research for enterprise system development. They cannot implement the analysis and evaluation phase of the research alone for the same reason.
2. Unlike in the case of consumer product development, engineers alone cannot implement idea generation in the field of enterprise system development. it is difficult for engineers alone to fully achieve a detailed understanding of users. The first step of the idea generation phase is to group users with similar behavioral patterns into user groups based on the behavioral patterns identified in the work model analysis described above. These behavior patterns are based on users' business tasks and skills. In the field of consumer products and service, engineers can develop ideas by themselves, because user behavior is simple. In the field of enterprise system development, user behavior is often triggered by individual reasons such as tasks,

work hours, and work environment. Therefore, it is necessary to examine in detail the causal relationships. Although engineers have knowledge of the business tasks and skills of users as the background of their behavior, it is difficult for them to master how to organize the obtained information from the user perspective. There is another reason why engineers alone cannot brainstorm and select ideas in the field of enterprise system development. In this field, advanced technologies are often used. If engineers alone discuss and generate ideas, they are likely to lack the value-perspective of the users and will generate technical potential-oriented ideas.

3. Unlike in the case of consumer product development, UX designers alone cannot implement idea generation in the field of enterprise system development. In this field, user behavior often relies on specialized tasks and skills. Therefore, UX designers who have no special business or technical knowledge in the field cannot achieve a detailed understanding of users, brainstorm ideas, or select ideas.

3 Proposal Methods

Designing of UX in the field of enterprise system development requires UX designers and engineers to supplement each other's knowledge in '1.user research' and '2.idea generation' phases. In this study, two collaborative UX design Methods were proposed for UX designers and engineers.

UX Observation Tour. UX Observation Tour is a behavioral observation method of user research. In this Method, UX designers and engineers engage in brainstorming ideas [1] and field work to share their common views and experience of implementing a user research. This enables the engineers who are unfamiliar with user research methods to work with the UX designers and to obtain data on users' behavior and their psychological and/or physical characteristics. UX Observation Tour has been designed to focus on the planning and implementation phases of a user research. Analysis and discussion are carried out in UX Idea Mapping described below. It is important that engineers implement user research at the actual research site.

UX Idea Mapping. In UX Idea Mapping, engineers and UX designers work together to analyze and discuss obtained user research data to achieve a detailed understanding of users, associate user needs with unique ideas developed based on their expertise in systems, and select suitable ideas for a system using a UX map.

3.1 UX Observation Tour

Planning. The first step in this Method is brainstorming ideas for a 'tour' plan that will allow the UX designers and the engineers to work together and supplement each other's knowledge and experience. Note that brainstorming ideas also serves as a rehearsal for the collaborative work to be carried out by the UX designers and engineers later in the process. The UX designers and engineers select a theme for the UX experience in advance, and discuss and share information about themes 1 and 2 below:

Theme 1: Project goal: Ideas are brainstormed for a top-down assigned project goal, project success, expected effects, desirable direction, background, and issues. Then, the ideas are shared among the members.

Theme 2: Research subjects: The following items about the research subject are discussed: type of system, role of the system, preceding events, and competing systems and/or services. In general, in the field of enterprise system development, engineers are able to select prospective research participants based on their expertise in specific business tasks and skills. It is, however, difficult for those who have no UX knowledge to come up with preceding events or competing systems and/or services because these events or systems and/or services must have value that is equal to that to be provided to users. Here are some examples of events listed by UX designers that have equal value, 1) Events with a similar business task requiring selection of an appropriate product in accordance with given conditions such as 'customer service desk for insurance products' and 'cosmetic product counter', 2) Events with a similar mission requiring a device to endure long hours of operation such as 'monitoring system in a flight control room' and 'game arcade', 3)Events with a similar desired attitude in customer interactions to achieve customer satisfaction such as 'store support system' and 'hotel concierge'.

For this reason, the UX designers are in charge of listing the subject events and providing ideas on research subjects based on engineer comments. The UX designers then request feedback from the engineers.

The results of discussions of theme 1 and 2 above are then put together into a research plan. The research plan must include information on the research subjects and schedule such as subjects and observation points at each observation site, Time table, information on observation sites and where to meet, important points of the research. Also, it should include the following information so that the engineers who are not familiar with user research can check it during the research.

Implementation. The UX designers and engineers participate in the user research as UX Observation Tour. As described above, this research requires engineers to fully understand the user needs and generate ideas for a system. For this reason, it is desirable to invite engineers with as many attributes as possible, such as different specializations or roles, to the research group. The duration of the tour should be shorter than half a day in consideration of the busy schedule of engineers. Note that the research should focus more on the number of observation points than duration. Here is a example of the schedule for a half-a-day tour: 30 minutes: orientation / 2 to 4 hours: research / 60 minutes: review.

The research members repeat the cycle of conducting the research for 15 to 20 minutes and sharing the research results within the team for the next 10 minutes.

Opinion exchanges will allow discovery of new perspectives, and information sharing will clarify the details to be recorded. Each team consists of up to six members. Note, however, a team can be reduced to the size of two or three members if needed because a smaller number of individuals might be better suited to discussions and less likely to pressure or discomfort the research subjects. Note that each team should include at least one UX designer to check how the engineers conduct the observations and to share the check result with the team members. Each member carries the research plan and checks it before entering an observation site. It should be understood that it may be difficult for engineers to conduct the research as planned because they are not used to conducting observations. For this reason, UX designers must check how engineers are conducting observations. They must give advice to the engineers if any of the following applies in order to encourage the engineers to conduct the research autonomously.

Here are some examples of cases in which the UX designer should give advice to the engineer :

- The engineer does not have a general understanding of the subjects or the individuals who have business relationships with the subjects. Example advice: "Keep a record of people who talked with your research subjects and also the individuals who were near them."
- The engineer focuses only on the product and service provider perspective or on the user perspective. Example advice: "Fill in the observation sheet for both of the perspectives."
- The engineer focuses only on objects such as work environment, including interior, or a work tool, and it is therefore necessary to guide him or her to focus on how a person interacts with another person or an object. Example advice: "What is the user doing? Why is he or she doing it?"
- It is necessary to guide the engineer to establish a hypothesis on the psychological and/or environmental background for the user's behavior during the observation.
- The engineer acts like a spectator or a critic, and it is therefore necessary to show him or her how to act like the users. Example advice: "Ask a question as if you were a user, 'What would you do if you were a user like XXX?'"

Preparation of Analysis and Evaluation. After the research is completed, a 60 minute review session is held so that the members will not forget the research results. This session also serves as a preparation for the analysis and evaluation to be conducted in UX Idea Mapping. The members then put all the facts observed, estimated backgrounds of the behavior, and findings during the research on an observation summary sheet (Fig. 2). An observation summary sheet is provided for each observation site or scene, and the members are expected to spend at least 15 minutes filling in each sheet. On each sheet, information must be provided in the following order: Each information item should be written on a sticky note for later use in UX Idea Mapping. The members then affix the photos and memos that they took to each observation summary sheet. It is important that these sheets contain as much information as possible for the later task: understanding users in detail.

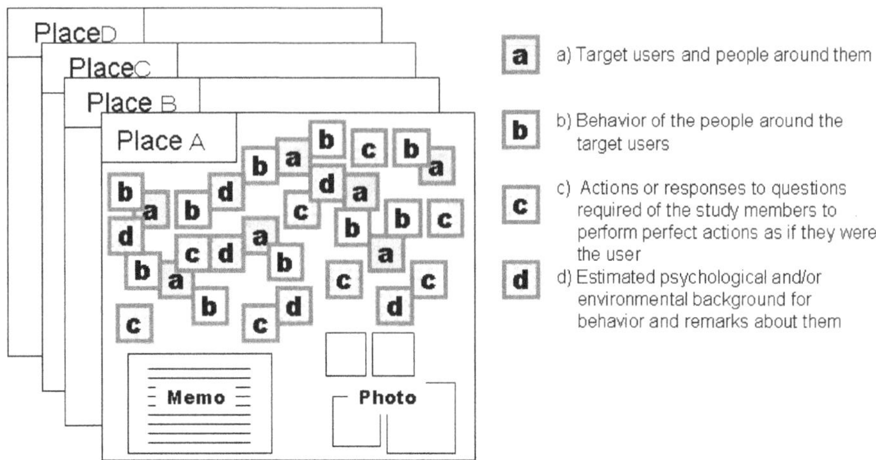

Fig. 2. Observation summary sheet

3.2 UX Idea Mapping

In UX Idea Mapping, engineers and UX designers work together to analyze and evaluate the obtained research data to achieve a detailed understanding of users, associate user needs with unique ideas developed based on their expertise in systems, and select suitable ideas using a UX map.

In collaborative work, visualization and sharing of research details are important. Therefore, teams of 5 to 6 members are created for effective and efficient discussions. The members implement UX Idea Mapping using a large map by sharing the analysis and evaluation results, detailed understanding of the users, and information on the selected ideas.

Analysis and Evaluation of the Research Results. Referring to the observation summary sheets (Fig2), the background of the user behavior is modeled. Work model analysis [2] is then conducted to find potential user needs. Also, both the research subjects and individuals who have business relationships with the subjects are analyzed for each observation site. Engineers tend to focus on individuals who regularly use systems, but in this process, they must consider the value and business significance of a system for those who have business relationships with the subjects. To achieve this, UX designers must pay attention to the individuals around the users who have business relationships with the users so that no information about them is missed.

Understanding the Users in Detail. Based on the behavioral patterns identified in the work model analysis described above, users are classified into user groups according to the types of behavior patterns. For each user group, behavioral goals, higher needs, and the highest needs are examined. The members then create essential value identification sheets containing data on each user group's ideal and required state. The sheets are shared among the members. During this process, the engineers must review their research results to carefully examine what the users want from their business operations and why they feel so. Meanwhile, during this collaborative work, the UX designers must check whether or not the engineers have properly incorporated their research results into the examination and have gained an insight into the nature of the research.

The next step is to create a persona sheet [3] for the target user groups based on the results of work model analysis and the data in the essential value identification sheets. On the persona sheet, an image of a hypothetical user is created based on the results of UX Observation Tour. Each sheet must contain not only the users' names, ages, careers, and preferences but also their 'user characteristics', which include the users' final goals and their roles when using a product and service. The sheet must also provide the task and skill characteristics of the users, which describe what greatly influences user behavior in terms of their business tasks and skills. Note that the task and skill characteristics are merged from artifacts created during the work, influencers and the extent and level of their influence, and physical environment and tools that were examined in work model analysis.

In this Method, all processes and specific ideas are visualized and shared on the UX map. For this, a Then UX map framework must first be created (Fig.3). The vertical axis is the user axis, and the horizontal axis is the time axis. The user axis is divided according to combinations of user characteristics and business characteristics and technical potential described in the persona sheet. In the field of consumer product development, a user scenario could only be created by using the user axis. In the field of enterprise system development, however, it is difficult to understand user behavior based only on the user characteristics, because user behavior relies heavily on tasks and skills. For this reason, task and skill characteristics must also be considered. The time axis must be divided into three or four levels indicating steps to reach the goal. Here, the rightmost column is for the highest user needs, which indicates the ideal situation that the users aspire to, as identified from the essential value identification sheet.

Engineers usually find it difficult to divide the axes when creating a UX map framework. If the divisions are rough and inappropriate, user scenarios and ideas cannot be properly mapped. Therefore, this process requires the experience of UX designers. They must work closely with engineers because dividing the user axis needs an engineer's knowledge on business tasks and skills.

Once the framework is completed, a user scenario is created and shared among the UX designers and engineers. 'Needs' shown in the essential value identification sheet are mapped onto appropriate locations with respect to the user and time axes of the framework. Then, referring to the observation summary sheet (Fig.2), the following items are mapped as the 'Fact': a) target users and people around them, b) behavior of the people around the target users, c) tasks worked on, responses to questions, and situations in which the questions are asked, and d) estimated psychological and/or environmental background for behavior and remarks about it. The user scenario creation process up to this point can be systematically and quickly carried out by engineers because they can use the information that they developed. This process does not require as much time for engineers compared to a process in which they are required to write a user scenario in sentences. At this point, all team members review the behavior of individual users to avoid missing information or mistakes. When doing so, they should have the persona sheet at hand so that they can read it while reviewing the characteristics or values of individual user groups. Finally, the needs and the current state are compared, discrepancies between them are examined, and 'Issues' to be resolved are mapped. (Fig.3)

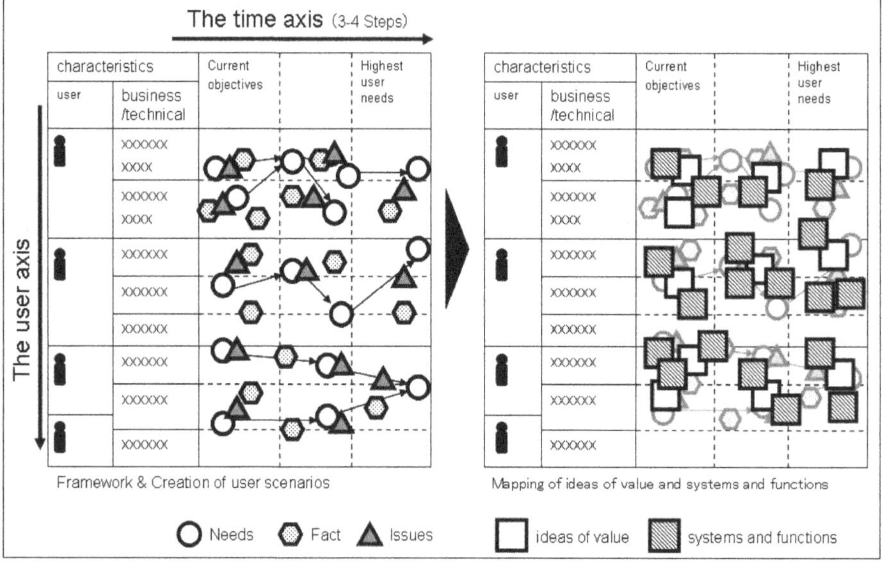

Fig. 3. UX map: Creation of Framework and user scenario / Mapping Ideas

Brainstorming Ideas. Focusing on the needs, current state, and issues for the target users, the members brainstorm for value that a system can provide. Since engineers tend to provide ideas on specific functions or systems, UX designers must guide them to talk about value. Here are some examples of ideas about value. "A user who is XXX becomes able to do YYY.", A user who wants to do YYY becomes able to prevent or reject XXX.". After value is discussed, the members brainstorm ideas for systems and functions that can realize the value. These ideas of value, systems and functions are mapped to user scenarios. An idea assessment sheet is created to assess and select ideas based on value for the users and for the company.

4 Result and Effect

The proposed collaborative Methods were applied to the following enterprise system development projects, agent system for carriers, conference system for executives, door-to-door insurance sales system, store visitor service system, projector for business use and broadcasting system.

Application of the collaborative Method to the projects listed above resulted in the following effects:

1. Effect of applying UX Observation Tour to the user research phase
In UX Observation Tour, the UX designers and engineers were able to jointly create a user research plan, and the research enabled sufficient information to be collected for the engineers to achieve a detailed understanding of the users. Application of this Method indicated that the UX designers and engineers worked together to examine the task- and skill-dependent behavior of the hypothetical user (subject of the research) and observation points, create the research plan, and appropriately implement the user research.
2. Effect of Applying UX Idea Mapping to the idea generation phase
In the post-project interviews, the engineers stated that they learned to think from the perspective of a selected type of user in their daily work. Therefore, participating in even only one project allowed the engineers to understand the users in detail.

Before participating in the project, the engineers were unable to determine the quality of their own ideas. By associating value that can be provided to the users with ideas about systems and functions, the engineers became able to examine the value of ideas for the users such as "this idea may suit this scene that a user may encounter". Also the engineers improve the specificity and accuracy of ideas in early stages due to an enhanced ability to assess from many perspectives their ideas developed for a particular type of user. And they improve the value of their own ideas.

5 Conclusion

In this paper, two UX research methods, UX Observation Tour and UX Idea Mapping, for enterprise system development were applied to internal projects. As a result, the UX designers and engineers jointly designed UX, and both of the methods were effective in promoting understanding of users and development of ideas. Both methods required all members to stay in a project from the beginning to end. This meant that we needed to call our engineers to all the meetings. As a result, for some of our projects, we could not apply the same methods. Many engineers could not help cancelling meeting attendance due to work pressures. Therefore, exploring more efficient ways to share and deliver information should be addressed.

References

1. Osborn, A.F.: Applied imagination: Principles and procedures of creative problem solving. Brainstorming, 3rd revised edn. Charles Scribner's Sons
2. Beyer, H., Holtzblatt, K.: Contextual Design: Defining Customer-Centered Systems (Interactive Technologies). In: Work Models, ch. 6, pp. 89–120. Morgan Kaufmann (1997)
3. Cooper, A.: The Inmates Are Running the Asylum: Why High Tech Products Drive Us Crazy and How to Restore the Sanity. In: Designing for Pleasure. Persona, ch. 9, pp. 123–144. Ind. Sams Publ., Indianapolis (2004)

Part II
Evaluation Methods and Techniques

An Estimation Framework of a User Learning Curve on Web-Based Interface Using Eye Tracking Equipment

Masanori Akiyoshi and Hidetoshi Takeno

Hiroshima Institute of Technology, Miyake 2-1-1, Saeki-ku, Hiroshima, 731-5193 Japan

Abstract. This paper addresses an estimation framework of a user learning curve on Web-based interface. Recent Web-based interface has rich features such as "dynamic menu", "animation" and so forth. A user sometimes gets lost in menus and hyperlinks, but gradually improves the performance of his/her task that is to find target information during the session. This performance change is in a sense considered to be "learning curve" as to the Web-based interface. To estimate the "learning curve" is necessary to evaluate the Web-based interface from the viewpoint of a user's task achievement. Our proposed estimation framework consists of two steps; One is to identify the relationships among the processing time, eye tracking log, and Web structure. The other is to identify the estimated formula as a "learning curve". This paper reports the relationship from preliminary experiment using several Web pages and eye tracking log.

1 Introduction

Recent Web-based applications have rich interface by using new technology such as "Ajax", multimedia plug-in and so forth. This movement will be enhanced when "HTML5" is practically used on Web browsers. On the other hand, such interface may become complicated appearance against problem-solving environment for a user's tasks. Therefore rich Web interface using new technology has trade-off on good-looking and ease-of-use from a user's viewpoints.

Usability of Web pages has been argued mostly from results of subjective questionnaires, error count measurement, processing time and so forth. Moreover "eye tracking" technology makes it possible to evaluate such interface design from ergonomics viewpoints. Even if such usability evaluation is well-executed by interface designers, practical situation by a user is still under fog, that is, the user learning curve is properly ascending one or not. Though the learning curve is considered to be significant indicator in several domains [1][2][3], Web-based interface is not enough to be evaluated by this viewpoint.

This paper addresses how to estimate the learning curve on user operations when using Web-based interface. Collected data of the processing time and eye tracking log against trial tasks are fused for identifying the estimation formula by using sysntheszing mathematical expression elements.

M. Kurosu (Ed.): Human-Computer Interaction, Part I, HCII 2013, LNCS 8004, pp. 159–165, 2013.

2 Estimation Framework

2.1 Problem Definition

As mentioned in the introduction, Web-based interface design process needs to be evaluated the usability from "learning curve" The learning curve has been argued mostly about productivity under repetitive tasks such as assembling work, practicing exercise and so forth. Of course tasks by Web-based interface include repetitive operations to some extent, however, most tasks have slight variations to achieve. This fact causes a user to feel complexity and stress when using such interface.

Even if some experimental evaluation concerning the Web-based interface design shows good usability, the variation of tasks may lead to impair such usability in practical usage phase. Therefore it seems to be indispensable to estimate the learning curve for practicability. If such evaluation based on the learning curve is allowable from usability viewpoints, the interface design is endurable in spite of having some complexity. We believe this is significant for re-designing the Web-based interface.

2.2 Proposed Framework

Fig.1 shows an overview of our proposed framework. Given a Web-based interface and typical tasks, several trial operation logs by test users are collected. Collected data are the processing time of each task and eye tracking log. In addition to these data, structural information on Web pages is also significant. Since these data interrelate each other, statistical calculation identifying such relationship is firstly done. Then a certain interval data are used to estimate each user's learning curve and finally summarize the learning curve evaluation for the interface.

As indicated in Fig.1, there exist two S/W modules; statistical analysis module and estimation module. The key issue is how to estimate each user's learning curve, which are inherently non-linear characteristics. Therefore it is slightly hard to assume template formulas with parameters. Our idea is to prepare a set of arithmetic operators and basic mathematical functions and derive a formula by using a certain synthesizing method, for instance, genetic programming technique.

3 Preliminary Experiment

We executed preliminary experiments as follows in order to investigate what types of relationship could be induced by using the processing time, eye tracking log and Web structural data.

3.1 Web Pages and Trial Tasks

Table1 shows Web pages for trial tasks and Fig.2 shows an example of the Web page for tourists. These web pages are mostly provided by tourist offices.

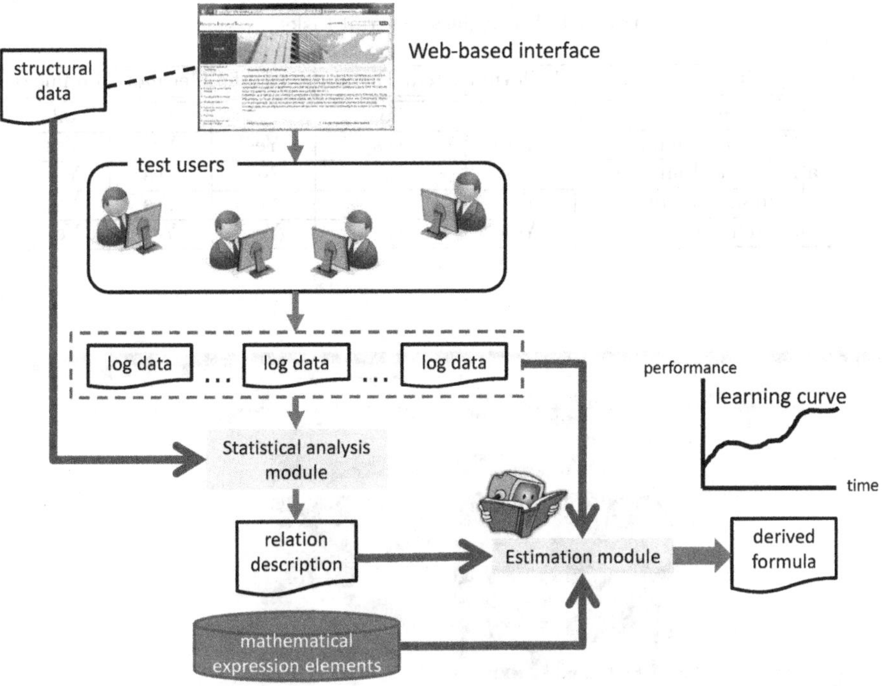

Fig. 1. Overview of estimation framework for the learning curve

Trial tasks are to search the appropriate information on "historical spots", "cultural spots", "adventure spots", "commercial area" and "trip information". As indicated in Table1, these pages are similar to each other. The layouts as shown in Fig.2 are also similar.

3.2 Result on Trial Tasks

The left-hand graph in Fig.3 shows the processing time concerning each site. In this experiment, the Web page of "California" is used to have a user understand the tasks and operations. During the task, the traversal time from one task to the other is recorded.

The right-hand graph in Fig.3 shows the detailed processing time concerning each site. Fig.4 shows the overlapped result of California Web pages and its eye tracking log as to the "historical spots" search task.

From this right-hand graph in Fig.3, a user learns the Web page structure from the first task of searching the information on "historical spots of California", which needs more processing time than the rest of tasks. After that a user smoothly executes the tasks on the rest of site Web pages.

Table 1. Web pages for trail tasks

Site		California	Great Britain	Australia	Germany	Jamaica
Web data	Total links	73	33	162	91	52
	Category menu	Yes	Yes	Yes	Yes	Yes
	Explicit Home menu	Yes	No	No	Yes	Yes
	Dynamic menu	Yes	Yes	Yes	Yes	Yes
	Search box	Yes	Yes	Yes	Yes	Yes

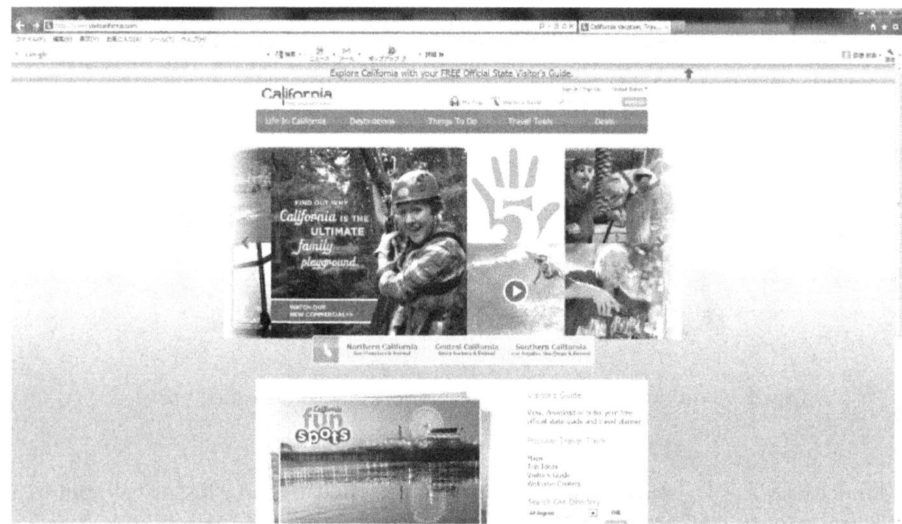

Fig. 2. An example of Web page for trial tasks

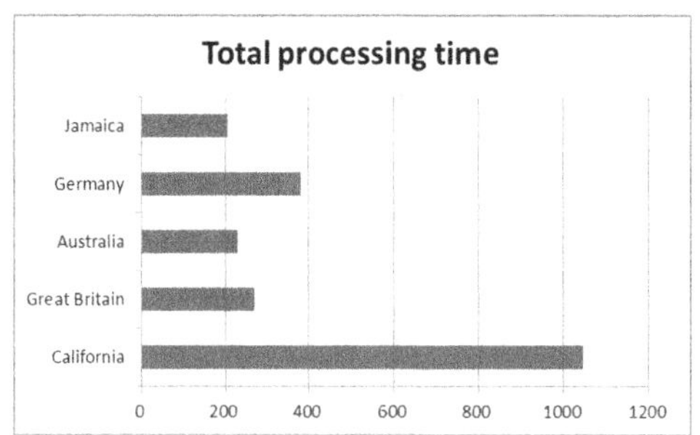

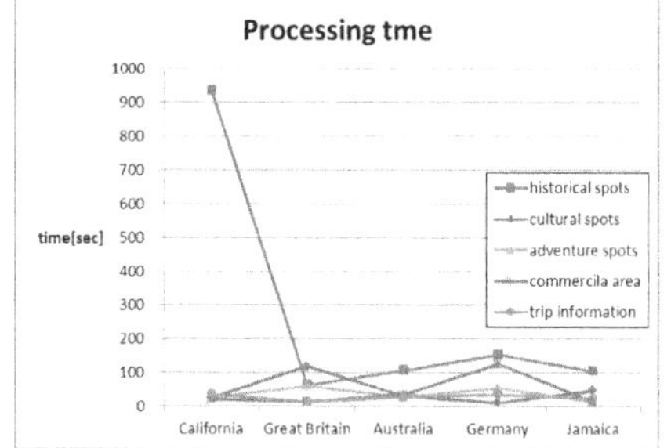

Fig. 3. Result for trial tasks

Fig. 4. An overlapped Web page and eye tracking log of "California"

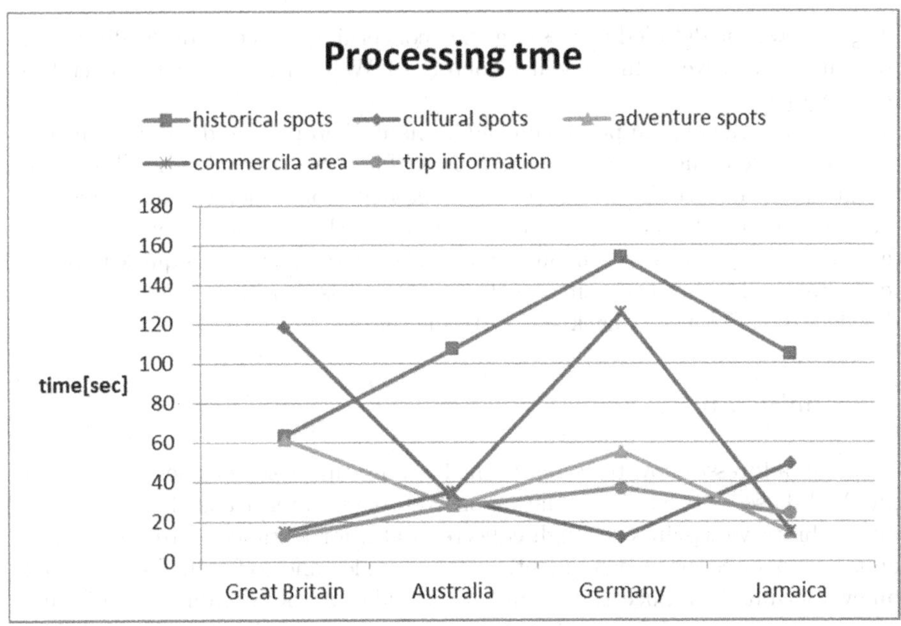

Fig. 5. Comparison result for trial tasks

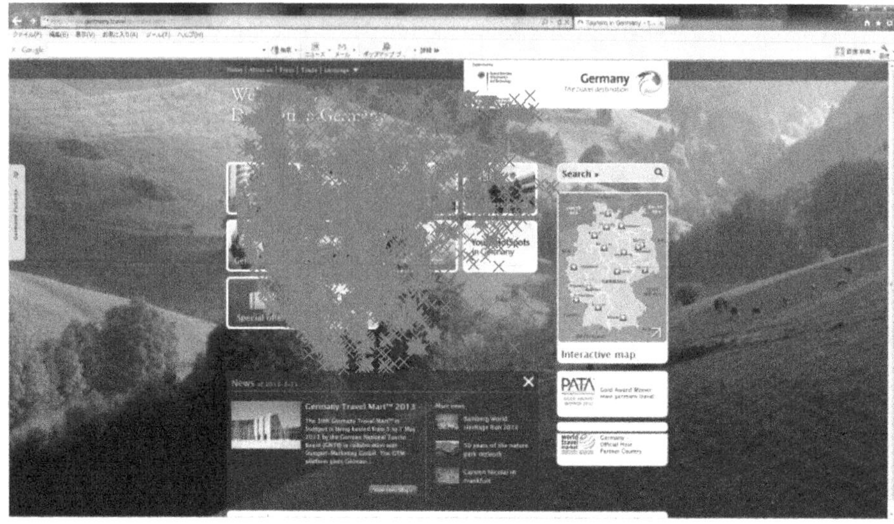

Fig. 6. An overlapped Web page and eye tracking log of "Germany"

Fig.5 shows the detailed processing time concerning sites except "California". From this result, we induced which factors of Web structural data affect the processing time.

Fig.6 shows the overlapped result of Germany Web page and its eye tracking log as to the "commercial area" search task. The "eye tracking log" shows the movement towards the menus including "Explicit Home menu item". This eye movement sometimes happens during a user's back and forth traverse of the Web pages. "Explicit **Home** menu item" is considered to provide quick jump to the starting point, however, this result indicates it is considered to make worse side-effect during a user's back and forth operations.

4 Conclusion

This paper addresses how to estimate the learning curve of user operations when using Web-based interface. Evaluation on Web-based interface is often discussed from usability viewpoints through collected data, for instance, subjective questionnaires, error count measurement, eye tracking log and so forth. The proposed framework aims to induce the estimated formula for the learning curve by using test users tasks which record each processing time, eye tracking log and Web structural information. Through trial tasks, there exists relationship which affect this approach.

References

1. Gu, H., Takahashi, H.: How bad may learning curves be? IEEE Trans. on Pattern Analysis and Machine Intelligence 22(10), 1155–1167 (2000)
2. Huang, G., Man, W.: Learning Curve: Principle, Application and Limitation. In: Proc. of International Conf. on E-business and E-government, pp. 1840–1843 (2010)
3. Hou, R.-H., Kuo, S.-Y., Chang, Y.-P.: Applying various learning curves to hypergeometric distribution software reliability growth model. In: Proc. of 5th International Symposium on Software Reliability Engineering, pp. 8–17 (1994)

A Grounded Procedure for Managing Data and Sample Size of a Home Medical Device Assessment

Simone Borsci[1], Jennifer L. Martin[2], and Julie Barnett[1]

[1] Brunel University, School of Information Systems, Computing and Mathematics, Kingston Lane, Uxbridge, Middlesex UB8 3PH, UK

[2] University of Nottingham, Department of Electrical and Electronic Engineering, University Park, Nottingham NG7 2RD, UK

Simone.borsci@brunel.ac.uk

Abstract. The selection of participants for usability assessment, together with the minimum number of subjects required to obtain a set of reliable data, is a hot topic in Human Computer Interaction (HCI). Albeit, prominent contributions through the application of different *p* estimation models argued that five users provide a good benchmark when seeking to discover interaction problems a lot of studies have complained this five-user assumption. The sample size topic is today a central issue for the assessment of critical-systems, such as medical devices, because lacks in usability and, moreover, in the safety in use of these kind of products may seriously damage the final users. We argue that rely on one-size-fits-all solutions, such as the five-user assumption (for websites) or the mandated size of 15 users for major group (for medical device) lead manufactures to release unsafe product. Nevertheless, albeit there are no magic numbers for determining "a priori" the cohort size, by using a specific procedure it is possible to monitoring the sample discovery likelihood after the first five users in order to obtain reliable information about the gathered data and determine whether the problems discovered by the sample have a certain level of representativeness (i.e., reliability). We call this approach "Grounded Procedure" (GP). The goal of this study is to present the GP assumptions and steps, by exemplifying its application in the assessment of a home medical device.

Keywords: discovery likelihood, medical device, sample size, usability testing.

1 Introduction

The current trend of technology manufacturing is to propose new concepts, shapes and functioning of devices that aim to go toward an even more integrated and simplified use of the products. As Streitz [1] states, this trend produces a physical and mental disappearance of the technologies that result in what is known as ubiquitous computing. Ubiquitous computing can be considered as a new evolutionary line of the human artifact interaction in which technology is designed to be pervasive, context-aware and adaptive [2].

This ubiquitous approach is going to re-conceptualize the everyday use of the technologies not only for common interactive devices (e.g., computers, mobile phones

M. Kurosu (Ed.): Human-Computer Interaction, Part I, HCII 2013, LNCS 8004, pp. 166–175, 2013.

etc.), but also for critical-life systems, such as medical devices. In addition, as Herman and Devey [3] have noted, there is a growing trend to transform specialized devices in home care technologies. The diffusion in our everyday environments (i.e., work places, home, etc.) of these integrated technologies forces manufacturers to strongly focus their attention on the usability of the product, especially for those products, such as medical devices, that can seriously affect the user's well-being.

The usability and use-related safety of medical devices are strongly regulated [4-9] and manufacturers are required by authorities to take a user-centred design approach, where usability is integrated into the entire development cycle. The processes recommended by IEC 62366 [4] and ANSI/AAMI HE75 [9] require manufacturers to conduct multiple cycles of design and evaluation during development in order to identify and address any serious use-related risks associated with the device use. Nevertheless, as recent research suggest [10, 11], many manufacturers do not have the necessary expertise or knowledge about usability and human factors, and therefore can delay evaluation of a product until just before the release of the device in order to confirm the effectiveness of their design.

A further issue related to usability testing of medical devices is the difficulty of using the results to make appropriate design or business decisions [12]. A possible consequence of this may be that devices reach the market that pose a risk to users or patients. The safety of medical devices is an important factor , as Heneghan [13] shows, every year a large number of device release on the market have to be recalled because of safety concerns.

One of the most important concerns of manufactures when planning a usability test is deciding on which kind, and how many participants should be included. On one hand if an insufficient number of participants are included, manufacturers run the risk of not identifying all usability issues, on the other hand, however, if manufacturers conduct more testing than is necessary they waste valuable resources.

Recently the Food and Drug Administration (FDA), in response to demands from manufacturers for more clarity about the involvement of final users in usability testing, published guidance that stated that: "The most important aspect of sampling may be the extent to which the test participants correspond to the actual end users of the device" [14]. The FDA guidance suggests that while in HCI field a set of estimation models have been created, for determining the number of users needed for usability testing, these models do not reflect the real world. On the basis of this, the guidance recommends that validation testing of medical devices should include 15 users from each major user group, basing this figure on an empirical study by Faulkner [15].

Despite the guidance highlighting the limitations of the estimation models, at the end the FDA suggest that manufacturers rely on a one-sample-size-fits-all solution (i.e., to test the device with 15 users), similar to what happened in the HCI field when in the nineties it was proposed that a sample of five users could be considered sufficient for a reliable analysis of a web site (i.e., the five-user assumption) [16-20].

The aim of this paper is to critically discuss, in light of recent HCI studies, the previous one-sample-size fits all solutions and propose a new procedure for calculating usability testing sample sizes based on the data emerging from the usability assessment.

2 From One-Size Fits All Solutions to a Procedure for Managing and Checking the Sample Behavior

The reliability of the five-user assumption for the assessment of websites was shown by Nielsen [16, 18], in tune with Virzi studies [19, 20], in the nineties through the use of an estimation model, called Return on Investment (ROI). However, this model, together with the five-users assumption, was strongly criticized as too optimistic by a large set of studies [21-25]. Today in HCI, a sample of five users is only considered as a good starting point for an usability assessment, and at least others three well-tested models that addressed the optimistic results of the ROI model have been developed by researchers for estimating the number of users needed for a usability test: the Good-Turing model (GT) [23, 26], the Bootstrap Discovery Behavior model (BDB) [21] and the Monte Carlo re-sampling method [27]. All these models aim to esteem a specific index called the *p*, which represents the average percentage of errors discovered by a user. The final number of users for an evaluation sample can be calculated by inserting the *p* into the following *Error Distribution Formula* :

$$D = 1 - (1 - p)^N \tag{1}$$

When manufacturers start the evaluation neither *p* nor *D* (the total number of usability problems) is known, although clearly given one, the other can be readily calculated. This leaves those wishing to evaluate the usability of a product or service the inverse problem of whether the number of users involved in the test (N) have identified a sufficient number of problems to ensure that a given threshold percentage (i.e, D_{th}) has been met. This threshold will vary according to the type of product: for medical devices where the risks of usability errors are much greater than the website, an appropriate threshold is likely to be 97% or even higher for particularly high-risk devices [14].

The only way to check whether the evaluation of a medical device has reached the desired threshold (i.e., D_{th}) is by estimating the *p* of the total sample and then calculating how each *p* changes when a new user is added to the sample. Every time that a user is added to a sample, the overall *p* of the cohort may increase or decrease, depending on the added user's performances in terms of identifying problems. At the same time, in tune with the new user's performances the possibilities of the manufacturers to achieve a high percentage of identified problems may decrease or decrease.

By applying the estimated *p* to the *Error Distribution Formula* (1) it is possible to construct a curve of discoverability, by examining when the threshold is reached by the sample. This allows the estimation of the minimum number of participants that can represent the ability of a larger population of final users to identify all the interaction issues during an assessment.

The most recent research [21, 24-26] agrees on the fact that there are no fixed sample sizes that may guarantee beforehand the reliability of the evaluation. In fact, the variability of the users' answers and reactions during the interaction analysis is unpredictable. Moreover, all devices are different and may have different levels of complexity. In sum, the number and the kind of the problems identified by participants may vary substantially. This means that the best size of a sample is the one that can allow practitioners to gather the larger percentage of problems (D), with the minimal economic investment. Finally, for medical device manufacturers to blindly rely on a mandated size is a risk as it is not possible for them to know when it is possible to stop the assessment because the desired D_{th} is reached, or when a supplementary investment in evaluation is needed because the threshold is not achieved. The only pragmatic solution to help manufacturers take appropriate decisions during usability testing is to check in an iterative way the sample behavior, as suggested in the Grounded Procedure (GP) [28] proposed by the researchers of the Match programme (founded by the EPSRC Grants: EP/F063822/1 EP/G012393/1).

In the GP manufacturers start by assuming a specific range of p standard (e.g., for medical 0.40-0.50 to reach the 90-97% of the problems), and use this value as a comparator against which the behavior of the real population of subjects can be assessed. In light of this, practitioners have to compare the p of their actual tested sample (e.g., four or five users) to the standard to make the following two main judgments, leading to the associated decisions and actions:

- *If the sample fits the standard*: report the results to the client and determine whether the product should be re-designed or released.
- *If the sample does not fit the standard*: add more users to the sample and re-test the p in a cyclical way until the pre-determined percentage of problems (D_{th}) is reached.

The manufactures, by applying the GP, aim to obtain reliable evidence for deciding whether to extend their evaluation by adding users or whether they can stop the evaluation because they have sufficient information. The GP consists of three main steps:

- *Monitoring the interaction problems (step 1)*: a table of problems is constructed to analyze the number of discovered problems, the number of users that have identified each problem (i.e., the weight) and the average p of the sample;
- *Refining the p of the cohort (step 2)*: a range of models are applied and then the number of users required reviewed in the light of the emerging p;
- *Taking a decision based on the sample behavior (step 3)*: the p is used to apply the *Error Distribution Formula* and take a decision on the basis of the available budget and evaluation aim.

Each of these steps is now discussed using an exemplar evaluation case.

3 Description of the Evaluation Case

We conducted an evaluation of a blood pressure monitor (BPM) gathered in September 2011. We tested 12 users (6 male; Age M: 29.16; SD: 1.85) each with more than one year of experience of using different kinds of BPM. We applied a think-aloud protocol where each user was asked to verbalize the problems they experienced during the use of the device. During the test session the participants completed three simple tasks: i) Preparing the monitor for use; ii) measuring blood pressure and writing down the result; iii) Switching off the monitor.

We are not interested here in describing the quality of the device, but in demonstrating the value of the GP for conducting the evaluation and making decisions about the results. Since, the researchers did not use the GP during this study, we will discuss what their results in terms of the problem identified by their sample, as well as the additional analysis and conclusions that would have been enabled by applying the GP.

3.1 The Behavior of the Evaluation Casa Cohort

The participants identified an amount of 12 different problems. For each one of these problems we coded the users' behavior (see Table 1) as 0 when a user did not identify a problem and with 1 when a user did identify it.

Table 1. Problems identified by each participant. The individual *p* represents the number of problems discovered by each participant divided for the total problems discovered by the sample. The weight of problems represents the percentage of the sample that have identified the same problem.

	Task 1			Task 2							Task 3		Individual
Problems	**1**	**2**	**3**	**4**	**5**	**6**	**7**	**8**	**9**	**10**	**11**	**12**	***p***
P1	0	0	0	0	0	1	0	1	1	0	0	0	0.25
P2	0	0	0	1	1	1	1	1	1	1	1	1	0.75
P3	0	0	0	0	0	1	0	0	1	0	1	1	0.33
P4	1	1	0	0	1	1	1	1	0	1	1	1	0.75
P5	1	1	0	1	0	1	0	1	1	1	0	0	0.58
P6	1	1	1	0	1	1	1	1	0	1	0	1	0.75
P7	0	0	0	1	1	1	1	0	1	1	1	1	0.66
P8	1	1	1	1	1	0	0	1	1	1	0	0	0.66
P9	1	0	0	1	0	0	0	1	0	0	1	0	0.33
P10	0	1	0	0	0	0	0	0	0	0	1	1	0.25
P11	0	0	0	1	0	1	1	0	0	1	0	0	0.33
P12	0	1	1	1	1	1	1	1	1	1	0	0	0.75
Weight	**42%**	50%	**25%**	58%	50%	75%	50%	67%	58%	67%	50%	50%	

The weight of the problems can be used by manufacturers as an indicator of the sample behavior homogeneity or heterogeneity in discovering the problems. Usually in HCI, a sample can be considered heterogeneous when more than 50% of the problems are identified by only one participant. For instance, a sample of 10 users which identified a set of 10 problems, can be consider heterogeneous, whether 5 out of 10 of the identified issues are been experienced only once during the test. Nevertheless in medical device field, by looking for a most restrictive limit to increase the safety of the device, a sample can be considered heterogeneous when more than 50% of the problems are discovered by less than a half of the participants. For instance, whether 5 problems out of 10 are been identified by less than 5 users in a sample of 10.

In our evaluation case the sample is homogeneous as only two problems out of 12 are identified by less than 6 users (see Table 1). We estimate the p of the sample by applying three estimation models (Table 2): the ROI, the GT and the BDB. We do not report here the MC, because the results of this model are the same of the BDB one.

Table 2. Discovery likelihood of the sample (p) estimated by the Return of Investment (ROI) model, Good-Touring (GT) model and Bootstrap Discovery Behavior (BDB) model

	Estimation models		
	ROI	GT	BDB
P of the cohort	0.53	0.43	0.51

The sample shows a range of p from 0.43 to 0.53 (M: 0.49), by applying these values to the Error Distribution Formula (1), we may report that this cohort of 12 participants discovered between 98% to 99.9% problems of the device with a homogenous discovery behavior (fig. 1).

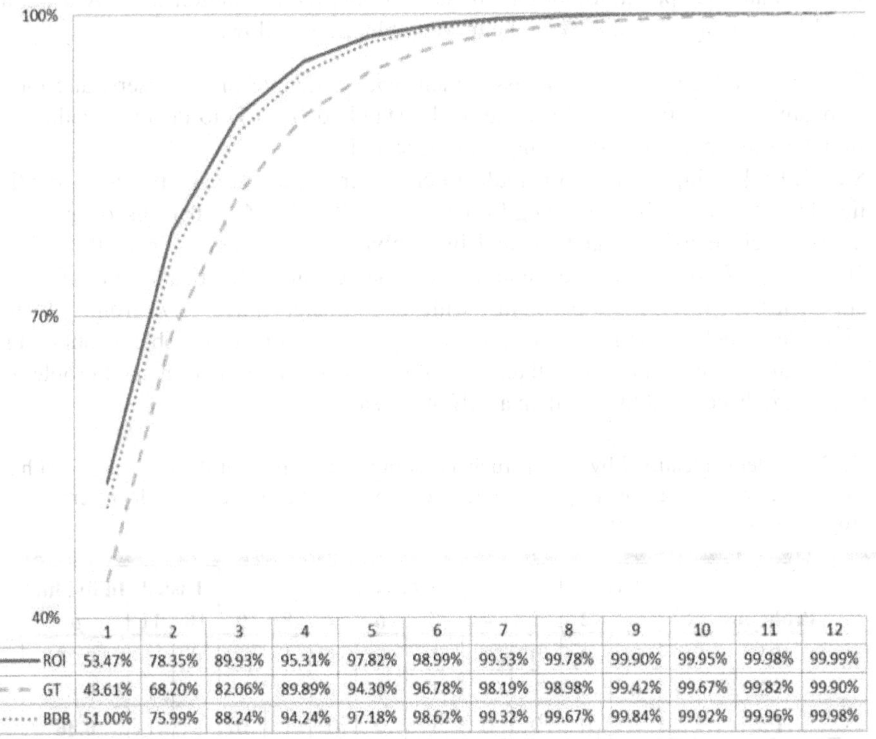

	1	2	3	4	5	6	7	8	9	10	11	12
ROI	53.47%	78.35%	89.93%	95.31%	97.82%	98.99%	99.53%	99.78%	99.90%	99.95%	99.98%	99.99%
GT	43.61%	68.20%	82.06%	89.89%	94.30%	96.78%	98.19%	98.98%	99.42%	99.67%	99.82%	99.90%
BDB	51.00%	75.99%	88.24%	94.24%	97.18%	98.62%	99.32%	99.67%	99.84%	99.92%	99.96%	99.98%

Fig. 1. Percentage of problems discovered by the sample on the base of the sample p changes after each participant analysis, estimated by the Return of Investment (ROI) model, Good-Touring (GT) model and Bootstrap Discovery Behavior (BDB) model

In light of our analysis, it is clear that more users do not need to be added to the evaluation as this would be a waste of resources; the probability of any new user identifying new problems whilst completing the same the three tasks is between 0.1% to 2% problems.

3.2 Save Your Investments and Guarantee the Reliability of the Assessment by the Grounded Procedure

As in the classic estimation studies [18], we can assign an arbitrary cost of £100 to each analysis and therefore conclude that to discover 12 problems the investment of the manufacturers was £ 1200.

Nevertheless, by using the average values of p of the three estimation models, we can estimate that evaluators reached 90% of the problems after the analysis of the first four users (i.e., D(p_{ROI},p_{GT},p_{BDB})=93.14%) and 97% after the first six (i.e., D (p_{ROI},p_{GT},p_{BDB}) =98.13%). In light of this, if the GP had been applied during the assessment of this BPM, after 6 users the manufacturers would have stopped the assessment, thereby obtaining a reliable results and saving 50% of the budget (£600).

We simulate the application of the GP steps during the evaluation case, by using a threshold percentage (D) of 97% of the total problems, as follow:

- Step 1: Manufacturers start the assessment with a sample of five users, and they compare the p of this initial sample to the standard (p=0.5) to decide whether to stop the assessment or add new users to the sample.
- Step 2: By looking at Table 3 manufacturers observe that the first five users identified 11 problems with a p ranging from 0.42 to 0.58 (M: 0.49). This discovery likelihood is close to the standard, and by applying the average p in to the *Error Distribution Formula* (1), the manufacturers may estimate that this sample of 5 users identified 96% of the problems, with an estimated range of D from 93% to 98%. Nevertheless, the sample is quite homogeneous, in fact, 6 problems out of 11 (55%) are discovered by more than 50% of the users, while the remained problems (45%) are discovered by less than a half of the sample.

Table 3. Problems identified by each participant during the analysis of the three tasks, with a sample of 5 users. This sample is quite homogeneous (55%), albeit there is a high percentage of heterogeneity (45%).

	Task 1		Task 2							Task 3		Individual
Problems	**1**	**2**	**3**	**4**	**5**	**6**	**7**	**8**	**9**	**10**	**11**	***p***
P1	0	0	0	0	1	0	1	1	0	0	0	**0.27**
P2	0	0	1	1	1	1	1	1	1	1	1	**0.81**
P3	0	0	0	0	1	0	0	1	0	1	1	**0.36**
P4	1	1	0	1	1	1	1	0	1	1	1	**0.81**
P5	1	1	1	0	1	0	1	1	1	0	0	**0.64**
Weight	**40%**	**40%**	**40%**	**40%**	100%	**40%**	80%	80%	60%	60%	60%	

- Step 3: Since the sample is quite homogeneous, manufactures could decide to stop the assessment. Nevertheless, by considering that the percentage of heterogeneity is high (45 %); practitioners may decide to add at least another user to increase the reliability of the evaluation data.

The manufacturers include a new user (i.e., number 6) in the sample. Finally, after another cycle of GP analysis (i.e., steps 1, 2 and 3), this new user increases the cohort p ($0.46<p<0.56$, M: 0.51), and as table 4 shows, a new usability problem is identified, and the sample becomes more homogeneous (2 problems out of 12 are discovered by less than 50% of the sample). On the basis of this data manufacturers have enough information to stop the assessment and report that the participants have identified a total amount of 12 problems, which represents 98.7% (97.7%<D<99.3%) of the possible issues that can be identified by a larger sample of end users interacting with the product during the three evaluation tasks.

Table 4. Problems identified by each participant during the analysis of the three tasks, when the user number 6 is added to the sample. This sample shows a behavior in tune with the cohort analyzed in table 1. The participants discover 12 problems and, the new user increases the homogeneity of the cohort; in fact, only 2 problems out 12 are identified by less than 50% of the sample.

	Task 1			Task 2							Task 3		Individual
Problems	1	2	3	4	5	6	7	8	9	10	11	12	p
P1	0	0	0	0	0	1	0	1	1	0	0	0	0.25
P2	0	0	0	1	1	1	1	1	1	1	1	1	0.75
P3	0	0	0	0	0	1	0	0	1	0	1	1	0.33
P4	1	1	0	0	1	1	1	1	0	1	1	1	0.75
P5	1	1	0	1	0	1	0	1	1	1	0	0	0.58
P6	1	1	1	0	1	1	1	1	0	1	0	1	0.75
Weight	50%	50%	17%	33%	50%	100%	50%	83%	66%	66%	50%	66%	

In this case, both the overall p and the homogeneity of the sample are greatly increased when user 6 is added to the cohort. However, sometimes adding a new user may decrease both the homogeneity and the p of the cohort. This could happen for different reasons, such as selecting inappropriate users. In these cases, the manufactures have to reconsider the selection criteria, and restart the GP analysis after a new user analysis.

4 Conclusion

The GP helps manufacturers to decide when to stop the evaluation of a device when the optimal sample size is reached, thereby preventing wasting resources. Of course, the results of our evaluation case are not generalizable to the assessment of any other BPM or medical device. This is because the GP only indicates the reliability of the data gathered during a specific evaluation process, meaning that with other participants or with other evaluation conditions, the GP outcomes will vary. As a result, there is no one single magic number of users for reliably testing a certain kind of device, and, as a consequence, the manufacturers should apply the GP for each evaluation, whether it be formative or summative. Finally, the diffusion of the GP in medical device field could significantly improve the possibility of manufacturers to release usable and safe product on the market by taking decisions during the life-cycle on the basis of the real data at hand.

References

1. Streitz, N.: From cognitive compatibility to the disappearing computer: experience design for smart environments. In: Proceedings of the 15th European Conference on Cognitive Ergonomics: the Ergonomics of Cool Interaction, pp. 1–2. ACM, Funchal (2008)
2. Soylu, A., Causmaecker, P.D., Desmet, P.: Context and Adaptivity in Pervasive Computing Environments: Links with Software Engineering and Ontological Engineering. Journal of Software 4, 992–1013 (2009)
3. Herman, W.A., Devey, G.B.: Future Trends in Medical Device Technologies: A Ten-Year Forecast. Food and Drug Administration, Center for Devices and Radiological Health (2011)
4. IEC: IEC 62366: 2007 Medical devices – Application of usability engineering to medical devices. CEN, Brussels, BE (2007)
5. ISO: ISO 14971:2000 Medical devices – Application of risk management to medical devices. CEN, Brussels, BE (2000)
6. ISO: ISO 13485:2003 Medical devices – Quality management systems – Requirements for regulatory purposes. CEN, Brussels, BE (2003)
7. ISO: ISO 14971:2007 Medical devices – Application of risk management to medical devices. CEN, Brussels, BE (2007)
8. ISO: ISO 15223-1:2012 Medical devices – Symbols to be used with medical device labels, labelling and information to be supplied – Part 1: General requirements. CEN, Brussels, BE (2012)
9. ANSI/AAMI: HE75: Human factors engineering-Design of medical devices. Association for the Advancement of Medical Instrumentation, Arlington, VA (2009)
10. Martin, J., Norris, B.J., Murphy, E., Crowe, J.A.: Medical device development: The challenge for ergonomics. Applied Ergonomics 39, 271–283 (2008)
11. Money, A., Barnett, J., Kuljis, J., Craven, M., Martin, J., Young, T.: The role of the user within the medical device design and development process: medical device manufacturers' perspectives. BMC Medical Informatics and Decision Making 11, 15 (2011)
12. Martin, J., Barnett, J.: Integrating the results of user research into medical device development: insights from a case study. BMC Medical Informatics and Decision Making 12, 74 (2012)
13. Heneghan, C., Thompson, M., Billingsley, M., Cohen, D.: Medical-device recalls in the UK and the device-regulation process: retrospective review of safety notices and alerts. BMJ Open 1 (2011)
14. Food and Drug Administration (FDA): Draft Guidance for Industry and Food and Drug Administration Staff - Applying Human Factors and Usability Engineering to Optimize Medical Device Design. U.S. Food and Drug Administration, Silver Spring, MD (2011)

15. Faulkner, L.: Beyond the five-user assumption: Benefits of increased sample sizes in usability testing. Behavior Research Methods 35, 379–383 (2003)
16. Nielsen, J.: http://www.useit.com/alertbox/20000319.html
17. Nielsen, J.: http://www.useit.com/alertbox/number-of-test-users.html
18. Nielsen, J., Landauer, T.K.: A mathematical model of the finding of usability problems. In: Proceedings of the INTERACT 1993 and CHI 1993 Conference on Human Factors in Computing Systems, pp. 206–213. ACM, Amsterdam (1993)
19. Virzi, R.A.: Streamlining the Design Process: Running Fewer Subjects. In: Proceedings of the Human Factors Society 34th Annual Meeting, vol. 34, pp. 291–294. ACM, Santa Monica (1990)
20. Virzi, R.A.: Refining the test phase of usability evaluation: how many subjects is enough? Human Factors 34, 457–468 (1992)
21. Borsci, S., Londei, A., Federici, S.: The Bootstrap Discovery Behaviour (BDB): a new outlook on usability evaluation. Cognitive Processing 12, 23–31 (2011)
22. Caulton, D.A.: Relaxing the homogeneity assumption in usability testing. Behaviour & Information Technology 20, 1–7 (2001)
23. Lewis, J.R.: Evaluation of Procedures for Adjusting Problem-Discovery Rates Estimated From Small Samples. International Journal of Human-Computer Interaction 13, 445–479 (2001)
24. Schmettow, M.: Heterogeneity in the usability evaluation process. In: Proceedings of the 22nd British HCI Group Annual Conference on People and Computers: Culture, Creativity, Interaction, vol. 1, pp. 89–98. British Computer Society, Liverpool (2008)
25. Schmettow, M.: Sample size in usability studies. Communications of the ACM 55, 64–70 (2012)
26. Turner, C.W., Lewis, J.R., Nielsen, J.: Determining Usability Test Sample Size. In: Karwowski, W. (ed.) International Encyclopedia of Ergonomics and Human Factors, vol. 2, pp. 3084–3088. CRC Press, Boca Raton (2006)
27. Lewis, J.R.: Validation of Monte Carlo estimation of problem discovery likelihood (Tech. Rep. No. 29.3357). IBM (2000)
28. Borsci, S., Macredie, R.D., Barnett, J., Martin, J., Kuljis, J., Young, T.: Reviewing and Extending the Five–user Assumption: A Grounded Procedure for Interaction Evaluation (manuscript submitted for publication, 2013)

Usability Guidelines for Desktop Search Engines

Manuel Burghardt, Tim Schneidermeier, and Christian Wolff

Media Informatics Group, University of Regensburg, Regensburg, Germany
{manuel.burghardt,tim.schneidermeier,christian.wolff}@ur.de

Abstract. In this article we describe a usability evaluation of eight desktop search engines (DSEs). We used the heuristic walkthrough method to gather usability problems as well as individual strengths and weaknesses of the tested search engines. The results of the evaluation are integrated into a set of 30 design guidelines for user-friendly DSEs.

Keywords: usability testing, heuristic evaluation, desktop search engines, usability guidelines.

1 Introduction: Desktop Search Engines and the Case for Usability

While *web search engines* (WSEs) have long since become a useful tool to fulfill everyday information needs on the web, so called *desktop search engines* (DSEs) are often inadequate to meet information needs on a user's private computer (Cole 2005). Strangely enough, many available systems do remarkably well in terms of performance and quality of search (Chang-Tien et al. 2007): That is why we believe that *usability* plays an important and oftentimes neglected role in the design of DSEs. Although there are many studies on the usability of WSE (Thurow & Musica 2009) and guidelines for the general design for search user interfaces (Hearst 2009, Wilson 2012, Russell-Rose & Tate 2013), the area of DSE has not been the subject of extensive usability research so far. While there are many similarities between web and desktop search, there are also some substantial differences: On the web, we usually search for new, mostly unseen information, but on our private desktops we search for "stuff we've seen before" (Dumais et al. 2003). The different information behavior for WSEs and DSEs (Bergman 2008) has implications for the design of a desktop search system, i.e. existing guidelines for the design of user-friendly web search systems (cf. Leavitt et al. 2006) cannot be adopted to the area of DSEs without further ado. In this paper we propose a set of guidelines for the design of user-friendly DSEs which has been derived from an expert-based usability inspection of existing desktop search systems.

2 Evaluation Design

The guidelines presented in this article are the result of a *heuristic walkthrough* (Sears 1997) for a total of eight available DSEs, including platform-specific systems such as

M. Kurosu (Ed.): Human-Computer Interaction, Part I, HCII 2013, LNCS 8004, pp. 176–183, 2013.

Windows Search 4.0 and *Apple's Spotlight*, but also individual search engines such as *Copernic* or *xFriend* (cf. Table 1 for an overview of all the DSEs that were subject of this evaluation study, cf. Figure 1 for an overview of the methodological approach). The heuristic walkthrough is an analytic evaluation method that relies on usability experts who perform an inspection of the subject of evaluation and document positive as well as negative usability and interaction issues. It is a combination of the rather unstructured, free-form *heuristic evaluation* (Nielsen 1994), and the more structured, task-based *cognitive walkthrough* (Wharton et al. 1994).

Table 1. Overview of all tested desktop search engines

Name	Source
Apple Spotlight	part of the Apple operation system since Mac OS X 10.4
Archivarius 3000	http://www.likasoft.com/de/document-search/index.shtml
Copernic Desktop Search	http://www.copernic.com/en/products/desktop-search/index.html
Everything Search Engine	http://www.voidtools.com/
Filehand Search	http://www.filehand.com/
Windows Search 4.0	http://www.microsoft.com/de-de/download/details.aspx?id=23 (part of the MS Windows operation system since Windows 7)
X1	http://www.x1.com/
xFriend	http://www.xfriend.de/

Each DSE was tested by an independent pair of evaluators[1], each trying to accomplish a common information retrieval task with the respective search system. The evaluations revealed individual strengths, but also weaknesses of the respective DSE, which were documented as usability problems and categorized according to Nielsen's (1994) renowned framework, which consists of ten generic usability heuristics[2] (cf. Table 2). In some cases, one identified usability problem was classified as violating several heuristics, which makes for a total of 70 usability problems[3], and 92 violations of the usability heuristics in all.

---

[1] The evaluators were undergraduate students from the information science (`http://iw.ur.de`) and media informatics (`http://mi.ur.de`) B. A. degree programs at the University of Regensburg. They were trained in the heuristic walkthrough method in advance, and they also had knowledge about existing guidelines for the design of user-friendly WSEs (e.g. Leavitt et al. 2006 and Quirmbach 2012)

[2] Online version available at <`http://www.useit.com/papers/heuristic/heuristic_list.html`>, last accessed on 1.10.2013.

[3] We do not report the exact number of usability problems for each DSE, as the evaluation was not about comparing several systems to find out which one is best, but rather to analyze why a system is bad with regards to its usability.

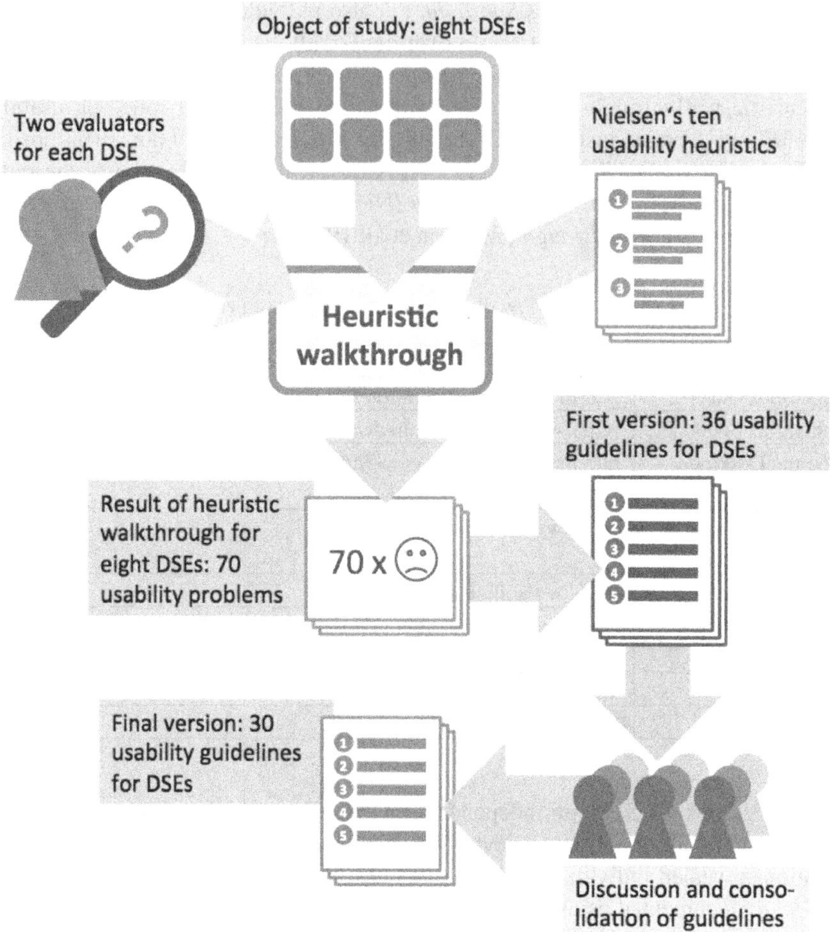

Fig. 1. Overview of the methodological approach used to gather usability guidelines for DSEs

After the heuristic walkthrough, we clustered some of the redundant usability problems and also considered specific strengths which had been evaluated positively by the testers. We integrated the reported problems as well as the positive aspects of the evaluated DSEs into an initial set of 36 usability guidelines.

In a next step, these guidelines were discussed with the participants of the previous heuristic walkthrough in order to get feedback on the appropriateness of the suggested guidelines for the respective DSE they had tested before. The group discussion revealed some interesting wording problems and also showed that some guidelines were formulated redundantly or put in the wrong heuristic category. After this first, theoretical validation round we reduced our set of guidelines to a total of 30, and also did some rephrasing to make them more comprehensible. The final set of guidelines is presented in the next section.

Table 2. Overview of the heuristics used during the evaluation, and the number of violations for each heuristic

Usability heuristic (Nielsen 1994)	Violations
(1) Visibility of system status	12
(2) Match between system and the real world	9
(3) User control and freedom	8
(4) Consistency and standards	12
(5) Error prevention	11
(6) Recognition rather than recall	6
(7) Flexibility and efficiency of use	7
(8) Aesthetic and minimalist design	8
(9) Help users recognize, diagnose, and recover from errors	9
(10) Help and documentation	10
	Total: 92

3 Guidelines for the Design of User-Friendly Desktop Search Engines

This section presents the results of a heuristic walkthrough for eight DSEs: a set of 30 guidelines for the design of user-friendly search engines for the desktop context, categorized according to Nielsen's (1994) ten usability heuristics.

Visibility of System Status

The guidelines in this category ensure that the user of a DSE knows what the software is doing at a given point in time. These guidelines are all about comprehensibility and transparency of the system status, which includes appropriate feedback on specific operations and the coming about of certain results.

- **G1.1** It should be obvious to the user which areas of the system are indexed and thus included in the search scope at a given point in time.
- **G1.2** It should be obvious to the user when the DSE is busy, building or updating the index, which may have effects on search performance.
- **G1.3** It should be obvious to the user how many files are actually searched, and how many relevant documents were finally retrieved.

Match between System and the Real World

The DSE should speak the language of the user, i.e. it should use words and metaphors the user is already familiar with. Information, especially on the results list, should be presented in an intuitive and comprehensible order.

- **G2.1** If there is an explicit button to submit a query, it should be labeled unambiguously with "search".

- **G2.2** If there are identical documents in the results list, i.e. documents that are stored redundantly on different locations of the system, these should be marked as duplicates.
- **G2.3** On the results list, it should be obvious for the user where the respective documents are stored (make the document path available).

User Control and Freedom

The user should be free to control certain functionalities of the DSE. For the designer, this is often a tightrope walk between hiding certain functions to reduce complexity, but at the same time provide access to these functions at any point in time, to ensure full user control and freedom.

- **G3.1** If necessary, the user should be able to access advanced search options, which are hidden per default to reduce unnecessary complexity in a simple and intuitive way.
- **G3.2** The user should be able to define the scope of the search in a simple and intuitive way.
- **G3.3** If a search takes exceptionally long, the user should be able to cancel it manually.
- **G3.4** If necessary, the user should be able to filter the list of results by different criteria such as file format, date or name.

Consistency and Standards

The DSE should be consistent in itself with regard to design and wording as well as functionality and operations. It should also adhere to standards that are known from typical desktop applications and to conventions that have been established in the area of WSE.

- **G4.1** Standards and conventions that are known from the area of desktop applications (e.g. design of icons or menus) should be observed.
- **G4.2** Colors, layout and font should be used in a consistent way.
- **G4.3** Basic user interface elements, like for instance the search field or the search button, should be used consistently in different situations.
- **G4.4** The DSE should support truncation and search operators (e.g. AND / OR / NOT), or their conventionalized shortcuts, that may be known from WSEs.

Error Prevention

This category contains guidelines for a pre-emptive system design that reduces potential interaction errors.

- **G5.1** The user should not be required to set any advanced search parameters to enter a simple query.
- **G5.2** If the user has not configured it otherwise, the DSE should search all areas of the system on default.

- **G5.3** The DSE should prevent the user from misspelling the query and actively support query formulation by providing *search as you type* functionality as known from many WSEs.
- **G5.4** The DSE should translate special characters on the query side as well as on the indexing side into the platform specific encoding.

Recognition Rather Than Recall
The DSE should support recognition rather than recall, which first and foremost is relevant for the query a user formulates at the beginning of his search. After submitting the query to the DSE, the user usually sees a results page: To evaluate the results, it is vital to compare it with the original query, thus the query should be visible at this stage of search.

- **G6.1** The DSE should display the original query on the results page.
- **G6.2** The search field should be big enough to display complex queries.

Flexibility and Efficiency of Use
The search engine should provide shortcuts that accelerate the interaction for experts, but do not obfuscate novice users. Frequently used functions should be easily accessible for any user group.

- **G7.1** The user should be able to open the search dialogue at any time with a single action (e.g. a mouse click or a keyboard shortcut).
- **G7.2** The user should be able to save complex queries for later reuse (personalized search history).
- **G7.3** The user should be able to jump to the target documents directly by clicking on the items in the results list.
- **G7.4** A query should be processed in less than two seconds, as the user is accustomed to high speed information retrieval from the web context.

Aesthetic and Minimalist Design
Interaction should be kept simple, i.e. the interface should not contain irrelevant or information used rarely.

- **G8.1** The items in the results list should hide inadequate metadata from the user.
- **G8.2** The user interface is functional and only consists of the necessary interaction components, such as search field, search button, and advanced search options.

Help Users Recognize, Diagnose, and Recover from Errors
If an error occurs, the DSE should provide feedback on the problem cause, and also suggest a potential solution. In the case of DSE, the most frequent problems that occur are queries which do not return any results.

- **G9.1** If a query returns zero results, the DSE should provide hints on how to reformulate or improve the unsuccessful query.

Help and Documentation

Ideally, a user should be able to use the basic functions of a DSE without having to read a manual or a documentation. The DSE should be self-explanatory or provide useful information to understand complex interaction behavior (e.g. in the form of tooltips or meaningful icons). Nevertheless, advanced and complex functions should be described in some kind of documentation. The documentation should be easy to use, and focus on potential user problems and questions.

- **G10.1** The DSE should describe and explain the advanced search options.
- **G10.2** There should be a document that describes and explains the indexing function in detail.
- **G10.3** The DSE should provide search templates (i.e. exemplary queries) that illustrate how to use the search syntax to formulate successful queries.

4 Outlook

We believe that our set of guidelines can help future developers of DSEs to build more usable systems, and that it may serve as an evaluation tool for users who have to decide which system to choose from the abundance of available search engines. It must be stressed, however, that the guidelines presented here are not meant to be exhaustive for any usability aspect of DSEs, but rather serve as a basic collection of hints and guidelines, that may be adjusted and extended for specific scenarios if necessary. In addition, the concept of *desktop search engines* needs some serious reconsideration, as the traditional *desktop metaphor* is slowly fading away in the face of ubiquitous and mobile computing, and the increasing availability of cloud storage services. We are planning to further validate, extend and refine the usability guidelines for DSEs, and to eventually adapt them for the domain of mobile search (Tan et al. 2008) in consecutive studies.

References

1. Bergman, O., Beyth-Marom, R., Nachmias, R., Gradovitch, N., Whittaker, S.: Improved search engines and navigation preference in personal information management. ACM Transactions on Information Systems (TOIS) 26(4), 1–24 (2008)
2. Chang-Tien, L., Shukla, M., Subramanya, S.H., Yamin, W.: Performance Evaluation of Desktop Search Engines. In: IEEE International Conference on Information Reuse and Integration, pp. 110–115 (2007)
3. Cole, B.: Search engines tackle the desktop. IEEE Computer 38(3), 14–17 (2005)
4. Dumais, S., Cutrell, E., Cadiz, J.J., Jancke, G., Sarin, R., Robbins, D.C.: Stuff I've seen: a system for personal information retrieval and re-use. In: Proceedings of the 26th Annual International ACM SIGIR Conference on Research and Development in Information Retrieval, pp. 72–79 (2003)
5. Hearst, M.A.: Search User Interfaces. Cambridge University Press (2009)
6. Leavitt, M., et al.: Research-Based Web Design and Usability Guidelines. U.S. Dept. of Health and Human Services (2006)

7. Nielsen, J.: Heuristic evaluation. In: Nielsen, J., Mack, R. (eds.) Usability Inspection Methods, pp. 25–62. John Wiley & Sons, New York (1994)
8. Russell-Rose, T., Tate, T.: Designing the Search Experience. The Information Architeture of Discovery. Morgan Kaufman, Waltham (2013)
9. Sears, A.: Heuristic walkthroughs: finding the problems without the noise. International Journal of Human-Computer Interaction 9(3), 213–234 (1997)
10. Tan, C., Sheng, B., Wang, H., Li, Q.: Microsearch: When search engines meet small devices. In: Indulska, J., Patterson, D.J., Rodden, T., Ott, M. (eds.) PERVASIVE 2008. LNCS, vol. 5013, pp. 93–110. Springer, Heidelberg (2008)
11. Thurow, S., Musica, N.: When Search Meets Web Usability. New Riders, Indianapolis (2009)
12. Quirmbach, S.: Suchmaschinen. X-media-press, Springer, Heidelberg (2012)
13. Wharton, C., Rieman, J., Lewis, C., Polson, P.: The cognitive walkthrough method: A practitioner's guide. In: Nielsen, J., Mack, R. (eds.) Usability Inspection Methods, pp. 105–140. John Wiley & Sons (1994)
14. Wilson, M.L.: Search User Interface Design. Morgan & Claypool Publishers, San Francisco (2012)

Analyzing Face and Speech Recognition to Create Automatic Information for Usability Evaluation

Thiago Adriano Coleti, Marcelo Morandini, and Fátima de Lourdes dos Santos Nunes

University of Sao Paulo, Brazil
{thiagocoleti,m.morandini,fatima.nunes}@usp.br

Abstract. Observe users perform their tasks in a software is an important way to performing usability evaluation due to the reason that provides real data about the interaction between user and system. Filming and verbalization are very used techniques and they must be a concern for all designers. However, the needs of reviewing all registered data manually became these techniques slow and difficult. This paper presents an approach that uses face recognition and speech processing to generate relevant information about a system under test such as what moments the user had specific reaction and which ones. The ErgoSV software supported the experiments that were performed using an e-commerce website. The results showed that this approach allows the evaluator identify interfaces with usability problems easily and quickly as well as present information using percentages that supported the evaluator making decision.

Keywords: Usability Evaluation, Human-Computer Interaction, Speech Recognition, Face Recognition.

1 Introduction

Evaluating software usability is one of the most important activities of the design development process and performing it with real users should be a concern to all developers. In some sense, this task should be irreplaceable since it provides real information about the interaction between user and software and how one interferes in other to the evaluator [2].

This strategy to evaluate Human-Computer Interaction (HCI) usability is also known as usability test, and usually is performed by observing the user performing their tasks in a prototype or in a full software release. Two techniques are widely used to supporting the test: filming and verbalization. Filming consists in the positioning of one or several cameras near the user in order to collect images of face, keyboard, mouse, environment and other locations that can be considered important by the evaluator. In verbalization tests, the participant is encouraged to verbalize (pronounce) what he is thinking about the system and the evaluator can collect this data writing or registering them in audio files. The participant can verbalize during the evaluation (simultaneously verbalization) or verbalize after the test (consecutive verbalization). These techniques are widely used by researchers and developers and both of them

M. Kurosu (Ed.): Human-Computer Interaction, Part I, HCII 2013, LNCS 8004, pp. 184–192, 2013.

may present either qualitative or quantitative results for analyzing the recorded interaction. However, they are considered slow and expensive techniques due to the reason that evaluators and designers should review all the images and voice data as a film or a music to identifying whether happens some usability problem. According to Nielsen [2,3] this task can take two to three times the time of evaluation.

This paper presents the development, implementation of a usability evaluation approach based on observation method, filming and verbalization techniques and supported by face recognition and speech recognition. In this approach software collects face images and words pronounced by participants. Then, it processes these data and indicates what time specific user's face reaction occurs or when they pronounced a word. Thus, these data can be used to produce other relevant information about the interaction such as level of confidence and satisfaction on the results presented and efficiency/efficacy of the interactions performed.

2 Bibliographic Review

This section presents the bibliographic review performed in order to collect data about the subjects dealt with this research. Three issues are discussed: Usability evaluation supported by face and speech recognition; Image Processing/Face Recognition; and Speech Processing.

2.1 Usability Evaluation Supported by Face Recognition and Speech Recognition

The usability evaluation is a systematic process aimed to collect data in order to produce qualitative and/or quantitative information about the interface, users and interaction process, allowing the evaluator to provide corrections or establish a interface pattern [2,4]. Two methods are used by the designer to perform usability evaluations: (1) Usability inspection, where an interface is compared with guidelines, such as Ergonomic Criteria [1] or Heuristics [2,3]; (2) Usability Test, where real users are encouraged to use a software prototype or a full release and submit it to real situations in order to analyze whether the interaction between user and software has problems [1]. Filming the interaction process using one or several cameras or request to user for verbalizing what they are thinking about the software are two widely used techniques. The first technique aims to register images about the interaction between user and software. The evaluator places one or several cameras in strategies position in order to collect images from user, software, computer and environment. The images are used as data and analyzed by evaluator in order to identify interfaces with usability problems. The analysis is performed manually and consists in watch all the video since the first recorded second until finishing the test. The second technique is known as verbalization and consist in encourage the user (participant) verbalize what they are thinking about the software and consequently, the evaluator registers it in note or audio files [1,2,4]. The analysis of audio files or notes is performed in the same way of filming technique [1]. Due to this reason these techniques are considered slow and this difficulty leads some evaluators ignore this stage of usability test causing interaction problems.

2.2 Face Recognition/Image Processing

An digital image is the representation of a physic object that can be recorded, processing and interpreted according to user's needs. Image processing is composed by a set of techniques aiming at manipulating images using computational algorithms in order to extract information from them [6].

The image processing is an activity usually used in several areas such as medicine, geography, physical and human-computer interaction. In medicine area the image process has being highlighted in several activities such as X-Ray and ultrasound as a resource to supporting the medical decision-making. Beyond medicine, the image processing is used in other studies and task, such as entertainment, design, security and aviation and involves a broad class of software, hardware and theory [5].

The face detection/face recognition is one of the most important and known image processing activities. This technique use algorithms to identify were a face is located in a image where a human being is represented. [7].

The image processing and more specifically the face recognition could be an important resource in order to support usability evaluation to collect and processing user´s face images during the evaluation and processing it to generating information about test.

2.3 Speech Processing

The human being has several mechanisms to express their emotions and one of the more important ways is the voice. Due to the importance in human life, the voice became an important area of research in computing [12]. Speech processing is the process of voice interpretation by computer, receiving an external signal and through computational algorithms performing the transformation in an output like a text [9,10]. The approach of converting voice signal in a text is also defined by authors as Automatic Speech Recognition (ASR).

There are several methods and techniques to perform the speech recognition such as Linear Predictive Coding (LPC), Perceptual Linear Prediction (PLP) and Mel-Frequency Cepstral Coefficient (MFCC) and Hiden Markov Models (HMMs). The main difference among them is the number of processes performed to transforming the voice signal in text, but the basic activities are the same: (1) collect sounds using a resource such as microphone; (2) processing the signal and generating the text; (3) display the final result [9, 10].

The use of speech processing in different areas such as software development and biometrics raised the needs of tools to supporting the recognition activities easily and quickly in such waythat developers do not need to know models. Aiming solving this gap, the Laboratório de Processamento de Sinais (LAPS) in Federal University of Para – Brazil has developed the Coruja Application [11]. This application allows the use of speech processing functions easily and quickly in development environments such as Visual C# and can recognize both English and Brazilian Portuguese language. Researches using this tool [1,12] concluded that the Coruja Application recognizes between sixty and ninety percent of tested words. Tests were also performed before starting the ErgoSV development that also had the recognition rate greater then seventy percent. Due to this reason the Coruja Application was chosen to supportthe ErgoSV development.

3 Usability Evaluation Supported by Face and Voice Recognition

The usability evaluation framework supported by face and voice recognition was developed in order to support observation method. The main novelty of this approach is the use of face recognition, image processing and speech recognition as a resource to collect and process data, generating relevant information such as confidence and satisfaction on the results presented, efficiency/efficacy of the interactions performed, the interfaces and moments when the user had specific reactions. In this way, evaluator does not need review all data storage in order to obtain these data.

Aiming analyzing the effectiveness of the approach, experiments were performed using two specifics software developed for this research, called ErgoSV Software and ErgoSV Analyzer [8]. These applications aimed to collect data about user such as face image and words pronounced beyond collecting screenshot images, processing the data and generating relevant information. Figure 1 presents the ErgoSV Software Approach.

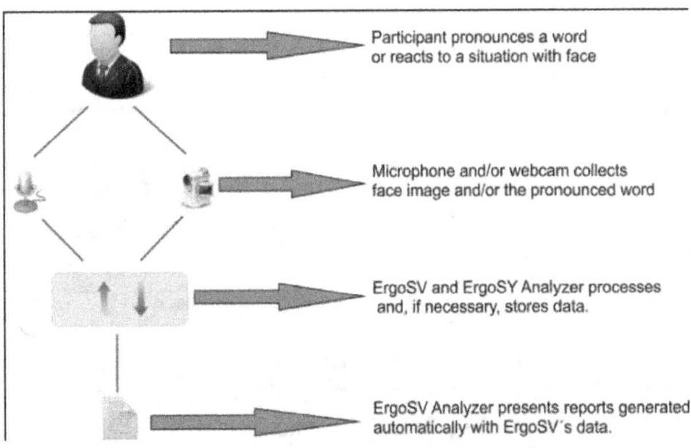
Participant pronounces a word
or reacts to a situation with face
Microphone and/or webcam collects
face image and/or the pronounced word
ErgoSV and ErgoSY Analyzer processes
and, if necessary, stores data.
ErgoSV Analyzer presents reports generated
automatically with ErgoSV's data.

Fig. 1. ErgoSV ErgoSV Approach

3.1 ErgoSV Software

The first application was called ErgoSV and aimed to collect evaluation data. This software was installed in a computer and used to performing observation in a website usability test. In order to develop this software two resources were used to support face and speech recognition: (1) OpenCV Library: a free computational library that has several image processing functions and is easily integrated with development environment such as Visual C#. This library allows the easy access to face recognition function, avoiding the development of recognition algorithms [7]; (2) Coruja Library:a free library that allows developers to use speech recognition functions easily and also allows the integration with development environments. This tool is able to recognize any pronounced word and/or specific words configured in a word files (specific dictionary) [11].

Therefore, to perform the approach experiments, we choose the user face as a data to be collected and configured the ErgoSV and the OpenCV Library in order to collect only the face image and register it. Regarding to speech data collection, we choose four words that represent quality concepts: Excellent, Good, Reasonable and Bad.

Besides these settings, before start any test, the evaluators configured other parameters such as application name, approach (Only Filming, Verbalization, Both), Images Interval (for screen and face collecting) and Words. A face image was requested for all participants in order to collect a default picture to be compared to others face images collected during the test.

We used an e-commerce website and we established a series of activities to be performed by participants. The activities were related with the buying process such as Searching for a product, Visualizing Products, Buying Process and Informing payment details. Figure 2 presents the ErgoSV interface used to performing the tests and collecting data.

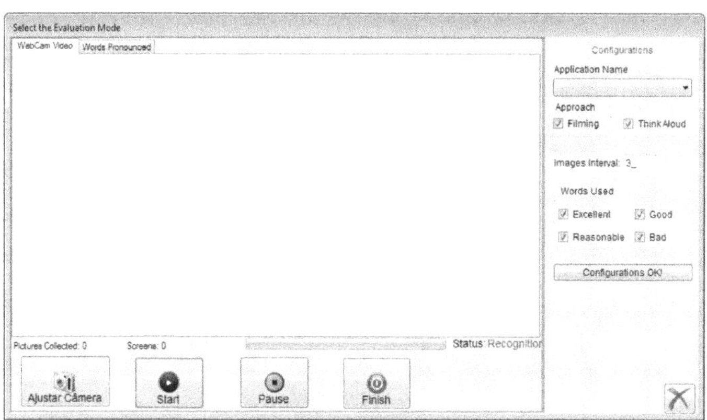

Fig. 2. ErgoSV Interface

A series of experiments was performed by four participants using ErgoSV who executed several tasks provided by evaluators. Each test took about fifteen minutes and in all tests the ErgoSV collected one face image and one screen image per second and all the pronounced word. The test data, processing and results are present in next subsection.

3.2 ErgoSV Analyzer

The ErgoSV Analyzer is a software developed in order to make the processing of collected data and displaying relevant information about software tested such as the words pronounced, the face and screenshot images collected, the words confidence and the software usability rate.

This application is also used to analyze whether the face image, words pronounced and screenshot images are adequate to generating usability information, mainly considering which moments the user had specific reactions.

The information exhibition was divided in three parts: the first interface is related with Words Pronounced and displays which words were pronounced, the confidence rate and the time (minutes after starting test) the specific reaction has happened. Also, this interface presents a chart containing the percentage of each word pronounced during the test. When the evaluator selects a pronounced word, he/she can access some images of screenshot that were used by participant when they had that reaction. The quantity of images displayed is configured according to user needs who must inform how many seconds before and after the word is pronounced he/she hope see the screens. Figure 3 presents the Words Pronounced Interface and Figure 4 presents the Results Interface.

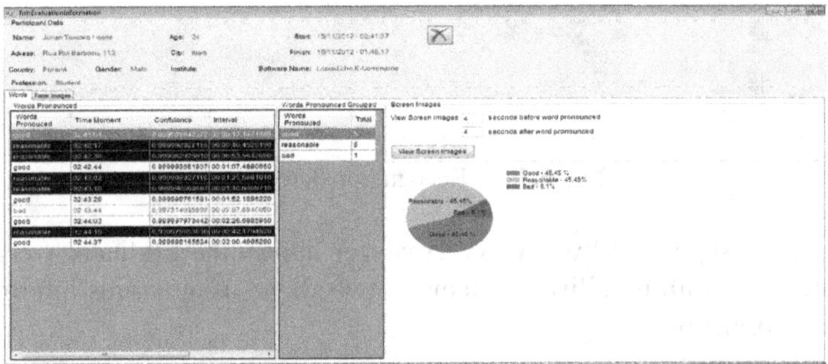

Fig. 3. Words Pronounced Interface

Fig. 4. Results Interface

The interface showed in Figure 4 displays information about the face images collected in the test such as Time Moment, Situation of the image (whether the interface is different from default image), Status (Discarded or Face Recognized). The Status Information refers to the capacity of recognizing or not a face and it was necessary because due to several reasons such as distractions, phone calls and others, the participant can be not looking for the camera and thus, the system is not able to recognize the face. Initially these images are discarded; however it must be important to analyze what moment the participant was not looking to computer. Two charts present the percentage of discarded images and faces that were recognized.

As well as the words pronounced, the face images displayed also allow the evaluator access the screen images that presents what the participant has did when the system collected that image. Figure 5 presents the Face Recognition Screens.

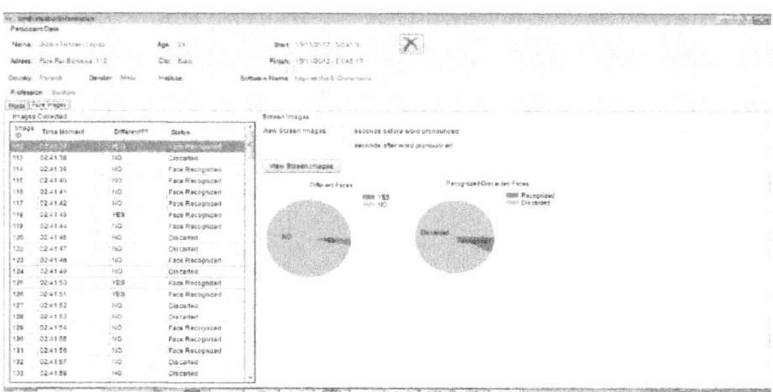

Fig. 5. Face Recognition Screens

The approach supported by ErgoSV Analyzer allows the evaluator (re-searcher) identify interfaces with usability problems in two ways: using words information or using faces information:

(1) Using words pronounced information: words such as Reasonable and Bad are highlighted calling attention of evaluator to possible usability problems and providing a series of interfaces in order to be analyzed. This resource avoids the need of reviewing all registered data to finding problems. For example, whether the participant pronounced the word "Bad" after ten minutes from starting the test, this word will be presented in the ErgoSV information allowing verify some interfaces before and after the pronunciation. In this way it is not necessary to review ten minutes of registered data to finding this information. In this case, in less than one minute the evaluator can know what interface have usability problems. Charts presenting quantitative information using the percentage of each word pronounced can provide real inputs about the general user opinion about the application;

(2) Using Face Recognition Information: after performing the evaluation, an image processing is performed to compare the captured face image to the default image, captured on the beginning of the test. A specific algorithm of image processing is used to performing the images comparison. Thus, two different images can be an important parameter that the participant had some reaction in this moment and so, something happened with this user. A series of screen images and words pronounced

can be accessed from the image register, supporting the evaluator to identifying the problems. Similarly, the information that the user was not looking for the camera highlights that some action had turned the user's attention and this situation may have been caused by the interface. Percentages of images collected, face recognized and images discarded can support evaluator making decisions quantifying the user's behavior through face image. The experiments also presents that face reaction is more involuntary then the pronouncement of a word leading the system processing a large number of different faces.

4 Discussion

The use of Speech and Face Recognition was considered satisfactory due the reason that it facilitates the data collecting processing allowing the participants perform their tasks without have to to note or mark something in a book or other software. The processing of pronounced words generated relevant information about software usability and allows user to identify problems interface in an easy and fast way.

The same results were noted in speech recognition similarly to face recognition. The ability to recognize different faces and whether the user was not looking for camera allowed the evaluator to identify possible problems interfaces beyond identify situation that distracted the participant. However the algorithm used to compare images still needs some calibration because it indicates some similar images as different. An improvement in this resource is being performing in order to provide a better image comparison.

Therefore, the results of proposed approach and the application used to support the experiments were considered satisfactory due to the reason that usability problems were identified based on specific user reactions, providing what moment and/or interface that needs improvement, beyond relevant information generated automatically by software avoiding the full registers review.

5 Conclusion

The observation method is an important and effective way to perform usability evaluation, mainly because it allows that real users test the application submitting it to situations similarly to real environment. Filming and Verbalization are two techniques widely used due to reason that collect the opinion and behavior of participants during the software using.

This paper presented the first results of a research to automate the generating information process using face and speech recognition. The use of these resources allowed identify easily and quickly which interfaces had usability problems due by processing specific user's reactions collected during the test, reducing time and cost in the review process. The data processing also allowed quantifying the usability test through the percentage of words and images, providing to evaluator a general idea about the users' opinion and their reactions. Currently we work in order to improve the cross reference information based on parameters such as age, gender, education and other that can be created in the future. Also we intend to use the ErgoSV and ErgoSV Analyzer to performing evaluation in other software such as prototypes and Ecological software.

Acknowledgment. Financial Supported by FAPESP.

References

1. Cybis, W.A., Betiol, A.H., Faust, R.: Ergonomia e Usabilidade: conhecimentos, métodos e aplicações, 2nd edn. Novatec, São Paulo (2010)
2. Nielsen, J.: Usability Engineering. Morgan Kaufmann, Moutain View (1993)
3. Nielsen, J.: Designing Web Sites - Designing Web Usability. Campus (2000)
4. Preece, J., Rogers, Y., Sharp, H.: Interaction Design Beyond Human-Computer Interaction (2005); John-Wiley & Sons, Ltd. (2011)
5. Gonzalez, R.C., Woods, R.E.: Digital image processing. Addison-Wesley, Reading (1992)
6. Nunes, F.L.S.: Introdução ao processamento de imagens médicas para auxílio a diagnóstico – uma visão prática. Livro das Jornadas de Atualizações em Informática, 73–126 (2006)
7. Lima, J.P.S.M., et al.: Reconhecimento de padrões em tempo real utilizando a biblioteca OpenCV. Técnicas e Ferramentas de Processamento de Imagens Digitais e Aplicações em Realidade Virtual e Misturada, 47–89 (2008)
8. Coleti, T.A., Morandini, M., Nunes, F.L.S.: The Proposition of ErgoSV: An Environment to Support Usability Evaluation Using Image Processing and Speech Recognition System. In: IADIS Interfaces and Human Computer Interaction 2012 (IHCI 2012) Conference, Lisbon, vol. 1, pp. 1–4 (2012)
9. Neto, N., Patrick, C., Klautau, A., Trancoso, I.: Free tools and resources for Brazilian Portuguese speech recognition. In. J. Braz. Computing Society, 53–68 (2011), doi:10.1007/s13173-010-0023-1
10. Shariah, M.A., et al.: Human computer interaction using isolated-words speech recognition technology. In: International Conference on Intelligent and Advanced Systems 2007 (2007)
11. `http://www.laps.ufpa.br/falabrasil/` (accessed in December 2011)
12. Silva, P., Batista, P., Neto, N., Klautau, A.: An open-source speech recognizer for Brazilian Portuguese with a windows programming interface. In: Pardo, T.A.S., Branco, A., Klautau, A., Vieira, R., de Lima, V.L.S. (eds.) PROPOR 2010. LNCS, vol. 6001, pp. 128–131. Springer, Heidelberg (2010)

Linking Context to Evaluation in the Design of Safety Critical Interfaces

Michael Feary[1], Dorrit Billman[2], Xiuli Chen[3], Andrew Howes[3], Richard Lewis[4], Lance Sherry[5], and Satinder Singh[4]

[1] NASA Ames Research Center, Moffett Field, California, USA
[2] San Jose State University Foundation at NASA Ames, Moffett Field, CA, USA
[3] University of Birmingham, Birmingham, England, UK
[4] University of Michigan, Ann Arbor, MI, USA
[5] George Mason University, Fairfax, VA, USA

{michael.s.feary,dorrit.billman}@nasa.gov, HowesA@bham.ac.uk, {rickl,baveja}@umich.edu, sherry@gmu.edu

Abstract. The rate of introduction of new technology into safety critical domains continues to increase. Improvements in evaluation methods are needed to keep pace with the rapid development of these technologies. A significant challenge in improving evaluation is developing efficient methods for collecting and characterizing knowledge of the domain and context of the work being performed. Traditional methods of incorporating domain and context knowledge into an evaluation rely upon expert user testing, but these methods are expensive and resource intensive. This paper will describe three new methods for evaluating the applicability of a user interface within a safety-critical domain (specifically aerospace work domains), and consider how these methods may be incorporated into current evaluation processes.

Keywords: Work Analysis, Evaluation, Human Performance Modeling, Human – Automation Interaction.

1 Introduction: A Pressing Challenge for New Methods for Technology Evaluation

In many work domains, technology is designed to support users in carrying out functions and goals needed to do the work. Developing good user interfaces requires knowledge of what the work requires, knowledge of the environment in which the technology may be used and knowledge of human performance constraints. In this paper, we refer to this knowledge collectively as *context*.

The need to incorporate contextual information in evaluation of new technology in safety-critical domains is evident in incident and accident reports. There is recognition of this need in aviation and space domains as shown by changes to regulations and guidance material in aviation. Traditionally, these regulations have been written with the intent of removing as much context information as possible to allow for wide applicability; however the aviation regulatory community has recognized the

M. Kurosu (Ed.): Human-Computer Interaction, Part I, HCII 2013, LNCS 8004, pp. 193–202, 2013.

increasing need for context information to be included in the evaluation. A good example of the introduction of a requirement for context information is illustrated by European Aviation Safety Agency (EASA) Certification Specification 25.1302, below:

"This installed equipment must be shown, *individually and in combination with other such equipment,* to be designed so that qualified flight-crew members trained in its use can safely perform *their tasks associated with its intended function* by meeting the following requirements:

(a) Flight deck controls must be installed to allow accomplishment of these tasks and information necessary to accomplish these tasks must be provided.
(b) Flight deck controls and information intended for flight crew use must:

1. Be presented in a clear and unambiguous form, at resolution and precision *appropriate to the task.*
2. Be accessible and usable by the flight crew in a manner consistent with the *urgency, frequency, and duration of their tasks*, and
3. Enable flight crew awareness, if awareness is required for safe operation, of the effects on the aeroplane or systems resulting from flight crew actions.

(c) Operationally-relevant behaviour of the installed equipment must be:

1. Predictable and unambiguous, and
2. Designed to enable the flight crew to intervene in a manner *appropriate to the task.*

(d) To the extent practicable, installed equipment must enable the flight crew to manage errors resulting from the kinds of flight crew interactions with the equipment that can be reasonably expected in service, assuming the flight crew is acting in good faith." (EASA CS25.1302)

This new regulation presents challenges to the state of the art evaluation methods, by explicitly requiring context information (stated as task characteristics) to be included in the certification and approval process. In addition, this regulation calls for methods that can be used to demonstrate alignment between the task and the intended function of the technology under evaluation.

Given these requirements, this paper will provide a brief background of usability evaluation in safety-critical interface evaluation. We will then describe three candidate methods for evaluating the applicability of a user interface within a work context, and consider how these methods may be incorporated into current evaluation processes. We will also show how the three methods can be used independently or linked to provide different levels of resolution for the different evaluation requirements.

2 Human-Automation Interaction Evaluation and Safety Critical Domains

We begin by examining the characteristics of the aviation and space domains we have been involved in. We have noticed five characteristics that we believe place significant constraints on effective methods for evaluating Human-Automation Interaction methods.

The work is performed by experts, and access to experts may be limited. Analysts and designers may share a part of the domain expert's knowledge, but operational expertise is required for evaluation. Limited access can be a key constraint, particularly when simple observation is insufficient. In addition, the population of experts evaluators may be reduced to the point that that the overall evaluation has limited utility (Faulkner, 2003; Macefield, 2009). Access to static expertise in documentation or training materials may be of limited value for many reasons, including reliance on specific procedures that may change, be obsolete, or be operationally invalid. Further, even when usability assessments are conducted by usability experts, assessment done by different experts may vary considerably in both the nature and severity of problems identified (Molich et al 2010).

The systems are increasingly complex and interactive. The dynamics and complexity of interactive systems may make it difficult to identify and explicitly define and present situations for evaluation. (Feary, 2005)

The cognitive activity may be difficult to understand from observation. There may be few external cues about internal processes, although these hard-to-observe activities may be very critical parts of work. (Caulton, 2001)

It is often difficult to clearly separate the work to be done and the functionality used to accomplish it with new technology. Use of automation can change the nature of the work being accomplished to the extent that it is difficult to separate this work from the functionality provided by the new technology. For example, navigation is a critical work activity in aviation and space domains, and there are many different means available for accurate navigation. If the work, in this case finding one's way from point A to point B, can be separated from the functionality used to accomplish it (e.g. using a GPS navigation system), it is possible to generate evaluation methods which are more broadly applicable to new technologies. This characteristic is true in many information work domains.

There is a need for methods usable early in the development process. This is problem that is not unique to safety critical domains. In the aviation community, the FAA has recognized this need in its' 2012 workplan, by stating that "Consideration of the safety aspects must be embedded within the initial concept development – otherwise, whole aspects of the technology or operational concept may need revision in order to ensure safety." It can be difficult to provide functionality that behave enough like the final product early in the design process to be valid for user testing, and it may be too expensive to resolve issues discovered late. Therefore, user interface evaluation in safety-critical domains requires an increased emphasis on methods beyond user testing.

The need for improved evaluation methods is becoming more apparent when these characteristics are combined with the increasing pace of development of technologies. Specifically the rate of development of information automation being proposed in safety-critical domains has increased dramatically in the last decade. The volume of candidate automation concepts being presented also highlights the need for more efficient methods to meet the schedule requirements of the often large, expensive and complex safety critical design projects that typically allow limited time for evaluation. The need for methods that can respond to the increase in the number of technologies requiring evaluation—and their combinations in particular contexts—has been recognized by the safety-critical organizations, (US FAA, 2012; EASA, 2007).

3 Three Methods for Integrating Context into the Evaluation of Safety-Critical Interfaces

In the previous section, we discussed the need for new Human – Automation Interaction evaluation methods. In this section we will discuss three candidate methods, Work Technology Alignment Analysis, Task Specification Language and Optimal Control Modeling.

3.1 Work - Technology Alignment (WTA) Analysis

The first method, *Work-Technology-Alignment*, evaluates how well technology aligns with the structure of the work it is intended to support (Billman, et al., 2010, 2011, in preparation). Technology that is better aligned with a domain of work activity should support more effective performance, in that domain. Assessment of alignment depends on discovering the elements and organization of the work domain, and on assessing how well the entities and organization of the technology corresponds with that needed for the work domain. The method uses Needs Analysis to identify the elements and structure of the work and integrates proposals from several research traditions in HAI, Human Computer Interaction (HCI), Work Domain Analysis (WDA), and related disciplines to form the analysis. The goal of the analysis is to help identify where work and the functionality used to accomplish the work are not aligned, and to help provide insight into how to provide better alignment, and therefore improve Human-Technology performance.

High technology - work structural alignment means that there is a strong match at the level of particular elements (entities, relations, and operations), and that the organization of elements in the technological system (the "system") aligns with the organization of elements in the work domain. Conversely, a design might have weak WTA alignment for several reasons:

- Elements of the work are not represented in the system (missing functions);
- Elements of the system are unrelated to the work (system overhead or irrelevant "features"); or
- Elements in the work domain and elements of the system are organized differently.

We predict that systems with high alignment will provide multiple benefits: faster and more accurate performance; less training; better skill retention; and successful operation over a wider range of goals or situations, including novel, infrequent, or emergency conditions.

An initial study assessed alignment to evaluate the technology used in a space flight control work, specifically, software for planning flight activities of the International Space Station. This included a needs analysis of the work structure, an analysis of legacy technology, and redesign of software guided by the alignment to the work structure. Figure 1 illustrates the improved alignment of the redesigned system. Based on these analyses, performance differences were predicted using legacy versus redesigned systems. Predictions were tested in a comparative experiment using tasks and material closely matching a subset of real operator work. Performance using the revised prototype had half the errors and took half the time, for critical tasks revising the scheduled time of events.

This case study suggests the Work-Technology Alignment evaluation method should be further developed as a means for incorporating context information in evaluations of complex, safety-critical technology. Research in progress is developing more structured methods of representing work, representing the technology, and comparing these representations.

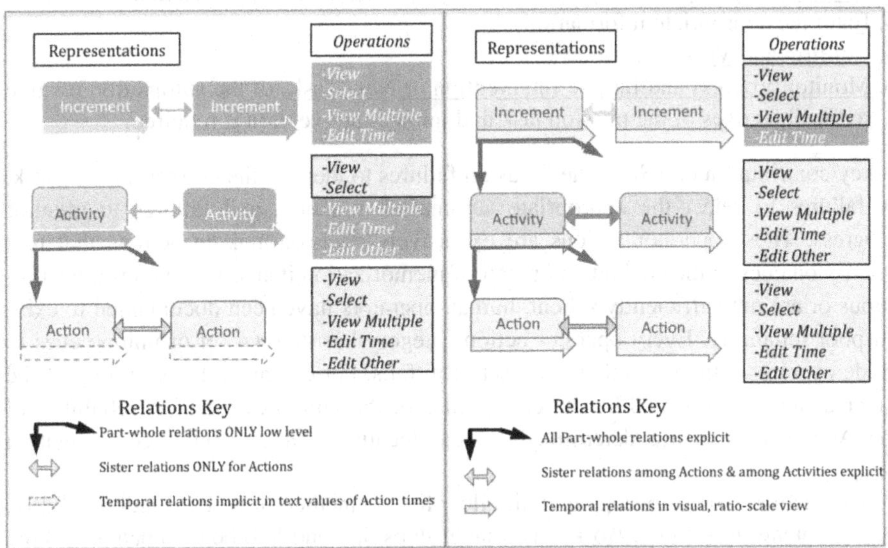

Fig. 1. Shaded representations and operations indicate aspects of the domain structure that are not expressed in the software. Differences in relations are noted in the key. The redesigned prototype aligns much better with the domain structure. Performance was better with the redesign, and particularly in tasks that tapped into points of greatest difference in alignment.

3.2 Task Specification Language (TSL)

The second method, analysis based on *Task Specification Language* (TSL) (Sherry et al., 2009) provides a task structure that can be applied to a wide variety of domains for detailed evaluation. This method maps traditional task analysis information into a more usable format, integrates contextual information, and responds to the need for methods and tools that do not require extensive expertise to implement and interpret.

The goal is to provide a framework for developers and evaluators to think about the work activity (task), how the task is triggered, and the cues provided to the user to enable task completion and monitoring of task completion. The method may be used independently to identify issues in development, or used to provide input to computational models.

TSL is an approach to documenting the cognitive operations required by the users to perform mission tasks providing a framework for a more structured Cognitive Walkthrough (Wharton et al., 1992) and can be enhanced to use recently available "affordable models of human performance," to emulate Simulated User Testing.

The TSL specifically categorizes operator actions into the following categories:

1. Identify mission task and objectives
2. Select appropriate automation function to perform the mission task
3. Access the appropriate display, panel, page for the automation function
4. Enter the appropriate information
5. Confirm and Verify entries
6. Monitor progress and Initiate Intervention or New Tasks of the automation relative to the objectives of the mission task and initiate intervention if required.

A key contribution of TSL is the focus on failures to identify the correct mission task, or failures to select the appropriate automation function, and failures to monitor progress. These operator actions are exclusively decision-making actions that rely heavily on cues in the cockpit and recall of memorization items. When cues are ambiguous or are not sufficiently salient, human operators have been documented to exhibit poor reliability. Every operator action category has its own set of unique cues to guide operator actions and their own set of pitfalls. For example, the reliability of the Enter actions are affected by the ergonomics of the input devices. The reliability of the Access actions are determined by the location and user-interface navigation design.

The inclusion of all 6 steps of TSL allow for the method to be used independently, but the intention of future work is to enable steps 3, 4 and 5 to be automated, and the information collected in steps in 1 and 2 to be used in computational methods to enable steps 3, 4 and 5 to be automated.

3.3 Optimal Control Modeling (OCM)

The third method makes use of *optimal control modeling* to predict the strategies that people will adopt given specifications of (1) human information processing architecture, (2) the subjective utility functions that people adopt, and (3) the person's experience of the task environment. This approach uses cognitive architecture in context, and generates strategies for interaction with automation (Howes, et al., 2009; Lewis et al., (2012); Payne et al., in press; Eng et al (2006)). This work utilizes the contextual information in the form of cognitive architecture constraints, and fits well with the specific characteristics that safety-critical domains tend to provide, such as a population of expert users as the basis for evaluation.

The approach is based on a theoretical framework for the behavioral sciences that is designed to tackle the adaptive, ecological and bounded nature of human behavior (Lewis et al., 2004; Howes et al., 2009). It is designed to help scientists and practitioners reason about why people choose to behave as they do and to explain which strategies people choose in response to utility, ecological context, and cognitive information processing mechanisms. A key idea is that people choose strategies so as to maximize utility given constraints. In this way, the method provides an analytic means to predict and understand behavior as a function of the elements of context identified at the outset of this paper: the goals of the work are represented in explicit utility functions; the environments of training and performance are represented in the ecological context, and the human performance constraints are represented in the explicit assumptions about cognitive mechanisms. Payne and Howes (in press) and Lewis et al. (2004) illustrate the framework with a number of examples including pointing, multitasking, visual attention, and diagnosis. Importantly, these examples span from perceptual/motor coordination, through cognition to collaborative interaction.

Lewis et al's (2012) model of simple word reading brings together three threads that are critical to understanding cognition in the cockpit: (1) mathematical models of eye movement control (Engbert et al., 2005; Reichle, Rayner, & Pollatsek, 2003); (2) work on how higher-level task goals shape eye movement strategies (Rothkopf, Ballard, Hayhoe, & Regan, 2007; Ballard & Hayhoe, 2009; Salverda, Brown, & Tanenhaus, 2011); and (3) Bayesian sequential sampling models of lexical processing and perception (Norris, 2009; Wagenmakers, Ratcliff, Gomez, & McKoon, 2008). The model is an instantiation of a more general architecture for the control of active perception and motor output in service of dynamic task goals. The model decomposes the problem into *optimal state estimation* and *optimal control*, mediated by an information processing architecture with independently justified bounds.

Eng et al. (2006) report a model of the time taken and working memory loads required to perform simple tasks with Boeing Flight Deck of the Future (FDF) and existing 777 interfaces. Critically, optimal control modeling was used to select the strategies for both interfaces. The FDF performed better than the 777 for both time and working memory conditions. Across both tasks, the FDF consistently supported a strategy that allowed for a lower working memory load compared to the best case working memory load in the 777 (in one task by 175 milliseconds and in another by 1375 milliseconds). The FDF also performed better on time on task than the 777 (in one task by 100 milliseconds and in another by 500 milliseconds). These results validated the explicit design objectives behind the FDF interface. The interface comes at no cost to the time required to complete tasks while enabling a better distribution of working memory load. The success of the modeling was critically dependent on optimal control modeling to determine the predicted strategies because without this crucial constraint it is possible for the models to use almost any strategy on each of the two interfaces. Model fitting without such constraints, which is a more common means of modeling human behavior, could not make any predictive discriminations between the two interfaces.

In new work we are developing models and empirically investigating how pilots switch attention between aviation and navigation tasks. In the model Bayesian state estimation is used to maintain a representation of two variables: (1) the aircraft attitude and (2) the body-centric location of FMS buttons. The scheduling of eye-movements between attitude indicators and the FMS are determined by the utility associated with the accuracy of these state estimates. Inaccurate estimates of button locations leads to data entry errors. Inaccurate estimates of attitude lead to poor situation awareness. Depending on whether the pilot wishes to prioritize data entry, using the FMS, or awareness of attitude then an optimal schedule of eye-movements is selected by the control model. Future work will be focused on providing tools to support the use of the modeling approach in evaluation processes.

4 Summary

In this paper we presented the case for why context information is important in evaluation of Human-Automation interaction, why new evaluation methods are needed for safety-critical systems and the characteristics of the problem that make it challenging. We then briefly described three candidate evaluation methods that have some promise of meeting this challenge in different ways. Work Technology Alignment (WTA) analysis provides a mechanism and metric for overall assessment of technology against the work context. The intention of the WTA assessment process is to produce a body of structured information that enables comparing the technology, training and procedures to a representation of the work to assess fitness-for-purpose.

Task Specification Language (TSL) emphasizes the need to explicitly define the mission tasks, and the accompanying functionality to complete the tasks, with the means by which the human operator can monitor the task completion. TSL is designed to be used as an independent assessment tool, or in cooperation with a computational method, such as an OCM model.

Optimal Control Modeling (OCM) provides machinery to enable a more thorough evaluation of safety-critical Human-Automation Interaction in the time limited evaluation process. The approach is to provide the model with functionality and context information—including assumptions about human information processing constraints—and then computationally generate rational strategies that could be used to achieve the work goals given those constraints. The strategy information generated by the analyses could then be used within existing evaluation processes to help identify Human- Automation Interaction vulnerabilities. These methods collectively provide a path forward for including context information into safety-critical work domain evaluations.

References

1. Ballard, D.H., Hayhoe, M.M.: Modeling the role of task in the control of gaze. Visual Cognition 17(6-7), 1185–1204 (2009)
2. Billman, D., Feary, M., Schreckengost, D., Sherry, L.: Needs analysis: the case of flexible constraints and mutable boundaries. In: CHI 2010 Extended Abstracts on Human Factors in Computing Systems (CHI EA 2010), pp. 4597–4612. ACM, New York (2010), `http://doi.acm.org/10.1145/1753846.1754201`, doi:10.1145/1753846.1754201
3. Billman, D., Arsintescucu, L., Feary, M., Lee, J., Smith, A., Tiwary, R.: Benefits of matching domain structure for planning software: the right stuff. In: Proceedings of the SIGCHI Conference on Human Factors in Computing Systems (CHI 2011), pp. 2521–2530. ACM, New York (2011), `http://doi.acm.org/10.1145/1978942.1979311`, doi:10.1145/1978942.1979311
4. Billman, D., Arsintescu, L., Feary, M., Lee, J., Schreckenghost, D., Tiwary, R.: Product-Based Needs Analysis and Case Study of Attitude Determination and Control Operator (ADCO) Planning Work (in preparation as NASA Technical Memorandum)
5. Caulton, D.A.: Relaxing the homogeneity assumption in usability testing. Behaviour & Information Technology 20(1), 1–7 (2001)
6. Eng, K., Lewis, R.L., Tollinger, I., Chu, A., Howes, A., Vera, A.: Generating automated predictions of behavior strategically adapted to specific performance objectives. In: Proceedings of the Sigchi Conference on Human Factors in Computing Systems, pp. 621–630 (2006)
7. Engbert, R., Nuthmann, A., Richter, E.M., Kliegl, R.: SWIFT: a dynamical model of saccade generation during reading. Psychological Review 112(4), 777 (2005)
8. European Aviation Safety Agency, Certification Specification 25.1302 and Acceptable Means of Compliance 25.1302 Installed Systems and Equipment for Use by the Flight Crew (2007)
9. Faulkner, L.: Beyond the five-user assumption: Benefits of increased sample sizes in usability testing. Behavior Research Methods 35(3), 379–383 (2003)
10. Feary, M.: Formal Identification of Automation Surprise Vulnerabilities in Design. Doctorate Dissertation, Cranfield University (2005)
11. Federal Aviation Administration AVS Workplan for Nextgen. Federal Aviation Administration, USA (2012)
12. Howes, A., Lewis, R.L., Vera, A.: Rational adaptation under task and processing constraints: Implications for testing theories of cognition and action. Psychological Review (2009)
13. Lewis, R., Shvartsman, M., Singh, S.: The adaptive nature of eye-movements in linguistic tasks: How payoff and architecture shape speed-accuracy tradeoffs. Topics in Cognitive Science (to appear)
14. Macefield, R.: How To Specify the Participant Group Size for Usability Studies: A Practitioner's Guide. Journal of Usability Studies 5(1), 34–45 (2009)
15. Molich, R., Chattratichart, J., Hinkle, V., Jensen, J.J., Kirakowski, J., Sauro, J., Sharon, T., Traynor, B.: Rent a Car in Just 0, 60, 240 or 1,217 Seconds?-Comparative Usability Measurement, CUE-8. Journal of Usability Studies 6(1), 8–24 (2010)
16. Norris, D.: Putting it all together: A unified account of word recognition and reaction-time distributions. Psychological Review 116(1), 207 (2009)

17. Payne, S., Howes, A.: Adaptive Interaction: A utility maximisation approach to understanding human interaction with technology. Morgan Claypool lecture (in press)
18. Reichle, E.D., Rayner, K., Pollatsek, A.: The EZ Reader model of eye-movement control in reading: Comparisons to other models. Behavioral and Brain Sciences 26(4), 445–476 (2003)
19. Rothkopf, C.A., Ballard, D.H., Hayhoe, M.M.: Task and context determine where you look. Journal of Vision 7(14) (2007)
20. Salverda, A.P., Brown, M., Tanenhaus, M.K.: A goal-based perspective on eye movements in visual world studies. Acta Psychologica 137(2), 172–180 (2011)
21. Sherry, L., Medina-Mora, M., John, B., Teo, L., Polson, P., Blackmon, M., Koch, M., Feary, M.: System Design and Analysis: Tools for Automation Interaction Design and Evaluation Methods. Final Report NASA NRA NNX07AO67A (2010)
22. Wagenmakers, E.J., Ratcliff, R., Gomez, P., McKoon, G.: A diffusion model account of criterion shifts in the lexical decision task. Journal of Memory and Language 58(1), 140–159 (2008)
23. Wharton, C., Bradford, J., Jeffries, J., Franzke, M.: Applying Cognitive Walkthroughs to more Complex User Interfaces: Experiences, Issues and Recommendations. In: CHI 1992, pp. 381–388 (1992)

Environmental Evaluation of a Rehabilitation Aid Interaction under the Framework of the Ideal Model of Assistive Technology Assessment Process

Stefano Federci[1], Simone Borsci[2], and Maria Laura Mele[3]

[1] University of Perugia, Department of Human Science and Education
Piazza Ermini 1, Perugia, Italy
stefano.federici@unipg.it

[2] Brunel University, School of Information Systems, Computing, and Mathematics
Kingston Lane, Uxbridge, Middlesex UB8 3PH, UK
simone.borsci@brunel.ac.uk

[3] University of Rome La Sapienza, Department of Psychology
Via Dei Marsi, 00185, Rome, Italy
marialaura.mele@uniroma1.it

Abstract. Recently Federici and Scherer [1] proposed an ideal model of an Assistive Technology Assessment (ATA) process that provides reference guidelines for professionals of a multidisciplinary team of assistive technology (AT) service delivery centers to compare, evaluate, and improve their own matching models. The ATA process borrows a user-driven working methodology from the Matching Person and Technology Model [2] and it embraces the biopsychosocial model [3] aiming at the best combination of AT to promote customers' personal well-being. As Federici and Scherer [1] suggest, the multidisciplinary team, by applying the ATA process, may provide for users not only a device, but much more an assistive solution, which is the real outcome of a match process. An assistive solution is provided for the user only when the interaction dialogue between user, device, and environments of use improves the users' performances in participating in their everyday contexts. In this theoretical framework, the evaluation of the users' interaction with the AT in different kinds of environments is a key factor for the success of the ATA process, because, as Mirza, Gossett Zakrajsek, and Borsci [4] claim, the environment is antecedent to the AT and crucial for identifying how the AT works in relation to the users' needs. In the ATA process a specific Environmental Assessment (EA) model for testing the interaction of the user with the environments of use, through the AT, has been defined. The aim of this paper is to describe the EA model steps and discuss the dimensions that a practitioner has to consider for this assessment. Accessibility, universal design, and sustainability are used in the EA model as the dimensions for measuring the relationship between the AT and the environment [4]. The EA model steps and the trade-off among these dimensions are presented through a case example in which practitioners analyze the relationship between a communication aid used by a child and her classroom and home environments.

Keywords: accessibility, assistive technologies, sustainability, universal design, user-centered delivery process.

M. Kurosu (Ed.): Human-Computer Interaction, Part I, HCII 2013, LNCS 8004, pp. 203–210, 2013.

1 Theoretical Background

The term "assistive technology" (AT) is "an umbrella term for any device or system that allows individuals to perform tasks they would otherwise be unable to do or increases the ease and safety with which tasks can be performed" [5]. Moreover, an AT can be considered as "any item, piece of equipment, or product system, whether acquired commercially, modified, or customized, that is used to increase, maintain, or improve functional capabilities of individuals with disabilities" [6, 7]. In the light of these definitions, it is quite evident why in the last few years many researchers have studied the processes of AT assignment, by aiming to rate the success (in terms of increasing the people's well-being) and failure (in terms of AT non-use) of the AT delivered to the people.

In the AT industry, the term "service delivery" is used to identify the set of procedures and processes that act as intermediaries between the AT manufacturers and AT end-users [8]. The AT delivery process, carried out by a team of professionals with different areas of expertise [1, 2, 9, 10], is articulated in activities which include the physical delivery of the technical aid to the disabled person, the user's training, and the setting up of the technology. The overall process of an AT delivery system is oriented to obtain, through a well-designed and researched sequential set of assessments, the best match between the AT and the user (i.e., matching process).

A well-designed system of AT delivery in which the matching process is iteratively supported by the effort of a team of professionals in order to identify and adapt an AT to the user's needs is a central topic. In fact, many studies have clearly shown that a wrong or a not-user-centered process of matching, assignment, and delivery results in a high percentage of AT non-use (estimated from 30% to 33%) after the delivery [11-13].

As the United States Assistive Technology Act [6] indicates, the matching process differs from any other process of system delivery, because the professionals of an AT service have to provide not only the technology, but a set of services that directly assists an individual with a disability in the selection, acquisition, or use of an AT device. In tune with this complexity, as Federici and Scherer suggest, the team of professionals of an AT service delivery have to aim to deliver not the technology per se, but much more an assistive solution that acts "as a mediator of quality of life and well-being in a specific context of use. [...] An assistive solution does not coincide with assistive technology, since the first one is a complex system in which psycho-socio-environmental factors and assistive technology interact in a non-linear way by reducing activity limitations and participation restrictions by means of one or more technologies" [1].

Finally, the assistive solution is the outcome of a user-driven process, called by Federici and Scherer [1] the Assistive Technology Assessment (ATA) process, aimed at the improvement of individual functioning.

2 The Model of the Assistive Technology Assessment Process

The ATA process model is "a user-driven process through which the selection of one or more technological aids for an assistive solution is facilitated by the comprehensive utilization of clinical measures, functional analysis, and psycho-socio-environmental evaluations that address, in a specific context of use, the personal well-being of the user through the best matching of user/client and assistive solution" [1]. This process is usually represented as a flow chart that can be read either from the perspective of the user or from the perspective of an AT service delivery. For our aims we report here only a descriptive sketch of the user's and AT service delivery center's actions.

The user's actions in the ATA process can be grouped into three phases: (i) The user seeks a solution; (ii) The user checks the solution provided by the professionals; (iii) The user adopts the solution, and receives training and follow-up.

The actions of the AT service delivery center can be grouped into four phases: (i) Initial meeting with user and interviewer focused on gathering the user's background information and psycho-socio-environmental data; (ii) The multidisciplinary team evaluates the data and user's request and arranges a suitable setting for the matching assessment; (iii) The multidisciplinary team, along with the user, assesses the assistive solution proposed, tries the solution and gathers outcome data. When the assistive solution proposed requires an environmental evaluation, the team initiates a parallel assessment called the Environmental Assessment (EA) process. The multidisciplinary team evaluates the outcome of the matching assessment, then proposes the assistive solution to the user; (iv) When the technological aid is delivered to the user, a follow-up and ongoing user support are activated and the assistive solution is verified in the daily-life context of the user.

The ATA process model has placed the user at the center of the evaluation process, and it acknowledges that the environment is antecedent to the AT and crucial for determining an assistive solution [4]. In light of this, the evaluation of the environment is a key factor for identifying the best assistive solution "intended as individualized interventions providing users with appropriate environmental facilitators (AT products, personalized environmental modifications, personal assistance) to overcome disability and enable participation in all aspects of life" [14].

2.1 Assessing Environmental Factors

The World Report on Disability has recently confirmed an assumption in the field of disability studies: "Data on all aspects of disability and contextual factors are important for constructing a complete picture of disability and functioning. Without information on how particular health conditions in interaction with environmental barriers and facilitators affect people in their everyday lives, it is hard to determine the scope of disability" [7]. According to the ICF biopsychosocial model of disability [3], Environmental Factors (products and technology, the natural and constructed environment, support and relationships, attitudes and services, systems and policies) and Personal Factors (e.g., age, sex, race, motivation, and self-esteem) belong to the Contextual Factors. Therefore, we define the environment in the ATA process as any context in which the AT is used by a person, according to the World Health Organization's description of the environment as "the world in which people with different levels of functioning must live and act" [7].

The EA process aims to analyze the cost-benefit balance with regard to the impact of the AT on the environment to lead the multidisciplinary team and the user to either modify the environment, or change the AT, or both. This decision in the EA process is supported by measuring three dimensions of environment and AT impact on the user's performances [4]:

1. Accessibility (Access): This measures the level of environmental characteristics to permit entrance, exit, and internal movements. This measure also predicts how many changes are needed for rendering accessible the environment in use;
2. Universal design and usability (Use): This measures how much an environment and a human product are designed for all;
3. Sustainability (Sustainable): This measures to what extent an environment and AT are adaptable over time to a person's changing needs, with minimal impact on the natural environment and economic maintenance.

The dimensions of accessibility, sustainability, and universal design all exist along their own continuum and each decision about the environment or about the AT (or both) can be evaluated in terms of universal design, accessibility, and sustainability, falling into various places on the three continua. The evaluation of the three continua can help to focus a decision on a critical deciding factor for improving the person's performance.

As displayed in Fig. 1, we can identify three main phases in the EA process:

1. Checking the match (Fig. 1, point 1). The practitioners (such as engineers, architects and experts of human factors) assess the environmental impact on supporting or obstructing the full participation of the user. If there is a match between the environment, the user, and the AT, the assistive solution is achieved and the environment assessment process ends. However, if a match does not occur, it is necessary to estimate the impact of any possible modification to the environment or to the AT.
2. Checking the impact (Fig. 1, point 2). Practitioners have to check the economical and socio-cultural impact of the modifications to the climate.
3. Making a decision (Fig. 1, point 3). On the basis of the impact analysis, practitioners can make one of the following decisions: (i) Modify the environment: In this case, the ATA process restarts from the multidisciplinary team's evaluation for a new or the modified assistive technology. The match between the AT and the user only requires a minimal environmental adaptation. (ii) Modify the AT: In this case, the ATA process restarts with a new multidisciplinary team meeting in order to discuss: (a) The cost benefit of AT modifications; (b) The cost benefit of identifying another AT. In this case the process restarts from the beginning of the ATA process. (iii) Modify both the AT and the environment. In this case, the ATA process needs to restart with a new multidisciplinary team meeting in order to discuss the cost benefits of the proposed modifications.

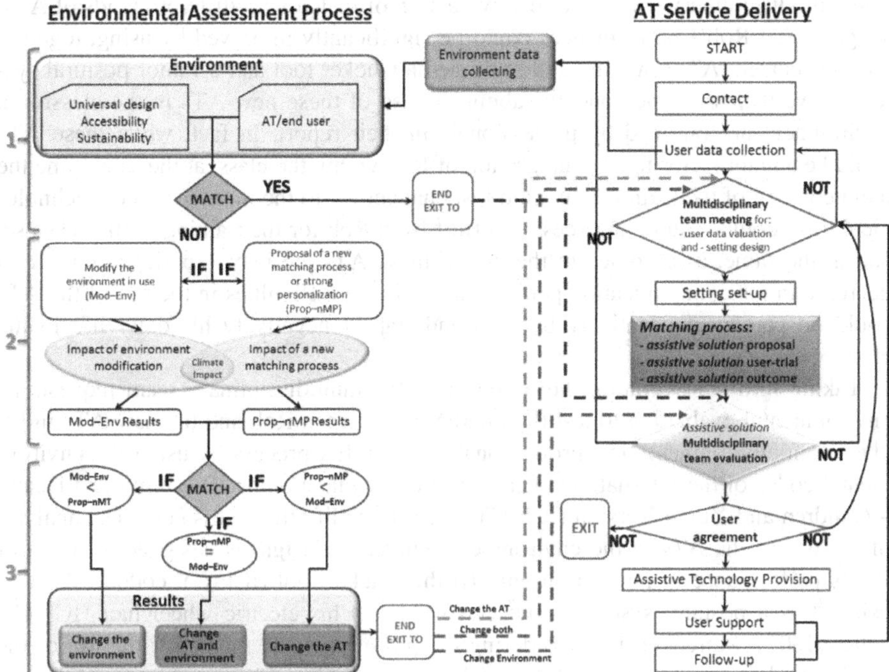

Fig. 1. Flow chart of the Environmental Assessment Process in the ATA process model. The phases of the environmental assessment (1, 2, and 3 on the right) are linked to the procedures of the AT Service Delivery process.

The environmental assessment, when needed, supports and integrates the ATA process driven by two main actors: the user and the multidisciplinary team.

3 Evaluation of the AT Interaction in the Environment: An Evaluation Case

For the aim of our paper we will report only a sketch of the subject profile as follows: Roberto (Rob) is 7 years old with a diagnosis of severe spastic quadriplegia with a dystonic component. His individual functioning can be summarized as follows:

- He attempts to grasp, but he has significant dystonia;
- He has standard visual performance (field of vision, visual acuity, sensitivity to contrast etc.). Moreover, he perceives and locates objects in both the proximal and distal distance, with good ability to fix and track;
- He has excellent cognitive resources and he is very communicative and participatory with the environment. He appears to understand any request about tasks ;
- He moves voluntarily within the room using a motorized wheelchair;
- He uses augmentative communications adequately.

The multidisciplinary team, after the evaluation of match with different kinds of ATs, suggests that Rob's performances could be significantly improved by using, together with his current AT, a writing and multimedia Clicker tool and a Junior postural system. Nevertheless, some concerns about the use of these new ATs in the classroom environment are outlined by professionals in their report. In fact, while these ATs could be a main factor for the integration of Rob within the class, at the same time the main concern of the team is that a too fast changeover to the most advanced technological tools could require an excessive effort from Rob for the training in the ATs use, and at the same, as a novice in the use of these ATs, he may experience initially a decrease in his communication performances. These difficulties in the use of the ATs could be perceived negatively by Rob and impact negatively his daily life in the classroom.

Taking into consideration these concerns, the multidisciplinary team requests an environmental evaluation to test the interaction between Rob and the new ATs in his classroom environment. The professionals run the EA process by using the environmental codes of the International Classification of Functioning, Disability and Health - Children and Youth Version (ICF-CY: [15]) to codify the assessment. The analysis of the use of the ATs in the environment (universal design) is designed as a test of Rob's performance in interaction with (i) the Clicker tool (ICF-CY code=e1251) by using it as a postural system in the classroom (ii) his electric wheelchair (ICF-CY code=e1201). Moreover, by considering the physical requirements for the use of the Clicker tool in terms of accessibility and sustainability, professionals arrange the test with Rob sitting (i) at his usual desk in a central position, and (ii) in a new desk position. The new position of the desk was selected by professionals for the following reasons: (i) it was more peripheral from the center of the classroom and closer to the wall (but still not isolated) than Rob's usual desk , reducing the possibility that his schoolmates accidentally damage the AT device; (ii) it had a higher level of illumination than the usual position (ICF-CY code=e2400); and (iii) it was close to an electrical outlet (ICF-CY code=e1501). Rob's performance time was assessed by using three different tasks for each trial; the performance time measured in the laboratory of the AT service delivery center (M=13.26 s; DS=4.02 s) was used by professionals as a comparative index of performances. The findings obtained were as follows:

- When the Clicker tool was tested in a central position, Rob's interaction was very slow (M=25.01 s, DS=5.73 s). The AT in this position decreased Rob's performance compared to the laboratory testing. In this context of use, the Clicker was not as good a facilitator (ICF-CY code=e1251.+0) as the electric wheelchair (ICF-CY code=e1201.+0). Moreover, the low illumination and the distance from the socket unit acted as severe environmental barriers (ICF-CY codes=e2400.3 and e1501.3). Finally, the test showed that the use of these ATs in the classroom environment caused problems in the dimensions of accessibility and universal design, while, from the sustainability point of view, the electric wheelchair did not support Rob's movements during the interaction.
- When the Clicker tool was tested in a peripheral position, Rob seemed more comfortable, due to the optimal level of illumination. Nevertheless, he was not driven

to control his hand movements by the electric wheelchair (M=19.55 s; DS=3.22 s). In that case, the illumination and the access to the sockets acted as facilitators (ICF-CY codes=e2400.8 and e1501.8), whereas the electric wheelchair and the Clicker tool had still not properly supported Rob in his movements (ICF-CY codes=e1251.+0 and e1201.+0). Therefore, although the accessibility problems were solved, and Rob's performances were slightly improved, his movements were still affected by the electric wheelchair.

Finally, Rob was invited to test the Clicker tool sitting in the Junior postural system previously tested in the laboratory of the AT service delivery center. This test was only run with the desk in the new peripheral position. With the use of this kind of postural system, the times of Rob's performances were very close to his performances at the center (M=14.05 s; DS=1.57 s).

At the end of their report, the professionals proposed that the Clicker tool could be used as a complete facilitator (ICF-CY code=e1251.+4) only when associated with the Junior postural system tested at the AT service delivery center (ICF-CY code=e1151.+3), also recommending that the position of the desk in the classroom should be modified in order to optimize Rob's performance in its use.

On the basis of this analysis, the multidisciplinary team decided to introduce gradually the new ATs in Rob's contexts of use and concurrently to modify the environment (his position in the classroom) as proposed by the environmental report.

4 Conclusion

An AT can be considered an assistive solution only when all the possible nuances of the user's interaction experience have been carefully analyzed under the lens of accessibility, universal design, and sustainability. When a trade-off among these three dimensions is identified by professionals, it is possible to match the needs of the users, the functioning of the AT, and the context of use by allowing users an efficient, effective, and satisfactory interaction with the technology in their environment. Nevertheless, the trade-off of the accessibility, universal design, and sustainability dimensions often requires one of the components to be modified in interaction with the user (the AT or the environment). In light of this, the EA process consists in the decision-making flow that could lead professionals to modify the environment, the AT or both for a successful matching between user and technology.

This decision process is carried out relying on measurements and methods that pertain to the interaction assessment, as shown in the evaluation case. Finally, in line with the AAATE/EASTIN indication [14], the EA process represents a new way to improve the efficiency and the effectiveness of the AT system delivery process that brings from the interaction framework a set of evidence-based practices and concepts to support professionals in taking critical decisions for the relationship between the users and the AT.

References

1. Federici, S., Scherer, M.J.: The Assistive Technology Assessment Model and Basic Definitions. In: Federici, S., Scherer, M.J. (eds.) Assistive Technology Assessment Handbook, pp. 1–10. CRC Press, Boca Raton (2012)
2. Scherer, M.J. (ed.): Assistive Technology: Matching Device and Consumer for Successful Rehabilitation. American Psychological Association, Washington, DC (2002)
3. World Health Organization (WHO): ICF: International Classification of Functioning, Disability and Health. WHO, Geneva, CH (2001)
4. Mirza, M., Gossett Zakrajsek, A., Borsci, S.: The Assessment of the Environments of Use: Accessibility, Sustainability, and Universal Design. In: Federici, S., Scherer, M.J. (eds.) Assistive Technology Assessment Handbook, pp. 67–81. CRC Press, Boca Raton (2012)
5. World Health Organization (WHO): A Glossary of Terms for Community Health Care and Services for Older Persons. Technical Report, WHO (2004)
6. United States Congress: Assistive Technology Act (Public Law 108-364) (2004)
7. World Health Organization (WHO), World Bank: World Report on Disability. WHO, Geneva, CH (2011)
8. Stack, J., Zarate, L., Pastor, C., Mathiassen, N.-E., Barberà, R., Knops, H., Kornsten, H.: Analysing and federating the European assistive technology ICT industry. Final Report. European Commission (2009)
9. Corradi, F., Scherer, M.J., Lo Presti, A.: Measuring the Assistive Technology Match. In: Federici, S., Scherer, M.J. (eds.) Assistive Technology Assessment Handbook, pp. 49–65. CRC Press, London (2012)
10. Scherer, M.J.: Living in the state of stuck: How technologies affect the lives of people with disabilities. Brookline Books, Cambridge (2005)
11. Federici, S., Borsci, S.: The use and non-use of assistive technology in Italy: A pilot study. In: Gelderblom, G.J., Soede, M., Adriaens, L., Miesenberger, K. (eds.) Everyday Technology for Independence and Care: AAATE 2011, vol. 29, pp. 979–986. IOS Press, Amsterdam (2011)
12. Philips, B., Zhao, H.: Predictors of Assistive Technology Abandonment. Assistive Technology 5, 36–45 (1993)
13. Scherer, M.J., Sax, C.L., Vanbiervliet, A., Cushman, L.A., Scherer, J.V.: Predictors of assistive technology use: The importance of personal and psychosocial factors. Disability and Rehabilitation 27, 1321–1331 (2005)
14. Aaate.net, `http://www.aaate.net/`
15. World Health Organization (WHO): ICF-CY: International Classification of Functioning, Disability and Health – Children and Youth Version. WHO, Geneva, CH (2007)

Towards Ergonomic User Interface Composition: A Study about Information Density Criterion

Yoann Gabillon[1], Sophie Lepreux[2], and Káthia Marçal de Oliveira[2]

[1] Centre de Recherche Public – Gabriel Lippmann
41, rue du Brill, L-4422 Belvaux, Luxembourg
gabillon@lippmann.lu
[2] UVHC, LAMIH, F-59313 Valenciennes, France
CNRS, UMR 8201, F-59313 Valenciennes, France
{sophie.lepreux,kathia.oliveira}@univ-valenciennes.fr

Abstract. One way to design new interactive system is to automatically compose from existing systems. An interactive system encompasses a functional core (FC) and a user interface (UI). Many studies of the software engineering community focus on design or runtime composition of FC through components or services. However, provide good quality UI is important to make the composed system acceptable to the users. To address this need, the HCI community has studied how to compose UI at different levels of granularity. The main challenge is how to choose the best composition option in order to provide UI of good quality from the user point of view. This paper presents a step towards this challenge by proposing the chosen of the best composed graphical UI considering quality ergonomic criteria that can be automatically measured. In particular, it focuses on the information density criterion. Information density concerns the users' workload from a perceptual and cognitive point of view with regard to the whole set of information presented to the users rather than each individual element or item.

Keywords: UI Composition, ergonomic, usability, criteria, metrics, measures, evaluation functions.

1 Introduction

One way to design new interactive system is to automatically compose from existing systems. An interactive system encompasses a functional core (FC) and a user interface (UI). In consequence, to compose an interactive system, it's necessary to compose FC and UI. Many studies of the software engineering community focus on design or runtime composition of FC through components [16] or services [11]. However, providing UI of good quality is essential to make the composed system acceptable to the users. To address this need, the HCI community has studied how to compose UI at different levels of granularity (see for example, UI generation [9], adaptive UI [17], Mashups [8], UI composition [3, 7, 13]). Several options of UI

M. Kurosu (Ed.): Human-Computer Interaction, Part I, HCII 2013, LNCS 8004, pp. 211–220, 2013.

composition are available in these works. The main challenge is how to choose the best composition option in order to provide UI of "good" quality.

Several ergonomic criteria (Nielsen [10], Scapin and Bastien [14], ISO/IEC 9241 [5] SQuaRE [6], etc.) can be found in the literature. In this paper we present our study about the information density criterion defined by Scapin and Bastien [14]. Information density concerns the users' workload from a perceptual and cognitive point of view with regard to the whole set of information presented to the users rather than each individual element or item. Therefore, it is an important criterion since it is directly worried about the user point of view. In addition, this criteria can be based on objective and digital information, such as screen size or the number of labels, which facilitates the automatic evaluation Finally, information density has a great influence on other criteria (for example legibility or prompting).

This paper presents a step towards this challenge by proposing the chosen of the best composed graphical UI considering quality ergonomic criteria that can be automatically measured. The paper is structured as follows. Based on the literature overview (serction 2) on UI composition and measures of usability, we propose new measures to evaluate information density automatically (section 3). These measures are illustrated in a case study (section 4). Section 5 presents our conclusions and future works.

2 Literature Overview

2.1 UI Composition

The **CAMELEON** European project [1] identified key levels of abstraction in UI design. These levels are based on the general architecture of Model-Based Interface Design Environment. They distinguish the domain level (user tasks and concepts), abstract user interface (AUI), concrete user interface (CUI) and final user interface (FUI). This architecture is useful for UI composition at different levels in order to generate the final interface.

Currently, different approaches developed in parallel focus in UI composition more or less directly. These approaches can be organized into two categories depending on when the composition takes place: design time or runtime.Works about **UI composition at design time** are structured according to the level of abstraction of the composition. Amusing [13] composes UI described at AUI. The composition is made by operators of composition (functions that produce UI from different UI). ComposiXML [7] allows the composition of UI by the designer. It composes trees representing the UI. The composition is performed at CUI then extended at AUI. ComposiXML proposes unary or binary operators of composition. Works about **UI composition at runtime** are structured according to different approaches: composition of the task model of the composed UI by automated planning, UI generation [4, 9], Mashups [8], adaptive/adaptable UI [17]. COMPOSE [3] focuses on the composition of the task model to fulfill the user's goal. The composition of the task model is made by automated planning. Works about UI generation are a form of composition although this term and composition operators are not explicit. For example, SUPPLE [4] generates automatically different UI for different platforms. In contrast, Mashups allows final user to manually compose applications based on data. UI are generated at FUI level. Works about UI composition at design time or runtime do not take into account UI quality. The UI quality is manually supported ether by the designer at design time, or by the user at run time. These works use functions e to compose the UI: operators of UI composition.

Operators of UI composition are central concepts for understanding how to compose UI. These operators consider temporal and spatial aspects for an UI [2]. Temporal relationships are studied through works about task models. [12] define 5 task operators: enabling, choice, concurrency, interleaving, and interruption. We will use these operators to identify different types of compositions. The spatial aspect considers spatial relationships between UI. In mathematics, spatial relationships between regions are studied by [2]. They define six possible spatial relationships between regions (and 3 inverse relationships): disjoint, meet, overlap, equal, covers and contains.

2.2 Evaluation of UI Quality

Different domains (Software Engineering, HCI and Usability/Ergonomic) propose quality standards, criteria and/or measures for evaluating the quality of a UI. In general, the UI evaluation is based on two main features [10]: utility and usability. In this context, usability is widely used by standards and models, and in general, the ergonomic criteria are associated with this feature.

ISO 9241-11 offers 27 examples of measures to meet this definiiton [5]. SQuaRE [6], in turn, proposed measures divided into four usability characteristics (ease of understanding, ease of learning, ease of use and power of attraction). Although the criterion of information density is not explicitly defined in these standards, it is clear, as explain below, that it has a real impact on the results for the questions proposed by the two standards.

Scapin and Bastien [14] proposed eight criteria for evaluating UI usability: guidance, workload, explicit control, adaptability, error management, consistency, significance of codes and compatibility. These criteria are structured in 13 sub-criteria and are accompanied by recommendations. The information density criterion "concerns the users'workload from a perceptual and cognitive point of view, with regard to the whole set of information presented to the users rather then each individual element or item" [14]. The authors argue that the users' performance is negatively affected when the informational load is too high or too low. We must remove elements unrelated to the content of the task and prevent the user memorizing long and numerous information or procedures. Five recommendations are proposed: (1) limit the information density of the screen, showing only necessary information;

(2) the information must not require translation units; (3) use the minimum quantifier, especially in query languages; (4) avoid the user having to remember data from one page to another screen; and, (5) data that can be computed from those must be automatically computed.

2.3 Measures of Quality about Information Density

QUIM (Quality in Use Integrated Measurement) [15] is a model and automatic measures of usability computed before interaction of the user. This model encompasses 10 factors decomposed into 26 criteria. These criteria are also decomposed into 127 measures. In this work, we find issues about information density on two following criteria: workload (one of the criteria proposed by Scapin and Bastien) and understandability (a characteristic of usability proposed by ISO9126). In QUIM, these criteria meet the efficiency factor (usability characteristics proposed by ISO9241-11 [5]). Table 1 presents the QUIM model and measures that seem relevant to the evaluation of information density.

Table 1. Measures relevant to information density criteria defined QUIM [15]

Criterion	Measure	Description
Workload	Depth of the interface	It measures the degree of heavy of cognitive load on users by considering the mean of display information
	Number of icons	The more number of icons, the more the memory load of the user increases to recognize and distinguish them.
	Uniformity of layout	It indicates how the visual elements of the interface are well arranged.
Ease of understanding	Local density	It measures the percentage of space used in each individual group of information.
	Global density	It measures the percentage of display used to present all information.

3 Proposed Measures of Informational Density

Based on the current related works and measures proposed by QUIM, we propose measures to evaluate automatically the quality of composed UI. Note that we mean by UI, a WIMP graphical UI composed from existing known components. Our approach is to define objective measures, i.e. measures that can be calculated automatically before UI composition and thus independent of subjective evaluation of a designer. Proposed measures are shown in Table 2. Measures 1 and 2 are based on criteria of Scapin and Bastien. Measures 3 to 9 are basic measures for the calculation of other measures (derived measures). Measures 6, 10, 11, and 12 are defined from QUIM (Table 1).

Table 2. Proposed measures of information density

Mesure	Definition/formula
M1. Memorizing rate	(Number of data that must be stored from one screen to the other) / Total number of data
M2. Mental calculus rate	(Number of data that require calculation of the user when it could be done automatically) / Total number of data
M3. Number of inputs	Number of fields where the user must enter a value (e.g. text field, list)
M4. Number of outputs	Number of fields where the software displays a value (e.g. resulting information as a result of user input).
Number of labels	Number of entire labels, i.e., the complete sentence and not every word.
M5. Number of buttons/ icons	Number of buttons and/or icons with its label
M6. Number of pictures	Number of pictures used
M7. Number of screens	Number of screens used to perform user task
M8. Size of the screen	Size of each screen used to perform user task
M9. Density rate	(Nb inputs + Nb outputs + Nb labels + Nb buttons/icons + Nb pictures) / Nb screens
M10. Global density	Used space / total space
M11. Uniformity	It indicates how the visual elements of the interface are placed evenly between screens. It corresponds to standard deviation of densities of each screen.

4 Validation of Measures

4.1 Case Study

We present in this section a case study as an illustrative example for the application of measures of information density defined in Table 2. Consider the following scenario: *Yoann lives in Valenciennes. Its main objective is to **find a travel** that could be viewed on a map. Options are needed to drive research and others are selectable by Yoann for booking the travel he wishes (locomotion, number of people, etc.). The system should be able to advise if it wants to access a service (doctor, hotel, etc.).*

These UI allow Yoann to get direction of his travel (UI1, Figure 1a), to choose preferences as the number of passengers, etc. (UI2, Figure 1b) and to select related services as doctor, bakery, etc (UI3, Figure 1c). We suppose that the UI of travel planning system useful to Yoann can be composed from these 3 existing UI with three different operators. The first operator composes UIs in the same frame (Figure 2). The second and the third operator compose UIs respectively in tabs (Figure 3), and in sequence (Figure 4). For the designer at design time or for an adaptive system at runtime, it is an important issue to choose the best composition to produce the UI for the travel planning system. To address user needs (find a travel), using these composition operators and the evaluation of measures, we evaluate the three potential composed UIs and choose the best one considering the information density criterion.

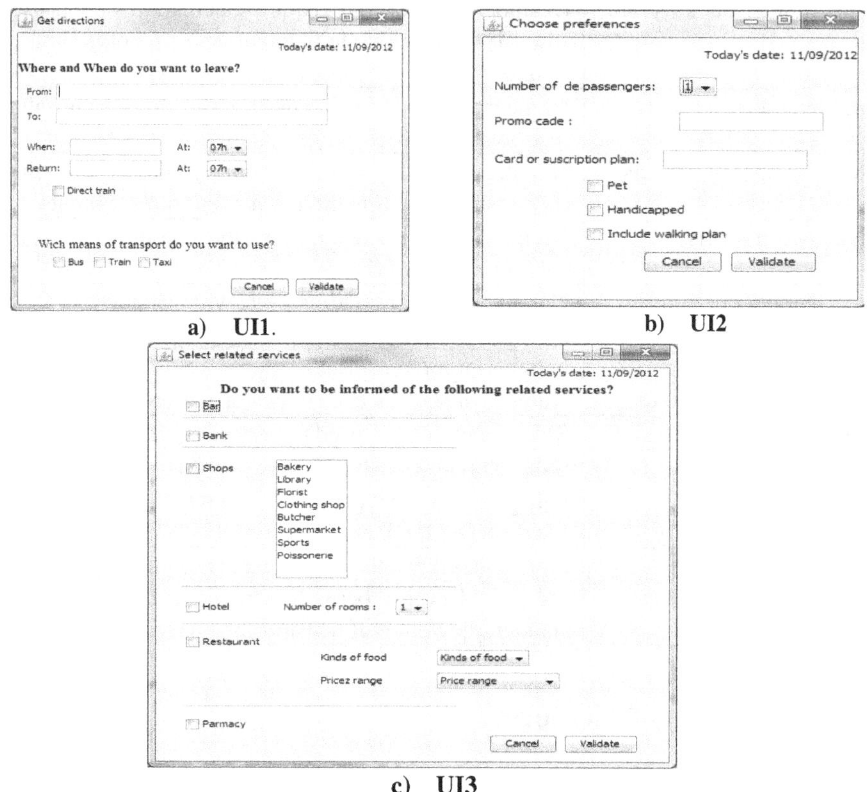

a) UI1. b) UI2 c) UI3

Fig. 1. UI 1 to get direction, UI 2 to choose preferences and UI3 to select related services

4.2 Application of Measures on Our Case Study

From the three UI to be composed, three operators of composition have been applied considering the spatial and temporal relationships. The first composition is computed by the operators {orderIndependance, meet} with an option for the vertical placement of components (corresponding to the operator union [7] and [13]). With these operators, all information are made in a single screen, duplicate information (in this example: today's date) were placed only once (Figure 2). The second composition is computed by the operators {interleaving, equals}. It provides tabs composed of three screens corresponding to the initial UI (Figure 3). The third composed UI {enabling, covers} provides a sequence of three UI components (Figure 4). Note that the final composite UI are generated according to selected operators with the tool composition called COMPOSE [3] that composes UI dynamically.

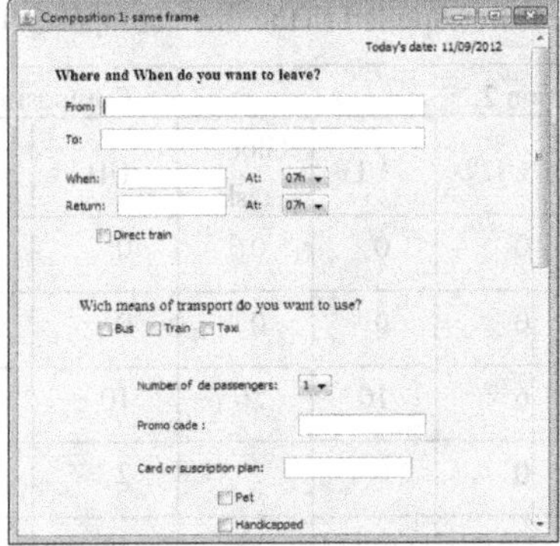

Fig. 2. Composition 1 {orderIndependance, meet}: in the same frame

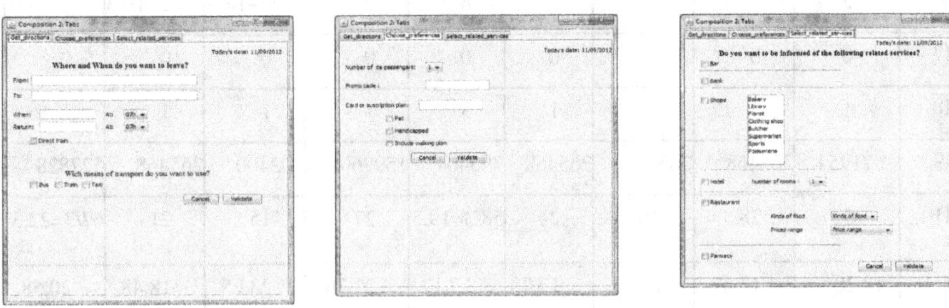

Fig. 3. Composition 2 {interleaving, equals}: a) UI'1, b) UI'2 and c) UI'3 in tabs

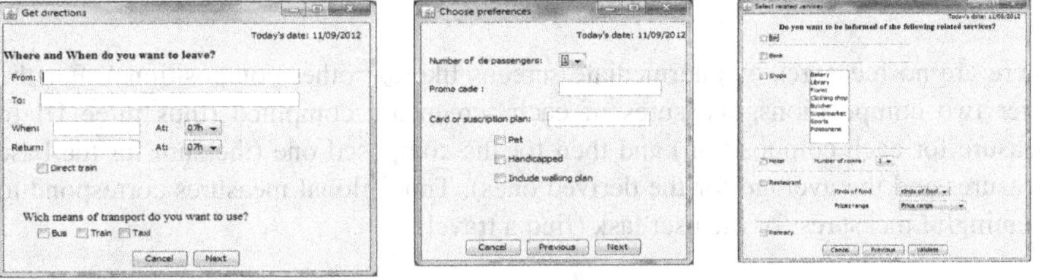

Fig. 4. Composition 3{enabling, covers}: a) UI'1, b) UI'2 and c) UI'3 in sequence

We apply the proposed measures to these three compositions to compare its quality according to the information density criterion. Table 3 presents the results of measurements for the three possible compositions. In the first interface composed (Figure 2), we observe that since it has a lot of information, we must consider the need for navigation on the screen (vertical scrolling). So, there are two main ways to measure this composed UI: considering (1) the number of information visible for each navigation, or (2) all information on a screen. Since it is difficult to anticipate the number of required navigation and their results, we chose the second way, i.e., measures are performed for all information available on a screen. In consequence, in Table 3, we consider a single screen: local density corresponds to the global density

Table 3. Proposed measures applied to the three composed UI of the case study

M.	Comp.1	Composition 2				Composition 3			
		UI1'	UI2'	UI3'	Global task	UI1'	UI2'	UI3'	Global task
M1	0	0	0	0	0	0	0	0	0
M2	0	0	0	0	0	0	0	0	0
M3	26	10	6	10	26	10	6	10	26
M4	2	2	0	0	2	2	0	0	2
M5	29	13+3=16	7+3=10	11+3=14	28	13	7	11	31
M6	2	2	2	2	6	2	2+1= 3	2+1= 3	8
M7	0	0	0	0	0	0	0	0	0
M8	1	1	1	1	3	1	1	1	3
M9	521954	265468	265468	265468	796404	159960	102400	265468	527828
M10	59	28	16	24	58/3=19,3	27	15	21	67/3=22,3
M11	18,28	13,47	8,27	17,78	13,17	22,26	23,25	18,48	20,58
M12					4,76				2,52

(there are no measures of intermediate screens like the other compositions). For the other two compositions, measures of each screen are computed (thus three UI to measure for each composition) and then for the composed one (the sum for the base measures and the average for the derived ones). Thus, global measures correspond to meaningful measures for the user task (find a travel).

4.3 Results and Discussion

As the result of our case study we identified that the composition 2 is the best one because it has the lowest global density percentage (composition 2=13.17%, composition 1 = 18.28% and composition 3= 20.58). However, this finding is not completely generalizable, because it depends on the number of UI to be composed. Indeed, we note that in the case where the number of UI is important, the number of labels will be more important and will involve an increase of the corresponding measure then there will be no impact the other compositions (that means, the stability of the other measures). Composition 1 does not add information (label or button), it just increases the size of the screen. Composition 3 does not increase the need of information except for the navigation buttons (next and previous).

Note that the measurement of information density of the composition 1 gives a good result in placing all information on the same screen that is enlarged according to the number of information. Adapting the screen size is proportional to the amount of information preserves the measure of this criterion. However, it generates increased perceptive users'workload (criterion not studied here). We remember that information density criterion is one of 8 criteria proposed by Scapin and Bastien [14]. These criteria are interrelated, an individual one cannot allow the choice of the best composition in absolute. In consequence, as a perceptive, we will extend this work for studying other usability criteria.

Concerning the composition 1, as we said earlier, we have chosen to consider all the information on the total size of the screen. The user should navigate to access all the information and it could be interesting to consider subsets of information and a number of different screens. We justified this choice by the fact that it is difficult to know automatically which is the number of navigations (screen) and related information. However, a study on this issue would be interesting to measure the global density of the composition.

Measurement of uniformity allows knowing the standard deviation between the densities of individual screens. This can be noted in the composition 2, where the density is lowest because the three screens provided and presented in tab have the same size. This final size is the size of the largest initial UI to be composed. Thus, the global density measurement of UI'1 and UI'2, and composed UI are decreased. While in the composition 3, screen sizes are independent and thus the densities remain close to initial densities.

Moreover, we do not want to remove measures 1, 2 and 7 because they seem important for this criterion, even they were not completely illustrated by the case study. Other examples could be analyzed involving this information to conclude on their impact on information density.

5 Conclusion

At design time to ease the works of designer, as at runtime to provide a quality UI, the need to compose ergonomic UI is central. This article is a first step towards ergonomic UI composition. Note that this study focuses on WIMP Graphical UIs composed by a central orchestrator (corresponding to service orchestration) from existing component. This work proposed and applied objective measures to evaluate information density criterion. These measures automatically predict what the best composed UI according to this criterion. We are aware that criteria are interrelated and should not be evaluated only individually. Therefore, we are now working on the definition of measures for other ergonomic criteria.

References

1. Calvary, G., Coutaz, J., Thevenin, D., Limbourg, Q., Bouillon, L., Vanderdonckt, J.: A Unifying Reference Framework for Multi-Target User Interfaces. Interacting with Computers 15(3), 289–308 (2003)

2. Egenhofer, M.J., Franzosa, R.D.: Point-Set Topological Spatial Relations. International Journal of Geographical Information Science and Systems 5(2), 161–174 (1991)
3. Gabillon, Y., Petit, M., Calvary, G., Fiorino, H.: Automated planning for user interface composition. In: Proceedings of the 2nd International Workshop on Semantic Models for Adaptive Interactive Systems (SEMAIS 2011) of the 2011 International Conference on Intelligent User Interfaces (IUI 2011), Palo Alto, CA, USA (2011)
4. Gajos, K., Weld, D.S.: SUPPLE: automatically generating user interfaces. In: Proceedings of the 9th International Conference on Intelligent User Interfaces (IUI 2004), pp. 93–100. ACM, New York (2004)
5. ISO. ISO/IEC 9241-11: Draft International Standard on Ergonomics Requirements for office works with visual display terminals (VDT), Part 11: Guidance on Usability (1994)
6. ISO. ISO/IEC WD 25023. System and Software Engineering – System and Software product Quality Requirements and Evaluation (SQuaRE) – Measurement of system and software product quality (2011)
7. Lepreux, S., Vanderdonckt, J., Michotte, B.: Visual Design of User Interfaces by (De)composition. In: Doherty, G., Blandford, A. (eds.) DSVIS 2006. LNCS, vol. 4323, pp. 157–170. Springer, Heidelberg (2007)
8. Lin, J., Wong, J., Nichols, J., Cypher, A., Lau, T.A.: End-user programming of mashups with vegemite. In: Proceedings of the 14th International Conference on Intelligent User Interfaces (IUI 2009), pp. 97–106. ACM, New York (2009)
9. Myers, B.: Engineering more natural interactive programming systems: keynote talk. In: Nicholas Graham, D.T.C., Calvary, G., Gray, P.D. (eds.) EICS, pp. 1–2. ACM (2009) ISBN 978-1-60558-600-7
10. Nielsen, J.: Usability engineering. Academic Press, Boston (1993)
11. Papazoglou, M.P.: Service-oriented computing: Concepts, characteristics and directions. In: WISE, pp. 3–12. IEEE Computer Society (2003) ISBN 0-7695-1999-7
12. Paternò, F., Mancini, C., Meniconi, S.: ConcurTaskTrees: A Diagrammatic Notation for Specifying Task Models. In: Proc. of the IFIP TC13 Int. Conf. on Human-Computer Interaction Interact 1997, London, pp. 362–369 (1997)
13. Pinna-Dery, A.M., Fierstone, J., Picard, E.: Component model and programming: a first step to manage human computer interaction adaptation. In: Chittaro, L. (ed.) Mobile HCI 2003. LNCS, vol. 2795, pp. 456–460. Springer, Heidelberg (2003)
14. Scapin, D.L., Bastien, J.M.C.: Ergonomic criteria for evaluating the ergonomic quality of interactive systems. Behaviour & Information Technology 16(4), 220–231 (1997)
15. Seffah, A., Donyaee, M., Kline, R., Padda, H.: Usability Measurement and Metrics: A Consolidated Model. Software Quality Journal 14, 159–178 (2006)
16. Szyperski, C., Gruntz, D., Murer, S.: Component software: beyond object-oriented programming. Addison-Wesley Professional (2002)
17. Tan, D.S., Meyers, B., Czerwinski, M.: Wincuts: manipulating arbitrary window regions for more effective use of screen space. In: Proceedings of ACM CHI 2004 Conference on Human Factors in Computing Systems, vol. 2, pp. 1525–1528 (2004), Late breaking result papers

Human-Machine Interaction Evaluation Framework

Hans Jander[1] and Jens Alfredson[2]

[1] Swedish Defence Research Agency (FOI), SE-164 90 Stockholm, Sweden
Hans.Jander@foi.se
[2] Saab AB, Aeronautics, SE-581 88 Linköping, Sweden
Jens.Alfredson@saabgroup.com

Abstract. The aim of the study reported in this paper was to use and evaluate a new methodological framework for Human-Machine Interaction (HMI) evaluation in system development for complex, high-risk and task-critical environments to assess overall HMI readiness. This has been conducted in the context of simulations in a state-of-the-art development simulator for fighter aircraft cockpit design in an industrial setting. The simulations included active and experienced military fighter pilots flying two civil navigational scenarios. The framework consists of already established evaluation methods and techniques combined with new influences inspired from risk management practices. A new HMI assessment survey has been developed and integrated into the framework. The results of the study are promising for the studied framework and also indicate some overlap when compared to existing practices regarding collected data. Applied within industry the framework can help leverage future HMI evaluations within system development.

Keywords: Usability, HCI, HMI, System evaluation, System Development.

1 Introduction

Within the domain of high risk and task critical environments there is a great need to incorporate end users iteratively in system development and design processes to be able to evaluate a suggested HMI-design in a relevant context (Hackos & Redish, 1998; Suchman, 2007; ISO 9241-210, 2010; Jander, Borgvall & Castor, 2011; Jander, Borgvall & Ramberg, 2012). This paper focuses on the evaluation step in the system development and design process. HMI-evaluations are not always prioritized and when evaluations are conducted the result from evaluations often comes in too late and suggested issues/improvements/changes in design are not always implemented due to time and budget constraints within projects. There are several reasons for this. One potential reason, that evaluations not always are integrated per default in the design process, is that there are no standardized evaluation procedures.

There is a need to develop evaluation methods that can be used, applied and adapted in system development and design to enhance overall system efficiency and meet the end user needs. Every millisecond that can be saved, every mental workload

M. Kurosu (Ed.): Human-Computer Interaction, Part I, HCII 2013, LNCS 8004, pp. 221–230, 2013.

decrease will improve the operator capability to perform their task in a faster, safer, and more accurate way.

Cost benefits aspects of using different evaluation methods needs to be considered before implementation within the industry.

This paper describes a study performed at Saab Aeronautics in PMSIM in Linköping, Sweden. PMSIM is a state-of-the-art development simulator for fighter aircraft cockpit design. The aim of this study was to evaluate a new methodological evaluation framework that has been developed within a research project in cooperation between Swedish Defence Research Agency (FOI), Saab Aeronautics, and Stockholm University. The project overall sponsor is the Swedish Governmental Agency for Innovation Systems (VINNOVA), within the National Aviation Engineering Program 5 (NFFP5). The focus of this study is not to evaluate the system that was tested, but rather to evaluate the developed the methodology.

The methodological evaluation framework developed in the project is further described in Jander, Borgvall, & Castor (2011), and Jander, Borgvall, & Ramberg (2012). The framework uses a variety of already established Human Factors (HF) and Human-Machine Interaction (HMI) evaluation methods and techniques such as think aloud protocol, mental workload measures, surveys and interviews combined with new influences inspired from risk management practices. A new HMI assessment survey has been developed and is integrated into the framework.

One of the new things within this methodological framework is the concept of use subjective weighting of parameters evaluated in the so called HMI assessment survey.

2 Objective

The overall objective of the reported study was to evaluate a new methodological framework for evaluating and assessing HMI in a fighter aircraft cockpit. Parameters investigated where:

- Time to perform evaluations
- Time for evaluation setup
- Time for analysis
- Type of data captured/collected
- "Know-how" needed to perform evaluation from the test leader perspective
- Test leader acceptance
- Test person (participant acceptance)
- Overall applicability of the methodological framework

3 Method

Two different evaluation methods approaches were used to evaluate characteristics of the systems HMI and was later compared. Method 1) New methodological evaluation framework; Method 2) A predefined survey addressing specific questions concerning

HMI functionality (benchmark). More specifically Method 1 was first used and was in the end complemented with Method 2.

Two test leaders conducted the evaluations. The evaluation was simulation based with three participants performing two missions in the flight simulator including the use of new functionality relating to HMI while performing predefined tasks using the system. On a meta-level an overall analysis were made to evaluate the two methods used to describe characteristics, e.g. pros and cons and give recommendations for future work.

3.1 Participants

All together five subjects, all male, participated in the study. Three were active or former fighter pilots from the Swedish Air Force and two persons with experience of system evaluation, one from Saab Aeronautics and one from the Swedish Defence Research Agency. The pilots were all classified as experienced fighter pilots with rudimentary experience in civil navigations procedures. The fighter pilots represented different experience levels. The first with approximately 8 years of working experience, the second with approximately 15 years of working experience, and the third with approximately 30 years of working experience. The two test leaders conducting the evaluation were both classified as experienced HMI-specialists, each with more than ten years of relevant working experience in the field. One was considerably more of an HMI generalist with expertise in HMI evaluation methods and the other was also considered as a specialist in the fighter aircraft domain. The two test leaders lead the evaluation procedure, but also in the end analyzed the result on a meta-level, e.g. describe method characteristics. Also, the role of an Air Traffic Controller (ATC) was used during the simulations to increase validity in the study.

3.2 Apparatus

The study was conducted in PMSIM (Display and Control Simulator) at Saab Aeronautics in Linköping. PMSIM is a state-of-the-art development simulator for fighter aircraft cockpit design. The simulator is a fixed base, dome simulator, where the visual surroundings are displayed on a dome with a radius of three meters, with a field of view of +/- 135 degrees azimuth and +90/-45 degrees evaluation. The simulated aircraft was a top-modern fighter aircraft.

3.3 Scenarios

Two pre-defined civil navigational scenarios was set up with the purpose of testing new system functionality to support pilots in civil navigation procedures including take off, holding, and landing. Especially new visual presentation of information regarding Area Navigation (RNAV) was displayed. Functionality and visual presentation regarding SID (Standard Instrument Departure) and STAR (Standard Terminal Arrival Route) were displayed, and the pilots interacted based on this information in the two scenarios.

3.4 Analysis

The interpretation of the results is made on a meta-level and is focused on the characteristics of the two different methods rather than the results of the specific system evaluation. More detailed descriptions of the analysis approach are described in the result section below.

3.5 Procedure

Each participant was given a short written description about the experiment, e.g. purpose, aim, and procedure. Then, each participant was presented and briefed about the new system for civil navigation procedures by a simulator instructor. Before entering the flight simulator cockpit the participants was informed how to use the Bedford rating scale for mental workload and how to think aloud when performing tasks in simulator.

Each participant performed two scenarios in the simulator using new system functionality and was asked to think aloud and highlight event-triggered events, and rate mental workload (MWL) according to the test leader instructions during the whole scenario. In average each participant were asked make MWL-ratings every fourth minute. Event-triggered comments and MWL-ratings were noted by the test leaders.

After completion of the simulation, participants were asked to report some spontaneous reactions and comments of the simulations and the new system used.

The participants were then asked to complete the HMI survey, facilitated by the test leader. They answered the survey by rating the importance of each of the 24 HMI criteria and rated the perceived criteria fulfillment of each criterion. The participants were also asked to make comments, give examples, make diagnoses on potential issues clarifying and motivating their choice of ratings. The ratings where based on the task performed and the system used in the simulator. This was explicit to the participants with the purpose of catching contextual aspects of use. An example of a criterion from the HMI survey is: Menus, symbols and texts are grouped in a logical way.

The participants were then asked to answer 8 questions survey regarding specific functions and displays of the system evaluated, also referred to as method 2. These questions were used as benchmark and comparison measure. An example of a question is: What are your comments on how data is presented on the center display?

There was no difference in the test procedure between the two evaluated methodological approaches except the tools used for data collection in the sense that both methods use fighter pilots as participants performing the same task scenario in the simulator.

In the end the participants were asked some questions regarding experiences of the overall applicability of the evaluation method and procedure just conducted.

All steps in the evaluation procedure was timed, think aloud and event triggered comments and MWL was noted by the test leaders. The test leaders were using predefined test protocols.

After the system evaluation sessions with the three fighter pilots, data was analyzed.

4 Results and Analysis

4.1 Time to Perform Evaluation

The average time to conduct on evaluation was 3 hours and 25 minutes. Some more time was needed (in average 40 min) to perform the HMI-survey (method 1) compared with the benchmark evaluation survey (method 2).

4.2 Time for Preparation

The preparation time for the evaluation is very dependent on the apparatus and test scenarios needed and personnel involved. Test scenarios already existed and the simulator was up and running. The total preparation time for the evaluation time is estimated to 3 working days for the evaluation team. If new test scenarios needs to be designed more time is needed.

4.3 Time for Analysis

The results collected from the benchmark evaluation survey are relatively straight forward and easy to interpret due to the design of the specific questions. Most of the answers referred mostly to describing and guiding specific system characteristics. The results from the HMI evaluation framework require more time for analysis. There are many more dimensions of the HMI that are investigated and the results from MWL-ratings, event-triggered events, and HMI-survey all needs in depth analysis that are further described below. The results from the HMI evaluation framework is not only describing and guiding specific system characteristics, but also describes more general system characteristics complemented with potential prioritizing of identified issues (as described under the section 4.10 "Comparison of data from HMI assessment survey and baseline survey").

The time for analysis of the results from the HMI evaluation framework is approximately 1 day per participant and 1-2 hours per participant for the benchmark evaluation.

4.4 Mental Workload Measures

Bedford rating-scale were used to rate Mental Workload (Castor, 2009). The scale consists of ten steps (1=very low MWL and 10 very high MWL). See Table 1 for the three pilot participants' MWL-ratings.

Due to the lack of a control group performing the test scenarios without using the new system to support civilian procedures at take-off, holding, and landing it is hard to make any conclusions how the evaluated system specifically affected MWL. In a few cases MWL-rating were high but considering participants additional comments (think aloud) these MWL-ratings cannot directly be deduced to this specifically system functionality, rather to overall system functionality (which is an interesting finding) and different participants experience levels.

Table 1. Mental Workload ratings

Participant (P)/Scenario (S)	Number of ratings	Mean	Standard Deviation
P1/S1	10	4.2	1.5
P1/S2	8	4.9	2.2
P2/S1	14	4.2	1.2
P2/S2	9	5.2	0.8
P3/S2	10	4.6	1.4
P3/S2	9	4.3	0.9

4.5 Think Aloud Event Triggered Events

Only a few relevant event triggered comments referring to system characteristics were articulated during the test scenarios. Due to the relatively non-complex tasks and low dynamics in the scenario, very few frustrations or other events were highlighted. A few times the participants raised questions how to navigate in system menus. Also some comments were made that referred to specific design solutions and suggestions regarding the interface.

4.6 HMI-Survey

The participants experienced some redundancy between some criteria in the HMI-survey. For example, the criterion statement "The system empowers me to complete the assigned task in the best possible way" is similar to the criteria statement "I feel that the system fulfills my needs". Overall, all criteria were rated as important on the six-grade rating scale. This indicates that almost all criteria in the survey were considered relevant for the system tested in this specific context with very few exceptions.

4.7 Participant´s Comments and Justifications on HMI-Ratings

The rated criteria value and the rated criteria fulfillment value was complemented with comments with the purpose of motivating, clarifying, and justifying ratings. An example was when one participant rated the criterion "I have a feeling of achieving high task effectiveness when using the system" as 4 (rather important) on the importance scale and as 2 (almost totally fulfilled) on the fulfillment scale. An additional comment made by the participant on the rating was; "I prefer accuracy prior to efficiency in the context of civil navigation". This example illustrate that the importance of the different criteria might differ in another context and this aspect is captured in the evaluation framework.

The comments made by the participant added great value and meaning to the criteria ratings in the survey. In some cases spontaneous design issues were addressed and some specific design suggestions were articulated.

4.8 HMI Assessment Matrix (Analysis Tool)

The product of the rated criteria value and the rated criteria fulfillment value from the HMI-survey resulted in a number from 1-36. Low numbers was assumed to indicate that there are no design issues, e.g. HMI is ok. High numbers indicate that there are some design issues that needs to be considered, e.g. HMI is not ok. Though, the result of the study indicates that it is very hard to draw any conclusions from just a number from 1-36. There are several reasons for that. For example, if two criteria have the same product value it is hard to choose which of them is the most important to consider. Also, in some cases in the study the product value was relatively high but considered additional comment made by the test person indicated that there actually was no issue. Therefore, it is very important to consider the column of comments made by the test person for each of the criteria. The result of using the HMI-matrix as an analysis tool shows that it is just a complement to other collected quantitative data. The quantitative data gives power to the qualitative data and the qualitative data dress the quantitative data with meaning. To give a meaning and make conclusions of just a number between 1-36 alone is in this case inappropriate and even hazardous.

4.9 Benchmark Survey

The benchmark survey (method 2) consisted of eight specific questions regarding the functionality of the tested system. Some of the questions were not answered by the participant due to that they did not use all the functions that the questions addressed. In general, given answers addressed specifically system characteristics.

4.10 Comparison of Data from HMI Assessment Survey (Method 1) and Baseline Survey (Method 2)

In order to compare the results of the data collected from comments made in the HMI-survey with the answers from the benchmark survey, a taxonomy was created to classify comments from the HMI-survey and answers from the benchmark survey. Four classes were created (see table 2). Class 1, 2, A, and B: were class 1 refer to comments and answers on general system characteristics; and class 2 refer to comments and answers on specific system characteristics; and class A refer to describing comments and answers; and B refer to guiding comments and answers.

Table 2. Taxonomy used for analyzing results of the HMI-survey (method 1) and benchmark survey (method 2)

Class	1	2
A	Describing general system characteristics	Describing specific system characteristics
B	Guiding general system characteristics	Guiding specific system characteristics

When comparing the results from the HMI-survey and the benchmark survey it is obvious that most of the answers referring to guiding and describing specific system characteristics was collected from the benchmark survey but the comments from the HMI-survey also give some guidance regarding specific system characteristics. On the other hand, the HMI-survey also describes and gives guidance on specific system characteristics and also describing general system characteristics. When conducting system evaluation specific functionality is hard to isolate from the overall system and this is probably not always even desirable. There were also some overlap and redundancy in answers between the HMI-survey comments and the benchmark-survey answers.

4.11 Know-How Needed to Perform Evaluation from the Test Leader Perspective

To be able to interpret result accurately it was vital to have at least on test leader with domain experience. It also leverages the credibility in the relation with the participants. For practical reasons it also helps with experimental setup and administration to have some "inside" the organization were the evaluation will take place. The know-how needed could also consider the three different stages when conducting system evaluation: 1) Preparation; 2) Performing; 3) Analyzing. For preparation someone from the organization were the evaluation will take place is vital to make necessary arrangements (scenario design, simulator set up including simulator operator/s). Some domain expertise is needed to design questions referring to this study benchmark test. For preparation of test protocol of the HMI assessment framework, domain expertise is not necessarily needed. When performing the evaluation two test leaders are needed. At least one should have domain expertise and at least one should have experience of HMI-evaluations. During the analysis it is desirable to include the test leaders who have conducted the evaluation with the motivation of capture details during the evaluation in order to transform the result to valid conclusions and communicate to the design team.

4.12 Participants' (Pilots and Test Leaders) Acceptance

Both the test leaders and the pilots experienced positive acceptance of the new methodological evaluation framework and judged the framework as relevant, valid and easy to conduct.

5 Conclusions

The study shows promising for the studied HMI evaluation framework and also indicated a few overlaps with existing practices within the industry regarding results in identification of specific describing and guiding system characteristics data. The HMI evaluation framework also identified more general system characteristics data, referring to the whole system used, not only the evaluated system tested in isolation.

The use of a combination of qualitative (survey comments, think aloud, and interview) and quantitative (survey and MWL ratings) measures suggested in the new framework will leverage HMI-evaluations and help system designers to find, describe and prioritize potential design issues into further design iterations. Additional comments on each criterion are vital to consider before making conclusions of numerical values in isolation. More studies needs to be conducted to validate the applicability of the suggested evaluation framework evaluating other systems in different contexts within the studied domain. The studied framework can both be used for benchmark and acceptance tests, but also for formative and diagnostic testing. The frameworks ability of considering contextual aspects and the combination of using both quantitative and qualitative data gives considering advantages.

6 Discussion and Future Research

The new methodological evaluation framework approach (method 1) investigated in this study shows promising results in system evaluation. Some of its advantages are the explicit use of the concept of weighting which is rather new in systems evaluation, even though the use of weighting sometimes is used more implicitly in evaluations. One way of catching the right context of use of a system in evaluations is the assumption that the importance of identified HMI criteria might differ between different systems, tasks, and users (Frokjaer, Hertzum, & Hornbaek, 2000). The use of weighting considers these aspects and gives valid results in evaluations. The evaluated methodological evaluation framework is generic and can be used for evaluating a variety of systems within the domain.

One potential problem using specific questions (method 2) about system functionality is that the answers tend to be quite isolated and just relate to the specific system tested. In a complex system HMI like a fighter aircraft cockpit there is always other interactions needed that relate to other overall system functionality as well. Therefore, there is a need to conduct systems evaluation using the new functionality integrated with the overall system in a relevant scenario to capture the right context of use. However, the use of specifically addressed questions can on the other hand give valuable insights about specific system characteristics and these questions can serve as a complement to the methodological evaluation framework.

Most of the HMI criteria were rated as important and that might lead to problems when identifying design issues when using the HMI assessment matrix alone referring how to in the best way prioritize identified issues in further iterations. Therefore additional comments need to be carefully considered during the analysis.

The study setup and experiment design could use a control group performing the same task without using the system new system in order to make comparisons regarding how the new system affected ratings and comments. However, this was not possible due to lack of participants and time constraints.

In this case the evaluated system was not very complex and the task performed in the simulator was relatively simple. A new study is needed to evaluate another system, preferably in a highly dynamic scenario with increased task complexity to further evaluate the new methodological approach.

During the analysis phase in this study no end users (i.e., the pilots) received feedback and were consulted to validate the test results. Due to lack of access of the participated pilots in the analysis phase this was not done. It would have been recommended to consult the end users for a double check to make sure the results and analysis is valid, also from the end users perspective before writing final test report.

The benchmark survey (method 2) used in this study requires some extra time to prepare compared with the survey used in the evaluation framework. The benchmark survey also addresses very specific system characteristics and sometimes missed to catch more general system characteristics that were identified using the evaluation framework.

The evaluated framework puts focus on both finding pros and cons regarding system characteristics. The classification/taxonomy described just describes system characteristics in four dimensions. However, each of the system characteristics could also describe the identification of both positive and negative aspects of the system. Traditionally HMI-evaluations are primarily concerned with identifying problems, while both negative and positive system characteristics were identified in this study. This is of great importance to designers who also needs to know what the systems strengths are.

References

1. Castor, M.: The use of structural equation modeling to describe the effect of operator functional state on air-to-air engagement outcomes. Doctorial Thesis No. 1251, Linköping University, SE-581 83 Sweden (2009)
2. Frokjaer, E., Hertzum, M., Hornbaek, K.: Measuring usability: Are effectiveness, efficiency, and satisfaction really correlated? In: Conference on Human Factors in Computing Systems (CHI 2000), N.Y., April 1-6 (2000)
3. Hackos, J., Redish, J.: User and task analysis for interface design. Wiley, New York (1998)
4. ISO 9241-210:2010. Ergonomics of human-system interaction, Part 210, Human-centred design for interactive systems, Geneva, Switzerland (2010)
5. Jander, H., Borgvall, J., Castor, M.: Brain Budget- Evaluation of Human Machine Interaction in system Development for High Risk and Task Critical Environments (FOI-R–3272–SE) (2011)
6. Jander, H., Borgvall, J., Ramberg, R.: Towards a Methodological Framework for HMI Readiness Evaluation. In: Proceedings of the Human Factors and Ergonomics Society Annual Meeting, vol. 56 (2012)
7. Suchman, L.: Human-Machine Reconfigurations, Plans and Situated Actions. Cambridge University Press, NY (2007)

Supervisory Control Interface Design for Unmanned Aerial Vehicles through GEDIS-UAV

Salvador Lorite[1], Adolfo Muñoz[1], Josep Tornero[1], Pere Ponsa[2], and Enric Pastor[3]

[1] Design and Manufacturing Institute (IDF), Polytechnic University of Valencia, CPI, Edif. 8E, Camino de Vera s/n, 46022 Valencia, Spain
{slorite,amunyoz,jtornero}@idf.upv.es

[2] Automatic Control Department, UPC BarcelonaTech University, Av. Víctor Balaguer s/n, 08800 Vilanova I la Geltrú, Barcelona, Spain
pedro.ponsa@upc.edu

[3] ICARUS Research Group, UPC BarcelonaTech University, C/ Esteve Terradas 7, 08860 Castelldefels, Barcelona, Spain
enric@ac.upc.edu

Abstract. This paper reflects the state of art in the field of human factors for unmanned aerial vehicles. It describes the GEDIS-UAV guide, which is a modification of the GEDIS guide. It also shows the evaluation of the Sky-eye project graphical user interface as an example of the methodology. The analysis and evaluation method reflected in this paper may be used to improve the graphical user interface of any unmanned aerial vehicle.

Keywords: Supervisory Control, Unmanned Vehicles, Ergonomics, GEDIS.

1 Introduction

This paper aims to advance the research on guidelines to design and implement interfaces for monitoring unmanned aerial vehicles (UAVs). Today the UAVs have become a fashionable topic in the world, but we must be aware of the risks associated with a failure of these flying machines, the consequences can be disastrous, even more when these machines are for civilian use. Some failures occur during teleoperation [1], [3], [5], [7], [13], [25]. Twenty percent of the failures are attributed to human error [24]; therefore improving the control interface can decrease the failures considerably [4], [26]. There are not specific regulations or guidelines oriented to the design of interfaces for UAVs, however there is one guideline we consider can be helpful after some adaptations, It is the human factors guide for human supervisory control display design GEDIS [18]. Taking into account aspects of human computer interaction of UAVs, this guide has been adapted in order to make it fully functional for UAV's graphical user interfaces (GUIs), here lays the main contribution of the present work.

M. Kurosu (Ed.): Human-Computer Interaction, Part I, HCII 2013, LNCS 8004, pp. 231–240, 2013.

2 Previous Research on Human Interface Design Guidelines

This section refers to the state of the art of standards and guidelines related with the design of GUIs for UAVs: ARINC 661 [2], STANAG 4586 [4], [11], DO-178B [20], JAUS [23], ISO 9241-11 [8] and GEDIS [18]. Table 1 shows a comparison of the standards and guidelines.

Table 1. Standards and guidelines comparison

	User Centered	Focused on the system	Focused on interaction
JAUS	NO	YES	NO
STANAG	NO	YES	NO
ARINC 661	NO	NO	NO
DO-178B	NO	NO	NO
ISO 9241	YES	NO	YES
GEDIS	YES	NO	YES

To date the unmanned systems architectures vary considerably from one system to another, this situation complicates the creation of a guideline or a standard. There are guidelines and standards that can be used but they present limitations because they do not meet all the needs of each unmanned system architecture, for example GEDIS should be modified in order to be useful for other types of unmanned vehicles or for other types of missions.

3 GEDIS-UAV Guideline

From the initial point of view of strategies for effective human-computer interaction applied to supervision tasks in industrial control rooms [12], [21], GEDIS-UAV has adopted GEDIS guideline method to cover all the aspects of the GUI design [18 - 19]. GEDIS-UAV offers design recommendations in the moment of creating the interface and it also offers recommendations of improvement for interfaces already created. The guide is composed by indicators and subindicators. The method consists in analyzing and measuring each indicator in order to obtain a global evaluation index.

3.1 Indicators List

The GEDIS-UAV indicators have been defined from concepts extracted of other generic human factors guidelines [18] and the subindicators have been defined from the same sources but taking into account specific ergonomic criteria, like the level of situational awareness in UAVs, here lays the main contribution of the present work. The indicators are: architecture, distribution, navigation, color, text font, status of the devices, process values, graphs and tables, data-entry commands, and alarms.

3.2 Evaluation

The evaluation is expressed with a quantitative numeric form and with a qualitative format that reflects the operator experience using the interface or the analysis criteria of the evaluator. The evaluation method is the same as in GEDIS guide. Each subindicator is punctuated numerically in a scale from 1 to 5. The indicator value is calculated by solving the following formula:

$$\text{Indicator} = \frac{\sum_{j=1}^{J} w_j Subind_j}{\sum_{j=1}^{J} w_j} \tag{1}$$

Where, J = number of Subindicators of the indicator, Subind = subindicator assessment value and w = weight. For this study each subindicator has the same weight ($w1 = w2\ldots = wJ = 1$).

The indicators values are used to calculate the global evaluation by solving the following formula:

$$\text{Global Index} = \frac{\sum_{i=1}^{10} p_i ind_i}{\sum_{i=1}^{10} p_i} \tag{2}$$

Where, ind = indicator and p = weight. As explained before in this first approach all indicators have the same weight ($p1 = p2\ldots= p10 = 1$). The guide recommends that the global evaluation index should not be lower than 3 points. A positive evaluation should reach at least 4 points.

4 Applying the GEDIS-UAV Guide: The Sky-Eye Project Case

Sky-eye project is part of the work being conducted by the research group ICARUS (Intelligent communications and avionics for robust unmanned aerial systems) of the UPC BarcelonaTech University. Among the group´s work, the project Sky-eye [14] aims to research improvements in unmanned aerial systems (UAS) for fire eradication missions, building flexible and generic missions designed for an efficient execution, one of the objectives in order to facilitate the operation is to achieve the appropriate level of automation [22] over all the UAV's work processes; this goal includes the development of a good supervisory control interface. The embedded hardware/software architecture developed by the ICARUS group includes the GCS [15 – 16]. The GCS has been designed to fulfill the following functions: mission planning, mission control, manual and/or supervised control of the UAV and data manipulation. The design of the console that incorporates the graphical interface of the GCS is based on the standard ARINC 661, comprises a display mounted on a control panel similar to a conventional aircraft cockpit. The GUI consists of a TFT (thin film transistor) screen that displays the flight instruments, the flight controls, the local map, the global map for the control of the mission, the artificial horizon and the navigation camera aboard the vehicle. The local map is in the bottom left of the screen and the global map on the right side just above the engine rpm, fuel and oil pressure gauges. Both the local map and global map can zoom in and out the pictures.

Figure 1 depicts the GUI developed by the research group ICARUS. Although the design is based on the ARINC 661 standard, the GUI has a high complexity in the sense that almost all the features have been included in one screen. GEDIS-UAV structures all the functionalities in a multi-layer application and it allows the tasks to be distributed between different operators. Starting from this information, it is possible to make an assessment that will lead to identify and propose crucial improvements to the supervisory control interface layout.

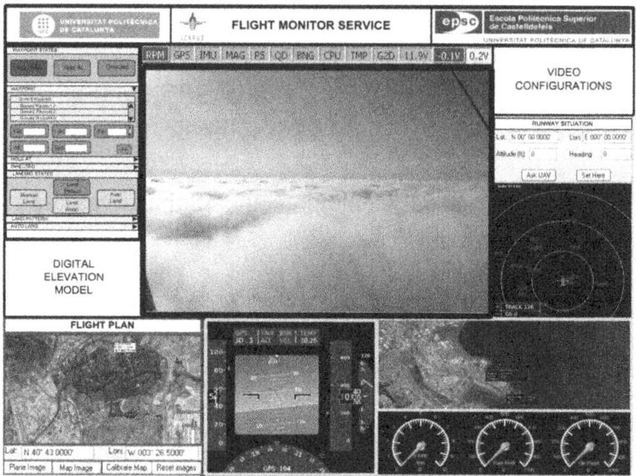

Fig. 1. GUI developed by the research group ICARUS

5 Current Interface Evaluation through GEDIS-UAV

The guide detects a group of anomalies and numerically quantifies each of the components and indicators for a global assessment index. As follows the Sky-eye interface end user evaluation (where A=appropriate, M=medium, N.A. = Not appropriate):

Table 2. Architecture

A: Architecture	A	M	N.A.	Specific criteria
A1: Division in areas	5	3	0	---
A2: Screens number "sn"	---	---	---	3<sn<9=5, n<4=0,

The division (A1) got a "3" because the mission control module is not appreciable, but it keeps relation with the rest of the modules: UAV, global map, local map, avionics sensors, vehicle control, mission planning and data manipulation. Because there is only one screen that displays all the information together, the number of screens (A2) got a "0", having "1.5" points in total for the architecture indicator (A). Figure 2A depicts the original GUI schematic division by areas.

Table 3. Distribution

B: Distribution	A	M	N.A.	Specific criteria
B1: Model comparison	5	3	0	---
B2: Flow process	5	3	0	---
B3: Density	5	3	0	---

The model comparison subindicator (B1) got a "3" because the interface is similar to the model, except for some items to display. For certain tasks, the process flow is not entirely clear then flow process subindicator (B2) got a "3". All the elements are in close proximity therefore the subindicator density (B3) got a "0", having "2" points in total for the distribution indicator (B).

Table 4. Navigation

C: Navigation	A	M	N.A.	Specific criteria
C1: Navigation between screens	5	3	0	---

The interface has only one screen where all the information is displayed to the operator, this design allows the operator to navigate between different parts of the system but this characteristic limits radically the operator's capability of navigation, one of the main reasons is because every time the operator explores a specific part of the system, another part gets hidden. Another limitation is that the interface does not display the navigation buttons correctly. Therefore the subindicator navigation between screens (C1) got a "0", having "0" points in total for the navigation indicator (C).

Table 5. Color

D: Color	A	M	N.A.	Specific criteria
D1: Absence of non-appropriate	---	---	---	Yes=5, No=0
D2: Colors number "cn"	---	---	---	cn<4=5, cn>4=0
D3: Blink absence	---	---	---	Yes=5, No=0
D4: SC contrast vs GC	5	3	0	---
D5: Relationship with text	5	3	0	---

The absence of non-appropriate combinations subindicator (D1) got a "5". There are more than 9 colors then the subindicator colors number (D2) got a "0". The subindicator (D3) blink absence got a "5" because the interface does not have visual alarms. In general there is a good contrast between the graphical contrast and the screen contrast therefore the subindicator (D4) got a "5" and the subindicator relationship with text (D5) got a "5" because the relationship with the text color in general is appropriate. All this subindicators lead to "4" points in total for the color indicator (D).

Table 6. Text font

E: Text font	A	M	N.A.	Specific criteria
E1: Font number "fn"	---	---	---	fn<4=5, fn>4=0
E2: Absence of small fonts	---	---	---	Yes=5, No=0
E3: Absence of N.A. combinations	---	---	---	Yes=5, No=0
E4: Abbreviation use	5	3	0	---

The number of fonts used in the interface is 3 then the subindicator font number (E1) got a "5". There are some fonts with size 6; therefore the subindicator (E2) got a "0". There are not non-appropriate combinations therefore the subindicator (E3) got a "5", and since the interface uses too many abbreviations the subindicator (E4) got a "0", having "2.5" points in total for the text font indicator (E).

Table 7. Status and devices

F: Status of the devices	A	M	N.A.	Specific criteria
F1: Uniform icons and symbols	---	---	---	Yes=5, No=0
F2: Status team representativeness	---	---	---	le<4=5, le>4=0

There is no use of symbols therefore the uniform icons and symbols sub-indicator (F1) got a "0" and the status team representativeness (F2) got a "5", having "2.5" points in total for the status and devices indicator (F).

Table 8. Process values

G: Process values	A	M	N.A.	Specific criteria
G1: Visibility	5	3	0	---
G2: Location	5	3	0	---

The visibility subindicator (G1) got a "3" because not all the required values are visible (for example is not easy to find the altitude value) and in general the process values could be better visualized. The location subindicator (G2) got a "3" because the process values are relatively well located, but it could be easier for the operator. These values lead to "3" points in total for the process values indicator (G).

Table 9. Graphs and tables

H: Graphs and tables	A	M	N.A.	Specific criteria
H1: Format	5	3	0	---
H2: Visibility	5	3	0	---
H3: Location	5	3	0	---
H4: Grouping	5	3	0	---

The format of the graphs and tables is appropriate therefore the subindicator (H1) got a “5”, the visibility (H2) and location (H3) subindicators got a “3” because some graphics could be a supplement, like displaying the advanced distance that depends of the speed and the time and the graphs and tables are relatively well located. Since there is not any suitable grouping the subindicator (H4) got a “0”, having “2.75” points in total for the graphs and tables indicator (H).

Table 10. Data entry commands

I: Data entry commands	**A**	**M**	**N.A.**	**Specific criteria**
I1: Visibility	5	3	0	---
I2: Usability	5	3	0	---
I3: Feedback	5	3	0	---

The visibility (I1) got a “3” because the input commands could be better visualized, the usability (I2) got a “5” and the feedback (I3) got a “3” because the feedback is indirect, the operator must enter a command to know about a new situation, when it should be automatic. These values lead to “3.67” points in total for the data entry commands indicator (I).

Table 11. Alarms

J: Alarms	**A**	**M**	**N.A.**	**Specific criteria**
J1: Visibility of alarms	5	3	0	---
J2: Location	5	3	0	---
J3: Situation awareness	---	---	---	Yes=5, No=0
J4: Alarms grouping	5	3	0	---
J5: Information to the operator	5	3	0	---

The visibility of alarms (J1) got a “3” because the alarms could be better visualized; the location (J2) got a “3” because the alarms are relatively well located. The alarms could give better parameters or instructions to let the operator have a better understanding of the situation, therefore the situation awareness (J3) got a “3”. In general the alarms grouping and how the alarms are showed to the operator are correct therefore the subindicators (J4) and (J5) got a “5”. All these values lead to “3.8” points in total for the alarms indicator (J). The final result of the Sky-eye graphic user interface evaluation, taking into account that each indicator has the same weight, stands in 2.572 (rounded = 2.6). After applying some corrections to the detected anomalies, the global evaluation index can be stood between 4 and 5 which are the maximum values of the numeric scale.

6 Proposals for Interface Improvements

The GEDIS-UAV analysis and evaluation made possible to identify an interface limited in structure, distribution and navigation. These three first indicators show the errors that occur more often in the design of GUIs for UAVs.

Among other things it was detected that the text size is not right, the interface does not show the status of the devices in a suitable manner, the process values could be better visualized as well as the data-entry commands; all this increases the operator response time and the delays inside the control loop. Another important anomaly detected is that the interface's alarms could give more information in case of failures in order to improve the operator situational awareness [6]. Figure 2 depicts the distribution analysis of the Sky-eye project GUI. Figure 2A depicts the original GUI distribution and figure 2B shows the proposed distribution.

SPACE RESERVED FOR TITLES
ALARMS
DATA ENTRY GRAPHS
STATUS AND DEVICES
DATA ENTRY
DATA ENTRY AND STATUS
LOCAL MAP
STATUS AND DEVICES
GLOBAL MAP
STATUS AND DEVICES

(A) Original GUI distribution

ALARMS
STATUS AND DEVICES
FRONTAL CAMERA WITH HUD OVERLAY
THERMAL CAMERAS AND OTHER SENSORS RELATED WITH THE MISSION
DATA ENTRY COMMANDS
LOCAL MAP
GLOBAL MAP
MISSION CONTROL AND DATA MANIPULATION

(B) Proposed distribution

Fig. 2. Distribution analysis of the Sky-eye project GUI

As part of the recommendations the following screens were proposed: Data entry commands, alarms, UAV systems status and process values, local map, global map, frontal video with HUD (head-up display) overlay, thermal cameras and mission control/ data manipulation (shown in figure 3). Each screen represents one of the zones that the interface is supposed to have, and should meet specific ergonomic criteria.

Fig. 3. Proposed GUI for Sky-eye two-wing UAV

At a glance is possible to note the difference and the level of improvement. The evaluation of the proposed interface through GEDIS-UAV guide is 5, which is the maximum value of the numerical scale; this means that the implementation of the GUI will minimize at maximum the possibility of human error.

7 Conclusions and Future Work

As a result and based on GEDIS-UAV recommendations, the students of the BarcelonaTech improved the interface design for the "Shadow MK1" UAV [10], [17]. For more details about the work conducted in order to design the graphical user interface refer to "Diseño de Interfaces de Supervisión de Vehículos Aéreos No Tripulados - Supervisory Control Interfaces Design for UAVs" [9].

Although there are some standards regarding security for human machine interface systems that keep relation with physical ergonomics and interface design aspects through style rules, it is remarkable the absence of human centered designs in interactive systems. At this point, our contribution is to apply usability engineering, using techniques like the measurement of the operator mental workload, improvement of the GUI design and others related with usability techniques like the cognitive walkthrough. The application of GEDIS-UAV guide on a real project, demonstrates the functionality and applicability of the guideline. Future work will try to establish more specific ergonomic criteria to design supervisory interfaces by adding, deleting or modifying some indicators. Another line of research will try to improve the guide assessment techniques, in the present work, the evaluation methodology assigns the same weight to all the indicators, but maybe this could be improved if it is taken into account the importance of some indicators over others. Important efforts of future research will take into account the use of new input devices like multi-touch screens, speech recognition engines and brain wave sensors in order to improve the design and implementation process of interfaces for unmanned vehicles.

References

1. Air Force Research Laboratory. Wright-Patterson Air Force Base (October 2007), `http://www.wpafb.af.mil/shared/media/document/AFD-070418-024.pdf`
2. ARINC: Aeronautical Radio. Incorporated (2010), `http://www.aviation-ia.com/aeec/projects/cds/index.html`
3. Carrigan, G.P., Long, D., Cummings, M.L., Duffner, J.: Human Factors Analysis of Predator B Crash. In: Proceedings of AUVSI 2008: Unmanned Systems North America, San Diego, California (June 2008)
4. Cummings, M.L., Kirschbaum, A.R., Sulmistras, A., Platts, J.T.: STANG 4586 Human Supervisory Control Implications. In: Proceedings of UVS Canada Annual Conference, Montebello, Quebec, Canada (2006)
5. Cooper, J.G.: Cognitive Engineering Research Institute (June 2007), `http://www.cerici.com/documents/2007_workshop/6-1-BYU-Cooper.pdf`

6. Endsley, M.: Measurement of situation awareness in dynamic systems. Human Factors (1995)
7. Foundation, F. S. Flight Safety Digest, Alexandria, Virginia, United States (May 2005), http://flightsafety.org/fsd/fsd_may05.pdf
8. ISO: International Organization for Standardization (2000), http://www.iso.org/iso/iso_catalogue/catalogue_tc/catalogue_detail.htm?csnumber=30030
9. Lorite, S.: Diseño de interfaces de supervisi6n de vehículos aéreos no tripulados (2008), http://www.institutoidf.com/instituto/downloads/user_center_design_interfaces/Interfaces_Vehiculos_Aereos_No_Tripulados.pdf
10. Martinez, J.: AutoNAV4D. A co-simulator for Unmanned Aircraft Systems. Barcelona-Tech, Castelldefels (2008)
11. NATO: The North Atlantic Treaty Organization (2007), http://www.nato.int/structur/AC/224/standard/AEDP2/AEDP2_Documents/AEDP-02v1.pdf
12. Nimmo: Designing control rooms for humans. Control Magazine (2004)
13. Owen, D.: Air Accident Investigation, New Edition. PSL Patrick Stephens Limited, Somerset England (2001)
14. Pastor, E., Royo, P., Lopez, J., Barrado, C., Santamaria, E., Prats: Project SKY-EYE. Applying UAVs to Forest Fire Fighter Support and Monitoring. In: UAV 2007 Conference (2007)
15. Pastor, E., Lopez, J., Royo, P.: A Hardware/Software Architecture for UAV Payload and Mission Control. In: 25th Digital Avionics Systems Conference (2006)
16. Pastor, E., Lopez, J., Royo, P.: An Embedded Architecture for Mission Control of Unmanned Aerial Vehicles. In: 9th EuroMicro Conference on Digital Systems (2006)
17. Pastor, E., Prats, X., Royo, P., Delgado, L., Santamaria, E.: UAS Pilot Support for Departure, Approach and Airfield Operations. In: Proceedings of the IEEE Aerospace Conference, Montana, United States (2010)
18. Ponsa, P., Díaz, M.: Creation of an Ergonomic Guideline for Supervisory Control Interface Design. In: Harris, D. (ed.) HCII 2007 and EPCE 2007. LNCS (LNAI), vol. 4562, pp. 137–146. Springer, Heidelberg (2007)
19. Ponsa, P., Vilanova, R., Amante, B.: Human intervention and interface design in automation systems. International Journal of Computers, Communications & Control 6(1), 166–174 (2011)
20. RTCA: Radio Technical Commission for Aeronautics, and the European Organization for Civil Aviation Equipment EUROCAE (1992), http://www.do178site.com/
21. Schneiderman, B.: Designing the user interface. Strategies for effective human-computer interaction, 3rd edn. Addison-Wesley (1998)
22. Sheridan, T.B.: Telerrobotics, automation and human supervisory control. M.I.T. Press (1992)
23. Society of Automotive Engineers SAE, Unmanned Systems Technical Committee AS4 (2010), http://standards.sae.org/as5684a/
24. Strauch, B.: Investigating Human Error: Incidents, Accidents and Complex Systems. Ashgate Publishing (2002)
25. Terrence Fong, C.T.: Vehicle Teleoperation Interfaces. Autonomous Robots 11, 9–18 (2001)
26. William, T.: U.S. Military Unmanned Aerial Vehicle Mishaps: Assessment of the Role of Human Factors Using Human Factors Analysis and Classification System (HFACS) (2005), http://www.wpafb.af.mil/shared/media/document/AFD-090226-154.pdf

Remote Usability Evaluation of Mobile Web Applications

Paolo Burzacca and Fabio Paternò

CNR-ISTI, HIIS Laboratory, via G. Moruzzi 1, 56124 Pisa, Italy
{paolo.burzacca,fabio.paterno}@isti.cnr.it

Abstract. Recent proliferation of mobile devices has made it important to provide automatic support for usability evaluation when people interact with mobile applications. In this paper, we discuss some specific aspects that need to be considered in remote usability of mobile Web applications, and introduce a novel environment that aims to address such issues.

Keywords: Remote Evaluation, Logging Tools, Mobile Usability.

1 Introduction

In usability evaluation, automatic tools can provide various types of support in order to facilitate this activity and help developers and evaluators to gather various useful pieces of information.

Several approaches have been put forward for this purpose. Some tools allow users to provide feedback on the considered applications through questionnaires or reporting critical incidents or other relevant information. Other proposals have been oriented to providing some automatic analysis of the user interface implementation in order to check its actual conformance to a set of guidelines. A different approach consists in gathering information on actual user behaviour and helping evaluators in analysing it in order to identify possible usability problems.

In remote usability evaluation evaluators and users are separated in time and/or space. This is important in order to analyse users in their daily environments and decrease the costs of the evaluation by avoiding the need to use specific laboratories and to ask users to move.

The purpose of this paper is to discuss the possibilities offered by remote usability evaluation of mobile applications based on logging user interactions and supporting the analysis of such data. We describe the novel issues raised by this type of approach and provide concrete indications about how they can be addressed, in particular when Web applications are accessed through mobile devices.

In the paper we first discuss related work; next we provide a discussion of the important aspects that have to be considered when designing support for remote evaluation of mobile application; and then introduce examples of possible solutions to such issues provided by a novel version of a remote evaluation environment. Lastly, we draw some conclusions and provide indications for future work.

M. Kurosu (Ed.): Human-Computer Interaction, Part I, HCII 2013, LNCS 8004, pp. 241–248, 2013.

2 Related Work

Ivory and Hearst [1] provided a good discussion of tools for usability evaluation according to a taxonomy based on four dimensions: method class (the type of evaluation); method type (how the evaluation is conducted); automation type (the evaluation phase that is automated: capture, analysis, re-design, ...); and effort level (the type of effort required to apply the method for the evaluators and the users). In this work we plan to consider usability testing solutions based on user interactions logs, and discuss how to provide automatic support for analysis of such information and a number of visualizations to ease the identification of any usability issues. Extracting usability information from user interface events has long been considered [2], and stimulated the development of various tools for this purpose, but previous work has not been able to adequately support usability evaluation of mobile applications.

Google Analytics [3] is a widely used tool, which has not been proposed in particular for usability evaluation but can be configured to capture general and custom events at client-side, and offers a number of statistics information and reports. However, it is rather limited in terms of the number of events that it is able to capture for each session, and is not able to capture various events that only mobile devices can generate through their sensors. Model-based approaches have been used to support usability evaluation exploiting user logs. One example was WebRemUsine [4], which was a tool for remote usability evaluation of Web applications through browser logs and task models. The basic idea was to support an automatic analysis based on the comparison of the actual use of a system, represented by the logs, with the expected use described through a task model. This approach was mainly used to analyse desktop applications. It was useful to find usability problems but it also required some effort, since evaluators had first to develop a complete task model of the considered application. A version of this approach aiming to compare the designers' task model with the actual use detected through a logging of mobile applications in Windows CE mobile devices was presented in [5]. In that case the logging tool had to communicate with the operating system to detect events and track the user's activity. In this way it was also able to log events related to environmental conditions, such as noise, battery consumption, light, signal network, and position. It also contained some early attempt to graphically represent when the logged events deviate from the expected behaviour. In this paper we will discuss a different approach in which the user-generated logs will be compared with optimal logs created by the application designers in order to demonstrate the best way to perform the tasks. This approach was introduced in [6], even if that solution was limited in terms of intelligent analysis and how to represent the usability data collected.

Previous work, such as WebQuilt [7], performed logging through a dedicated proxy server able to intercepts the HTTP requests to the application servers. However, this type of approach was not able to detect local events generated by the users (e.g. clicks, zoom, scroll events), which can provide useful information in usability evaluation. WELFIT [8] is a tool that performs logging through JavaScripts that are manually included in the analysed Web pages, it is relevant to the discussion presented, even if the representations provided for the usability analysis are not easy to interpret.

W3Touch [9] is a recent tool that performs some logging of interactions with Web applications in touch-based smartphones, still through JavaScripts, and the collected information is used to assess some metrics important for usability in such devices. The two main metrics considered are related to the number of zooming events and to the missed links in touch-based interaction. According to the values obtained from the metrics the designers can apply some adaptation to the user interface considered in order to improve it.

3 Important Dimensions in Remote Evaluation of Mobile Applications

In remote evaluation based on logging tools of mobile applications we can identify three main aspects to address:

- what can be logged,
- how the information gathered can be processed,
- how the usability data can be represented for the analysis by evaluators and designers.

In this section we discuss these aspects, in particular when the evaluation focuses on Web applications accessed through mobile devices. In this case we have to consider that the context of use can be dynamic, the interaction resources (e.g. screen size) can vary in a broader range, and such devices are usually equipped with a number of sensors (GPS, accelerometer, gyroscope, ..) that can provide additional useful information about the actual user behaviour. Indeed, a logging tool for mobile applications should be able to detect any standard, touch, gestures, and accelerometer events. It should also consider form-related events (e.g., change, select, and submit), system related events, and customizable events. Such custom events are various types of composition of basic events in terms of their ordering or standard events on specific parameters (e.g. a pageview event is triggered when a specific page is shown to the user), and it should be possible to associate them with specific events names that can then be visualized in the reports.

Regarding how to support an automatic analysis of the user-generated logs various solutions are possible. In this type of processing a concrete reference point in terms of good user behaviour during the interactive session would be useful. Previous work has considered task models to represent the expected user behaviour. However, task models require some time and effort to be developed, in particular if the entire interactive application considered should be modelled. Another possibility is to use logs representing examples of good sequences of events to perform some given tasks with the user interface considered. Such logs can be created by the designers of the user interfaces. Thus, by comparing the logs representing the actual behaviour with the optimal logs it is possible to automatically identify their differences and analyse them to understand whether they are indicators of usability problems. Such differences can show user errors, which are actions not necessary for achieving the current goals or inability of the user to perform some actions or the misinterpretation of the correct navigation path. An automatic comparison between these two sequences of events can be performed in various ways, an example is the application of the Sequence Alignment Method (SAM) [10], in which the difference between sequences is given by the number of operations necessary to make them the same, where each operation has a different weight, which depends on the importance associated to it. The operations necessary to equalize two sequences are reordering, insertion, deletion. While the first involves elements that belong to both sequences, the other two address elements that appear only in one sequence.

Regarding the issues related to how to represent the relevant information in order to facilitate the identification of usability problems various options are possible as well. It is clear that a raw visualization of all the events gathered would easily generate a huge amount of events that cannot be analysed. The first aspect to consider is to provide the evaluators with tools to filter the data according to the type of event. Further filtering can be done based on the time when the events occurred. Even with this type of filtering it is still possible to gather large amount of data difficult to interpret. In order to better analyse the logged events it is thus important to understand what the user intentions were when such logs were generated. For this reason various tools ask the user to explicitly indicate what task they wanted to accomplish and even when they finished its performance. This information is usually included in the logged session and provides useful context in order to filter the events shown, to help in the interpretation, and also to provide information about task completion time. In the case there is the possibility to compare the actual logs with an optimal log then it would be important to show all of them at the same time with the possibility of lining up the sequences in such a way that important events appear lined up. Often graphical representations of the sequences of events that occurred, along with information regarding the event type, time, etc. still requires considerable effort from the evaluators who have to think about where the events occurred in the user interface. Thus, it is also important that the tools be able to provide graphically the user interface annotated with where the events occurred so that the evaluators have an immediate representation of the actual user interface state at that time, and the exact user interface part that was manipulated.

4 WUP: An Example Tool for Remote Evaluation of Mobile Web Applications

WUP is a tool that has been developed taking into account the requirements discussed in the previous section. Its new version addresses some of the limitations detected in its initial implementation [6] related to the visual representations provided for the usability analysis and the underlying processing of the data gathered.

WUP exploits a proxy server, which inserts into the accessed Web pages some JavaScripts, which are then used to log the user interactions and send such logs to the usability server. Various types of events can be detected, those related to forms, keyboards, mouse, touch, GPS, accelerometer, and semantic events. The latter group (semantic events) refers to the possibility of explicitly indicating when a certain event occurs on a specific element. These events can also be associated with pre- and post-conditions in order to better characterise them. Thus, for example, it is possible to use them to indicate when a form is submitted after all the mandatory fields have been filled in. Thus, the event is associated with clicking the button associated with sending the form data, and has preconditions indicating that that each of the mandatory input field has been filled in. This allows the tool to explicitly indicate whether and when this specific event occurs in the logs visual representations.

When evaluators want to start a remote usability study regarding a Web application, they have to indicate the list of tasks that will be proposed to the users through a dedicated panel, which is also used to indicate when the task performance starts and finishes. They can also indicate any custom events that they are interested in and which task they relate to. Moreover, evaluators can provide the environment with an example optimal log for each task, which they can create by performing what they consider the optimal sequence of actions associated with that task.

In order to support the usability analysis, various representations are provided. One is the timeline comparator (see Figure 1). It shows first the timeline associated with the optimal log, at the top, and then those corresponding to the logs generated by the various users. For each timeline the tool provides an identifier, the time when the log was created and the duration of the session, and the environment in which the log was created in terms of device, browser, and operating system.

It is possible to manipulate the list of timelines in various ways. Each can be selected, moved through drag-and-drop in order to close those that evaluators want to compare without having to be constrained by the original order, or hidden if it is not useful for the current analysis. Moreover, the timelines that are more meaningful can be added to a favourite group that can be directly accessed on demand. It is also possible to filter the types of events that are shown.

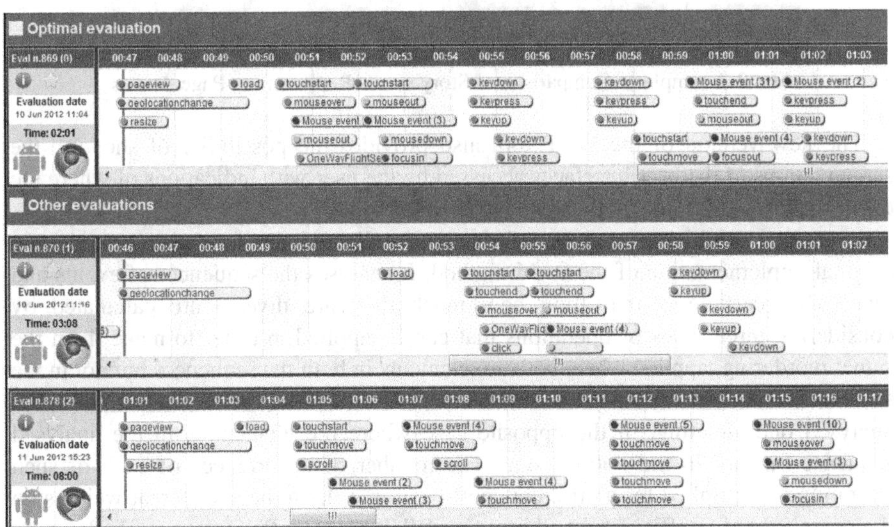

Fig. 1. Examples of Timelines Visualization

The events that appear in the timelines are identified by a label and a coloured bullet. Each event type is associated with a specific colour. For each event there are some pieces of associated information: occurrence time, the corresponding application element, and other specific information that depends on the event type. All such details appear in a text area in the bottom part of the tool user interface when the cursor hovers over the corresponding label. It is also possible to search for specific events or event types. The results of the search show only the events satisfying the query parameters. It is also possible to display in the timelines vertical bars indicating when there has been a page change in the navigation.

The tool also allows comparisons at the page level instead of the event level. Thus, it is possible to show storyboards that for each session show one element for each page accessed (see an example in Figure 2) with arrows indicating the navigation flow. For each page the visit time is reported as well. The nodes representing the navigated pages are blue if they are associated with Web pages that are not accessed in the other sessions in the comparison.

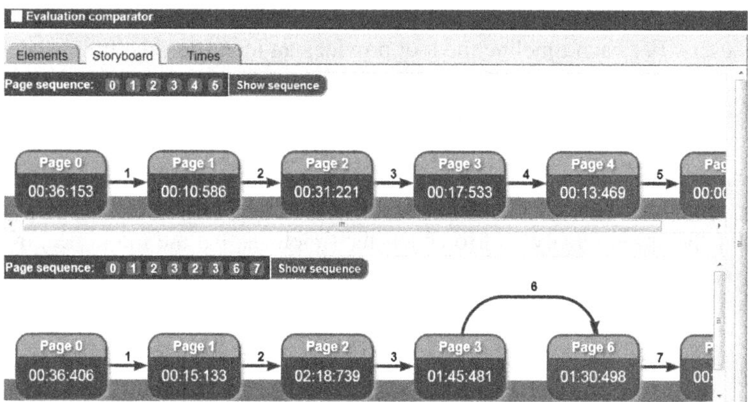

Fig. 2. Example of Comparison of Storyboards Representing Page Access

The new version of the WUP tool also provides the possibility of showing the screen dumps of the user interfaces accessed by the user with indications of where the events occurred highlighted by small red icons.

Regarding intelligent analysis of the data collected the tool also provides an original implementation of the SAM method. It analyses the sequences of events and the SAM coefficients indicating how much they are diverse are calculated by considering three types of operations that can be applied in order to make them the same: reordering, applied when there are elements in both the sequences but not in the same position, insert, when there is an element in the optimal sequence but not in the analysed one, deleting, in the opposite case where the element is in the analysed sequence but not in the optimal one. The number of occurrences of each of such operation is multiplied for a different coefficient in order to have different weights on the overall SAM coefficient. In addition, in WUP such coefficients are calculated by analysing both the sequences of events and the sequences of pages accessed, with different weights. The choice of the coefficient is customizable by the evaluator in order to indicate the aspects that they think have more or less impact in the comparison analysis. In the end, the tool calculates some values that for each user sessions provide some summary quantitative indication about how far they are from the optimal session.

We have conducted a first user test about the tool and its results. In this first test we considered two types of users: end users who carried out the remote usability test with WUP and people with some experience in usability evaluation. We considered a set of tasks to carry out on the mobile version of the Web site of an airline for this purpose. Then, we compared the usability issues identified by the evaluators though the WUP support with those really reported afterwards by the users through some questionnaires. In general, there was a good match of the problems identified that were often related to the use of link texts not sufficiently clear, excessive navigation depth, ambiguous labels associated with some commands, and forms not very clear.

A further integration that we have designed is an App for Android mobile devices, obtained through an instance of a WebView object, which is a kind of Web browser in a Java application. Then, through this browser it is possible to include the scripts for logging in the accessed Web pages. The scripts then send the logs in the format that can be exploited by our usability server for providing all the relevant visualizations to the evaluators. The advantage of this additional solution is that it does not require access through the proxy server, thus it can be faster and more secure. The disadvantage is that it is specific to a mobile platform.

5 Conclusions and Future Work

This paper provides a discussion of the issues in remote evaluation of applications accessed through mobile devices and indicates possible solutions, also reporting on experiences with a tool that has been developed for this purpose, describing its architecture, possible use and briefly reporting on example applications.

Future work will be dedicated to further increasing the underlying intelligent analysis in order to facilitate the identification of potential usability problems. We also plan to exploit the logging of some physiological sensors in order to combine the analysis of the user interactions with information about the user emotional state, and to apply the tool to a wider set of applications.

References

1. Ivory, M.Y., Hearst, M.A.: The state of the art in automating usability evaluation of user interfaces. ACM Comput. Surv. 33(4), 470–516 (2001)
2. Hilbert, D.M., Redmiles, D.F.: Extracting usability information from user interface events. ACM Comput. Surv. 32(4), 384–421 (2000)
3. Google: Google Analytics, `http://www.google.com/analytics/index.html`

4. Paganelli, L., Paternò, F.: Tools for Remote Usability Evaluation of Web Applications through Browser Logs and Task Models. Behavior Research Methods, Instruments, and Computers 35(3), 369–378 (2003)
5. Paternò, F., Russino, A., Santoro, C.: Remote Evaluation of Mobile Applications. In: Winckler, M., Johnson, H. (eds.) TAMODIA 2007. LNCS, vol. 4849, pp. 155–169. Springer, Heidelberg (2007)
6. Carta, T., Paternò, F., Santana, W.: Support for Remote Usability Evaluation of Web Mobile Applications. In: ACM SIGDOC, pp. 129–136. ACM Press, Pisa (2011)
7. Santana, V., Baranauskas, M.: Summarizing observational client-side data to reveal web usage patterns. In: SAC 2010: Proceedings ACM Symposium on Applied Computing, pp. 1219–1223. ACM Press (2010)
8. Waterson, S., Landay, J.A., Matthews, T.: In the lab and out in the wild: remote web usability testing for mobile devices. In: CHI Extended Abstracts 2002, pp. 796–797. ACM Press (2002)
9. Nebeling, M., Speicher, M., Norrie, M.C.: W3Touch: Metrics-based Web Content Adaptation for Touch. Proceedings CHI 2013, Paris (2013, to appear)
10. Hay, B., Wets, G., Vanhoof, K.: Mining Navigation Patterns Using a Sequence Alignment Method. Knowledge and Information Systems 6(2), 150–163 (2004)

Design and Implementation of ErgoIdentifier: A Tool for Automated Identification of Websites Interaction Elements

Oscar Francisco dos Santos and Marcelo Morandini

University of Sao Paulo, Brazil
{oscar.f,m.morandini}@usp.br

Abstract. The purpose of this work focuses on the development of an environment that will is called *ErgoIdentifier*. This environment is responsible for performing automatic collection of websites' interaction elements and thus, support the usability evaluation process by presenting important features and routines for future usability evaluation automatic tools. The ErgoIdentifier will use the website's implementation code to automatically identify the elements of interaction of its pages. Once identified, these interaction elements must be mapped to the same key characteristics that may influence the usability as color, exact location on the page, size and format. So, this environment can also be used by the evaluator by presenting him/her initial basis for consideration. The Human Computer Interaction, or HCI, aims to provide developers ways of designing and evaluating systems in which there is interaction between user and system. Usability can be considered as a key concept within the context of HCI and is focused on creating systems that are easy to learn and use. Therefore, it is possible to assess the quality of interactive systems according to factors that define its designers as priority. The ErgoIdentifier provides overall overviews of the evaluation processes starting with an identification of the website's source code files and the web pages architecture. These information and the features of the interaction elements must be stored in a Database for presenting special resports to the evaluator. These reports should include the features of the interaction elements, number of repetition of specific ones, such as frames, icons and links. This proposed environment is composed by the following processes: (a) Website architecture definition; (b) Interaction Elements Definition; (c) Interaction Elements Visualization; and (d) XML Files Generation. So, the ErgoIdentifier will consist of a database containing information from the pages and elements of interaction that should be used in a usability evaluation process. It also contains forms for queries characteristics of pages and elements found on the website to be viewed through a terminal where the environment is installed. They can also be obtained this information using text file formats, HTML and XML that can be used as input for tools to support usability evaluation. Also, the proposition of the ErgoIdentifier is based on a stimulus for the design and development of other usability evaluation tools that would be using it as a basis for defining the website's architecture and also to have information about each webpage that are part of the website. Concerning the webpages, it is important that all of interaction elements should be automatically recognized and identified. This will allow the usability evaluation tools to be more efficient in their

M. Kurosu (Ed.): Human-Computer Interaction, Part I, HCII 2013, LNCS 8004, pp. 249–255, 2013.

purpose as this task (interaction elements recognition) is no longer needed to be performed by the tool. We intend to develop specific tools that should present meaningful usability evaluation reports by using the ErgoIdentifier and also present this environment for the HCI community.

Keywords: Tools Usability and Interaction, User Interfaces, Ergonomics Criteria, Usability.

1 Introduction

According to the ACM (2009), the Human Computer Interaction, or HCI, aims to provide developers mechanisms and strategies for designing and evaluating systems in which there are interaction between user and system. Also according to the ACM (2009), usability as a key concept within the context of HCI, has focus on creating systems that are easy to learn and use, because with this concept is possible to assess the quality of interactive systems according to factors that define its designers as priorities.

Considering the International Organization for Standardization (ISO 9241-11, 1998), usability is the extent that a product can be used by specified users to achieve specified goals with effectiveness, efficiency and satisfaction in a specific use. Effectiveness means that the user is able to perform the desired task, efficiency refers to the time spent on task performance and satisfaction defines how the system is acceptable by users.

Although usability should be measured, verifying whether the system was produced attending good usability patterns, it needs to be evaluated and the evaluations should be done with well defined processes and methods, formerly known and tested by specialists and experts on the subject. For such methods the use of specific supporting tools can be really necessary to avoid personal aspects of the evaluators and can also cover a greater range of criteria to be evaluated.

According to Sharp et al (2007), there are two main methods for collecting data on the usability evaluation of interactive systems: tests and questionnaires of satisfaction with users. They must measure the extent to which the system meets the needs of users, i.e., the efficiency and effectiveness for the purposes that have been proposed. The goal of these measures is to provide information for those designers can increasingly improve the usability of the same. These measures, still according to Sharp et al (2007), may be obtained with quantitative metrics using performance data such as: time to complete a given task, time to complete a task from a specified time, number and type of errors per task, number of errors per unit time, frequency of use of online help or manual, number of users who commit a certain type of error and number of users who completed a task successfully, among others.

One way to facilitate and expedite these measurements is to obtain this information in an automated manner, i.e. using some mechanisms to obtain the same speeds and facilitating the work of the evaluator to the use of certain assessment tools usability as tools: Bloodhound, ISEtool, MESA, CoLiDes, CogTool, among others (Katsanos et al, 2010).

This paper presents specific features about the development of an environment that will is called ErgoIdentifier. This environment is responsible for performing automatic collection of websites' interaction elements and thus, supoport the usability evaluation process by presenting important features and routines for future usability evaluation automatic tools. The ErgoIdentifier will use the website's implementation code to automatically identify the elements of interaction of its pages. Once identified, these interaction elements must be mapped to the same key characteristics that may influence the usability as color, exact location on the page, size and format. So, this environment can also be used by the evaluator by presenting him/her initial basis for consideration. This proposed environment is composed by the following processes: (a) Website architecture definition; (b) Interaction Elements Definition; (c) Interaction Elements Visualization; and (d) XML Files Generation.

This paper is divided as the following: Section 2 presents specific concepts that were relevant for the development of the ErgoIdentifier environment; Section 3 presents the design aspects of this environment presenting some database tables (or part of them), snapshots of some interface screens and other features; Section 4 presents some conclusions that can be considered about the design and future utilization of the ErgoIdentifier; and finally Section 5 presents the bibliographic references used in the production of this paper.

2 General Concepts

Usability, as pointed by the ISO/IEC 9241, can be defined as: the *effectiveness*, *efficiency*, and *satisfaction* with which users achieve specified goals in particular environments. Effectiveness can be defined as the accuracy and completeness with which specified users can achieve specified goals in particular environments. Efficiency as the resources expended in relation to the accuracy and completeness of goals achieved. And, finally, user satisfaction as the comfort and acceptability of the work system to its users and other people affected by its use [2]. Specifically, some web sites usability evaluation techniques use previous evaluations approaches that produce qualitative reports, which might lead to subjectivity problems.

So, evaluating is one of the main stages of the design development process and aim to certify if the interface is according with the specification and whether it allows users to perform their task with efficiency, effectiveness and satisfaction, i.e., with high levels of usability. The evaluation activities should be performed in all stages of usability engineering such as analysis, development and evaluation. So, specific techniques that are appropriated for each stage were developed, such as usability inspection and usability tests (Cybis et al., 2010).

Usability can be measured during user interactions with the system and evaluated by evaluators and/or inspectors that may judge how well the user interface aspects are, *a priori*, fitted to users, tasks and environments. In doing so, they judge the *ergonomics* of that user interface. Usability and ergonomics are linked to a cause-effect relationship. The more ergonomic (or fitted) the interface is the higher is the level of usability it can afford to its users [8].

Methods aimed to measure usability (usability tests) are known to be usually expensive and complex [8]. Alternatively, ergonomics of the user interfaces can be evaluated or inspected faster and at lower costs. A simple differentiation between *evaluations* and *inspections* can be established based on the type of the knowledge applied to the judgments involved with both techniques. Evaluators apply mainly implicit knowledge they accumulated from study and experience, while inspectors apply primarily the explicit knowledge supported by documents, such as checklists. Inspectors cannot produce fully elaborated or conclusive diagnosis, but their diagnoses are comparatively coherent and generally obtained at low cost.

2.1 Support for the Information Collection from Websites

The ErgoIdentifier is graphically presented on Figure 1 that shows a general overview of all the processes involved in this environment starting with the website's source files identification that contains the information about the web pages, storing not Just these information in a database but also the web pages structure and all the interaction elements presented on each one of them.

Having these information, the ErgoIdentified generates XML (standard markup language) files that can be used as entries for usability evaluation supporting tools and may also be used by the usability evaluators to perform specific evaluations based on questionnaires or ckecklists. An Extensible Markup Language (XML) is a markup language that defines a set of rules for encoding documents in a format that is both human-readable and machine-readable. It is defined in the XML 1.0 Specification produced by the W3C [9], and several other related specifications, all free-to-use standards. The design goals of XML emphasize simplicity, generality, and usability over the internet. Although the design of XML focuses on documents, it is widely used for the representation of arbitrary data structures, for example in web services. Many application programming interfaces (APIs) have been developed to aid software developers with processing XML data, and several schema systems exist to aid in the definition of XML-based languages.

The environment ErgoIdentifier comprises several processes which are:

Identification of the Source File and Write HTML Page Site. This process reads the page's HTML source file in question and writes it to a text file and later in a database, where they will be asked to research all the information on the elements and attributes assigned to them.

Identification of Interaction Elements and Attributes of Each. This process reads the source HTML file saved in the database and makes the research of interaction elements within it such as links, frames, buttons and images, and also all the attributes defined for each of these elements that may have some influence on the usability of the site and saves them in the database for later retrieval and delivery tools for usability evaluation.

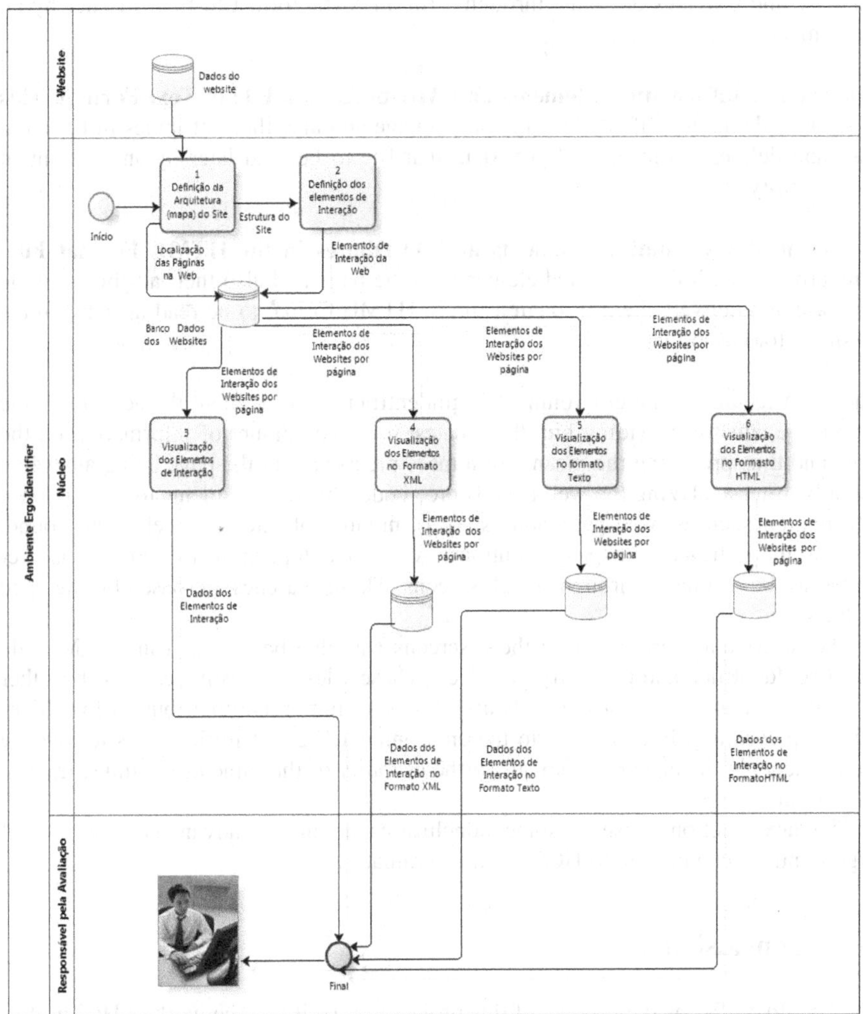

Fig. 1. ErgoIdentifier Structure

Visualization of the Interaction of Elements and Their Attributes. This process reads the identified elements on the page and also their attributes in the database and available through the same set of forms in HTML using PHP, also identifying the meaning thereof, to facilitate the analysis by evaluating usability.

Provision of Information Elements and Attributes in the XML Format File. This process reads the identified elements on the page and also their attributes in the database and provides the same through a file in XML format to be read later by an assessment tool usability.

Provision of Information Elements and Attributes in a File in Text Format. This process reads the identified elements on the page and also their attributes in the database and delivers them through a text format file to be read later by an assessment tool usability.

Provision of Information Elements and Attributes in the HTML Format File. This process reads the identified elements on the page and also their attributes in the database and delivers them through a file in HTML format to be read later by an assessment tool usability.

The main feature of the environment Ergoidentifier is to facilitate the activity of the usability evaluator providing him the greatest possible amount of information on the page and thus providing the means for a more precise about the page being analyzed. Initially, after analyzing the web page source code, this environment stores important information such as: web page address (url), number of interaction elements found, such as links, frames, images or buttons. After this step, these information is presented to the evaluator through search screens. These searches are based on the page addresses.

The information presented on these screens can also be obtained in a .XML file that ErgoIdentifier automatically produces. These files are easily readable by other usability evaluation supporting tools and this is an important contribution ErgoIdentifier is presenting. In this scenario the environment Ergo Identifier seeks to identify the elements in the page that may affect the usability of the same as the links, frames, buttons and images.

The next section presents some conclusions about the advantages the use of ErgoIdentifier can present to HCI usability evaluators.

3 Conclusion

The ErgoIdentifier as the product of this project will facilitate the work of HCI usability evaluators, since it is expected that its use may produce important data according to the information found on the pages of websites – more specifically, according to the interactions elements presented on each page of the website under evaluation.

Using this environment may be accomplished in various ways, namely by referring elements found on the website using screens on a terminal where the environment is installed, and also receiving information elements using text files and XML format that can be employed as entry into tools to support usability evaluation.

The proposal is that it is a stimulus for other solutions that may be developed or updated and, thus, facilitate the work of the usability evaluators, making it more transparent and less subject to errors, contemplating, yet, increasingly, the characteristics to be evaluated. Another aspect to be considered is that the ErgoIdentifier may support the production of direct evaluation mechanisms, more precisely supporting the questionnaires or checklists production, according to the characteristics of the elements and found that the final assessment of the usability of website pages is the responsibility of the evaluator.

Finally, it is relevant to inform that the Ergo Identifier was not designed to replace the assessment instruments usability of websites, but basically it supports this assessment process facilitating the work of evaluators in the search for interaction elements and their characteristics that may somehow influence usability.

Acknowledgment. Financial Supported by FAPESP.

References

1. ACM. Sigchi Report, New York (2009), Disponível em: `http://sigchi.org/cdg` (acesso em Maio de 15 de, 2012)
2. BIZAGI LMTD. (2012), Disponível em: `http://www.bizagi.com` (acesso em Maio de 15 de, 2012)
3. ISO 9241-11. Ergonomic requirements for office work with visual display terminals (VDTs). Part 11 — Guidelines for specifying and measuring usability. International Organization for Standardization, Genève (1998)
4. Katsanos, C., Tselios, N., Avouris, N.: International Journal on Artificial Intelligence Tools 19, 755–781 (2010)
5. Nielsen, J.: Usability Engineering. Academic Press, Boston (1993)
6. Patton, R.: Software Testing. Sams Publishing, Indianapolis (2006)
7. Sharp, H., Rogers, Y., Preece, J.: Interaction Design: beyond human-computer interaction. Wiley, England (2007)
8. Scapin, D.L., Bastien, J.M.C.: Ergonomic Criteria for Evaluating the Ergonomic Quality of Interactive Systems. Behaviour and Information Technology 16(4/5) (1997)
9. World Wide Web Consortium's (W3C) Web Accessibility Initiative, `http://www.w3c.com` (accessed on January 2013)

A Self-Evaluation Tool for Quantitative User Research within the digital.me Project

Andreas Schuller[1], Rafael Giménez[2], and Fabian Hermann[1]

[1] Fraunhofer-Institute for Industrial Engineering, Stuttgart, Germany
{andreas.schuller,Fabian.Hermann}@iao.fraunhofer.de
[2] Barcelona Digital Centre Tecnològic, Barcelona, Spain
rgimenez@bdigital.org

Abstract. For upcoming validations within the di.me project, the technical evaluation components will be an important instrument for monitoring overall key usage indicators and serve as the basis for the further analysis of usage data. Consolidated findings acquired from the evaluation components shall serve as the basis for further improvements on the developed clients and overall di.me system. This paper states a list of related requirements as well as a technical overview of the employed system.

Keywords: Quantitative user research, Self-Evaluation, User Feedback, User Research, Usability, User Experience, Requirements.

1 Introduction

The self-evaluation system as described here is targeted to enable the gathering of relevant client usage data for upcoming validations within the project. In particular, this shall address validations that might involve larger usage numbers and a setting, which cannot be directly controlled by any of the project partners. The acquired data will serve as the basis for evaluation and the measurement of key indicators regarding usability and user experience. There are two di.me clients developed, a web application and an Android application for mobile devices. Both clients are supported by the *Self-Evaluation Tool.*

For the *Self-Evaluation Tool* (*SET*), a number of requirements have been collected. Since the di.me software is especially concerned with safeguarding the user's privacy and personal data, there have been special considerations for related functions. All gathered requirements are listed in section two "System Requirements Analysis".

As stated in for the project MyExperience, Fröhlich et al. [1] mention two important factors of such a *Self-Evaluation Tool*, which are also central for the system employed in di.me:

1. Implicit logging of device usage, user context and environment context.
2. Explicit questionnaires to collect subjective user feedback in the particular situation.

M. Kurosu (Ed.): Human-Computer Interaction, Part I, HCII 2013, LNCS 8004, pp. 256–264, 2013.

For the shown di.me system, the decision has been made to also divide these two aspects on a technical level. Implicit interaction is using the existing di.me architecture to gather this data on a customized di.me *Evaluation Server Service*; explicit data acquisition is employing an existing open source application. A detailed description is given in section three "Overview of the employed system".

1.1 Considerations of Related Tools

For the gathering of implicit user data, there are some frameworks and established software solutions on the market that were considered. A well-known analysis tool is offered by Google Analytics [2]. There exist versions for analyzing both web sites and mobile Android applications. However, the usage of Google Analytics servers would not be suited for the di.me project's decentralized server architecture. Mozilla offers its own test suite, Mozilla Test Lab Test Pilot [3] where users can get involved in testing future versions of a browser. The Mozilla Test Lab is strongly related to Mozilla's related projects and does not support usage by external projects. Another similar project is the open source project Piwic [4], which offers steadily growing features, but does not support native Android applications at the moment.

2 System Requirements Analysis

Derived from the aforementioned main objectives of the evaluation tool, the following table illustrates several derived requirements. The right column illustrates how these requirements are met by the developed technical solution.

Table 1. General requirements table

REQUIREMENT	DEVELOPMENT PROTOTYPE
Allowing participating di.me users to *send interaction data* and system status information for evaluation purposes to a consortium *Evaluation Server* on a voluntary basis.	The amount of usage data sent can be set up in the client. According to the settings, the raw data sent contains different sets of user and interaction data (see table 2 for details).
Presenting participating di.me users *short questionnaires or single questions in particular use situations* (like e.g. first system use, closing of the system, use of interesting functionality, at particular time points).	Online questionnaires can be filled out by the user at all times, independently by the running di.me system. Although for the moment this does not allow for automated triggering of questionnaires, special user groups can be addressed explicitly through the di.me central web-portal during beta tests. The possibility of automating the allocation of questionnaires according to user behavior is planned for future releases.

Table 1. (*continued*)

Allowing participating di.me users to *send their feedback* on the di.me system, on specific functionality, or on particular use situations.	The developed di.me portal and community websites will allow for a general contact, allowing the users to give their feedback to the system or towards a particular functionality.

Additionally, for the technical development of the *SET* functionality, these key decisions have been taken:

- Usage data will be sent along with REST calls to the *Personal Server* (*PS*): this means that the interaction recording functionalities will rely on the same communication protocol as for the transmission of other data.
- All data reaching the *Evaluation Server* will have to pass the security infrastructure of the *PS*. If this is enabled by the user, this data is being sent in intervals to an *Evaluation Server*.
- The data will be anonymized by the *Personal Server* or contain no personally traceable data: Since all usage data has to pass the *PS*, it will be justified that the data is anonymized and obfuscated there. Therefore the *Evaluation Server* has no possibility to analyze mass clear user data.
- Evaluation questionnaires will be conducted online, through an external tool: since there are a multitude of questionnaire systems available, the decision had been taken to employ an existing open source tool for this purpose.

2.1 Data Privacy Levels

The following sections will give an impression, in which ways the usage of the *SET* can be utilized for evaluating the developed di.me system prototypes. The following table gives an overview of relevant usage data, a potential privacy classification, and

Table 2. Distinction of interaction data by privacy levels

PRIVACY LEVEL	INTERACTION DATA	ANALYZED INDICATORS
no or little concerns	• Timestamp of transaction • Reference to current client type (mobile or desktop) • Reference to current View on the UI (encoded) • Reference to concrete action taken on the UI (encoded)	• Average Time to follow interaction sequences (e.g. setting up group, adding different users) • Average number of interaction steps for conducting certain functions
	• Reference to particular call made (e.g. new group or changed existing group) without any content	• Preferred ways of interaction (if there are more than one)

Table 2. *(continued)*

More detailed usage data but anonymized, not directly traceable	• Reference to current client type and machine (e.g. Phone Version, Browser type) • Reference to situational or contextual data (current place, current situation encoded) • Encoded Identifier of current user without any clear information (to distinguish the same user) • Obfuscated payload of transmitted REST-call • Generally personal, but not directly identifiable information (e.g. Gender, Birthday)	• Average number of different objects per type (e.g. average number of groups) • Statistics about technology used • user groups (e.g. old – young, male – female) • Different general behaviours according to different situations or places • Detection of covariance between situations and actions taken • Detection of longer sequences of actions taken (long-term usage, cycles of usage intensiveness, etc.) • Detection of similarities between users at certain events
Personally traceable data, potential privacy concerns	• Identifier of the user linked with clear identification information (e.g. Name or Nickname) • Reference to concrete situations and places • Plain text payload of transmitted REST-call	• Reconstruction of movement profiles at events • Reconstruction of time profiles of individual users • Linking between different contacts, deducing knowledge from concrete personal networks

examples of possible relevant higher level indicators that could be deduced from the raw data. The di.me *SET* only collects data from the first and second privacy levels where there is no directly traceable data involved. Furthermore, approval has to be given by the user for both levels explicitly as *opt-in*.

3 Overview of the Employed System

Relevant software parts of the *SET*-components are within the di.me clients and in the di.me (service) gateway, which includes a service adapter particularly for the *Evaluation Server*. On the client, user interaction data is being tracked if the functionality is enabled by the user. Further settings for information tracking can be adjusted.

The transmitted data is stored within the *Personal Servers* temporarily, and then sent anonymously to the *Evaluation Server* in fixed time intervals. The *Evaluation Server* is able to permanently store data from multiple *Personal Servers*. For a more thorough overview of the complete di.me system, see [7].

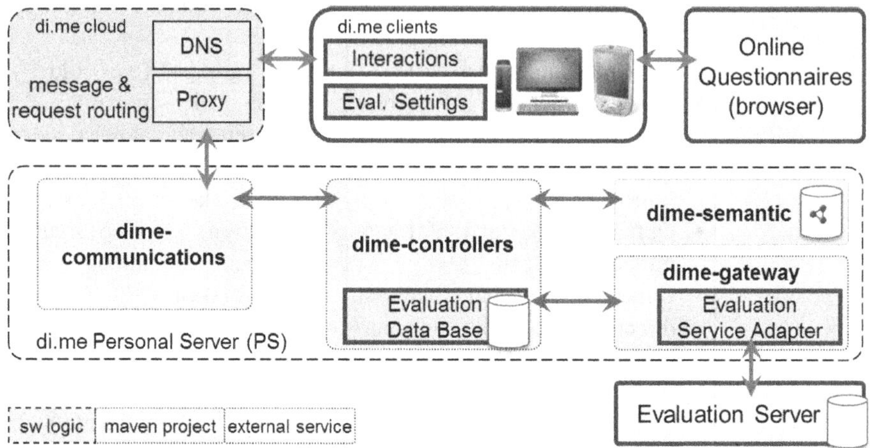

Fig. 1. Relevant components in the di.me system architecture for the *SET* are marked with a thick border (red)

Online questionnaires are stored on a different external sever, running the open source implementation of Limesurvey [5]. These questionnaires are accessed through the client's browsers directly and not through the *PS*. The data transmitted through the online questionnaires (which is of course voluntary and where only provided answers are sent) is completely separated from the tracking data, and therefore direct linking between these two data sets is being avoided.

Since the direct proposal of questionnaires towards the user is covered externally through the respective browser on the client platform, the functional documentation describes the set up and communication of the interaction tracking of the users.

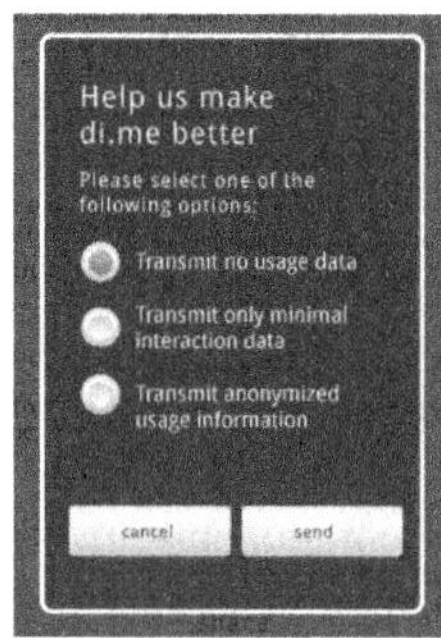

Fig. 2. Early concept screenshot of the mobile user interface showing different options for the transmission of interaction usage data

3.1 Communication through the di.me REST-API

Evaluation calls are routed through the REST-API interface, following the technical documentation. The decision had been taken to introduce this as a separate call for this (in contrast to providing additional evaluation information with each REST-call), in order to keep the communication flexible and independent of future changes of the API. The payload is using the same standard envelope for the transmission of the data, as most of the other sent objects. For readability purposes, the standard payload envelope is omitted in the following example:

```
"guid":"<Unique ID for reference of this call>"
"timestamp": 1326386999037,
"client":<di.me mobile, desktop...>,
"view": <REFERENCE TO VIEW>,
"action": <REFERENCE TO ACTION TAKEN>,
"currPlace": <OPTIONAL CONTEXT REFERENCE>,
"currSituation": <OPTIONAL SITUATION REFERENCE>
```

The *client* points to the type of di.me client that was used. *View* and *action* references are described in the following section. The References to current context information (*currPlace* and *currSituation*) are optional, according to the user settings.

3.2 Encoding of Views and Actions

For the storing different views and the according actions, an encoding scheme has been set up. The following image contains a showcase example of the general structure of the encoding for the mobile client. References are named according to their position within the information architecture. The naming convention takes into account the initially chosen element (e.g. *people*) and also the activated tab (e.g. *people.groups* and *people.all*).

Fig. 3. Example drill down through different view hierarchies on the mobile client, numbers indicate the clicked or touched areas

For the general encoding of different view areas, the descriptive string is following the actual structure within the UI. Examples of referencing views according to the scheme would be:

- `people.groups.detail` (the detail view of the selected group)
- `data.databox.detail.resource` (an individual resource of a particular databox or folder)

The coding scheme resembles a kind of navigation breadcrumb as would be used in web sites. All references are strongly related to the class or package identifiers used in the client's code. Therefore, the identifiers between mobile and web-UI can differ slightly.

The references of the functions executed by the user can take on a related name to the caption within the UI (e.g. "*new*", "*add*", "*delete*") and can be the same for a number of screens. Using this naming scheme, the combination of client reference with view and action reference are unique for each chosen UI-function. This way, user preferences for alternative ways of executing the same function can be detected.

3.3 Tracking Explicit User Feedback

Limesurvey is an online evaluation tool and server, which provides the possibility to create and configure online questionnaires and users to register and complete online surveys. It offers a rich set of options and configurations for editing and setting up questionnaires (e.g. different question types, multi-language support, and unlimited number of participants). The tool has been used in many previous studies within scientific and industry-related projects.

Fig. 4. Screenshot of a test questionnaire on a mobile setup

Rationale for Using Limesurvey

Apart from previous experiences of using the Limesurvey tool, there are certain particular characteristics that speak for the application within this scope of the di.me project because it meets the associated requirements:

- Both the web-application and the hosting server are under an open source license. A server can be easily set up for this purpose by the project partners. No other unauthorized party has access to this server.
- Anonymized questionnaires: Questionnaires can be set up without storing any personally identifiable information from the users (unless users provide this information by themselves).
- A multitude of different question types are pre-set within the application.
- Stylesheets can be employed to include a certain look and feel to adapt to the other user interfaces. Increasing mobile support.

For the usage in the di.me project, Limesurvey seems as optimal option regarding open source solutions, and servers allowing for self-hosting. This way, the data flows can still be controlled and matched within the overall di.me system, and the project can benefit from the various features already implemented and offered.

4 Conclusion

Within this paper it was tried to show some of the essential requirements, fundamentals and an initial technical overview of some aspects of the implemented *SET* in the di.me project

Although no real usage data could be acquired with the *SET* yet, first implementations and prototypical test runs have yielded to first promising results. As for the planned di.me validations and beta tests, the first aim is to robustly collect the most general information, and iteratively include more sophisticated usage data later on. Further publications on the analyzed usage data and derived conclusions for the di.me system and possible improvements of the *SET*, are planned.

As described by Sellner [6] there is the possibility to expand the *Self-Evaluation Tool* suite by (mobile) widgets, and to increase the technical support of the *SET* to other user research methods (like a usage diary with possibilities to include rich media like videos). Also, the automated triggering of particular questionnaires according to different interactions or user groups is currently being evaluated. With the inclusion of these additional aspects and further improvements, the *SET* will allow for more and more autonomous and sophisticated analysis of usage data in diverse application areas.

Acknowledgments. This work is funded by the European Commission under the Seventh Framework Program FP7/2007-2013 (digital.me – ICT-257787).

References

1. Fröhlich, J., et al.: MyExperience: a system for in situ tracing and capturing of user feedback on mobile phones. In: Proceedings of the 5th International Conference on Mobile Systems, Applications and Services (MobiSys 2007). ACM, New York (2007)
2. Google, Google Analytics, https://developers.google.com/analytics/
3. Mozilla Labs, Mozilla Test Pilot, https://testpilot.mozillalabs.com/
4. Piwic Project Team, Piwic Open Source Web Analytics, http://piwik.org/
5. LimeSurvey Project Team, Carsten Schmitz: LimeSurvey: An Open Source survey tool LimeSurvey Project Hamburg, Germany (2013), http://www.limesurvey.org
6. Sellner, T.: Konzeption und prototypische Entwicklung eines kontextbezogenen Evaluierungssystems für mobile Anwendungen. Master-Thesis Fakultät Informatik Studiengang Medien- und Kommunikationsinformatik Hochschule Reutlingen (2011)
7. Thiel, S., et al.: A Requirements-Driven Approach Towards Decentralized Social Networks. In: Park, J.J.(J.H.), Leung, V.C.M., Wang, C.-L., Shon, T. (eds.) Future Information Technology, Application, and Service. LNEE, vol. 164, pp. 709–718. Springer, Netherlands (2012)

Priming Categorization in a Card Sort

Camie Steinhoff and Jeremiah D. Still

Missouri Western State University, Saint Joseph, MO, USA
{csteinhoff1,jstill2}@missouriwestern.edu

Abstract. When using the card sorting technique, the goal of a user experience researcher is to determine the user's expected information architecture. Card sorting is a knowledge elicitation method where users are given labeled cards and are asked to place them into groups. This method is commonly used to determine a natural navigation structure for a group of users. We examine the impact of priming, an implicit memory effect in which exposure to a stimulus influences response to a later stimulus, on this popular user-centered design method. A control group did the card sort only, while the experimental group watched a short presentation before performing their card sorts. The dependent measure was the percentage of agreement of each card sort against the *typical sort*. The primed group sort was significantly more similar to the typical response than the control group. This study provides evidence that card sorting can be modulated by priming.

Keywords: Evaluation methods and techniques, Human Centered Design and User Centered Design, Card Sorting, Priming, Knowledge elicitation.

1 Introduction

Card sorting is a user-centered design technique where users are given labeled cards and are asked to sort them into groups. This method is commonly used to determine a natural navigation structure for a group of users. We examine the impact of priming on this popular knowledge elicitation method. If card sorting is affected by a simple priming manipulation, there could be considerable implications for effective use of this technique.

1.1 Card Sorting

Websites are filled with large amounts of information, which users must navigate through making their search tasks difficult. According to Usability.gov, when seeking information on a website, 60% of the time people cannot find what they are looking for [26]. In order to provide better navigation for users, information needs to be organized appropriately. According to Pirolli and Card [19], users ought to be viewed as information foragers (a.k.a., infomavores). They navigate through information trying to find a familiar scent or "good scent", which correctly leads them to what they are searching for. Website links have labels that are semantically related to content on the

M. Kurosu (Ed.): Human-Computer Interaction, Part I, HCII 2013, LNCS 8004, pp. 265–272, 2013.

target page. Thus, labels carry a scent of the linked content. Weak or misleading scents produce indecision (e.g., slow click through), frustration (e.g., do not continue along the link chain), and confusion (e.g., follow multiple links on a single page) for our informavore users. However, providing a good scent leads to more efficient and accurate navigation. Effective information architecture is built with a broad, shallow structure. The top levels must provide scent for all levels down the link chain. This is a tricky design task, but appropriate web page groupings can be easily determined through the employment of a card sorting methodology.

Card sorting is a technique used to see how people categorize information; the results are used to infer users' navigation expectations. In the task, participants are given various cards with information on them and asked to group them. Although target users are typically presented with text, pictures and objects can also be placed on cards [21]. There are two major types of card sorts. In an open card sort the participants are asked to write their own titles for each of the groups, while in a closed card sort titles are provided [8, 24]. This grouping procedure ought to help designers determine a familiar information structure for their users, rather than depending on their own life experiences. While card sorting has clear value, it is subject to shortcomings. Miller [15] examined some of these issues revealing that the number of categories used in the card sort, the distribution of cards and sample selection methods can affect its performance. Findings like these raise questions about what else could harm or improve the performance of this popular knowledge elicitation method.

There are several ways to analyze the results from a card sort. We present a few commonly used methods. The *edit distance technique* [5] compares the similarity of card sorts against each other based on the smallest number of card moves to make the sorts identical. Using the *pathfinder* [25], a network of links are used to represent cards that were grouped together with each link reflecting the weight of the relationship between the cards. In contrast, Hudson [9] describes how *quality of fit* can provide additional information from a card sort. When performing in a card sort, participants are sometimes instructed to omit a card if it does not fit anywhere. Interestingly, Hudson observed people were reluctant to omit cards. One way to capture this reluctance is to ask participants to assign a "quality of fit" score to each item based on how well it fit into the group. These scores were used to strengthen how well an individual card fit into the whole card sort by averaging the scores of that card and including confidence of the placements.

In addition to physical card sorting, there are online versions which we have found to be easier to employ. These online tools appear to streamline traditional methods and offer built-in analyzes [3]. The EZSort tool uses Usort to group cards by direct manipulation and EZCalc software to perform analysis [6]. Optimal Sort [18] shows results in a similarity matrix, dendogram, and a participant-centric analysis. The participant-centric analysis specifically tests the participants' card sorts against each other's to find the most acceptable top submissions. UXPunk's Websort [27] shows results as category summaries, tree graph, categories by items matrix, and items by items matrix.

The user experience literature contains many applications of card sorting. Some applications include: improved web navigation, prioritization of information, measurement for learning, and classification of problems. When Google AdWorks Help Center was restructuring their website, a card sort containing over 500 cards was used. After their website redesign users found information faster and with fewer errors [16]. A card sort and an informal one-on-one interview protocol were used to develop the loyalty program for Wells Fargo. Participants grouped cards that represented purchase types (clothes, groceries, vacation, etc.) into categories and subcategories and marked their top 10 cards that would encourage them to join. This card sort allowed them to create their first loyalty program that provides maximum incentives to users by taking advantage of both occasional luxuries and everyday necessities [13]. The way cards are sorted can also be used as a quantitative measure of learning outcomes [e.g., 7]. When using the same one-word programming-related cards in a sort they found statically significant differences distinguishing novices from graduates of their computer science department. Being able to sort the cards in several meaningful ways corresponded with participants' knowledge acquisition in the field. Card sorting can also be used to understand and classify problems. A usability evaluation compared four New Zealand university online library catalogues. There were too many problems detected to easily determine a solution. Interestingly, by using a card sort, they were able to understand and classify the problems [28].

1.2 Priming

Priming describes the implicit memory effect in which exposure to a stimulus influences response to a later stimulus [10]. To prime a card sort, the researchers must influence how participants organize the cards without their explicit realization of the influence. Nisbett and Wilson [17] found that participants in experiments often misjudge the logic behind their thought processes. Bargh, Chen and Burrows [1] experiment used priming and found participants were unaware of the fact that had been influenced. Participants were primed with either a neutral, polite, or rude word list and then taken to a room where two facilitators were deep in conversation and ignored them. The proportion of interrupters from each group was related to the word list they had been given with individuals in the "rude" group being faster to interrupt than those in the "polite" group.

After priming, information is retrieved from memory for use. The retrieval theory of priming in memory "assumes that a prime and target are combined at retrieval into a compound cue that is used to access memory. If the representations of the prime and target are associated in memory, the match is greater than if they are not associated, and this greater match facilities the response to the target" [20, p. 385]. Activation theories of priming propose that exposure to a prime activates the conceptual representation of the prime; that activation persists for a given amount of time allowing the concept to be accessed more quickly in the future if the same concept or a related concept is encountered. From either perspective, priming may directly influence the ease of retrieval during a knowledge elicitation task like a card sort.

Priming can affect relatively simple cognitive processes as well as more complex processes; priming can occur for individual letters, words, semantic structure, concepts, decision making, and physical actions. As an example of the scope of priming, consider the effects of priming on creativity. If given samples before completing a generative task (e.g., create something novel), participants will demonstrate less creativity, tending to adopt features that were shared across the samples into their own creations [14, 23].

A card sort is the visual representation of how an individual mentally perceives the categorization [12, 22]. "Categories are not 'out there in the real world,' external to people. Rather, mental representations depend on factors specific to each person including experience in the world, perception, imaging capabilities, and motor capabilities" [11, p. 284]. Participants in cards sorts are given the instruction to organize the information using a "feels right approach" [2]. Priming of categorization would change how participants' feel the cards should be grouped. Chi and Koeske [4] examined the relationship of interlinking networks of information – the subject was dinosaurs – and how easily the information was remembered. The networks were created using two tasks, production and a clue game, to elicit the participant's prior dinosaur knowledge. Mapping the semantic network was done using the follow links: dinosaur-dinosaur, dinosaur-property, and nine-categories based on general knowledge of dinosaurs. They found that the higher interlinking and better structured network of dinosaurs was more easily remembered and retained over a year later than the less structured network

The ease with which it seems one can be primed, lead to the question of whether participants can be primed to organize cards a certain way. For example, could recently presented marketing material like commercials or brochures prime a user's card sort? If so, does this priming statistically impact their behavior? Card sorting was developed to focus on how people really think when designing a user interface, but priming could influence those results in an unnatural manner.

2 Methods

Ninety undergraduates participated for course credit. The card sort contained 40 items that participants sorted into nine groups for a fictional zoo website. A control group did the card sort only, while the experimental group watched a short presentation before performing their card sorts. The card sorts were completed using WebSort.net, an online card sorting tool that allows participants to drag and drop each item into the different groups. A sample sort is shown in Figure 1.

The priming presentation consisted of a series of slides that contained picture representations of the cards the participant was about to sort. Figure 2 provides an example of a slide in the presentation that shows pictures of a wedding, cocktail party, birthday party, family reunion, and catered food to implicitly suggest these items are associated with each together.

The dependent measure was the percentage of agreement of each card sort against the *typical sort*. This measure allows us to capture the impact on group agreement variability. The typical sort was determined by conducting a frequency count of card categorization across all participants. The category a card was placed in with the most frequency was determined to be the "typical" sort for that card.

Plan Your Visit
Zoo Calendar
Hours
Zoo Etiquette
Hotels/Lodging
Guided Tours
Parking
Admission
Directions
Zoo Map

Teacher's Lounge
Request a School Assembly
Wildlife Sponsorship Program
Planning a Fieldtrip

Kid's Corner
Youth Day Camps
Little Critter Kid's Club
Printable Coloring Pages

Habits
Safari Park
Desert Dome
Australian Outback
Scott's Aquarium

Media Outreach
Like us on Facebook
Press Releases
Follow us on Twitter
Zoo Blog

Animals
Birds
Amphibians
Reptiles
Fish
Mammals

Zoo Extras
Realtime ZooCam
Photo Gallery Archive
ZooMAX Theater
Animal Keeper Chats

Events
Cocktail Parties
Family Reunion
Birthday Parties
Zoo-Nique Catering
Weddings

Give to the Zoo
Careers
Donate Today
Volunteer

Fig. 1. Representation of a participant's card sort

Fig. 2. Sample slide from the priming presentation

3 Results

This experiment utilized a between-subjects experimental design. The percentages of agreement were compared using an independent samples *t*-test. The primed group ($M = .83$, $SEM = .014$) sort results were significantly more similar to the typical response than sort results for the control group ($M = .78$, $SEM = .018$); $t(88) = 2.499$, $p < .05$. Therefore, priming was found to reduce variability within a card sort. Not only does this demonstrate potential card to category changes, but it can give researchers a false sense of security as most participants categorize the cards in the same way.

4 Conclusion

Card sorting essentially ask participants to sort labeled cards into groups. This method is used to visually represent a natural navigation structure for a group of participants. The goal of card sorting is to determine participants' natural expectations, but priming could affect participant card sorting independent of the expectations they otherwise might have had. This study examines how priming possibly impacts participants' card sorting behavior.

We provide evidence that a card sort can be primed. Card sorting is intended to capture natural expectations. However, we showed that priming decreases card sorting effectiveness by nudging participants toward a typical response. From a practical perspective, this means that when designers introduce their company, build scenarios, or creating orientation scripts they need to be careful not to prime participants' responses to the upcoming task. Therefore, we need to be careful not to decrease the effectiveness of our card sorts through unintentional priming.

References

1. Bargh, J.A., Chen, M., Burrows, L.: Automaticity of social behavior: Direct effects of trait construct and stereotype activation on action. Journal of Personality and Social Psychology 71(2), 230–244 (1996), doi:10.1037/0022-3514.71.2.230
2. Brucker, J.: Playing with a bad deck: the caveats of card sorting as a web site redesign tool. Journal of Hospital Librarianship 10(1), 41–53 (2010), doi:10.1080/15323260903458741
3. Bussolon, S., Russi, B., Missier, F.D.: Online card sorting: As good as the paper version. In: Proceedings of the 13th European Conference on Cognitive Ergonomics: Trust and Control in Complex Socio-Technical Systems (2006), doi:10.1145/1274892.1274912
4. Chi, M.T.H., Koeske, R.: Network representation of a child's dinosaur knowledge. Developmental Psychology 19, 29–39 (1983)
5. Deibel, K., Anderson, R., Anderson, R.: Using edit distance to analyze card sorts. Expert Systems 22(3), 121–128 (2005)
6. Dong, J., Shirely, M., Waldo, P.: A user input and analysis tool for information architecture. In: Proceedings of the CHI 2001 Extended Abstracts on Human Factors in Computing Systems (2001), doi:10.1145/634067.634085

7. Fossum, T., Haller, S.M.: A new quantitative assessment tool for computer science programs. In: Proceedings of the 10th Annual SIGCSE Conference on Innovation and Technology in Computer Science Education (2005), doi:10.1145/1151954.1067489
8. Gaffney, G.: What is Card Sorting? Information & Design (2000), http://www.infodesign.com.au/ftp/CardSort.pdf (retrieved October 28, 2011)
9. Hudson, W.: Playing your cards right: getting the most from card sorting for navigation design. Interactions 12(5), 56–58 (2005), doi:10.1145/1082369.1082410
10. Johnston, W.A., Dark, V.J.: Selective attention. Annual Review of Psychology 37, 43–75 (1986)
11. Lakoff, G.: Women, Fire and Dangerous Things: What Categories Reveal about the Mind. University of Chicago Press, Chicago (1987)
12. Maiden, N.M., Hare, M.M.: Problem domain categories in requirements engineering. International Journal of Human-Computer Studies 49(3), 281–304 (1998), doi:10.1006/ijhc.1998.0206
13. Makoski, D.: Vacations or groceries? Purchase modeling and loyalty programs. In: Proceedings of the 2003 Conference on Designing for User Experiences (2003), doi:10.1145/997078.997086
14. Marsh, R.L., Bink, M.L., Hicks, J.L.: Conceptual priming in a generative problem-solving task. Memory & Cognition 27(2), 355–363 (1999)
15. Miller, C.: Item sampling for information architecture. In: Proceedings of the 2011 Annual Conference on Human Factors in Computing Systems (2011), doi:10.1145/1978942.1979264
16. Nakhimovsky, Y., Schusteritsch, R., Rodden, K.: Scaling the card sort method to over 500 items: restructuring the Google AdWorks Help Center. In: CHI 2006 Extended Abstracts on Human Factors in Computing Systems (2006), doi:10.1145/1125451.1125491
17. Nisbett, R.E., Wilson, T.D.: The halo effect: Evidence for unconscious alteration of judgments. Journal of Personality and Social Psychology 35(4), 250–256 (1977), doi:10.1037/0022-3514.35.4.250
18. Optimal Workshop, http://www.optimalworkshop.com/optimalsort.htm
19. Pirolli, P., Card, S.: Information foraging. Psychological Review 106(4), 643–675 (1999), doi:10.1037/0033-295X.106.4.643
20. Ratcliff, R., McKoon, G.: A retrieval theory of priming in memory. Psychological Review 95(3), 385–408 (1988), doi:10.1037/0033-295X.95.3.385
21. Rugg, G., McGeorge, P.: The sorting techniques: A tutorial paper on card sorts, picture sorts and item sorts. Expert Systems 14(2), 80–93 (1997)
22. Sanders, K., Fincher, S., Bouvier, D., Lewandowski, G., Morrison, B., Murphy, L., Petre, M., Richards, B., Tenenberg, J., Thomas, L., Anderson, R., Anderson, R., Fitzgerald, S., Gutschow, A., Haller, S., Lister, R., McCauley, R., McTaggart, J., Prasad, C., Scott, T., Shinners-Kennedy, D., Westbrook, S., Zander, C.: A multi-institutional, multinational study of programming concepts using card sort data. Expert Systems 22(3), 129–138 (2005)
23. Smith, S.M., Ward, T.B., Schumacher, J.S.: Constraining effects of examples in a creative generations task. Memory & Cognition 21(6), 837–845 (1993)
24. Spencer, D., Warfel, T.: Card Sorting: a Definitive Guide (2003), http://www.boxesandarrows.com/archives/card_sorting_a_definitive_guide.php (retrieved October 28, 2011)

25. Stevens, S.M., Dornburg, C.C.: Utilizing pathfinder in the design of an intranet website. In: Proceedings of the 27th International Conference Extended Abstracts on Human Factors in Computing Systems (2009), doi:10.1145/1520340.1520622
26. Usability.gov, http://www.usability.gov/
27. UX Punk, http://uxpunk.com/websort/
28. White, H., Wright, T., Chawner, B.: Usability evaluation of library online catalogues. In: Proceedings of the 7th Australasian User Interface Conference. Australian Computer Society, Inc., Darlinghurst (2006)

Part III

User Interface Design and Development Methods and Environments

Case Study for Experience Vision – Application for PC

Kanako Ariya

Fujitsu Design Ltd.
Kamiodanaka 4-chome, Nakahara-ku Kawasaki, Japan 211-8588
ariya@jp.fujitsu.com

Abstract. In order to examine the new value of photo management software preinstalled on personal computers to develop a model for the next photo management software, I have to utilize the Experience Vision method. I will introduce the process from gathering information from the activity of novice users, structuring of their real user demands, to scenario creation.

1 Introduction

There are many novice users among customers who purchase Fujitsu PCs. On the other hand, software developers are skilled PC users, and therefore, it is often the case that development is started without grasping beginners' actual use condition. The resulting software may be too difficult for beginners to use.

By grasping requirements in the early stage of development, improved quality and increased efficiency are expectable. The solution of those problems was tried by applying a vision centered design Experience Vision method.

2 Process

2.1 Behavior Observation of Novice Users

The project members started with collecting features and results of novice users' photograph life by observing and conducting interviews.

For this observation and interview, I prepared a "Novice Interview Template" [fig.1].

As a result, I was able to collect a series of the beginner's actions from taking a photograph, saving it to a personal computer, to arranging, editing, and printing. I was also able to obtain a lot of other notices.

2.2 Structuration of Notices and Configuration of Personas

Next, in order to retrieve the beginners' intrinsic value from the behavior observation that was conducted by the project members, the gathered keywords were written out to cards.

M. Kurosu (Ed.): Human-Computer Interaction, Part I, HCII 2013, LNCS 8004, pp. 275–280, 2013.

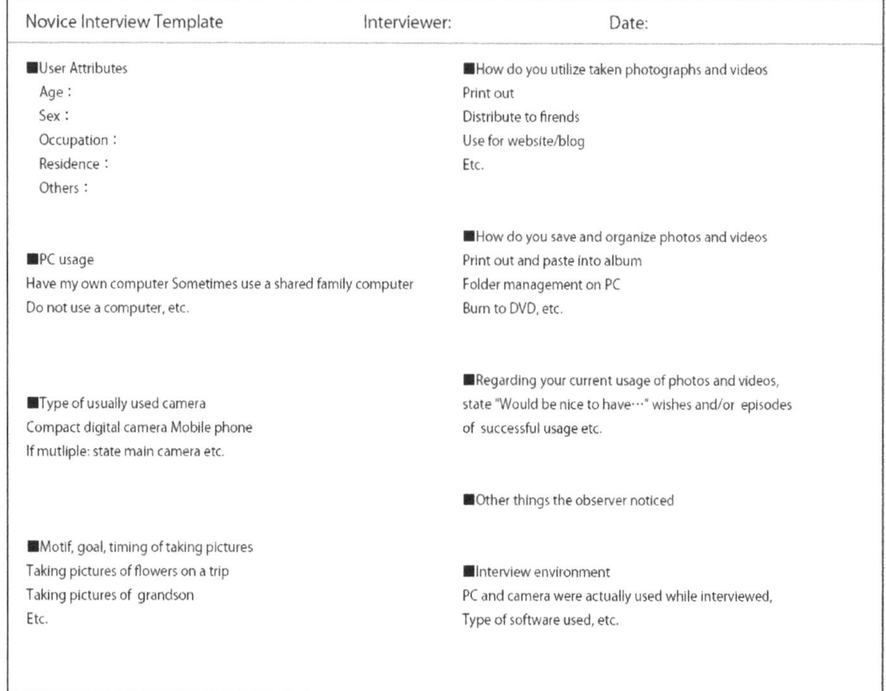
Novice Interview Template | Interviewer: | Date:

■User Attributes
Age :
Sex :
Occupation :
Residence :
Others :

■PC usage
Have my own computer Sometimes use a shared family computer
Do not use a computer, etc.

■Type of usually used camera
Compact digital camera Mobile phone
If mutliple: state main camera etc.

■Motif, goal, timing of taking pictures
Taking pictures of flowers on a trip
Taking pictures of grandson
Etc.

■How do you utilize taken photographs and videos
Print out
Distribute to firends
Use for website/blog
Etc.

■How do you save and organize photos and videos
Print out and paste into album
Folder management on PC
Burn to DVD, etc.

■Regarding your current usage of photos and videos, state "Would be nice to have…" wishes and/or episodes of successful usage etc.

■Other things the observer noticed

■Interview environment
PC and camera were actually used while interviewed,
Type of software used, etc.

Fig. 1. Novice Interview Template

Demands and tasks were structured depending on whether gathered information was the user's goal, or rather a mean to achieve a purpose by analyzing their relationship to each other.

Through this structure I clarified the cause and effect of problems novice users face.

Moreover, I made three personas based on the interviewed people and shared them between the project members at this time.

2.3 Laddering Up to the Intrinsic User Value

From the structured notices, I formed three intrinsic user values "pleasure to photograph", "pleasure to see", and "pleasure to show" based on statements, such as "I will not delete it, even if it is blurred, as long as the expression is good, ", "I want to take pictures of important events properly", "I want to make sure it is saved", These helped to create the overall structure.

2.4 Consideration of the Advantage as a PC Maker (Business Offering Policy)

In case of Fujitsu personal computer, the Insertion of a SD card automatically starts the importing tool.

When automation helps beginners to achieve his purpose without being confused by difficult messages and choices of the OS, it is an important aspect in the development of easy-to-use software.

Since this interaction is a strong point unique to a PC maker who is developing both hardware and software, I decided to consider concrete scenarios based on the given interaction.

Moreover, individual users think of ease of use as an important factor in the purchase of a personal computer. When buying a personal computer, the percentage of users purchasing at a shop front of mass home electronics retailers, that ask the salesperson for an easy-to-use personal computer, is high.

Therefore, software that promise ease of use and meets the expectations when used becomes important.

2.5 Using Structured Scenarios

Activity Scenario

Since in the case of this example the target for the development was clear, I started from the activity scenario.

For each of the three persons' persona, usage scenes of their photo life from taking a picture to printing and the corresponding actions taken were described as an activity scenario [fig. 2].

Interaction Scenario

To some activity scenarios, I did the breakdown how things can be realized and created a detailed interaction scenario [fig. 3].

I then evaluated if the flows suit our persona, and prioritized depending on the user, and chose the scenario for prototyping.

Activity Scenario	Author	Ariya	Date		No.	
	Title	He takes photos with the collector disposition and is arranged simply, and use.				

Persona		
Name	Feature	There are lots of photos of travel, hobby, grandchild, a pet dog, etc. and settlement does not stick.
Mr. M. Nakatani	Basic Info	65 years old, living in Ichikawa-shi, Chiba with his wife, sometime his daughter come with a grandchild.
	Target	I would enjoy the sense of fulfillment of long activity, or would like to give it to a grandchild.

Scene	activity scenario	Task
1) Arrange important photos	Mr. Nakatani is a person in which a thing is saved up from ancient times, and he collected pottery, and has also taken and collected the photos of a travel or a hobby. It was a trouble that there is a photo collected for years in large quantities, and it is confused. He had to put the photos of the pottery whose picture was taken while traveling into both category "trip" and "pottery." However, will not an extra copy of two sheets increase many photos more. Mr. Nakatani was serious. If a photos are arranged, it will become easy to look for the target photos. The photos forgotten is found, and he remembers that time longingly, or he enjoys himself together with a grandchild, and came to think that taking photos was good.	1) Connect PC with a camera. 2) Import 3) Manage 4) Look 5) processes and rectifies. 6) Output

Fig. 2. Activity Scenario

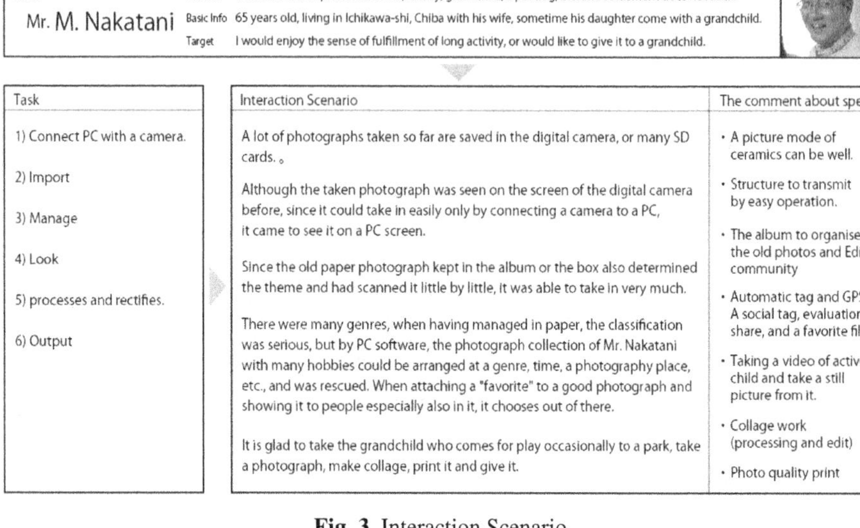

Fig. 3. Interaction Scenario

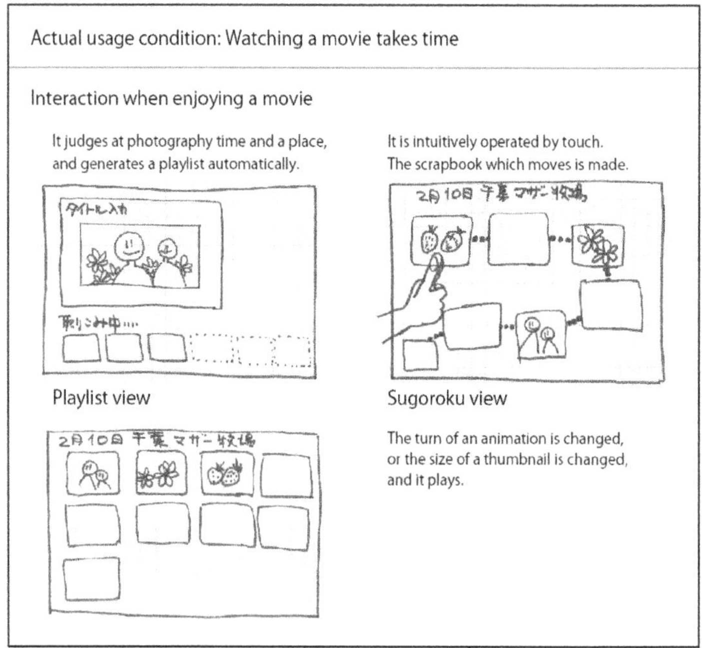

Fig. 4. User Interface Ideas

Prototyping

From these work I extracted the user requirements for photograph software, developed the user interface design based on it, and created prototype ideas for user interface [fig. 4], [fig. 5].

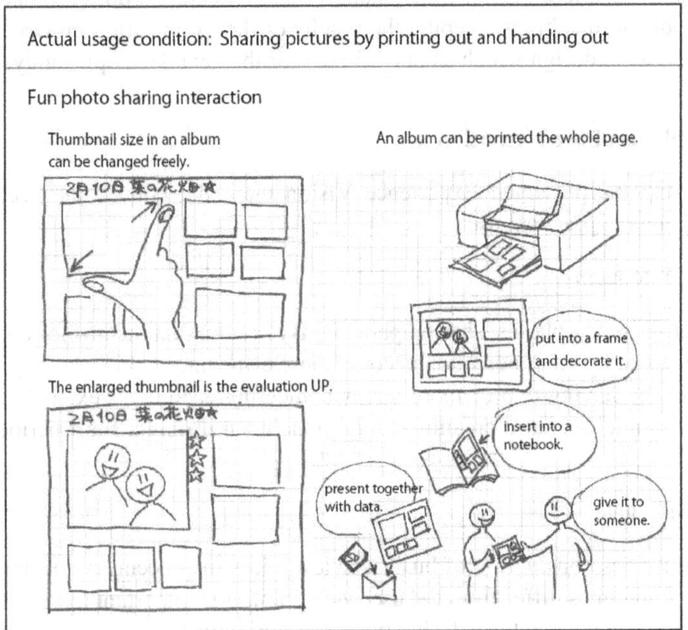

Fig. 5. User Interface Ideas

3 Conclusion

3.1 The Advantages for the Mounting Process

Vision centered design method is a technique applied in the planning phase of a product, a system, or a service. However, since it also has positive side effects in the implementation phase, an example has been introduced.

- The overview of the whole user experience by visualizing the thinking process helped to discover that the photograph experience starts from "taking a picture". A fact that I did not consciously consider in the development of previous photograph software

Since the user wants to take a picture well, displaying additional information when looking at photographs for reference, such as settings the picture has been taken with or a map of the location is appreciated. This shows how the presented method has effectively helped to gain overview of the whole User Experience of photograph browsing by clarifying the user values and actions.

- Minimization of the redo due to change of requirements

In actual development is not rare to be obliged to a change of design.

If it is only underlying technology that changes, I can respond by only making adjustments to the interaction scenario.

In commercialization, even if functionality's implementation does not make it into the product due to deadlines, keeping the results of the examination process, helps to not forget the ideal design which can be utilized for the next development cycle.

3.2 Problems of the Execution

When utilizing the presented Experience Vision method I noticed the need for the following points in practical use.

- Dividing into teams

Taking photos, seeing photos, sharing photos – By dividing into teams for each activity, discussions and scenario creation become more efficient.

Moreover, by having two or more teams competing each other examine the same activity, substantial scenario creation can be done even if only a short period of time is given.

- Raising facilitators

During discussions considering of business viewpoints may occur. As business viewpoints may sometimes differ from the user viewpoint, it is important to raise a reliable facilitator who can cope with such situations appropriately.

- Rooting the value creation process

For successful examination of this method it is important to be useful for the improvement of a product, and that all stakeholders of the development process to understand that the method helps to guide a product to business success, and that the method is integrated into the development process. Therefore, the development related members also need to change their mind to successfully adopt the presented method.

Using the Common Industry Format to Document the Context of Use

Nigel Bevan

Professional Usability Services, 12 King Edwards Gardens, London W3 9RG, UK
mail@nigelbevan.com

Abstract. The ISO/IEC 25063 standard provides a Common Industry Format for documenting the context of use. It defines the context of use as the "users, tasks, equipment (hardware, software and materials), and the physical and social environments in which a system, product or service is used", and specifies what should be included in a description of the context of use. This paper explains the importance of identifying the context of use as part of the human centred design process, provides an outline of the information that needs to be included in a description of the context of use, and explains how the scope of the context of use needs to be identified and how multiple contexts of use can be differentiated.

Keywords: Standards, context of use, usability, common industry format.

1 Introduction

ISO 9241-210 emphasises the importance of understanding and specifying the context of use as part of the human-centred design process. The characteristics of the users, tasks and organizational, technical and physical environment define the context in which the system is used. The objective of ISO/IEC 25063 "Common Industry Format for Usability: Context of Use Description", is to explain the various roles of context of use descriptions in systems development, and to specify in detail the information that needs to be identified. This will provide a source of guidance for people responsible for documenting the context of use, and could also be used to specify the information about context of use that should be provided as part of a contract for systems development. ISO/IEC 25063 is currently being finalized, with publication expected in late 2013 or early 2014.

2 What Is the Context of Use?

The phrase "context of use" has been used in a general sense in HCI for many years [15], and is currently defined by the Interaction Design Foundation as "the actual conditions under which a given artefact/software product is used, or will be used in a normal day to day working situation" [2].

M. Kurosu (Ed.): Human-Computer Interaction, Part I, HCII 2013, LNCS 8004, pp. 281–289, 2013.

In ISO 9241-11, developed at the same time as the MUSiC method [1,14], "context of use" has a more precise meaning: the characteristics of the users, tasks and the physical, social and organizational environments in which a product, system or service is used. As this includes all the factors that influence the usability (effectiveness, efficiency and satisfaction) when a product is used, this definition provides a more rigorous framework than traditional approaches to user and task analysis that may, for example, overlook the influence of the technical, physical and social environment. The definition also explicitly includes the characteristics of the user that will influence usability.

In a design situation, the characteristics of the product will determine the usability in a given context of use. For an existing product, the characteristics of the context of use determine the usability of the product.

The most recent version of the ISO definition of context of use is in ISO/IEC 25063: "the users, tasks, equipment (hardware, software and materials), and the physical and social environments in which a system, product or service is used".

3 Context of Use in Systems Development

As usability depends on the context of use, detailed knowledge about the context of use is an essential prerequisite for requirements definition, design and evaluation. In the early stages of product conception, information about the context of use complements information about user needs. Many user requirements can be derived directly from the context of use, as the system needs to be usable in all the intended contexts of use. Requirements identified from the context of use could for example include the need to use terminology that is familiar to the identified user groups, to support commonly occurring task flows, and for the interface to be usable in unusual physical environments.

During design and development, the context of use description will become more detailed as more information is obtained and design decisions are taken. It may be necessary to identify and describe the context of use for some or all of following situations (which are explained in more detail in ISO/IEC 25063):

- **Initial high-level description of the context of use.** This information can provide an initial basis for identifying user needs (and could for example include lists of user groups and their tasks).

More **detailed descriptions of the context of use** are needed to support particular stages of the design and development process:

- **Current context of use.** Information about the currently existing context of use can be used to identify needs, problems and constraints that might otherwise be overlooked, but which design of the future system should take account of.
- **Intended context of use.** Defining the intended context of use provides a basis for designing the new product or system by describing the types of users who are intended to use it, the tasks that are to be undertaken and the environment(s) in which it is intended to be used.

- **Context of use specified as part of user requirements.** The context of use should be included as part of a user requirements specification to clearly identify the conditions under which the requirements apply and the contexts in which the system needs to be usable.
- **Intended context of use of the implemented system.** This documents how and when the implemented system is intended to be used. The context in which the implemented product or system has been designed to be used may differ from the context that was originally intended (for example as a result of compromises made during design and development).
- **Context of use of the deployed system.** The context of use of the system after deployment can be identified through follow-up evaluation, and includes any new ways the system is actually being used (for example by unanticipated types of users for new tasks in different environments).

Two other applications of context of use descriptions are:

- **Context of use used for evaluation.** To obtain valid results, it is important that the context of use that is used for the evaluation is so far as possible a realistic representation of the actual or intended context of use, using users with similar skills and abilities carrying out typical tasks in a representative environment. Documenting the context of use to be used for evaluation helps plan a realistic evaluation and subsequently provides evidence that the results are valid.
- **Context of use information included in a product description.** To help potential purchasers or users of a product or system, the product description should include a description of the intended context of use of the product.

4 Content of a Context of Use Description

ISO/IEC 25063 specifies the particular items that are required and recommended for inclusion in different types of context of use descriptions. The items in the standard were derived from those previously described in ISO 9241-11 and ISO 20282-1, and they were refined through discussion in the working group (that includes experts in ergonomics, usability and software quality) taking account of feedback received on draft versions of the standard. The items are summarized below.

Subject of the context of use description:

- The system, product, service or concept for which the context of use is being described.
- The purpose of the system, product, service or concept.
- A summary of any preconditions and/or constraints that affect the design of the interactive system.

User groups and stakeholders:

- Each distinctly different user group.
- Other stakeholders who could have an impact on the use of the system, product or service.

- The relationship between each relevant user group and the system, product or service in terms of key goals and constraints.
- The characteristics of each user group.
- If the actual or intended users will include people whose physical or psychological characteristics are at the extremes of the normal range, these characteristics should be included in the description of context of use description.

User characteristics that could affect usability:

- Demographics such as such as age, gender or education.
- Psychological and social characteristics such as cognitive abilities, cultural background, language, literacy, knowledge and skills, motivation and attitude.
- Physical and sensory characteristics such as body dimensions, handedness and visual and auditory abilities.

Goals and responsibilities of the user group and the organization (in which the user group works):

- A list of the goals of the different user groups described as intended outcomes that people are trying to accomplish (including personal goals when relevant).
- Any goals defined by the organization that provides and/or develops the interactive system that are likely to affect usability.
- Any responsibilities that are judged to be likely to affect usability.

Tasks of the users:

- For each task, the characteristics that are likely to affect usability, which could include the goal of carrying out the task, the task result or outcome, whether there is discretion in how to carry out the task, the duration and frequency, and the complexity.
- Tasks will usually need to be analysed and described. While task analysis is logically part of a context of use description, it is usually documented separately.

Technical, social and physical environment(s):

- The technical and technological environment that could for example include tools, equipment, hardware configuration, input device(s), network connection, and assistive technologies.
- The social and organizational environment that could for example include availability of assistance, responsibilities, group dynamics, time pressures, and interruptions.
- The physical environment that could for example include the time, location, workplace, lighting and temperature.

Problems:

- The description of an existing context of use can include any identified problems that are observed or reported, which can help identify user needs and potential improvements.

5 What Should Be Included in a Context of Use Description?

To decide what to include in a detailed context of use description, the following decisions need to be made:

a) What is the focus of the context of use?
b) What is the scope of the context of use?
c) How many different contexts of use are there?
d) Which characteristics of the context of use should be described?

5.1 What is the Focus of the Context of Use?

The context of use represents the users, tasks and environments for which a system, product or service will be used. The system, product or service is the focus of design or evaluation in predefined contexts of use.

The boundary between the system, product or service and the technical environment depends on the scope of what is being designed or evaluated. This is represented by Equipment that could be part of the System, Product or Service. For example, if designing software for a digital alarm, the product is the software, and the hardware is part of the technical environment, but if designing the whole alarm, both the hardware and software are part of the product. Figure 1 shows four categories of the context of use that can influence the usability of a system, product or service: Users, Tasks, a Physical and social environment, and a Technical and technological environment (including Equipment).

Although the context of use is most commonly used with the focus on designing or evaluating a system, product or service, any element can be the focus. For example when employing staff to operate an existing system, the focus could be on evaluating whether the staff have (or could acquire) the skills needed to operate the product in specific contexts of use.

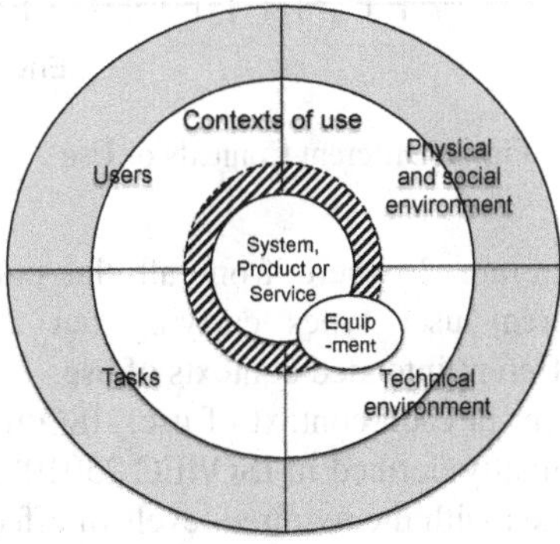

Fig. 1. Scope of the Context of Use

5.2 What Is the Scope of the Context of Use?

It is important to decide the specific types of users, tasks and environments that are within the actual or intended contexts of use. In Figure 1, the outer shaded area represents the users, tasks and environments that are not part of the context in which the product is being or is expected to be used. The inner part is those contexts of use in which the product is used, or is intended to be used.

5.3 How Many Different Contexts of Use Are There?

For how many different combinations of users, tasks and environments is the product or system being used, or intended to be used?

A context of use description can be of one instance of a context of use, or could include a range of contexts of use in which the product, system or service is used, or in which it is intended to be used. Different contexts of use are differentiated by subsets of user groups, tasks or types of environment that are known or judged to be likely to result in significant differences in usability. The overall context of use of interest will then be composed of a set of potential contexts of used defined by all the relevant permutations of the subsets.

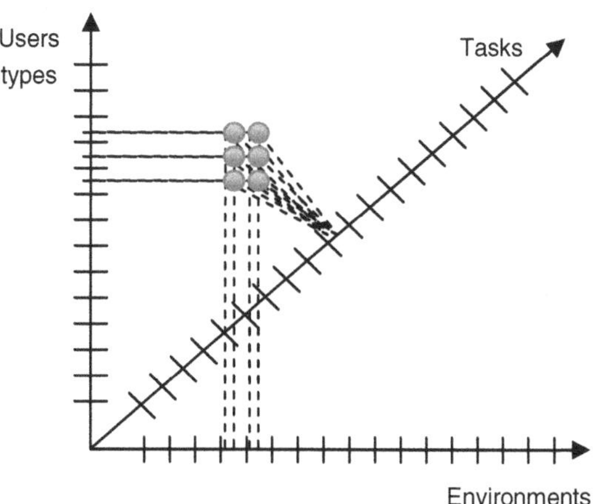

Fig. 2. Different Contexts of Use

This is illustrated in Figure 2 where from all the potential users, tasks and environments, three different user types carrying out a task in two different environments define six different intended contexts of use.

Usability may be different in each context of use. ISO/IEC WD 25022 describes context completeness (originally defined in ISO/IEC 25010) as the extent to which a product or system can be used with the required levels of effectiveness, efficiency and satisfaction (and freedom from risk) in each of the specified contexts of use. This quality characteristic is intended to be used to highlight the need to specify the required level of usability in each context of use included in a user requirements specification, and subsequently to provide a profile of the extent to which requirements have been met when evaluating the actual usability achieved in each context of use.

5.4 Which Characteristics of the Context of Use Should Be Described?

A detailed description of the context of use should identify all the attributes that will have a significant impact on usability, but descriptions of the context of use can become very long and complex if every characteristic of every attribute is described in detail. Only those characteristics of the context of use that are judged to be likely to affect usability need to be included, although it may also be useful to describe any other variations in characteristics that could potentially also affect usability. So for example when selecting participants to evaluate a product, previous experience of using the product, or another product with the same interaction style, may have a much bigger influence on usability than conventional demographics such as age, gender or education level.

Some user characteristics can be identified in different ways: either by describing the specific psychological, social, physical and sensory characteristics, or by identifying groups with specific tasks, job roles or demographics that are associated with particular characteristics.

Characteristics that will not affect usability need not be included (for example the temperature in an office environment that is within normal ranges). Making the judgement of which characteristics are likely to affect usability requires some expertise, and to conform to ISO/IEC 25063, an explanation of the basis for the judgement has to be provided.

6 Conclusions

The description of the context of use provides common information that is needed to help maintain a human-centred design focus within a project. It is intended for use in conjunction with the other information that is to be produced relating to human centred design. The description of the context of use is intended to be used as part of system-level documentation resulting from development processes.

Inadequate knowledge about the context of use can result in the development of products, systems or services that do not meet user needs, and evaluation results that do not represent how a system will actually be used. The lack of a shared understanding of the context of use in development teams is a common failing in systems development ([14]). The ISO/IEC 25063 standard is intended to highlight the importance of describing the context of use, and to help ensure that appropriate information is included in descriptions of a context of use.

Additional Common Industry Format standards are planned for documenting other deliverables in user centred design:

- User needs report (ISO/IEC 25064)
- User requirements specification
- User interaction specification
- User interface specification
- Usability evaluation report (ISO/IEC 25066 under development)
- Field data report

These will complement the existing ISO/IEC 25062 Common Industry Format for Usability Test Reports.

If you would like to contribute to development of the Common Industry Format standards, or to comment on drafts, you can either do this via your national standards body [3], or if you are a member of one of the ISO TC159/SC4 liaison organisations [4] such as UXPA [16] you can participate through the liaison organisation.

Acknowledgements. ISO/IEC 25063 was developed by the ISO working group "Common Industry Formats for Usability Reports" that is joint between ISO/IEC JTC1/SC7/WG28 and ISO TC159/SC4/WG28. Particular thanks are due to Thomas Geis, Susan Harker, Karsten Nebe, Mary Theofanos, and Shin-ichi Fukuzumi for their feedback on this paper, and to the other members of the working group who have contributed to development of ISO/IEC 25063 that include Jonathan Earthy, Clemens Lutsch, Jim Williams and Brian Stanton.

References

1. Bevan, N., Macleod, M.: Usability measurement in context. Behaviour and Information Technology 13, 132–145 (1994)
2. Interaction Design Foundation: Context of use, http://www.interaction-design.org/encyclopedia/context_of_use.html
3. ISO: Members, http://www.iso.org/iso/home/about/iso_members.htm
4. ISO: TC159/SC4 Ergonomics of human-system interaction, http://www.iso.org/iso/home/standards_development/list_of_iso_technical_committees/iso_technical_committee.htm?commid=53372
5. ISO 9241-11: Ergonomic requirements for office work with visual display terminals (VDTs) - Part 11 Guidance on usability (1998)
6. ISO 9241-210: Ergonomics of human-system interaction – Part 210: Human-centred design for interactive systems (2010)
7. ISO 20282-1: Ease of operation of everyday products – Part 1: Design requirements for context of use and user characteristics (2006)
8. ISO/IEC 25010: Systems and software engineering – Systems and software product Quality Requirements and Evaluation (SQuaRE) – System and software quality models (2011)
9. ISO/IEC WD 25022: Systems and software engineering - Systems and software Quality Requirements and Evaluation (SQuaRE) - Measurement of quality in use (2013)

10. ISO/IEC 25062: Software Engineering – Software product Quality Requirements and Evaluation (SQuaRE) – Common Industry Format (CIF) for Usability Test Reports (2006)
11. ISO/IEC DIS 25063.3: Systems and software engineering – Systems and software product Quality Requirements and Evaluation (SQuaRE) – Common Industry Format (CIF) for usability: Context of use description (2013)
12. ISO/IEC FDIS 25064: Systems and software engineering – Software product Quality Requirements and Evaluation (SQuaRE) – Common Industry Format (CIF) for usability: User needs report (2013)
13. ISO/IEC WD 25066: Systems and software engineering – Software product Quality Requirements and Evaluation (SQuaRE) – Common Industry Format (CIF) for usability: Evaluation report (2013)
14. Macleod, M.: Usability in Context: Improving Quality of Use. In: Bradley, G., Hendricks, H.W. (eds.) Human Factors in Organizational Design and Management - IV (Proceedings of the International Ergonomics Association, 4th International Symposium on Human Factors in Organizational Design and Management), Stockholm, May 29-June 1. Elsevier / North Holland, Amsterdam (1994)
15. Maguire, M.: Context of Use within usability activities. Int. J. Human-Computer Studies 55, 453–483 (2001)
16. UXPA. User Experience Professionals Association liaison with ISO, `http://www.uxpa.org/standards`

V&V of Lexical, Syntactic and Semantic Properties for Interactive Systems through Model Checking of Formal Description of Dialog

Guillaume Brat[1], Célia Martinie[2], and Philippe Palanque[2]

[1] NASA Ames Research Center, MS-269-1 Moffett Field, California, USA
guillaume.p.brat@nasa.gov
[2] IRIT, Université Paul Sabatier, 118, route de Narbonne
31062 Toulouse Cedex 9, France
{martinie,palanque}@irit.fr

Abstract. During early phases of the development of an interactive system, future system properties are identified (through interaction with end users in the brainstorming and prototyping phase of the application, or by other stakeholders) imposing requirements on the final system. They can be specific to the application under development or generic to all applications such as usability principles. Instances of specific properties include visibility of the aircraft altitude, speed… in the cockpit and the continuous possibility of disengaging the autopilot in whatever state the aircraft is. Instances of generic properties include availability of undo (for undoable functions) and availability of a progression bar for functions lasting more than four seconds. While behavioral models of interactive systems using formal description techniques provide complete and unambiguous descriptions of states and state changes, it does not provide explicit representation of the absence or presence of properties. Assessing that the system that has been built is the right system remains a challenge usually met through extensive use and acceptance tests. By the explicit representation of properties and the availability of tools to support checking these properties, it becomes possible to provide developers with means for systematic exploration of the behavioral models and assessment of the presence or absence of these properties. This paper proposes the synergistic use two tools for checking both generic and specific properties of interactive applications: Petshop and Java PathFinder. Petshop is dedicated to the description of interactive system behavior. Java PathFinder is dedicated to the runtime verification of Java applications and as an extension dedicated to User Interfaces. This approach is exemplified on a safety critical application in the area of interactive cockpits for large civil aircrafts.

1 Introduction

Nowadays interactive applications are more and more required to handle the complexity of command and control systems for safety critical applications. Formalisms,

M. Kurosu (Ed.): Human-Computer Interaction, Part I, HCII 2013, LNCS 8004, pp. 290–299, 2013.

processes and tools are then required to bring together several properties such as reliability, dependability and operability. In addition to standard properties of computer systems (such as safety or liveness), interaction properties have been identified. Properties related to the usage of an interactive system are called external properties [2] [9] and characterize the capacity of the system to provide support for its users to accomplish their tasks and goals, potentially in several ways, and prevent or help to recover from errors. Although all types of properties are not always completely independent one from each other, external properties are related to the user's point of view and usability factor, whereas internal properties are related to the design and development process of the system itself (modifiability, run time efficiency). Interactive systems have to support both types of properties and dedicated techniques and approaches have been studied for this purpose, amongst them are formal methods. Formal languages have proven their value in several domains and are a necessary condition to understand, design and develop systems and check their properties.

Formal methods are studied since several years in the field of HCI as a mean to analyze in a complete and unambiguous way interactions between a user and a system. Several types of approaches have been developed [8], which encompass contributions about formal description of an interactive system and/or formal verification of its properties. Amongst these approaches, ICO description technique and associated Petshop CASE tool, provide augmented support for describing the conceptual model of the system but also for analysis and validation at earlier stage in the process [10]. This kind of approaches provide support for describing exhaustively interactive systems and their behavior, as well as prototyping, testing and verifying synchronously certain types of properties. However, as existing notations to produce executable models are quite expressive, models cannot be verified until they have been translated into more abstract models in order to perform properties verification. This paper proposes to associate Petshop to JPF, a framework for runtime verification of Java programs. This association provides support for complete and non-ambiguous description of an interactive application (with Petshop) as well as formal verification of the ICO specification based interactive application (with JPF). Next section is dedicated to the presentation of the tool suite. Third section illustrates the use of this tool suite for the example of the Weather Radar aircraft cockpit application. Fourth section is dedicated to related work.

2 A Tool Suite for the Validation and Verification of Interactive Systems

This tool suite is composed of two software tools: Petshop and JavaPathFinder. Petshop [3] is dedicated to the description of interactive system behavior. JavaPathFinder [4] is dedicated to the runtime verification of Java applications and as an extension dedicated to User Interfaces.

2.1 Petshop

The CASE tool Petshop[1] is Java based and provides support for editing ICO models. Interactive Cooperative Object (ICO) [16] is an object-oriented formal notation dedicated to interactive systems. It provides support for describing: the events to which the application can react, the set of functions it can perform and the implicit set of states in which the system can be. This formalism encompasses both the "input" aspects of the interaction (i.e. how user actions impact on the inner state of the application, and which actions are enabled at any given time) and its "output" aspects (i.e. when and how the application displays information relevant to the user). ICO notation is based on Petri nets and Petshop tool then allows classical manipulations on the Petri nets add/remove/modify (Petri net items, marking, code within transitions, etc.) and offers classical editing services (copy/cut/paste, undo/redo, navigation amongst the models, etc.). Petshop also enables to execute simultaneously the interactive application as well as its underlying models. Furthermore, it is possible to modify the models while the modeled interactive application is running. This list of features enables to formally specify, test and validate an interactive application in early stages of the development process, using Petshop as a high-fidelity prototyping tool [19]. However, properties verification activities require transformation of the high-fidelity prototype. Fig. 1 represents diagrammatically the current existing process for verifying properties of interactive applications running in the Petshop environment.

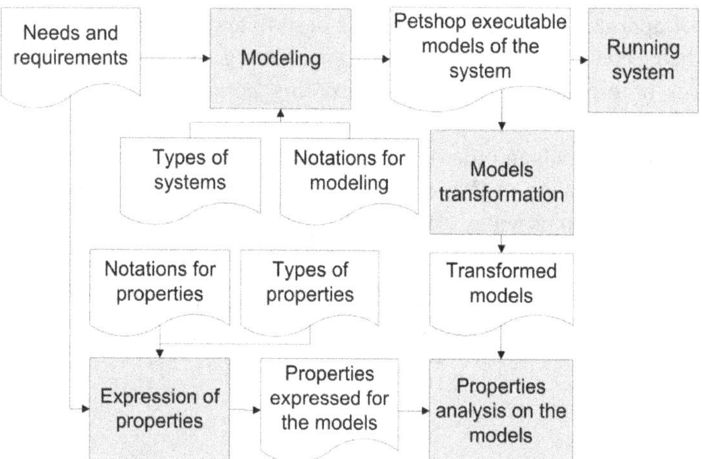

Fig. 1. Existing process for verifying properties of Petshop running interactive applications

The analysis performed at runtime within Petshop environment is executed on translated version of ICO models. The translated models are low-level Petri nets and the Petshop analysis module performs an invariant Analysis (P/T invariants) of the underlying Petri net. Previous work has shown that it is also possible to perform formal manual analysis of interactive system properties [17] as well as ergonomic rules

[1] `http://www.irit.fr/recherches/ICS/softwares/petshop/`

[18], both using ACTL notation for expressing properties. However, as previously described, ICO notation is quite expressive and ICO models cannot be verified until they have been translated into more abstract models in order to perform properties verification.

2.2 JPF

Java PathFinder[2] (JPF) [4, 23] is a framework for the runtime verification of Java programs. It can be used as an explicit-state model checker that works directly on Java bytecode. JPF specializes in finding deadlocks, verifying assertions, and checking temporal logic specifications through the use of listeners, which monitors the exploration of all possible paths in a Java program and continuously check that the specifications are met. JPF explores all possible interleavings in multi-threaded programs as well as all possible choice points (both in terms of control logic and data values) corresponding to a specific environment.

JPF has many extensions, which can be used to process various languages (e.g., UML-style Statecharts, Scala), the use of specific Java libraries (e.g., network communciations, java.awt or javax.swing), or, to switch from model checking to a less exhaustive form of verification (e.g., symbolic execution, concolic execution or runtime analysis). In our case, we are using mostly jpf-awt, which provides convenient abstractions of user interface libraries (awt or swing) and means to model interacting users through scripts [24].

Complex functional properties, corresponding to LTL [21] safety properties, can be expressed and checked using JPF listeners. Listeners are Java programs that run in parallel with the execution done by JPF, monitor the states of the application under test at every step, and check them against the specified formal property. JPF listeners are commonly referred to as observers in the model checking community. So, using listeners does not require any modification of the original application code; it does require knowledge of that code though. Listeners can easily encode LTL safety properties such as the Property *P* described above. However, they cannot express liveness properties (in layman's terms, asserting that something good eventually happens), e.g., stating that a value is eventually displayed. Liveness properties can be checked by JPF only using the jpf-ltl extension, which has not been tested extensively. This capability can be useful to check properties such as checking that a progression bar keeps moving or that a button eventually gets reset.

2.3 Process for Formal Description and Verification of Interactive Applications

Fig. 2 summarizes the proposed process. Functional as well as non-functional needs and requirements are identified at the beginning of the process (top left part in Fig. 2).

[2] `http://babelfish.arc.nasa.gov/trac/jpf/`

Interactive application is then formally described using Petshop tool. In parallel, properties that have to be verified by the application are represented using temporal logic notations. JPF is then used to verify properties directly on the running interactive application.

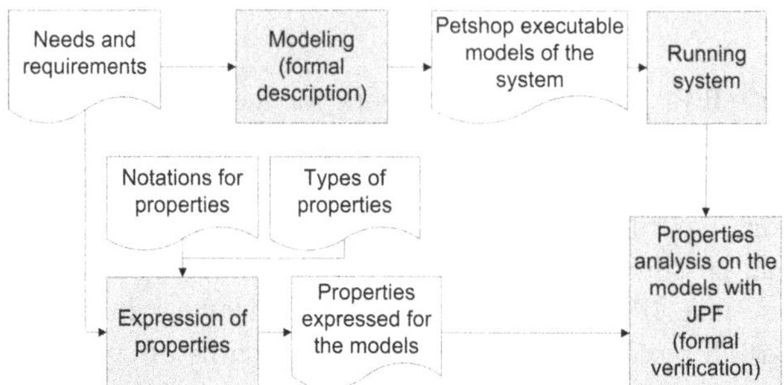

Fig. 2. Proposed verification process integrating Petshop and JPF

Following section provides an example of applying the tool suite for the implementation and verification of a civil aircraft cockpit interactive application.

3 Illustrative Example: WXR Application

Weather Radar application (also named WXR) has been modeled taking into account ARINC 661 [1] standard, which aims at defining software interfaces to the Cockpit Display System (CDS) used in all types of aircraft installations.

3.1 Weather Radar Presentation

Weather radar is an application currently deployed in many cockpits of commercial aircrafts. It provides support to pilot's activities by increasing their awareness of meteorological phenomena during the flight journey, allowing them to determine if they may have to request for a trajectory change, in order to avoid storms or precipitations for example. Fig. 3A shows screenshots of weather radar displays. Fig. 3B presents a screenshot of the weather radar control panel. This panel provides two functionalities to the crew members. The first one is dedicated to the mode selection of weather radar and provides information about status of the radar, in order to ensure that the weather radar can be set up correctly. The second functionality, available in the lower part of the window, is dedicated to the adjustment of the weather radar orientation (Tilt angle). This can be done in an automatic way or manually. Additionally, a stabilization function aims at keeping the radar beam stable even in case of turbulences. It shall not be possible to manually edit the Tilt angle if the application is in automatic mode or if the stabilization functionality is on.

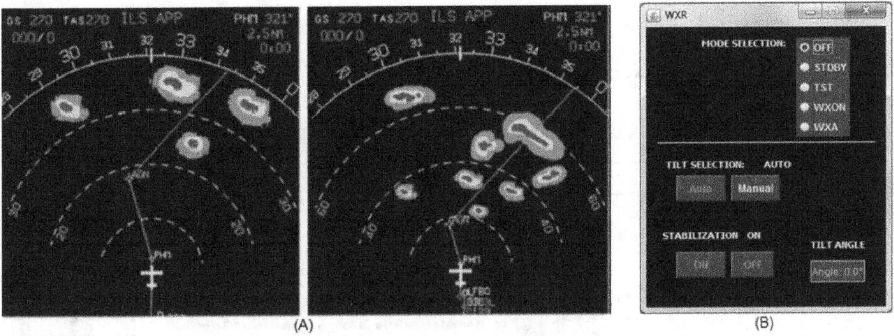

Fig. 3. A - Screenshot of weather radar displays, B - Screenshot of the weather radar control panel

3.2 Formal Specification of WXR Application with Petshop

Fig. 4 presents a diagrammatic overview of the WXR application running in the Petshop environment. The following parts of the application are represented distinctively: the presentation part of the application (User Interface), the behavioral part of the application (Cooperative Objects models) and the functions that bind the presentation part to the behavioral part: activation and rendering functions.

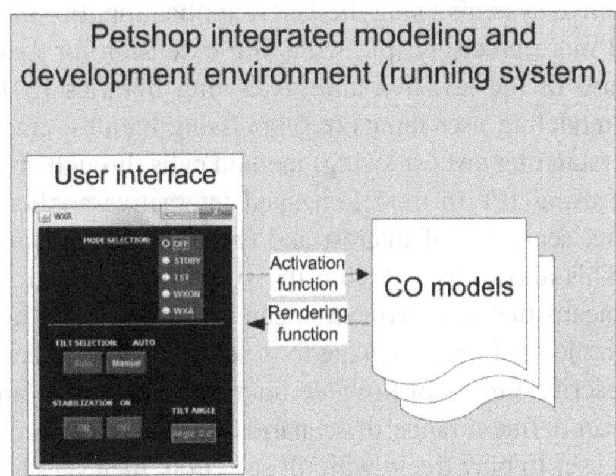

Fig. 4. Overview of the WXR application running in the Petshop environment

The weather radar control panel application is composed of the presentation part (shown in Fig. 3B), the Cooperative Object (CO) model (shown in Fig. 5), and the activation and rendering functions. Activation and rendering functions are not presented in this article and the interested reader can find example in [16]. The Cooperative Object shown in Fig. 5 is the formal description of the WXR application's behavior. This formal description is used as part of the specification for developing the final application running on the targeted system. JPF tool is then used to verify properties against the final application as described in the following paragraphs.

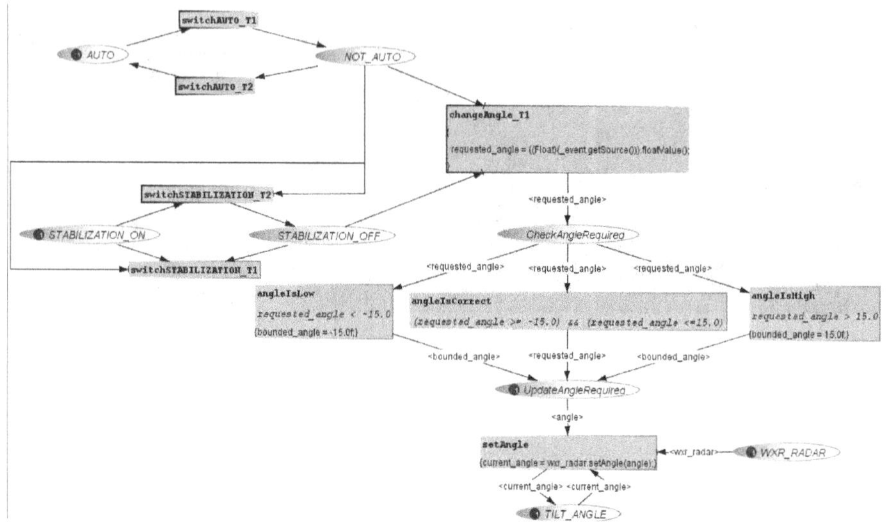

Fig. 5. Cooperative Object (CO) model of the weather radar control panel

3.3 Formal Verification of WXR Application with JPF

Our goal is to demonstrate that we can automate the exhaustive verification of formal properties on interactive systems using the WRX application. For that we use the JPF model checker, and more precisely jpf-awt, a JPF extension for model checking applications making use of the java.awt and java.swing libraries [24]. This extension provides means of modeling user inputs (e.g., pressing buttons, entering text, selecting items) and understanding awt (or swing) method calls through abstractions.

The first step in using JPF to model-checked interactive applications consists of identifying user input scenarios of interest and capturing them using scripts that are passed to *jpf-awt*. This allows us to "close the system" (in model checking jargon), which in this case means that the verification can be done without human interaction. The scripts use a simple scripting language to describe input sequences of interest; in some ways, they describe ranges of possible interactions with the application. In the case of WRX, we can define a range of scenarios starting with some mode selection and then allowing a user to play freely with tilt selection, then stabilization and finally setting a range of tilt angle. This corresponds to the following script, in which the ANY keyword indicates a random choice between different options:

```
ANY {$MODE_SELECTION.select()}
ANY {NONE | $MANUAL.doClick() | $AUTO.doClick()}
ANY {NONE | $ON.doClick() | OFF.doClick()}
$TILT_ANLGE:input.setText("whatever")
```

The second step consists of capturing a formal property representing functional or non-functional requirements. Non-functional, systemic, requirements such as requiring the absence of deadlocks or other "Java language issues" are checked automatically by JPF. Functional requirements can be expressed, and thus checked, by various means. Assertions are simple instructions, which can be inserted at any point in the user interface code. They simply monitor the value of complex conditions over the values or states of any user interface object. For example, the property, say *P*, stating that "it shall not be possible to manually edit the Tilt angle if the application is in automatic mode or if the stabilization functionality is on" can be checked by placing the assertion based on the following condition

```
(lbl_Selection.getText()!="AUTO") && (lbl_Stabilization.getText()!="ON)
```

in the method that displays a new tilt angle. If *P* can be violated by some of sequence allowed by the input script, then JPF reports the violation and demonstrates it by displaying a trace expressed in terms of the elements described in the script. Assertions are also very useful to check that an entered numerical value is within a specific range, e.g., checking that a title angle value is indeed between 0° and 360°. Assertions are also convenient for expressing some simple safety (in layman's term, asserting that nothing bad happens) properties. However using assertions requires instrumenting the code of the application, which is not always desirable.

The third step consists of running JPF and waiting for its report. If the property is verified, JPF returns some statistics about the analysis time and the number of states and threads explored by the analysis. If the property can be violated by the application, JPF returns a counter-example showing a possible violation sequence. This counter-example is produced as a trace of events corresponding to the events used in the script, thus facilitating the understanding of the counter-example by the developer; displaying a trace as a full Java execution trace would be overwhelming to the developer and would be hard to relate to the application.

4 Related Work

Paterno and Santoro [20] proposed an approach based on formal model-checking (with CADP[3] toolset) of LOTOS specifications of dialogue between the user and the system. Another set of approaches are based on the formal verification of state charts. Campos and Harrison [5] proposed an approach based on SMV [15] model-checking of Interactor specifications. Kamel and Ait Ameur [13] also propose an approach to verify properties for multimodal interactions with SMV model checker. Combéfis et al. [7] propose to translate state chart models into Java programs which can then be verified using Java PathFinder model checker. All of these approaches based on state chart models of interactive application behavior do not provide support for complete and non-ambiguous description of concurrent events driven applications (such as multimodal interactive systems). Furthermore, they do not provide support for simultaneous execution of the application prototype from the models, as actually provided

[3] http://cadp.inria.fr/

by Petshop. Approaches based on the executability of models provide augmented support for describing the conceptual model of the system and for analysis and verification at earlier stage in the process [10]. This kind of approaches provides support for describing exhaustively interactive systems and their behavior, as well as prototyping, testing and verifying synchronously certain types of properties. APEX-CPN Tools [22] is a framework based on colored Petri nets [22], which provides support for rapid prototyping of ubiquitous environments and a predefined set of algorithms for properties verification. However the underlying notation of this framework is less expressive than the ICO one.

5 Conclusion and Future Work

We presented an approach for supporting validation and verification of interactive applications throughout the whole development process. This approach relies on the synergistic use of Petshop tool for producing formal specification of the application and of JPF tool for formal verification of the developed application. This framework provides support for validation and verification of internal and external properties of an interactive application. Petshop tool is used to produce formal specifications of complex interactive critical applications. JPF tool is then used to verify that the final application built from the specification meets the properties requirements.

The presented work will be followed by an investigation on how to verify properties on ICO models. As they are the formal specification of the interactive application and they are also used as the source code of the application prototype, they could be used as the deployed interactive application itself. Future work is to investigate to which extent JPF tool can be used to directly perform model-checking on ICO running models.

References

1. ARINC 661 specification: Cockpit Display System Interfaces to User Systems, Prepared by AEEC. Published by Aeronautical Radio, Inc. (April 22, 2002)
2. Bass, L., John, B., Juristo Juzgado, N., Sánchez Segura, M.I.: Usability-Supporting Architectural Patterns. In: ICSE 2004, pp. 716–717 (2004)
3. Bastide, R., Navarre, D., Palanque, P.: A Tool-Supported Design Framework for Safety Critical Interactive Systems. Interacting with Computers 15(3), 309–328 (2003)
4. Brat, G., Drusinsky, D., Giannakopoulou, D., Goldberg, A., Havelund, K., Lowry, M., Pasareanu, C., Venet, A., Washington, R., Visser, W.: Experimental Evaluation of Verification and Validation Tools on Martian Rover Software. Journal on Formal Methods in Systems Design 25(2-3) (September 2004)
5. Campos, J.C., Harrison, M.D.: Model Checking Interactor Specifications. Journal of Automated Software Engineering 8(3-4), 275–310 (2001)
6. Clarke, E.M., Emerson, E.A., Sistla, A.P.: Automatic verification of finite-state concurrent systems using temporal logic specifications. ACM Transactions on Programming Languages and Systems 8(2), 244–263 (1986)

7. Combéfis, S., Giannakopoulou, D., Pecheur, C., Feary, M.: A Formal Framework for Design and Analysis of Human-Machine Interaction. In: Proceedings of IEEE System, Man and Cybernetics (SMC), Anchorage, USA, pp. 1801–1808 (2011)
8. Dix, A.: Upside down As and algorithms – computational formalisms and theory. In: Carroll, J. (ed.) HCI Models Theories and Frameworks: Toward a Multidisciplinary Science, ch. 14, pp. 381–429. Morgan Kaufmann, San Francisco (2003)
9. Gram, C., Cockton, G.: Design principles for Interactive Software. Chapman & Hall, London (1996)
10. Fuchs, N.E.: Specifications are (preferably) executable. Journal on Software Engineering 7(5), 323–334 (1992)
11. Hewelt, M., Wagner, T., Cabac, L.: Integrating verification into the PAOSE approach. In: Proceedings of the Petri Nets and Software Engineering. International Workshop PNSE 2011, Newcastle upon Tyne, UK, pp. 124–135 (June 2011)
12. Jensen, K., Kristensen, L.M., Wells, L.: Coloured Petri Nets and CPN Tools for modelling and validation of concurrent systems. International Journal on Software Tools for Technology Transfer 9(3-4), 213–254 (2007)
13. Kamel, N., Ait Ameur, Y.: A Formal Model for CARE Usability Properties Verification in Multimodal HCI. In: Proceeding of IEEE International Conference on Pervasive Services, Istanbul, Turkey, July 15-20, pp. 341–348 (2007)
14. Mascheroni, M., Wagner, T., Wüstenberg, L.: Verifying reference nets by means of hypernets: A plugin for Renew. In: Proceedings of the International Workshop on Petri Nets and Software Engineering, PNSE 2010, Braga, Portugal, pp. 39–54 (2010)
15. McMillan, K.L.: Symbolic Model Checking. Kluwer Academic Publishers (1993)
16. Navarre, D., Palanque, P., Ladry, J.-F., Barboni, E.: ICOs: a Model-Based User Interface Description Technique dedicated to Interactive Systems Addressing Usability, Reliability and Scalability. Transactions on Computer-Human Interaction, ACM SIGCHI 16(4), 1–56 (2009)
17. Palanque, P., Bastide, R.: Verification of an Interactive Software by analysis of its formal specification. In: Proceedings of the IFIP TC13 Interact 1995 Conference, Lillehammer, Norway, June 27-29, pp. 191–197 (1995)
18. Palanque, P., Farenc, C.: Embedding Ergonomic Rules as Generic Requirements in a Formal Development Process of Interactive Software. In: Proceedings of IFIP TC 13 Interact 1999 Conference, Edinburg, Scotland, September 1-4 (1999)
19. Palanque, P., Ladry, J.-F., Navarre, D., Barboni, E.: High-Fidelity Prototyping of Interactive Systems Can Be Formal Too. In: Jacko, J.A. (ed.) HCI International 2009, Part I. LNCS, vol. 5610, pp. 667–676. Springer, Heidelberg (2009)
20. Paternó, F., Santoro, C.: Integrating model checking and HCI tools to help designers verify user interface properties. In: Paternó, F. (ed.) DSV-IS 2000. LNCS, vol. 1946, pp. 135–150. Springer, Heidelberg (2001)
21. Pnueli: The temporal logic of programs. In: Proceedings of the 18th IEEE Symposium on Foundation of Computer Science, pp. 46–57 (1977)
22. Silva, J.L., Campos, J.C., Harrison, M.D.: Formal Analysis of Ubiquitous Computing Environments through the APEX Framework. In: EICS 2012: Proceedings of the 4th ACM SIGCHI Symposium on Engineering Interactive Computing Systems, pp. 131–140 (2012)
23. Visser, W., Havelund, K., Brat, G., Park, S.: Model Checking Programs. In: Proceedings of the 15th IEEE International Conference on Automated Software Engineering (ASE 2000). IEEE Computer Society, Washington, DC (2000)
24. Mehlitz, P.C., Tkachuk, O., Ujma, M.: JPF-AWT: Model checking GUI applications. In: ASE 2011, pp. 584–587 (2011)

Formal Pattern Specifications to Facilitate Semi-automated User Interface Generation

Jürgen Engel[1,2], Christian Märtin[1], Christian Herdin[1], and Peter Forbrig[2]

[1] Augsburg University of Applied Sciences, Faculty of Computer Science, An der Hochschule 1, 86161 Augsburg, Germany
{Juergen.Engel,Christian.Maertin}@hs-augsburg.de
[2] University of Rostock, Institute of Computer Science, Albert-Einstein-Strasse 21, 18059 Rostock, Germany
Peter.Forbrig@uni-rostock.de

Abstract. This paper depicts potentialities of formal HCI pattern specifications with regard to facilitate the semi-automated generation of user interfaces for interactive applications. In a first step existing proven and well accepted techniques in the field of model-based user interface development are highlighted and briefly reviewed. Subsequently it is discussed how we combine model-based and pattern-oriented methods within our user interface modeling and development framework in order to partly enable automated user interface generation. In this context a concrete pattern definition approach is introduced and illustrated with tangible examples from the domain of interactive knowledge sharing applications.

Keywords: HCI patterns, model-based user interface development, pattern-based development, formalized pattern specification, user interface generation.

1 Introduction

There are many valuable pattern collections available for user interface (UI) designers and software developers. However, most patterns lack standardized specification and are therefore hard to retrieve and often impractical to use. Due to this fact the Pattern Language Markup Language (PLML) has been introduced in the year 2003. But PLML in turn shows clear weaknesses when patterns are intended to be used for (semi-)automated UI generation. Therefore, we started from PLML as a basis and made several changes and enhancements to support automatic pattern processing. These efforts predominantly focus on features conveying pattern relationship modeling and provision of means for automated pattern treatment. This paper deals with well-known and widely accepted model-based techniques and how they can be combined with a pattern-based approach where emphasis is on the structured and formal specification of HCI patterns.

M. Kurosu (Ed.): Human-Computer Interaction, Part I, HCII 2013, LNCS 8004, pp. 300–309, 2013.

2 Related Work

Patterns were originally introduced by Christopher Alexander in 1977 as a means to accomplish reuse when solving problems in architecture and urban planning [1]. Eighteen years later, the pattern concepts were translated to the domains of software architecture and software engineering by the Gang of Four (GoF) [11]. Nowadays patterns are also applied to the fields of HCI [8], user experience (UX) [19], usability engineering [13], task modeling [10], and application security [21].

There exist many widely accepted pattern collections, for instance the ones of Jenifer Tidwell [18], Martijn van Welie [20], or Douglas van Duyne [5]. However, different pattern authors usually describe their patterns in different and inconsistent styles. This can be regarded as a clear shortcoming of patterns, because this makes it difficult or even impossible to search, choose and reference patterns across the various pattern collections. In a workshop held within the context of the CHI 2003 conference the participants aimed at unification of pattern descriptions and guidance for the authors. Hence the Pattern Language Markup Language (PLML) version 1.1 was constituted. According to PLML documentation of a certain pattern should consist of the following elements: a pattern identifier, name, alias, illustration, descriptions of the respective problem, context and solution, forces, synopsis, diagram, evidence, confidence, literature, implementation, related patterns, pattern links, and management information [8].

In [7] it is concluded that it is possible to map the pattern descriptions contained in the previously mentioned pattern collections into PLML compliant formats, however this cannot be done in a fully automated manner.

Extensions and changes were suggested in PLML version 1.2 [4]. These efforts strived to make PLML more feasible for Management of User Interface Patterns (MUIP). A second development is PLMLx [3]. Additional pattern description elements are introduced, including organization, resulting context, and acknowledgements. Further the <Management information> element is being extended and the <Example> and <Rationale> elements are separated from each other. A third approach is the XPLML framework which can be regarded as a bundle of specifications and tools to formalize HCI patterns. The framework is intended to close the gap between the textual pattern specifications and their application in user interface software. The XPLML framework is implemented on the basis of seven modules: unified HCI pattern form, semantic metadata, semantic relations among patterns, atomic particles of HCI design patterns, requirements engineering in HCI community, survey of HCI design pattern management tools, and specification documentation.

The basic idea to support user interface designers and software developers with a combination of both, model-based techniques and pattern-based methods is realized by the integrated framework for pattern-based modeling and generation of interactive systems (PaMGIS) [6]. PaMGIS is developed by the Automation in Usability Engineering group (AUE) at Augsburg University of Applied Sciences. As illustrated in Figure 1, this framework allows for creation of abstract user interface models (AUI) on the basis of diverse fundamental information about the users, the users' tasks, used devices, and environment. Additionally the AUI designer can make use of patterns stored in a pattern repository. The AUI is iteratively transformed into a semi-abstract

UI model which in turn is used to generate respective user interface source code. The framework has been continuously improved. Patterns are now available in a modified PLML format and seamless pattern hierarchies can be modeled [7].

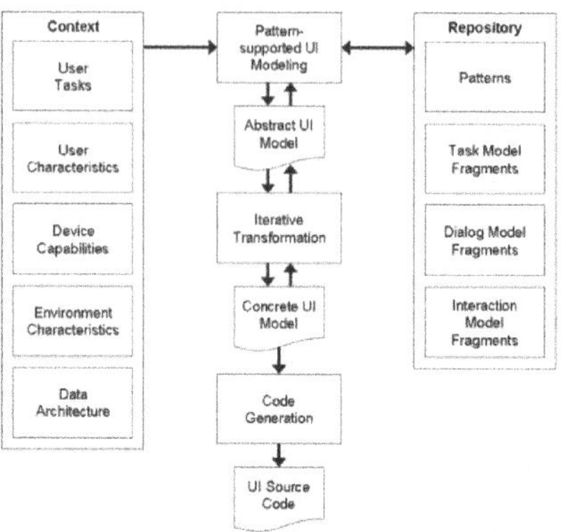

Fig. 1. Functional overview of the PaMGIS framework

Task models play an important role in the area of HCI in general and, in particular, for model-based user interface development. They represent the logical activities of users executed in order to reach their goals [16]. Therefore, knowing the necessary user tasks is fundamental to the design process [15]. A well-known approach for representing task models is ConcurTaskTrees (CTT). CTT provides a graphical syntax and is organized in a strictly hierarchical structure, so that complex tasks can be iteratively decomposed into less complex subtasks until a certain level of granularity is reached. Thus, the logical structure of the task models is represented in a tree-like manner. CTT distinguishes four different task types, i.e. user, interaction, application, and abstract tasks. Temporal relationships between tasks can be expressed by a variety of temporal operators, i.e. hierarchy, enabling, choice, enabling with information passing, concurrent tasks, concurrent communicating tasks, task independence, disabling, and suspend-resume. Additionally tasks can be defined as optional or iterative [15]. ConcurTaskTrees are used for task model specifications within the PaMGIS framework. An illustrated example can be viewed in chapter 3.

Besides task models, dialog models comprise essential information for user interface generation. Dialogs can be directly derived from the related task model [2]. Here, it is assumed that all tasks which are active at a certain point in time are to be visualized within a common dialog. This can be regarded feasible for relatively small task models, but fails for more complex models since related user interfaces tend to be overloaded [9]. This phenomenon can be avoided by explicitly designing navigation specifications on the basis of abstract dialog graphs [17] and assigning individual tasks of the task model to the dialog specification nodes. Using this technique it is possible to define platform-specific navigation models [9]. The nodes of the dialog graph represent dialogs of different types, i.e. single, multiple, modal, and complex. The edges indicate whether dialog transitions are of sequential or concurrent nature [9]. Dialog graphs are used to define platform-dependent dialog models within the PaMGIS framework. Exemplary dialog graphs are provided in chapter 3.

3 Formal Pattern Specifications

The intension of the PaMGIS framework is to combine model- and pattern-based methods and techniques in order to make user interface modeling and realization more easy and practicable even for users with less development skills. Once the relevant models are available the framework takes the job to at least semi-automatically transform the models iteratively and generate UI source code. One of the basic ideas is also to support the construction of the relevant models by means of patterns. In this sense PLML shows some deficiencies notably in terms of pattern relation modeling and provision of details required for automated pattern processing. Indeed PLML provides relevant description elements, i.e. <Pattern-link> and <Implementation>, but the former lacks of detail for appropriate pattern referencing and the latter is completely unstructured yet. Therefore, we started with PLML version 1.1 and made several changes and enhancements which mainly apply to the specification elements <Pattern ID>, <Pattern-link>, and <Implementation> as illustrated in Table 1. Further we introduced a new element named <Embedding-link> which is highlighted in [14]. The entire structure of the resulting PLML variant which we now call PaMGIS Pattern Specification Language (PPSL) is also summarized in [14].

Table 1. Selected pattern specification elements of the PaMGIS Framework

Specification Element	Brief Description
UPID	Unique pattern identifier
CollectionID	Identifier of the respective pattern collection
PatternID	Pattern identifier
Pattern revision	Revision of referenced pattern
InstanceID	Pattern instance identifier
Pattern-link	Relationship to other patterns or pattern instances
LinkID	Unique link identifier
Link-type	Type of link (i.e. PERMANENT or TEMPORARY)
Relationship-type	Type of relation
Pattern identification	UPID of the respective pattern
Label	Name of the pattern link
Implementation	Code or model fragments or details of technical realization
Task model fragment	Specification of pattern-intrinsic tasks and their relationships based on an modified CTT notation
Dialog model fragment	Context-specific definition of dialogs and their relations based on dialog graphs
Interaction model fragment	Abstract specification of the dynamic aspects of the user interface dialogs

Details of the PLML modifications are discussed and illustrated in the following by means of patterns identified during the p.i.t.c.h. project (pattern-based interactive tools for improved communication habits in knowledge transfers) that was conducted by AUE and two medium-sized enterprises and was focused at the knowledge management domain [12]. Within this context prototypical applications for individual platforms were developed.

3.1 Relationships of Patterns

As already elaborated in [7] automated pattern processing demands adequate and accurate pattern referencing. On one hand, this affects the PLML specification element <Pattern ID> which must allow for exact identification of an individual pattern. On the other hand, <Pattern-link> must be capable to address and describe particular pattern relations. Therefore, we have replaced PLML's <Pattern id> element by <UPID> which now is a composite of identifiers of the relevant pattern collection, the pattern itself, the particular pattern revision, and an individual pattern instance. This allows to distinguish individual pattern entities in the case a pattern is applied more than once in a certain context.

In terms of the PLML specification element <Pattern-link> there is a need to distinguish two fundamental types of pattern links. First, there exist kinds of permanent links to other patterns, which can be regarded as "hard-coded" and generally will not change for a long period of time. If a permanent link is considered to be changed this would normally lead to a new revision of the pattern. As soon as a respective pattern is applied, all related patterns referenced by permanent links are also applied automatically. Moreover, there must be a possibility to model temporary pattern links in case a relationship to an individual pattern is required just under certain circumstances or in a specific context. Hence we defined a sub-element of <Pattern-link> as outlined in Table 1, i.e. <Link-type>. A descriptive example is given in [7].

3.2 Support for Automated Pattern Processing

In order to equip HCI patterns with information facilitating automated pattern processing and user interface generation we render the so far unstructured PLML element <Implementation> more precisely. For this reason we store relevant task model, dialog model, and interaction model fragments together with the patterns. Thus, we have defined a sub-element of <Implementation> named <Fragment>. Fragments can be regarded as building blocks which can be used to improve the overall user interface model by applying a pattern in the design process.

Task models used within the PaMGIS framework are expressed in CTT syntax. Therefore, the task model fragment of a particular pattern is defined in CTT XML format. Figure 2 shows an excerpt of the task model of the p.i.t.c.h. pattern *Advanced Search* [7].

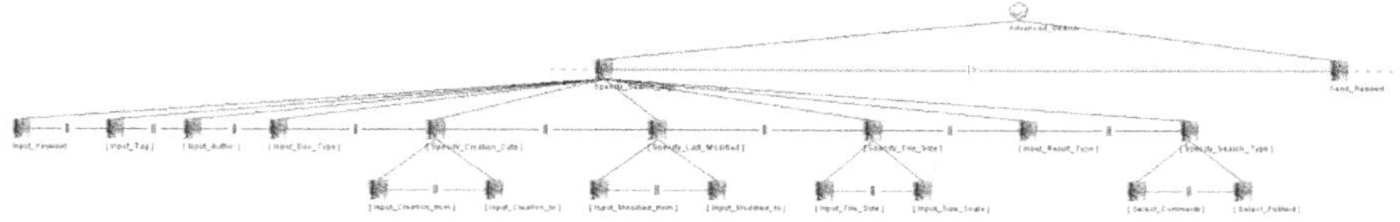

Fig. 2. Excerpt of the task model of the *Advanced Search* pattern

In this example we focus on interaction tasks which directly contribute to the resulting user interface while abstract tasks, user tasks and application tasks are less important within the scope of this paper. We iteratively refine the task model until the leaves of the task tree can be matched to exactly one interaction object. For this purpose we have introduced an additional specification element <IeRef> which establishes a link between the task and a certain interaction element specified within the interaction model fragment (see below). The XML representation of the above task model fragment is sketched in Figure 3.

```
<Fragment Type="TaskModel" Identifier="TMF_0001">
   <Task Identifier="PAS_0001" Category="abstraction" Iterative="false"
         Optional="false" Frequency=" ">
      <Name>Advanced_Search</Name>
      <Parent name=" "/>
      <SiblingLeft name=" " TempOp="Interleaving"/>
      <SiblingRight name=" "/>
      <SubTask>
         ...
         <Task Identifier="PAS_0003" Category="interaction"
               Iterative="false" Optional="false" Frequency=" ">
            <Name>Specify_Search_Args</Name>
            <TemporalOperator name="SuspendResume"/>
            <Parent name="Advanced_Search"/>
            <SiblingLeft name="Decide_Search_Args"/>
            <SiblingRight name="Send_Request"/>
            <SubTask>
               <Task Identifier="PAS_0013" Category="interaction"
                     Iterative="false" Optional="false" Frequency=" ">
                  <Name>Input_Keyword</Name>
                  <TemporalOperator name="Interleaving"/>
                  <Parent name="Specify_Search_Args"/>
                  <SiblingLeft name="Decide_Search_args"/>
                  <SiblingRight name="Input_Tags"/>
                  <IeRef>IE_0001</IeRef>
               </Task>
            </Subtask>
         </Task>
         ...
      </Subtask>
   <Task>
</Fragment>
```

Fig. 3. XML code snippet of the *Advanced Search* pattern's task model

Here, the subtask *Input_keyword* is linked to an interaction element with ID *IE_0001*. The content of the elements marked in bold have to be calculated and replaced when the pattern is applied respectively the model fragment is integrated into the overall task model. While the <Parent>, <SiblingLeft> and possibly <SiblingRight> elements are to be automatically aligned to the conditions inside the overall task model the data held within the <TempOp> attribute of the <SiblingLeft> element is destined to be moved to the <TemporalOperator> element of the left sibling task and deleted from the task model fragment. Note that dependent on the task types included in the task model fragment adjustments of the type of parent elements might be necessary, i.e. becoming abstract tasks. However, this can be covered automatically, too.

While one pattern usually possesses one particular task model fragment it might include several dialog model fragments. Dialog models represent target platform-specific navigations. In the mentioned example of the *Advanced Search* pattern all subtasks can be assigned to one single dialog on a desktop PC equipped with a large display. The related dialog graph can be viewed on the left and the resulting UI dialog on the right side of Figure 4.

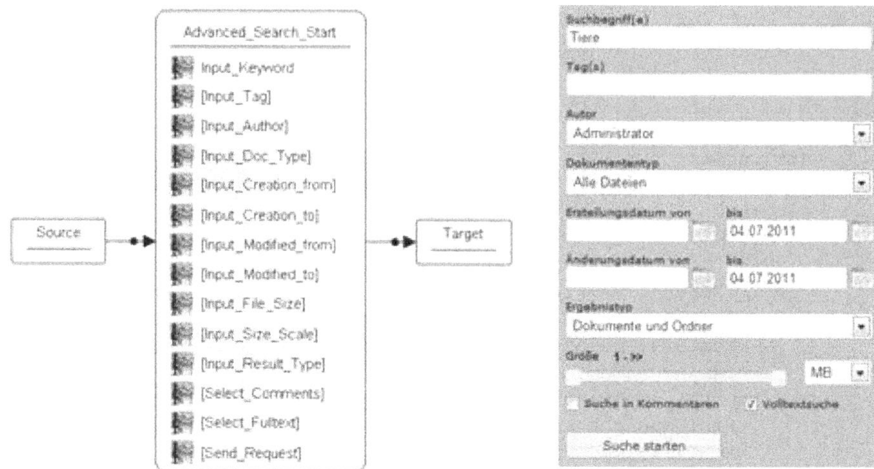

Fig. 4. Possible desktop PC dialog graph (left) and resulting UI (right)

The related XML representation of the PC desktop dialog model fragment is sketched in Figure 5. The assignment of tasks to the dialog is accomplished by means of the <Coverage> specification element.

```
<Fragment Type="DialogModel" Identifier"DMF_0001">
   <DMName>Advanced_Search_Desktop</DMName>
   <Dialog>
      <DID>00010001</DID>
      <DName>Prepare_Advanced_Search<DName>
      <Coverage>
         <Task>
            <TID>PAS_0003</TID
            <TName>Specify_Search_Args</TName>
            <Processing>recursive</Processing>
         </Task>
         <Task>
            <TID>PAS_0004</TID>
            <TName>Send_Request</TName>
            <Processing>exclusive<Processing>
         </Task>
      </Coverage>
   </Dialog>
</Fragment>
```

Fig. 5. XML code snippet of the desktop PC dialog model

The <Processing> element indicates whether solely the mentioned subtask itself (*exclusive*) or all subtasks shall also be included in the dialog specification (*recursive*). In contrast to this simple example the dialog model for mobile phones is more complex because owing to screen size limits the functionality has to be split into several dialogs. The various nodes in the task tree help to compose meaningful groups. Note that not all tasks are incorporated in the mobile dialog model. The respective dialog graph is illustrated on the left of Figure 6. The resulting UI dialog is shown on the right side.

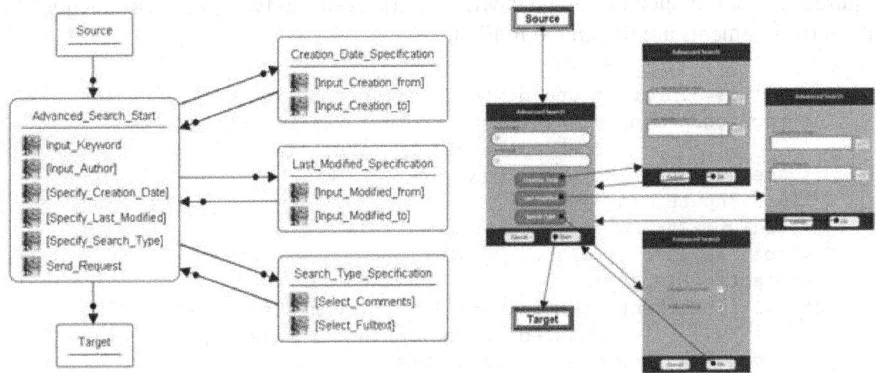

Fig. 6. Possible mobile phone dialog graph (left) and resulting UI (right)

Similar to the desktop version it is necessary to assign the tasks to particular dialogs using the <Coverage> element. But in addition it must be specified when and how a transition to a different dialog shall happen. For this purpose we introduced the <DialogFlow> element which allows for specification of respective successor dialogs and interaction elements triggering the dialog transition. As shown in Figure 7 both, the successor dialog and the interaction element are referenced via appropriate identifiers.

```
<Fragment Type="DialogModel" Identifier"DMF_0002">
   <DMName>Advanced_Search_Mobile</Name>
   <Dialog>
      <DID>00020001</DID>
      <DName>Advanced_Search_Start</DName>
      <Coverage>
         ...
      </Coverage>
      <DialogFlow>
         <Successor Type="sequential">
            <DID>00020002</DID>
            <Trigger>
               <IeRef>IE_0101</IeRef>
               <Event>On_Klick</Event>
            </Trigger>
         </Successor>
         ...
      </DialogFlow>
   </DialogFlow>
</Fragment>
```

Fig. 7. XML code snippet of the mobile phone dialog model

The three dialogs *Creation_Date_Specification*, *Last_Modified_Specification*, and *Search_Type_Specification* do yet neither directly nor indirectly possess an interaction element that could trigger the transition back to the *Advanced_Search_Start* dialog. This problem is fixed by applying the *OK_Cancel* pattern in each case.

Finally the interaction model fragment contains the abstract specifications of the required interaction elements. The XML definitions of the two previously mentioned interaction elements are illustrated in Figure 8.

```
<Fragment Type="InteractionModel" Identifier"IMF_0001">
   <InteractionElement Identifier="IE_0001" Visible="true"
                       Enabled="true" Optional="false">
      <Name>userInput_Keyword</Name>
      <Type>InputField</Type>
      <DataType>String</DataType>
      <Label>Keyword(s)</Label>
   </InteractionElement>
   <InteractionElement Identifier="IE_0101" Visible="true"
                       Enabled="true" Optional="false">
      <Name>userAction_CreationDate</Name>
      <Type>TransitionActivator</Type>
      <Event>OnKlick</Event>
      <Label>Creation Date</Label>
   </InteractionElement>
</Fragment>
```

Fig. 8. XML code snippet of the interaction model fragment

Some of the elements specified in the interaction model address user inputs and system outputs, e.g. the interaction element *userInput_Keyword* specified in the XML code snipped above. Such elements can be regarded as interface to the underlying business logic of the particular software.

During the model transformation process the defined abstract interaction elements are substantiated until they can be mapped to the particular widget sets appropriate for the present context of use and available on the target platform. For instance, an abstract *TransitionActivator* might become a link in a browser-based application or a button in a Windows-based fat client.

4 Conclusion

In this paper, we have introduced our approach to specify HCI patterns formally in order to support automatic respectively semi-automated pattern processing and user interface generation. We took PLML version 1.1 as basis and reworked the mechanisms for appropriate modeling of relationships between patterns, i.e. the specification elements <Pattern id> and <Pattern-link>. Additionally we have structured the <Implementation> element in order to hold fragments of task, dialog, and interaction models which can be used during the user interface model design process and for UI generation purposes. These enhancements are explained and illustrated by means of examples from experimental applications in the knowledge sharing domain.

In our current research we focus on further improvements of model design and code generation automation.

References

1. Alexander, C., et al.: A pattern language. Oxford University Press (1977)
2. Berti, S., et al.: A transformation-based environment for designing multi-device interactive applications. In: Proceedings of the 9th International Conference on Intelligent User Interfaces, Funchal (January 2004)
3. Bienhaus, D.: PLMLx Doc. (2004), `http://www.cs.kent.ac.uk/people/staff/saf/patterns/plml.html` (last website call on February 3, 2012)
4. Deng, J., Kemp, E., Todd, E.G. (Hg.): Focusing on a standard pattern form: the development and evaluation of MUIP. In: Proceedings of the 6th ACM SIGCHI New Zealand Chapter's International Conference on Computer-Human Interaction: Design Centered HCI (2006)
5. van Duyne, D., Landay, J., Hong, J.: The Design of Sites, Patterns for Creating Winning Websites, 2nd edn. Prentice Hall International (2006) ISBN 0-13-134555-9
6. Engel, J., Märtin, C.: PaMGIS: A Framework for Pattern-based Modeling and Generation of Interactive Systems. In: Jacko, J.A. (ed.) HCI International 2009, Part I. LNCS, vol. 5610, pp. 826–835. Springer, Heidelberg (2009)
7. Engel, J., Märtin, C., Herdin, C.: Exploiting HCI Pattern Collections for User Interface Generation. In: Proceedings of PATTERNS 2012, the 4th International Conferences of Pervasive Patterns and Applications, Nice, France, pp. 36–44 (2012)
8. Fincher, S., et al.: Perspectives on HCI patterns: concepts and tools. In: CHI 2003 Extended Abstracts on Human Factors in Computing Systems, Ft. Lauderdale, Florida, USA, pp. 1044–1045. ACM (2003)
9. Forbrig, P., Reichart, D.: Spezifikation von "Multiple User Interfaces" mit Dialoggraphen. In: Processdings of INFORMATIK 2007: Informatik Trifft Logistik, Beiträge der 37, Bremen. Jahrestagung der Gesellschaft für Informatik e.V., GI (September 2007)
10. Gaffar, A., et al.: Modeling patterns for task models. In: TAMODIA 2004 Proceedings of the 3rd Annual Conference on Task Models and Diagrams. ACM, New York (2004)
11. Gamma, E., et al.: Design Patterns. Elements of Reusable Object-Oriented Software. Addison-Wesley, Reading (1995)
12. Kaelber, C., Märtin, C.: From Structural Analysis to Scenarios and Patterns for Knowledge Sharing Applications. In: Jacko, J.A. (ed.) Human-Computer Interaction, Part I, HCII 2011. LNCS, vol. 6761, pp. 258–267. Springer, Heidelberg (2011)
13. Marcus, A.: Patterns within Patterns. Interactions 11(2), 28–34 (2004)
14. Märtin, C., Herdin, C., Engel, J.: Patterns and models for automated user interface construction – in search of the missing links. In: Kurosu, M. (ed.) Human-Computer Interaction, Part I, HCII 2013. LNCS, vol. 8004, pp. 401–410. Springer, Heidelberg (2013)
15. Paternò, F.: ConcurTaskTrees: An Engineered Approach to Model-based Design of Interactive Systems. ISTI-C.N.R., Pisa (2001)
16. Paternò, F.: Model-based Design and Evaluation of Interactive Applications. Springer, London (2000)
17. Schlungbaum, E., Elwert, T.: Dialogue Graphs – A Formal and Visual Specification Technique for Dialogue Modelling. Springer (1996)
18. Tidwell, J.: Designing Interfaces. Patterns for Effective Interaction Design, 2nd edn. O'Reilly Media Inc. (2011) ISBN 978-1-449-37970-4
19. Tiedtke, T., Krach, T., Märtin, C.: Multi-Level Patterns for the Planes of User Experience. In: Proc. of HCI International, July 22-27. Theories Models and Processes in HCI, vol. 4. Lawrence Erlbaum, Las Vegas (2005)
20. van Welie, M.: Patterns in Interaction Design, `http://www.welie.com` (last website call on November 25, 2012)
21. Yoder, J., Barcalow, J.: Architectural patterns for enabling application security. In: International Conference on Pattern Language of Programs, PLoP (1997)

A Mobile Application Flow Representation for Mutual Understanding of IT and Healthcare Professionals

Yusuf Nasuh Erturan[1], Semih Bilgen[2], Gul Tokdemir[3], Nergiz E. Cagiltay[4], Ekrem Yildiz[5], and Esra Özcebe[6]

[1] Department of Medical Informatics - METU, Ankara, Turkey
nasuherturan@gmail.com
[2] Electrical Engineering Department - METU, Ankara, Turkey
bilgen@metu.edu.tr
[3] Department of Computer Engineering, Cankaya University, Ankara, Turkey
gtokdemir@cankaya.edu.tr
[4] Department of Software Engineering, Atılım University, Ankara, Turkey
nergiz@atilim.edu.tr
[5] Department of Information Sciences, METU, Ankara, Turkey
ekrem.yildiz@live.com
[6] Faculty of Education, International Cyprus University, Lefkosa, Cyprus
eozcebe@gmail.com

Abstract. Ever since mobile applications were developed and became popular, they have started to take part in almost every field of our lives. Healthcare is one of the most popular fields that mobile applications have become a part of. However, development of mobile healthcare applications requires an inter-disciplinary work on which people from different domains should communicate. To do so efficiently, mobile application instructions should be provided as clearly as possible so that mutual understanding can be achieved. This study, aims to provide a methodology to provide the common grounds for healthcare and IT specialists so that to improve the satisfaction level of all the stakeholders of the system from the provided IT services and the end-user interfaces. In other words, by providing a better communication medium for the stakeholders during the design phase, we believe that software development process will be improved, so do their satisfaction from the developed system.

Keywords: Mobile healthcare, Communication gap, Representation guideline.

1 Introduction

Ever since the mobile applications were developed and became popular, they have started to take part in almost every field of our lives. Healthcare is one of the most popular fields that mobile applications have become a part of. According to a report written by Heather Clancy and published by Mobile Healthcare in 2011, over the next four years, mobile healthcare applications will change the way doctors communicate with each other, their work operations and also the way how healthcare organizations

M. Kurosu (Ed.): Human-Computer Interaction, Part I, HCII 2013, LNCS 8004, pp. 310–319, 2013.

interact with patient communities (Clancy, 2011). The vision of Clancy has already started to come true. A study which was conducted by "Pyramid Research Group" (HealthcareITNews, 2010) in 2011 showed that, more than 200 million mobile health applications were in use by doctors and patients and this number would be tripled in 2012. Another result from that study is that, 70 percent of people worldwide are interested in having access to at least one m-health application and they are willing to pay for it (HealthcareITNews, 2010). Furthermore, mobile healthcare application market was $718 million in 2011 and it would reach $1.3 billion in 2012 (Research2guidance, 2012). Another report which was prepared by Arthur D. Little Co. in 2011 also stated that mobile health potential value will be $10 billion within the next five years (Arthur, 2011).This is a great appetizer for IT companies, so they develop new strategies to add mobile healthcare into their future plans.

Healthcare IT is an interdisciplinary field and it is much more complicated than other interdisciplinary fields, because health issues are critical in terms of patients' lives. Moreover, integration of mobile technologies into healthcare (especially into mobile healthcare applications) is one of the hot topics in the field. It is because the market share of mobile health applications is so huge, that the numbers are expressed in billions of dollars. In such a profitable market, IT companies have started to invest in mobile healthcare to get a market share.

'Mobile healthcare IT applications'; just the phrase itself includes different domains: Mobile, healthcare, IT and application domain. As it can be inferred, developing a mobile healthcare IT application requires gathering of people from different expertise. Gathering those people is the easy task; however, making them work on the same subject and communicate through the same language may not be that easy. Uniting all those people in a team requires utmost commitment to overcome the communication gap, since the application developers do not have the related medical knowledge and the medical staff don't understand the software code unless they are provided a human-readable visualization (Ongenae, 2010). To overcome this problem, a document, which facilitates mutual understanding, should be provided to all those people. There are different kinds of guidelines developed for this purpose. However, if the guidelines are in a mass detailed format, the size of the guidelines may become a problem and if they are superficially prepared, they can be vague to interpret (Backere, Steurbaut, Colpaert & Decruyenaere, 2010).

People from different domains – in our case IT people and healthcare specialists – usually have different ways of thinking. Studies show that people from healthcare domain and technical domain are from different cultures, they use different languages to communicate, they do not know each other's domains and because of this reason the technology integration in medical domain requires these people to come together and work closely (Dankelman, Grimbergen & Stassen, 2007). However people from healthcare domain are usually too busy to spend time on such collaborations and it is not always possible these two groups of people come together and work together effectively. Kilov and Sack (2007) state that communication of experts from different domains is only possible through a joint ontology and creation of this ontology requires a common system of concepts which are applicable and extensible to any specific viewpoint (Kilov & Sack, 2009). At this point the question is how these common concepts will be created and what these common concepts will be.

In this study, we aim to provide a methodology to provide the common grounds for healthcare and IT specialists. The main idea behind this developed methodology is to improve the satisfaction level of all stakeholders of the system from the provided IT services and the end-user interfaces. In other words, by providing a better communication medium for the stakeholders during the design phase, we believe that software development process will be improved, so do their satisfaction from the developed system.

Specifically in this study, the mobile application development process is analyzed with this aim. We provide a clear and efficient MAFR that can be used by IT professionals as well as healthcare professionals during mobile healthcare application development process, to ensure mutual understanding of the functionality and the interface specifications of the mobile application. In order to illustrate the application of our proposal, a mobile healthcare application developed specifically for speech and language therapy of children with Speech Sound Disorder has been examined. The effectiveness and usability of the proposed MAFR is tested during the design of a mobile health application, which involves four domain experts. In this study, the development stages of the system are well documented to better understand the communication problems of these specialists and how the proposed approach addresses these problems. Additionally, an observer observed all communication stages during the application of the proposed methodology and interviews with stakeholders are conducted to better understand the effectiveness of the proposed representation. The study analyses the collected data to explore the effect of proposed approach to improve the communication between these groups of people and to increase the success of the project in terms of development time and effectiveness.

The data collected from this study is analyzed descriptively to better understand the effect of the proposed communication tool on the quality and success of the developed software system.

2 Mobile Application Flow Representation (MAFR)

Mobile Application Flow Representation (MAFR) includes representation elements, explanation of these elements, and the MAFR methodology that is used during mobile application design phase.

2.1 Representation Elements

Representation elements are the shapes that are shown to the users about the mobile application interaction design. These elements consist of gestures, pages, buttons, pictures, videos, text fields as presented in Table 1.

Table 1. Representation Elements

Notation	Name	Explanation
	Touch	Touch on the related element.
	Touch and Hold	Touch on related element and hold your finger for a while
	Slide right or Slide left	Touch on the element and with the finger touched on it; slide it to the right or to the left.
	Zoom in	Touch on the related element with two fingers and with the fingers touched on it, zoom in the related element.
	Zoom out	Touch on the related element with two fingers and with the fingers touched on it, zoom out the related element.
	Drag object	Touch on the related element and with the finger touched on it, drag the related element.
	Action lines	Action line direct the user to the related page based on the users actions. This line shows that what the application will display next.
< text >	Explanation for the action line	Used for explaining the action line. For example, if the related item is a touchable item, the explanation will be <touched>.
	Touchable button	Shows that user can touch on the button.
	Touchable combobox button	Shows that user can touch on the combobox therefore, the list in the combobox will be showed to the user.
	Touchable radio button	Shows that user can touch on the items listed, i.e. user will mark the item by touching on it.
	Touchable checkbox button	Shows that user can touch on the items listed, i.e. user will mark the item by touching on it.
A	Touchable input text button	Shows that user can touch on the textbox and make an input.

Table 1. (*continued*)

A	Text Field	Shows the content as simple text format so that user can read what is written in it. For example, the content of a web page.
	Touchable Image	Shows that user can touch on the image.
	Touchable Video	Shows that user can touch on the video.
<< Others >>	Others	Special buttons for specific applications. It can be unique for that application and can be shown as what it is look like.

For clarification, explanations should be as detailed as possible. For instance, if the application has a main page with 5 touchable buttons on it, they are pictured and coded as follows:

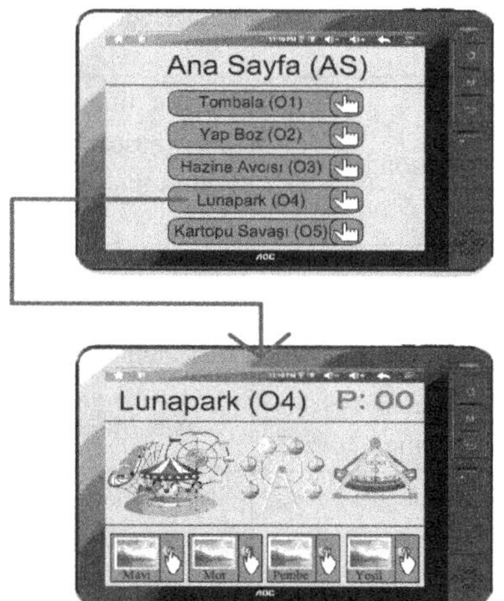

Fig. 1. Example Notation

This example shows that there is a main page including 5 touchable buttons on it. When a user touches a button, the flow goes to the related page. In this example when the user touches on 4th touchable button the flow goes to "Lunapark (O4)" game page.

Action line directs the user to the related page based on the user's actions. This line shows that what the application will display next. In figure 1, there are two interfaces. First one is the main page and the other one is the page activated based on the user's action. Transitions are showed with the arrows. Second page, which is named as "Lunapark (O4)", has 3 images, 4 drag objects and the score.

3 Case Study

The proposed MAFR approach is applied in development of a mobile application for speech and language disorder domain. The case study aims to test the proposed MAFR that aims to eliminate the communication gap between therapist and mobile software developers especially for a speech and language disorder application. Speech and Language disordered patients refers to a group of people who have deficits in both speech (fluency, rate, or articulation) and language (comprehension, expression, or usage) (Dennis & Baker, 2002). Patients who have speech and language disorder need to perform some practices which are guided by therapists to eliminate the disorder effects. In order to carry out those practices patients should meet with their therapist very often. However, some patients especially who live in rural areas do not have an opportunity to meet with therapists frequently. Speech and language disorder mobile application helps to solve this problem for the patients and therapists. The mobile application for this purpose should be developed same as what the subject matter exactly does in practices. Therefore, the application should reflect the real practice as much as possible, which requires broad communication of therapist and application developers. For the case study, a mobile application design is performed using the proposed MAFR with the aim of providing a common communication medium between therapist and developers.

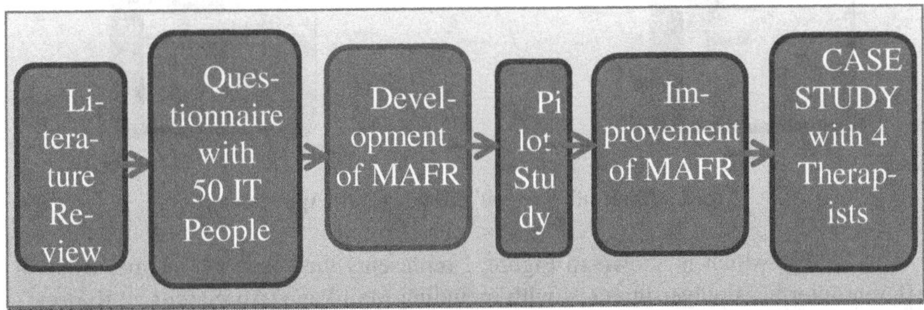

Fig. 2. Research Flow

As shown in Figure 2, first of all, a literature study on mobile application design guidelines was performed. After the analysis of literature review, a questionnaire was conducted to 50 people from IT domain and gathered their experiences about the problems that they had faced with people from other domain during development process. Then, MAFR was developed and a pilot study with one therapist was performed to evaluate MAFR and the methods that are applied to the patients during the therapy. According to the results of the pilot study, MAFR was improved and then a case study with four therapists was conducted and after the interviews therapists' views about MAFR were collected. One of the therapists has 20 years of experience in language and speech disorder area, who was also a child development and education specialist. The second therapist has 12 years of experience in language and speech disorder area who was a hearing-impaired teacher. The third therapist has 9 years experiences in language and speech disorder area. The fourth therapist has

3 years experiences in language and speech disorder area and she had four year experience in teaching of mentally disordered people.

3.1 MAFR of the Pilot Application

MAFR of the pilot application which was used during the interviews with therapists is given below. These representations were shown to the therapists and their opinions were collected.

Fig. 3. MAFR of "Kartopu" Mobile Game Application

The MAFR which is shown in Figure 2 represents the "Kartopu" game. It has 6 different interfaces player interacts with including MainPage (AnaSayfa). "Kartopu" game is aimed to improve patients' vocabulary. Moreover, as they play the game their perception will also be improved since they will learn more objects. In the game, questions like "Which one is a book?", and four pictures are shown to the patients. When patient drag the snowball onto the correct object, the application will give a feedback as "Congratulations" and the patient gets 10 points, and then the new question comes to the screen. If the patient drags the snowball to the wrong object the application will give a feedback as "Wrong answer" and the patient does not get any point, and then the new question follows. At the end of the game, score and logs will be recorded to see the improvement of the patient.

4 Results

According to the questionnaire conducted to 50 people from IT domain, they are facing with different kinds of problems during development process. Results of the questionnaire showed that 50% of the attendees need new tools and models to describe the process to the customers easily. Moreover, 70% of the attendees said that those kinds of tools and models can decrease both development process of the application and cost of the software. Furthermore, 45% of the attendees mentioned that customers should be in the software development process. Besides, 71% of the attendees stated that the reason why the software projects last more than the project time and exceeds the project cost is requirements not clearly identified by the customers. 80% of the attendees stated the problem between them and customers. They said that they have communication problem because of the fact that they either can't express themselves to customers or customers can't express what they what to them. 60% of the attendees think that there is a communication gap between customers from different domains and people from IT domain. Also in open-ended questions of the questionnaire, most of the attendees mentioned about the importance of software requirements as the problems between customers and software developers are caused by unclear requirements and having difficulty in communication. Moreover, as a model used in development process, most of the attendees use pictures, slides and storyboard. So, they need a simple model that can learly understandable by both customers and people from IT domain.

From the questionnaire, it can be concluded that there is a communication gap between customers and people from IT domain when they tried to identify the requirements of the software application which will cause the exceeding of project cost and time. In order to full this gap, it would be better to have new tool or model which will not only decrease the project time and cost but also increase the effective software application since the requirements are clearly identified.

As to interviews, the interviews with four subject matter experts have lasted 30 minutes each. The questions used during the interviews are provided in Appendix A. The proposed mobile application design has included a brief explanation of the application and its design in MAFR. Each interview is recorded and transcribed for analysis. Four interviewees were asked to examine MAFR document in 10 minutes separately. After then, the interview questions were asked to the therapists to get their ideas about MAFR.

The results showed that the proposed MAFR is considered to be very important during such kind of development process in terms of effectiveness, and efficiency of the process.

A 12-year-experienced interviewee said that "using such kind of a model during development process is very effective". A 9-year-experienced interviewee told that "conversations are not always a good way and can be understood differently from person to person".

All of the interviewees stated that they are fully satisfied with this development process and using this model makes the process efficient. During the usual development process, 20-year-experienced interviewee stated that it is pointless to get subject matter experts' ideas after the development is over. She mentioned that the efficient way is correcting misunderstandings during the process. For instance, in our case all the four therapists corrected different parts of our misunderstandings and neither therapists nor software experts have to do the development twice.

Finally, two of the interviewees stated that representation elements of this MAFR are so easy to understand that they don't even need to look at the explanations. They said that most people can easily understand the elements.

"Have you ever been in a development process of a software or application?" was one of the questions directed to interviewees. None of the therapists have been in a development process of a software or application. They just face with the application after it is developed. They stated that most of the applications they have faced with have serious problems which have to be taken into consideration in terms of relevance to subject, relevance to exercises used in the field and need of people in the target group.

"What do you think about the MAFR?", "Did you understand the representation easily?" were other questions. Therapists said that the representation elements of the MAFR are so easy to understand that they didn't even need to read the explanations.

"What are the positive and negative parts of the MAFR?" All of the interviewees stated that subject matter experts should definitely be included in the development process. However, most of the times they can't tell precisely what they want to tell the IT professionals and most of the times they don't understand what the IT professionals tell them. The positive part of this MAFR is that it is a common conversation platform for different professions. When it comes to the negative part of the MAFR, two of the interviewees stated that it shouldn't be like a storyboard and there is no need to represent all pages of the application with the MAFR. It should be as simple as it can be.

5 Conclusion

During the development process, IT companies have serious communication problems while facing with customers. These problems are because of either they can't efficiently express themselves to customers or customers can't tell what they really want from them. To overcome this problem they mostly use UML representations but they are not very well understood by customers, in our case healthcare professionals. Healthcare professionals on the other hand try to tell what they want verbally but since they are in a specific field and people from IT field don't understand what they want to say to them. Therefore, a commonly used representation is needed to be used by people from both fields. MAFR, proposed in this paper, can provide a solution for the communication gap between healthcare professionals and IT developers. The proposed method is applied in speech and language disorder therapy and a mobile application design for the practices were developed. The usefulness and effectiveness of the MAFR were verified through interviews with four therapists. From the results, MAFR happens to be a very useful method that can be applied in healthcare field. It is an effective and efficient model for developing mobile applications in the areas that need special expertise.

References

1. Little, A.D.: Capturing Value in the mHealth Oasis: An Opportunity for Mobile Network Operators (2011), http://www.adlittle.com/viewpoints.html?&view=519 (retrieved)
2. Backere, F., Steurbaut, K., Colpaert, K., Decruyenaere, J.: On the Design of a Management Platform for Antibiotic Guidelines in the Intensive Care Unit. In: Fifth International Conference on Software Engineering Advances, Nice, France, August 22-27 (2010)
3. Clancy, H.: The Mobile Health Application Ecosystem: Primary Categories & Development Consideration. MobileHealthcareToday, Virgo (2011)
4. Dankelman, J., Grimbergen, C.A., Stassen, H.G.: New Technologies Supporting Surgical Interventions and Training of Surgical Skills. IEEE Engineering in Medicine and Biology Magazine, 47–52 (May/June 2007)
5. Dennis, P.C., Baker, L.: Prevalence and type of psychiatric disorderand developmental disorders in three speech and language groups. UCLA Neuropsychiatric Institute, USA (2002)
6. HealthcareITNews, mHealth apps forecast to increase threefold by 2012 (2010), http://www.healthcareitnews.com/news/mhealth-apps-forecast-increase-threefold-2012 (retrieved)
7. Kilov, H., Sack, I.: Mechanisms for communication between business and IT experts. Computer Standards & Interfaces 31, 98–109 (2009)
8. Ongenae, et al.: Towards computerizing intensive care sedation guidelines: design of a rule-based architecture for automated execution of clinical guidelines. BMC Medical Informatics and Decision Making 10(3) (2010), doi:10.1186/1472-6947-10-3
9. Research2guidance, US$ 1.3 billion: The market for mHealth applications in 2012 (2012), http://www.research2guidance.com/us-1.3-billion-the-market-for-mhealth-applications-in-2012/ (retrieved)

Communicating Ideas in Computer-Supported Modeling Tasks: A Case Study with BPMN

Juliana Jansen Ferreira and Clarisse Sieckenius de Souza

Departamento de Informática – PUC-Rio
Rua Marquês de São Vicente 225, Rio de Janeiro – RJ, Brasil
{jferreira,clarisse}@inf.puc-rio.br

Abstract. The communication role of models in Software Engineering is widely acknowledged. Models tell model users what model builders propose. Computer-supported modeling (CSMod) traditionally concentrates on helping users build models with various kinds of notations. Although such focus on 'representation' is obviously important for the overall 'communication' goal, some design features in CSMod tools may be yet unexplored. This paper presents a study with the use of ARIS EXPRESS in modeling tasks with Business Process Modeling Notation (BPMN). We report on how we combined various methods to analyze the way in which this tool supports 'communication through models'. Our findings articulate semiotic and cognitive aspects of notations with evidence provided by study participants during tasks and interviews. Our contribution lies not only in the findings, and how CSMod design can evolve in relatively unexplored ways, but also in our methodology, which we believe can be used in similar contexts.

Keywords: Computer-supported modeling, Semiotic engineering methods, Cognitive dimensions of notations, Discourse analysis, Communication, Modeling notation, BPMN.

1 Introduction

In software development professional practice, one of the main roles of models is to create and express common ground, that is, shared basic understanding of the essence of the modeled object, entity, event, or other. [1] Common ground is needed because software development is typically a group undertaking, where different people are responsible for completing different parts of the overall goal.

Computer modeling tools have been built and evolved to increase the ease, speed, notational standardization and quality of modeling tasks. As a result, today serious software development is normally carried out with the aid of computer-supported modeling (CSMod) tools. [2]

Although CSMod tools have been extensively analyzed from a software engineering perspective [1] [3] [4], they haven't been as often analyzed from an HCI perspective. In particular, to the best of our knowledge, there haven't been studies about the 'communicability' of models produced with CSMod tools. Why is this important?

M. Kurosu (Ed.): Human-Computer Interaction, Part I, HCII 2013, LNCS 8004, pp. 320–329, 2013.

Because the ultimate purpose of models in the context of software development activities is to 'communicate' meanings and to 'signify' common ground.

This paper reports on research based on Semiotic Engineering [5], a theory of HCI which focuses on how well producers of software artifacts communicate their intent to their consumers through user interface signs and patterns of interaction. We want to understand how CSMod tools support the ultimate goal of model building, namely: communication through models. Such an investigation will deal not only with how modeling notations respond to the expressive needs of model builders, but also on how the context of communication is made available to the model builder. In this way he should be able to explore how his message can be received by other software development team members, across space and time.

We have done a qualitative study of a small-size modeling case using BPMN with ARIS EXPRESS (AE). [6] This in-depth study had two major phases. In the first one we carried out an inspection of AE using SIM, the Semiotic Inspection Method [7], along with a cognitive analysis of the notations that can be used with it. For this we used CDN, the Cognitive Dimensions of Notations Framework [8]. The second phase, in which we collected empirical data and additionally used discourse analysis (DA) [9], served as an internal triangulation for our research findings. We registered and analyzed four participants' modeling activities with AE and then interviewed them about their thoughts in relation with the task they had been asked to perform.

Our findings suggest that CSMod design can evolve in relatively unexplored directions, helping users (modelers) to gain greater awareness of the communication-through-models process. This is the main contribution of this paper. Moreover, we believe that the methodology that we have used - which we have been testing in totally different contexts - has yielded valuable results and can, therefore, be considered an additional contribution of this paper.

The next four sections present and discuss our research in detail. We begin with a brief description of BPMN and AE. Then we outline the methodology we have used: a two-phased analysis combining SIM, CDN and DA. Next we present our findings in each phase and our conclusions about what they mean when compared to each other. In the last section we conclude the paper and point at some of the implications of this work and the opportunities for future work.

2 BPMN and ARIS EXPRESS

We used the BPMN and AE for the experiment because together they support the business modeling, which can be used as the starting point for software development, thus a means of communication between business stakeholders and software development professionals. Based on these models, the group defines the scope and context where technological support is meant to be applied. [4] [10]

BPMN is said to be readily understandable by all business players, from business analysts to technical developers [11] and it has been the object of several studies aiming at investigating its capability and suitability to represent the business context through modeling as well as exploring its capability to communicate and visualize business contexts. [4] [12] Because of its research history, we decided to use BPMN in our investigation, combining the cognitive and semiotic power of CSMod tools in building communicative models.

AE [6] is a free modeling tool that offers a small subset of features from the professional ARIS Platform products[1]. It has been chosen because participants of our study knew how to use it, which allowed us to focus on how the tool supports business modeling activities, rather than on other issues having to do with novice user interaction with new software. Our research question in this study was: how does this tool support the process of communication through models?

3 Semiotic-Cognitive Combined Methodology

We used a combined semiotic-cognitive methodology because it allows us to analyze a very heterogeneous yet tightly related collection of data. Evidence collected for this research was registered in audio recordings of interviews and verbal protocols produced by participants of empirical test experiments, in various versions of models used in test tasks, and the researcher's annotations made throughout the experiments. Another important piece of evidence was the AE interface itself, which in this research is considered a key piece of empirical evidence of the CSMod tool design intent as communicated to the users via software.

The whole set of collected data allowed us to investigate aspects of both the emission and the reception of the designer-user computer-mediated communication. This hybrid set of data was analyzed using a combination of three methods: SIM [7]; the CDN framework [8] and discourse analysis (DA) [9]. The method we used is a two-phased analysis with a final diagnose phase. All three phases were performed by the same researcher, as described below.

3.1 SIM and CDN Analysis of the CSMod Tool

The first phase of the method was carried out to give the researchers an in-depth understanding of AE as used for modeling business processes with BPMN. AE also supports other modeling notations, but the focus of this research lies solely on BPMN.

SIM helps us to identify the various sign systems and notations with which AE' designers communicate their entire design vision to users. This method allows us to characterize how interface designers organize various signs (like words, images, layout, widgets, animations, screen patterns and sequences, etc.) to communicate to the users their interactive message, which we can paraphrase as this:

"Here is my understanding of who you are, what I've learned you want or need to do, in which preferred ways, and why. This is the system that I have therefore designed for you, and this is the way you can or should use it in order to fulfill a range of purposes that fall within this vision."

[1] http://www.softwareag.com/corporate/products/bis/recognition/default.asp

In this message the first person "I" refers to the designer, whereas the "you" refers to the user. In accordance with Semiotic Engineering [5], this method frames human-computer interaction as a special case of computer-mediated human (designer-user) communication and analyzes how this communication is emitted, that is, sent from designers to users.

Since SIM frames communication in the context of computer-supported modeling (i. e. taking into consideration the fact that the model is produced under the influence of CSMod tool features), we used CDN to inspect cognitive dimensions of BPMN with AE notations (i. e. we also studied the cognitive characteristics of representations with which users have to deal, given that modeling is in essence an intellectual task).

CDN proposes a set of design principles for creating or evaluating notations. In practice, it provides a common vocabulary for discussing many cognitive factors of such representation systems. CDN have been conceived to be combined with other methods and approaches. [8] Therefore, our intent to expand the results of semiotic inspection using CDN is totally legitimate.

After this first phase of analysis, we examined the indications we got and designed the internal triangulation experiment to investigate computer-mediated designer-user communication in BPMN modeling tasks using AE. This procedure provided the necessary cohesiveness between method's phases and allowed us to investigate aspects of both the emission and the reception of the designer-user computer-mediated communication.

We recruited four participants with experience in business modeling, but none of them had really used BPMN in *professional* practice. This an explicitly targeted user profile for AE (beginners or occasional users). The profile of the main researcher herself was similar, which increased her awareness in identifying what kinds of aids and scaffolds would be helpful to fulfill the proposed test tasks.

The domain selected for the experiment was known by all four participants, so the investigation could be totally focused on the modeling tasks using BPMN with AE. The process chosen for the experiment was the submission of a paper to a conference. This was a simple process, purposefully selected to keep the focus of the investigation on BPMN and AE.

3.2 Triangulating Results with Empirical Observation and Discourse Analysis

After the execution of test experiments with all participants, the collected data (audio recording of the verbal protocols during the tasks performed, the modified version of the model used in the tasks, audio recording of interviews and the researcher's annotations made throughout the experiments) was analyzed.

We looked for empirical evidence of occasional discrepancies between the designer's communicative intent and the users' interpretation. We used DA to analyze the participants' discourse and collect signs of how they received the designers' message. While listening to the audios, guided by additional annotations made throughout the experiments, the researcher identified symptoms of communication breakdowns regarding the interpretation and use of notations deployed by AE. These symptoms were detected and technically characterized according to the AE designer's communication strategies (SIM) and their presumed cognitive impact on users (CDN). Upon finding such elements we then examined two factors that together connect CDN and SIM, that is, they allow us to relate semiotic characteristics of communication through interface signs and notations with the empirical evidence of cognitive processes that are in place when the communication is received. The two factors are:

- Presence or absence of a corresponding CDN feature. For example, upon finding discourse evidence that the participant was talking about '*visibility*' in BPMN with AE notations, we checked whether he or she was referring to the presence or absence (lack) of visibility in the notation.
- The perceived impact of presence or absence of CDN features. For example, once in the presence of evidence regarding '*visibility*', we looked for discourse evidence of value judgment: did this have a positive (+) or negative (-) impact on the participant's performance during the proposed task?

In the final diagnose step of the method, a categorization of perceived symptoms of communication breakdowns (phase 1) along with the relations between semiotic/cognitive characteristics and the participants discourse about their experience (phase 2) contributed to indicating significant aspects of the communication-through-models process in this case study.

4 Tasks and Findings

Two tasks were used in this experiment: 1) To narrate one's understanding of a proposed business model built with AE using BPMN; and 2) To propose and execute a modification of this specific business model using BPMN with AE.

4.1 Findings from Semiotic and Cognitive Inspections

We identified the targeted user that AE' designers are addressing through the interface by looking at AE documentation. It says that this is a tool for beginners in business process modeling and also for occasional users. There is a large amount of documentation available (video tutorial, manual, etc.), but when it comes to actually supporting modeling tasks *in line*, AE is not as helpful as one would expect. The basic constraints of business modeling are communicated to the user (e. g. constraints for connecting types of elements), but active orientation and support for using the BPMN language in modeling process are not available. This would not only be expected, given the targeted users, but also perfectly feasible (technologies providing *over the shoulder* task-related help are used in most office applications, for example).

During semiotic and cognitive inspections, we also identified that AE relies heavily on the OMG[2] specification of BPMN [11] to support the understanding and modeling

[2] The Object Management Group (OMG) is a non-profit computer industry consortium responsible for the UML and BPMN specification.

tasks. In other words, AE designers delegate help and support to OMG. Since our participants, didn't have much experience in modeling with BPMN, we looked specifically for notational support material. Two complementary resources were found: the AE poster[3], provided by AE documentation, and the BPMN poster[4], provided by OMG specification, which according to AE is "responsible for BPMN". The latter seemed very useful for participants with little practice in using BPMN. To investigate communicability aspects in this particular case, we decided to inspect representations for two types of tasks pertaining to the context of our experiment's process model: manual process tasks and user process tasks (Fig. 1). Their meaning could only be completely clarified when the poster was combined with the complete OMG BPMN specification.

Fig. 1. User and Manual process task elements

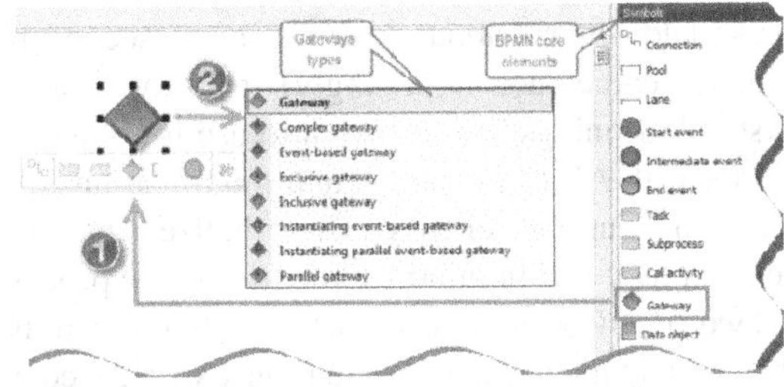

Fig. 2. Core element and type definition

Manual tasks are defined as those whose achievement is assigned to a person or group of people, never actually being executed by an IT system. *User tasks* are those performed by a human being with the assistance of some IT system. Because the latter pointed at a potentially ambiguous situation (is it a user's or a system's task?), and the reception of the message sent through the interface (where this task is represented by a "puppet" icon) would probably need more notational support, not provided by the AE, we concluded that this case would be particularly interesting to explore in our subsequent experiment test. We also concluded that, to support participants fairly while they would be trying to interpret interface signs, we should give them access to the OMG BPMN specification, the BPMN poster and the AE poster.

In the initial inspection phase, we also identified a core set of model elements defined by the OMG BPMN specification [11] that were the most salient elements offered by AE interface. Such elements could be further detailed by subsequent typing, if applicable. For example, regarding the gateway element, once the user adds the core element into the process model (Fig. 2-1) AE "asks" the user which type he wishes to assign to this element (Fig. 2-2). This is an interesting strategy of communication in AE, to present BPMN elements in increasing levels of detail. However, we did not know how this strategy would be received by users.

---

[3] `http://www.ariscommunity.com/aris-express/poster`

[4] `http://www.bpmb.de/index.php/BPMNPoster`

Guided by findings of phase one, we thus completed the design of the test experiment. The experiment was divided in three parts: 1) an explanation about the experiment's objective, duration, data collection methods, and a presentation of support resources for notations; 2) a presentation of the business process model to be used in the experiment and the tasks to be performed, an understanding what it means and how to modify it; and finally 3) an interview to discuss aspects of the experiment, the notations for business modeling, the participant's experience with BPMN, the use of support resources, their comments about the executed tasks, and free conversation about additional relevant aspects spontaneously raised during the interview.

4.2 Findings from Empirical Observations and Discourse Analysis

We should remark about findings in the second phase of our study that most of the evidence came (not surprisingly) from the *modification* task, when supposedly understood meanings had to be put to use for objective purposes. When it came to using BPMN with AE to *execute* actual modifications, participants either needed some kind of external support, or they just verbalized that they did not know how to express the idea that they had in mind for modifying the process using BPMN with AE.

Two broad meaning categories emerged from the data: 1) "*Previous experience*" - The participant narrates a situation experienced by him regarding business process modeling, which guided his choice to perform the proposed tasks; and 2) "*Aha! moment*" - The participant has a sudden insight about AE and how it would serve his purpose to represent what he intends to do with the business process model. Although finer meaning categories were clearly detectable, for the purposes of the research reported in this paper, the broad categories just mentioned are sufficiently expressive.

Participants gave us evidence of the importance of defining the model's purpose (the builder's intent) and the targeted model users. This powerful kind of evidence for an investigation about communication though models was categorized as "*Previous experience*". Here is a piece to illustrate it:

> "*...for small processes like this there is no problem in using these elements (* Data object *), which are great to convey the understanding about the process. But when a process is too big, this kind of details pollutes the model ... it might actually prevent [one from] understanding the process 'overview'.*"

This piece of evidence refers to the large set of elements provided by BPMN, contrasted with the lack of orientation or support about how they are going to be combined to *mean* something. The evidence suggests that there should be some protocol (between modelers themselves and between modelers and users) defining which elements should be used or not, when, why, and so on.

Using Ellis and Gibbs's distinctions between social and technological protocols frequently used in groupware [13], we found evidence from interviews that modelers occasionally resort to social protocols when trying to compensate for the lack of technological communication and task-supportive inter-user protocols encoded into the CSMod tool. For example, since BPMN goal is to account for many different levels of representation [11], there are in this notation cognitive challenges associated with

CDN's *diffuseness* dimension, *the complexity or verbosity of the notation in expressing meaning*. In order to make efficient and effective use of BPMN, we learned that model builders need to know which "vocabulary" they should use so that the targeted model users can understand it and wield it for their own purposes. This was taken as evidence that the presence of *diffuseness* has a negative (-) impact (social protocol overheads) on the completion tasks.

The manual and user process tasks used in our experiment led to further evidence of communicability issues. Because issues were revealed by participants' insights that corrected previous misinterpretations, we categorized them as "*Aha! moment*". Typically participants did not understand a number of visual language elements. Some queried the support material for more information. When they got to the section with task type descriptions, they suddenly gained a new understanding, which helped them make a better sense of the model they were working with. This has to do with the cognitive dimension called *closeness of mapping, closeness of the representation to the domain.* BPMN is designed to communicate that the "puppet icon" (Fig. 1) represents a task performed by an individual or group *with* IT support necessarily. Since there are processes that are done by users *without* IT intervention, the notation, depicting a single human figure, was very confusing. Participants only *got the message* when they went over the BPMN specification.

A work-around for trouble with the visual representation of IT support was further evidenced when one of the participants reported on the lack of a model element to represent the IT system: "*...I saw two ways to do it: one is to use the data store (Data store) [the other is] the text annotation ([Text annotation) element...neither BPMN, nor AE restrict the use of those elements...this needs to be agreed prior to modeling, so that everybody modeling and using the models knows that the element represents an IT system...*".

This evidence fell into the "*Previous experience*" category, because the participant reported and implemented a solution based on previous experience in modeling projects. This piece of evidence is associated with the cognitive characteristics of CDN's *secondary notation, the ability to use notations beyond the formal syntax for expressing information or meaning*. In this case, one element was used to represent what the user needed to communicate, even if further social protocol agreements had to be made to achieve effective communication. The *secondary notation* cognitive characteristics were present and had a positive (+) impact on the proposed task.

The use of AE to perform the modification task played an "educational role" with respect to BPMN. It provided scaffolds to help users in getting to know more about BPMN. In the AE interface, when users choose an element to be placed in the process model, the list of this element's types are displayed, letting users know that they can be more specific in building the model. Evidence of how this was used (Fig. 2) was categorized as "*Aha! moments*". The corresponding cognitive characteristic was *visibility, ability to view all components simultaneously or two related components side by side at the same time*. In the illustrated situation in Fig. 2 the user needs a gateway, and AE leads him to think about what kind of gateway should be used. CDN's *visibility* characteristics were present and had a positive (+) impact on the achievement of the proposed task.

Another importantly revealing evidence in this case is that the AE interface design supports model builders better than model readers, in the sense that the interactive scaffolds like gradual unfolding of elements are offered only to the user who engages in model modification (or creation). Readers, however, would benefit much from unfolding the meaning and purpose of models built by others in very similar ways.

5 On Communication through Models

This research has shown that there are mismatches between the user profile that AE supposedly targets (occasional users and beginners) and the one that emerges from an analysis of emission and reception of its designers' message. Our study shows that the designers of the CSMod we used in experiments have in fact adopted a partial and more limited perspective than technology enables. In spite of agreeing that models are communication artifacts playing a critical role in software development, evidence indicates that they apparently believe that it suffices to support the *expression* of communication and *interpretation* will take care of itself. In other words, the reception phase of the overall communicative process is left almost completely unattended, except for the occasional support that model readers can get if they try to tinker with the model (e. g. click on elements as if they were about to edit them).

We should remark that many resources that could be used to improve model reading are already in place for model creation, or should be. For a flavor, a BPMN CSMod tool interface could be so designed as to highlight the user task and IT system relation when the model is being *used* (not *built*). Since this is a critical feature for this type of task and the conventional "puppet" icon representation doesn't help understanding, the interface could easily show the name of the IT system that supports the tasks when the user hovered the mouse over it.

A large volume of evidence pointed to the need of a protocol outside the notation domain, so that the model builder would be able to build understandable representations. The participants reported that in their experience, a *social protocol* among those who are building or making use of the models is indispensable. We believe that the use of social protocols to overcome representational limitations is a path to investigate in trying to further the communicability of CSMod tools. The question to be addressed is: can such tools use existing representational resources and support model building, reading and editing? Can information about signification agreements established in social protocolsbe at least partially encoded in technology?

In the course of research towards the answer to the questions above, we think that the combination of semiotic, cognitive and discourse analysis methods we have used conveniently covers the wide range of phenomena that must be investigated if we want to discover the power of communication through models. Together, they can not only tell us about how the CSMod design message is composed and how it affects the users as they build, edit or read models with it, but also about the cognitive challenges associated with the supported notations.

Acknowledgments. The authors want to thank the Brazilian funding agencies that support this project, namely CAPES, CNPq and FAPERJ.

References

1. Tortora, G.: UML in software engineering practice: Does the experience level matter? In: International Conference on Advances in ICT for Emerging Regions (ICTer), p. 88 (2011)
2. OMG, Unified Modeling Language (UML), V2.4.1- Infrastructure specification, Object Management Group (OMG), OMG Document formal/2011-08-05 (2011)
3. Moody, D.L.: The "Physics" of Notations: Toward a Scientific Basis for Constructing Visual Notations in Software Engineering. IEEE Transactions Software Engineering 35(6), 756–779 (2009)
4. Zhao, L., Letsholo, K., Chioasca, E., Sampaio, S., Sampaio, P.: Can business process modeling bridge the gap between business and information systems? In: Proceedings of SAC 2012, pp. 1723–1724. ACM, USA (2012)
5. De Souza, C.S.: The Semiotic Engineering of Human–Computer Interaction. The MIT Press, Cambridge (2005)
6. AG Software, ARIS EXPRESS, `http://www.ariscommunity.com/aris-express`
7. De Souza, C.S., Leitão, C.F.: Semiotic engineering methods for scientific research in HCI. Morgan & Claypool, Princeton (2009)
8. Blackwell, A., Green, T.: Notational systems: The cognitive dimensions of notations framework. In: Carroll, J.M. (ed.) HCI Models, Theories and Frameworks: Toward a Multidisciplinary Science, San Francisco, pp. 103–134 (2003)
9. Gee, J.P.: An Introduction to Discourse Analysis: Theory and Method. Routledge, London (2005)
10. Gruhn, V., Laue, R.: Reducing the cognitive complexity of business process models. In: 8th Cognitive Informatics, ICCI 2009, pp. 339–345 (2009)
11. OMG, Business Process Model and Notation (BPMN), Version 2.0, Object Management Group (OMG), OMG Document formal/2011-01-03 (2011)
12. Wohed, P., van der Aalst, W.M.P., Dumas, M., ter Hofstede, A.H.M., Russell, N.: On the suitability of BPMN for business process modelling. In: Dustdar, S., Fiadeiro, J.L., Sheth, A.P. (eds.) BPM 2006. LNCS, vol. 4102, pp. 161–176. Springer, Heidelberg (2006)
13. Ellis, C., Gibbs, S.: Groupware: some issues and experiences. Communications of the ACM 34 (1991)

Semantic Execution of Subject-Oriented Process Models

Albert Fleischmann[1], Werner Schmidt[2], and Christian Stary[3]

[1] Metasonic AG, Münchner Str. 29, D-85276 Pfaffenhofen, Germany
Albert.Fleischmann@metasonic.de
[2] University of Applied Sciences Ingolstadt, Esplanade 10, D-85049 Ingolstadt, Germany
Werner.Schmidt@haw-ingolstadt.de
[3] University of Linz, Freistädterstraße 315, A-4040 Linz, Austria
Christian.Stary@jku.at

Abstract. Workflow Management Systems (WFMS) are becoming increasingly important as tools to support people involved in the execution of business processes and to automate parts of it. As business processes involve several actors with varying backgrounds, workflow engines need to offer appropriate interfaces in order to be accepted and deliver the expected benefits. In this paper we present a structural interface design based on general user interface requirements and special properties of workflow systems, in particular of a subject-oriented workflow engine.

Keywords: Business process management, workflow systems, user interface, structural design, Subject-oriented BPM.

1 Introduction

Workflow Management Systems (WFMS) support the management of business processes both at design and at runtime. A modeling component allows specifying the process, while a Workflow or Process Engine (WE, PE) controls the execution of process instances according to the model. The WE navigates users through the steps of a process they are involved in and might integrate IT applications to accomplish process-related tasks. WFMS require a well-designed user interface (UI) as a critical factor for their success. Interface design is no longer considered to be art, but 'a kind of joint computer-cognitive engineering, that is, science-based techniques to create interactive systems satisfying specified requirements' (see Card's foreword in [6]). Consequently, a user interface needs to meet specified requirements in order to be accepted by its users. In section 2 we outline general guidelines for designing user interfaces and then look at domain-specific requirements for workflow engines (section3). Based on the requirements in section 4.2 the design proposal is worked out, recognizing the properties of Subject-oriented Business Process Management (S-BPM) (section 4.1). The design is validated and modified according to the evaluation results (sections 4.3 and 4.4). The contribution concludes in section 5.

M. Kurosu (Ed.): Human-Computer Interaction, Part I, HCII 2013, LNCS 8004, pp. 330–339, 2013.

2 General Design Guidelines for User Interfaces

There are many publications available on guidelines for user interfaces and websites (e.g., see [1] [6] [7] [9] [12] [13]). They do not precisely describe design activities, but define goals. The guidelines do not give special recommendations for particular application classes like WFMS, and they are 'quite similar if we ignore differences in wording, emphasis and the state of computer technology when each set was written' [6]. In his book 'Designing with the mind in mind' Johnson describes the most important aspects of psychology underlying user interface and usability guidelines. Figure 1 shows them together with the corresponding design principles [5] [6].

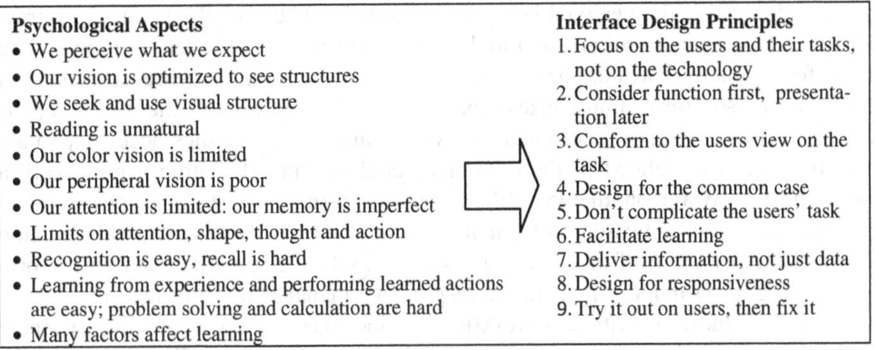

Psychological Aspects
• We perceive what we expect
• Our vision is optimized to see structures
• We seek and use visual structure
• Reading is unnatural
• Our color vision is limited
• Our peripheral vision is poor
• Our attention is limited: our memory is imperfect
• Limits on attention, shape, thought and action
• Recognition is easy, recall is hard
• Learning from experience and performing learned actions are easy; problem solving and calculation are hard
• Many factors affect learning
Interface Design Principles
1. Focus on the users and their tasks, not on the technology
2. Consider function first, presentation later
3. Conform to the users view on the task
4. Design for the common case
5. Don't complicate the users' task
6. Facilitate learning
7. Deliver information, not just data
8. Design for responsiveness
9. Try it out on users, then fix it

Fig. 1. Psychological aspects and design principles for user interfaces

The principles in the figure are mainly of static nature. They do not refer to operational aspects relevant for interfaces in use. Nievergelt proposes to consider these aspects by coining the following questions that should be answered for each situation in interaction: Where did I come from? Where am I? Where can I go from here? [11]. Users of workflow engines when executing sequences of tasks need orientation and navigation support to know where they are, where they have been, and where they can go. Although support for visualizing navigation structures is essential (cf. [9]), many applications lack, e.g., the 'you are here' indication. When Nievergelt's design issues are tackled several concepts facilitate answering the questions: Trails refer to past actions (i.e. orientation w.r.t. to the past), sites correspond to the current action or information to give (i.e. orientation w.r.t. to the current situation), and modes are about possible actions to come (i.e. orientation w.r.t. to future activities). Trails have also been called feedback, sites have been called responses, and modes have been called openings ('What can you do?'). When users carry out more than a single task when communicating with interactive systems, so-called field tasks, reached thanks to the responses, have been distinguished from so-called interaction tasks including feedbacks and openings [3]. Hence, trails, sites and modes reflect interaction patterns with certain meanings that correspond to handling workflows interactively. Workflow systems may engage users in several tasks in a certain period of time requiring trails, sites, and modes to act in line with active business processes. We will refer to trail (Now), site (Needed), and modes (Next) in our design approach - see section 4.

3 User Interface Requirements for Process Engines

As we are talking about user interfaces the focus is on how workflow engines integrate humans in the execution of instances of various process types with participants diverse in hierarchical position, education, computer literacy etc. (from CEO to blue collar worker). The PE should reduce cognitive overload by providing an intuitive and easy to use interface (process portal), framing both its own functionality to execute process instances and the embedded applications with their particular user interfaces. The UI requirements can be derived from the functions a WE needs to provide for actors in processes. For illustrating those, the typical work at a conventional office desk can serve as a metaphor. The desk is equipped with many tools helpful for all types of processes like personal computer, notepad, inhouse-mail envelopes, in-tray, out-tray, stapler etc. There are also tools which are specific for a certain process like forms for purchase orders or vacation requests. When working on process instances at the desk a person for example takes inhouse-mail envelopes out of the in-tray, opens them, selects one (e.g. price calculation request) and starts activities necessary to accomplish the tasks related to the case. This could mean calculating a price with a spreadsheet software on the PC, fill the result in the request form, put it in an envelope, add the addressee and put it into the out-box. Another typical situation might be the person itself instantiating a process by filling in a vacation request form and sending it via inhouse-mail to the responsible manager for approval. In addition to supporting those activities, a workflow engine, due to its overarching of single work places, can also deliver functions like status reporting etc. The following list contains major functions which set the requirements for a user interface properly presenting them.

- **Instantiating processes and tracking.** A user needs to be able to select and start processes he/she is allowed to initiate (according to organizational settings). He should be able to observe the status of instances once they have been started.
- **Receiving and Selecting.** A user requires a quick overview of and an easy access to open instances he needs to work on (work list).
- **Working.** A user needs to be able to accomplish the steps he is responsible for in the process, e.g., directly starting an application system out of the WE user interface when needed in a step. The applications (or single transactions) possible to call are process-specific and therefore need to be embedded and offered according to the context (e.g., a CRM system in a marketing process). Aborting or suspending the instance execution should be possible as well as continuing it later.
- **Sending.** A user needs to be able to easily pass his work results on to the next actor in the process in row. This includes the system's support by determining or suggesting the right addressee(s).
- **Orientation and Navigation.** While processing instances the user should always be able to obtain information about the whole process in terms of which steps already have been finished, which tasks are his/hers and which are the steps still to go afterwards by other actors. The UI should help deciding on and carrying out activities at each execution state by setting the right defaults and providing possible options.

These requirements correspond to Nievergelt's operational aspects (see section 2), as a user wants to know: Where am I now? What do I need to do? What needs to be done next by whom? We term this the Now – Needed - Next (3N) approach.

4 Designing a User Interface for a Subject-Oriented Process Engine

Based on the considerations in section 3 we propose a particularly structured user interface design, tailored for the domain of workflow systems and focused on the runtime part. It should serve as a blue print for interaction design on various devices (mobile and static), allowing up-to-date technologies for implementation. The UI functions for handling a workflow engine depend on the method in which processes are modeled at design time. Functions especially for navigation through a workflow at runtime (process execution) might differ according to the approach used - e.g., BPMN models can include about 160 symbols [14] which might lead to extensive navigation features. To demonstrate the Now-Needed-Next approach we stick to a straight-forward BPM technique, namely Subject-oriented BPM. Before giving the design structure, we briefly outline the approach (for details see [2]).

4.1 Properties of Subject-Oriented Business Process Management (S-BPM)

The subject-oriented description of a process starts with the identification of process-specific roles involved, the subjects, and the messages exchanged between them (see fig. 2). When sending messages, required data is transmitted from sender to receiver via simple parameters or more complex business objects if necessary.

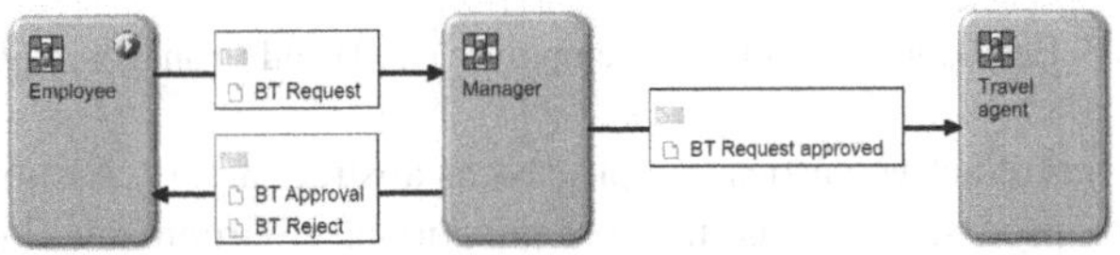

Fig. 2. Interaction structure of the process (BT=Business Trip)

In a refinement step, the modeler describes which activities and interactions the subjects have to perform in which order during process execution, i.e., he defines the behavior of individual subjects. He also specifies business objects as data structures being exchanged with the messages and being manipulated in the subject behavior.

The subject behavior diagram in the left part of figure 3 shows the order in which the employee sends and receives messages, or executes internal actions (functions), and the states he is in during his business trip request process. The initial state is a function state in which the employees complete their business trip request. The state transition 'Fill in BT Request done' leads to a send state in which they send the request to the manager, before entering the receive state, in which the applicants wait for the manager's response. In case they receive a rejection message, the process comes to an end. In case the employees receive the approval message from the manager, they go on the trip on the agreed date and the business trip application process is completed.

The behavior of the manager is complementary to that of the employee (see right part of fig. 3). The manager waits in a receiving state for a request from the employee. After receiving one, he goes to the state of decision, leading either to the approval or rejection. In the second case, a state follows to send the rejection to the employee. In the first case, the manager first moves to a send state for transmitting the approval to the applicant, and then proceeds to a state of informing the travel agent about the approved request. The behavior of the travel office can be described analogously.

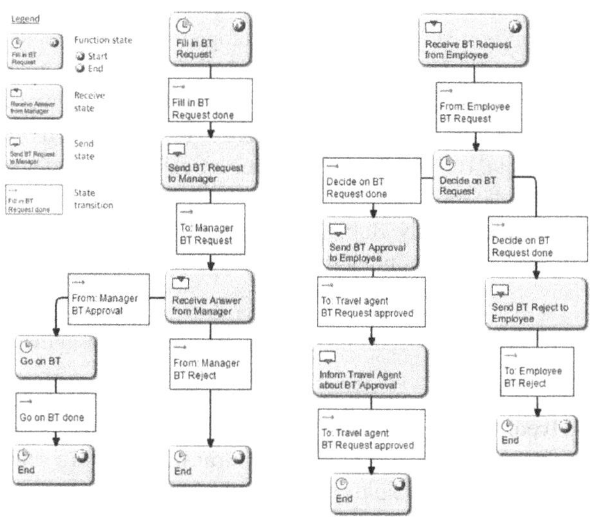

Fig. 3. Behavior of the subjects 'employee' (left) and 'manager' (right)

Subjects represent active parties in a process as abstract actors. Assigning people to subjects embeds processes in a certain organizational environment. For example all members of a department can execute the behavior of the subject 'employee' while the 'manager' behavior is reserved for the department head and deputy. Such various embodiments of a business process in an organization are called process contexts.

If a business event (e.g., need for visiting a customer in Berlin) in a certain context (e.g., by Bob Miller from the sales department) has to be handled, an instance of the corresponding process (e.g., business trip application) is initiated.

4.2 Structuring User Interfaces for Semantic Execution Support

When structuring a UI for a S-BPM-based workflow system we focus on function and not on graphical aspects (principle 2 in fig. 1). According to the nature of S-BPM only two types of screens are required for execution support: a screen for starting a process instance or selecting existing instances. The second type are screens for the basic workflow operations (do, receive, send). They can be based on one template.

Figure 4a shows the first screen type. The left part lists instances grouped by processes which contain tasks to be accomplished by the user currently logged on (personal work list). In the example he or she has to work on three business trip and two vacation requests (may be as the supervising manager). The right part offers the processes the particular user can start instances of according to the responsibility rules specified in the organization. Selecting one of the four processes listed creates a new instance of the process type chosen, e.g. a request for a certain business trip.

After initiating such a new process instance the user has to execute either a function, a send operation or a receive operation. For that type of operations a common template for the user interface is used. This template (see figures 4b-4d) is based on the Now - Needed - Next (3N) properties described in section 3.

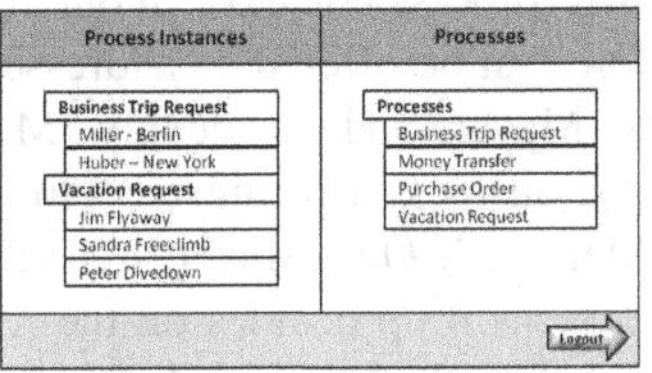

a) Selecting open task or start new process instance

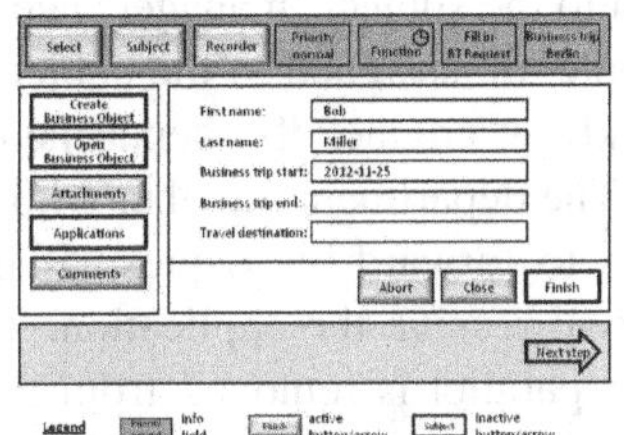

b) Executing a function: Fill in business trip request

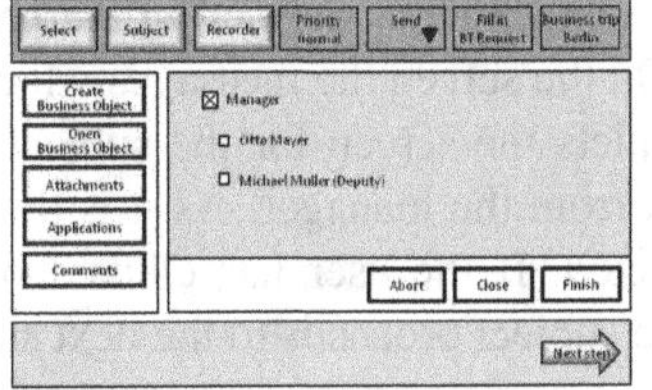

c) Selecting a person assigned to subject 'manager'

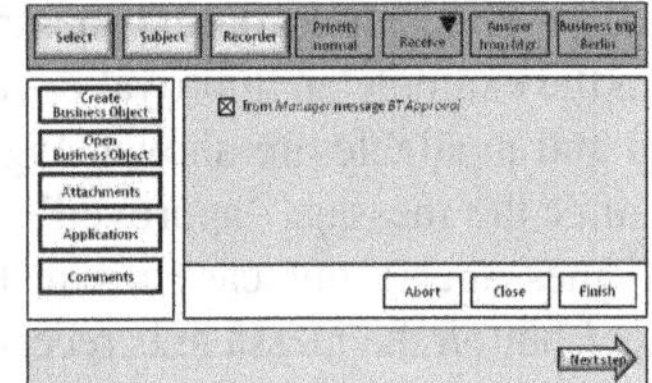

d) Selecting an expected and available message

Fig. 4. Screen types

- **Now.** The row on top (dark grey background) contains functions to inform the user about the current status of the process instance. They are identical to all screens.
- **Needed.** The middle part (white background) contains all functions which are required for executing internal functions specific to a certain process. They include creating new business objects, opening existing ones or starting an integrated application (arranged on the left). The remainder of the middle part displays the work area in which the user can work on open business objects and finds functions to suspend, abort and finish his activities.
- **Next.** The row on the bottom (light grey background) shows all operations for defining what is coming next.

Figure 4b depicts the screen for executing the function 'Fill in BT Request' as modeled in the behavior diagram for the subject the user represents (here employee, see fig. 3). This information is presented on top together with the priority and name of the instance. Pushing the button 'Subject' displays the entire behavior model of the subject with the current execution state being highlighted. 'Recorder' activates a feature of the process engine, showing the steps already taken in the instance by all subjects involved in the process. 'Select' brings the user back to his work list (fig. 4a).

The business object modeled as belonging to the current function is already open as a form. The user needs to type in the required information. The business object form is part of the process specific aspects of the UI. Filling it in can be aborted without saving the inputs ('Abort') or suspended with storing the data put in so far ('Close'). Once all required fields are filled finishing is possible ('Finish'), activating the functions in the bottom row (here 'Next step'). By clicking the 'Next step' button the workflow proceeds to the subsequent action. In our example this is a send operation which transfers the application form to the manager.

Figure 4c shows the UI for such a send state in which the person or organization assigned to the subject 'manager' needs to be known (process context). In our context two people are assigned to the subject and therefore can be offered as addressees by the workflow engine: the department head, Otto Mayer, and his deputy, Michael Müller. The department member who applies for the business trip can select to whom he wants to forward his request. If he selects 'Manager', Otto Mayer and Michael Müller will receive the application. The first who picks it up decides on the request which in parallel is removed from the work list of the other person. As soon as an addressee is selected, the message can be sent by clicking 'Next step'.

The subsequent state in the 'employee' behavior is waiting for the manager's answer. In a receive state different messages can be expected as defined in the process model, in the example an approval or rejection. On the screen the messages which are expected and available are shown. Figure 4d depicts the screen for the subject 'employee' after the message 'approved' has arrived from the manager. As it is the only expected message in our case it can be preselected. If the user has clicked on the 'Next step' button the message is received and the subject proceeds to the next state.

4.3 Evaluation

The design has initially been provided in form of Microsoft PowerPoint slides and then transferred to a portlet-based user interface in order to validate it. The design prototype has been evaluated using several items. In table 1 we relate them to the psychological aspects and the design principles described by Johnson (see section 2). The list has also been influenced by [4]. Evaluating a user interface is more or less the only way to find out whether it has a chance to get accepted, which lays ground for the economic success of an entire product (see [7, p. 134]). In nearly all principles for good user interface design testing is required (see [6, p. 176] or [5]). Once testing is mentioned developers often refer to expensive usability labs. However, Jakob Nielsen showed following certain principles produces very good results with much less effort [8]. According to Nielsen five testers are sufficient for usability testing [10]. Based on this work Krug has developed a 'lost our lease, going-out-of-business sale usability testing' methodology as an alternative to expensive testing labs (see [7, p. 137]). Krug states 'Testing only three users helps ensure that you will do another round soon'. Testing should be done in short intervals because testing is an iterative process.

Following those recommendations we organized test sessions with 3 users, starting with a short intro. The testers received the list of items, but we did not explicitly ask them the questions.

Table 1. Evaluation items

Psychological aspects	No.	Items
1, 2	1	Are the functions grouped according to the tasks to be executed?
1, 2	2	Is the user interface designed from normal user's perspective?
1, 2, 3	3	Are the functions described understandable?
3, 4, 5, 6	4	Are related functions grouped reasonably?
7	5	Can the user always identify his current position in the task flow?
4, 5, 6	6	Can the user always identify his next step in the task flow?
5	7	Are there needless clicks for activating important functions?
4, 5, 6	8	Are there functions supporting the repetitive execution of tasks?
3, 8	9	Does the interface allow finding required functions directly and fast?
2	10	Is there a common principle visible/sensible behind the user interface?
6	11	Is the user always informed what is going on and what needs to be done next?
5, 6	12	Does the user need to memorize many data in order to execute functions?
3, 4	13	Are the mostly used functions directly accessible?
7, 8	14	Is there a quick overview about the available functions?
1, 2, 5	15	Is there a general handling concept?
6	16	Does it take the user a long time to learn the user interface?

We explained that we just expected their recommendations on how to improve the UI according to the items list. Then we exposed the testers to the first version of the interface based on the design presented in section 4.2.

Tester 1 was a 56 years old sales person for (subject-oriented) BPM solutions. He brought in a lot of user interface experience collected from customers. The second proband was a 34 years old product manager for a BPM suite, and the third person, also 34 of age, works as a principal consultant for introducing BPM in companies.

The evaluation focused on the functional aspect (principle 2 in figure 1). Table 2 shows most significant test results and most important insights.

Table 2. Evaluation results

- The start screen is too complicated to understand, especially the wording (process instance, process) is confusing.
- Users want to work rather than to administer tasks or process instances
- Users want to quickly grasp what they have to do and once a task is finished they want to be informed instantly what the next steps are. This was not clear enough in the evaluated version.
- The business object to be worked on in the current task needs to be visible once the user opens a task (see figure 4b in section 4.2).
- If there is an application needed in the task its UI should be visible on the screen.
- The users need to be able to configure the interface on their own, including rearranging function groups on the screen and adapting the wording of functions as companies want to use their own labels for functions.
- Function arrangement is not consistent: Functions related to subsequent tasks should be located at same positions e.g. selecting the receiver of a message should be found at the bottom. The top line should first display information fields, followed by functions to visualize the state of a subject and of the whole process instance.

4.4 First Structural Redesign

Based on the test results we have adapted the interface structure. We show only the functional redesign due to space limits. Figure 5a depicts the modified structure for completing business object forms (function state in the behavior model). Compared to the initial design shown in figure 4b we rearranged and relabeled functions.

- **Now.** In the top line information fields on the left show the type of action (internal function), followed by information of the process instance (process type, creation date, priority). The orientation functions on the right lead to screens revealing the status of the process instance, either for the subject (where am I?) or for the entire process (where are we?). The new labels better express the meaning than 'Subject' and 'Recorder' in the previous version.
- **Needed.** In the left column functions for creating new business objects (in our example business trip request form) or adding attachments etc. can be found. The business object to be worked on is positioned in the middle part. In case a single business object is used in the process the form is opened automatically. Editing can be aborted – in this case all inputs are removed. The activity can also be interrupted – data already filled in are stored. Upon completion the form finishing is possible.
- **Next.** Activates the transition to the next state 'fill in business trip request done' in the bottom line. If the process model had specified other transitions in this state the UI would present them as additional arrows. The 'back' button leads back to the work and process list.

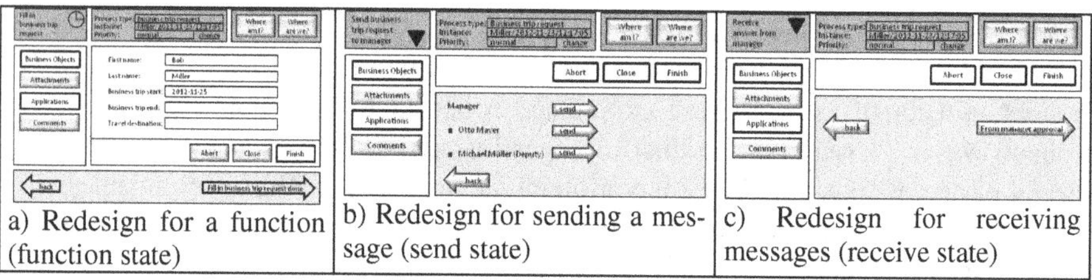

a) Redesign for a function (function state)

b) Redesign for sending a message (send state)

c) Redesign for receiving messages (receive state)

Fig. 5. Redesigned user interface

Figure 5b shows the screen for sending messages. The only activity a user needs to perform in that state is selecting the person assigned to the receiving subject in case there is more than one option. Whereas in the previous interface the user needed to check boxes and then push 'Next step' (see figure 4c), now clicking the right arrow is sufficient. If there is only one person the sending operation is executed automatically. The behavior model specifies the messages to be expected in a receive state ('Approval' or 'Rejection' in the example). At runtime it is only necessary to select one of the messages available in the current state and accept it. The arrow on the screen in figure 5c shows the approval message. If there were more messages available, the user could choose by clicking the right arrow, causing the reception. Like in the send state this procedure saves one user action (checking a box) compared to the initial interface.

5 Conclusions

Workflow engines have two UI parts: Process-independent and process-specific functions. Process-independent functions form the framework and 'infrastructure' in which the required tasks of a process are executed by users. The original UI of an existing design has been evaluated using agile user testing. Improvement potential has been identified and the UI has been changed accordingly and can be evaluated again. In future work based on the user interface approach, corresponding application programming interfaces need to be defined allowing a flexible alignment of user interfaces for workflow systems with corresponding workflow system functionality. Furthermore it has to be investigated how the agile user testing approach proposed by [8] and [7] can be integrated in a scrum-driven software development cycle, allowing for seamless interactive application development.

References

1. Cheriton, D.R.: Man-machine interface design for time-sharing systems. In: Proceedings of the ACM National Conference, pp. 362–380 (1976)
2. Fleischmann, A., Schmidt, W., Stary, C., Obermeier, S., Börger, E.: Subject oriented Business Process Management. Springer, Berlin (2012)
3. Horchami, M., Fréard, D., Jamey, E., Nigay, L., Panaget, F.: A platform for designing multimodal dialogic and presentation strategies. In: Decalog 2007: Proceedings of the 11th Workshop on the Semantics and Pragmatics of Dialogue, pp. 169–170 (2007)
4. ISO 9241-110: Beurteilung von Software auf Grundlage der Internationalen Ergonomie-Norm DIN EN ISO 9241-110, `http://people.f3.htw-berlin.de/Professoren/Pruemper/instrumente/ISONORM%209241-110-L.pdf` (last access November 2012)
5. Johnson, J.: GUI bloopers 2.0: Common User Interface Design don'ts and dos. Morgan-Kaufmann Publishers, San Francisco (2007)
6. Johnson, J.: Designing with the Mind in Mind. Elsevier Publishing, Amsterdam (2010)
7. Krug, S.: Don't make me Think. New Riders Publishing, Berkley (2006)
8. Nielsen, J.: Guerrilla HCI: Using Discount Usability Engineering to Penetrate the Intimidation Barrier, `http://www.useit.com/papers/guerrilla_hci.html` (last access November 2012)
9. Nielsen, J.: User interface directions for the web. Comm. of the ACM 42(1), 65–71 (1999)
10. Nielsen, J.: Why You Only Need to Test with 5 Users, `http://www.useit.com/alertbox/20000319.html` (last access November, 2012)
11. Nievergelt, J., Weydert, J.: Sites, modes and trails: Telling the user of an interactive system where he is, what he can do, and how to get to places. In: Guedj, R., Hagen, P., Hopgood, F., Tucker, H., Duce, D. (eds.) Methodology of Interaction, pp. 327–338. North Holland (1980)
12. Norma, D.A.: Design Rules based on Analysis of human error. Communications of the ACM 26(4), 254–258 (1983)
13. Shneiderman, B.: Designing the user Interface: Strategies for effective human-computer interaction. Addison-Wesley, Reading (1987)
14. Silver, B.: BPMN Method and Style, BPMN Implementer's Guide: A Structured Approach for Business Process Modeling and Implementation Using BPMN 2, Cody-Cassidy (2011)

Special Challenges for Models and Patterns in Smart Environments

Peter Forbrig, Christian Märtin, and Michael Zaki

University of Rostock, Department of Computer Science,
Albert Einstein Str. 21,
18055 Rostock, Germany
{peter.forbrig,christian.maertin,michael.zaki}@uni-rostock.de

Abstract. Smart environments aim at inferring the intention of the user and based on that information, they offer optimal assistance for the users while performing their tasks. This paper discusses the role of supportive user interfaces for explicitly interacting with the environment in such cases where implicit interactions of the users fail or the users want to get informed about the state of the environment. It will be shown by small examples how patterns help to specify the intended support with implicit and explicit interactions. A notation for presentation patterns will be introduced that allows users dynamically to change the presentation style. It will be discussed how extended task models can be combined with presentation patterns and how this information can be used in supportive user interfaces on mobile devices.

Keywords: Smart Environment, model-based design, pattern, supportive user interface, task migratability, task pattern, presentation patter.

1 Introduction

During the last few decades a lot of work has been accomplished by different research teams to study prototypes of environments of assisting users performing their daily life tasks. This research was often focused on elderly people but sometimes also focuses on children (e.g. [3] and [16]).

Our paper is based on research within our graduate school MuSAMA (Multimodal Smart Appliance Ensembles for Mobile Applications). The experimental basis is a smart meeting room. The room is equipped with a lot of sensors, projectors and cinema screens (see Fig. 1.).

Bayesian algorithms are informed by sensors and try to infer next possible actions of the users. Based on that information, convenient assistance has to be provided.

"This creates complex and unpredictable interactive computing environments that are hard to understand. Users thus have difficulties to build up their mental model of such interactive systems. To address this issue users need possibilities to evaluate the state of these systems and to adapt them according to their needs." [13]

M. Kurosu (Ed.): Human-Computer Interaction, Part I, HCII 2013, LNCS 8004, pp. 340–349, 2013.

Meta-UIs are mentioned by the authors of paper [13] as a solution for this problem. This means that users are able to configure user interfaces that can be visible (explicit interaction) and invisible (implicit interaction via sensors).

Fig. 1. Smart meeting room

As a result of the SUI 2011 workshop participants agreed on the following more specific and precise definition for this kind of user interfaces:

"A supportive user interface (SUI) exchanges information about an interactive system with the user, and/or enables its modification, with the goal of improving the effectiveness and quality of the user's interaction with that system." [7].

The most important aspect of this definition is the fact that the user interface should be adaptable in order to give the user the opportunity to interact with the system in a more appropriate way according to the specific encountered context of use.

This idea of a "Meta-User Interface" approach for controlling and evaluating interactive ambient spaces was also suggested by [2].

We will focus our discussion in this paper on the role of supportive user interfaces in smart meeting rooms. The paper is structured in such a way that first, existing approaches for supportive use interfaces in ubiquitous environments are discussed. Afterwards, models are studied that help to develop supportive user interfaces. Additionally, it will be discussed how specific patterns might help to assemble models and are helpful during run-time.

2 Models and Supportive User Interfaces

Within our graduate school MuSAMA (Multimodal Smart Appliance Ensembles for Mobile Applications) we have the opportunity to study research questions for supporting users while performing their tasks in a smart meeting room. We already mentioned that one approach for such environments is the usage of Bayesian networks. These networks describe possible activities of users. Algorithms are available that infer next possible actions. Based on this information it is possible to provide convenient assistance to the user.

Unfortunately, it is not easy to create such a Bayesian network. Additionally, such networks have to be trained. In this way a lot of meetings with similar goals and participants have to be observed. Even when this was possible it is not easy to provide the user with information about the current state of the environment. Roscher et al. discuss in [13] a functional model and system architecture for Meta-User Interfaces. Such interfaces allow users to control devices in the smart environment in an explicit way. In this way it is possible to "manually overrule" the decision of the environment.

"The Migration menu provides possibilities to redistribute a UUI (ubiquitous user interface) from one interaction resource to another, e.g. transfer the graphical UI to a screen better viewable from the users' current position. Through the Distribution menu the user can control the distribution on more fine grained levels by distributing selected parts of the UI among the available IRs." [13].

For ubiquitous user interfaces the five features shapeability, distribution, multimodality, shareabilty and mergeability are specified and presented in [14]. These results are originally from [2].

1. **Shapeability:** Identifies the capability of a UI to provide multiple representations suitable for different contexts of use on a single interaction resource.
2. **Distribution:** Identifies the capability of a UI to present information simultaneously on multiple interaction resources, connected to different interaction devices.
3. **Multimodality:** Identifies the capability of the UI to support more than one modality.
4. **Shareability:** Denotes the capability of a UI to be used by more than one user (simultaneously or sequential) while sharing (partial) application data and (partial) interaction state.
5. **Mergeability:** Denotes the capability of a UI to be combined either partly or completely with another UI to create combined views and input possibilities."

These results reflect in a wonderful way necessary technical properties of user interfaces in given ubiquitous environment. They also underline the necessity of having explicit interactions in smart environments.

In our discussion we will focus on two main aspects:

1. What kind of models can help to specify user interfaces for smart environments in detail?
2. What kind of patterns can support the modeling of smart environments?

3 Models for Smart Environments

In conjunction with modeling efforts for smart environments the collaborative task modeling language (CTML) was developed in our group. This language consists of models specifying the activities of stakeholders and the whole team by task models. Additionally there are models for devices and the room as well. Details can be found in the PhD thesis of Maik Wurdel [21].

In this paper we will concentrate on the models that help us to generate user interfaces for explicit interactions. Task models are most important for this aspect. CTML uses task tress in the notation of CTT [12] extended by constrains in an OCL-like style. This notation was extended in [22] by new task types that are recalled in Fig. 2.

Type	Symbol	Description
User Output task		The user is providing output (information) to other users in the environment, without interacting with the system.
User Input Task		The user is receiving input (information) from other users in the environment, without interacting with the system.
Display Application Task		This task is performed by the system, after receiving some internal information. This task results in an output to be displayed to the user.
Computational Application Task		This task symbolizes an internal computation performed by the system without providing any output to the user.

Fig. 2. New task types introduced in [22]

Additionally, a development process for assistive user interfaces was suggested. The model of this process is shown in Fig. 3. One can see that based on a severe analysis of the tasks that have to be performed and supported some kind of task model is designed. This model is very important for the further development. It is the basis of the further development of implicit and explicit interactions. Implicit interactions are specified within task models. Explicit interactions are designed by the combination of tasks and dialogs. The navigation between different dialogs is specified by a so called dialog graph. It allows the automatic generation of supportive user interfaces.

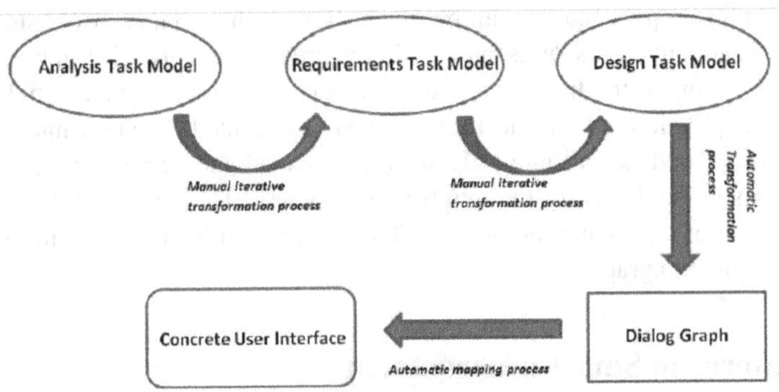

Fig. 3. Our application's development flow from [22]

Dialog graphs were introduced some years ago for the development of interactive systems. It was extended in [22] to fulfill the special needs for supportive user interface design in smart environments by introducing implicit concurrent and implicit sequential transitions.

Initially, a dialog graph had only explicit concurrent and sequential transitions. They are activated by the user when interacting with the system and performing certain task. Sequential transitions result in a hiding of the old dialog and appearing the new dialog whilst concurrent transitions do not hide old dialog but give the activity to the new one.

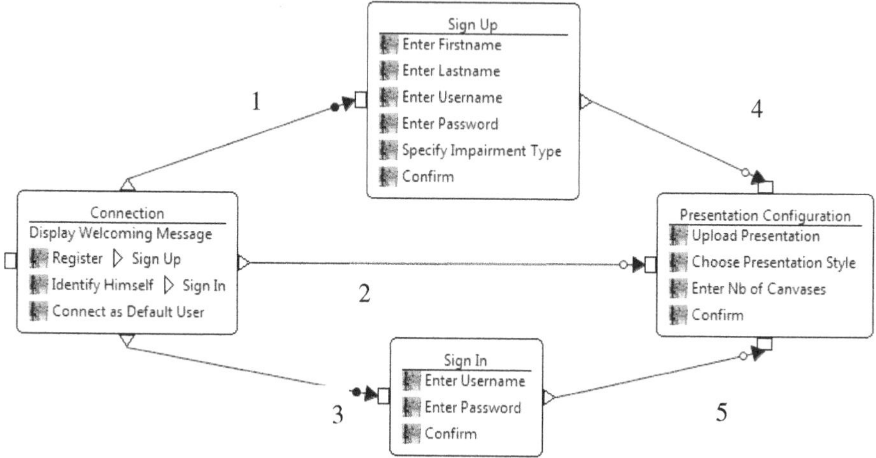

Fig. 4. Part of a dialog graph for a role presenter

The dialog graph of Fig. 4. consists of four dialogs with five transitions. Transition 1 and 3 are explicit transitions while all the others are implicit. They are related to activities that are part of the task model but are identified by sensors. In the example of the dialog graph of Fig. 4. there is a task "going to the front". This task has to be performed before a presentation can be given. In case that some sensors signal that a person that is announced as "presenter" is in the presentation area, it can be concluded that the task "going to the front" was executed depending on the current dialog ("Sign in" or "Sign up") an implicit transition (4 or 5) is executed. The user interface of the presenter is updated accordingly. He or she can load the presentation, choose the presentation style and specify the number of canvases. This input can be considered as the selection of a presentation pattern. This aspect will be discussed in more detail in the following paragraph.

4 Patterns in Smart Environment

Design patterns have proved [10] to be a good tool to represent knowledge in software design. They spread through computer science domain despite the fact that patterns were first discussed in architecture [1]. Additionally, many approaches take benefit of the usage of patterns in the HCI area [17]. Breedvelt-Schouten et al. [4] introduced task patterns that inspired our work. Sinnig [15] provided generic task patterns to be able to adapt a pattern to the context of use.

In a given smart environment numerous actors try to achieve a common goal that can be characterized as team goal. For the meeting room example, the ultimate goal is the efficient exchange of information among the actors in the room. Every task executed by an actor in its role is in a way a contribution to the team goal. It is a step towards this goal. Additionally, the task helps to reach the own individual goal (e.g. to make a good presentation).

A first step to develop patterns in the context of smart meeting rooms was to identify possible team goals (a certain state that the team wants to reach). First results were presented in [23] by providing six abstract team goals. These goals were (I) conference session performed, (II) lecture given, (III) work defended, (IV) topic discussed, (V) debate managed and (VI) video watched.

Some further patterns were identified in the meantime. One of these patterns is presented in Fig. 5. This pattern was identified in an institute of climate research. It is a team pattern for discussing weather phenomena.

Usually during meetings at this institute there is first a general presentation. Later on participants split into two subgroups and discuss some pictures and data. At the end the combined results from both groups are presented to the whole plenum.

This kind of patterns can help to structure an application in an appropriate way. The pattern follows a user-centered approach. It can be considered as static. There will be no changes for the pattern instance at run-time.

However, there are other types of patterns that have to be instantiated during run-time and different instances are used. This is especially true for presentation patterns. Each presenter might have a different style for presenting his ideas. Some stakeholder might give a presentation in the classical way of presenting one slide after another. If more than one projector is available it might make sense to use one for the outline of a talk and the others for the slides.

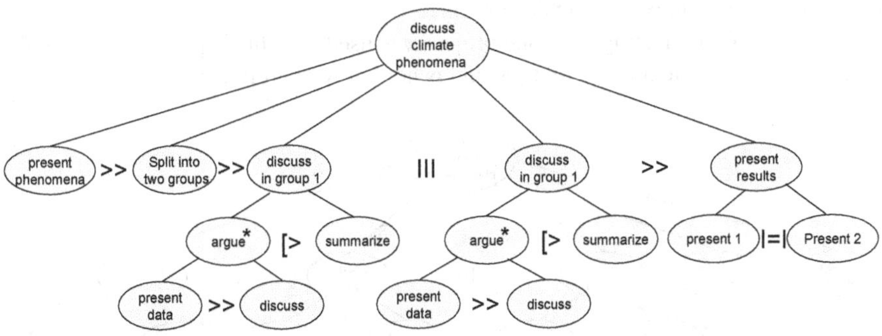

Fig. 5. Goal Pattern for discussing climate phenomena

This led us to the identification of information-distribution patterns. We will describe such patterns by concentrating on projectors but similar patterns are applicable to the general distribution of information to different devices. First, we tried to identify the generic parts of such a pattern. This is at least the name of the file where the information comes from, the number and the identification of the projectors. Finally, the presentation style is necessary. This generic part can be specified by four parameters. This can be represented by the notation given in Fig. 6.

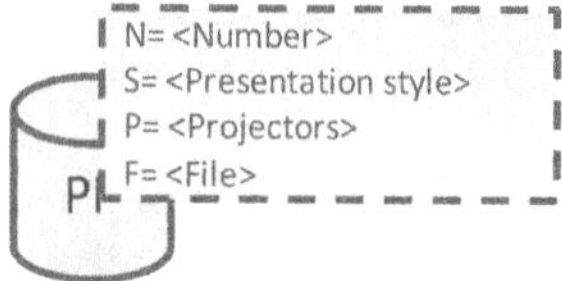

Fig. 6. Presentation Pattern

Instances of such a pattern are interpreted during run-time. All generic parameters missing an assigned value will be displayed by a supporting user interface for a mobile device. In this way the current presenter is asked to interactively provide the necessary information.

One can imagine that instances of patterns can be since the modeling stage. In this case values can already be assigned to parameters of these pattern instances. The file or the number of projectors might have been known during at the design phase.
We attached several instances of the information distribution pattern to the team goal pattern of Fig. 4. The result is presented in Fig. 7.

First (left hand side of the model) only projector 1 is used to show the data from file X.ppt. Later in the discussion phase two projectors are used by each subgroup. The number of available projectors is two and the projectors are already explicitly assigned. Group 1 is sitting in one corner of the room using projector 1 and 2 and group 2 is sitting in another corner using projector 3 and 4. The presentation style is sliding window (sw), which means that always the current and the previous slide are presented. In case there were more projectors more slides are shown. The file that has to be shown is not known during design time.

At the end of the meeting only one projector is used and this is projector 1. The file name will be available during run time and is not known beforehand.

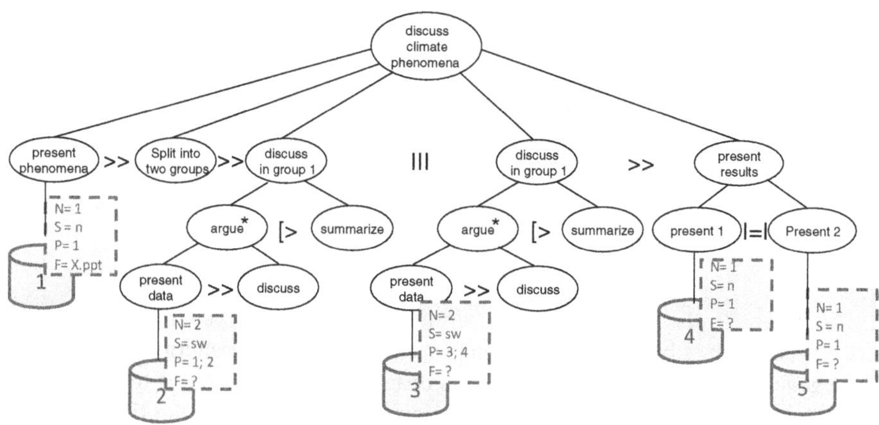

Fig. 7. Information-Distribution Pattern as part of a Goal Pattern

5 Task Migratability in Smart Environments

Task migratability is one of the usability criteria of interactive systems. It specifies the transfer of control for tasks execution between user and system. "It should be possible for the user or system to pass control of a task over to the other or promote the task from a completely internalized one to a shared and cooperative venture" [9].

Many interactive systems are static in this respect. The software designer decides often already during the development phase which task is to be allocated to which actor. In our discussion we will especially focus on the dynamic allocation of tasks (task migratability) and the possibility to influence this allocation by a supportive user interface.

Currently task migratability seems to be not a big issue in smart environments. In general the systems try to support users as much as possible. Sometimes it is possible to explicitly configure the environment via a user interface [13]. However, the concept of a Meta-UI is not directly related to task migratability. Often user interfaces are only distributed in a different way while the allocation of tasks remains the same. However, the concept of Meta-UIs can also be applied in such a way that a new configuration of a system results in a different task allocation. Consequently, Meta-UIs combined with supportive user interfaces can then be employed to make task migratability conceivable and possible in smart environments.

Tangible user interfaces seem to be an interesting option for supportive user interfaces. Tracked objects can help to identify the desired kind of support based on the inferred meeting type (brain storming session, workshop, business meeting, coffee break, etc.). The environment can be configured in such a way that a coffee pot on the table announces a business meeting. If the coffee pot is placed on the side board a workshop is performed. A coffee pot on the windowsill signals a brainstorming session and finally during a coffee break the pot has to be placed on a small table next to the big meeting table.

In this case, the coffee pot plays the role of the supportive user interface. Its location configures the provided support.

Additionally, objects can also be used to signal the environment level of support that is appreciated. On the one hand, a coffee pot standing on the big meeting table might express that all available support in the environment should be provided. On the other hand, if the pot stands on the window sill no assistance is needed. Users want to control everything in a manual way. Certain states in between these both extreme states can be specified as well.

However, the usage of tangible user interfaces in smart environments raises new challenges which are formulized in the following set of questions:

a) Should already existing objects from the domain be used or specific new objects be introduced?

While existing objects might be more convenient, they might have the disadvantage that they are used for their original purpose and thus placed somewhere. New introduced objects like stones seem to be safer and less confusing because the manipulation of those objects will not be performed often since they do not play another role in the room.

b) Should one object in different states/locations or several objects be used to specify the input to the environment?

There seems to be context dependent learnability problem. Is it easier to memorize the different states of one object or different objects?

c) Should existing metaphors in favor of new introduced metaphors be used?

There is again the question of learnability. Does the metaphor fit to the mental models of the users? Is it convenient for the users to act according to the metaphor?

There seems to be no general answer for all of those questions. Based on a thorough analysis of the application domain, design decisions have to be made like in classical interactive systems

6 Summary and Outlook

In this paper we argued for a model-based approach for smart environments. We presented some details of our specification language CTML that allows specifying the tasks of different actors and the cooperation of a team. It is argued to split the specification into a cooperation model and a configuration model. The cooperation model specifies general knowledge of activities of a specific domain. This knowledge is long lasting. The configuration model has to be specified according to the current instance of a session. Who are the participants that take part and which roles do they play?

References

1. Alexander, C., Silverstien, M.: A Pattern Language. In: Alexander, C., Ishikawa, S., Silverstein, M., Jacobson, M., King, I.F., Angel, S. (eds.) Towns, Buildings, Construction. Oxford University Press, New York (1977) ISBN 0195019199
2. Blumendorf, M.: Multimodal Interaction in Smart Environments A Model-based Runtime System for Ubiquitous User Interfaces. Dissertation. Technische Universität Berlin (2009)
3. Bobick, A.F., Intille, S.S., Davis, J.W., Baird, F., Pinhanez, C.S., Campbell, L.W., Ivanov, Y.A., Schtte, A., Wilson, A.: The kidsroom: Perceptually based interactive and immersive story environment. In: PRESENCE, pp. 367–391 (1999)
4. Breedvelt-Schouten, I.M., Paterno, F., Severijns, C.: 00000. In: Proceedings of DSV-IS, pp. 225–239 (1997)
5. Coutaz, J.: Meta-User Interfaces for Ambient Spaces. In: Coninx, K., Luyten, K., Schneider, K.A. (eds.) TAMODIA 2006. LNCS, vol. 4385, pp. 1–15. Springer, Heidelberg (2007)
6. Demeure, A., Lehmann, G., Petit, M., Calvary, G. (eds.): Proceedings of the 1st International Workshop on Supportive User Interfaces: SUI 2011, Pisa, Italy, June 13 (2011), http://ceur-ws.org/Vol-828/
7. Demeure, A., Lehmann, G., Petit, M., Calvary, G.: SUI 2011 Workshop Summary Poster. In: [6]
8. Dittmar, A., Forbrig, P.: Selective modeling to support task migratability of interactive artifacts. In: Campos, P., Graham, N., Jorge, J., Nunes, N., Palanque, P., Winckler, M. (eds.) INTERACT 2011, Part III. LNCS, vol. 6948, pp. 571–588. Springer, Heidelberg (2011)

9. Dix, A., Finlay, J.E., Abowd, G.D., Beale, B.: Human-Computer Interaction, 3rd edn. Prentice-Hall, Englewood Cliffs (2003)
10. Gamma, E., Helm, R., Johnson, R., Vlissides, J.: Design Patterns. Elements of Reusable Object-Oriented Software. Addison-Wesley (1995)
11. Ishii, H., Ulmer, B.: Tangible bits: towards seamless interfaces between people, bits, and atoms. In: Proceedings of the CHI 1997 Conference on Human Factors in Computing Systems, Atlanta, Georgia, pp. 234–241 (March 1997)
12. Paterno, F., Meniconi, C., Meniconi, S.: ConcurTaskTrees: A diagrammatic Notation for Specifying Task Models. In: INTERACT 1997, IFIP TC13, pp. 362–369 (1997)
13. Roscher, G., Blumendorf, M., Albayrak, S.: Using Meta User Interfaces to Control Multimodal Interaction in Smart Environments. In: Proceedings of the IUI 2009 Workshop on Model Driven Development of Advanced User Interfaces (2009), `http://ceur-ws.org/Vol-439/paper4.pd`
14. Roscher, D., Lehmann, G., Blumendorf, M., Albayrak, S.: Design and Implementation of Meta User Interfaces for Interaction in Smart Environments. In: [6]
15. Sinnig, D.: The Complexity of Patterns and Model-based Development, Computer Science. Concordia University, Montreal (Thesis (2004)
16. Srivastava, M., Muntz, R., Potkonjak, M.: Smart kindergarten: sensor-based wireless networks for smart developmental problem-solving environments. In: Proceedings of the 7th Annual International Conference on Mobile Computing and Networking, MobiCom 2001, pp. 132–138. ACM, New York (2001)
17. Tidewell, J.: Interaction Design Patterns: Twelve Theses. In: Proc. Conference on Pattern Languages of Programming, PLoP 1998, Monticello, Illinois (1998)
18. Zaki, M., Wurdel, M., Forbrig, P.: Pattern Driven Task Model Refinement. In: Abraham, A., Corchado, J.M., González, S.R., De Paz Santana, J.F. (eds.) DCAI 2011. AISC, vol. 91, pp. 249–256. Springer, Heidelberg (2011)
19. Molina, A.I., Redondo, M.A., Ortega, M., Hoppe, U.: CIAM: A Methodology for the Development of Groupware User Interfaces. Journal of Universal Computer Science 14, 1435–1446 (2008)
20. Mori, G., Paternò, F., Santoro, C.: CTTE: Support for Developing and Analyzing Task Models for Interactive System Design. IEEE Trans. Software Eng. 28(8), 797–813 (2002)
21. Wurdel, M.: An Integrated Formal Task Specification Method for Smart Environments. PhD Thesis, University of Rostock (2011)
22. Zaki, M., Forbrig, P.: Making task models and dialog graphs suitable for generating assistive and adaptable user interfaces for smart environments. In: PECCS 2013, Barcelona, Spain, Feburary 19-21 (2013)
23. Zaki, M., Wurdel, M., Forbrig, P.: Pattern Driven Task Model Refinement. In: Abraham, A., Corchado, J.M., González, S.R., De Paz Santana, J.F. (eds.) DCAI 2011. AISC, vol. 91, pp. 249–256. Springer, Heidelberg (2011)

Parallel Rendering of Human-Computer Interaction Industrial Applications on Multi-/Many-Core Platforms

Sven Hermann, Arquimedes Canedo, and Lingyun (Max) Wang

Siemens Corporation, Corporate Technology
Princeton, NJ, USA
{sven.hermann,arquimedes.canedo,max.wang}@siemens.com

Abstract. Industrial Human Computer Interaction (Industrial HCI) devices are beginning the transition from single-core to multi-/many-core technology. In practice, improving the real-time response time of graphical user interface (GUI) applications in multi-/many-core is difficult. This paper presents a novel parallel rendering approach targeted to improve the performance of Industrial HCI applications in multi-/many-core technology. This is accomplished through the identification of coarse-grain parallelism during the application design, and the exploitation of fine-grain parallelism during runtime using a dynamic scheduling algorithm and true parallel execution of GUI workloads. Using a real benchmark application, we show that response time can be reduce by up to 217% in a quad-core processor.

1 Introduction

Industrial HCI (Human Computer Interaction) devices are real-time embedded computer systems, based on Graphical User Interface (GUI) applications, which allow humans to interact with and control complex industrial processes such as power plants, manufacturing lines, chemical processes, and transportation systems. The performance gap between high-end and low-end Industrial HCIs is quite substantial, and this causes additional design, development, manufacturing, and maintenance costs for Industrial HCI manufacturers. For example, multimedia and video processing in Industrial HCIs requires high-performance CPUs and GPUs, while basic input/output processing requires low-power embedded processors. The technological shift from single-core processors to multi-/many-core processors is very attractive for Industrial HCI vendors because the performance gap in multiple products can be eliminated by consolidating a line of Industrial HCIs with the same multi-/many-core processor rather than having different custom processors for different product configurations. While it is clear that multi-/many-core processors provide better performance, energy efficiency, scalability, consolidation, and redundancy than single-core processors, it is still an open question how to best utilize the additional cores for improving the performance and response time of GUI applications.

M. Kurosu (Ed.): Human-Computer Interaction, Part I, HCII 2013, LNCS 8004, pp. 350–360, 2013.

This paper presents a novel "**parallel rendering approach for GUI applications**", defined as the process by which an image is generated **cooperatively** and **concurrently** by independent computation threads running on different cores. **Our approach aims at accelerating the response time of Industrial HCI Devices through parallel execution of GUI-related workload in multi-/many-core processors.** Finding parallelism at the GUI object level is challenging and we identify three steps that are necessary to expose and exploit it. First, the application is analyzed for object dependencies using data flow analysis in a process we refer to as dependency-based load balancing where independent clusters of GUI objects are scheduled into different cores. Second, the worker threads execute workload in parallel and are allowed to modify the objects' data directly. Third, after the worker threads have finished, or a display update event is received, the "flush thread" optimizes the sequential access to the display by minimizing the number of pixels and the number of draw function calls. Our original contributions are:

- A method for parallel rendering of GUI applications in multi-/many-core based Industrial HCI devices.
- The extraction of object-level parallelism based on a dependency-based load balancing algorithm.
- The execution of GUI objects' in parallel through privatized memory.
- The reduction of display access through a flush call optimization.
- An implementation of our method on a quad-core system and its evaluation using an Industrial HCI benchmark.

The rest of this paper is organized as follows. Section 2 describes the limitations of the current Industrial HCIs and motivates the need for multi-/many-core-based Industrial HCIs. Section 3 presents the parallel rendering method including the load balancing, parallel execution, and flush optimization algorithms. Section 4 presents our experimental results on a soft real-time quad- core-based Industrial HCI. Section 5 concludes the paper and sets the direction for future work.

2 Industrial HCIs – A Review of the State-of-the-Art

Industrial HCI applications have two phases: the engineering phase, and the runtime phase. The *engineering* refers to the design of the screen and the definition of its functionality. For example, buttons to trigger certain actions, image display, drawings, status bars, file system menus, communication with Programmable Logic Controllers (PLC), etc. The *runtime*, on the other hand, refers to the actual execution of these programs in an embedded computer system and it is necessary for users to interact with the GUI. In this Section, we present the state-of-the-art in engineering and runtime implementations of Industrial HCIs to motivate and highlight the need for parallel computing.

2.1 Engineering System

Industrial HCI vendors hide the complexity of the underlying architecture to the Industrial HCI application designer for various reasons. First, a single engineering system is used for multiple Industrial HCI devices with different capabilities and this level of abstraction allows the same application to have the same look and feel in all the Industrial HCIs. Second, the job of the designer should be focused on dealing with GUI objects and their associated actions and attributes, and not on dealing with the underlying computer system. **The programming abstractions introduced by the current engineering systems, unfortunately, are not suitable for the next generation of computation elements because they assume that the underlying computation element is always a single-core processor**. Embedded processor manufacturers are moving towards multi-/many-core technology [1–3] and we expect the next-generation Industrial HCI devices to adopt parallel processing technology. Typically, Industrial HCI screens consist of several objects positioned and configured by the application developer. Each object may include a list of Actions that, on every cycle or when an event occurs, the Industrial HCI runtime will execute. These Actions range from changing values (e.g. SetValue) of variables (Tags), to changing the appearance and properties of the objects themselves (e.g. color, X-position, Y-position). In a single-core implementation, the runtime system executes all the objects' Actions, one by one. Clearly, this approach does not scale anymore as single-core processors have reached a speed plateau. In a multi-/many-core system, the runtime can implicitly exploit parallelism by assigning these Actions to different threads and scheduling these into different cores. However, it is critical that the parallelization is done carefully in order to obtain performance benefits from multi-/many-core. Poor parallelization of multi-threaded programs often leads to performance degradations when compared to single core due to excessive synchronization and communication overhead.

2.2 Runtime

The runtime is responsible for executing the Industrial HCI application created with the engineering system in a timely manner in order to comply with the real-time requirements. Figure 1 shows the conventional implementation of runtime systems for GUI applications. GUI applications are driven by user triggered events such as a mouse click and/or system events such as timer and alarms. These events are detected by a single "GUI thread" responsible for handling all events and managing all the GUI-related objects and operations such as updating the display. To maintain the application response time as short as possible, the GUI thread runs under an infinite loop that detects and dispatches events to the event handling functions allocated to worker threads that perform the handling of the event. Whenever the GUI thread is not processing events in a timely manner, the users may experience an unresponsive application that "freezes". Although this model decouples event detection from event handling in multiple worker threads, it does not scale well in multi-/many-core processors because these worker threads must use the GUI thread to modify GUI objects' data and the display as shown in Figure 1. **Unfortunately, this creates a serialization bottleneck that eliminates any possibilities of improving the response time with multi-/many-core because all the GUI related workload is concentrated on a single thread.** The main observation is that the existing runtime model suffers from a performance bottleneck when executed in multi-/many-core processors because worker threads are not allowed to modify GUI objects directly. Instead, the GUI thread is responsible for all GUI-related data and this inhibits scalability in modern multi-/many-core processors. Worker threads have to enqueue 'Update object Events' back to the GUI thread which then will handle all the GUI object related workload, e.g. updating the color change of a pressed button, in a serialized manner.

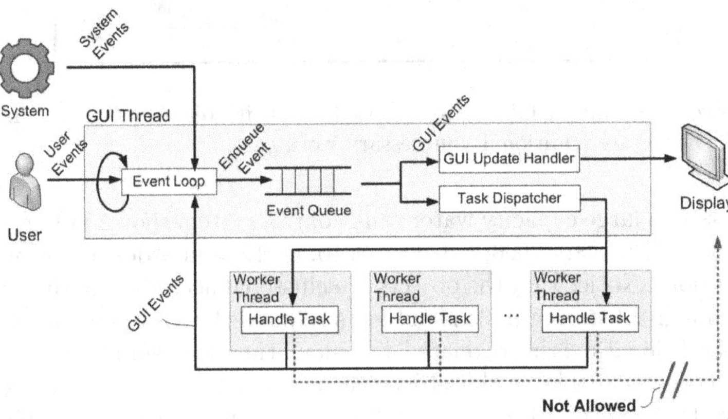

Fig. 1. The existing GUI application model suffers from a performance bottleneck in multi-/many-core processors because worker threads are not allowed to modify GUI objects

Current Industrial HCI runtime systems are also affected by their limited ability to transfer GUI objects to the screen after all the tasks are executed and the data has been updated by the worker threads. This transfer, referred to as *flushing*, can be performed one object at a time, or bundling several objects into a single flush call. Both approaches have advantages and limitations. Flushing single objects is simpler and faster but the number of flush calls can be a performance penalty in some systems. Bundling multiple objects and flushing once reduces the number of flush calls but increases the memory bandwidth requirements. Unfortunately, the flushing strategy greatly depends on the underlying hardware configuration. Current Industrial HCI runtime systems often perform the flush operations based on the objects' bounding boxes and clustering them according to the order by which they were created during the engineering phase. For example, existing runtime systems would group the 12

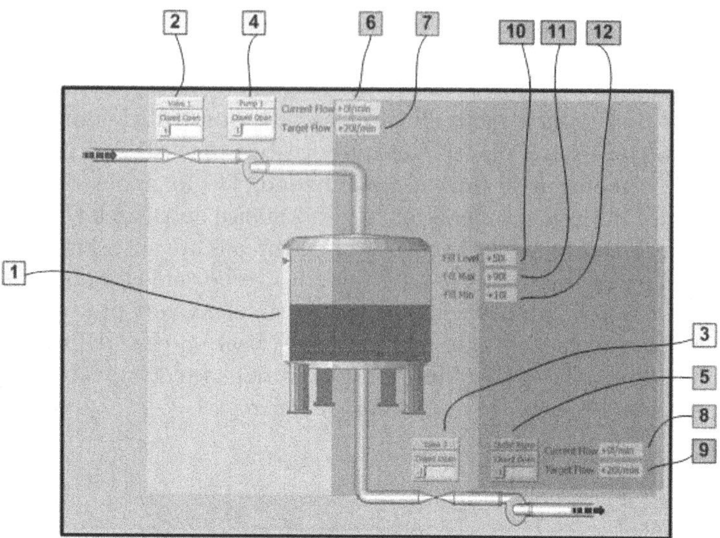

Fig. 2. Naive clustering of GUI objects based on their creation order incurs in area overlaps that generate additional unnecessary work

GUI objects in a large capacity water tank control system shown in Figure 2 into three sets $< 1, 2, 3, 4 >$, $< 5, 6, 7, 8 >$, $< 9, 10, 11, 12 >$ in order to perform three flush operations. Notice that the objects are clustered according to their creation index. Although clustering multiple objects reduces the total number of calls, it incurs in additional overhead related to calculating the size of the aggregated bounding box that encloses the objects in a set. Also, notice that there may be clusters that overlap in space and this creates unnecessary and redundant flushing. This shows that a redesign of the runtime system for Industrial HCIs is also necessary for the adoption of multi-/many-core technology. In this paper, we focus on two key aspects of the design: effective multi-threading in multi-/many-core, and optimization of the flushing operations.

2.3 Related Work

Our work relates to the desktop application parallelization research. In [4], the authors present an object-oriented parallel programming library for GUI applications and a dynamic runtime system that allows the parallelization of image processing applications in multi-/many-core processors. Due to the streaming nature of multimedia applications, other researchers have demonstrated that vectorization [5, 6] and custom parallel hardware [7] are other effective means to accelerate desktop applications. The common aspect to all the related work is the focus on the parallelization of non-real-time multimedia applications that are known to take advantage of parallel processing [8]. Our work, on the other hand, focuses on the parallelization of real-time sub-millisecond applications with tight dependencies between user-actions and data processing.

3 Parallel Rendering for Industrial HCIs

In order to improve the performance, energy efficiency, scalability, consolidation, and redundancy in Industrial HCIs, we propose a novel parallel rendering technology that effectively uses multi-/many-core processor technology to reduce the response time of GUI applications bound to real-time requirements. To overcome the sequential computation limitations inherent to the current Industrial HCI programming (See Section 2), we propose a parallel rendering method in both the engineering system and the runtime system to exploit parallelism in these applications.

3.1 Identifying Coarse-Grain Parallelism in the Engineering System

In our system, parallelization may begin at the engineering system. The GUI designer is often the best person to identify coarse-grain parallelism opportunities because the layout and functionality of an Industrial HCI screen is closely related to the underlying industrial automation pyramid [9] consisting of sensors, actuators, controllers, SCADA (Supervisory Control and Data Acquisition), MES (Manufacturing Execution Systems), and ERP (Enterprise Resource Planning) systems. We strongly believe that this intuition provides an excellent opportunity for our system to expose an initial coarse-grain concurrency. Figure 3 shows the process of identifying coarse-grain parallelism at the engineering system. The *execution group* (EG) selection step is introduced to the GUI design process to bind the Actions in the objects on the screen to *suggested* logical threads. It must be noted, however, that these are simply hints provided by the Industrial HCI designer and the ultimate execution of Actions in specific cores is up to the runtime scheduling algorithms. In addition to the list of available EGs, the "Default" setting is the default assignment for Actions and it implies that the designer is unsure about the assignment and it is completely up to the runtime to decide how Actions are executed in the available cores in the system.

3.2 Exploiting Fine-Grain Parallelism in the Runtime System

Although our engineering system exposes coarse-grain parallelism, this parallelism is still subject to the existing runtime system limitations discussed in Section 2.2. Even though multiple threads exist in the application, these are not allowed to modify GUI objects' data directly. Thus, a serialization bottleneck prevents threads to take advantage of multi-/many-core processors. To eliminate this serialization bottleneck, we propose a runtime system that allows different threads to access a privatized memory area and this allows the application to truly execute GUI applications in parallel. The responsibility of our runtime system is to schedule the execution of Actions of the objects to different CPU in such a way that the response time of the Industrial HCI application is reduced.

Figure 4 highlights the three main differences between our parallel rendering runtime system and conventional runtime systems. Although our approach also uses a GUI thread to enqueue input events (e.g. user inputs, system events,

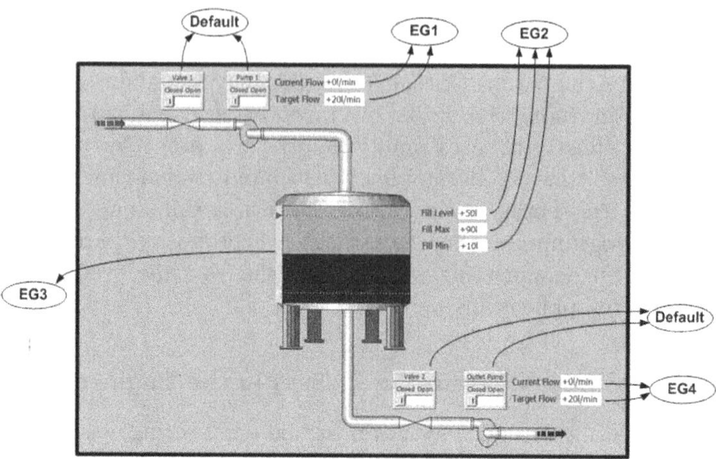

Fig. 3. Identifying coarse grain parallelism through EG selection during application engineering

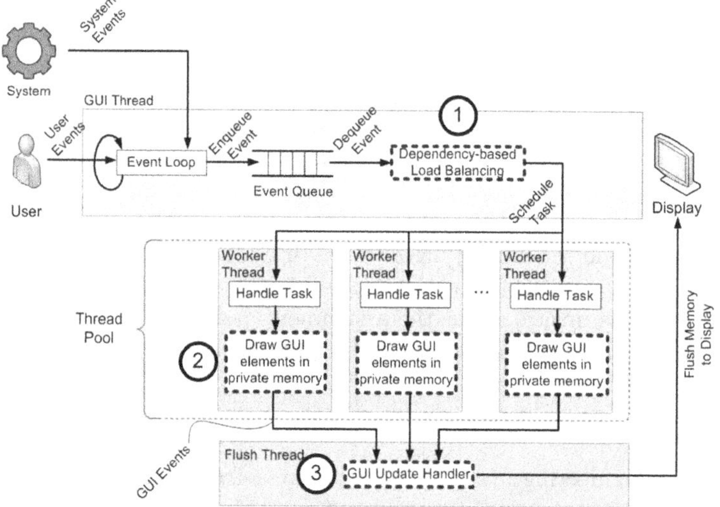

Fig. 4. Our parallel rendering method eliminates the serialization bottleneck in the GUI thread by ① performing a dependency analysis at the GUI object-level and distributing the workload to multiple worker threads,② allowing the worker threads to modify GUI objects directly, and ③ optimizing the flush of the internal memory to the display

interrupts, etc.), the first difference is that this thread is now also responsible for performing a dependency-based load balancing ① to distribute the workload to multiple worker threads. Second, the worker threads now use a privatized memory area ② to truly parallelize the execution of objects' Actions and eliminate the serialization bottleneck created in the conventional systems. Third, a dedicated flush thread ③ optimizes the data transfer between the worker threads private memory and the display in order to reduce the data size and the function call frequency.

The dependency-based load balancing is the first critical step for exploiting parallelism in Industrial HCI applications running on multi-/many-core. The key observation about the dependency-based load balancing algorithm is that it uses runtime information, in addition to the static coarse-grain information provided by the engineering system, to determine the data dependencies between GUI objects. As shown in Figure 5, this is accomplished through a dynamic data dependency analysis that groups the dependent GUI objects into clusters that are dispatched to different cores.

Maintaining data dependent objects in the same core minimizes synchronization and communication among cores because worker threads only access their private memory area and this ultimately helps to reduce the response time. The private memory area mechanism guarantees that only one CPU accesses that area, and in combination with the data dependency analysis, it enables the possibility of parallel execution of GUI applications as shown by ② in Figure 6.

Since the worker threads now run under different time constraints, caused by uneven workloads of each GUI object, it is necessary to synchronize them after their execution cycle completes. As shown in Figure 6, the "flush thread" ③ optimizes the sequential access to the display by minimizing the number of pixels and the number of draw function calls in order to reach the maximum performance gain when transferring the GUI data to the display. The fundamental optimization mechanism is to minimize both the size of the bounding box of multiple GUI objects and the number of calls necessary to flush them while avoiding the creation of overlapping bounding boxes. For example, Figure 6 shows that the algorithm determines that 4 non-overlapping clusters consisting of elements$< 1, 3, 8, 6 >$, $< 7, 4 >$, $< 2, 9 >$, and $< 5 >$ is the optimal strategy for flushing the screen in a particular system. It is important to note that the optimal balance between number of calls and size is highly influenced by the underlying hardware configuration. Nevertheless, compared to existing approaches, our method effectively eliminates the overlap regions and therefore unnecessary workload, and also reduces the size resulting in shorter flush times.

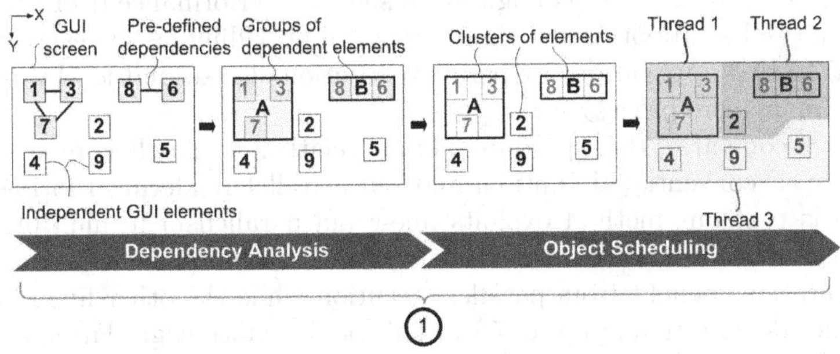

Fig. 5. Dependency-based object scheduling ①

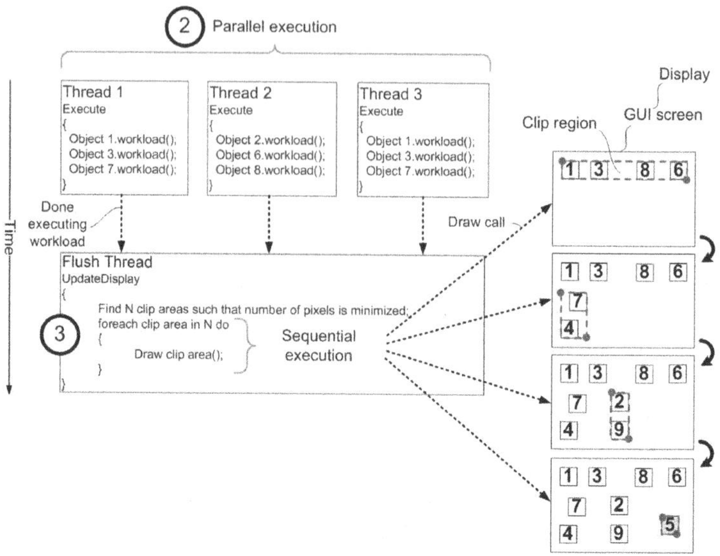

Fig. 6. Parallel workload execution ② and flushing optimization ③

4 Experimental Results

To validate our concepts, we implemented a parallel rendering system for Industrial HCIs in a commercial-off-the-shelf quad-core processor. Using a realistic benchmark used to test the response time of existing runtime systems, we focus on characterizing our parallel rendering system in terms of two key design aspects: the scalability of multi-/many-core based Industrial HCI systems against single-core implementations, and the effects of multi-/many-core scheduling in the performance of GUI applications.

Figure 7 shows the rendering time of six configurations of the benchmark when executed in a single and four cores. Our parallel rendering framework is capable of reducing the rendering time on five of the six configurations from 36% to 217%. The "1 Rectangle" configuration shows a performance degradation of -3%. These results support our main objective of providing faster response time on Industrial HCI applications by parallel execution of μ-second-level workloads on multi-/many-core processors.

Figure 8 compares the speedup factors relative to single-core execution obtained by a conventional runtime and our parallel rendering runtime. The difference is that our method exploits fine-grain parallelism in multiple-cores. Notice that using a conventional straightforward scheduling, only one out of six configurations benefit from parallel execution while the other five represent performance degradation of up to -58%. This performance degradation is due to the fact that the current runtime systems are incapable of effectively exploiting parallelism and a simple scheduling policy is not sufficient for taking advantage of

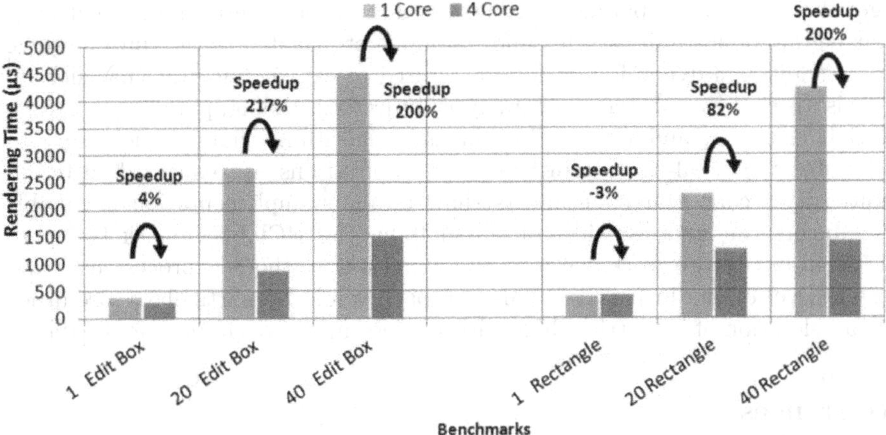

Fig. 7. Sub-millisecond level workloads can be reduced by up to 217% when executed by our method in a quad-core processor

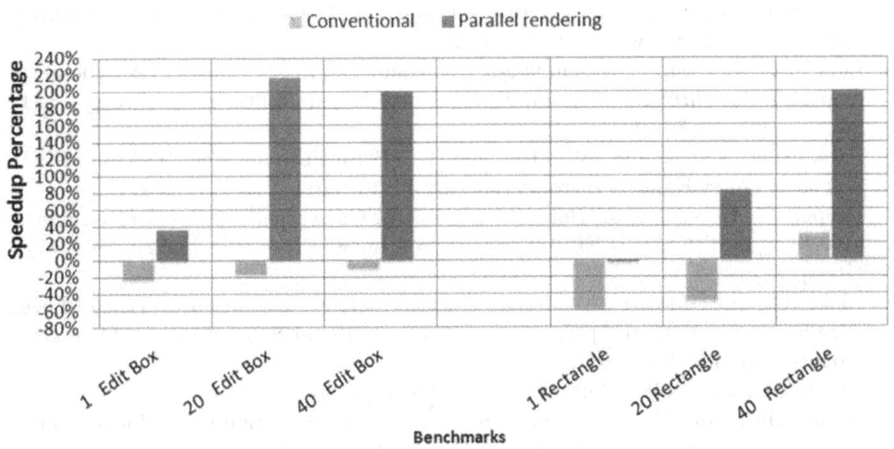

Fig. 8. Speedup percentages of existing runtimes and our parallel rendering method relative to execution on single core

multi-/many-core Industrial HCIs. The parallel rendering method, on the other hand, shows improvements of up to 217%.

5 Conclusion

To facilitate the transition from single-core to multi-/many-core Industrial HCIs, we developed a parallel rendering method to eliminate the serialization bottleneck that exists in state-of-the-art engineering and runtime systems. Our algorithm uses a static parallelization method at the engineering stage to identify coarse-grain opportunities. This information is propagated to the runtime stage where additional dynamic information is used to exploit fine-grain parallelism. This is assisted by a dependency analysis, object scheduling, parallel processing of GUI elements, and non-overlap flushing algorithms that are necessary to guarantee that real-time Industrial HCI applications are executed faster in multi-/many-core. Our experiments show that our implementation is capable of reducing the response time of a real Industrial HCI benchmark by up to 217%. In our future work, we plan to extend our method to process user and system-level events in parallel. This approach would be particularly useful for the acceleration of industrial HCIs with modern multi-touch interfaces [10].

References

1. Intel: Technical Resources for Embedded Designs with Intel Architecture, `http://www.intel.com/`
2. Freescale: QorIQ Processing Platforms - Industrial, `http://www.freescale.com`
3. Texas Instruments: Stellaris MCU for industrial automation, `www.ti.com`
4. Giacaman, N., Sinnen, O.: Object-Oriented Parallelization of Java Desktop Programs. IEEE Software (1), 32–38 (2011)
5. Luk, C.K., Newton, R., Hasenplaugh, W., Hampton, M., Lowney, G.: A Synergetic Approach to Throughput Computing on x86-Based Multicore Desktops. IEEE Software (1), 39–50 (2011)
6. Pankratius, V., Schulte, W., Keutzer, K.: Parallelism on the Desktop. IEEE Software: Guest Editors' Introduction (1), 14–16 (2011)
7. Draper, B., Beveridge, J., Bohm, A., Ross, C., Chawathe, M.: Accelerated image processing on FPGAs. IEEE Transactions on Image Processing 12(12), 1543–1551 (2003)
8. Blake, G., Dreslinski, R.G., Mudge, T., Flautner, K.: Evolution of Thread-Level Parallelism in Desktop Applications. In: International Symposium on Computer Architecture, ISCA (2010)
9. Nof, S.Y.: Handbook of Automation. Springer (2009)
10. Beaudouin-Lafon, M.: Instrumental interaction: an interaction model for designing post-wimp user interfaces. In: Proceedings of the SIGCHI Conference on Human Factors in Computing Systems, CHI 2000, pp. 446–453 (2000)

A Logical Design Method for User Interface Using GUI Design Patterns

Ichiro Hirata[1] and Toshiki Yamaoka[2]

[1] Product Innovation Department, Hyogo prefectural Institute of Technology, Yukihira Cho 3-1-12, Suma Ku, Kobe City, Hyogo, Japan
[2] Wakayama University, Faculty of Systems Engineering, Sakaedani 930, Wakayama City, Wakayama, Japan
tyamaoka@gmail.com, ichiro@hyogo-kg.jp

Abstract. This paper presents a discussion of method for user interface design using graphical user interface (GUI) design patterns. GUI design patterns are defined as "general operation and expression of embedded system products". Purpose of this study is to develop a user interface design efficient. GUI design patterns were extracted in embedded system products. Then, interviews were conducted with students and researchers in which the practical applicability of the extracted GUI design patterns. This process allowed the number of GUI design patterns to be narrowed down to 81 patterns. 81 patterns were analyzed using the cluster analysis, between them and classifies these objects into different 7 groups. The GUI design patterns, which were composed of 7 groups, divided into 4 layers. Finally, Design method using GUI design patterns was discussed. This proposed method is based on the Human Design Technology (HDT). HDT is a logical product development and UCD method easily accessible to anyone.

Keywords: User Interface, Design Pattern, Human Design Technology.

1 Introduction

User Centered Design (UCD) is a type of user interface design and a process in which the needs, wants, and limitations of users of a product are given extensive attention at each stage of the design process. UCD is defined as "a user interface design process that focuses on usability goals, user characteristics, environment, tasks, and workflow in the design of an interface; it is an iterative process, where design and evaluation steps are built in from the first stage of projects, through implementation" [1]. Since UCD method has been recognized as a powerful tool, large enterprises have been introducing UCD method and facilities. But, it is hard to introduce present UCD methods to middle/small enterprises because introducing UCD method is rather expensive. Thus, we have studied a design method to introduce UCD into middle/small enterprises.

M. Kurosu (Ed.): Human-Computer Interaction, Part I, HCII 2013, LNCS 8004, pp. 361–370, 2013.

In this paper, we suggest a method of screen design with the GUI design patterns. The design patterns were developed by Christopher Alexander, in collaboration, as a method to allow anyone to design and build at any scale [2]. They based on the idea that users know more about the buildings they need than any architect could, idea that has been exported to the design of websites [3]. The GUI design patterns are defined as "general operation and expression of embedded system products". So, the GUI design patterns are noticeably different from software design patterns, which are focused on the source code and software structures. Designers tend to utilize GUI design methods based on individually accumulated knowledge and experience. Designers are offered patterns that help them to design usable interfaces using proposed GUI design method. This method is based on the Human Design Technology (HDT) [4]. HDT is a logical product development and UCD method easily accessible to anyone. So, this method makes it possible to introduce UCD into middle/small enterprises.

2 Design Process Based on Human Design Technology

2.1 Human Design Technology (HDT)

The Human Design Technology (HDT) is a design method for product design. It is defined as "Method to integrate ergonomics, industrial design, marketing research, cognitive science, usability engineering, and statistics, to review process of product development to rely on intuition in the past by aspect of quantification as much as possible, and to support product making with charm of man priority that examines" [5]. The HDT process has 5 phases that assist the product development. The HDT design process is as follows.

1. Gather user requirements

User requirements are extracted to product problems. Extract problems using group interviews, observation and task analysis.

2. Grasp current circumstances

Investigate how users perceive a target product in the market using correspondence analysis.

3. Formulate structured concepts

Constructing structured concepts based on user requirements and other types of information. Since the main specifications must be determined at this stage, structured concept should be structured for logical continuity among their various items, thereby avoiding any omissions. The weighting of the different concept items is particularly important as a measure to ensure logical continuity among them. This is also significant for revealing the items that are important. Once the items are weighted, those that should take precedence may be determined automatically when certain design items must be traded off against one another.

4. Design (synthesis)

Visualize a product based on the structured concepts. HDT requires that the design be based on the seventy predetermined design items.

5. Evaluate the design

The design idea is evaluated by user test. A protocol analysis, questionnaires were made on 5 people.

Figure 1 depicts the clusters in HDT's design process. HDT is a design method for product design. So, HDT needed to customize for GUI design. When product was designed in HDT process, designer visualized using the 70 design items. Proposed GUI design method is visualized using 2 items instead of the 70 design items as follows.

- Concept target table
- GUI design patterns

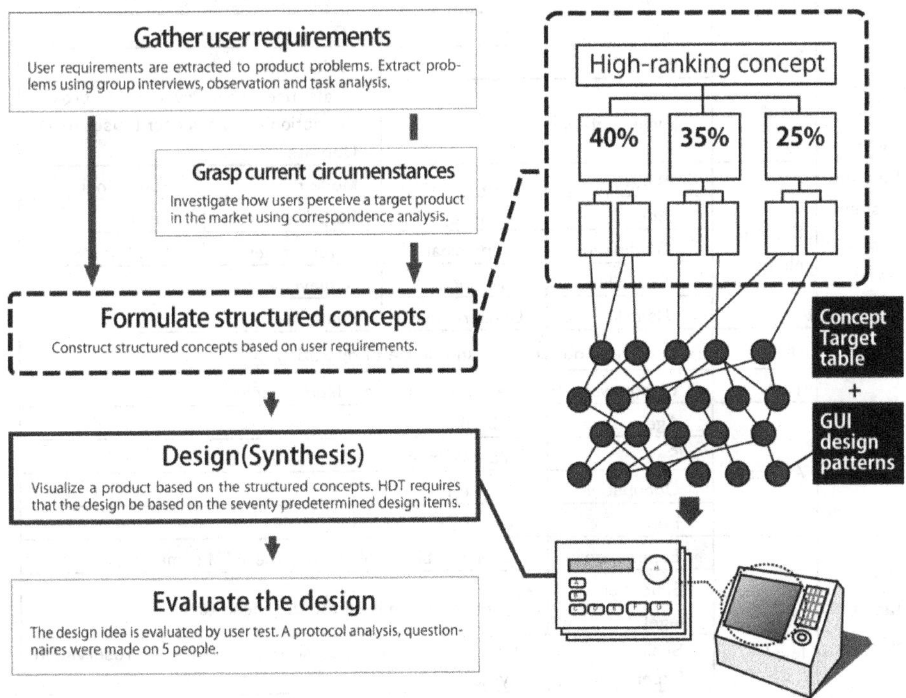

Fig. 1. Design process of Human Design Technology (HDT)

2.2 Concept Target Table

Table 1 shows the concept target table, which is one of the system's specifications. For the modeling of user interface, we must consider the target user and system's spec. GUI design required information to system specs and user. The concept target table could define target system and users clearly. The contents of target system and target users are included as follows.

- System: Function, Device, Space, Hours, and Implementation
- System's element: User decided 3-4 elements among the 18 elements.
- User Interface
- Task
- Attribute: Age, Sex, Occupation, and Earn
- User level: Experience, Education level, Similarity experience, Life style
- User's mental model: Functional model, Structural model

Table 1. Concept target table

<table>
<tr><td rowspan="12">Clear targeted system</td><td rowspan="5">System</td><td colspan="2">Function</td><td colspan="2">Exclusive</td></tr>
<tr><td colspan="2">Device</td><td colspan="2">Touch pad</td></tr>
<tr><td colspan="2">Space</td><td colspan="2">Bank, Public space</td></tr>
<tr><td colspan="2">Hours</td><td colspan="2">9:00-17:00</td></tr>
<tr><td colspan="2">Implementation</td><td colspan="2">・Staff use when system is broken
・Receptionist guides user if user don't Operate</td></tr>
<tr><td rowspan="5">System's element</td><td>Safety</td><td>Convenience</td><td>Modern</td><td>Functional</td></tr>
<tr><td>Security</td><td>Efficiency</td><td>Surprise</td><td>Legible</td></tr>
<tr><td>Confidence</td><td>Economical</td><td>Entertainment</td><td>Aesthetic</td></tr>
<tr><td>Reliability</td><td>Tolerance</td><td>Achievement</td><td></td></tr>
<tr><td>Usability</td><td>Conservative</td><td>Emotional</td><td></td></tr>
<tr><td>UI</td><td colspan="4">User need not get new knowledge of operation</td></tr>
<tr><td>Task</td><td colspan="4">Withdrawals, Remittance, Contributed, Money received</td></tr>
<tr><td rowspan="10">Clear targeted user</td><td rowspan="4">Attribute</td><td>Age</td><td colspan="3">18 - 65</td></tr>
<tr><td>Sex</td><td colspan="3">Man, Woman</td></tr>
<tr><td>Occupation</td><td colspan="3">General</td></tr>
<tr><td>Earn</td><td colspan="3">General</td></tr>
<tr><td rowspan="4">User level</td><td>Experience</td><td colspan="3">User has been able to use the ATM some time</td></tr>
<tr><td>Education level</td><td colspan="3">User is able to read the Japanese text</td></tr>
<tr><td>Similarity Experience</td><td colspan="3">User has been able to use the station ticket reservation system some time</td></tr>
<tr><td>Life style</td><td colspan="3">Various</td></tr>
<tr><td rowspan="2">Mental model</td><td colspan="2">Functional model</td><td colspan="2">Model to understand How-to-use it</td></tr>
<tr><td colspan="2">Structural model</td><td colspan="2">Model to understand How-it-works</td></tr>
</table>

2.3 GUI Design Patterns

To develop a user interface design efficient, the GUI design patterns were extracted. Generally, designers use guidelines to good solutions in order to ensure to their systems. These guidelines are offered as general sentences that have to be determined in each case. General sentences have various meaning. Thus, this diversity is also introduced complexity in the process of GUI design. On the other hand, the GUI design patterns are offered as concrete examples that have to be determined in each case.

The GUI design patterns are defined as "general operation and expression embedded system products" [6]. Each GUI design pattern is composed of summary, utility and examples (Fig. 2). For instance, the GUI design pattern "Various expressions" was as follow.

- Summary: Information design is changed by situation.
- Utility: icon, List, preview, etc.

This study used the following process to identify and select GUI design patterns that are applied to practical design situations.

First, we extracted GUI design patterns in embedded system products.

Then, selecting useful device "touch panel" for further examination further narrowed these GUI design patterns.

Finally, interviews were conducted with students and researchers in which the practical applicability of the extracted GUI design patterns to artifact GUI design were discussed. This process allowed the number of GUI design patterns to be narrowed down to 81 patterns.

Table 2 shows 81 patterns, which were selected as samples for classification by aforementioned process.

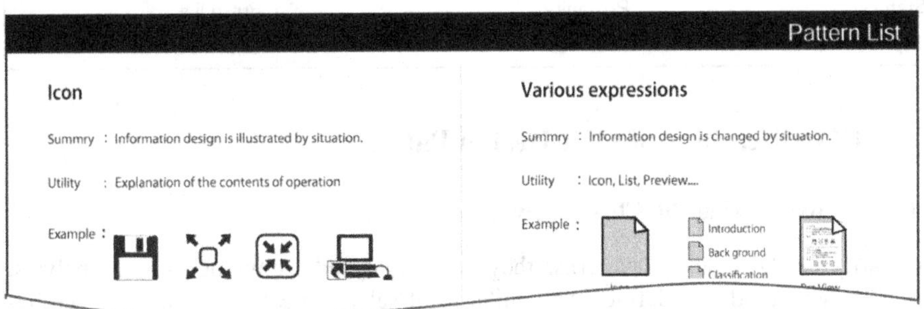

Fig. 2. Example of GUI design patterns

Table 2. GUI design patterns list

Display zoon out/in	Rearrangements of items	Move items using tab key
Undo	Item editing	Drop-down menu
Cloze items	Menu bar	Tree structure
Structural input	Adjust text size	Guidance of input area
Direct operation	Continuous filtering	Aggregation structure
Default indicate	All select by one click	Drag
Gray display	Searching	Procedural operation
Right down enter	Keyword sorting	Hub structure
Metaphor selection	Shortcut key	Gradual addition
Free input	One click enter	Visible and Un visible
Tool menu	Scroll bar	Auto complete
Round button	Re-layout	Guidance
Setting	All process display	Tab button
Double click	Cancel along the way	Enter after selection
Resize	List operation	Top navigation
Icon	Hierarchical information	Waiting time indicate
Various icons	Rectangle	Emphasis
Consistency color	Information of top class	Model display
Color information	One display	Modal dialog
Picture information	Simple line	Two windows
Current position	Center information	Three windows
Footer information	Flexible screen	End of task
Common header	Dual display	Tab
Complement of change	Stripe background	Base display
Pop Up	Emphasis of selection	1/()
Stand in	Proximity	Ruled line
Top with impact	Look flow	Check selection

3 Classifications of GUI Design Patterns

3.1 Analysis Using the Cluster Analysis

To clarify the GUI design patterns, they were analyzed using the cluster analysis, which is a method that defines the similarity of select objects from the distance between them and classifies these objects into different groups. We analyzed relationship between GUI design patterns and the user interface (UI) design items. The UI design items are prepared expert designer's know-how by precedence research [7]. Problem of how to select GUI design patterns can be fixed using the UI design items. Table 3 shows the UI design items.

Table 3. UI design items

Flexibility	Simplicity	Minimization of physical load
Customization for different user levels	Ease of information retrieval	Sense of operation
User protection	At a glance interface	Efficiency of operation
Accessibility	Mapping	Emphasis
Application to different cultures	Identification	Affordance
Provision of user enjoyment	Consistency	Metaphor
Provision of sense of accomplishment	Mental model	System Structure
The user's leadership	Clue	Feedback
Reliability	Term/Message	Help
Presentation of various information	Minimization of users' memory load	

We found 7 groups as a result of the cluster analysis. The results are as follows.

1. "Output" group's pattern

Gray display, Complement of change, color information, Footer information, All process display, Current position, 1/(), Guidance of input area, Hierarchical information

2. "Operation" group's pattern

Right down enter, Undo, Incremental search, Searching, Item editing, Shortcut key, Setting, Default indicate, Cancel along the way, Continuous filtering, Top navigation, Adjust text size,

3. "GUI parts" group's pattern

Scroll bar, Tab button, Close items, Switch, Slider, Drop-down menu, Menu bar, Metaphor selection, Drum menu

4. "Screen Layout" group's pattern

One display, Dual display, Model display, Modal dialog, center information

5. "Design Guideline" group's pattern

Consistency color, Proximity, Rectangle, Alignment, Common header, Blank effect, Top with impact, Icon, Picture information, Round button, Stripe background, Emphasis of selection, Unified color's bar, Emphasized label, Simple line, Various icons

6. "UI Guideline" group's pattern

Look flow, Support of users' memory load, Gradual addition, one click enter, Aggregation structure

7. "Operation's Structure" group's pattern

Right down enter, Undo, Incremental search, Searching, Item editing, Shortcut key, Default indicate, Setting, Cancel along the way, Continuous filtering, Top navigation, Adjust text size, Tool menu

The GUI design patterns, which are composed of 7 groups, can be divided into 4 layers (Fig. 2). GUI design patterns are connected between them by a hierarchical structure, so designers can resolve complex design solutions as simple.

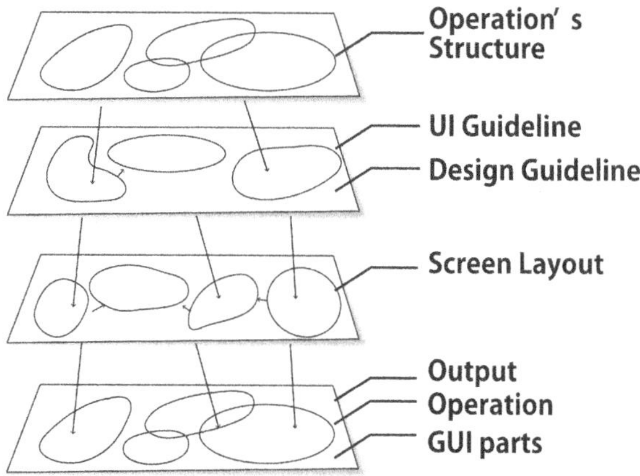

Fig. 3. The GUI design patterns can be divided into 4 layers

3.2 Applying GUI Design Patterns to Design Process

This chapter outlines design method using GUI design patterns. GUI design patterns were characterized the relationship between the structured design concept and the concept target table. The concept item that is a part of the structural design concept and the target device that is a part of the concept target table select these GUI design patterns. The procedure to apply GUI design patterns on presented method is as follows.

1. Constructing the structured concept: The structured concept is constructed based on user requirements. Relation to make hierarchy grouped concept items. After that, weight is put to each item and total weight of the items becomes 100. The priority of each item was described as the weight in this process.

2. Making the concept target table: The concept target table is able to define target systems and target users clearly. All items are related to the design structure concept.
3. Select GUI design patterns (Operation's structure): Operation's structure patterns are selected to the concept target table and concept item's weight. Pattern that is related to the concept item is assigned at least one.
4. Select GUI design patterns (UI guideline, Design guideline): As shown in Figure 3, second layer consists of 2 groups: UI guideline and Design guideline. These groups are related to concept item's weight and target user that is a part of the concept target table.
5. Select GUI design patterns (Screen Layout): GUI design patterns are selected to the concept target table and second layer patterns.
6. Select GUI design patterns (Output, Operation, GUI parts): As shown in Figure 3, second layer consists of 3 groups: Output, Operation and GUI parts. GUI design patterns are related to the concept target table and third layer patterns.
7. Visualize user interface based on the GUI design patterns.

4 Conclusions

In this paper, a method of screen design with the GUI design patterns is discussed. The design process for GUI design was described based on HDT and the GUI design patterns. We extracted GUI design patterns in embedded system products. Selecting useful device "touch panel" for further examination further narrowed these patterns. Then, interviews were conducted with students and researchers in which the practical applicability of the extracted GUI design patterns to artifact GUI design were discussed. This process allowed the number of GUI design patterns to be narrowed down to 81 patterns. 81 patterns were analyzed using the cluster analysis, between them and classifies these objects into different 7 groups. The GUI design patterns, which were composed of 7 groups, divided into 4 layers.

Logical design approach is needed for middle/small enterprises. As the usual traditional design method depends on designer's intuition or skill, it takes a lot of time to achieve design. But, beginner designers don't know GUI design items systematically. When they started GUI design, they tried to collect suitable GUI design items taking a lot of time. When they know the structure of the systematizing GUI design patterns, they collect suitable GUI design items quickly. In addition, design representation could be described quite clearly. The methodology used in GUI design pattern can be as follows.

1. GUI design representation could be described quite clearly.
2. GUI design process could be clearly.
3. Designer's ability is little influence.

Acknowledgments. This work was supported by Grant-in-Aid for Scientific Research(C: 23611055).

References

1. Henry, S.L.: Just Ask: Integrating Accessibility Throughout Design. ETLawton, Madison (2007)
2. Alexander, C., Ishikawa, S., Silverstein, M.: A pattern language: Towns, Buildings, Construction. Oxford University Press, New York (1977)
3. Van Duyne, D., Landay, J., Hong, J.: The Design of Sites: Patterns, Principles, and Processes for Crafting a Customer-centered Web Experience. Addison-Wesley, Boston (2002)
4. Yamaoka, T: Human-Centered Design Using Human Design Technology - Applications to Universal Design and so on–, Plenary Speech. In: 13th Triennial Congress of the International Ergonomics Association, vol. 4 (2003)
5. Yamaoka, T.: Introduction of Human Design Technology, vol. 4. Morikita Publisher, Tokyo (2003) (in Japanese)
6. Hirata, I., Mitsutani, K., Yamaoka, T.: Systematizing GUI bPatterns Base on Formal Concept Analysis and Application. Bulletin of Japanese Society for the Science of Design 58(2), 27–36 (2011)
7. Yamaoka, T.: Introduction of Human Design Technology, pp. 15–19. Morikita Publisher, Tokyo (2003) (in Japanese)

Developing Mobile Apps Using Cross-Platform Frameworks: A Case Study

Shah Rukh Humayoun, Stefan Ehrhart, and Achim Ebert

Computer Graphics and HCI Group,
University of Kaiserslautern,
Gottlieb-Daimler-Str., 67663, Kaiserslautern, Germany
{humayoun,ebert}@cs.uni-kl.de, s_ehrhart@gmx.net

Abstract. In last few years, a huge variety of frameworks for the mobile cross-platform development have been released to deliver quick and overall better solutions. Most of them are based on different approaches and technologies; therefore, relying on only one for using in all cases is not recommendable. The diversity in smart-devices (i.e. smartphones and tablets) and in their hardware features; such as screen-resolution, processing power, etc.; as well as the availability of different mobile operating systems makes the process of mobile application development much complicated. In this work, we analyze few of these cross-platform development frameworks through developing three mobile apps on each of them as well as on the native Android and iOS environments. Moreover, we also performed a user evaluation study on these developed mobile apps to judge how users perceive the same mobile app developed in different frameworks and environments, from the native to the cross-platform environment. Results indicate that these frameworks are good alternative to the native platform implementations but a careful investigation is required before deciding to check whether the target framework supports the needed features in a stable way.

Keywords: Cross-platform development, mobile apps, iOS, Android, smart-device, smartphone, tablet, user evaluation.

1 Introduction

The rate of smartphones amongst cell-phones was expected to exceed the 50% boundary in the year 2012 [11] with the amount doubling each year [3]. Nowadays smart-devices, which include smartphones and tablets, are a vital platform for people to access services in their daily life, not only in developed countries but in developing countries too [2]. Due to great variations in smart-device types (from mobiles to tablets), in their hardware (different screen sizes, resolutions, and computation power), and in the underlying operating systems (e.g., Android, iOS, Windows Phone 8) make it a big challenge for software developers to develop applications (called *mobile apps* or just *apps*) for them. Developing mobile apps separately for each platform or device is costly and time consuming process while keeping focus on just one platform or device reduces the number of accessible users. This problem leads to a solution where

M. Kurosu (Ed.): Human-Computer Interaction, Part I, HCII 2013, LNCS 8004, pp. 371–380, 2013.

the mobile apps are developed through frameworks, called *cross-platform development frameworks*. In these frameworks, the apps are developed just once and then can be deployed on those platforms and devices that are supported by the underlying framework. However, one of the main problems the industry is facing nowadays in this solution is that the apps developed on these frameworks normally provide not as good interaction and functionalities compared to the apps developed on the native development environments.

In last few years, plenty of frameworks for mobile cross-platform development have been released to deliver overall cost-effective and better solutions. Most of these frameworks use different underlying approaches and technologies; therefore, relying only on one for using in all cases is not recommended. In this work, we analyze few of these cross-platform development frameworks through developing three apps on each of them as well as on the two most widely used native environments, i.e., the Google Android and the Apple iOS. Moreover, we also performed a user evaluation study on these developed apps to judge how users perceive the same app developed in different frameworks and environments, from the native to the cross-platforms.

The remainder of this paper is structured as follows. In Section 2, we highlight the background. In Section 3, we describe the three scenarios for developing apps and details of the development of these apps in different frameworks and environments. In Section 4, we provide details of the user evaluation study. In Section 5, we analyze from the software evaluation perspectives. Finally, we conclude in Section 6.

2 Background

Smartphones and tablets are getting more and more popular since after launch of the Apple iPhone and iPad even though the first smartphone, the IBM Simon, was built in 1992 and then released in 1993 by BellSouth [1]. Nowadays, a number of operating systems from different vendors are available for these smart-devices. Few examples of the most famous ones are Google Android, Apple iOS, Microsoft Windows Phone, Symbian OS, and RIM Blackberry OS. Developing mobile apps separately for each platform is quite costly as it needs the same number of development time for each target platform. Moreover, it also makes the maintenance more costly and time-consuming. To resolves these issues, many cross-platform development frameworks have been developed in which developers write code once and then the resulting app can be deployed on different platforms and environments. Each of these frameworks targets a number of different platforms and environments starting at least from two. A study by Vision Mobile [8] pointed out over one hundred different mobile cross-platform frameworks. The availability of these frameworks on one-side gives developers the freedom to choose amongst them according to their requirements, but on the other side also makes it difficult to choose the right one.

Many people from the industry and academia have already analyzed and categorized the available cross-platform development frameworks. An example form the industry is a report by Vision Mobile [8] that discusses the tools for mobile cross-platform development. In academia, some studies [4, 9, 10] have also been done that analyze the frameworks and tools for mobile cross-platform development. Each of these studies analyzed different frameworks and tools and highlighted their advantages and disadvantages. They also tried to find out the better option amongst the selected ones against their chosen criteria.

In comparison to the previous work on the issue of cross-platform mobile development, the work behind this paper differs from two aspects. First, we implemented several sample applications derived from the interaction schema of mobile environment. Secondly, we verified the results through a user evaluation study to find out if users from different backgrounds are even satisfied enough with the cross-platform solutions, in order to make these solutions worth considering in the first place. The frameworks in which we were interested are: Appcelerator Titanium [5], which is an open source (under Apache License) runtime interpreter using HTML and JavaScript; RhoMobile Rhodes [6], which is a Ruby and HTML based open source (under MIT license) runtime interpreter; and MoSync [7], which is a C++ based open source (under GPL) mixture of a runtime interpreter, a source code translator and a web-to-native wrapper.

3 The Testing Scenarios and The Developed Apps

We choose three frameworks out of a variety of frameworks as well as the native iOS and Android environments for developing apps' versions and then for detailed testing based on our targeted criteria. We did not take into account the web app frameworks due to their reduced functionality as well as the app factory frameworks. Appcelerator Titanium [5] and RhoMobile Rhodes [6] were selected as these cross-platform development frameworks are based on completely different web programming languages. While the third framework MoSync [7] was selected because it combines the three approaches of hybrid frameworks and supports a number of platforms.

The sample scenarios (i.e. *MovePic, BubbleLevel,* and *AnnotatePic*) for developing the apps were derived from the perspective of interaction-schema of smart-devices, which mostly consists of touch-events (such as *tap, drag, pinch,* etc.), accelerometer, localization services, camera access, file system access, etc. Our focus was towards touch-events, accelerometer, camera access, and the file system access. We left other interaction-schema elements, such as localization services, due to their behavior complexity. For each scenario, we developed apps using the above-mentioned frameworks as well as the native iOS and Android development environments. The developed apps for the scenarios target towards not only the smartphones but also the tablets in order to consider the scalability issues. Following subsections provide the description of each scenario and the corresponding developed app's versions.

3.1 The *MovePic* Scenario

The *MovePic* scenario's goal was to test the support and processing of multi-touch gestures in smart-devices. This was done by hardcoding an image through the image-view in the underlying device. The presented image could be manipulated with multi-touch gestures such as panning, pinch zooming, rotating and dragging.

The native iOS version was developed using the built-in gesture recognizers in which the attached gestures can only be used inside the image, because in iOS the gesture recognizers are assigned to the image view only. At the time of the development, Android native environment did not have built-in gesture recognizers for multi-touch gestures, needed for this app; therefore, the functionality was realized through the manual implementation. This was done through the *OnTouchListener* interface and its *onTouch* method, which receives all the touch events recognized by the screen. MoSync did not support the rotation of elements inside a native or a web view, so an OpenGL view was used for the implementation. Due to OpenGL 3D environment and the usage of a different coordinate system than the screen coordinate system, the translation of the image was not as accurate compared to the native implementations. Appcelerator Titanium provided modules to enable multi-touch and gesture recognizers for iOS only. Therefore, the scenario was implemented only for the iOS using the free gesture recognizer module. At the time of development, the RhoMobile Rhodes lacked the handling of multi-touch gestures and the accessing of accelerometer. Hence, we skipped the first two scenarios for it. Figure 1 shows a screen-shot of the *MovePic* app, developed in the native iOS environment.

Fig. 1. The MovePic app (developed in the native iOS environment) on iPad 2

3.2 The *BubbleLevel* Scenario

The *BubbleLevel* scenario simulates a spirit level on the screen using the accelerometer data. A spirit level is a tool to measure if some object is parallel or orthogonal to the ground. The scenario's goal was to test the support and processing of the accelerometer in the device as well as checking its request rate. All the developed versions of this scenario have three different screens; i.e., a round spirit level (as shown in Figure 2.a) and a one-dimensional rectangular for vertical and horizontal (as shown in Figure 2.b and Figure 2.c respectively); which switch according to the device orientation. The round spirit level is displayed when the device lies flat. This provides a two-dimensional surface leveling. Tilting the device over 45 degree in any direction displays the vertical or horizontal bars, which are one-dimensional rectangular shapes. The accelerometers in smart-devices return three values representing the gravity vector in the device's left-handed coordinate system. The developed versions used these three values for simulating the desired spirit level.

The native iOS environment drawing functions were used to outline and to fill the circle and rectangles in all three views of the app for the native iOS implementation. The native Android version used a nested thread class for drawing the circle and the rectangles, which resulted a quicker drawing compared to the native iOS version. The MoSync's functions for drawing shapes were used to draw the circle and rectangles. While the simulating of spirit level was implemented using a Moblet, which provides interfaces for getting from the accelerometer and then using it accurately. The MoSync version looks quite similar to the native versions. The Appcelerator Titanium version used a web view showing a HTML5 document for realizing the UI of the app, as the framework itself did not have the functionality of drawing UIs. The accelerometer values were passed to the web view through events. A square was drawn instead of the circle due to the slow processing of the circle drawing.

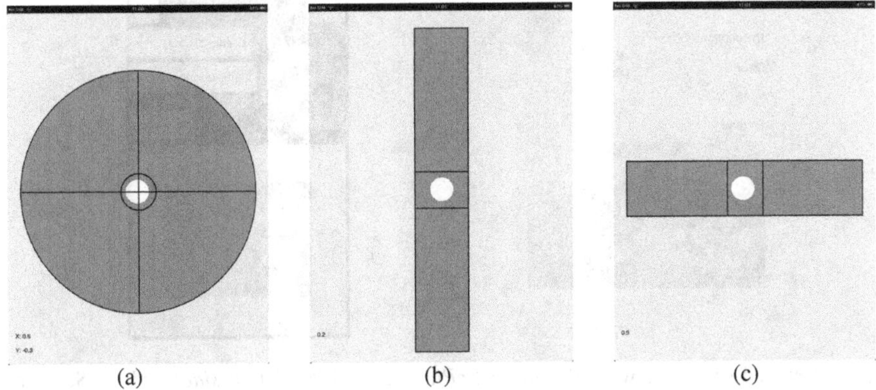

Fig. 2. BubbleLevel app on iPad 2: *(a)* a round spirit level when the device lays flat, *(b)* one-dimensional vertical spirit level, and *(c)* one-dimensional horizontal spirit level

3.3 The *AnnotatePic* Scenario

The *AnnotatePic* scenario's goal was the utilization of complex interaction-schema such as camera access, file system access and phone-specific services. The basic task was to take image from the device's camera, adding some additional information (name, description and date), and then saving the image and the data in the device's internal memory. The main screen of all the developed versions contains a list-view for showing all saved images in small-view along with their names, while the detailed screen consists of information-taking form and an image-taking button. Figure 3 shows the detailed-screen view on iPad 2 and on Samsung Galaxy S Plus.

The native iOS implementation used the *master-detail* template of iOS, which generates an app with two screens. The captured images are saved directly in the document folder of the app, while their data is saved using the core data framework of the iOS. The native Android implementation was done through a set of classes. These classes provide functionalities for generating the database, managing memory variables, saving and loading images, and managing activities for the two views. The MoSync version consisted of two sample apps for testing the camera functionality and the *master-detail* functionality with the data storage. Due to some technical issues in MoSync iOS version, only the MoSync Android version was evaluated in the user study. The Appcelerator Titanium versions were implemented through the *master-detail* application with database access. Due to the technical difficulties occurred at the IDE level, both versions were not included in the user study. The RhoMobile Rhodes targets towards data-driven business apps, so frameworks' automatically generated components were useful for the scenario. But, it also takes time to get rid of the extra-generated components. RhoMobile Rhodes custom data models in addition to own defined data models were used to implement the scenario. Due to the technical difficulties in image storing, the implementations were not included in the user study.

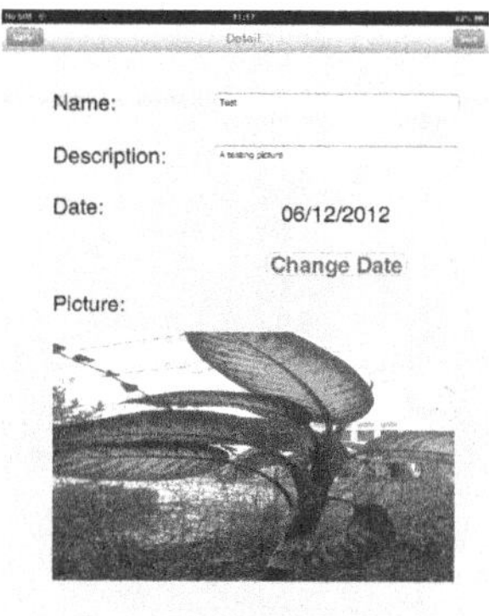

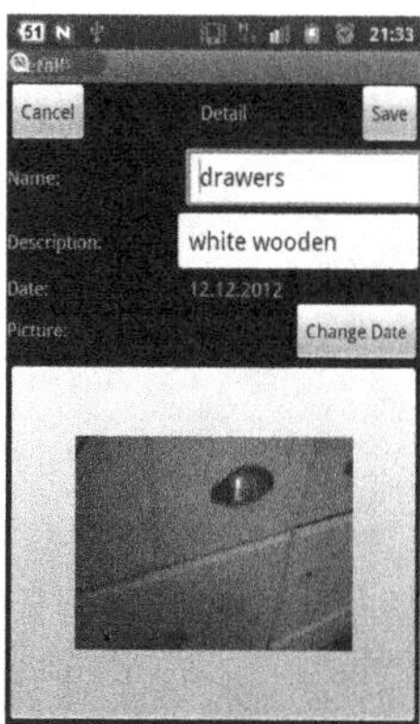

Fig. 3. Detailed-screen view of the *AnnotatePic* app on iPad 2 (*left-side*) and on Samsung Galaxy S Plus *(right-side)*

4 The User Evaluation Study

We performed a user evaluation study in a controlled environment, where the focus was on checking the interaction response of different versions of the three mentioned scenarios using different devices and operating systems. The purpose was to analyze whether normal users from different backgrounds feel any difference if the same app is presented to them, even though it is built through different frameworks and for different platforms.

The Experiment Settings

The test devices were a Samsung Galaxy S Plus and a Samsung Galaxy Tab for Android, and an iPhone 3GS and an iPad 2 for iOS. The tested versions were 12 implementations of the three scenarios for both kinds of devices (smartphones and tablets). Six of these versions were developed in native environments (i.e., Android and iOS). The remaining six implementations were: the MoSync implementations of MovePic for Android and iOS, the MoSync implementations of BubbleLevel for Android and iOS, the Appcelerator Titanium implementation of BubbleLevel for Android only, and the MoSync implementation of AnnotatePic for Android only. Due to the technical difficulties in other developed versions, we did not include them in the study. Table 1 shows those versions that were evaluated in the user study.

Table 1. The tested versions in the user evaluation study

	Native platforms		MoSync		Appcelerator Titanium	
	Android	*iOS*	*Android*	*iOS*	*Android*	*iOS*
MovePic	✓	✓	✓	✓		
BubbleLevel	✓	✓	✓	✓	✓	
AnnotatePic	✓	✓	✓			

The User Groups and The Experiment Layout

We performed the evaluation study with 9 users (2 females, 7 males). We categorized them according to their experience with smart-devices where 3 were expert in using Android based devices, 3 were expert in using iOS based devices, while the remaining 3 had no experience at all with smart-devices. The age of users was between 23 and 31 years old with a mean of 25.88. For each tested version, users were asked to judge the interaction-response time and the overall satisfaction with the app on a scale from 1 to 5. After testing different versions of the same scenario, each user was asked to name the version they would prefer for future use with multiple answers possibility.

Results and Discussions

The conducted user evaluation study provided some interesting results that could be useful for deciding the right environment(s) for developing mobile apps. In the MovePic scenario, the native iOS implementation received the best results (as it would be used by 7 users out of 9 users, see Figure 4) but the native Android and MoSync implementations too achieved comparable and good results. The reason that most users preferred iOS version was probably due to the usage of iOS built-in gesture recognizer in the implementation, which provided a better interaction response than the others. Moreover, users who were expert with smart-devices preferred the MoSync version of their own used platform instead of the other one, although both MoSync versions were identical.

In the BubbleLevel scenario, the MoSync Android version received the best results, as 7 users preferred it (see Figure 4), while the MoSync iOS and Android native versions received well appraisals too. On the other side, the iOS native and Appcelerator Titanium versions received just moderate ratings as none of the users showed any interest for using them in future. One thing that needs to be considered while comparing an app having the accelerometer functionality in Android-based devices is the quality of accelerometer in the underlying devices, as the device with high power processor might give better output than the others.

In the AnnotatePic scenario; the native iOS and Android versions received slightly better estimation in terms of the overall satisfaction, while in the interaction response time all the three versions achieved comparable and good results. The native implementations were chosen by most users for future use with 4 votes for the Android version and 5 votes for the iOS version, as shown in Figure 4. Figure 4 provides a graph overview of users preference for future usage of the tested versions.

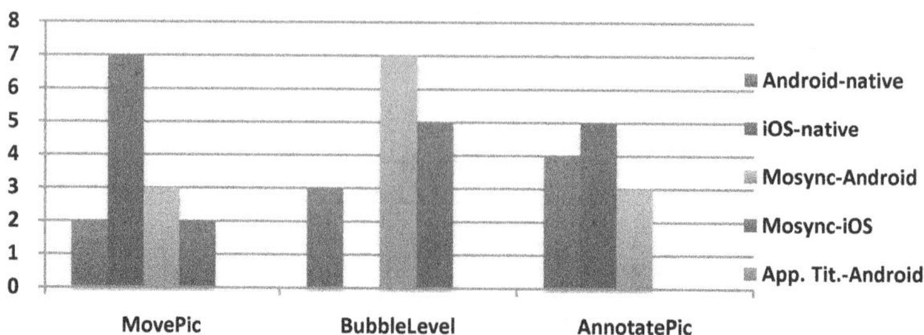

Fig. 4. Users preference for future usage of the tested versions

Overall, we analyzed that in case of those scenarios where the interaction-response time was very critical, i.e. in MovePic and BubbleLevel scenarios, users liked more the native versions because they received more quick response, but even so the cross-platform versions also gained good results. While in the case of scenarios where the interaction-response time was not so critical (i.e. in AnnotatePic scenario), all the versions received approximately the same kind of user satisfaction. Hence; we can conclude that where the quick response time is not so important, the better option is to use the cross-platform development as it saves time and cost and at the end achieves nearly the same user satisfaction level. While in the cases where the interaction response time plays an important role, if the quick response is not very critical then cross-platform development could be the alternative option; otherwise, the native-platforms are slightly better than the cross-platform frameworks. This is because the native implementation environments provide better solutions for the critical interaction response, which enhances the user satisfaction level. Overall, we can conclude that the mobile applications developed using the cross-platform frameworks provide approximately the same user satisfaction level as the ones developed in the native environments.

5 The Software Evaluation

We also performed evaluation of the developed versions of the three scenarios against software quality measurements to check the required development time between different platforms and frameworks. Moreover, we estimated their conformity against the style guides.

In the MovePic scenario, the native Android and iOS versions performed better. However, the image was following the fingers interaction slightly better in iOS. While the MoSync version's performance was the worst one due to the transformation between the 2D screen and the 3D OpenGL coordinate system. In the BubbleLevel scenario, the iOS version had the worst performance followed by the Appcelerator version. The reason behind Appcelerator version's low performance was the drawing of circle through a set of circular lines by the provided function, which seems to be not so efficient. While in the case of native iOS version, it was due to the technical difficulty occurred in the implementation for getting the quick request rate of the accelerometer data. The MoSync version had a far better performance but the best one was given by the native Android due to using a separate thread for the drawing. The AnnotatePic is not an interaction-response time critical scenario; hence, all the developed versions provided approximately the same performance level.

The implementations of the MovePic had a slightly different functionality for each version. The functionality provided by the native iOS version was better compared to the others, as it had the most natural interaction with the image and it also prevented the image from moving out of the screen, followed by the native Android version. In the BubbleLevel scenario, all implementations provided the same level of functionality due to the limitation of the scenario. In the AnnotatePic scenario, only the native Android version was without any errors while the iOS native version performed well until we updated it to the iOS 5.1. The MoSync version had problems during saving the images and was showing just half of the screen for the camera view.

From the maintainability perspective, the iOS-based versions were better compared to Android-based versions as much of the functionality was provided by the platform; hence, it shortens the code and reduces the time to develop. But as it is just for one platform only, so we felt the cross-platform development as the better solution. We also noticed that working with RhoMobile Rhodes framework saved development time compared to other frameworks as it provides many facilities for data-driven applications built-in from the start, followed by the iOS as it also provides much built-in functionality for utilizing many device features. In the case of cross-platform, we noticed that implementation time on MoSync was little bit faster than the others.

Lastly from the style-guide perspective, most of the cross-platform frameworks had not adopted the Android style guide. It is because the Android released its style-guide just few months before the time of our implementations. Moreover, we considered only the Android 2.2 and 2.3 versions during the development while some of the style-guide elements, like the action bar, work only on and above the Android 3.0. With regard to iOS based devices, we found out that all the tested cross-platform development frameworks provided pretty good adaptions to the iOS environment. Results of most of these frameworks conformed the style-guide of the iOS efficiently.

6 Conclusion

In this study, we performed a comparison between the native development environments and the cross-platform development environments. Apps were developed against three scenarios using the Android and iOS and native development environments as well as three selected cross-platform development environments (i.e. MoSync, Appcelerator Titanium, and RhoMobile Rhodes). The evaluation results from the software perspective and from the user study show that in many terms the results of cross-platform frameworks are as good as the native ones and in some cases even better. But the striking of Appcelerator Titanium has shown that relying on only one cross-platform development framework may lead to failures, because the whole smart-device market is evolving pretty fast and is in a constant flow. Also, when developing using the cross-platform approach, it is always better to think twice before updating an SDK to the newest version. It could be possible that the underlying cross-platform framework may not be able to build anymore on the new SDK version, as the developers of these frameworks need time for the adaption of the new SDKs.

The hybrid cross-platform frameworks provide much functionality today and it is surely further emerging. They also allow basic adaption and scalability to the tablets. The main difficulty for developers, who want to build cross-platform applications, is to find the solution best fitting their needs. But in most cases, it is not easy to find out what functionality a particular framework provides better than the others. In the forums of these frameworks many questions, which were posted one year ago or longer for asking some functionalities, are still looking for the answers or the answers are "coming soon functionality".

Overall, it can be said that the hybrid cross-platform frameworks are a good alternative to the native implementations with definite better cost-efficiency. But before choosing a particular framework, it is a must to find out if the underlying framework supports the needed features in a stable way. Moreover, the possibilities for porting existing applications between Android and iOS automatically are not fully developed, yet. The manual porting has some issues to remind but when considering them from the start, the process is manageable. In the near future, web cross-platform frameworks may compete the hybrid frameworks more and more, because of the fact that HTML5 is already capable of a few hardware access features and will perhaps evolve to replace the hybrid frameworks partially or totally. So, keeping eye on both technologies will help in deciding the better options for the underlying scenario.

References

1. A Look Back in Time at the First Smartphone Ever Business 2 Community, `http://www.business2community.com/mobile-apps/a-look-back-in-time-at-the-first-smartphone-ever-040906`
2. Di Giovanni, P., Romano, M., Sebillo, M., Tortora, G., Vitiello, G., Ginige, T., De Silva, L., Goonethilaka, J., Wikramanayake, G., Ginige, A.: User centered scenario based approach for developing mobile interfaces for Social Life Networks. In: UsARE 2012, pp. 18–24 (2012)
3. Gartner Says Android to Become No. 2 Worldwide Mobile Operating System in 2010 and Challenge Symbian for No. 1 Position by 2014, `http://www.gartner.com/it/page.jsp?id=1434613` (last accessed February 21, 2013)
4. Heitkötter, H., Hanschke, S., Majchrzak, T.A.: Evaluating Cross-Platform Development Approaches for Mobile Applications. In: Cordeiro, J., Krempels, K.-H. (eds.) WEBIST 2012. LNBIP, vol. 140, pp. 120–138. Springer, Heidelberg (2013)
5. `http://webinos.org/crossplatformtools/appcelerator-titanium/`
6. `http://webinos.org/crossplatformtools/rhomobile-motorola/`
7. `http://webinos.org/crossplatformtools/mosync/`
8. Jones, S., Voskoglou, C., Vakulenko, M., Measom, V., Constantinou, A., Kapetanakis, M.: VisionMobile Cross-Platform Developer Tools (2012), `http://www.visionmobile.com/blog/2012/02/crossplatformtools/`
9. Paananen, T.: Smartphone Cross-Platform Frameworks A case study. Bachelor's Thesis. Jyväskylän Ammattikorkeakoulu - JAMK University of Applied Sciences (2011)
10. Palmieri, M., Singh, I., Cicchetti, A.: Comparison of cross-platform mobile development tools. In: ICIN 2012, October 8-11, pp. 179–186 (2012)
11. Smartphones setzen Siegeszug fort - Kalenderwoche 07 - 17. Februar - aetka Partnerforum (February 17, 2012), `http://partnerforum.aetka.de/index.php?page=Thread&postID=993`

EMIL: A Rapid Prototyping Authoring Environment for the Design of Interactive Surface Applications

Johannes Luderschmidt, Nadia Haubner, Simon Lehmann, and Ralf Dörner

RheinMain University, Wiesbaden, Germany
{johannes.luderschmidt,nadia.haubner,simon.lehmann,ralf.doerner}@hs-rm.de

Abstract. Interactive surfaces (IS) like digital tabletop systems offer a cornucopia of input possibilities like touch gestures or interaction with physical objects. Additionally, multiple users can interact simultaneously allowing for a collaborative setting. These aspects have increased the complexity of designing such interfaces as compared to WIMP interfaces. However, existing UI design approaches fall short of taking these aspects into account and existing design approaches for IS focus on software development. We introduce the EMIL environment that allows authors of design teams to create multi-touch and tangible user interfaces. In its core, EMIL consists of a software framework that provides interaction components (for instance, widgets like images or maps as well as interaction concepts like gestures) that are especially suited for IS. Authors like UI designers collaboratively create software prototypes directly at the IS without the need to write code. For this purpose, they use and adapt the components of the software framework in an authoring application. Authors collect and retrieve information about the interaction components in a knowledge database employing a tablet computer app. In a qualitative evaluation interview, EMIL has been well received by a design team of an advertising agency.

Keywords: interactive surfaces, multi-touch, tangible user interfaces, engineering of interactive systems.

1 Introduction

So far, research in the area of interactive surfaces has concentrated on hardware, gestural interaction and software frameworks. In contrast, approaches how typical design teams of a software company handle creating IS applications have not been researched well.

In this paper, we present the EMIL (**E**nvironment for **M**ulti-touch **I**n the **L**aboratory) environment that offers a rapid prototyping approach based on libraries and tools allowing design teams to collaboratively develop IS prototypes. In its core EMIL consists of a UI framework providing building blocks of IS applications. To be more precise, it employs specialized multi-touch and tangible user interface interaction components and application templates. However, simply providing a software framework would only satisfy developers' needs when

M. Kurosu (Ed.): Human-Computer Interaction, Part I, HCII 2013, LNCS 8004, pp. 381–390, 2013.

it comes to creating interactive surface software. Furthermore, programming IS applications on a desktop computer in an integrated development environment makes testing of interaction on the actual IS hardware difficult and is therefore performed infrequently [5]. Hence, our EMIL authoring application (EAA) allows collaboratively creating IS applications directly at the surface without the necessity to write code. Authors can as well use the components of the UI framework as build widgets easily themselves at the surface employing resources they imported in EAA. EMIL enables a prototyping process in which different kinds of authors (UI and interaction designers as well as programmers) form a design team and build the prototype in iterative, alternating design cycles. In one cycle, UI and interaction designers shape the concept of the prototype's UI and interaction and create graphical resources at their desktop computers employing their accustomed tools like Photoshop. Programmers adapt and enhance components of the UI framework according to designers' needs in their IDE. In the other cycle, the authors meet at the surface to build and refine the prototype. Created prototypes can be used for initial user tests, for client feedback and as a foundation for the actual application.

However, simply providing design tools would fall short of handling design knowledge that is necessary to build an IS prototype. Therefore, another part of the EMIL environment is the EMIL pattern authoring and browsing system (EPABS). EPABS constitutes a database of IS design knowledge. This database stores experience reports, user study results and examples of component's application fields in the form of interaction patterns [1]. Authors retrieve and enhance interaction patterns in the database employing the EPABS app on a tablet computer.

EMIL's component library, the authoring tool and application templates facilitate have the potential to speed up IS prototype creation. The knowledge browser allows systematically building and retrieving corporate IS software design knowledge. In an expert interview we qualitatively evaluated EMIL with a design team. In this interview, EMIL's basic concepts were received well.

This paper is structured as follows. In section 2, we present related work. We introduce the EMIL environment in section 3. Section 4 presents the results of the qualitative evaluation. Finally, section 5 gives a conclusion and presents future work.

2 Related Work

There exist several frameworks, toolkits and libraries which enable programmers to develop interactive surface applications. reacTIVision [4] provides a toolkit consisting of a computer vision tracking application and a network-based dialect to build IS hardware and software. TISCH [2] presents a similar approach but additionally introduces a so called widget layer with which multi-touch applications can be built. Pure software frameworks like PyMT [3] and MT4J [9] enable the creation of IS applications. The mentioned frameworks and toolkits offer powerful tools for system builders and programmers, but are less fitted for

UI or interface designers [6]. Therefore, in the following, we focus on concepts assisting programmers on the one hand and supporting visual development (for UI and interaction designers) on the other hand.

In [8], Landay and Myers present an interactive user-interface design tool that allows designers to build WIMP UI prototypes based on the recognition of electronic sketches. However, their concept is based on WIMP UIs and not on IS. The OpenInterface (OI) Framework [10] allows for a multimodal UI creation process that allows to include input channels into an OI component. Such a component can be used in OI's graphical authoring application SKEMMI to rapidly build multimodal interfaces based on a data flow graph. However, OI's focus lies on the creation of a flexible input channel architecture and not on the process of building the GUI itself.

Squidy [7] is a zoomable environment for the design of natural user interfaces (NUIs). Squidy differs from OI in that it addresses the issue that authors involved in the authoring process of NUIs often use multiple toolkits or frameworks to create the desired UI and its behavior. This is achieved by tying together relevant frameworks and toolkits in a common library while a visual language is introduced to create NUIs. To see the current development status as a whole, Squidy introduces the concept of semantic zooming, making it possible to control the level of complexity shown to the particular author developing the application. Squidy provides a way to take input data of hardware devices (e.g., movement data recorded by a Kinect), process the data and send it to listening applications, e.g., via Tuio [4]. The focus on technical aspects is important to develop the actual available NUI input alternatives for a specific application. Therefore, Squidy's focus is not on the creation of IS software in design teams.

The Designer's Augmented Reality Toolkit (DART) [12] is based on the multimedia development environment Director and allows authors to build augmented reality (AR) applications. It supports early design activities, especially a rapid transition from low-fidelity prototypes to working applications. Hence, DART allows to test prototypes early and often. The authors gained the experience that designers need to use their own tools for content creation. They provide so called behaviors that can be easily attached to content created by authors and can be easily extended if necessary. Although authoring experience made in the field of AR cannot be directly transferred to IS, DART's promising design approach that supports designers in the prototype creation can also be applied to IS design.

To sum up, the introduced visual prototyping approaches allow to rapidly build interface prototypes in the field of WIMP, post-WIMP and AR interfaces. However, interactive surfaces and their characteristics are not covered by this related work.

3 EMIL Environment

EMIL is an authoring environment for the creation of interactive surface prototypes. It supports design teams in their efforts to collaboratively build software for target platforms like multi-touch tables or touchable wall displays.

A design team in the sense of EMIL typically comprises designers creating the look and feel of the UI and programmers developing the actual code (see figure 1). To support such design teams, EMIL offers the EMIL authoring application (EAA) with which prototypes can be created out of a set of components provided by the EMIL UI framework. To inform the team about existing solutions and to store prototyping results, the EMIL Pattern Authoring and Browsing System (EPABS) offers a design knowledge database represented by interaction patterns that can be accessed with a tablet computer app.

Fig. 1. Three authors modifying a prototype in the EMIL authoring application on a tabletop system. In the foreground, a UI designer modifies the image of a map marker in Photoshop on his computer. As soon as the UI designer saves the Photoshop file on his laptop to the cloud storage, the changes become available in the prototype and all components that contain the marker resource from Photoshop can be updated.

Section 3.1 introduces the EMIL UI framework. In section 3.2, we present EAA. Finally, section 3.3 describes EPABS.

3.1 EMIL UI Framework

The EMIL UI framework provides visual and non-visual components for the prototyping process. Visual components can be widgets like lists, geographic maps, browsers, media like images and videos et cetera. Another kind of visual components are so called views. A prototype can contain several views which themselves contain widgets. A view navigation allows switching between views. Furthermore, application templates are a combination of prepared views and widgets. For instance, a consulting application template comprises specialized views and widgets tailored for user scenarios in which, for instance, a bank consultant wants to use an IS as support medium in a mortgage consultation of a customer.

Non-visual components are controls and behaviors. Controls provide gestural input to widgets like multi-touch transformation controls that allow dragging, rotating and scaling based on standard gestures (see also [11]) and flick controls that allow for a momentum that keeps widgets moving after they have been released. Behaviors on the other hand encapsulate complex functionality that are connected to certain interactions. Figure 2 illustrates the concept of EMIL behaviors. To employ behaviors, they can be added to widgets.

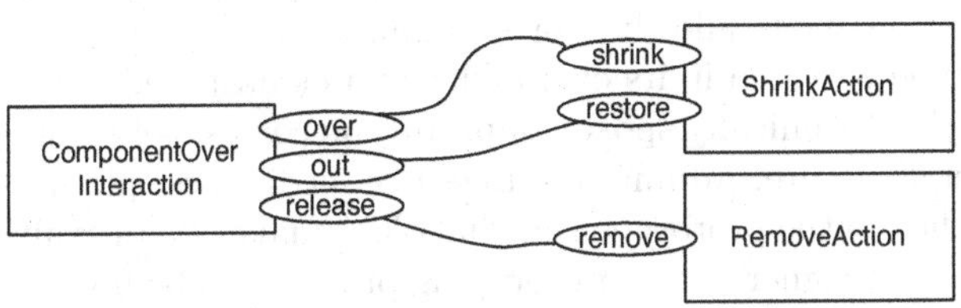

Fig. 2. The trash bin behavior is an example for an EMIL behavior. It basically shrinks a component that is dragged over the component that contains the trash bin behavior and restores the original size as soon as the component is dragged out. Shrinking and resizing gives a visual cue for the behavior's functionality. If the dragged component is released, it will be removed. The design of a behavior connects so called 'Interactions' with 'Actions': The interaction ElementOverInteraction has three outlets: 'over' which is fired whenever a component is dragged, 'out' whenever it is dragged out and 'release' whenever the dragged component is released above the component. These outlets are connected to inlets of actions. ShrinkAction shrinks and restores the size and RemoveAction removes the released component from the containing view.

The EMIL UI framework builds the foundation for the authoring application and programmers can enhance existing visual and non-visual components as well as create new ones.

3.2 EMIL Authoring Application

The center of prototyping in the EMIL process is the EMIL authoring application (EAA). In EAA, prototypes can be created and modified without coding. EAA knows two modes: The live mode allows using the application (see figure 3(a)) and the authoring mode enables designers and users to modify the prototype (see figure 3(b)). The authoring mode can be started by putting the so-called authoring tangible object on the surface or by using a key combination on the hardware keyboard. As soon as a user removes the authoring tangible or enters the key combination again, the authoring results will be saved and the live mode will be re-entered.

To actually create prototypes, designers gather around the IS in a collaborative work setting. Figure 1 illustrates such a prototyping session. After starting EAA, designers load an existing prototype or create a new one. A new prototype opens with an empty view. In the course of the prototyping, designers add new views and widgets to a prototype and configure those views and widgets.

The authoring process is based on a building block principle. Visual and non-visual components can be dragged out of menus onto the surface. For instance, a designer may drag a map widget out of the widget library menu onto the surface and edit its built-in map behavior by tapping the appropriate behavior plug (see figure 3)). Dragging a behavior out of the behavior menu onto a widget adds it. A new plug appears visualizing that the behavior has been added. The behavior can be customized similar to the built-in behavior. Tapping the behavior plug opens its properties menu allowing for manipulation.

Each prototype is stored in its own folder in a cloud-based storage (currently in the Dropbox[1]). Technically spoken, a prototype consists of resources stored in a file and folder structure. Adding resources like media files (pictures, photoshop files, video, audio) to the prototype's media folder makes them available in EAA. As every involved designer in the prototyping process can be invited to share the prototype folder in the cloud storage, they can create, modify or delete resources in the folder from every device connected to the cloud storage.

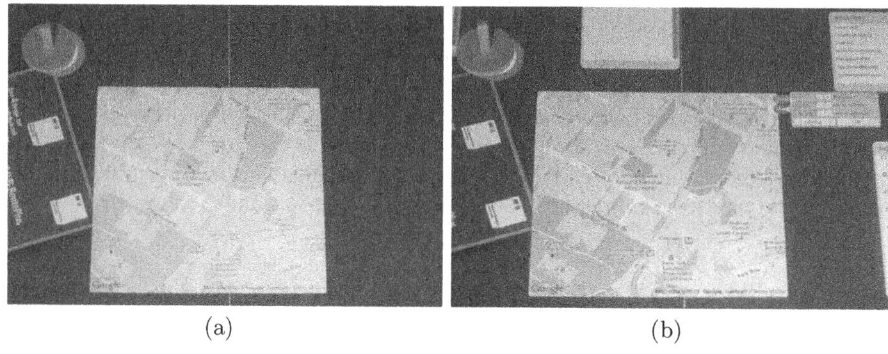

(a) (b)

Fig. 3. (a) A cutout of an EMIL prototype in the live mode in which two documents connected to tangible objects and a map widget are visible. (b) The same cutout as in (a) but in the authoring mode. On the right of the widgets, plugs allow accessing the widgets' properties menu. For instance, the map widget shows the menu of its built-in map functionality. In the authoring mode, additional menus appear on the surface that allow to add widgets, behaviors and views to the prototype.

Out of media resources stored in the cloud storage, designers can build their own widgets combining them with EMIL behaviors. For instance, dragging the image of a trash bin out of the Dropbox menu and subsequently adding a trash bin behavior to it creates a fully functional trash bin widget. Therefore, designers can prepare media resources in advance and use them in EAA. As Photoshop[2] is a popular application amongst UI designers, EMIL supports importing Photoshop files. Hence, designers can use their accustomed tools to create resources for

[1] `https://www.dropbox.com`

[2] `http://www.adobe.com/products/photoshop.html`

EMIL. During and after the prototyping session involved authors can iteratively refine the resources in the cloud storage.

3.3 EMIL Pattern Authoring and Browsing System

We introduce the EMIL Pattern Authoring and Browsing System (EPABS) that enables systematically building up and retrieving IS design knowledge. EPABS constitutes a database that stores information about the visual and non-visual components of the EMIL UI framework and prototypes created with EAA. We prepare this information in EPABS in the form of interaction patterns [1] and hierarchically arrange them to form an IS interaction pattern language similar to [13]. In the sense of [1], each EPABS pattern describes amongst others the problem that lead to its creation, its solution and examples for its usage in existing prototypes.

EMIL authors can browse and extend EPABS by using a tablet computer app (see figure 4(b)). In this app the pattern language is visualized by a node link graph (see figure 4(a)). Authors can apply visual filtering algorithms to the graph in order to narrow down the search for relevant patterns. After selecting a pattern, authors can read the pattern information or watch example videos or photos of its application in existing prototypes. If authors reuse an EPABS pattern in their own prototype they can attach videos and photos of its usage to the pattern's example section. Such videos and photos can be created employing the tablet computer app. Using the app, authors also add new patterns to the pattern language.

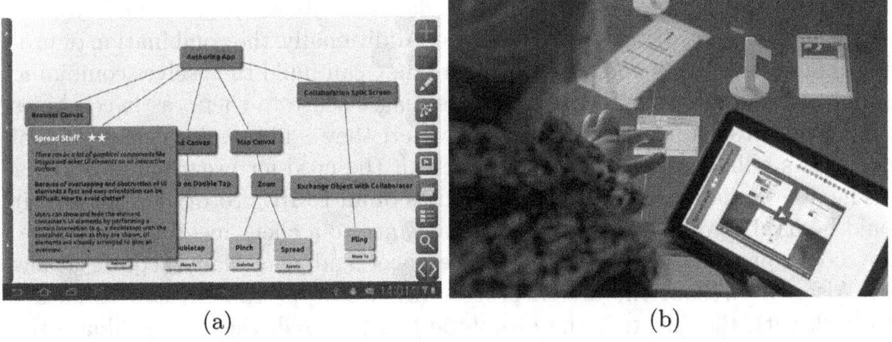

(a) (b)

Fig. 4. (a) Screenshot of the EPABS app on a tablet computer. It shows EPABS' pattern language represented by an interactive node link graph. In the graph, the 'SpreadStuff Behavior' has been selected showing its short description. (b) A designer add a SpreadStuff behavior to an image canvas after watching an example video of its usage in the EPABS app on the tablet computer.

4 Evaluation

We presented EMIL to a design team to gather qualitative feedback. This team consisted of a UI designer, a programmer and a concept designer from an advertising agency. This team had so far created four interactive surface applications. After the presentation, we interviewed them.

In their IS design process, the team usually creates prototypes for first tests that a programmer codes from scratch. This approach has at least three disadvantages. Firstly, it takes too long to create such a prototype. Secondly, the designers have to communicate their ideas to a programmer that has to convert them into code. Thirdly, they discover erroneous design decisions too late as the testing on the actual target platform comes too late in the process. With EMIL, they can quickly create prototypes themselves using the authoring tool without the need to communicate their ideas to a programmer and without writing code. This allows designers to "get their noses out of photoshop" and create prototypes themselves at an early design stage. In their opinion, EMIL provides a set of standard components for multi-touch and tangible user interfaces. Such components would already exist for mobile applications but not for IS. Such a set in combination with the authoring tool allows for the rapid prototyping of usable IS software. Instead of coding the prototype, the programmer involved in the design process can enhance EMIL's set of components and behaviors if necessary.

They embraced the iterative approach that allows alternately creating a prototype at the surface and preparing resources with their desktop tools allowing for quick design – test cycles. This offers to instantly see design results on the surface of resources created with accustomed tools like Photoshop giving a quick feedback to design decisions. They especially liked that authors involved in the design process meet in front of the IS to collaboratively assemble and modify the results of their work directly at the surface. Additionally, the combination of provided complex widgets and simple widgets they can build themselves combining graphical resources with EMIL behaviors makes sense to them, as it combines standard with custom functionality. However, they additionally desired a tool that allows building complex widgets without the need for programming.

The design team considered multiple uses of an EMIL prototype. Initially, it could be used to prepare a prototype in advance to a client meeting. Therefore, they could present this prototype to the client and potentially acquire a new job. Also, throughout the design process the prototype can be used to gather feedback with the client. If the prototype has matured, they can evaluate the prototype in a user test. Lastly, as the agency usually develops their IS software also in Flash, they can use the prototype's code and resources as a foundation for the final product development.

They suggested to provide EMIL to the open source community. Building blocks like behaviors or widgets could be easily extended by other Flash developers. This, however, led to their main criticism. They assume that there are currently too few building blocks like behaviors, widgets and application templates available in the EMIL UI framework. Additionally, they deem it necessary to try out EMIL in a real project. Pertaining the UI of the authoring tool, they demand fewer windows for a better visual overview.

5 Conclusion and Future Work

The EMIL environment presents a rapid prototyping authoring approach for the creation of interactive surface software in design teams. It comprises UI and interaction components, an authoring tool and a database that provides storing and retrieving design knowledge using a tablet computer app.

Authors create the IS prototypes directly at the surface employing the EMIL authoring application (EAA) without the need to possess programming skills. Therefore, created software is tested early and frequently on the target hardware. Using EAA, designers configure components and their behavior. Additionally, simple components can be easily created based on resources that authors prepare and store in a cloud-based storage system.

In an expert interview we gathered qualitative feedback from a design team. The design team especially liked the iterative approach provided by EMIL and the possibility to create prototypes without programming knowledge using a 'standard' set of components. The team sees the potential to facilitate and speed up their own IS software design process employing EMIL.

In future work, we need to evaluate EMIL in a real design project. However, as the evaluation has shown, there are still too few components in the UI framework. Therefore, we need to enhance our set of components.

Acknowledgements. This research work has been financially supported by the BMBF-FHProfUnt grant no. 17043X10.

References

1. Borchers, J.O.: A Pattern Approach to Interaction Design. In: Proceedings of the 3rd Conference on Designing Interactive Systems: Processes, Practices, Methods, and Techniques, DIS 2000, pp. 369–378. ACM, New York (2000)
2. Echtler, F., Klinker, G.: A Multitouch Software Architecture. In: NordiCHI 2008: Proceedings of the 5th Nordic Conference on Human-Computer Interaction, pp. 463–466. ACM, New York (2008)
3. Hansen, T.E., Hourcade, J.P., Virbel, M., Patali, S., Serra, T.: PyMT: a Post WIMP Multi-Touch User Interface Toolkit. In: Proceedings of the ACM International Conference on Interactive Tabletops and Surfaces, ITS 2009, pp. 17–24. ACM, New York (2009)
4. Kaltenbrunner, M.: reacTIVision and TUIO: a Tangible Tabletop Toolkit. In: ITS 2009: Proceedings of the ACM International Conference on Interactive Tabletops and Surfaces, pp. 9–16. ACM, New York (2009)
5. Khandkar, S.H., Sohan, S.M., Sillito, J., Maurer, F.: Tool Support for Testing Complex Multi-Touch Gestures. In: Proceedings of the ACM International Conference on Interactive Tabletops and Surfaces (2010)

6. Klemmer, S.R., Li, J., Lin, J., Landay, J.A.: Papier-Mache: Toolkit Support for Tangible Input. In: Proceedings of the SIGCHI Conference on Human Factors in Computing Systems, CHI 2004, pp. 399–406. ACM, New York (2004)
7. König, W.A., Rädle, R., Reiterer, H.: Squidy: A Zoomable Design Environment for Natural User Interfaces. In: CHI EA 2009: Proceedings of the 27th International Conference Extended Abstracts on Human Factors in Computing Systems, pp. 4561–4566. ACM, New York (2009)
8. Landay, J.A., Myers, B.A.: Sketching Interfaces: Toward More Human Interface Design. Computer 34(3), 56–64 (2001)
9. Laufs, U., Ruff, C., Zibuschka, J.: MT4j - A Cross-platform Multi-touch Development Framework. In: ACM EICS 2010, Workshop: Engineering Patterns for Multi-Touch Interfaces, pp. 52–57 (2010)
10. Lawson, J.-Y.L., Al-Akkad, A.-A., Vanderdonckt, J., Macq, B.: An Open Source Workbench for Prototyping Multimodal Interactions Based on Off-The-Shelf Heterogeneous Components. In: Proceedings of the 1st ACM SIGCHI Symposium on Engineering Interactive Computing Systems, EICS 2009, pp. 245–254. ACM, New York (2009)
11. Luderschmidt, J., Bauer, I., Haubner, N., Lehmann, S., Dörner, R., Schwanecke, U.: TUIO AS3: A Multi-Touch and Tangible User Interface Rapid Prototyping Toolkit for Tabletop Interaction. In: Dörner, R., Krömker, D. (eds.) Self Integrating Systems for Better Living Environments: First Workshop, Sensyble 2010, pp. 21–28. Shaker Aachen (November 2010)
12. MacIntyre, B., Gandy, M., Dow, S., Bolter, J.D.: DART: A Toolkit for Rapid Design Exploration of Augmented Reality Experiences. In: Proceedings of the 17th Annual ACM Symposium on User Interface Software and Technology, UIST 2004, pp. 197–206. ACM, New York (2004)
13. Remy, C., Weiss, M., Ziefle, M., Borchers, J.: A Pattern Language for Interactive Tabletops in Collaborative Workspaces. In: Proceedings of the 15th European Conference on Pattern Languages of Programs, EuroPLoP 2010, pp. 9:1–9:48. ACM, New York (2010)

Extending the Information of Activity Diagrams with a User Input Classification

Cindy Mayas, Stephan Hörold, and Heidi Krömker

Ilmenau University of Technology, Ilmenau, Germany
{cindy.mayas,stephan.hoerold,heidi.kroemker}@tu-ilmenau.de

Abstract. This paper presents an extended notation of actions in activity diagrams. The suggested method combines activity diagrams with a user input classification in order to support interdisciplinary teams, particularly in the early phases of development. In this way, the user input classification serves as a communication basis for user requirements, which is adapted to the needs of software engineers. The method is evaluated within a case study in a nationwide research project for public transport.

Keywords: activity diagram, actions, user input classification, public transport.

1 Introduction

These days usability is an important quality for software engineering [1], [2] and a key factor for successful and profitable products [3]. Integration processes of human-computer interaction (HCI) in software engineering (SE) are widely discussed. But the communication between usability engineers and software developers often occurs too late in the development process, though key decisions are made in the early development phases. Consequently, changes in the later development process are difficult and cause a higher development effort [4].

In order to provide usability information for key decisions of the development as early as possible, an adequate communication and integration of the results of user requirements analysis into the software engineering workflow is essential. Therefore, the existing and detailed knowledge about the user requirements have to be adapted to the requirements documentation of SE. Along these lines, the development processes require a more user-oriented documentation regarding software engineers.

Existing approaches to bridge this gap between HCI and SE are presented and analyzed in chapter 2 and advantages of UML are covered. Consequently, an approach to enrich UML activity diagrams with usability information and the according case study is presented in chapter 3 and 4.

The key contribution of this paper to bridge this gap is the suggested approach, which supports the interdisciplinary communication about usability requirements in early development phases. The included user input classification (UIC) can serve as a guide for early architectural decisions and in this way increases the usability quality of software products.

M. Kurosu (Ed.): Human-Computer Interaction, Part I, HCII 2013, LNCS 8004, pp. 391–400, 2013.

2 Background

2.1 Bringing HCI and SE Together

Addressing the integration of HCI in SE processes, many authors focus on combining the methods of HCI and SE. Exemplary here, only some approaches can be mentioned: the usage-centered design of Constantine[5], the user-centered software development process of Ferre [6] or Nebe's approach to integrate software engineering and usability engineering [7]. Other solutions prefer separate procedures to analyze the usability during a software engineering process, such as Folmer's SALUTA [1].

But in contrast to an adaptation of methods and procedures, the presented approach of integrating a user input classification to UML diagrams suggests an adaptation of communication tools. Actually, the communication of user requirements is focused on the workflow of usability engineers, despite of the workflow of software engineers.

According to Bruegge [8] an appropriate communication notation has to meet the following three criteria: well-defined semantics, well suited for representing, and well understood. Established kinds of analysis documentation in HCI [9], which depend on the solution and can be used through the development process, have strengths and weaknesses according to these criteria as shown in table 1.

Table 1. Overview of established kinds of analysis documentation

Representation form (examples)	*Semantics*	*Represen-tativity*	*Under-standability*
Mainly narrative (e.g. Personas [10], Scenarios [11])	loosely defined	moderate	high
Mainly pictoral or artifactual (e.g. Mood boards, Culture Cards [12])	undefined	high	high
Mainly tabular (e.g. user needs, usability goals [13])	partly defined	low	moderate
Mainly diagrammatic (e.g. contextual workflow [14], UML [15])	well-defined	high	moderate

Mainly narrative, pictoral, and artifactual forms of representation benefit from a general understandability, but they lack of well-defined semantics. In addition, the mainly tabular forms of representation have some partly defined semantics, such as the use of signal verbs to prioritize user requirement and usability goals.

The Unified Modeling Language (UML) is one kind of diagrammatic representation. The advantages of well-defined semantics of diagrams cause a moderate understandability, particularly for users without the basic knowledge of the semantic. But diagrams are well understood tools for users with prior knowledge of the semantic. Regarding UML, which is widely common in several disciplines, such as SE and HCI, we agree with Bruegge [8], that UML meets the three criteria very well.

2.2 UML in HCI and SE

Due to the flexibility of UML, the use of UML in HCI and SE is very multifaceted. UML is widespread in the software industry, especially for object-oriented software engineering [8]. The use of UML for HCI was intensively discussed and extended in TUPIS2000 workshop, see [17-19]. Nowadays, especially the UML behavioral diagrams became established tools for usability engineers.

Several kinds of diagrams are available to describe the structure, behavior, and interaction of concepts [15]. But the use of diagrams depends on the elaboration of the solution. While an abstract idea of the solution is sufficient for some diagrams, such as use case diagrams, e.g. sequence diagrams require a more detailed idea of the solution. Thus, not every artifact is suitable to serve as a basis for user input classification. For instance, tasks are hierarchic and abstract descriptions of user goals, which are independent from the solution [9]. In contrast, the description of activities and actions bases on the tasks and requires a detailed idea of the solution up to a certain extend.

For this reasons, activity diagrams are used after the requirements analysis in HCI and SE processes as well. We choose the action nodes of activity diagrams to integrate the additional information about the user input.

3 Approach

3.1 User Input Classification (UIC)

Based on the results of user requirements analysis, an interdisciplinary team develops first ideas for technical solutions for possible background systems and interaction devices. For each solution schematic activity diagrams display the required interactions for the user. Thus, each action can be analyzed according to user input. Some examples of possible user interaction should be collected per action and build the bases for the classification.

The user input classification (UIC) bases on a pre-tested 5-point-scale, which displays the interaction task and the semantic design of a user input according to Foley [20]. Foley defines an interaction task as "the entry of a unit of information by the user" and distinguishes "position", "text", "select", and "quantify" as the four basic interaction tasks [20]. In addition to the four interaction tasks, we enrich this set with the "confirmation" interaction, which is defined as a special kind of selection with only one or two alternatives and is often used to accomplish other input interactions or an information output.

3.2 Stereotypes in UML

In order to transfer the suggested UIC into UML, according UML stereotypes were defined. UML stereotypes are a kind of profile to classify UML elements with a "virtual meta-model concept" [20]. For instance, the Wisdom Approach of Nunes [19] provides stereotypes for interaction modeling with UML and Lieberman [21] presents stereotypes for activity diagrams detailing the user interface navigation.

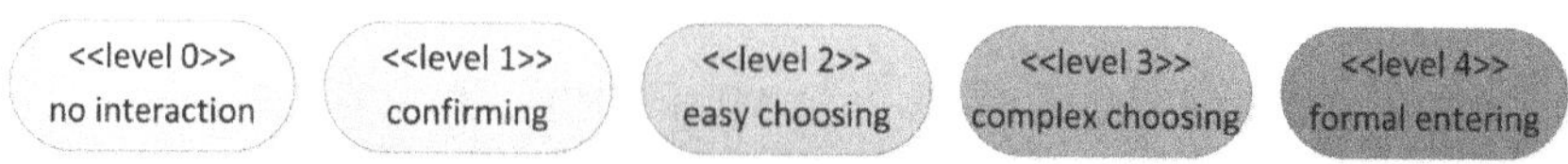

Fig. 1. Proposal for a UIC coloring concept for actions

We predefined a set of coloring information in grey shades for the background of the actions, as shown in figure 1, in order to display the different meaning between the actions with identical structure [15]. Lower stages are colored with a lighter grey than higher stages, according to defined shades. By these means, the density of user input is visualized by the lightness of the activities and provides further information about the users' interaction, in addition to the number of actions. The suggested set of stereotypes consists of five stereotypes, one per each level of UIC:

- <<Level 0>> The basic level requires no input interaction from the user. Information, which is already documented within the software or can be derived from, does not require an additional user input.
- <<Level 1>> The first level includes easy interactions, which do not require an input information, but rather confirmation of the user to proceed. Confirming actions are used at the end of a dialog box to return to the main page or in more complex interaction sequences to display the next dialog.
- <<Level 2>> The second level includes selecting tasks for small-sized choices, for example yes/no decisions or small menus with less than seven items, which are familiar and structured according to the knowledge of the user.
- <<Level 3>> The third level of UIC includes both, more complex selections with semantically well elaborated content, e.g. the choice of the home country from a list, as well as easy data entering, e.g. numeric quantities within a defined range or well-known text input, e.g. my name.
- <<Level 4>> The highest level 4 displays very complex interactions, particularly with semi-formalized or formalized input. For example entering the long and unfamiliar passport number in a visa tool is a very complex entering task, according to its formalized structure.

3.3 Procedure Model to Identify the Classification Level

Figure 2 shows the suggested procedure model to identify several classification levels of user interfaces. A conducted task analysis is the precondition to start the classification. We also recommend collecting some examples for user input for each action as a common classification basis. The following stages have to be passed through for each action:

- identifying the user interaction task,
- refining the user input for selection and entering tasks,
- identifying the dimension of semantic, which is used for the interactions,
- attributing the results to the UML stereotypes.

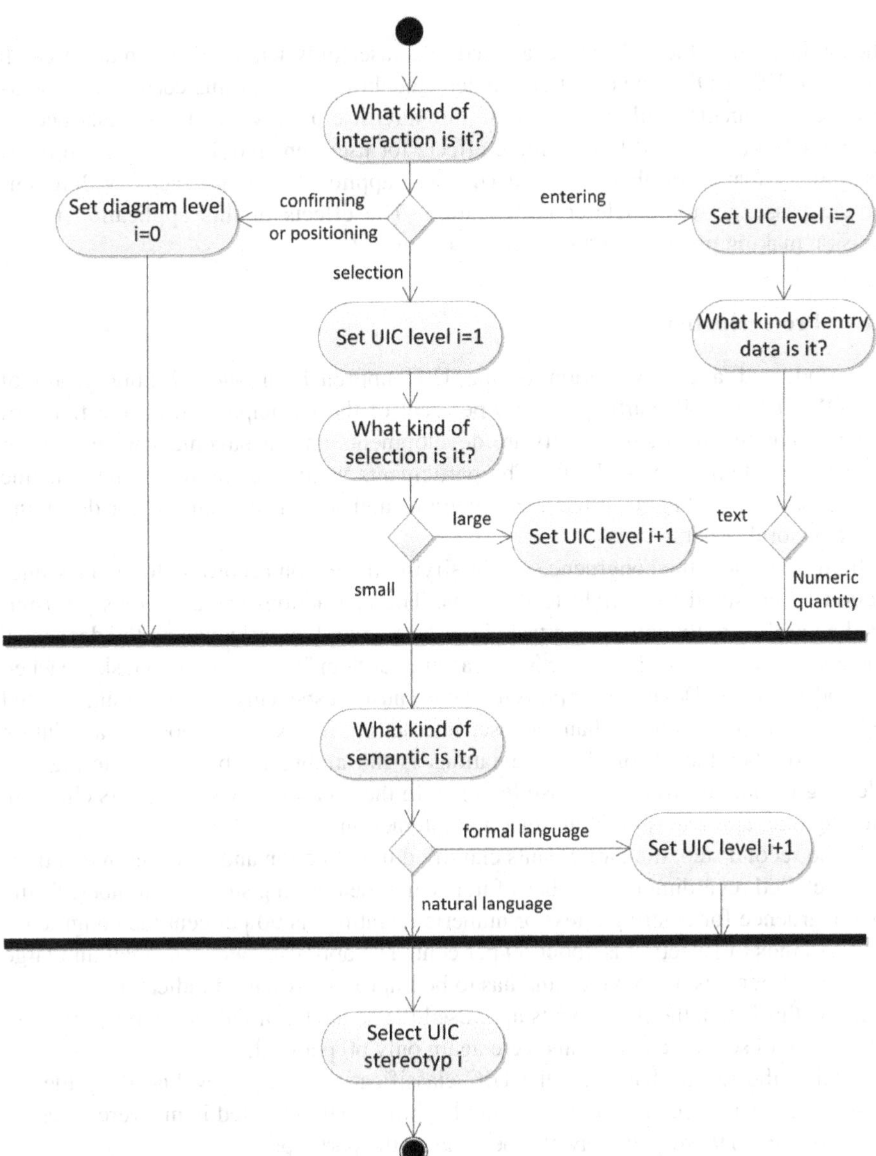

Fig. 2. Suggested procedure model to define UIC classes

4 Case Study

The application of the UIC was evaluated in a case study within the German research project IP-KOM-ÖV. The effort and understandability were evaluated with a standardized questionnaire with members of the interdisciplinary team, as described in section 4.1, and revealed first positive effects for user-centered development in interdisciplinary teams. Furthermore, the UIC was applied to evaluate activity diagrams for the passenger-to-vehicle-communication. The effects of this application to the decision making process are discussed in section 4.2.

4.1 Pre-evaluation

We conducted a pre-evaluation of the UIC approach in one working group of IP-KOM-ÖV with 10 participants. 90 per cent of the participants from the fields of human-computer interaction, software developments and management were familiar or even very familiar with UML. The participants were most used to state machine diagrams, activity diagrams, use case diagrams and sequence diagrams for designing the behavioral structure.

In the first step, the congruence of classifying the action according to the task interaction is measured with eight test actions. The test actions are consciously formulated neutral from the interaction task, in order to avoid an influence on the decisions. The congruence of six of eight actions was greater than 70 per cent, two tasks reached only 60 per cent. Deviating appraisals were caused especially by two multi-faceted tasks, which required more than one user interaction, for example choosing a point on a map. Another factor for slight deviations is the ambiguity between entering and selecting for larger groups of possible items. In these cases, few participants chose an entering interaction despite of an selection interaction.

In the second step, the participants classified the selection and entering interactions more detailed regarding the number of items and the entering string or number. While the congruence for entering a text or numeric quantities is 90 per cent the congruence of most kinds of selection is about 60 per cent. The appraisal between small and large numbers of items is not obvious and has to be improved by a hard indicator.

In the third step, the participants appraised the semantic of the user input. The congruence of all semantic appraisals were again only 60 per cent.

Finally, the result chart with the UIC classification was pre-evaluated by the assessment of clarity, intelligibility, and applicability. All evaluated items were assessed as positive from 90 respectively 100 per cent of the participants.

These results indicate, that the classification of user input is comprehensible to interdisciplinary teams. In contrast, the process of classification should be passed by usability experts in order to obtain more reliable data.

4.2 Application in the Decision Process

We evaluated the practical applicability of the UIC in another working group of IP-KOM-ÖV by applying the UIC to a decision process. Subsequent to the requirements analysis [22],[23], alternative proposals for the passenger-to-vehicle-communication were developed and analyzed by activity diagrams with UIC.

In one meeting we compared activity diagrams for the build-up of a WLAN connection by manual selection, ad hoc network selection, QR-code scan, or NFC support, see exemplary diagrams in figure 3. In addition, we considered different initial situations in order to vary user input.

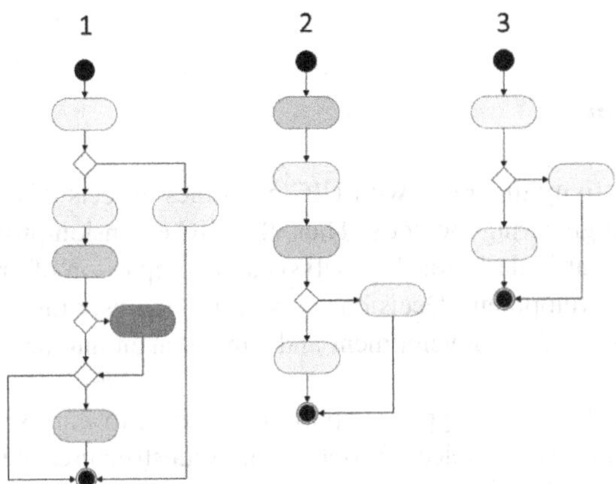

Fig. 3. Exemplary activity diagrams with UIC stereotypes within IP-KOM-ÖV

Subsequent to the discussion of several actions and exemplary user input, we used the criteria number of actions, maximum level of UIC, and mean level of UIC to compare the solutions. While the number of actions showed only slight differences for some solution, for instance between example (1) and (2) in figure 3, the mean level of UIC, and especially the required maximum revealed considerable differences between the suggested solution. While example (3) consists of level-1-actions only, example (2) requires level-1- and level-2-actions. At least, example (1) also contains level-3-actions.

As a consequence, possible improvements for the usability for technical solutions, which contained level-3- or level-4-interactions were discussed intensively. The impact of the UIC was intuitively understood with less explanations by all participants of the discussion. Next to the technical requirements, the information about the user requirements was directly taken into consideration for the decision process, according to the UIC.

5 Discussion

The UIC presupposes a task structuring process such as HTA [24] or provided by Martinie [25]. It is not possible to classify ambiguous tasks which are broadly defined and might include several different user inputs. Hence, the results of the classification depend on the results of the task analysis.

Target products with more than one user group, might evoke ambiguities of the UIC, due to the fact that the semantic model of the content depends on the users' mental models and daily routines. In relation to the user descriptions, the UIC value might differ for several user groups and require more than one value for one activity and additional information, at the same time. Furthermore, the requirements of handicapped users have to be considered separately, particularly in regard to user input technologies. This adaptation to differing user groups should be the subject in further research.

6 Conclusions

The extension of activity diagrams with UIC combines aspects of usability engineering with software engineering methods. Thus, the UIC extension provides an interdisciplinary approach, particularly for the analysis and comparison of proposed solutions in early phases of development. Decisions concerning the user interaction can be discussed in early phases of the development and can be taken into account for technical key decisions.

Furthermore, the UIC stereotypes support conclusions to improve a required user input. For instance, a level-3-selection out of many unstructured items could be improved by a hierarchical level-2-selection or a level-4-entering task with formal text input could be supported by proposals of the most frequent terms. Thus, according to the UIC stereotypes, recommendations for improvements could be given to the actions, in the future.

According to the positive first evaluation results in theory and in the field, the application of the classification should be evaluated more detailed in an entire workflow process with interdisciplinary teams. In this paper the UIC approach is applied solely to activity diagrams. In a next step we have to proof, if the UIC can be transferred to other behavioral diagrams.

Acknowledgements. Part of this work was funded by the German Federal Ministry of Economy and Technology (BMWi) grant number 19P10003L within the IP-KOM-ÖV project. The project develops an interface standard for passenger information in German public transport with focus on the connection between personal mobile devices, vehicle systems and public transport background computer systems.

References

1. Folmer, E., van Gurp, J., Dannenberg, R.B.: Software architecture analysis of usability. In: Bastide, R., Palanque, P., Roth, J. (eds.) EHCI-DSVIS 2004. LNCS, vol. 3425, pp. 38–58. Springer, Heidelberg (2005)
2. Jerome, B., Kazman, R.: Surveying the Solitudes. An Investigation into the relationships between Human Computer Interaction and Software Engineering in Practice. In: Human-Centered Software Engineering — Integrating Usability in the Software Development Lifecycle, pp. 59–70. Springer, Heidelberg (2005)

3. Williams, J.P., Bias, R.G., Mayhew, D.J.: Cost Justification. In: Seras, A., Jacko, J.A. (eds.) The Human-computer Interaction Handbook. Fundamental, Evolving Technologies and Emerging Applications, pp. 927–947. Taylor and Francis Group, New York (2008)
4. Hackos, J.T., Redish, J.C.: User and task analysis for interface design. Wiley, New York (1998)
5. Constantine, L., Biddle, R., Noble, J.: Usage-Centered Design and Software Engineering: Models for Integration. In: ICSE 2003 Workshop on Bridging the Gap Between Software Engineering and Human-Computer Interaction, Portland, Oregon (2003)
6. Ferre, X.: Integration of Usability Techniques into the Software Development Process. In: ICSE 2003 Workshop on Bridging the Gap Between Software Engineering and Human-Computer Interaction, Portland, Oregon (2003)
7. Nebe, K., Zimmermann, D., Paelke, V.: Integrating Software Engineering and Usability Engineering. In: Pinder, S. (ed.) Advances in Human Computer Interaction. InTech (2008)
8. Bruegge, B., Dutoit, A.H.: Object-Oriented Software Engineering – Using UML, patterns and Java. Pearson, Boston (2010)
9. Courage, C., Redish, J.G., Wixon, D.: Task Analysis. In: The Human-Computer Interaction Handbook. Fundamental, Evolving Technologies and Emerging Applications, pp. 927–947. Taylor and Francis Group, New York (2008)
10. Cooper, A., Reimann, R., Cronin, D.: About face 3, the essentials of interaction design. Wiley, Indianapolis (2007)
11. Rosson, M.B., Carroll, J.M.: Usability engineering –Scenario –based development of humen-computer interaction. Morgan Kaufmann (2002)
12. Foucault, B.E.: Contextualizing cultures for the commercial world: Techniques for presenting field research in business envirnoments. In: Salvendy, G. (ed.) Proceedings of the HCII Conference, Las Vegas (2005)
13. Mayhew, D.: The Usability Engineering Lifecycle. Morgan Kaufmann, San Francisco (1999)
14. Beyer, H., Holtzblatt, K.: Contextual design: defining customer-centered systems. Morgan Kaufmann, San Francisco (1998)
15. OMG: Unified Modeling Language (OMG UML), Infrastructure Version 2.4, http://www.omg.org/spec/UML/2.4.1/Infrastructure
16. Nunes, J.N.: What drives software development: Bridging the gap between software and usability engineering. In: Seffah, A., Vanderdonckt, J., Desmarais, M.C. (eds.) Human-Centerd Software Engineering, Software Engineering Models, Patterns and Architectures for HCI. HCIS, pp. 9–25. Springer, London (2009)
17. Markopoulos, P.: Modelling user tasks with the unified modeling language. In: Proc. of Workshop TUPIS 2000 in < <UML2000> > International Conference
18. Cook, S.: The UML Family: Profiles, Prefaces and Packages. In: Evans, A., Caskurlu, B., Selic, B. (eds.) UML 2000. LNCS, vol. 1939, pp. 255–264. Springer, Heidelberg (2000)
19. Jardim Nunes, N., Falcão e Cunha, J.: Towards a UML Profile for Interaction Design: The Wisdom Approach. In: Evans, A., Kent, S., Selic, B. (eds.) UML 2000. LNCS, vol. 1939, pp. 101–116. Springer, Heidelberg (2000)
20. Foley, J.D., van Dam, A., Feiner, S.K., Hughes, J.F.: Computer Graphics – Principles and Practice. Addison-Wesley, Boston (1997)
21. Lieberman, B.: UML Activity Diagrams: Detailing User Interface Navigation, http://www.ibm.com/developerworks/rational/library/4697.html (February 22, 2013)

22. Mayas, C., Hörold, S., Krömker, H.: Meeting the Challenges of Individual Passenger Information with Personas. In: Stanton, N. (ed.) Advances in Human Aspects of Road and Rail Transportation, pp. 822–831. CRC Press, Boca Raton (2012)
23. Hörold, S., Mayas, C., Krömker, H.: Identifying the information needs of users in public transport. In: Stanton, N. (ed.) Advances in Human Aspects of Road and Rail Transportation, pp. 331–340. CRC Press, Boca Raton (2012)
24. Annet, J.: Hierarchical Task Analysis (HTA). In: Handbook of Human Factors and Ergonomics Method, pp. 33–37. CRC Press, Boca Raton (2005)
25. Martinie, C., Palanque, P., Winckler, M.: Structuring and Composition Mechanisms to Address Scalability Issues in Task Models. In: Campos, P., Graham, N., Jorge, J., Nunes, N., Palanque, P., Winckler, M. (eds.) INTERACT 2011, Part III. LNCS, vol. 6948, pp. 589–609. Springer, Heidelberg (2011)

Patterns and Models for Automated User Interface Construction – In Search of the Missing Links

Christian Märtin, Christian Herdin, and Jürgen Engel

Augsburg University of Applied Sciences
Faculty of Computer Science
Automation in Usability Engineering Group
An der Hochschule 1
86161 Augsburg, Germany
{Christian.Maertin,Christian.Herdin,
Juergen.Engel}@hs-augsburg.de

Abstract. This paper starts with an analysis of current or proven model and pattern-based user interface development methods and techniques. It discusses how these approaches facilitate the construction process and enhance the overall flexibility, usability and user experience of the resulting software. It is shown that HCI patterns meanwhile can contribute heavily to all development aspects of interactive systems. In order to integrate patterns, task, dialog, and object-oriented models to further automate user interface construction, the paper tightly couples these seemingly disparate development paradigms to allow a more powerful interplay. Thereby some of the missing links are identified for letting the pattern-based automated generation of complex parts of high-quality and media-rich applications become a routine job. A well-known smart phone app is examined to demonstrate some steps of the new approach.

Keywords: Model-based user interface development (MBUID), HCI patterns, task models, object-oriented models, dialog models, embedded patterns, user interface generation.

1 Introduction

Model-based user interface development (MBUID) has affected HCI since the nineteen eighties. However, over the years, the initial confidence in the efficiency and generative power of model-based development processes and tools has given way to a more unemotional view on the advantages and shortcomings of the model-based paradigm. The wide spectrum of end-users with differing levels of expertise and preferences, the heterogeneous working contexts and workflows, the variety of development environments and languages used for interactive system development, and the different target computing platforms from desktops to smart phones, with novel interaction techniques and modalities make it quite hard to define a generic and open-ended architecture for future MBUID environments [20].

M. Kurosu (Ed.): Human-Computer Interaction, Part I, HCII 2013, LNCS 8004, pp. 401–410, 2013.

Current trends in the area of interactive system design and user-centered development seem mostly to be aimed at providing a high degree of context-awareness, designer creativity and developer flexibility in order to produce high-quality interactive software with adequate user experience levels. The new social media with their intuitive, easy to use interfaces and the massive trend towards mobile applications and ubiquitous computers has directed the focus rather on rapid and agile user interface development methods than on detailed modeling environments.

On the other hand, research in the field of model-based and model-driven development is widespread and over the years has led to various approaches for automated GUI generation by interpreting semi-abstract and concrete models written in detailed user interface description languages [1], [29]. Model-based approaches also have proven to be valuable for approaching key challenges in HCI modeling and development, e.g. in the field of detailed modeling of real time control systems [19].

It is the goal of this paper to highlight some of the major contributions of MBUID and to pave the way for an interactive system development paradigm that leaves enough room for individual media-oriented design and development practices, but at the same time keeps in mind the benefits made available by MBUID, like high quality and usability through detailed modeling, platform independence, and efficiency through automated generation of non-trivial parts of the interactive target software.

HCI patterns could play a major role to more flexibility in MBUID. Therefore we propose a combined development approach that tightly couples the MBUID paradigm with HCI patterns for various interactive system modeling aspects.

The paper is structured in the following way: Chapter 2 will examine relevant work in the area of MBUID that is time-proven and in our opinion should make it into the combined approach. In chapter 3 we review the potential of pattern-based development approaches, introduce the notion of embedded patterns, and define the various pattern categories for pattern-based user interface modeling. Chapter 4 defines the structure and the major steps of the combined new development process and demonstrates some of its features by reengineering a popular media app. Chapter 5 concludes the paper and discusses the directions of our planned future work.

2 MBUID Accomplishments

Model-based user interface development environments introduce models to the development process of interactive applications [4]. The models are the carriers of the specified target system´s functional and data requirements and may serve to map these requirements to the structure and properties of the user interface in order to allow for effective and usable interaction of the user with the final target system implementation. The role of the models varies with respect to the modeling purpose. Typically more than one model is used interactively or parsed during the development process to construct the desired solution. Some ways in which models are exploited provide information for controlling highly-automated development processes for interactive systems. In the following we examine some major directions in model exploitation.

2.1 Task Models

Task models specify interaction goals, the sequence of user actions, and the collaboration of tasks and subtasks between users and the modeled system. They are in the center of many model-based development approaches. The CTT notation [23] is widely used in the HCI community for designing graphical tree specifications of the task structure and substructure of interactive applications. It depends on the level of detail, how complex task models may become for non-trivial applications.

As the static notation of task models to a certain degree describes the interactive behavior of the system under development, it is common to enable the execution of the task model together with a separately developed prototype or a mockup of the user interface in order to give an assessment of the quality of the modeled user-system interaction [2]. An executable task model can also be used as a starting point for deriving the user interface structure. In [25] so-called dialog graphs are derived directly from the task model. They allow for dynamic simulation of semi-abstract representations of the interactive application within various device contexts. The lifespan of task models can also encompass the runtime of the interactive application. Such task models can be used to implement context-aware dynamic user interfaces that behave differently at runtime, depending on the device type on which the application is executed [14].

In order to specify the detailed interactive behavior of highly sophisticated user interfaces and to design novel interaction techniques precisely, the approach presented in [22] combines task models, scenarios extracted from the task models, and detailed ICO models. ICO models are based on Petri nets [19] and allow the modeling of asynchronous and concurrent input/output actions as well as event-based state changes of interactive applications. Executable prototypes can be constructed from ICO models.

A recent approach for automatic generation of device-specific user interfaces from discourse models is presented in [24]. Discourse models are device and modality independent and define the sequence of questions and answers, i.e. the dialog, to solve a given problem. Together with a Domain-of-Discourse model that provides domain classes and their attributes, and the Action-Notification Model they form a communication model that represents the tasks and concepts of the interaction and serves as the basis for user interface generation.

2.2 Object-Oriented Models for User Interface Construction

Like task models, object-oriented models have a long history in MBUID environments. The survey in [4] compares several development environments of the first and second generation. In the last decade of the 20th century software engineering methods and tools were mainly based on object-oriented technologies. Some of the MBUID systems of this time-span, e.g. AME [15] and TADEUS [26] therefore chose the object-oriented modeling paradigm and notations for defining models of the interactive target system during its different lifecycle phases. Several systems were able to automatically define the window structure, choose abstract and concrete interaction objects for the user interface, and generate layout prototypes [28], [12], [15].

One aim of these MBUID environments was the tight coupling of the software engineering lifecycle with the user interface development process. Although most systems were targeted at the construction of traditional GUI-based applications, the technology and philosophy behind some of these environments today could again serve as one key technology for efficiently creating and generating web services and mobile apps.

The *Application Modeling Environment (AME)* [15], [16], e.g., applied a model refinement process and started modeling with an object-oriented analysis model that contained the domain classes (business logic) of the application, class attributes and attribute types, names and calling parameters of the class methods, and inter-class relations. The OOA model could also include the inter-class communication structure, i.e. the message-based calling structure of methods between domain classes that could later automatically be transformed into platform independent dialog sequencing code.

The OOA model was exploited by parsing the classes and inter-class relations (inheritance, aggregation, different types of associations) and by applying rules in order to define the hierarchical window structure of the user interface, abstract interaction objects, and the dynamic invocation structure for activating user interface elements and accessing the business logic. This information was collected in an OOD model. The OOD model included both, domain classes and their objects, and user interface classes and their objects (e.g. abstract windows, dialog boxes, and interaction objects). Typically one domain class was mapped to many user interface classes. Associations between the domain and user interface classes were used for communication and for transferring data between domain classes and the still abstract user interface.

The OOD model could be manually enhanced by browsers and editors. It served as the data model for an executable and fully functional prototype of the user interface. The UI and layout prototype was generated automatically by mapping the abstract interaction objects onto concrete interaction objects available within the simulation environment and by applying rules for interaction object grouping.

In order to arrive at a user interface prototype with satisfying usability characteristics, a user profile as well as a profile of the target environment could be interpreted by the generator. The resulting prototype could then be inspected with respect to correctness of the interaction design and usability and visual appearance of the user interface. From this, it was only a small remaining step to generate the C++ code for the user interface and the bindings to the business logic for different then state-of-the-art target platforms, e.g. Windows 95 and X-Window.

AME therefore was a quite flexible system that combined automation with explicit developer interaction during all phases of the development life cycle. One advantage of AME was the representation of the user interface as abstract OOD classes. These classes could serve as a stable user interface model and for communication with the business logic, without selecting concrete interaction objects too early. Instead, they were only defined during the final generation steps. The model was flexible enough to undo the selection decision and assign other concrete IOs with their inherent interaction techniques when the prototype was already being executed. This allowed the simulation and evaluation of different versions of the user interface before the target code was generated.

Model-driven architecture (MDA), a software engineering trend that evolved some years after MBUID [21], also is built on the transformation of abstract into more and more concrete model-representations with the final generation of domain and user interface code. As a starting point, typically, different UML models of the application are created and then exploited by automated model-transforming tools. MDA approaches provide UML models for all parts of the system under development. In contrast, in an MBUID environment like AME, as a starting point only such parts of the business logic that later would interact with the user interface had to be included into the OOA model [16]. Non-interactive parts of the application kernel could be developed independently by using the interactive business classes as their interface to the OOD user interface classes.

3 HCI Patterns

HCI patterns and pattern languages [18], [3], [27], [17], [5] recently have raised much interest in the MBUID community. Structural and behavioral information contained in HCI patterns can be used for modeling many different aspects of interactive systems or fine-tuning the properties of user interfaces derived from task or object-oriented models. Patterns also can be transformed into executable user interfaces by automated transformation processes [30], [9].

Within the PaMGIS framework [7] we have developed the *PaMGIS Pattern Specification Language (PPSL),* a powerful pattern description language based on PLML that can directly be exploited for user interface generation and for linking patterns with other modeling components. Table 1 shows the structure of PPSL pattern descriptions. There are many categories of HCI patterns [13], some of which are briefly discussed here. All pattern types can be specified with PPSL [6], [8], embedded into object-oriented models and linked to task and dialog models.

Structural Patterns. Such patterns resemble classic design patterns [11] and specify the class/object structure and the static and dynamic inter-class relations of parts of the interactive application.

Domain Patterns. Such patterns specify those parts of the business model that directly interact with the user interface.

GUI Patterns. Such patterns specify one or more abstract interaction objects, their relationships, and their interactive behavior. GUI patterns are primarily aimed at good usability.

Media Patterns. Such patterns specify (reusable groups of) media-specific interaction objects and their interaction techniques (e.g. multi touch input, speech input/output).

Infrastructural Patterns. Such patterns specify context and platform-specific reusable design information.

Table 1. Pattern description elements of the PaMGIS Framework

Specification Element	Brief Description
UPID	Unique pattern identifier as defined in [6]
Name	Name of the pattern
Alias	Alternative names, also known as
Illustration	Good example of instantiation of the pattern
Problem	Description of the problem to be solved
Context	Situations and circumstances in which the pattern can be applied
Forces	Description of forces in the environment that the use of the pattern will resolve
Solution	Description of how to resolve the problem
Synopsis	Summary of the pattern description
Diagram	Schematic visualization of the pattern
Evidence	Verification that it is in fact a pattern by
Example	at least three known uses of the pattern
Rationale	discussion and any principled reasons
Confidence	Rating of how likely the pattern provides an invariant solution for the given problem
Literature	References to related documents or papers
Implementation	Code or model fragments or details of technical realization as defined in [6]
Pattern-link	Relationship to other patterns or pattern instances as defined in [6]
Embedding-link	Back-link to object-oriented analysis and/or design model
ELinkID	Unique embedded link identifier
Reference class ID list	OO model classes from which the pattern is referenced
UML relationship-type list	Relation types between classes and referenced pattern
Label	Name of the embedding link
Management Information	Authorship and change management
Authors	Name of the pattern author
Credits	Merits
Creation-Date	Date of pattern compilation
Last-modified	Date of last change
Revision-number	Version of the pattern definition

UX Patterns. Such patterns specify rule-based or algorithmic knowledge for designing specific user experience characteristics for the interactive system.

Pattern Transformation Patterns (PTP). Such patterns contain rule-based or algorithmic descriptions for transforming patterns to different device contexts (e.g. from desktop to mobile device) [9].

4 Coupling HCI Patterns with Task- and Object Modeling

The discussion of important contributions to the fields of task modeling, object-oriented modeling, and patterns for interactive application development clarifies that it does not seem possible to arrive at an effective solution for user interface design automation, if one of the mentioned areas is neglected. Therefore we propose a tightly-coupled modeling paradigm which uses HCI patterns – specified in PPSL – as pivotal points to both integrate task modeling and object-oriented modeling aspects into the final design. This allows three different views onto the interactive system under construction: the pattern view, the task model view, and the object model view. The "missing links" can now be identified as the attributes `Implementation`, `Pattern-link`, and `Embedding-link` of PPSL specifications that relate each pattern with modeling components in the task and object models. Figure 1 shows the resulting combined model structure.

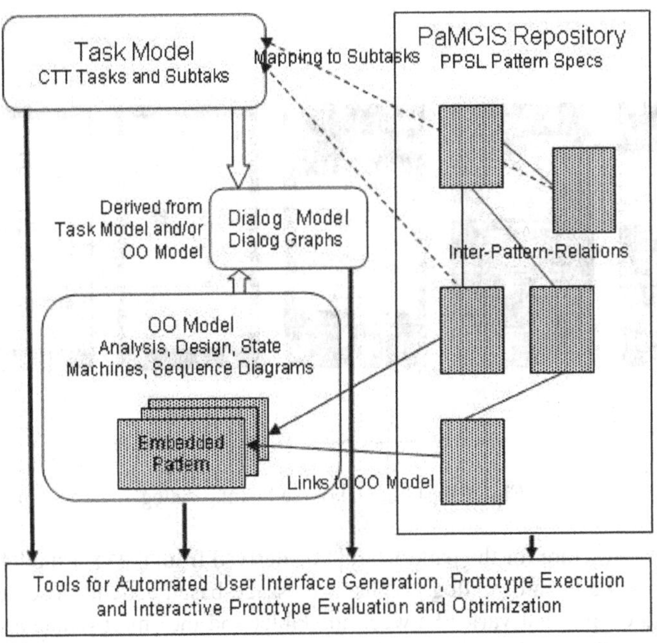

Fig. 1. A tightly-coupled modeling approach

As an example, we use the CNN smart phone application for Android to briefly demonstrate a small part of the proposed approach. Figure 2 shows the CTT task model for the *News Sharing pattern* found in many news apps for smart phones and tablets. In the user scenario the user wants to share some news from the CNN-App with his or her follower at google+. In the repository the pattern could be represented as a domain pattern with several domain classes each of which would be related to a user interface pattern. The domain pattern could be embedded into the OO model where it would be associated with one or more domain classes defining the actual aggregation and intra class structures.

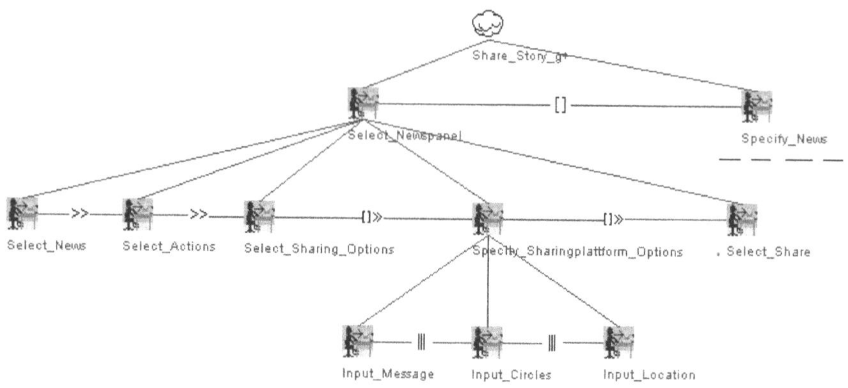

Fig. 2. Excerpt of the task model of the *News Sharing* pattern

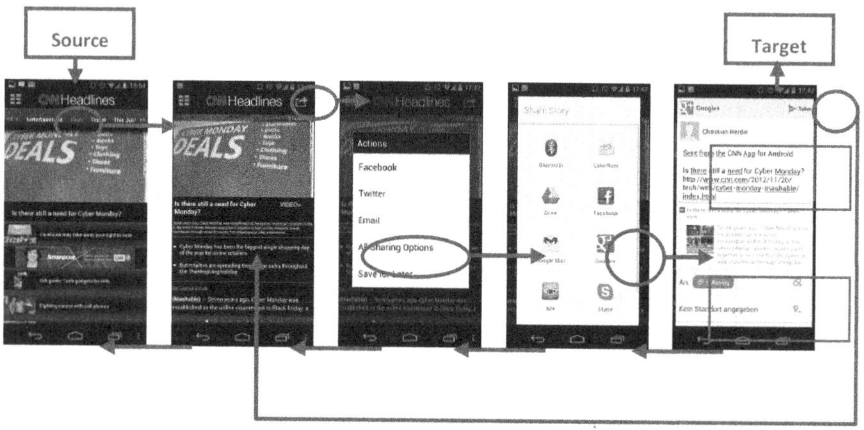

Fig. 3. Resulting UI of the Sharing dialog

The dialog structure for the pattern could be derived from the task model and/or the OO models in the form of dialog graphs or message-based activation sequences. The visual screen design that varies between the tablet and the smart phone app could be available as platform-independent and/or device-specific user interface patterns in the repository. These patterns could be directly referenced by the domain pattern embedded in the OO model during the refinement process executed by the interactive prototyping and automated generation tools. This could lead to the resulting user interface shown in figure 3.

5 Conclusion

This paper has reviewed proven approaches in task-, object-oriented, and pattern-based modeling of interactive systems. All three areas contribute heavily to the quality and flexibility needed for real-world, state-of-the art interactive applications. By centering a combined modeling approach around powerful PPSL HCI pattern specifications and defining the most important inter-model-relationships, it becomes possible to integrate the strengths of the three modeling paradigms and to allow automated prototyping and generation tools an easier exploitation of the so far distributed modeling knowledge.

Thus, in future implementations of such combined modeling approaches, even detailed system modeling information, low-level interaction specifications, and creative user experience design suggestions could contribute to widely automatically generated prototypes of the interactive target applications.

References

1. Abrams, M., et al.: UIML: An Appliance-Independent XML User Interface Language. In: Proc. Eighth International World Wide Web Conference (WWW 1998). Elsevier Science Pub. (May 1999)
2. Bomsdorf, B., Szwillus, G.: Early Prototyping Based on Executable Task Models. In: Proc. CHI 1996, pp. 254–255. ACM, Vancouver (1996)
3. Breiner, K., et al. (eds.): Proc. of the 1st Int. Workshop on Pattern-Driven Engineering of Interactive Computing Systems (PEICS 2010), Berlin, Germany, June 20. ACM Int. Conf. Proc. Series (2010)
4. da Silva, P.P.: User Interface Declarative Models and Development Environments: A Survey. In: Paternó, F. (ed.) DSV-IS 2000. LNCS, vol. 1946, pp. 207–226. Springer, Heidelberg (2001)
5. Engel, J., Märtin, C., Forbrig, P.: Tool-support for Pattern-based Generation of User Interfaces. In: [3], pp. 24–27 (2010)
6. Engel, J., Märtin, C., Herdin, C., Forbrig, P.: Formal Pattern Specifications to Facilitate Semi-Automated User Interface Generation. In: Kurosu, M. (ed.) Human-Computer Interaction, Part I, HCII 2013. LNCS, vol. 8004, pp. 300–309. Springer, Heidelberg (2013)
7. Engel, J., Märtin, C.: PaMGIS: A Framework for Pattern-Based Modeling and Generation of Interactive Systems. In: Jacko, J.A. (ed.) Human-Computer Interaction, Part I, HCII 2009. LNCS, vol. 5610, pp. 826–835. Springer, Heidelberg (2009)
8. Engel, J., Herdin, C., Märtin, C.: Exploiting HCI Pattern Collections for User Interface Generation. In: Proc. Patterns 2012, Nice, France, pp. 36–44. IARIA (2012)
9. Engel, J., Märtin, C., Forbrig, P.: HCI Patterns as a Means to Transform Interactive User Interfaces to Diverse Contexts of Use. In: Jacko, J.A. (ed.) Human-Computer Interaction, Part I, HCII 2011. LNCS, vol. 6761, pp. 204–213. Springer, Heidelberg (2011)
10. Fincher, S., et al.: Perspectives on HCI Patterns: Concepts and Tools (Introducing PLML). In: CHI 2003 Workshop Report (2003)
11. Gamma, E., et al.: Design Patterns. Elements of Reusable Object-Oriented Software. Addison-Wesley, Reading (1995)
12. Janssen, C., Weisbecker, A., Ziegler, J.: Generating User Interfaces from Data Models and Dialog Net Specifications. In: Proc. INTERCHI 1993, pp. 418–423. IOS Press, ACM, Amsterdam (1993)
13. Kaelber, C., Märtin, C.: From Structural Analysis to Scenarios and Patterns for Knowledge Sharing Applications. In: Jacko, J.A. (ed.) Human-Computer Interaction, Part I, HCII 2011. LNCS, vol. 6761, pp. 258–267. Springer, Heidelberg (2011)

14. Klug, T., Kangasharju, J.: Executable Task Models. In: Proc. TAMODIA 2005, Gdansk, Poland, pp. 119–122. ACM (2005)
15. Märtin, C.: Software Life Cycle Automation for Interactive Applications: The AME Design Environment. In: Vanderdonckt, J. (ed.) Proc. of CADUI 1996, pp. 57–73. Presses Universitaires de Namur (1996)
16. Märtin, C.: Model-Based Software Engineering for Interactive Systems. In: Albrecht, R. (ed.) Systems: Theory and Practice, pp. 187–211. Springer, Wien (1998)
17. Märtin, C., Roski, A.: Structurally Supported Design of HCI Pattern Languages. In: Jacko, J.A. (ed.) Human-Computer Interaction, Part I, HCII 2007. LNCS, vol. 4550, pp. 1159–1167. Springer, Heidelberg (2007)
18. Marcus, A.: Patterns within Patterns. Interactions, 28–34 (March+April 2004)
19. Martinie, C., et al.: Formal Tasks and Systems Models as a Tool for Specifying and Assessing Automation Designs. In: Proc. ATACCS 2011, Barcelona, Spain, pp. 50–59 (2011)
20. Meixner, G., Paterno, F., Vanderdonckt, J.: Past, Present, and Future of Model-Based User Interface Development. i-com (3), 2–11 (2011)
21. Mellor, S.J., Scott, K., Uhl, A., Weise, D.: Model-Driven Architecture. In: Bruel, J.-M., Bellahsène, Z. (eds.) OOIS 2002. LNCS, vol. 2426, pp. 290–297. Springer, Heidelberg (2002)
22. Palanque, P., et al.: A Model-based Approach for Supporting Engineering Usability Evaluation of Interaction Techniques. In: Proc. EICS 2011, Pisa, Italy, pp. 21–29. ACM (2011)
23. Paternò, F.: Model-Based Design and Evaluation of Interactive Applications. Springer (2000)
24. Raneburger, D., et al.: Automated Generation of Device-Specific WIMP UIs: Weaving of Structural and Behavioral Models. In: EICS 2011, Pisa, Italy, pp. 41–46. ACM (2011)
25. Reichart, D., Forbrig, P., Dittmar, A.: Task Models as Basis for Requirements Engineering and Software Execution. In: Proc. TAMODIA 2004, Prague, Czech Republic, pp. 51–58. ACM (2004)
26. Schlungbaum, E., Elwert, T.: Automatic User Interface Generation from Declarative Models. In: Vanderdonckt, J. (ed.) Proc. of CADUI 1996, pp. 3–17. Presses Universitaires de Namur (1996)
27. Seissler, M., Breiner, K., Meixner, G.: Towards Pattern-Driven Engineering of Run-Time Adaptive User Interfaces for Smart Production Environments. In: Jacko, J.A. (ed.) Human-Computer Interaction, Part I, HCII 2011. LNCS, vol. 6761, pp. 299–308. Springer, Heidelberg (2011)
28. Vanderdonckt, J., Bodart, F.: Encapsulating Knowledge for Intelligent Automatic Interaction Objects Selection. In: Proc. INTERCHI 1993, pp. 424–429. IOS Press, ACM, Amsterdam (1993)
29. Vanderdonckt, J., et al.: UsiXML: a User Interface Description Language for Specifying multimodal User Interfaces. In: Proc. W3C Workshop on Multimodal Interaction (WMI 2004), July 19-20 (2004)
30. Wendler, S., et al.: Development of Graphical User Interfaces based on User Interface Patterns. In: Proc. Patterns 2012, Nice, France, pp. 57–66. IARIA (2012)

Evaluation of User Interface Description Languages for Model-Based User Interface Development in the German Automotive Industry

Gerrit Meixner[1], Marius Orfgen[2], and Moritz Kümmerling[2]

[1] Heilbronn University
Max-Planck-Str. 39, 74081 Heilbronn, Germany
Gerrit.Meixner@hs-heilbronn.de
[2] German Research Center for Artificial Intelligence (DFKI),
Trippstadter Str. 122, 67663 Kaiserslautern, Germany
{Marius.Orfgen,Moritz.Kuemmerling}@dfki.de

Abstract. Developing human-machine-interfaces (HMI) in the automotive industry is a time-consuming and complex task, involving different companies (car manufacturers, suppliers, translators, designers) and teams with different backgrounds. One way to improve the current problems arising from communication and documentation deficits is to formalize the specification to make it easier to read, to structure and to analyze. The project automotiveHMI aims to create a domain-specific modeling language for HMI development in the automotive industry. As part of the project, current specification processes and artifacts as well as the related roles were analyzed. During the analysis 18 criteria which should be fulfilled by a domain-specific modeling language have been identified. The criteria are used to evaluate existing modeling languages and to set objectives for the development of a new modeling language focusing the cross-company and cross-team development of model-based HMIs in the automotive industry.

Keywords: Automotive User Interface, Model-Based User Interface Development, Task Analysis, User Roles.

1 Introduction

Different studies show (e.g., [1]) that over 80% of today's innovations in the automotive industry are based on car electronics and its software. These innovations can be categorized into hidden technologies (e.g., ASP, ESP), comfort functions (e.g., navigation, communication, entertainment) or driver assistance (e.g., distance checking). Especially the last two categories have to be configurable by the driver and therefore require a certain amount of driver interaction. This results in a need for a modern and consistent human-machine-interface (HMI) which on one hand allows the configuration of these systems but which on the other hand conforms to the specialized requirements of the automotive industry. Some of these requirements are:

M. Kurosu (Ed.): Human-Computer Interaction, Part I, HCII 2013, LNCS 8004, pp. 411–420, 2013.

the interaction devices have to be integrated into a limited space; the HMI has to be intuitively usable and adaptable, since drivers generally do not get an extensive explanation and the HMI has to be very easy to use and should distract the driver as little as possible from his main task of driving.

Additionally to the growing number of configurable systems in a modern car, there is a need for shorter release cycles and lower costs for the development of HMIs. One main source of problems in the development of HMIs is the communication overhead caused by informal specifications [2]. This overhead is needed to reduce the ambiguity and the incorrectness of the specification document. A more formal approach to specification might reduce this overhead dramatically, leading to shorter development times, cost savings and fewer problems.

(Semi-)Formal specification of HMIs is researched in the context of model-based user interface development (MBUID) [3] and resulted in a vast number of specification languages for different aspects of HMIs in the last years. To find out which of the existing modeling languages suits the purpose of describing an HMI in the context of the automotive industry (if such a language even exists), a large-scaled analysis was performed in the German automotive industry.

The rest of the paper is structured as follows: In section 2, related work concerning description languages for HMIs are discussed. In section 3, an introduction to the project automotiveHMI will be given. Section 4 will shortly present the results of a process analysis that was undertaken in cooperation with the different project partners. Section 5 will discuss criteria for HMI modeling languages that were derived from the analysis. These criteria are then used to analyze existing modeling languages for their suitability in future HMI development processes in the automotive industry. In section 6 we will give a summary and an outlook on future work.

2 Related Work

A vast number of (XML-based) User Interface Description Languages (UIDLs) exist already in the field of MBUID. Some of the UIDLs are already standardized by e.g., OASIS, currently being standardized by e.g. W3C[1] and are subject of a continuous development process. Numerous projects and applications prove their practical suitability. Examples of a UIDL are UsiXML [4] or XIML [5].

The purpose of using a UIDL to develop a HMI is to systematize the HMI development process. UIDLs enable the developer to systematically break down a HMI into different abstraction layers and to model these layers. Thus it is for example possible to describe the behavior, the structure and the layout of a HMI independently of each other. Existing UIDLs differ in terms of the supported platforms and modalities as well as in the amount of predefined interaction objects that are available to describe the elements of the HMI. In the relevant literature several authors

[1] `http://www.w3.org/2011/mbui`

struggled with the challenge of a clear comparison of existing UIDLs (e.g., [6], [7]). These comparisons were mostly done on a theoretically basis by checking the language against some defined criteria. However, a comprehensive comparison focusing the state-of-the-practice (especially concerning real-world usage of model-based user interface development) in the industry with underlying real projects is yet to be drawn [8].

The aim of MBUID is to describe the properties of an HMI in sufficient detail and formality so that (semi-)automatic model transformations can be applied to generate the final HMI. The Cameleon Reference Framework (CRF) [9] identifies four different layers of a HMI in a MBUID process.

3 The Project AutomotiveHMI

The publicly funded research project automotiveHMI (http://www.automotive-hmi.org) consists of eleven partners of the German automotive industry, two research institutes as well as one association. The industry members are car manufacturers (Original Equipment Manufacturer - OEM), suppliers and tool developers which together cover the complete development chain for automotive HMI-systems [10].

Current HMI development processes are characterized by different, inconsistent workflows and heterogeneous tool chains. The exchanged requirements are often inconsistent, redundant, incomplete and in general not machine-readable. These circumstances lead to tremendous communication efforts between OEMs and their suppliers until both get the same understanding of the new HMI-system. Mistakes and bugs are often first noticed when the supplier delivers the first software-version back to the OEM. At that late time modifications are very cost intensive and change-request negotiations become a common annoyance. A further problem is the wide range of actors from many different branches that are involved in the automotive HMI development: Computer scientists and electrical engineers work together with designers, ergonomists and psychologists in interdisciplinary teams. The HMI modeling language that is to be developed shall serve as the connective link (lingua franca) between these actors. On this account the modeling language has to be domain specific. Domain specific languages (DSL) are dedicated to a particular problem domain and their “vocabulary” is generally based upon common expressions that are typical for the domain. Thus DSLs are far more expressive in their domain than general-purpose languages would be.

The project goal of automotiveHMI is to create a modeling language that will allow the different members of the development chain to specify and exchange the requirements and artifacts for HMI development. This modeling language forms a common data interface for the different process members. It allows bridging the “digital gap” currently found in today’s HMI development due to the document-driven exchange of specification data. Building on this data interface, it is possible to exchange digital information for use in development tools without information breaks.

This results in a more efficient collaboration of development members and allows further the digital convergence of different HMI subsystems (e.g. navigation, communication, car systems). Furthermore, the modeling language provides domain-specific benefits [11], since it is tailored to the specific needs of the automotive industry: it uses terms and meanings of the domain; it allows domain experts to create and review the specification; code and domain are being brought closer together and the productivity is increased, since changes are done on the domain level, not the code level.

4 Analysis of the Development Process

As a prerequisite to the creation of the specification language, a certain selection of project and associated partners (OEMs as well as suppliers and tool developers) were interviewed first to get a comprehensive insight into the automotive HMI development processes and second to identify specific roles and requirements for the specification language. Nine partners (who are representative for the German automotive industry) were questioned in a three-step process using a questionnaire with over 160 questions as well as a day-long workshop with 2 to 10 stakeholders per partner. The overall manpower invested by all partners in the analysis phase is more than 25 person months. The results were then combined into documents that were send to the partners for review and validation. The questionnaire ranged from questions about the used software and methods, specifics about the specification and test processes and personal experience with model-based approaches. A larger part of the analysis was devoted to a free-form discussion about likes and dislikes regarding software tools, personal wishes for a future development process and currently unsolved problems in the HMI development. The reviewed results were then combined to form the abstract reference process [12] as well as the partner-independent roles and criteria.

In total we identified 7 different partner-independent roles in the development process: Interaction Designer, Screen Designers, Hardware Developer, Software Developer, Tester, Reviewer and Translator.

5 Criteria and Their Application on UIDLs

This section presents the identified and validated industrial criteria derived from the results of the analysis as well as their application on existing UIDLs.

5.1 Criteria

Table 1 describes the derived criteria as well as the roles that require them. Criteria with "General" as requiring parties are those which cannot be mapped to specific roles but were mentioned as part of overall innovations.

Table 1. The 18 criteria

C1: Versioning (Required by: Interaction Designers, Software Developers, Reviewers)
One of the main problems currently perceived is that there are different versions of the specification that are simultaneously been used. Interaction Designers refine or even change requirements that have an impact on many parts of the implementation. Screen Designers make changes to screens (affecting the implementation of that screen) or screen elements (affecting every screen that incorporates these elements). Meanwhile, Software Developers implement according to an older version and Testers derive test cases also according to the older version. Reviewers also analyze the specification and currently face the problem of either restarting the whole review activity or overlook subtle changes if a new version is released. With subcontractors of the automotive supplier added to the picture, there are multiple versions of the specification being used as a base for development activities during the project. Currently, there is no systematic way to identify the differences between these versions, which results in changes being overlooked or old problems remaining unresolved. A modeling language that allows automatic identification of these differences would reduce the inconsistency problems.

C2: Management of Variants (Required by: Interaction Designers, Screen Designers)
In the early phases of specification but also every time major changes are required, there might be different design alternatives being discussed. The discussions result in one of the variants being picked and the others being discarded. These decisions are not documented systematically and therefore are not traceable. If a certain design decision is questioned later in the development process, it is difficult to argue why this was done. Also later high-level changes (e.g. to remove or alter features) might make those design alternatives interesting again. It should therefore be supported to annotate parts of the specification as variants that were discarded or to document groups of design alternatives together with the decision systematically.

C3: Definition of State Machines (Required by: Interaction Designers)
The dynamic properties of an HMI are typically modeled as a state machine. Each state relates to a screen of the final HMI and is annotated with information about interaction elements or information shown to the driver. Each transition stands for a change from one screen to another either as the result of driver interaction (e.g., pressing a button or making a selection) or a system event (e.g., a popup indicating a warning). The state machine contains information that is both easy to formalize and can be used to automatically derive data for other roles (e.g., testing). Currently, state machines are specified using presentation or spreadsheet programs, resulting in specifications that cannot be automatically checked or transformed.

C4: Support for Abstract Screens (Required by: Interaction Designers, Screen Designers)
An important part of the communication between Interaction and Screen Designers is the definition of abstract screens. These screens describe the available interaction

Table 1. *(continued)*

elements (e.g. selecting a radio station or informing the driver about traffic) without restricting the Screen Designer to a specific modality or layout. These abstract screens are currently specified in documents, limiting the readability and therefore the usefulness for automatic transformations. Also, finding the required abstract elements for a screen in a specification document is more difficult compared to a possible plug-in for the Screen Designer's graphics editing program.

C5: Support for Concrete Screens (Required by: Screen Designers, Software Developers)
Screen Designers provide examples for layout and design as part of the specification. Currently, the different formats (standard graphics formats or sound formats) are difficult to integrate in the word-processor-written specification, resulting in consistency problems since these examples are stored externally. Automatic tracking of the consistency of the examples with the rest of the specification could solve these problems.

C6: Annotations (Required by: Interaction Designers, Software Developers, Reviewers)
The main goal of the modeling language is to reduce media breaks, therefore keeping a consistent body of information related to HMI specification and development. Informal notes and annotations on different parts of the specification allow designers and reviewers keep reminders, questions and to-dos in place with the related information. It can also be used to extend the informal parts of the specification on demand to make up for formal constructs that the language currently lacks.

C7: Definition of Informal Requirements (Required by: Interaction Designers, Screen Designers)
An ideal specification would be completely formal, with no need for interpretation, no inconsistencies and no duplicate information. In a real development process, this level of formality is neither feasible nor desired. Sometimes it is easier to add informal text to a transition or screen than to specify it exactly instead of conveying the intent. It is therefore important to be able to annotate formal information like state machines or requirements with pictures, drawings or informal text. This high-level information also helps the creators of the specification in the creation process, since it allows to mark parts of the specification for later revisiting or to document intermediary results.

C8: Metadata for Requirements (Required by: Interaction Designers, Software Developers)
Currently, specification documents are very large and therefore difficult to handle. This includes checking for consistency, checking for changes between versions and finding of relevant parts for a certain activity. To improve the first and last point, metadata for requirements could help to sort and filter requirements based on properties such as author, change date, related parts of the HMI or type of requirement. Metadata could also be used to keep outdated requirements or design alternatives in the specification for traceability, decision management and documentation reasons.

Table 1. *(continued)*

C9: Traceability for Requirements (Required by: Interaction Designers, Software Developers, Reviewers)
Since the specification is subject to frequent changes of varying severity, quickly identifying the affected parts of the specification when changing or removing a requirement helps in ensuring consistency and making sure that no outdated information remains in the specification. A way to allow this is to include traceability information in the specification. Artifacts of the development process are related to one another (e.g. if a requirement is refined, links to its refinements are created), allowing automatic retrieval of all affected parts.

C10: Referencing External Data (Required by: Interaction Designers, Software Developers)
The specification of an HMI consists of several types of information, including examples, like animations, prototypes and mockups. Since the examples are too informal to be integrated into the modeling language, they have to be referenced unambiguously. Generally, there are different types of information in the development of an HMI which allow different levels of abstraction or formalization. It is useful for automatic transformation to formalize those where it makes sense. Less formal information should generally be allowed to be stored in an external location and be referenced where appropriate.

C11: Open, Standardized and Free Modeling Language (Required by: General)
There have been efforts in the past (e.g., [2], [14] [15] [16]) to define modeling languages tailored for the automotive industry. Most of these failed because they had no support from tool vendors. An important requirement for a language that can be used in industrial development is that the language is open, standardized and free. Standardization allows different companies to create tools or plug-ins to other tools that allow interoperability. Since adopting a standard requires changes, the transition can be made easier when the language carries no license costs. Openness guarantees that the language can be extended to contain additional information that might become useful in the future.

C12: Simple Integration with Tools (Required by: Interaction Designers, Screen Designers, Software Developers, Reviewers, Translators)
Currently, exchange of information between roles is achieved through text, images or example programs. Even if specialized tools that support modeling exist, the models have to be exported as text or pictures, hindering automatic import at the receiver's side. A modeling language that can hold all the information of the HMI design process needs to be easily integratable with current generic and specialized tools to be useful.

C13: Support for Iterative Approach (Required by: Interaction Designers, Hardware Developers, Software Developers)
Even without drastic high-level changes like the addition or removal of features, HMI development is iterative in nature. A modeling language for HMI specification must therefore support different versions as well as an easy way to compare or merge these versions.

Table 1. *(continued)*

C14: Support for Prototyping (Required by: Interaction Designers)
Currently, when specifying the dynamic behavior of a user interface, interaction developers have no way to actually experience what they specified. They have to wait until the implementation is done to evaluate the usability and to suggest improvements, which results in higher costs, since it occurs late in the development process.

C15: Support for Different Modalities (Required by: Interaction Designers, Hardware Developers, Software Developers)
Current HMIs already support different input and output modalities. While visual output is the main output modality, warning signals, tactile feedback and speech output is also used in current automobiles. Speech input is a newer feature that complements buttons and touchscreens as a further way to interact with the HMI. Since the future is likely to improve these modalities or even add further ones, a modeling language should support specifications for different modalities.

C16: Flexibility of Processes (Required by: General)
Industry processes are subject to continuous improvement. Also different vendors or suppliers use different development processes. A modeling language should therefore be flexible enough to be used with any process. It is important that the language puts no constraints on the development process. It would otherwise hinder innovations which would result in poor acceptance.

C17: Sufficient Abstraction of the Modeling Language (Required by: Hardware Developers, Software Developers, Testers)
A current problem of HMI languages is their concrete applicability. They are either very specialized (e.g. to support specific development processes or to be used as an exchange format for developer tools) or they are too generic (e.g. to describe abstract user interfaces (AUI). For a language to be usable in an industrial development process, it has to describe dynamic and static properties of a user interface on different abstraction levels without imposing unnecessary constraints on the development process.

C18: Referencing of Information (Required by: Interaction Designers)
Redundant information in a specification decreases maintainability and increases the chance for contradictions. Information should therefore not be repeated, but instead referenced. For example, instead of defining the position of a widget that appears on a number of screens, the position could be put into a template that serves as the base of these screens.

5.2 Application of the Criteria and Evaluating Existing Approaches

The 18 criteria were applied to a number of current available UIDLs, including those with a focus on the automotive industry as well as domain-independent ones.

Four UIDLs developed by the automotive industry (Infotainment Markup Language (IML) [15], OEM XML [14], AbstractHMI [16] and ICUC XML Daimler

[2]) and seven general UIDLs (e.g., Dialog and Interface Specification Language (DISL) [13] and USer Interface eXtensible Markup Language (UsiXML) [4]) were analyzed. The modeling languages were analyzed using the 18 criteria. A summary of the results are shown in Fig. 1. Generally, OEM-XML met the most criteria (9 of 18), followed by ICUC and UsiXML. However, this means that the most suitable language only met half of the criteria required by the industry.

None of the languages supported C1, C7, C8 or C9. While the automotive languages matched more criteria than the general ones, they still did not provide enough features to be used in all stages of the actual development. It was therefore concluded that a new language is required by the industry that matches all 18 requirements.

	C1: Versioning	C2: Management of variants	C3: Definition of state machines	C4: Support for abstract screens	C5: Support for concrete screens	C6: Annotations	C7: Definition of informal requirements	C8: Metadata for requirements	C9: Traceability for requirements	C10: Referencing external data	C11: Open, standardized and free modeling language	C12: Simple integration with tools	C13: Support for iterative approach	C14: Support for prototyping	C15: Support for differetnt modalities	C16: Flexibility of processes	C17: Sufficient abstraction of the modeling language	C18: Referencing of information	Sum
IML					X					X			X		X	X		X	6
OEM-XML		X	X		X					X			X	X	X	X		X	9
ICUC			X		X					X			X	X		X		X	7
AbstractHMI			X		X					X			X			X		X	6
Teresa-XML				X								X							2
UIML					X					X	X				X	X		X	6
useGUI					X						X		X	X		X		X	6
DISL			X	X															2
UsiXML				X	X					X	X		X		X	X			7
XIML				X	X	X				X						X		X	6
SEESCOA XML				X						X						X			3
Sum	0	1	4	5	8	1	0	0	0	8	3	1	6	3	4	9	0	7	

Fig. 1. Results of the criteria application

6 Summary and Outlook

This paper presented (parts of) a large-scale analysis performed on automotive HMI development processes in the context of the project automotiveHMI. The analysis led to the identification of representative roles and requirements (criteria) which are relevant for the definition of a HMI modeling language in the automotive industry. After presenting the criteria, it was discussed how today's domain-specific as well as general-purpose UIDLs do not match these criteria, which led to the need for a new, domain-specific language that could become an industry standard for the (German) automotive industry. The project automotiveHMI is currently working on the realization of this domain-specific language.

Acknowledgements. The research described in this paper was conducted within the project automotiveHMI. automotiveHMI is funded by the German Federal Ministry of Economics and Technology under grant number 01MS11007.

References

1. Danneberg, J., Burgard, J.: A comprehensive study on innovation in the automotive industry, http://www.oliverwyman.com/pdf_files/CarInnovation2015_engl.pdf
2. Huebner, M., Gruell, I.: ICUC-XML Format. Format Specification Revision 14. Elektrobit (2007)
3. Hussmann, H., Meixner, G., Zuehlke, D. (eds.): Model-Driven Development of Advanced User Interfaces. SCI, vol. 340. Springer, Heidelberg (2011)
4. Vanderdonckt, J., Limbourg, Q., Michotte, B.: USIXML: A User Interface Description Language for Specifying Multimodal User Interfaces. In: Proc. of the W3C Workshop on Multimodal Interaction, Sophia Antipolis, France (2004)
5. Puerta, A., Eisenstein, J.: XIML: A Universal Language for User Interfaces. RedWhale Software, http://www.ximl.org/pages/docs.asp
6. Souchon, N., Vanderdonckt, J.: A Review of XML-Compliant User Interface Description Languages. In: Jorge, J.A., Jardim Nunes, N., Falcão e Cunha, J. (eds.) DSV-IS 2003. LNCS, vol. 2844, pp. 377–391. Springer, Heidelberg (2003)
7. Guerrero García, J., González Calleros, J., Vanderdonckt, J.: A Theoretical Survey of User Interface Description Languages: Preliminary Results. In: Proc. of Joint 4th Latin American Conference on Human-Computer Interaction, Los Alamitos, USA (2009)
8. Meixner, G., Paternó, F., Vanderdonckt, J.: Past, Present, and Future of Model-Based User Interface Development. i-com 10(3), 2–11 (2011)
9. Calvary, G., Coutaz, J., Thevenin, D., Limbourg, Q., Bouillon, L., Vanderdonckt, J.: A Unifying Reference Framework for Multi-Target User Interfaces. Interacting with Computer 15(3), 289–308 (2003)
10. Kuemmerling, M., Meixner, G.: Model-Based User Interface Development in the Automotive Industry. In: Proc. of the 3rd International Workshop on Multimodal Interfaces for Automotive Applications, Palo Alto, USA, pp. 41–44 (2010)
11. Ghosh, D.: DSL for the Uninitiated. Communications of the ACM 54(7), 44–50 (2011)
12. Hess, S., Gross, A., Maier, A., Orfgen, M., Meixner, G.: Standardizing Model-Based IVI Development in the German Automotive Industry. In: Proc. of the 4th International Conference on Automotive User Interfaces and Interactive Vehicular Applications, Portsmouth, USA, pp. 59–66 (2012)
13. Bleul, S., Schaefer, R., Mueller, W.: Multimodal Dialog Description for Mobile Devices. In: Proc. of the Workshop on XML-based User Interface Description Languages, Gallipoli, Italy (2004)
14. Brunhorn, J.: XML-Sprache zur Beschreibung von HMIs für Infotainmentsysteme und Kombiinstrumente. Language Specification 1.0. OEM Arbeitskreis HMI Methodik (2007)
15. Jud, A.: Präzise Syntaxdefinition einer Modellierungstechnik für Infotainment-Systeme. Master-Thesis, Technische Universität Berlin (2007)
16. Reich, B.: Abstrakte Beschreibung automobiler HMI-Systeme und deren Erweiterung für neue Dienste. Master-Thesis, Universität Ulm (2008)

An Empirical Study on Immersive Prototyping Dimensions*

Samuel Moreira[1], Rui José[2,3], and José Creissac Campos[1,4]

[1] Departamento de Informática/Universidade do Minho
[2] Departamento de Sistemas de Informação/Universidade do Minho
[3] Centro Algoritmi
[4] HASLab / INESC TEC

pg17627@alunos.uminho.pt, rui@dsi.uminho.pt, jose.campos@di.uminho.pt

Abstract. Many aspects of the human experience of ubiquitous computing in built environments must be explored in the context of the target environment. However, delaying evaluation until a version of the system can be deployed can make redesign too costly. Prototypes have the potential to solve this problem by enabling evaluation before actual deployment. This paper presents a study of the design space of immersive prototyping for ubiquitous computing. It provides a framework to guide the alignment between specific evaluation goals and specific prototype properties. The goal is to understand the potential added-value of 3D simulation as a prototyping tool in the development process of ubiquitous computing environments.

Keywords: 3D environments, prototyping, ubiquitous computing.

1 Introduction

Ubiquitous computing technologies provide exciting new opportunities for enhancing physical spaces to support the needs and activities of people within them. However, many aspects of the human experience of ubiquitous computing in built environments can only be explored in the context of the target environment. In evaluating these systems it is not only necessary to explore conventional properties of usability, but also properties of the environment that contribute to the experience of its users. Fielding such systems for testing purposes, however, is in many cases not feasible because of the potential disruption to the target environment. Consider, for example, an emergency evacuation scenario. Additionally, developing the system to a deployable state can imply commitment to design decisions that will be expensive to reverse. Nevertheless, the potential impact of a system in user practice, justifies that its design should be explored as early as possible [18]. It should be possible to use prototypes to explore the

* This work is funded by the ERDF through Programme COMPETE and by the Portuguese Government through FCT - Foundation for Science and Technology, project ref. FCOMP-01-0124-FEDER-015095.

M. Kurosu (Ed.): Human-Computer Interaction, Part I, HCII 2013, LNCS 8004, pp. 421–430, 2013.

consequences that different design decisions might have, while promoting the identification of new solutions.

Simulated 3D environments offer an interesting solution to immersive prototyping [5,12,22,20]. 3D Application Servers and game engines provide a fast track to developing virtual worlds that replicate the type of environments that needs to be prototyped. The use of these 3D Application Servers as the basis for a immersive prototyping framework enables agile development of simulations of the ubiquitous environment. However, to be successful, immersive prototyping requires a thorough alignment with the key properties of the target environment, both at the technical and social level, and a strong focus on the specific evaluation goals and they can be met while considering the specific limitations of immersive prototyping. With this in mind, we have carried out a study of the design space of immersive prototyping based on 3D simulation, in order to define a framework to guide the alignment between specific evaluation goals and particular prototype properties.

A similar study was carried out by Ostkamp et al. [17]. In it the authors were interested in studies about public displays. They introduced the AR-Multipleye, a system that visually highlights items on a personal device that is pointed towards a public display. They, additionally, carried out an evaluation of the existing approaches according to a set of criteria to classify highlight methods for public displays.

In our case, the key issue that was addressed is "what are the relevant dimensions that prototypes should exhibit to better support evaluation of the envisaged design?". The paper presents the two groups of characteristics identified as a result of this work. The first relates to the immersive prototyping ubiquitous systems, and includes topics such as Fidelity of immersion, Embodied interaction support or Hybrid prototyping. The second addresses the different perspectives on evaluation (from evaluation centered on the system and its functional qualities, to evaluation centered on the user's experience of the system), and the methods to gather feedback about user experience. A discussion on how the framework was applied to the development of a prototype used to aid the design of a concrete ubiquitous environment ends the paper.

2 Methodology

In order to establish the relevant analysis dimensions we performed a review of the research literature on the topic of ubiquitous computing immersive prototyping. Most of the papers are related to the rapid development and evaluation of ubiquitous systems in the early stages of the development life cycle. Examples include 3DSim [12], TATUS [15], the work of O'Neill et al. [16], UBIWISE [1], the work of Reynolds [19] or APEX [20,21]. Others papers, as UbiWorld [5] and the work of Pushpendra et al. [22], are focused in creating immersive environments for users, and testing their applications, using CAVEs and other immersive technologies. VARU [6], CityCompiler [11], UbiREAL [14], and the work of Brandherm et al.[2], focus their study in hybrid prototyping approaches, integrating services (e.g. Internet services) and devices in their ubiquitous systems. A few papers are more concerned with the analysis of user behavior when confronted with different situations (this is the case of Siafu [10] and the work of Maly et al. [9]), while Topiary [7] and the work of Li et al. [8] are more concerned with the context awareness behavior of ubiquitous applications.

The papers were analyzed in search of codes for two groups of characteristics of ubiquitous computing that we initially defined as: (1) Properties of the simulation; and (2) Requirements for evaluation and evaluation objectives.

Open Coding [23] was used to analyze the contents of the papers. Each paper was read in order to identify phrases or paragraphs containing references to the two groups of characteristics of ubiquitous computing aforementioned. A code was assigned to each piece of text identified. At this stage, the goal was to generate as many codes as possible without much consideration of how they related with each other. The MAXQDA10 tool was used to aid the open coding process. A total of 33 different codes were identified: 20 in the first group, and 13 in the second. The number of code instances identified was 220.

An affinity diagram was then created to synthesize the data. The goal here was to find the key dimensions, based on the natural relationships between codes. In a brainstorming session we grouped similar properties into logical groups. As we analyzed more codes, we discussed whether to place each of them in one of the existing groups, as also the possibility of creating more groups or the creating of subgroups.

3 Dimensions

This section presents the results of the study. A total of eleven main dimensions was identified. Seven in the first group of characteristics (Prototyping) and four in the second (Evaluation). Two of the dimensions in the latter group are further divided in sub-dimensions, creating a total of thirteen. For each group we present the identified dimensions and provide illustrative examples from the literature.

3.1 Prototyping

The first group characterizes the relevant features of the immersive prototyping of ubiquitous systems. The seven dimensions are described below.

Fidelity of immersion can be described as the degree to which a virtual environment represent (in terms of appearance, sound, etc.) the real world, making the user feel immersed in the virtual environment. Techniques to immerse users within virtual environments go from the use of head-mounted displays to the use of CAVEs [3] (see, for example [22,5]), or other CAVE-derived techniques as presented in [5], the ImmersaDesk and the Infinity Wall [4]. An example of immersion is the case of immersive video inside a CAVE. This approach eases the evaluation and prototyping of mobile applications before its actual deployment, providing a high fidelity recreation of a user's experience [22].

3D modeling and simulation is a means to build virtual environments and/or devices. This is typically achieved through the use of game engines or 3D application servers. A key factor is to make the virtual environment realistic. It should be noted however, that creating a realistic simulation extends beyond its physical and graphical qualities. For example, [1] points out that creating a realistic simulated wireless device, implies being realistic in terms of connection latency, bandwidth, screen size, and battery life. According to [16] the use of game engine allows for a greater flexibility in the type of sensors that are used. Half-Life, Unreal, and Quake are the most used game engines. In [20] the OpenSimulator 3D application server is used. According to the author one advantage of using a 3D application server is to enable the remote and simultaneous connection of many users over the internet.

Embodied interaction support refers to the ability of the simulation to enable the reproduction of interactions that we use every day in the real world. Embodied interaction can be achieved through the use of interactions technologies such as motion tracking and gesture, or speech recognition. Users may, for example, interact with the virtual environment through the use of 3D gestures to point to devices and room objects [12], allowing for a more interactive and immersive experience. In [11] a scenario is built where a camera captures the size and location of human shadows and, based on that, triggers appropriate events (e.g. displaying a video).

Controlled Environment Manipulation. Ubiquitous systems' simulation can be molded to best serve the objectives of the designers and developers. We can define the behavior of the system and its objects, by programming them, by the use of models, or we can manually control/influence this behavior. The most common method, for expressing behavior is programming it through the use of scripts [1,20]. Another approach to attach behavior and functionalities to the system and its objects, is through the use of models [20,16]. Wizard of OZ can also be used to give behavior to the system [8] . The need to use people to realize the tests, and the fact that these tests are never realized in the exact same circumstances, are problems associated with the technique [22].

Context driven behavior happens when the system/prototype is able to capture the state of the environment and its relevant data, adjusting its behavior to that data. (e.g., a door opens, when a user gets close to it). This feature is present in many systems [7,15,5,16,1]. Approaches to gather context data include the use of sensors or other devices such as GPS systems [8], systems with information about networks, or specialized tools to extract information from the virtual environment [12,9]. Sensors, in particular, are very common in ubiquitous systems. According to [19], sensors can be classified as active or passive, i.e., they can detect values internally or from the virtual environment, respectively. Sensors can act as listeners for the system, enabling it to react to the environment [12] and store relevant sensor information for later use [22].

Multi-user Support. Enabling multiple users to explore the ubiquitous system allows for faster testing and assessment of the behavior of the system. This can be achieved by supporting the connection of multiple real users, or supporting the use of bots in the system. Supporting multiple real users enables evaluation of their behavior and their interactions in the system, but also evaluation of the system's behavior. In [20,16,15], this is an important dimension to integrate in the development of the ubiquitous system. Supporting the use of bots (i.e. AI expert software systems), enables the configuration of environments featuring multiple user using a limited numbers of real users, or to systematically explore an environment (e.g. to automatically identify unwanted behaviors) [16,15].

Hybrid prototyping takes advantage of a combination of simulated and real components to generate a mixed reality which can be used to assess the envisaged system. In [11], a mix of physical miniature prototyping and virtual prototyping is used. Two basic types of hybrid prototyping were found: one focusing on devices, another on services. Virtual devices enable testing specific systems (e.g., smartphones or sensors), and their integration in the ubiquitous environment, without actual physical deployment. In [1], images of the device's physical interface are used to create the virtual device. The embedding of sensors in virtual devices is addressed in [2]. A emulation framework allowing simulated hardware devices to interact with emulated software is described in [19]. Hybrid prototyping of services provides higher realism, accuracy and precision, since it can use real services. The most common cases are the integration of internet services, or the use of Bluetooth or similar protocols to integrate real devices [20,1]. Many systems tend to create their own communication components, using protocols such as TCP-IP or UPnP [12], or resorting to proxies [15], while other systems integrate existing network simulators into their framework [19] (thus reducing cost while providing users and developers an enhanced experience).

3.2 Evaluation

Evaluation is a key motivation in the immersive prototyping of a system. This second group of dimensions characterizes the different perspectives on ubiquitous systems evaluation. Two types of interests could be identified. Evaluation focused on the system and its developers, and evaluation focused on the users. Additionally, codes related to how to conduct experiments and collect data were also found.

System-centric evaluation is focused on evaluating the prototypes and the supporting frameworks, and is divided in two sub-dimensions.

Developer-Centric Evaluation. This evaluation is mainly concerned with knowing how easy it is for developers to develop accurate ubiquitous environments. This can be accomplished by collecting their feedback while performing a predefined prototyping task [16,20,7]. Other possibility is to use developers as test users, in order to determine if they can identify problems in ubiquitous environment.

Environments-Centric Evaluation. Immersive prototypes have the goal of creating virtual environments that are accurate enough replicas of real environments. These virtual environments must have the same properties that the real environments have, in order to give to the users a more realistic experience. To assess these environments, users that regularly explore the real environment should supply feedback to the developers, for them to know if the environment is accurate enough. At a more fundamental level, environments also need to be tested and evaluated regarding how the models react to user interactions or to context changes, in order to check if the prototype is behaving correctly.

User-centric evaluation focuses on how the users react to the ubiquitous system. Evaluating the users' behavior and their feelings when interacting with it, or evaluating if they can interact with the system efficiently and perform the tasks they were assigned.

Evaluating User Experience. User experience can be characterized by how well a person feels, when she interacts with the system. Through user experience evaluation, developers can know if the system that they are building will create a positive impact in people's lives. User experience evaluation techniques are widely used in many of the studies that were analyzed. Particularly in [7,20,9], a big importance is given to analyzing and comparing user experience and behavior, allowing redesign of the systems depending on the users' feedback.

Evaluating Usability. Usability is also a key goal on the process of developing ubiquitous systems. The more common approach to usability testing is through observation and recording users while they perform tasks. Others usability test methodologies are described in [13]. Maly et al. [9] built a framework for testing the usability of applications in virtual environments. The method consists in conducting specific tasks to evaluate usability. The approach builds on usability testing methodologies for desktop applications, combined with the evaluation of user behavior in ubiquitous environments.

Controlled experiments enable carrying out interaction tests under varied environment settings and context changes. A possibility is to replicate the exact same experiment with different users. All experiments will have the same system configurations, e.g., the events generated by sensors or the way the system adapts to context changes must be the same for any user that interacts with the ubiquitous system. Increasingly, ubiquitous systems are being developed to function and adapt to different scenarios [12,5,20]. A possibility, to assess what can happen when the system is deployed in different scenarios is to change one or several ambient settings in each experiment. These manipulations can go from re-positioning objects and avatars, to the manipulation of actuators and devices

Table 1. Relation between each evaluation dimension and each prototyping dimension

	Developer evaluation	Environments evaluation	Evaluating user experience	Evaluating usability
Fidelity of immersion	2	3	3	2
3D modeling and simulation	2	2	2	2
Embodied interaction support	2	1	3	3
Controlled env. manipulation	3	2	1	1
Context driven behavior	3	3	2	2
Multi-user support	2	2	1	1
Hybrid device prototyping	2	2	2	2
Controlled experiments	3	3	1	1

such as, lights, temperatures or displays [12,20,14]. The more common examples were the manipulation of lights and temperatures. In [12], the authors evaluate the suitability of the Philips iPronto device to new environments and their adaptability to different interactions.

Data collection is an increasing concern in the evaluation of ubiquitous systems. Developers can gather user feedback, either by allowing the user to freely explore virtual environments, or by making him or she follow or perform a list of tasks and storyboards [5]. Video recording or user observation are examples of methods to gather data about user behavior/performance, while performing tasks. The use of sensors to collect user performance, and save this data in log files, is another method that can be used. Conducting a series of interviews with users, or using surveys, are methods used to collect user feedback after the completion of the experiment.

3.3 Discussion

The relationships between the four evaluation dimensions and the dimensions related to the development of ubiquitous systems is presented in Table 1. The table should be read having in consideration that the primary point of analysis are the several types of evaluation. Evaluation dimension are assessed against each prototyping dimension, and also to the controlled experiments dimension. With this we want to highlight which dimensions are more critical for each evaluation dimension. The scale of values chosen to measure the relationship was: (1) - little influential, (2) - influential, and (3) - very influential. The values in Table 1 are derived from the analysis of the papers. They reflect the percentage of codes collected for each of the evaluation dimensions, when compared with the percentage of codes for each of the prototyping dimensions in the papers.

From Table 1 several conclusions can be reached. Developer-centric evaluation is more concerned with how to give behavior to the system, and how it reacts to change (be it context changes or user interactions). The ability to support multiple users with the purpose of realizing experiments is also an influential aspect of developer centric evaluation. Nevertheless, the other dimensions are also influential in this type of evaluation. Regarding the assessment of environments, the more realistic is the environment the better is the ability to evaluate the envisaged design. The realization of controlled experiments in the virtual environment, and how ubiquitous applications or smart objects react to changes are also among the most influential dimensions to assess environments. Allowing multiple users to interact with the environment, and supporting the use of virtual/real devices/services are the remaining influential dimensions in environment evaluation. For the user to have a good user experience, he should feel able to use most of the interactions that he usually uses in reality. The environment should be as realistic as possible, so that the user feels as embedded as possible in the environment. Regarding usability, the way users interact with the system and how much they feel immersed in the virtual environment are the more important dimensions to make user more connected with the environment, thus providing them a better way to accomplish their tasks. The possibility of interaction with virtual or real devices/services, and the way the ubiquitous system reacts to the user, are other influential dimensions to usability evaluation.

4 Case Study

The motivation to carry out the study described above appeared in the context of using immersive protoyping to support the design of a specific ubiquitous systems. The bar of a art gallery in Guimarães, Portugal has been equipped with public displays featuring the Instant Places system[1]. By default, users can interact with the system via their smartphones. The goal now is to enrich the system with new interaction capabilities. To study the viability of different alternatives prototypes will be developed in the APEX framework. The developers of the APEX frameworks, and the designers and developers of Instant Places, felt the need to identify what were the relevant prototyping dimensions that should be considered, and how they related to specific evaluation goals.

Considering that the main goal of the prototype to be developed is evaluating a number of new interaction techniques, and their influence the experience of being in the bar, the most relevant dimensions are: the Fidelity of immersion and support for embodied interaction. However, other features like Context driven behavior and Hybrid prototyping should also be considered as relevant. Indeed Hybrid prototyping is also quite relevant since the goal is to integrate Instant Places into the prototype, adding only the new interactions techniques. In the current case, it was decided to experiment with a table top interface. Hence, a prototype of the space was built (see Figure 1) that integrates virtual screen connected to the Instant Places service. Users are able to interact with the service both through their physical smartphones, or through a virtual table top interface in the simulated environment. The prototype was tested with users and while, due to space constraints it is not possible to discuss the results herein, they indicate that the table top interface was found useful.

[1] `http://www.instantplaces.org/` (Accessed: 29/1/2013)

Fig. 1. The art gallery prototype

5 Conclusions

This paper has presented a set of dimensions that address the immersive prototyping of ubicomp systems and their evaluation. Starting from a review of the sate of the art the relevant dimensions were identified. They characterize both the features that can be used to build immersive prototypes of ubiquitous environments, and the types of evaluation that can be carried out. By establishing a relation between these two groups, it becomes easier to decide which type of prototype to use given specific evaluation needs. Identifying the dimensions that should be the focus of a prototyping exercise provides two main advantages: it helps both reduce the costs of the process, and it helps focus the prototype on those features that will provide better results.

The approach is being used in a concrete example, where a public space has been equipped with ubicomp technology. In order to explore the impact of introducing new technology in the environment (e.g. tabletop interfaces) an immersive prototype has been developed. We are currently comparing the experience of using the prototype with the experience of being in the actual space.

References

1. Barton, J.J., Vijayaraghavan, V.: UBIWISE, A Ubiquitous Wireless Infrastructure Simulation Environment. Technical Report HPL-2002-303, HP Laboratories, Palo Alto (October 2002)
2. Brandherm, B., Ullrich, S., Prendinger, H.: Simulation framework in second life with evaluation functionality for sensor-based systems. In: UbiComp 2008 Workshop W2 – Ubiquitous Systems Evaluation, USE 2008 (2008)
3. Cruz-Neira, C., Sandin, D.J., DeFanti, T.A.: Surround-screen projection-based virtual reality: the design and implementation of the cave. In: SIGGRAPH 1993, pp. 135–142. ACM (1993)
4. Czernuszenko, M., Pape, D., Sandin, D., DeFanti, T., Dawe, G.L., Brown, M.D.: The immersadesk and infinity wall projection-based virtual reality displays. SIGGRAPH Comput. Graph. 31(2), 46–49 (1997)

5. Disz, T., Papka, M.E., Stevens, R.: Ubiworld: An environment integrating virtual reality, supercomputing, and design. In: Heterogeneous Computing Workshop, pp. 46–57 (1997)
6. Irawati, S., Ahn, S., Kim, J., Ko, H.: VARU Framework: Enabling Rapid Prototyping of VR, AR and Ubiquitous Applications. In: Virtual Reality Conference, VR 2008, pp. 201–208. IEEE (2008)
7. Li, Y., Hong, J.I., Landay, J.A.: Topiary: a tool for prototyping location-enhanced applications. In: UIST 2004, pp. 217–226. ACM (2004)
8. Li, Y., Landay, J.A.: Rapid prototyping tools for context-aware applications. In: CHI 2005 workshop – The Future of User Interface Design Tools (2005)
9. Maly, I., Curin, J., Slavik, P., Kleindienst, J.: Framework for visual analysis of user behaviour in ambient intelligence environment. In: Ambient Intelligence, pp. 85–107. InTech (2010)
10. Martin, M., Nurmi, P.: A generic large scale simulator for ubiquitous computing. In: Mobile and Ubiquitous Systems, pp. 1–3. IEEE Computer Society (2006)
11. Nakanishi, Y.: Virtual prototyping using miniature model and visualization for interactive public displays. In: Proceedings of the Designing Interactive Systems Conference, pp. 458–467. ACM (2012)
12. Nazari Shirehjini, A.A., Klar, F.: 3DSim: rapid prototyping ambient intelligence. In: Proc. Joint Conference on Smart Objects and Ambient Intelligence, pp. 303–307. ACM (2005)
13. Nielsen, J.: Usability Engineering. Morgan Kaufmann Publishers Inc., San Francisco (1993)
14. Nishikawa, H., Yamamoto, S., Tamai, M., Nishigaki, K., Kitani, T., Shibata, N., Yasumoto, K., Ito, M.: UbiREAL: Realistic Smartspace Simulator for Systematic Testing. In: Dourish, P., Friday, A. (eds.) UbiComp 2006. LNCS, vol. 4206, pp. 459–476. Springer, Heidelberg (2006)
15. O'Neill, E., Klepal, M., Lewis, D., O'Donnell, T., O'Sullivan, D., Pesch, D.: A testbed for evaluating human interaction with ubiquitous computing environments. In: First International Conference on Testbeds and Research Infrastructures for the DEvelopment of NeTworks and COMmunities, pp. 60–69. IEEE Computer Society (2005)
16. O'Neill, E., Lewis, D., Conlan, O.: A simulation-based approach to highly iterative prototyping of ubiquitous computing systems. In: 2nd International Conference on Simulation Tools and Techniques, pp. 56:1–56:10. ICST (2009)
17. Ostkamp, M., Bauer, G., Kray, C.: Visual highlighting on public displays. In: 2012 International Symposium on Pervasive Displays, pp. 2:1–2:6. ACM (2012)
18. Reilly, D., Dearman, D., Welsman-Dinelle, M., Inkpen, K.: Evaluating early prototypes in context: Trade-offs, challenges, and successes. IEEE Pervasive Computing 4(4), 42–50 (2005)
19. Reynolds, V., Cahill, V., Senart, A.: Requirements for an ubiquitous computing simulation and emulation environment. In: InterSense 2006. ACM (2006)
20. Silva, J.L., Ribeiro, Ó.R., Fernandes, J.M., Campos, J.C., Harrison, M.D.: The APEX framework: Prototyping of ubiquitous environments based on petri nets. In: Forbrig, P. (ed.) HCSE 2010. LNCS, vol. 6409, pp. 6–21. Springer, Heidelberg (2010)
21. Silva, J.L., Campos, J.C., Harrison, M.D.: Formal analysis of ubiquitous computing environments through the apex framework. In: ACM Symposium on Engineering Interactive Computing Systems (EICS 2012), pp. 131–140. ACM (2012)
22. Singh, P., Ha, H.N., Olivier, P., Kray, C., Kuang, Z., Guo, A.W., Blythe, P., James, P.: Rapid prototyping and evaluation of intelligent environments using immersive video. In: MODIE Workshop at Mobile HCI 2006, September 12-15 (2006)
23. Strauss, A.L., Corbin, J.M.: Basics of Qualitative Research: Techniques and Procedures for developing Grounded Theory. Sage Publications Inc. (1998)

From Multicultural Agents to Culture-Aware Robots

Matthias Rehm

Faculty of Engineering and Science
Aalborg University
9200 Aalborg, Denmark
matthias@create.aau.dk

Abstract. In our work on developing multicultural agents we have primarily relied on the analysis of video recordings of multimodal face to face interactions between humans, where the videos have been collected in different cultures. This posed some questions concering the cultural biases of the analysis due to the cultural background of the annotators. For the development of culture-aware robots we have now adopted a strategy that takes this cultural bias into account as a feature of the development process by integrating the potential user groups from different cultures into this process. We exemplify this approach with a case study on affective body movements for a humanoid robot.

1 Introduction

In previous research we showed how a cross-cultural multimodal corpus of human face to face interactions can serve as empirical foundation for implementing multicultural agents (e.g. [13]). To this end, video recordings have been annotated in relation to a number of communicative phenomena like gestures, postures, proxemics, communication management, etc. Based on these annotations, statistical models have been derived and implemented in embodied conversational agents in order to simulate culture-specific communicative behavior in these agents. Although this was a successful approach, there have always been some discomforts about it due to the following reasons:

- Subjectivity of the annotation: Although there are measures that can be taken to ensure a certain degree of objectivity in the annotation of the video data (e.g. ensuring high inter-rater agreement by calculating kappa values, restricting free text annotations, training of annotators), manual annotations will always contain a certain degree of subjective interpretation of the phenomena that are under observation. This subjective interpretation may become a liability if the number of annotators is limited (which is often the case due to costs), meaning that single subjective interpretations get more weight in the models derived from the annotations.
- Cultural bias of the annotation: Our cultural background influences to a large degree how we behave in and how we interpret situations involving social

M. Kurosu (Ed.): Human-Computer Interaction, Part I, HCII 2013, LNCS 8004, pp. 431–440, 2013.

interactions. Thus, apart from being subjective, annotations of behavior will be (unconsciously) biased by the cultural background of the annotator because what they deem "normal" in social interactions will be structured by those unconscious shared heuristics from the cultural group they belong to.
- Cultural bias of the design and the implementation of the agents: The same unconscious cultural bias might also influence the design and implementation of the agents. Which kinds of gestures look "normal" and how gestures are performed have for instance been shown to vary between cultures, and thus cultural heuristics are likely to influence how movements and behaviors of an agent are realized on the surface.

Meanwhile, we have moved to physical agents, i.e. robots. Here the difference between humans and robots is more apparent, due e.g. to limited expressive channels or reduced degrees of freedom. For instance the Nao platform which we are using has less joints in arms and legs then a human, making movements look different, independent on how careful movements have been designed.

Thus, we suggest a new methodological approach for modeling the behavior of robots and for making them culture-aware, which could also be of benefit for the use in multicultural agents. Instead of collecting data from human interactions, potential users of the system have to create the behavior themselves, allowing us to collect a cross-cultural database of behavioral parameters for the robotic system under development. This reduces subjective or cultural biases that were previously introduced. Instead, the cross-cultural database of behavioral parameters allows data-mining the statistical models that will drive the generation of communicative behavior in the robot based on informants that are immersed in the target culture.

In this paper, we are first looking at cultural influences on the developement and evaluation process (Section 2), before we propose our method of co-creation which is loosely based on ideas from classical participatory design in HCI (Section 3). Then we report on the results of our co-creation experiment for affective body movements (Section 4) before we discuss how this method might resolve some of the discomforts discussed above (Section 5). The paper ends with a short conclusion (Section 6).

2 Related Work

In recent years, culture has been identified as an important variable that influences not only the development of interactive systems, but more fundamentally also experimental work that often serves as an empirical basis for interactive systems like virtual agents or robotic companions. Henrich and colleagues [7] present a thought provoking analysis of experimental work in psychology covering an analysis of the top journals in Psychology over four years (2003–2007) that shows that general conclusions about human psychology are pre-dominantly based on a very specific sample which is only representative for small fraction of society. They called this the WEIRD sample for Western, Educated, Industrialized, Rich, and Democratic, and highlighted that 68% of all samples were from the US, and overall 96% from Western industrialzed societies, although WEIRD societies represent only 12% of the world population. To put it bluntly, current claims about general human psychology e.g. concerning cooperation, moral reasoning or visual perception, are based solely on Western university and college students, making these universal claims seem at least be very questionable.

Following this argument, Blanchard [1] examined research in the field of educational systems and analyzed contributions to the two main conference in the area (ITS and AIED) over the last decade (2002–2010) focusing on the origin of first authors as well as samples used in evaluations and shows that there is a similar WEIRD tendency to be found in this area of research.

Earlier, Elfenbein and Ambady [5] showed the importance of taking participants cultural background into account as one variable in experimental settings when they investigated in-group advantages for the production and recognition of emotional facial expressions. In earlier work, we have taken these suggestions into account for a cross-cultural examination of the interpretation of emotional facial expressions in virtual agents [8] that also showed an in-group effect concerning the designers' as well as the observers' cultural group. Moreover, we have presented an in-depth analysis of the challenges of developing multicultural agents focusing on the problem of implicit biases by the developers' and the users' cultural backgrounds [11].

3 Users as Co-creators

The method we are proposing here is inspired by "classical" HCI work on participatory design (e.g. [3]; [2]). This design paradigm claims that it is necessary to involve users early on in the development process to ensure an optimal solution in terms of usability and features of a product. The PD process allows potential users (as well as stakeholders) bringing their perspective into the development process. In recent work we have shown that especially in cross-cultural developments it is an absolute requirement to involve the target group and let them become co-designers of the envisioned system [14].

Here we report on our adoption of the approach for the development of culture-aware robots. In our case study, we focus on affective body movements for humanoid robots. Instead of analyzing culture-specific human face to face interactions like we did in previous work on culture aware agents, we allow users to design affective body movements for the robots directly by manipulating a set of well defined movement parameters. Result of this co-creation experiment is a cross-cultural data base that can be used to derive a probabilistic model to drive the behavior of the robot.

3.1 Affective Body Movements in Humanoid Robots

A particular challenge with robots is their restricted possibilities regarding expressive behaviors, which convey important information in human interactions. In embodied conversational agents for instance, facial expressions are prominent means for conveying affective information (e.g. [15]). But most humanoid robots so far are extremely limited in terms of facial expressions. In our case study, we worked with the Nao, a humanoid robot that allows no facial movements. Thus, affective information can best be displayed by bodily movements or robot specific means like sound or light. One set of parameters that is repeatedly mentioned in related work on affective body movements for robots is based on Laban's effort and shape dimensions [9]. Two recent examples highlight this use of Laban's movement analysis. Masuda and Kato [10] show that observers are able to distinguish between four different emotions when a basic movement is modified on the basis of Laban's parameters. Takahashi and colleagues [16] report on the design of emotional body movements based on Laban's parameters for a robot resembling a teddy bear. Despite its low expressivity (raising/lowering arms, moving arms to front of body, tilt/shake head), recognition rates for three emotions (joy, fear, sadness) are acceptable.

3.2 Experimental Design

The co-creation experiment is based on Laban's effort and shape dimensions [9]. Thus, by manipulating parameters on these dimensions, participants can create body movements that (from their perspective) exhibit affective information. The goal of this co-creation experiment is to locate the value ranges for the different dimensions that relate to the expression of emotions for several cultures. Following work by Gross and colleagues [6], the experiment concentrates on one single movement that has to be manipulated to make it affectively expressive.

So far the database consists of around 600 entries across 4 different cultures (Danish, German, Japanese, Greek) plus additional entries for other cultures that have not yet reached a critical mass. Participants demographics show that roughly a third are female (35%) and two thirds male (65%) with an age range from 20 to 45 (mean: 28.5, SD: 6.44). Most participants have no hands-on experience with robots.

Data collection was organized as a web experiment, where participants were randomly presented with the task of adding an affective connotation to a standard movement from the robot (knocking at a door). This follows the ideas presented by Gross and colleagues on isolating relevant parameters by focusing on a single movement [6]. Participants were presented with six tasks corresponding to the following six basic emotions [4]: anger, disgust, fear, happiness, sadness, and surprise. To create affective motions, participants could manipulate the Laban parameters weight, time, and space. Because the parameter names time, weight and space have been shown in a pilot test to be not readily understandable by participants, they were changed to speed, power and path for the experiment, where speed (time) denotes how fast the movement is performed, power (weight) denotes how much strength is put into the movement, and path (space) denotes if the motion is direct or indirect.

Figure 1 gives an impression of the web interface. Each parameter could be changed on a three point scale: speed (slow to fast), power (weak to strong), path (direct to indirect). For each movement, participants were then asked to

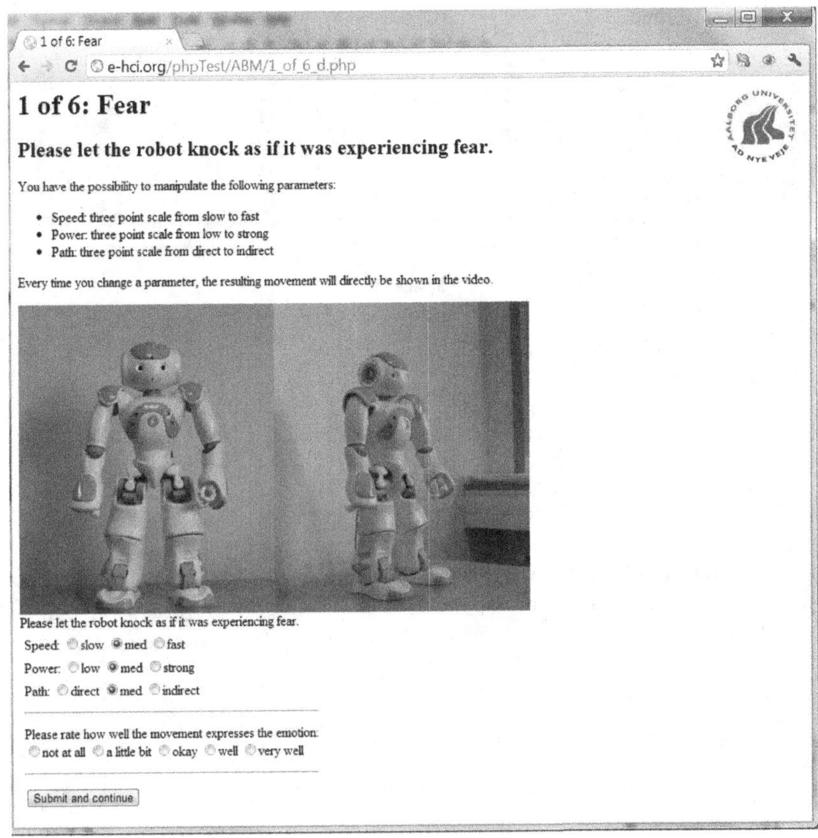

Fig. 1. Interface for the web experiment. Tasks are presented in random order.

indicate their satisfaction with the movement on a five point Likert scale. Each parameter modification is directly visible in the video window, which shows the robot's movement according to the current parameter values showing the robot from two perspectives (front view and side view) allowing for a better insight into how parameter modifications change the movement.

4 From Co-creation to Culture-Aware Behavior

Here we report on a comparison of German and Japanese data. More detailed results including Greek and Danish data can be found in [12].

Looking at the cross-cultural database, several significant differences are visible in the parameter values for some of the emotions. Figure 2 provides an overview of these differences for the two exemplary cultures German and Japanese. The results highlight that we find significant differences for all parameters, but not necessarily for all or even for the same emotions. For instance, speed of the gesture (time parameter) is important for happiness but not for any

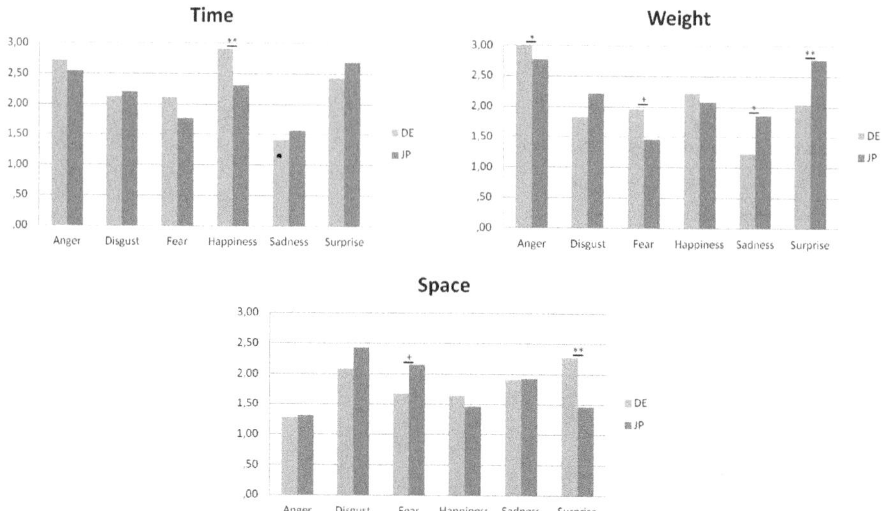

Fig. 2. Average values for time, weight and space parameter for the six emotions across two exemplary cultures (German, Japanese). Significance levels: +: p<0.1; *: p<0.05; **: p<0.01.

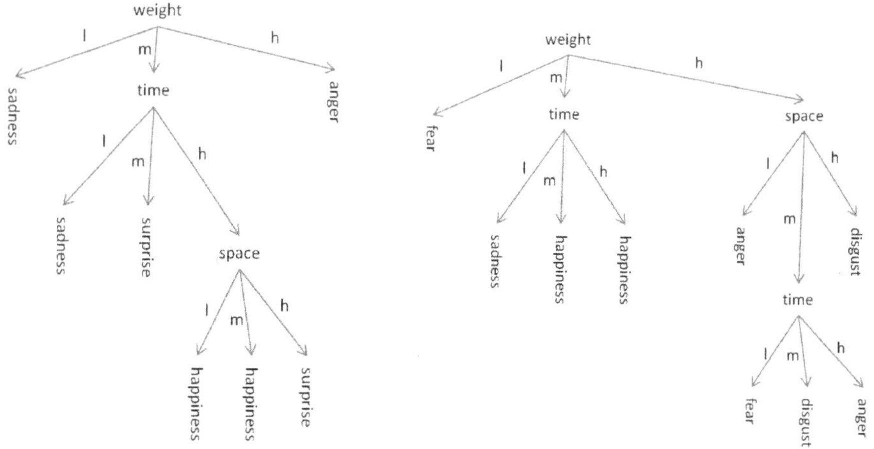

Fig. 3. Decisions trees (J48 pruned) for the two example cultures German and Japanese

of the other emotions, while the power of a gesture (weight parameter) effects the connotation of anger, fear, sadness, and suprise.

Data mining techniques are employed on the cross-cultural database collected by the web experiment. Decision trees allow for deciding for the relative importance of the different parameters in relation to the emotional content of the movement. Coming back to Figure 2 we see that by the significance of the differences between the cultures that the weight put into the movement seems to

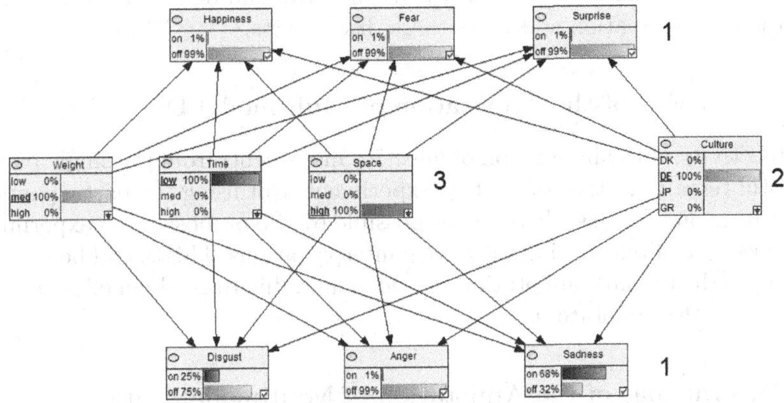

Fig. 4. Bayesian network modeling the relation between emotions (1), cultural background (2), and Laban parameters (3)

be differentiating the impression of fear as well as sadness. Figure 3 shows the two decision trees (J48) calculated on the German and Japanese data. What is apparent from the figure is that weight indeed is an important feature being at the root of both trees. Moreover, a cultural difference in attributing emotional connotation to a movement is apparent from the culture-specific decision trees. Low weight is attributed to sadness for the German sample independent of the values of the other parameters, whereas it is attributed to fear for the Japanese sample, again indepedent of the values of the other two parameters. Several other differences as well as similarties can be seen by comparing the two trees.

Calculating the decision trees allows for analyzing the relative importance of feature value combinations for the attribution of emotions to movements. Based on this information, a Bayesian network is build up (see Figure 4), which allows for reflecting the unreliability and ambiguity that is a trademark of phenomena like culture and emotions. It is used for generating movement patterns (Figure 4, 3.) based on the input information concerning the cultural background of the user (Figure 4, 2.) and the emotion that is to be conveyed by the body movement (Figure 4, 1.).

This allows us now to generate culture-specific affective body movements for the robot grounded in the unconscious heuristics of members of the respective cultures about affective body movements on the one hand but also of suitable body movements for robots (as compared to humans) on the other hand. Next step is to test the result with observers from the corresponding cultures.

5 Discussion

The motivation for exploring the the co-creation method were some discomforts we highlighted in the introduction regarding the empirical basis of our behavior models. In this section, we revisit these discomforts and discuss to what extent the method of co-creation addresses these discomforts.

5.1 Subjectivity of the Annotation of Multimodal Data

The subjectivity of the impression of affective movements from the single participant's still remains in the co-creation experiment. But using the participants as as co-creators on a large scale becomes possible by the proposed web experiment should take care of relativizing subjective interpretations. This would be difficult to achieve with standard annotations of video data due to the high effort needed on the side of the annotators.

5.2 Cultural Bias of the Annotation of Multimodal Data

In the co-creation experiment, this cultural bias was explicitely turned into a feature of the data collection by establishing a cross-cultural data base of movement parameters. Thus, instead of presenting a problem for the data analysis, the data collection is designed to be based on cultural bias allowing for exploring this effect for the interpretation of affective body movements. Compared to the annotation of cross-cultural video data, two layers of complexity are removed, because in case of the video data, there will be cultural bias in creating the videos (which is the target of the analysis) and there will be cultural bias in analyzing the videos by the annotators (which can be seen as unwanted noise).

5.3 Cultural Bias for the Design and the Implementation of Agents

Again by the method of co-creation, this cultural bias is turned into a feature of the development process, allowing for creating and comparing the culture-specific relevance of different movement parameters for the emotional connotation of movements. Thus, what the participants with a given cultural background deem as "normal" for executing an emotional gesture will be captured in the co-creation process and is generalized by the calculated models for movement generation.

Summing up, we can state that the approach presented in this paper has proven to be a promising direction for developing culture-aware robots by taking cultural biases of the intended user groups into account through a participatory development process.

6 Conclusion

In this paper we presented an approach that allows us to tackle the challenge of implicit cultural biases in the development of culture aware technology exemplified by affective body movements for humanoid robots. We claim that it is necessary to make these cultural biases explicit when developing multicultural applications and take them into account on several levels during the development process. Here we presented a co-creation experiment that allowed for collecting a cross-cultural database of movement parameters serving as a basis for deriving culture-specific behaviors for the robot. Future work includes validating the resulting behavior, again taking culture into account, this time as an experimental variable.

Acknowledgements. Special thanks go to Prof. Yukiko Nakano (Seikei University, Japan), Prof. Tomoko Koda (Osaka Institute of Technology, Japan), PD Dr. Katharina Rohlfing (Center of Excellence for Cognitive Interaction Technology, Germany), Amaryllis Raouzaiou (National Technical University of Athens, Greece), and Markus Häring (Augsburg University, Germany) for their recruiting efforts for the case study described in this paper.

References

1. Blanchard, E.: On the WEIRD Nature of ITS/AIED Conferences: A 10 Year Longitudinal Study Analyzing Potential Cultural Biases, pp. 280–285. Springer (2012)
2. Bødker, S., Iversen, O.S.: Staging a professional participatory design practice: moving pd beyond the initial fascination of user involvement. In: Proceedings of the Second Nordic Conference on Human-Computer Interaction, pp. 11–18. ACM, New York (2002)
3. Dearden, A., Rizvi, H.: Participatory design and participatory development: a comparative review. In: Proceedings of the PDC, pp. 81–91 (2008)
4. Ekman, P.: Basic emotions. In: Dalgleish, T., Power, M. (eds.) Handbook of Cognition and Emotion, ch. 3, pp. 45–60. John Wiley and Sons Ltd., Chichester (1999)
5. Elfenbein, H.A., Ambady, N.A.: When Familiarity Breeds Accuracy: Cultural Exposure and Facial Emotion Recognition. Journal of Personality and Social Psychology 85(2), 276–290 (2003)
6. Melissa Gross, M., Crane, E.A., Fredrickson, B.L.: Methodology for assessing bodily expression of emotion. Journal of Nonverbal Behavior 34, 223–248 (2010)
7. Henrich, J., Heine, S.J., Norenzayan, A.: The weirdest people in the world? Behavioral and Brain Sciences 33, 61–135 (2010)
8. Koda, T., Ishida, T., Rehm, M., André, E.: Avatar Culture: Cross-Cultural Evaluations of Avatar Facial ExpressionsAvatar Culture: Cross-Cultural Evaluations of Avatar Facial Expressions. AI & Society, Special Issue on Enculturating HCI 24(3), 237–250 (2009)
9. Laban, R.: The mastery of movement. Dance Books (2011)
10. Masuda, M., Kato, S.: Motion rendering system for emotion expression of human form robots based on laban movement analysis. In: Proceedings of the 19th IEEE International Symposium on Robot and Human Interactive Communication, pp. 324–329 (2010)
11. Rehm, M.: Developing Enculturated Agents — Pitfalls and Strategies. In: Blanchard, E.G., Allard, D. (eds.) Handbook of Research on Culturally-Aware Information Technology. IGI Global (2010)
12. Rehm, M.: Experimental designs for cross-cultural interactions: A case study on affective body movements for HRI, pp. 78–83. IEEE Computer Society Press (2012)

13. Rehm, M., Nakano, Y., André, E., Nishida, T., Bee, N., Endrass, B., Wissner, M., Lipi, A.A., Huang, H.-H.: From Observation to Simulation — Generating Culture Specific Behavior for Interactive Systems. AI & Society 24, 267–280 (2009)
14. Rodil, K., Winschiers-Theophilus, H., Jensen, K.L., Rehm, M.: Homestead Creator, pp. 627–630. ACM (2012)
15. Schröder, M., Bevacqua, E., Cowie, R., Eyben, F., Gunes, H., Heylen, D., ter Maat, M., McKeown, G., Pammi, S., Pantic, M., Pelachaud, C., Schuller, B., de Sevin, E., Valstar, M., Wöllmer, M.: Building Autonomous Sensitive Artificial Listeners. IEEE Transactions on Affecite Computing 3(2), 165–183 (2012)
16. Takahashi, K., Hosokawa, M., Hashimoto, M.: Remarks on designing of emotional movement for simple communication robot. In: Proceedings of the IEEE International Conference on Industrial Technology (ICIT), pp. 585–590 (2010)

Visual Interfaces Design Simplification through Components Reuse

Javier Rodeiro-Iglesias and Pedro M. Teixeira-Faria

School of Informatics Engineering, University of Vigo, Spain
jrodeiro@uvigo.es
School of Technology and Management - Polytechnic Institute of Viana do Castelo, Portugal
pfaria@estg.ipvc.pt

Abstract. One way to simplify a visual interface creating process is to give to the interface designer the ability of reusing pre-built visual components representations. In order to avoid premature commitment to specific presentations, and leaves open the prospect of alternative visual presentations for different environments, abstract interaction objects (AIOs) can be used. One of these AIOs is the *complex component*, which is a component representation having similarity properties with the object-oriented paradigm. This type of component embraces the reuse concept at semantic and functional levels, which contributes to reduce the complexity in the graphical user interface design process. Further advantages of using *complex components* are the possibility of visual and functional customization of these components, which greatly improves the versatility of them when compared with a *widget*.

Keywords: Abstract Interaction Objects, Complex Components, Visual User Interface Components Reuse.

1 Introduction

Most of the visual interfaces are created for the user to interact with them, using interactive visual components. Much work in the field of interactive graphics involves describing an interface in terms of a collection of *abstract interaction objects* (*AIOs*) [3][6][12]. An AIO represents a data structure of a user interface object without any graphical representation and independent of any implementation environment. The use of AIOs avoids premature commitment to specific presentations, and leaves open the prospect of alternative visual presentations for different environments. Therefore, in the interface designing process the selection of appropriate AIOs becomes necessary. In the study here described an AIO was selected: the *complex component (CC)*. The criteria considered to select it were by the fact that his representation supports visual appearance, topological composition and interaction [15]. It is also indicated that there exists a generic similarity between *(CC)* and *object-oriented paradigm* (*OOP*) which means that a relation between visual interface components (the *complex components*) and objects in OOP could be established. Knowing that OOP supports objects reusing (e.g. by association, aggregation or inheritance) [5] and

M. Kurosu (Ed.): Human-Computer Interaction, Part I, HCII 2013, LNCS 8004, pp. 441–450, 2013.

taking into account the comparable relation that exists between objects (in OOP) and *(CCs)*, the possibility of reusing *(CCs)* will be verified. The approach here proposed indicates the existence of a generic similarity between *(CCs)* and OOP [13] which means that a relation between these visual interface components and objects in OOP can be established (encapsulation, inheritance, polymorphism). For example, a *(CC)* has features that can be related with the *aggregation* concept existent in OOP, which differs from ordinary *object composition* in that it does not imply ownership. Thus, by eliminating one of the containers will not imply to eliminate the objects it contains (the same happens with *CCs*). Each container can be identified as a class, which keep a list of their child components, and allow adding, removing, or retrieving components amongst their children. In order to achieve this objective, we analyze the properties of component reuse at semantic and functional levels, based in one game visual interface prototype previously created [11].

1.1 Study Motivation

It is possible to establish the main scope of the study presented here. It is focused on the representation of self-contained visual interfaces based on the direct manipulation interaction style [10], supporting user freedom design features. The user interface designer can establish the shape, size, color, position, among other properties for each interface visual element. Thus, the user interface designer has the possibility to create a visual interface prototype based on visual components. Specifically, the contribution of this study is focused in verifying complexity reduction (simplification) in the visual interfaces design process, by using reuse features provided by *(CCs)* usage. The possibility of reusing *(CCs)* is of great importance since that contributes to simplify the interface design, which can be freely established by the interface designer. The visual elements to be used are independent of any platform or programming environment.

1.2 Defined Problem

In a previous study [15] the bases for characterizing a new AIO were established: this new AIO is called *(CC)*. Using this concept, an example of a game interface implementation was designed. And, after the interface has been designed, the idea of verifying the *(CC)* reuse features has emerged. It was decided to verify their reuse potential at both the semantic and functional levels. We understand the semantic level as the possibility to change *(CCs)* visual appearance, maintaining his functionality. And thus, allowing to use components on different platforms (e.g. to be possible to change the graphics of a game, while maintaining its functionality). The components reuse at functional level implies more profound changes in *(CCs)*, related with his functionality (e.g. more or less visual states and transitions between them). The problem that emerges is concerned with the validity of using these both reuse concepts. Thus, in order to verify that possibility, a relation with the OOP reuse concepts will be established, since it is a clearly stated and validated paradigm. Therefore, from an interface prototype designed using *(CCs)*, and assuming the existence of a particular *(CC)* (with a specific visual appearance and behavior) which the designer wants to reuse in another interface, it will be verified if it can be done under considering two perspectives. The first one is semantic, by keeping the component behavior and changing the visual appearance. The other perspective implies to change the component behavior while keeping (or not) the original visual appearance. Considering these two perspectives, an analysis will be made in order to validate them focusing in the OOP reuse concepts.

2 Components Specifications

Usually, the term *reusability* is related with OOP technology and most of the times specifically related to *reusing code* [1]. Other related term is *inheritance reuse* which refers to using the inheritance concept in an application, in order to take advantage of the behavior implemented in existing classes. Other term is *component reuse* which refers to the use of prebuilt, fully encapsulated components, usually called *widgets* (*WIndows gaDGETS*). They are typically self-sufficient and encapsulate only one concept. Usually, the component reuse concept differs from code reuse in that we don't have access to the source code and it differs from *inheritance reuse* in that it doesn't use *subclassing* (new classes based in existing ones). Common examples of reusable software components are *Java Beans* and *ActiveX* components. There are several advantages in component reuse. First, it offers a greater scope of reusability than either code or inheritance reuse because components are self-sufficient (typically, we plug them in and they work). The main disadvantage of component reuse is that because components are small and encapsulate only one concept, we may need a large library of them to create an application (although when a component encapsulates one concept, it is a cohesive component).

2.1 User Interface Description Languages (XML-UIDL)

During the last decade, new user interface specification tools have emerged, with special focus on *User Interface Description Languages Based on XML* (*XML-UIDL*).

To specify user interfaces using XML [17] is considered to be one solution for the standardization and interoperability between applications [9][14] and is the main reason for the constant emergence of new XML-UIDLs. It is possible to observe (Figure 1) the release year of XML–Compliant languages first versions (drafts in some cases). Each of them comes up with a specific purpose and application. For example, one of those description languages is the *XForms* [16]. It separates the presentation from the data, keeping the principle of separation of concepts, allowing component reuse and device independence. However, despite XML supports reuse, and some of the (XML-UIDL) allow visual presentation reusing, these languages are not designed to support functional reuse. Thus, this type of interface specifications is not considered in our analysis related with components reuse, and thus another approach was taken.

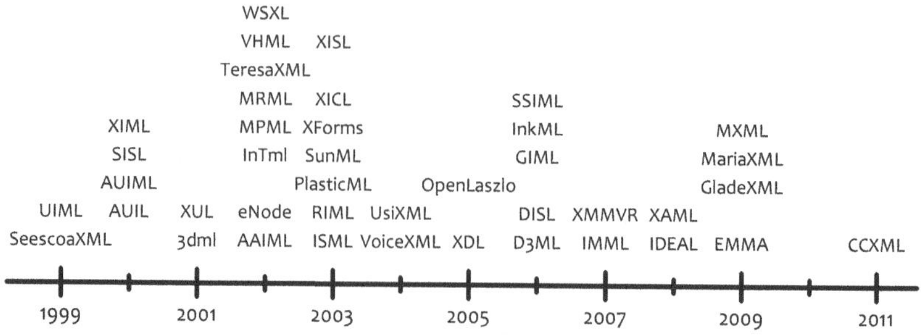

Fig. 1. XML-UIDL Evolution

2.2 Abstract Interaction Objects (AIOs)

A *Concrete Interaction Object* (CIO) represents any visible and manipulable user interface object that can be used to input/output information related to user's interactive task, and sometimes called widgets. These objects include some restrictions [2]:

- Lack of uniformity and standardization: concrete interaction objects induces a generalization problem as soon as a same object can be found in different physical environments with different names, different graphical presentations, but still with the same behavior;
- Absence of abstract representation: without such a representation, developers are submitted to specificities of several physical environments, designers are forced to not ignore low level details, and human factors experts are mainly focused on presentation aspects rather than behavioral aspects;
- Lack of compatibility with OO programming: in this programming paradigm most object classes' libraries encapsulate logically related classes with respect to inheritance relationship. Basic classes currently provide foundation classes, widget classes and graphical object classes. Any abstraction that is not compatible with OO dedicated mechanisms will be limited and useless;
- Difficulty of reusability: the reuse of existing objects leads to the acceptation of existing CIO's constraints which can be considered as insufficient under given circumstances. Creating new AIO from existing AIOs will be less hazardous as abstract properties (e.g., attributes) can be reused from one AIO to another.
- These shortcomings clearly motivate the need for an abstract interaction object AIO. Considering that, four AIOs have been analyzed: *interactor* [6][8][15], *abstract data view (ADV)* [4][15], *virtual interaction object* [12] and *complex component* [15]. The AIOs analysis considered here is focused in his visual appearance and interaction properties (Table 1). Concerning visual appearance, we verified that two of the AIOs don't support visual presentation and one of them doesn't consider visual states (interactor has states, but are not visual and are algebraically represented). Interaction refers to the bi-directional interaction from or to an *interaction object*. In general, three elements may interact with an interaction object: the

user, another *interaction object* and the *application*. After the four AIOs have been analyzed, considering several characteristics (Table 1) we decided to choose the *(CC)* to analyze its reuse properties. This choice took into consideration the *(CC)* be the AIO which agglutinated more features supported in part by the other AIOs. Basically, a *(CC)* is a component composed of other components (*simple* or/and *complex*) which interact with each other through its *self* and *delegate events/actions* working toward a common goal (e.g. a *toolbar* allows a user to select a specific tool to perform some task at a given time) [15]. The components follow a hierarchical topological structure and so each one can be contained within others. Thus, an analysis on semantic and functionality perspectives of (*CCs*) reuse is presented.

Table 1. AIOs comparison

	interactor	***abstract data view (ADV)***	***virtual interaction object***	***complex component***
Visual Presentation			×	×
Visual States		×	×	×
Input from User	×	×	×	×
Output to User	×	×	×	×
Input from the Application	×			×
Output to the Application	×			×
Input from Other Components	×		×	×
Output to Other Components	×		×	×

3 Semantic Perspective of Components Reuse

The visual interface of a game was designed and when the user looks at the interface he has at his disposal two perfectly distinct groups of visual elements (which correspond to three balls and three sport fields). The interface functionality was implemented using *(CCs)* at two abstraction levels: in one of them, 6 *(CCs)* were used (each one corresponding to one ball or one field) and in the other abstraction level, 2 *(CCs)* were used (one corresponding to a group of balls and the other corresponding to a group of fields). As previously mentioned, a characteristic resulting from using *(CCs)* to represent an user interface is related to the ease of components reuse. In a first perspective to that, the interface designer can create a new user interface maintaining its functionality. A new visual interface is immediately obtainable, due to the fact that *(CC)* concept to consider components reusability in his characteristics. If the interface designer wants to reuse a *(CC)* in another interface, keeping the functionality but with a different visual appearance, he can do it. This perspective is focused in drawing a new game interface by simply changing the component visual states, while still maintaining its functionality. Instead of the user (in this case a child) has to relate balls with sport fields, he could for e.g. to relate objects with colors or sport shoes with balls. In this semantic *(CCs)* reuse perspective, the designer only has to be care with changing visual presentation attributes.

4 Functionality Perspective of Components Reuse

Another perspective of components reuse can be analyzed considering changes in the functionality of the *(CCs)* used. In a first approach, the changes in the components functionality are related with the number of components contained inside a *(CC)* (number of visual elements to be used) (e.g. instead of using three balls and three fields, a reduction or an increase in the number of available components could be tested, maintaining the components functionality). With respect to this approach it will be important to verify and to assess the changes occurring in parameters associated with the new visual interface (events, states, visual transitions) according to the reduction or to the increase in the number of used components.

In OOP a *class* is defined as a base structure used to create instances of it (objects). We can identify a *(CC)* as an interface component (with visual appearance, composition properties and supporting user interaction) which can be compared to an OOP class. A general comparison was previously made [15]. However, this part of the study will be focused on verifying *(CCs)* reuse features comparing them with the OOP reuse provided by the concepts of *association*, *aggregation* and *inheritance* [7].

4.1 Components Creation by Association and Aggregation Approach

An association represents a relationship between classes, and gives the common semantics and structure for many types of “connections” between objects. Associations are the mechanism that allows objects to communicate to each other through messages. Analogously, the communication between *(CCs)* associated with each other is performed by using *delegate events/actions.*

Class Association. Each ball *(CC)* used to design the game previously referred can be compared with a class with 3 possible visual states (*normal*, *selected* and *correct*) and 3 methods responsible for changing those states (visual transitions). Also each field *(CC)* can be identified as having features like a class with 2 visual states (*normal* and *correct*) and one method (visual transition). The structure of a ball and a field is represented on Figure 2.

On Figure 2 we verify that each ball may receive 2 user events and triggers 1 *delegate event* (on other component). It is also verifiable that there are internal transitions between the states of the *(CC)* limited by restrictions. In the case of the field, it receives 1 user event and triggers 1 *delegate event.* It has an internal transition between the 2 states whose trigger is dependent on a restriction. Relating the *(CC)* concept with the class concept, 3 *CC_Ball* class instances and 3 *CC_Field* class instances need to be created to implement the referred game. The relation between these balls and fields classes can be established by the OOP *association*, which defines a relationship between classes of objects that allows one object instance to cause another to perform an action on its behalf. In this case we verify the similitude with OOP method invocation, by the action performed by a *delegate event* triggered from a *(CC)*.

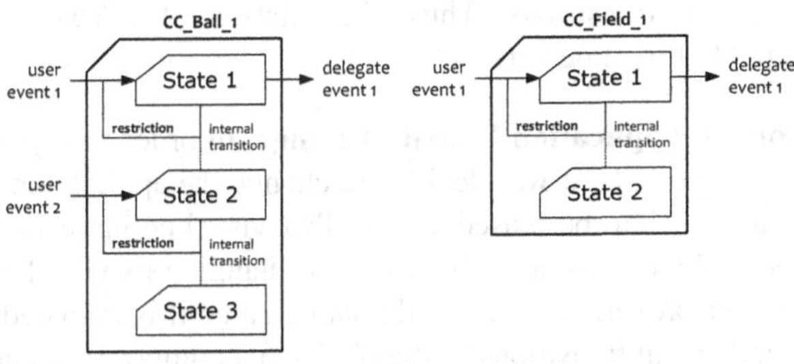

Fig. 2. Structure of a ball (left) and a field (right) used in the game interface

Class Aggregation. Aggregations are a special type of associations in which the participating classes don't have an equal status, but make a "whole-part" relationship. A *(CC)* also has features that can be related with the *aggregation* concept existent in OOP. The *CC_Balls* and the *CC_Fields* act as containers of 3 balls and 3 fields, respectively (Figure 3).

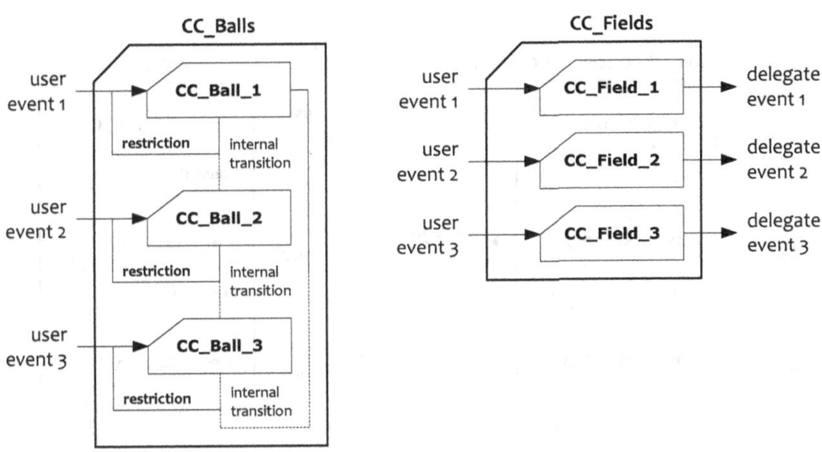

Fig. 3. Structure of the *CC_Balls* and *CC_Fields* containers used in the game interface

However, *aggregation* differs from ordinary *composition* in the perspective that it does not imply ownership. Thus, by eliminating one of the containers will not imply to eliminate the objects it contains. Each container could be identified as a class, which keep a list of their child components, and allow adding, removing, or retrieving components amongst their children.

4.2 Components Creation by Inheritance Approach

After analyzing *(CCs)* reuse approach by using the components, maintaining his original states and visual transitions, it seems to be adequate to analyze components reuse through another perspective, in which a *(CC)* is modified in order to contain more states and visual transitions. Thus, the relation of *(CCs)* design with the inheritance concept OOP will be verified.

Complex Component Application Domain Change. In order to expand and to verify the level of usage of a *(CC)* it was decided to change the application domain. Thus, *CC_Balls* has been chosen to be reused as a toolbar visual component. As previously mentioned, it is possible to reuse a *(CC)* by simply changing its visual appearance and hence his semantic. However, beyond the domain change it is intended to change the number of states and visual transitions of the *(CCs)* that compose the chosen container *CC_Balls (CC)*. In this way, the following changes were decided to perform:

– Increase the number of visual states: it is intended that each *(CC)* inside *CC_Balls* has one more visual state (e.g. each ball has three visual states and it is intended that each tool in the toolbar has four visual states);
– Increase the number of transitions between visual states: each *CC_Ball (CC)* inside *CC_Balls* contains three possible visual transitions between the three visual states. It is intended that each tool in the toolbar has five possible visual transitions between the four visual states.

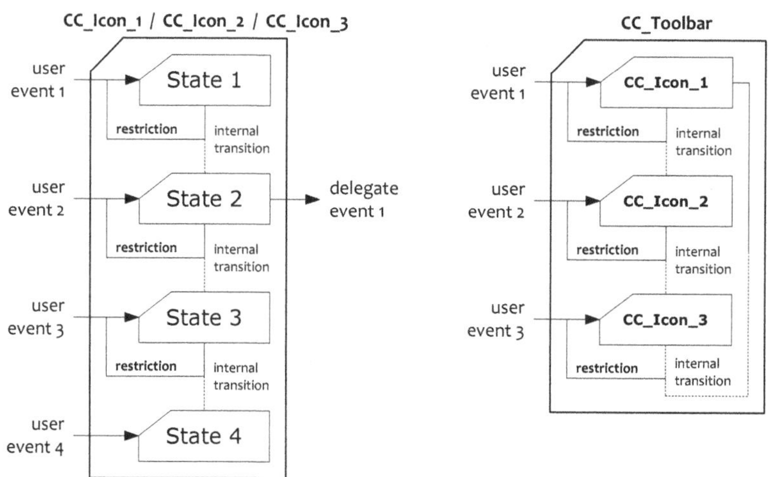

Fig. 4. The 3 icons (3 equal instances on the left) and the toolbar (on the right) represented as *complex components*

On Figure 4 are indicated the structures of each of the 3 tools (*CC_Icon_1*, *CC_Icon_2*, *CC_Icon_3*) which are inside (*CC_Toolbar*). Keeping in mind the possibility of reusing *(CCs)*, comparing it with reuse in OOP, we verify the similitude with the inheritance concept. Basically, considering a *CC_Balls (CC)* (which contains

3 balls) represented as a class, we may reuse it as a toolbar (with 3 tools) through the creation of a class by inheritance and extending it to support a new visual state and to redefine the existent transitions (by keeping some, eliminating and creating other). We verify a close relation between *(CCs)* and OOP. One of the important advantages of OOP is that it promotes reuse. Therefore, if we use *(CCs)* to design visual interfaces, similarly we can do component reuse of those components.

5 Conclusions

It is possible to design visual interfaces through various existent component specifications. One way to optimize the design process is through the reuse of components. During the last decade there has been a huge growth in the number of user interface description languages which uses XML as support language (*XML-UIDL*). However, those specifications need to be connected with high-level components provided by toolkits and usually referred as *widgets*. The use of those *widgets* limits the customization options available and because of that it limits the potential of reuse of this type of visual components. Additionally, even in spite of an increasing number of XML-UIDL enabling visual presentation reuse, such XML–Compliant Languages do not allow components functional reuse. Thus, we decided to increase the level of abstraction in the components specification by using AIOs. From those which were verified, the one which best supports features related with visual presentation, topological composition and component interaction is the *(CC)*. Thus, we sought to determine whether this type of component supports reuse. It was possible to verify the existence of a similitude between *(CCs)* features and OOP characteristics, considering in particular the reuse. This reuse characteristic can be applied by a *(CC)* under a semantic or a functional perspective. It contributes to reduce the complexity in a graphical user interface design process by reducing the number of components created and used. However, two envisaged limitations concerned with *(CCs)* reuse are:

- Identification of the issues that is necessary to change in *(CCs)* characterization in order to enable reusability;
- Classify/distinguish a new *(CC)* created by reusability.

In spite of those limitations, this advantage of being possible to reuse components simplifies the interface specification process also by being possible to specify (individually) each component and then, at the global interface level, only be necessary to specify the part that is not done yet with the *(CCs)*. Therefore, the obtained results confirm the hypothesis of being possible to simplify a graphical user interface design through the use of *(CCs)* which supports reusability. Thus, further advantages of using *(CCs)* are the possibility of visual and functional customization of these components, which greatly improves the versatility of a *(CC)*, when compared with a *widget*.

Acknowledgments. This work was supported by:

1. Grant SFRH/PROTEC/49496/2009 of MCTES – Ministério da Ciência, Tecnologia e Ensino Superior (Portugal).
2. Project TIN2009-14103-C03-03 of Ministerio de Ciencia e Innovación (Spain)
3. Project 10DPI305002PR of Xunta de Galicia (Spain).

References

1. Ambler, S.: A realistic look at object-oriented reuse. Software Development 6(1), 30–38 (1998)
2. Bodart, F., Vanderdonckt, J.: Widget Standardization through Abstract Interaction Objects. In: Proceedings of 1st International Conference on Applied Ergonomics, pp. 300–305. Springer, Istanbul (1996)
3. Carr, D.: Specification of Interface Interaction Objects. In: CHI 1994 – ACM Conference on Human Factors in Computer Systems, pp. 372–378 (1994)
4. Cowan, D., Lucena, C.: Abstract Data Views: An Interface Specification Concept to Enhance Design for Reuse. IEEE Transactions on Software Engineering 21, 229–243 (1995)
5. De Champeaux, D.: Object-Oriented Analysis and Top-Down Software Development. In: America, P. (ed.) ECOOP 1991. LNCS, vol. 512, pp. 360–376. Springer, Heidelberg (1991)
6. Duke, D., Harrison, M.: Abstract interaction objects. Computer Graphics Forum 12(3), 25–36 (1993)
7. Eck, D.: Introduction to Programming Using Java, 6th edn. (2011)
8. Faconti, G., Paternó, F.: An approach to the formal specification of the components of an interaction. In: Vandoni, C., Duce, D. (eds.) Eurographics 1990, pp. 481–494. North-Holland (1990)
9. Guerrero-Garcia, J., González-Calleros, J., Vanderdonckt, J., Muñoz-Arteaga, J.: A Theoretical Survey of User Interface Description Languages: Preliminary Results. In: Latin American Web Congress, pp. 36–43 (2009), doi:10.1109/LA-WEB.2009.40
10. Hutchins, E., Hollan, J., Norman, D.: Direct Manipulation Interfaces, vol. 1, pp. 311–338. Lawrence Erlbaum Associates, Inc. (1985)
11. Rodeiro-Iglesias, J., Teixeira-Faria, P.M.: User Interface Representation Using Simple Components. In: Jacko, J.A. (ed.) Human-Computer Interaction, Part I, HCII 2011. LNCS, vol. 6761, pp. 278–287. Springer, Heidelberg (2011)
12. Savidis, A.: Supporting Virtual Interaction Objects with Polymorphic Platform Bindings in a User Interface Programming Language. In: Guelfi, N. (ed.) RISE 2004. LNCS, vol. 3475, pp. 11–22. Springer, Heidelberg (2005)
13. Schlungbaum, E., Elwert, T.: Dialogue Graphs - A Formal and Visual Specification Technique for Dialogue Modelling. In: BCS-FACS Workshop on Formal Aspects of the Human Computer Interface. Sheffield Hallam University, Springer (1996)
14. Souchon, N., Vanderdonckt, J.: A Review of XML-compliant User Interface Description Languages. In: Jorge, J.A., Jardim Nunes, N., Falcão e Cunha, J. (eds.) DSV-IS 2003. LNCS, vol. 2844, pp. 377–391. Springer, Heidelberg (2003)
15. Teixeira-Faria, P.M., Rodeiro-Iglesias, J.: Complex Components Abstraction in Graphical User Interfaces. In: Jacko, J.A. (ed.) Human-Computer Interaction, Part I, HCII 2011. LNCS, vol. 6761, pp. 309–318. Springer, Heidelberg (2011)
16. W3C, XForms 1.0: The neXt generation of web FORMS, W3C Recommendation (October 14, 2003), http://www.w3.org/TR/2003/REC-xforms-20031014/
17. W3C Recommendation: XML, XML 1.0 (2008), http://www.w3.org/TR/REC-xml/

Established and Innovative Facets of Interactive Prototypes – A Case Study

Sebastian C. Scholz[1] and Dieter Wallach[2]

[1] Ergosign GmbH, Adams-Lehmann-Str. 44, 80797 Munich, Germnay

[2] University of Applied Sciences Kaiserslautern, Amerikastr. 1, Zweibruecken, Germany

scholz@ergosign.de, dieter.wallach@fh-kl.de

Abstract. In this paper we highlight four facets of interactive prototypes in user-centered design approaches. After reflecting on their established role in the design and validation phases, we consider recent innovative uses of prototypes in communicating with development/bidders and also to enhance training. To illustrate our experiences, we draw upon a recent successfully completed redesign project in the field of electrical engineering.

Keywords: user-centered design, prototyping, iterative design, empirical validation, delivery, education, e-Learning, innovation, integration, case study, development support.

1 Introduction

After a decade designing user interfaces, in these times of ubiquitous innovation it is reassuring to see the roots and pillars of one's own discipline still providing a sound foundation. Gould and Lewis' seminal paper *"Designing for Usability: Key Principles and What Designers Think"* [1] provided a significant contribution to the principles of user centered design (UCD). Almost three decades ago the authors postulated three principles for the (then) emerging field: (a) early focus on users, (b) empirical measurement using prototypes and (c) iterative design.

Despite their variety, the notions of iteratively designing (see Figure 1, facet 1) and validating (facet 2) prototypes with users are still established ingredients of virtually every flavour of UCD approaches. Two additional innovative facets of prototyping practice, have recently gained traction: Design prototypes are increasingly *not* thrown away after validation, but reused for outsourcing and delivering to development (facet 3). Design prototypes are also deployed to enrich e-Learning strategies with interactive materials, leading to more effective training (facet 4).

In this paper we will address all four facets — both established and innovative — to highlight the full integrative potential of interactive prototypes. To illustrate the discussed facets in a real-world project, a matching case study will be presented.

M. Kurosu (Ed.): Human-Computer Interaction, Part I, HCII 2013, LNCS 8004, pp. 451–459, 2013.

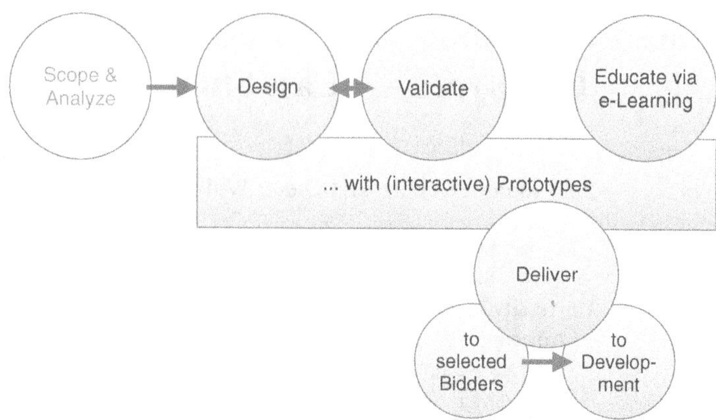

Fig. 1. Four facets of interactive prototypes

2 Established Facets: Design and Validate with Prototypes

UCD approaches include a thorough analysis of prospective users, their goals, workflows, contexts of use and their understanding of an interactive task [2]. Visions of future applications slowly become more concrete and tangible as rough storyboards that have been used to outline the ideas of the system are enhanced as higher fidelity visuals and interaction concepts are added through prototyping. Opposed to mostly static early screen incarnations, we reserve the term "prototype" for *interactive* artifacts. An emerging property of such artifacts is their ability to capture the dynamic interplay between a user and an application. In this sense a prototype literally depicts "the way products behave in response to the behavior that people behave" [4]. Being dynamic and concrete, prototypes foster effective communication between a project's stakeholders. Using prototypes potential design alternatives are communicated with palpable artifacts instead of discussing abstract and often foggy design ideas.

2.1 Disruptive Tools for Design Prototyping

Efficient prototyping calls for tools that adequately reflect the increasing maturity of achieved design stages. A designers' work from earlier design stages can rarely be reused in direct form when entering the next level of design maturity. All too often, a typical workflow is still described by a process that requires a sustained switching of tools. Starting with an adequate wireframe tool (e.g. *Balsamiq*), then moving to an appropriate mockup-tool (e.g. *Adobe Photoshop*) for creating an aesthetically pleasing visual design and finally using a prototyping tool (e.g. WYSIWYG HTML editors) for developing dynamic, interactive prototypes.

There are a growing number of innovative prototyping applications available that now help to prevent such process breakages (e.g. *AXURE, iRISE* or *ANTETYPE).* Using *ANTETYPE*, for example, designers can arrive at increasing prototype fidelity within a single tool. Coming from early static wireframes, different visual design alternatives can be explored, compared and easily shared between different stakeholders via a web viewer. Creating interactive prototypes in this tool neither presupposes coding efforts nor requires use of applications other than *ANTETYPE*. Depending on the implementation framework chosen, *ANTETYPE's* CSS export options also supports the reuse of prototype assets.

2.2 Continuous Validation

In addition to their use as reflective tools, interactive prototypes are also indispensable ingredients of empirical usability tests. They allow direct feedback to be gathered from prospective users thus informing subsequent design iterations – or even validating that an iteration cycle is complete, signaling that a validated interface artifact is ready to enter the implementation stage.

In their paper Gould and Lewis [1] differentiated between "understanding potential users, versus identifying, describing, stereotyping and ascertaining them". Methodologically, the authors stress the importance of bringing designers into an immediate exchange with potential users with methods such as contextual observation and/or interviews. The goal of a further design phase is then to distil captured insights about users, their tasks and context and to cast them into tangible artifacts that are validated with prospective users: "intended users should actually use simulations and prototypes to carry out real work, and their performance and reactions should be observed, recorded, and analyzed." [1]. Gould and Lewis also directly addressed the inherent character of iteration in UCD: "[…], when problems are found in user testing, as they will be, they must be fixed. This means design must be iterative: There must be a cycle of design, test and measure, and redesign, repeated as often as necessary" [1].

Modern prototyping tools enable the designer to significantly speed up iterations by facilitating rapid and extensive changes to a prototype. Risks and costs from this iterative approach are steadily decreasing: On the one hand recruiting prospective users is becoming easier over the internet (at least in the case of not highly-specialized consumer applications). On the other hand, technological advances in screen capturing and video-conferencing enable qualitative feedback not possible (and not usable) a couple of years ago.

3 Innovative Facets: Deliver and Educate with Prototypes

User-centered design endeavours can appropriately be characterized by a user interface first (UIF) approach: an application's (new) interface is researched, conceptualized, designed and validated without necessarily a single line of functional code in the final application's target language needing to be written.

3.1 Delivering to Selected Bidders

In an UIF approach, high-quality documentation of the designed interface concept is mandatory. When the implementation will be provided externally this is especially true because documentation is often the core and binding ingredient of a tender in a bidding process. Often the participating parties in a tender are distributed globally — and very competitive. Both tenderer and bidders thus share an inherent interest that the information provided in a tender is unambiguous. It is a fallacy to think that this leads to extensive documentations. Often the opposite is the case, putting enormous pressure on bidders.

High-fidelity prototypes can offer significant value to all participating parties in this situation. Interactive prototypes enhance the static, text-based documentation typically found in a tender. They grant vivid access to all crucial parts of an interface that are all too often neglected in textual documentations — and consequently underestimated in expected implementation efforts. Transitions, animations, the full set of button states, or interaction idioms such as the use of gestures – hard to describe verbally – are the hardest thing to implement in the originally intended and validated way.

3.2 Delivering to Development

Handing-over to development – no matter whether implementation is done in-house or outsourced – is generally a dreaded step in UIF approaches. Even when supplemented by some visual Mock-ups, static documentation offers broad potentials for misunderstandings between designers and developers. In the past years, however, technological advances opened up a chance for sharing more than just text files, bitmaps and icons between designers and developers. Modern development frameworks enable designers to cast their visuals in reusable Look & Feel code (e.g. CSS, QML or XAML resources), leading to a situation where both parties refer to the same language and potentially even use the same tool (e.g. *Microsoft Expression BLEND*). From a design perspective such an approach provides far-ranging control of the (visual) realization of validated concepts until shipping. Developers, on the other hand, can build upon an interface prototype for re-use during the development of full-fledged frontends.

A clear challenge when following the plan to reuse (parts) of a prototype is to find an appropriate balance between "letting creativity flow" and "correct (sustainable) coding". On the one hand, the design phase should not be (too) limited by efforts due to strict requirements for code reusability. Then again, dedicated code refactoring tasks should be planned when the general interface concept has been agreed upon.

3.3 Using Prototypes to Educate (Future) Users

A traditional requirement when redesigning applications is to minimize learning and training efforts for current and future users in order to stay competitive. For complex software, resulting ramp-up costs can easily drive a powerful interface concept out of consideration, especially when the user base has grown large. In some cases dedicated training is a (legal) prerequisite for using an application at all. Minimizing costs for the creation of training materials and for conducting training sessions is therefore an increasingly important goal for software vendors.

An interactive prototype that covers the core working scenarios for an application's central persona(s) is ideal for reuse in an e-Learning environment. In fact, participants in usability tests typically need to walk through the very same steps using an interactive prototype that learners will need to complete during hands-on training sessions with a released application (assuming meaningful prioritization of real-life scenarios for design and validation). Reusing an already available and validated interactive prototype that constituted the blueprint for the final application thus seems to be a logical step when conceptualizing a training approach. Its integration in a more comprehensive e-Learning environment would then allow for interactive exercises to enhance learning effectiveness.

4 The Four Facets: Case Study *ET**

We will depict the outlined four facets of prototyping deployment by referring to a recent redesign project. The project was targeted at an application to support electricians in the specification and configuration of home and building control installations. We will, for reasons of confidentiality, coin this application *ET*. To avoid confusion, *ET's* redesigned user interface will subsequently be labeled *ET**.

4.1 Design and Validate

In the *ET* project, prototypes of different fidelity were extensively advocated to gain common ground between a broad set of internationally distributed stakeholders. In a first design phase, general design decisions regarding the functionality, basic layout and workflow of *ET** were envisioned and successively refined through screen sketches and wireframe sequences. After finally settling on a stable design concept, a comprehensive interactive prototype of *ET** was developed using a Javascript-framework and illustrating representative working scenarios. The choice of a web-based approach for prototype creation was motivated mainly by the advantages provided when presenting artifacts to geographically widespread stakeholders.

Preceding contextual user/task analysis suggested that a careful distinction between two primary personas needed to be reflected in ET*'s interface concept: One identified persona covered the professional user, typically trained as an electrical engineer ready to configure commercial buildings as large as London's Heathrow airport with the help of ET*. The other pegged persona represented an occasional user, trained as an electrician who would mostly use ET* for configuring small, one-family residential buildings. The provision of two target personas with clearly different features needs and application scopes called for the introduction of distinct interface modes to be provided by ET*. While the "professional" mode provided full and flexible access to the broad range of functionality provided by ET*, the "novice" mode offered a restricted and guided process for common configuration tasks. This process comprised separate steps that were derived from gathered empirical evidence for simplified Mental Models [3] of occasional users, even providing automatic allocation of network addresses in the configuration process.

The distinction between two separate working modes of *ET**'s user interface made a comprehensive validation with prospective end-users absolutely essential. Collecting behavioral and Think Aloud data with user representatives in a usability lab as well as in informal interface walkthroughs in a total of four countries, led to iterative updates during the evolution of the *ET** prototype. The small-meshed validation studies avoided situations where innovation would happen just for the sake of innovation but ensured to serve substantial added value as evidenced by empirical feedback. Online access to the respective iterative stage of the interactive *ET** prototype allowed timely feedback from product management, developers and selected key customers.

4.2 Deliver

When designing *ET**, a UIF approach was executed. From the very beginning of the project it was planned to outsource *ET**'s actual software implementation after a design specification was derived. This specification was intended to serve as a core component of a tender for selecting an external development firm. The developed interactive *ET** prototype was initially planned to be used only for finalizing design and to support validation. During the process of writing the specification documents, however, the extended role of the prototype artifact as an important illustrative supplement for bidders and developers became obvious.

Deliver to bidders: In the case of *ET** the tender consisted of a comprehensive and detailed 300+ pages user interface specification that was accompanied by the implemented web-based prototype. The latter not only helped bidders to accurately estimate efforts by interactively investigating its features. It also granted them an easy entry to the complex domain of building control configuration by reflecting *ET*'s* key functionality that covered the application's most important scenarios.

Deliver to development: In the case of *ET** it would have been helpful if the technologies of the prototype (HTML / Javascript) and of its implementation in the final application (WPF, Windows Presentation Foundation) would have been the same. There were, however, two reasons why this was not feasible: The first reason being that two different frameworks were considered for the technical implementation of *ET** when the design activities started (WinForms vs. WPF). The second reason stemmed from the requirement of having an easy way of sharing iteratively refined prototypes with involved international stakeholders during the design phase — which was easily achieved by using web technologies for artifact creation.

To avoid a situation in which design vision, technological constraints and effort considerations of its realization might conflict, the functional capabilities of WPF and WinForms as potential implementation technologies were investigated at project start. The results of this analysis were continuously taken into account during all stages of design until the decision for the use of WPF was determined during the project. Repeated sanity checks of the prototype with regard to a WPF implementation ensured that no significant technological barriers would occur after handover to development.

4.3 Educate

When the *ET** application was finally released to the market, a high demand for efficient training arose. Whether for users being already acquainted with *ET*'s* predecessor or for those new to the system, training needed to be supplied for the new version. In order to train a high number of users efficiently and with a constant instructional quality, an e-Learning approach to training lessons was chosen. In these lessons learners are first exposed to declarative content sections regarding the basic theory of building control configuration. Animations were designed to illustrate relevant flows or relationships between system components. Screen casts, enhanced with spoken explanatory text, were integrated to exemplify user-system interaction. For each section, interactive quizzes were developed for individual self-tests to help learners to rank their progress and to detect potential knowledge gaps.

The interactive *ET** prototype that was applied and refined during formative usability testing — and which served as a companion to system specification during development — was finally reused as the core of the *ET** learning management solution (LMS, see Fig. 3).

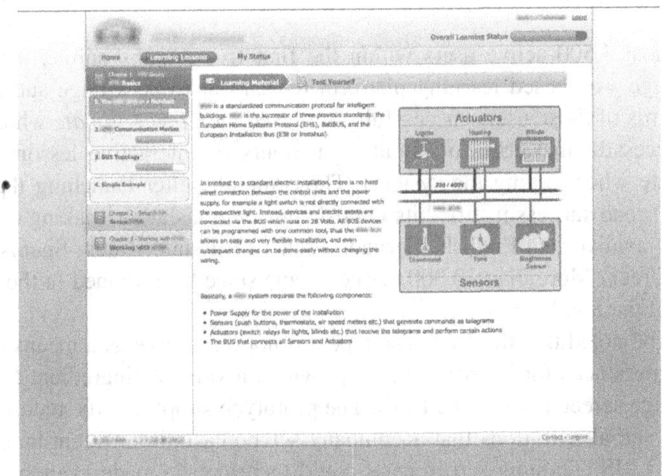

Fig. 2. ET* LMS solution

Challenging real-world task scenarios were introduced to provide learners with an interactive working experience using the *ET** web prototype in the LMS (see Fig. 4).

It is foremost the interaction with the *ET** prototype that provides learners with a highly effective learning experience. Hands-on tasks using the interactive prototype allowed a quite direct transfer of acquired procedural skills to real-life scenarios with the actual *ET** release that offers the very same user interface.

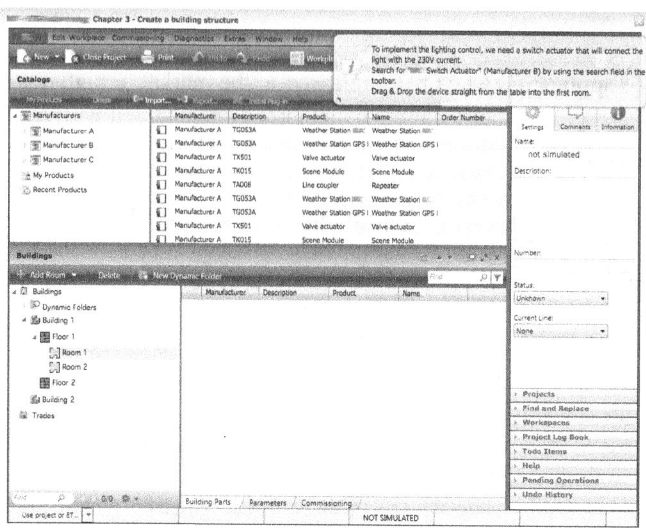

Fig. 3. Interactive prototype integrated in LMS

With almost 4.500 active users within the first five months online, the resulting multi-language web-based learning platform turned out to be a huge success. More than two-thirds of those users successfully achieved an *ET* certificate* which presupposed a successful mastering of about eight hours of interactive lessons (granting them a rebate when buying the system). Three months after launching the learning platform its broad success justified its multi-language translation, making the learning content now available in English, German, French, Russian, Dutch, Spanish, Italian, Czech and Greek. More than 10.000 learners have since been trained in the year after the release of the LMS.

It should be noted that the *ET** prototype did not only serve as a means to provide hands-on experiences for learners. It also provided a valuable ingredient for creating multi-language screen casts in the LMS. The prototype simplified the recording of the explanatory verbal narrations that accompany screen casts in different language versions of the LMS. Training screen casts could therefore be made available even before the corresponding national translations of the *ET** application were ready for release. The interactive simulation system was not the only reused element from the designs stages. Insights from contextual user/task analysis turned out to be also very helpful in the selection and creation of learning content. These insights were used to set the focus of e-Learning lectures on areas and concepts that were identified in the research phase of the project as being crucial to understanding *ET**.

5 Conclusion

In this paper we have outlined a project in which interactive prototypes were used as (1) reflective tools to envision the details of the future application during design,

(2) as a concrete artifact for validation with prospective users, (3) as a core element to first help substantiating formal bidding documents and then to support the application's implementation and (4) as an interactive simulation tool that forms the core of a comprehensive e-Learning system. Augmenting the view of prototypes from their common roles in design and validation towards additional roles in the deliver/educate facets has the potential to better integrate those involved in all stages of interactive system development. Even though challenges do exist, we think that great potential lies in these two latter uses. New use cases for prototypes facilitate a tighter integration of designers and developers and encourages innovation that can thoroughly be communicated to the end-user through highly effective e-Learning.

References

1. Gould, J.D., Lewis, C.: Designing For Usability: Key Principles and What Designers Think. Communications of the ACM 28(3), 300 (1985)
2. Holtzblatt, K., Wendell, J.B., Wood, S.: Rapid contextual design: A how-to guide to key techniques for user-centered design. Morgan Kaufmann, San Francisco (2005)
3. Young, I.: Mental Models. Aligning design strategy with human behavior. Rosenfeld Media, Brooklyn (2010)
4. Saffer, D.: Designing for interaction: Creating Innovative Applications and Devices. New Riders, Berkeley (2007)

Multi-level Communicability Evaluation of a Prototyping Tool

Vinícius Segura, Fabiana Simões, Gabriel Sotero, and Simone Diniz Junqueira Barbosa

Pontifícia Universidade Católica do Rio de Janeiro, Rio de Janeiro, RJ, Brazil
{vsegura,fpsimoes,gsotero,simone}@inf.puc-rio.br

Abstract. Semiotic engineering views human-computer interaction as a form of human communication between designers and users, mediated by a computer system. If we consider a design application, such as a prototyping tool, this communication is about the construction of a second communication, one between the user of the prototyping tool (in the role of the designer) and another user, who will interact with the system being designed. This article explores an extension to the Communicability Evaluation Method for design tools. This extension focuses not only on considering the kinds of communicability breakdowns, but also on what abstraction level they occur.

Keywords: semiotic engineering, communicability evaluation, prototyping tools.

1 Introduction

Semiotic Engineering studies Human-Computer Interaction from a communication-centered perspective, defining it as a form of human communication mediated by a computer system [9]. To Semiotic Engineering, computer systems are *meta-communication artifacts*, that is, artifacts that communicate the designer's meta-message.

When considering the case of interface design tools (DT), and more specifically the case of prototyping tools, the complexity level of this communication between designers and users increases. Apart from the aforementioned meta-communication between the designer of the DT and the user of the DT (about how the DT can and should be used), there is another meta-communication being defined during the use of the DT: one between the user of the DT, in the role of the designer of a new computer system, and the users of this new system.

The Communicability Evaluation Method (CEM) [5] evaluates the communicability of an interactive system, which is the quality of the designer's meta-message, not only in terms of the effectiveness of his direct messages to users, but also of the afforded conversational paths. CEM evaluates the reception of the meta-message, i.e., it identifies some interaction breakdowns that occur while a user interacts with a computer system.

In this paper, we studied how to apply the CEM in the evaluation of a DT, taking into consideration the fact that DTs comprise more than one meta-message during interaction time. The tool chosen for this analysis was UISKEI (User Interface Sketching and Evaluation Instrument) [8], focusing on its interaction behavior definition functionalities. Due to the plurality of meta-messages, while analyzing the collected data and

M. Kurosu (Ed.): Human-Computer Interaction, Part I, HCII 2013, LNCS 8004, pp. 460–469, 2013.

applying the CEM, we found it necessary to extend the method. The main change in the original method is that analysis is not only based on the exposition of the communicability breakdowns, but also on the abstraction levels in which they were observed.

The next section briefly describes UISKEI, the design tool we evaluated. Section 3 presents the original CEM and describes the evaluation scenario. Section 4 reports the results of a preliminary evaluation with the original CEM. Section 5 presents the extensions to CEM we found necessary to better evaluate user interface design tools, and section 6 presents the evaluation with the extended CEM. We conclude the paper with a discussion of the benefits of the extended CEM and point to future work.

2 UISKEI

UISKEI [7,8] is a pen-based prototyping tool developed to aid designers in the early stages of interactive systems design, namely: interface building; behavior definition; and prototype simulation. For this study, we focused only in its behavior definition functionalities. Behavior in UISKEI is defined according to an event-condition-action (ECA) model: when an *event* occurs, if all the *conditions* are met, then all the *actions* are executed. In its canvas, UISKEI shows the current selected ECA as a mind-map, and also all the created ECAs in the composition in an ECA Manager side-panel.

The pen-based interaction is maintained while defining behavior. To define an ECA, the user has to first select the element that will trigger the event and add an ECA to it. To do so, the user interacts with buttons in the top of the canvas, which allow him to add, remove, clone and navigate between ECAs. Given a selected ECA, the user may add conditions and actions. This is accomplished by drawing lines, with their starting and ending points determining not only if an action or a condition is being added, but also, in the case of an action, its kind. The final parameters of an action/condition being added are defined through a pie menu. This method allows the user to define an action/condition without raising the pen, in a single stroke.

3 CEM

CEM aims to evaluate the quality of the designer's meta-message reception by users [5,4]. Participants are invited to perform tasks using the system being evaluated and the interactions are recorded in videos. Later, evaluators analyze the recordings, aiming to understand how each user interacted with the system, which communication breakdowns happened, and when.

Communication breakdowns can be considered "moments of interaction in which the user demonstrates that he did not understand the metacommunication of the designer, or moments when the user finds difficulty to express his intention of communication in the interface" [9,5,4,1]. They are categorized by user utterances – expressions in natural language that allow the evaluator to presume what the user could have said when the breakdown occurred. CEM has 13 user utterances: Where is it? What now? What is this? Oops. Where am I? What happened? Why doesn't it? I can't do it this way. I can do it otherwise. Thanks, but no, thanks. Looks fine to me. Help! I give up.

3.1 Test Structure

The test was conducted with four participants, all of them interaction designers with no previous experience with UISKEI. The participants were divided in two different groups, according to their profile: those with programming experience, coming from a Computer Science background (P1 and P2); and those with no programming experience, coming from an Industrial Design background (D1 and D2).

The main objective of the experiment was to observe how (or if) UISKEI's ECA model was understood by users. Moreover, we also aimed at testing the hypothesis that the ECA model is easier to grasp by people with programming experience than by people without it.

In the experiment, during which both audio and video were captured, participants used a Wacom Cintiq 24 tablet and its provided stylus. Before starting the experiment, they were asked to complete a training session based on a step-by-step guide on how to define interaction behavior and use the simulation mode with UISKEI. Participants were encouraged to use the training material as a help resource during the tasks execution.

The test scenario read as follows:

An interaction designer is working in the design of a computer system and decides to create a functional prototype to present some of his ideas to his co-workers. He has already sketched the interface of this system and now wants to define how this interface behaves when a user interacts with it. He writes down a list of imagined behaviors of the system and now has to define it using UISKEI.

Each item in the imagined behavior list was presented to participants as a task. There were 5 tasks in total to be executed in sequence (T1-T5). With this scenario in mind, participants received an UISKEI project with the interface pre-drawn and some initial behavior defined. The tasks were chosen in order to cover most UISKEI's features regarding the creation and editing of behaviors. At any point in the test script participants could use the "Simulation" mode to evaluate the behavior they specified.

4 Evaluating UISKEI with the Original CEM

Participants did not experience operational difficulties creating ECAs, but had some problems in conceptually defining them. Only P1 and D1 executed all five tasks successfully. D2 had many problems and gave up in all tasks, except in T2. He spent a long time in T1 and T3, which made him quickly give up in T4 and T5. P2 created more ECAs than necessary in T1 and T5. Also, in T3, P2 did not add all the required conditions asked in the task description, because of wrong assumptions about UISKEI defaults. Additionally, as we encouraged participants to think aloud [3] during the experiments, the time they took to perform the tasks was not measured.

The results obtained with CEM are depicted in table 1. It is possible to see that most breakdowns were "Oops!" and "Looks fine to me.". The latter shows a big difference in number of occurrences between the two profiles. Other labels also show discrepancy between profiles, such as "Why doesn't it?", "I can't do it this way." and "What happened?".

During the test, P1 constantly mentioned that he missed an *else statement* to define ECAs. This clearly shows that he attempted to map basic programming structures he

Table 1. Number of utterances by profile and ordered by total number of occurrences

Utterance	P*	D*	Total	Utterance (cont.)	P*	D*	Total
Oops!	33	38	71	What is this?	8	8	16
Looks fine to me.	8	55	63	Where is it?	8	5	13
Why doesn't it?	16	26	42	What happened?	11	1	12
Help!	16	16	32	Where am I?	4	3	7
I can't do it this way.	5	15	20	I give up.	0	4	4
What now?	6	11	17	I can do otherwise.	0	1	1

knew onto ECAs. Another point raised by P1 was the lack of a clearer overview of the created ECAs. These missing features were tagged as "Where is it?"

P2 failed in 3 of the 5 tasks. However, he was not conscious of these failures, because the tests he made during the simulation did not cover enough cases. These failures were the result of a sequence of partial and temporary failures. For example, P2 did not notice the system response when he tried to clone an ECA. So he repeated the operation several times before realizing that he had already created several clones. This partial failure was tagged as "Why doesn't it?", and the final result (the total failure), as a "Looks fine to me."

When we examined the results of D1 and D2, it was clear to us that the main problems they faced were related to the underlying language of UISKEI, and not to its user interface. Their frame of mind and the way they modeled the problem, i.e., the solution they developed to the given task, were not easily mapped onto the ECA structure. This led us to consider abstraction levels when applying CEM, described in the next section.

5 Extensions to CEM

When analyzing the participants' utterances, we noticed that many of them occurred before the actual use of the tool. We were able to observe these utterances while participants were planning their solutions to the task at hand. This is related to the nature of the problem, since UISKEI is a tool to support interaction design, i.e., to create a new meta-communication message (developed by the user, in the role of designer of a new solution) within a meta-communication (the one between the UISKEI's designer to the UISKEI's user).

Building upon the work of Leitão and de Souza [2], we classified the communicability breakdowns not only by the utterances defined in CEM, but also by the abstraction levels in which they occurred. Figure 1 shows the abstraction levels model that we used.

To define this model, we considered that the behavior definition process with UISKEI happens as follows:

- The user receives the task and reformulates it using his own words. This happens at an **interpretative** level, since it relies on the user interpretation of the task description.

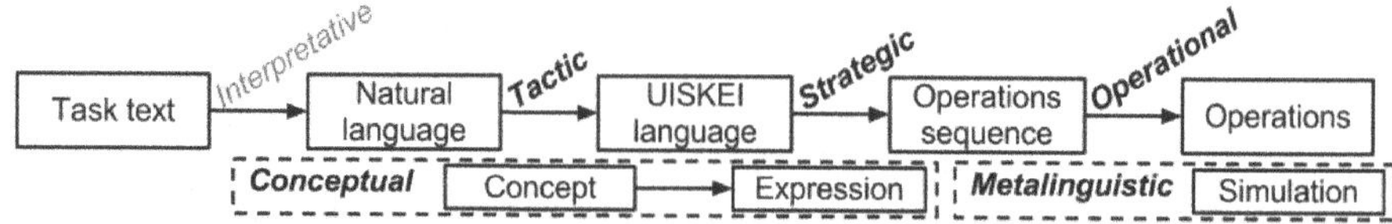

Fig. 1. Adopted abstraction levels

- The user's interpretation of the task is translated into the ECA model. This translation occurs at the **strategic** level, since this is related to the process of establishing objectives for using UISKEI.
- The user then reaches the **tactical** level, settling an action plan with a sequence of operations needed to reach the objective(s) defined at the strategic level.
- Finally, the user performs the previous planned operations. This stage happens at the **operational** level, focusing on the individual expression of each operation.

In this model, we also consider the problem of mapping a concept to a term in the user interface. For example, consider the definition of a condition for the status of a textbox (enabled or disabled). On the one hand, if the user does not know that enabling a textbox means making it possible to enter information, there is a concept problem in comprehending the effect of enabling a widget. On the other hand, if the user knows that effect, but refers to it as "activate" instead of "enable", we have an expression problem. We considered that concept problems are **strategic** problems, since it reflects the definition of the objectives. The expression problems were considered as **tactical** problems, because they reflect on how the user will describe the action plan to achieve his goals. In some cases we were not able to identify in which side of the concept/expression specter the problem occurred. When this happened, we said that the problem was at a **conceptual** level.

Once the user has defined a behavior, he has the possibility of verifying his solution using the simulation mode. By doing so, the user (in the role of the designer) evaluates whether the solution defined with UISKEI results in the expected behavior. Because the prototype simulation is a form of evaluating the prototype meta-communication, we considered problems found during the simulation to be at a **metalinguistic** level. Breakdowns at this level often cause the user to re-evaluate the products of the previous abstraction levels.

In addition to the need for different abstraction levels, the experiments revealed the recurrence of a phenomenon that did not fit any of the 13 user utterances of CEM. Participants often showed symptoms of uncertainty and insecurity when defining behaviors. We have observed that these symptoms occurred in three different situations:

- **Uncertainty of the project:** When the participant is not certain whether the defined behaviors will have the expected result. This symptom appears frequently and precedes the prototype simulation. Participants often attributed the expression "Will it work?" to this symptom. It was more common with participants with CS background.
- **Uncertainty of the product:** When the participant is not sure, even after the simulation, about the defined behaviors. Typically, this symptom came with the expression

"I think I'm done", in a doubtful tone. The participant defines the behavior, tests it in the simulation mode, apparently obtaining success, but still questions himself regarding the success of the task. In general, this symptom is followed by a new execution of the simulation mode, or by a revision of the created ECAs. It was also more common among participants with CS background. The difference between this utterance and "Looks fine to me." is that the participant has actually reached the goal, but is uncertain of that.

- **Insecurity about the adequacy of the tool:** When the participant manifests his belief that the tool is not for him. This symptom was perceived among participants with both backgrounds. Typically, it was presented with the expression "This is not for me." or similar. Participants with CS background, in general, presented this symptom when comparing the definition of ECAs and programming languages, manifesting that they "could do it much faster with Notepad". Participants with Design background presented this symptom as soon as they saw the mind-map structure. Comments like "this is a programmers' issue" were frequent.

Another interesting point is the use of the simulation mode for validating of the logic being defined. A comparison can be made with the discussion of *reflection in/on action* [6], since the participants chose to reflect about the created behavior after the simulation (*on action*) instead of being critical about it while they were defining the behavior (*in action*).

6 Evaluating UISKEI with the Extended CEM

We revisited the tagging from our first evaluation, this time considering the aforementioned abstraction levels, resulting in table 2. The table also describes the symptoms most commonly associated with the occurence of a given tag at a given abstraction level. In this analysis, breakdowns that occurred at an interpretative level were not considered, since they reflect problems outside the scope of the tool. Moreover, when a breakdown was perceived in more than one abstraction level, it was tagged only at the highest perceived level (the left-most cell in figure 1).

Table 2. Number of utterance occurrences separated by abstraction level and participants profile

Utterance	Lvl	P*	D*	Total	Symptoms
Oops!	conc	6	29	35	The user recovers himself of an error caused by an undesired effect or a wrong terminology choice.
	tat	1	2	3	The user quickly recovers from an action plan formulation error.
	op	31	35	66	The user quickly recovers from an error when executing an operation from the action plan.
Looks fine to me.	conc	6	29	35	The user expects wrong effects or uses a wrong terminology, without noticing the error.
	str	1	3	4	The user elaborates objectives that the designer can't comprehend, but is not aware of the problem.

Table 2. (*continued*)

Utterance	Lvl	P*	D*	Total	Symptoms
Looks fine to me.	tat	0	14	14	The user elaborates an incorrect action plan and doesn't notice the error.
	op	1	9	10	The user incorrectly performs an operation of the action plan and does not notice the error.
Why doesn't it?	str	1	0	1	The user doesn't understand why the designer can't comprehend his objectives.
	tat	1	1	2	The user insists in repeating an action plan that doesn't produce the desired results.
	op	8	1	9	The user insists in repeating an operation that doesn't produce the desired results.
	meta	6	24	30	The user, when checking the developed solution, notices that it isn't executing according to what he expected.
Help!	conc	2	0	2	The user can't understand what an interface expression means and searches for information through explicit meta-communication.
	str	2	2	4	The user doesn't know how to express his objectives and searches for information through explicit meta-communication.
	tat	3	9	12	The user does not understand the difference between the interface signs, staying unsure about which one he must use to build his action plan. After that, the user searches for information through explicit meta-communication.
	op	9	5	4	The user doesn't understand an interface sign and searches for information through explicit meta-communication.
I can't do it this way.	str	2	4	6	The user convinces himself that his formulation of objectives is wrong and tries do reformulate them.
	tat	2	10	12	The user gives up an action plan that he developed and decides to elaborate a new plan, restarting the task.
	op	1	1	2	The user tries to do an action several times, without getting the desired effects, convincing himself that he is doing something wrong.
What now?	str	0	2	2	–
	tat	6	8	14	The user knows what is the desired effect, but doesn't know how to define the action plan to accomplish it.
	op	0	1	1	The user does not know how to perform an operation from his action plan.
What is this?	conc	0	1	1	The user does not understand the meaning of an interface expression and searches information through implicit meta-communication.
	tat	0	1	1	The user doesn't understand the difference between the interface signs, ending up unsure of which one he will use to elaborate his action plan.
	op	8	6	14	The user doesn't understand the meaning of an interface sign and searches information through implicit meta-communication.

Table 2. (*continued*)

Utterance	Lvl	P*	D*	Total	Symptoms
Where is it?	str	0	2	2	–
Where is it?	tat	5	1	6	The user knows what he is trying to say, but does not know what term he should use among the system's options.
	op	3	2	5	The user knows what he is looking for, but can't find an interface element to do it.
What happened?	op	11	1	12	The user doesn't understand the system's answer to what it is told to.
Where am I?	tat	2	3	5	The user says something to the system that should be preceded by another utterance, not making sense when said without context.
	op	2	0	2	The user says something to the system that would be appropriate in another communication context.
I give up.		0	4	4	The user believes that he is not able to achieve his objective and interrupts the interaction.
I can do otherwise.	op	0	1	1	The user communicates his action with unexpected signs, since he does not understand what the system is saying about the solutions to reach his goals.

No occurrences of the "Thanks, but no, thanks!" utterance were observed. Despite the 4 occurrences of "I give up", we decided not to specialize it, since it represents a breakdown of the user interaction at all the levels of abstraction. For the original CEM, "Looks fine to me", as well as "I give up", characterizes a complete breakdown during which the user is unconscious of his failure. In a similar way, for this study, we used "Looks fine to me" as an utterance for when the user manifested unconsciousness of failure, however, without necessarily corresponding to a complete failure. The simulation mode made it possible for users that presented "Looks fine to me" symptoms to gain consciousness of their failure while testing the prototype. This utterance, therefore, was also used for classifying temporary failures as well.

The multi-level application of CEM let us identify in which communication context each breakdown in interaction occurs. On the one hand, breakdowns in operational and tactic levels were more frequently observed in the communication between UISKEI's designer and its user. On the other hand, breakdowns in strategic and metalinguistic levels were observed, in general, when the message of the participant was specified for the users of the system being prototyped (UISKEI's user in the designer's role). The problems at those levels reflect moments of the interaction in which the user demonstrates difficulties in expressing his communication intentions as a designer. Therefore, the multi-level application of CEM let us identify in which communication context each breakdown in interaction occurs. This information let us identify which role the user of the DT was playing when the breakdown occurred: user of the DT or designer of a new system.

The identification of these different types of problem takes us to different kinds of improvement suggestions to the DT being evaluated. For instance, considering the paraphrase of the designer meta-message [9] below, table 3 shows which parts of the designer's meta-message should be redesigned based on the level in which a communication breakdown occurs:

“Here is my understanding of *who you are* (1), what I’ve learned *you want or need to do* (2), in *which preferred ways, and why* (3). This is the system that I have therefore designed for you, and this is *the way you can or should use it* (4) in order to fulfill a range of purposes that fall within this vision”

Table 3. Relationship between the adopted abstraction levels and the meta-message parts.

	Conceptual	Strategic	Tactic	Operational	Metalinguistic
Passages	1	1, 2, 4	2, 3, 4	3, 4	1, 2, 4

6.1 Interpretation of Results

"Looks fine to me" occurred in 4 of the 5 levels of our model. Participants tended to recover more rapidly from the occurrence of "Looks fine to me" when this utterance occurred at the operational level. At the strategic and tactical levels, this recovery was harder, usually occurring only after the use of the simulation mode.

The "Why doesn’t it?" utterance stands out for its occurrences at the metalinguistic level, when the user first simulated his solution and then observed the existence of an error. This user utterance was usually followed by a recovery from previous failures of which the user was unaware – typically, the results of "Looks fine to me" user utterances. In most cases, this recovery spotted situations where the user was able to assimilate the strategic/tactical model of the tool. When this recovery did not happen, new failures were observed or even a new occurrence of the "Why doesn’t it" user utterance. The use of a multi-level CEM allowed us to observed that, at the metalinguistic level, the user was trying to reformulate his approach to the problem based on the results of the simulation.

"Help!" is another example of a user utterance that was observed at several levels of our model. At the operational level, its use is similar to its traditional use in CEM, that is to identify a situation where the user is trying to comprehend the communicative act of the system designer. With the multi-level approach to CEM, we could discern situations where the user tried to find out how to establish his own communicative act using the UISKEI language (*strategic*) or translating his own "speech" to the UISKEI language using a series of operations (*tactical*).

Each of the other utterances were more strongly characterized by one of the levels of the model. For example, the most frequent utterance was operational "Oops!", with more than 60 occurrences. Almost all participants had problems with the pen-based input, for example, inadvertently deselecting elements or misperforming the gestures for defining conditions and actions. The high frequency of this utterance shows that UISKEI lacks adequate feedback for user actions.

"I can’t do it this way." occurred around 20 times, especially at the tactical level. Participants took a wrong interaction path several times and this led them to reformulate their plan: they had to reformulate either an ECA (*strategic*), the sequence of actions needed to define it (*tactical*), or one operation on this sequence (*operational*). This utterance usually occurred only after the participant ran the simulation Mode, when he would stop and reflect on what could be wrong.

7 Conclusion

CEM investigates the breakdowns that occur in user-system communications. While evaluating a DT, however, the set of breakdown utterances had to be expanded in order to capture the context in which the breakdown occurs: if it is between the DT designer and his user, or between the DT user taking on the designer's role and the user of the system being designed. The multi-level approach of CEM proved to be useful when capturing this information, helping to shed light on the breakdown causes, the user's role when it occurred, and the part of the designer's meta-message that should be revised.

In order to apply the multi-level approach of CEM to other DTs, further revision of the levels schema is needed. The one discussed in this work was developed taking into consideration the inherent characteristics of UISKEI, which not only is a DT, but also explores pen-based interaction. Nevertheless, the evaluation at multiple abstraction levels showed itself promising while working with systems that are used to generate new systems.

Acknowledgements. We thank all study participants who selflessly devoted their time to our research. We also thank the financial support of CNPq (#313031/2009-6 and #308490/2012-6).

References

1. Barbosa, S.D.J., Silva, B.S.: Interação Humano-Computador, 1st edn. Campus-Elsevier (2010)
2. Leitão, C.F., de Souza, C.: Semiotic Engineering Methods for Scientific Research in HCI. Morgan and Claypool Publishers (2009)
3. Lewis, C.: Using the "thinking-aloud" Method in Cognitive Interface Design. Research report, IBM T.J. Watson Research Center (1982)
4. Prates, R.O., Barbosa, S.D.J.: Introdução à Teoria e Pática da Interação Humano Computador fundamentada na Engenharia Semiótica. In: Jornadas de Atualização em Informática (JAI), pp. 263–326. JAI/SBC, Rio de Janeiro (2007)
5. Prates, R.O., de Souza, C.S., Barbosa, S.D.J.: Methods and tools: a method for evaluating the communicability of user interfaces. Interactions 7(1), 31–38 (2000)
6. Schön, D., Bennett, J.: Reflective conversation with materials. In: Bringing Design to Software, pp. 171–189. ACM, New York (1996)
7. Segura, V.C.V.B., Barbosa, S.D.J.: Shape-based versus sketch-based UI prototyping: a comparative study. In: Proceedings of the 10th Brazilian Symposium on on Human Factors in Computing Systems and the 5th Latin American Conference on Human-Computer Interaction, IHC+CLIHC 2011, pp. 162–166. Brazilian Computer Society, Porto Alegre (2011)
8. Segura, V.C.V.B., Barbosa, S.D.J., Simões, F.P.: UISKEI: a sketch-based prototyping tool for defining and evaluating user interface behavior. In: Proceedings of the International Working Conference on Advanced Visual Interfaces, AVI 2012, pp. 18–25. ACM (2012)
9. de Souza, C.S.: The Semiotic Engineering of Human-Computer Interaction. Acting with Technology. MIT Press (2005)

Participatory Action Research in Software Development: Indigenous Knowledge Management Systems Case Study

Siang-Ting Siew[1], Alvin W. Yeo[2], and Tariq Zaman[2]

[1] Faculty of Computer Science and Information Technology
[2] Institute of Social Informatics and Technological Innovations
Universiti Malaysia Sarawak (UNIMAS)
{s.siangting,zamantariq}@gmail.com,
alvin@isiti.unimas.my

Abstract. Participatory action Research In Software Methodology Augmentation (PRISMA) is a software development methodology which has been amalgamated with Participatory Action Research (PAR). This paper justifies the inclusion of PAR in software development, and describes the PRISMA methodology vis-à-vis a case study. Specifically, the case study encompasses the development of eToro, an Indigenous Knowledge Management System for the Penans, a remote and rural community in Malaysian Borneo.

Keywords: Participatory Action Research, Software Development, PRISMA, Penans, Indigenous Botanical Knowledge Management, Remote Malaysian Borneo.

1 ICTs for the Underserved

It is generally acknowledged that providing Information and Communication Technologies (ICTs) to remote and rural communities can help in alleviating poverty and/or improving the socio-economic status of the communities. Among the many benefits of providing ICTs include giving access to unlimited knowledge (e.g. e-learning), providing health-related services (telediagnosis), offering businesses opportunities (e-commerce), employment opportunities, and access to government services (e-Government websites) [1]. Evidence suggests that rural dwellers have more to gain than urban dwellers from any increase in the density of communications capability [2], but the absence of relevant experience, local content and skills are major barriers for rural ICT usage [3,4].

Of importance is the need to build good quality and relevant ICTs (software included) which addresses the communities' needs. The local communities have their own concepts of knowledge and forms of communicating. As such, it is necessary that they should be able to use ICTs in such a way that their cultural identity is not compromised [5]. Furthermore, to prevent irrelevant "alien" conceptualizations from being carried forward into the implementation, the design and evaluation process need to be fully appropriated by the user community [6].

M. Kurosu (Ed.): Human-Computer Interaction, Part I, HCII 2013, LNCS 8004, pp. 470–479, 2013.

2 Problem Background

Literature is littered with failures and short term successes in the deployment of existing technologies that is mainly designed for urban settings but implemented in rural communities. These technologies would not work given that the target community of urban dwellers is very much different. For example, those living in the urban areas are more likely to be literate, have achieved a higher level of education, and have greater exposure to the use of technology. On the other hand, those who live in the rural (and remote) areas, are more likely to be illiterate, given the limited access to education, and lower exposure to technology-use. In addition, the context of use would be very different as well. With little or no technology appropriation, i.e. absence of input from local culture in the design of the system (be it hardware or software), the system has a greater likelihood of failure [6].

Furthermore, focus of technology appropriation must also be placed on the methodologies employed to build these ICTs. However, those methodologies invariably originate from the West (developed nations of North America and Europe) and are tailored towards the development of products and services for urban users in their urban settings [5]. Given the origin and the target markets, the context and cultural elements of urban developers and users would have been "infused" in the methodology and design.

The challenge is identifying and employing methodologies which allow development of relevant software for rural communities. The methodologies should not only encompass the technological aspects but also the complexities of the rural users, the contexts as well as addressing the needs of the target audience. As shown in projects involving target users [7-10], the acceptance and usage of technology would be greatly improved particularly if the community is involved in the process.

In the next section, we introduce the solution, and justify the use of Participatory Action Research in software development in the solution. In Section 4, we describe the solution vis-à-vis in the development of an Indigenous Knowledge System for a community in the remote area of Long Lamai in Malaysian Borneo.

3 Participatory Action Research in Software Development

Given the inappropriate methodologies, we propose using PAR amalgamated with a software development methodology. We believe community participation in rural projects is important, and more so in the development of technologies such as software which are to be used by indigenous communities. In this paper, the amalgamated methodology mooted is called Participatory action Research In Software Methodology Augmentation (PRISMA).

PAR has also been used successfully in numerous rural development projects such as in IDRC [14] and in Universiti Malaysia Sarawak's (UNIMAS) eBario Project and its replications [15]. As such, PAR provides the collaborative process of research and action targeted towards positive social transformation [16]. PAR established a two-way communication, which allows the researchers to be involved with the community and vice-versa; the researchers and community are actively involved in the development activities, to seek information, ideas, and generate knowledge to guide [17].

In PAR projects involving ICT development, we believe there are two goals. One is of course to develop the technologies or software (technology element), while the other is to learn and understand as much as possible from the implementation or deployment (knowledge element). With sufficient evidence from replications, best practices may then be developed which would be of use to other similar projects. Given the high costs of projects in rural areas, there is a need to maximize outputs and learnings from rural projects. Researchers also have to keep in mind, PAR is appropriate as it has a research component that seeks to engender positive change; and that participation "requires the equal and collaborative involvement of the 'community of research interest." [13].

As shown in Figure 1, PRISMA comprises two parts, a social change process (dotted circle) and software development process (solid line circle). The software development process encompass the formal and "hard (technological) aspects" which includes the formal components of software development, tools and techniques to carry out the requirements analysis, design, implementation, and testing. More important is the "soft (humanistic) aspects" which encompass the change the community wants, the reasons they want it, as well as the roles for people inside the indistinct world of political and social systems, multiple disciplines, environments and multiple stakeholders [17]. The soft aspects tend to be fuzzy, and will be outlined in detail. If we fail to address these non-technical factors, the user requirements may be affected, resulting in poor system design, un-usable user interfaces, over budget and delays in the project. The overlap between the social change and the software development involves merging of processes of both the hard and soft aspects.

PRISMA is a work in progress. In [13], PRISMA was described to augment the conventional Software Development Life Cycle employed to develop software for rural communities. A rural e-health initiative was developed using PRISMA [17]. Not all the phases of PRISMA was utilized in [13] and [17], however in this case study, the processes are further refined. For example, the first two steps of PRISMA in [17] are expanded to four steps in this paper.

4 Development of Indigenous Knowledge Management System, eToro

To illustrate PRISMA, we will apply its use in the development of an Indigenous Knowledge Management System. Before describing the different steps in PRISMA, we define some of the eToro terms that will be used within the context of developing software for a rural community. Typical stakeholders in the project include: Community (the group in which the project will be helping); researchers (those who are implementing the project and also trying to learn from it); sponsors (ones who are providing the funds, such as government agencies or industries).

eToro project is a collaborative effort of the Institute of Social Informatics and Technological Innovations (ISITI-CoERI), UNIMAS and the local community of Long Lamai, Sarawak. The project goal is to preserve the traditional knowledge of the community, given that the older generation is slowly dying out, knowledge is not being transferred to the younger generation. Also, the young are not as interested in learning and retaining the traditional knowledge. The community involved is located in Long Lamai, a very remote and rural village in Malaysian Borneo, situated near the Kalimantan border. From the nearest city, the journey comprises a 10-hour 4-wheel drive journey over logging road, and an hours' boat ride upriver. The community at Long Lamai consists of Penans, a small indigenous community which lives on subsistence farming. There are about 450 villagers [28]. There is no 24-hour electricity supply and no telecommunication service. Some families have generator sets to generate power, but few families can afford this. The Penans in Long Lamai were nomadic, but have settled down in the area for over 50 years. They still return to the forest to hunt and to gather jungle produce. There are still Penans in other villages who are nomadic, and depend totally on the forests for their livelihood.

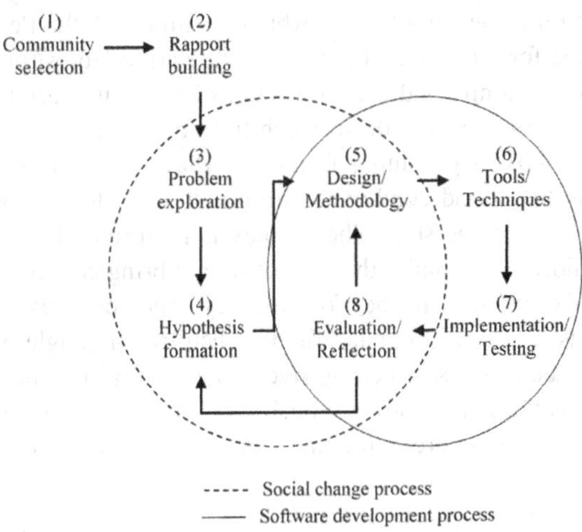

Fig. 1. Participatory action Research In Software development Methodology Augmentation (PRISMA)

4.1 PRISMA in eToro

The details below describe the use of PRISMA in developing eToro. Please refer to Figure 1 for the steps in PRISMA.

Step 1: Community Selection. The community was selected in 2007 to take part in a telecentre project. The Long Lamai community was chosen as it is a cohesive community, and it met the remoteness criteria (difficult to access and lacking infrastructure and communications).

Step 2: Rapport Building. There exists good rapport between UNIMAS and the community given the telecentre project. There is mutual respect between the two; both parties contributing their respective knowledge and expertise. The Long Lamai community has access to the Internet since 2009 after the inauguration of the eLamai telecentre. The majority of the younger generation are active users of Internet while the community elders consider the telecentre as major catalyst in boosting the local economy. The idea of documentation of Indigenous Knowledge (IK) has been initiated by the community elders during one of our visits in August 2011; they were aware that ICTs may be able to assist them to preserve their IK.

Step 3: Problem Exploration. Like other indigenous communities, the rapid change of the Penans' way of life has largely accounted for the loss of their IK [25]. Among other causes, elders were reluctant to transmit IK to younger generation who were not interested in learning and preserving the IK [26]. The community selected four elders and four youths as representatives to negotiate, discuss and help in the development of eToro. Through a series of meetings, the problem on IK was confirmed. They also discussed ways to capture and transfer the IK from old to the young, and settled on the idea of using the concept of Toro, which is familiar to the Penans. The Penans depend on the forest for hunting and for collecting various forest products. *Toro* is a joint activity of Penan family and it also works as an activity-based knowledge sharing and mentoring journey of the forest which links community elders to members of the younger generations in grooming future guardians of the rainforest. Mentoring includes lessons on livelihood combined with a notion of stewardship, incorporating conservation ethics and ownership. The journey is performed by a family including the parents and children. Normally, the parents do not bring children below the age of seven. There are six activities in the Toro journey. The activities start from leaving the *lamin toto* (house in the village) and finding the place in jungle which has enough food such as fruit trees, fishes in nearby river, sago plants, and animals for hunting. When a family finds the place, they establish their *lamin Toro*, or traditional temporary hut. The next activities are extracting sago, cooking food, catching fishes and hunting.

Step 4: Hypothesis Formation. Further discussions were held to decide which type of IK to focus on. They decided upon Indigenous Botanical Knowledge (IBK) and refer to it as the identity of the Penans. According to Garen Jengan, a local champion, "*if you don't know about the plants, you are not a Penan*". Another perceived benefit of eToro is to cover the knowledge gap between the young and old generations. The youths have ICT skills. Thus, they will be more confident in helping in the documentation process; ultimately, they will be a part of the learning cycle. The collected data, pictures and videos can also be used in tourism promotion activities. eToro can also help in training of young people so the community will have more trained human resource as guardians of the rainforest.

The researchers who were interested in the preservation of IK agreed on the focus on IBK. The research question used was: can an Indigenous Knowledge Management Sytems (eToro) be developed to capture the IBK, involve the young and is usable to the community? Expected outcomes of this exploratory study would include identifying current knowledge structures, existing/traditional intergenerational transfer processes, as well as, identifying how existing ICT knowledge can be employed in the development of eToro. The community will benefit (all going well) from having a system which would allow them to preserve the IBK, as well as an opportunity to bring the young and old together.

Step 5: Design/Methodology. Two activities, the design of the solution and identifying the approaches to achieve the solution, are conducted in this Step. The resulting design has to be acceptable to both the community and the researchers/developers; that the developers can build the eToro, and that the eToro will actually be used. In further discussions, it was realized that Penans are quite sensitive about their plants' knowledge and there is a strong social belief system which governs the knowledge management processes in the community. Through the various deliberations, a number of items was agreed upon. This discussion involves not only the community and researchers, but also software developers, knowledge engineers, botanists, environmentalists, as well as the diaspora of Long Lamai. The output of discussion includes the types of users of eToro, the access to this information (refer to Table 1), types of plant data to collect, as well as the processes needed for the collection, classification and verification of the plants.

Table 1. IKMS user types

User type	Rights.
IKM Manager	Full access.
Community elders	Browse all information.
Youth	Browse all information but have limited access to piousness plants information
Botanist	Browse the Pictures of the plant and enter the scientific name

From the researchers' perspective, a series of formalized methodology was identified (for details see [29]). These are: (1) Designing Process Flow Diagrams: For understanding processes, roles, actions & rights of stakeholders; (2) Developing Cultural Protocols (Free, Prior and Informed Consent agreement and guidelines): For community, researchers and data engagement. (3) Designing Data Instruments: For eliciting community needs and acquisition of IBK management system. (4) Developing Prototypes for Indigenous Knowledge Management System: For digital data collection and indigenous content management; the formats of the data (text, video, sound, images) and (5) Capacity Building Program: For participatory digital data collection and processing.

The researchers and developers also determined the datasets required, the Dublin Core [27] elements, and meta-data structure of IBK (which was translated to Penan, as not all Penans are literate and/or speak English or Malay, the national language of

Malaysia). The design of eToro will accommodate the characteristics of Penans IBK and also incorporate the social, cultural and belief systems which governs the Penans IBK.

Step 6: Tools and Techniques. Given the design, requirements and methodologies from Step 5, the tools employed and the techniques in the development and data collection processes were identified in Step 6. For instance, in data collection, we used Android based Tablet PCs and Open Data Kit (ODK). ODK is an extensible, open-source suite of tools designed to build information services for Android system. Created by developers at the University of Washington's Computer Science and Engineering Department and members of Change, Open Data Kit is an open-source project available to all (opendatakit.org). The Data collection form has been manually designed by the community so ODK is used to build function help in integrating the manual data collection form into the digital ODK survey form for mobile device.

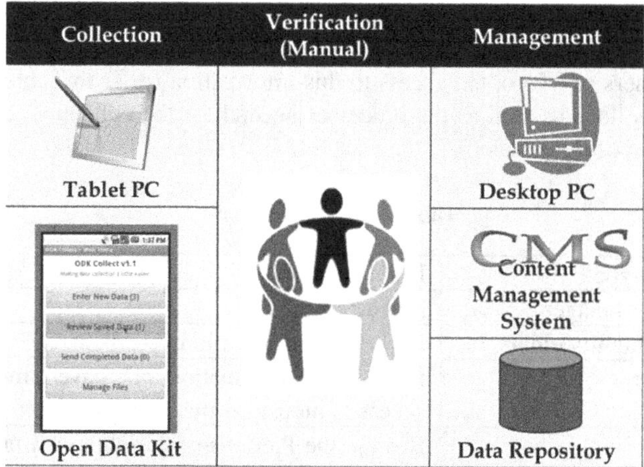

Fig. 2. Components and Services of IKMS

Step 7: Implementation and Testing. This step involves the implementation and the testing of the system. Figure 2 shows the components and services of eToro project which was implemented. The documentation activities consist of three phase. In the first phase, the young community members travelled to forest with the old folks to collect and document about plants data. Here the data is considered as part of knowledge which is shared by the old folks during the process of documentation. This data includes the text, images, video and Global Positioning System (GPS) coordinates of the plants. In the second phase, the collected information is manually verified in community meetings and in the third phase, an indigenous Content Management System (iCMS) is used to store the data on an external hard drive with e-*insitu* approach. The e-*insitu* approach is the facility for the community to have the physical control of the data and storage device in addition to logical data protection mechanisms.

Under e-*insitu* approach the hard drive would be kept under custodianship of a community appointed member.

After the prototype development, both the data collection software and iCMS have been tested on real data by collecting 30 plants information in three cycles (10 plants per cycle). The test has been conducted to confirm the usability of the software's functions. In the first two cycles, we accompanied the team in the data collection and data management process. The third cycle is performed in the absence of researchers. As the community language do not have a standard spelling system, in first cycle of data collection, 8 errors spellings have been reported in the data collection form. In second cycle, only 3 errors were reported and in the third cycle, no errors were reported; i.e. they are improving and learning to work independently.

Step 8: Evaluation/Reflection. The evaluation conducted in this step determines whether it has achieved the goals set. For example, the software is evaluated to determine if it is usable and accepted by the target community. In general, the team members for eToro were satisfied with the processes and features of eToro; as 67% of their responses are 'strongly agree' indicating that they were satisfied with eToro, while 15% 'agree', 11% 'undecided'. The responses of 'disagree' and 'strongly disagree' were negligible, as less than 1%. Among some of the feedback received, was that the system could be more interactive, and that it should be used deep in the jungle (i.e. need to resolve the power problem). From the researcher's response, the key difficulties were to understand how the local system works. There was also the language barrier, and the lack of equivalent terminology in Penan to describe the ICTs. The elders also had to be open to changes; not all community members were privy to all the data collected. Thus, with the system, the elders now had to explicitly state who should have access to what information.

eToro showed that an Indigenous Knowledge Management Systems (eToro) can be developed; and it can capture the IBK, involve the young and is usable to the community. Reflecting on how the project went, this study showed that ICTs can be employed to not only develop the IKMS but also with the right processes, develop a product that is accepted by the community, as well as bringing the young and old together. The project also underlined the importance of having a local champion to help to move the project along, and the importance of elders in supporting the project. The rapport UNIMAS has with the community also ensured that discussion about typically sensitive information was made available due to the trust that exists between the two parties. Community participation is also crucial, without whom, the project design would be unacceptable, and do not address the community's needs. Multidisciplinary teams were needed as the project involved not only IK experts, but also botanists, environmentalists in addition to the ICT experts.

5 Conclusion and Future Directions

This paper has demonstrated that working with the Penans, PRISMA can be employed to develop a usable Indigenous Knowledge Management System; a system that the community can and are using. PRISMA may also be applicable to other indigenous communities and be used to develop solutions in different domains. The next steps include refining the steps further, especially social component of PRISMA.

Acknowledgements. The authors are grateful for the institutional support and *Dana Principal Investigator* research funding from Universiti Malaysia Sarawak, as well as acknowledge and thank the continuous support from the community of Long Lamai.

References

1. United Nation Economic and Social Commission for Asia and the Pacific (UNESCAP). ICT for the economic and social development of rural communities. Policy Brief on ICT Applications in the Knowledge Economy 3 (2007), http://www.unescap.org/publications/detail.asp?id=1282 (retrieved)
2. International Telecommunication Union (ITU). World Telecommunication/ICT Development Report 2010: Monitoring the WSIS targets (2010), http://www.uis.unesco.org/Communication/Documents/WTDR2010_e.pdf (retrieved)
3. Pringle, I., David, M.: Rural community ICT applications: The Kothmale model. The Electronic Journal of Information Systems in Developing Countries (EJISDC) 8(4) (2002)
4. Gurstein, M.: Effective use: A community informatics strategy beyond the digital divide. First Monday 8(12) (2003)
5. Oyugi, C., Dunckley, L., Smith, A.: Evaluation methods and cultural differences: Studies across three continents. In: Proceedings of the 5th Nordic Conference on Human-Computer Interaction: Building Bridges (NordiCHI 2008), pp. 318–325 (2008), doi:http://doi.acm.org/10.1145/1463160.1463195
6. Winschiers-Theophilus, H.: Cultural appropriation of software design and evaluation. In: Whitworth, B. (ed.) Handbook of Research on Socio-Technical Design and Social Networking Systems. IGI Global (2009)
7. Batchelor, S., Sugden, S.: An analysis of InfoDev case studies: Lessons learnt. In: The Information for Development Program: Promoting ICT for Social and Economic Development (2003), http://www.sustainableicts.org/infodev/infodevreport.pdf (retrieved)
8. International Development Research Centre (IDRC). Networking institutions of learning – SchoolNet. Information and Communication Technologies for Development in Africa 3 (2004)
9. TeleCommons Development Group (TDG). Rural access to information and communication technologies: The challenge of Africa (2000), http://www.unbotswana.org.bw/undp/docs/bhdr2002/rural%20access%20to%20ICT%20the%20challenge%20of%20Africa.pdf (retrived)
10. United Nation Development Programme (UNDP), Accenture and Markle Foundation. Creating a development dynamic: Final report of the digital opportunity initiative. United Nations Development Program, New York (2001)

11. Oakley, P.: People's Participation in Development Projects, Oxford. Occasional Paper Series, vol. 7 (1995)
12. Munyua, H.: Information and communication technologies for rural development and food security: Lessons from field experiences in developing countries. Sustainable Development Department, Food and Agriculture Organisation of the United Nations, FAO (2000), http://www.fao.org/sd/cddirect/CDre0055b.htm (retrieved)
13. Siew, S., Yeo, A.: Employing participatory action research to augment software development for rural communities. In: Proceedings of the 25th BCS Conference on Human-Computer Interaction (BCS-HCI 2011), pp. 171–176 (2011)
14. IDRC Digital Library (2002-2010), http://idl-bnc.idrc.ca/dspace
15. Yeo, A.W., Faisal, S., Zaman, T., Songan, P., Khairuddin, A.H.: The telecentre replication initiative in Borneo Malaysia: CoERI experience. The Electronic Journal of Information Systems in Developing Countries (EJISDC) 50(3) (2012)
16. Kindon, S., Pain, R., Kesby, M.: Participatory action research: Origins, approaches and methods. In: Kindon, S., Pain, R., Kesby, M. (eds.) Participatory Action Research Approaches and Methods: Connecting People, Participation and Place, pp. 9–18. Routledge (2008)
17. Siew, S., Yeo, A.: Adapting PRISMA for software development in rural areas: A mobile-based healthcare application case study. In: Network of Ergonomics Societies Conference (SEANES), pp. 1–6 (2012), doi:10.1109/SEANES.2012.6299588
18. Rapoport, R.: Three dilemmas in action research. Human Relations 23(6), 499–513 (1970)
19. Kelles-Viitanen, A.: The role of ICT in governing rural development. In: IFAD Workshop: What are the Innovation Challenges for Rural Development, Rome, pp. 11–14 (2005)
20. Yakel, E., Torres, D.A.: Genealogists as a "Community of Records". American Archivist 20(1) (2007)
21. The Queensland Government, Aboriginal ceremonies. Queensland Studies Authority, Brisbane (2008)
22. Puri, S.K.: Integrating scientific with indigenous knowledge: Constructing knowledge alliances for land management in India. Management Information Systems Quarterly 31(2), 355 (2007)
23. Wenger, E., McDermott, R.A., Snyder, W.: Cultivating communities of practice: A guide to managing knowledge. Harvard Business School Press, Boston (2002)
24. Davis, W., Henley, T., Committee, W.C.W.: Penan: Voice for the Borneo Rainforest: Western Canada Wilderness Committee-Wild Campaign (1990)
25. Brosius, P.J.: What counts as local knowledge in global environmental assessments and conventions? In: Bridging Scales and Knowledge Systems: Concepts and Applications in Ecosystem Assessment, pp. 129–144 (2006)
26. Brown, E.H.: "Beyond" Gestalt Therapy. Journal of Contemporary Psychotherapy 5(2), 129–133 (1973), doi:10.1007/BF02111483
27. Weibel, S., Kunze, J., Lagoze, C., Wolf, M.: Dublin core metadata for resource discovery. Internet Engineering Task Force RFC, 2413, 222 (1998)
28. Zaman, T., Yeo, A.W., Kulathuramaiyer, N.: Harnessing community's creative expression and indigenous wisdom to create value. Paper presented at the Indigenous Knowledge Technology Conference 2011 (IKTC 2011): Embracing Indigenous Knowledge Systems in a New Technology Design Paradigm, Windhoek, Namibia (2011)
29. Zaman, T., Yeo, A.W., Kulathuramaiyer, N.: Augmenting Indigenous Knowledge Management with Information and Communication Technology. International Journal of Services Technology and Management (2013)

Enhanced 3D Sketch System Incorporating "Life-Size" and "Operability" Functions

Shun'ichi Tano[1], Naofumi Kanayama[1], Xinpeng Huang[1], Junko Ichino[1], Tomonori Hashiyama[1], and Mitsuru Iwata[2]

[1] University of Electro-Communications, Graduate School of Information Systems
1-5-1 Chofugaoka, Chofu-shi, Tokyo, Japan
[2] Tokyo Metropolitan College of Industrial Technology
1-10-40 Higashioi, Shinagawa-ku, Tokyo, Japan
tano@is.uec.ac.jp

Abstract. We have been studying the use of "rich media" to support creative and intelligent human activities. Over the past ten years we have focused on the 3D space as one of "rich media" and have developed many sketch systems that support the design of 3D objects. However, long-term evaluation has revealed that they are not used by designers in the field on an ongoing basis. Even worse, they are treated as if they were merely attractions in an amusement park. The fundamental problem was the lack of an indispensable function that needs a 3D space. To overcome this problem, we previously developed a system that incorporates two new functions, "life-size" and "operability," to make a 3D sketch system that is indispensable to designers. We have now enhanced the system by extending these two functions to overcome problems identified in the previous system.

Keywords: 3D sketch, Life-size, Operability, Professional designer, Mixed reality.

1 Introduction

"Media" is an artifact that expands our creativity and intelligence. The oldest media is words and numbers. The computer is now widely used as a media.

We have been studying a wide range of creativity-centered media to ensure that the systems fully support creative and intelligent human activities. They range from those used by knowledge workers to those used by car-exterior designers [1–9]. Specifically, for over ten years, we have been developing sketch systems that support the design of 3D objects because a 3D sketch cannot be realized without the power of advanced information communication technology (ICT) [6–9]. We regard the 3D sketch made possible by the power of ICT as a drastic extension of traditional "pen and paper" media. However, long-term evaluation has revealed that our 3D sketch systems were not being used by designers in the field. Even worse, they are treated as if they were merely attractions in an amusement park. This shows that while rich media may fascinate the ordinary user, it is often ignored by the professional user. This is a serious

M. Kurosu (Ed.): Human-Computer Interaction, Part I, HCII 2013, LNCS 8004, pp. 480–489, 2013.

problem because there are many systems that blindly utilize rich multimedia without long-term user evaluation.

Our analysis of the fundamental problems preventing 3D sketch systems from being used professionally revealed that it was the lack of an indispensable function that needs a 3D space. We thus developed a design concept inspired by "mixed reality" that makes the 3D sketch system indispensable to designers [10]. It extends the basic design concept by incorporating "life-size" and "operability" functions to better support human-computer interaction.

2 Related Work and Common Problem

Conventional research into 3D sketching can be categorized into two types. The first is generating 3D sketches from 2D sketches [16, 17]. The designer draws a 2D sketch, and then the system converts it into a 3D sketch on the basis of certain assumptions, and finally the system displays it in a 3D space. The second is drawing the 3D sketch directly in midair [11–15, 18]. The 3D lines are displayed as they are or as transformed smooth lines and converted into the model description in some systems [15, 18].

Although each type has its own strengths and has been successfully evaluated by the designers, there is a common problem—they are not utilized over the long term by professional designers for daily design tasks. They are missing something that would make them indispensable to professionals.

3 Motivation: Drawback of Previous 3D Systems

We have developed a series of 3D sketch systems [6–9] of both types. For example, our first prototype system, "Godzilla," was designed to support creative design, specifically that of car-exterior designers [6]. The designer draws a concept image on a 2D pad (a tablet with an LCD), grasps the sketch, and holds it in midair, and the image appears as a 3D image on a 3D pad.

The short-term user test we conducted for each system showed that the user interface was promising. All the evaluators welcomed the novel interaction. However, they stopped using the 3D space after a while. For examples, with Godzilla, the users were fascinated by the display of the 3D sketch. Some were even surprised by this function. Nevertheless, sooner or later, they realized that they did not need to look at it in the 3D space as a 3D sketch. They could look at it on the 2D pad and rotate it in a similar manner. The difference was whether the image was displayed in 3D (stereoscopic) or in semi-3D on the 2D plane (perspective 2D image).

The designers eventually stopped using the 3D space because they could do their work without it. In other words, our systems did not provide designers with an indispensable function that truly needs a 3D space.

4 3D Sketch System Incorporating Life-Size and Operability Functions [10]

4.1 Indispensable Functions in 3D Space

We identified two indispensable functions that need a 3D space. The first is a life-size 3D sketch function. If a 3D sketch is life-size, the user can evaluate its size by comparing his/her body with the sketch shown in midair in front of the user. Without this life-size presentation, the user cannot evaluate the sketch on the basis of a bodily comparison, so there is no need for a 3D sketch.

The second one is a function that enables the user to "operate" the 3D sketch, that is, touch it, push it, move it, and so on. If the 3D sketch is operable, the user can evaluate the ease of use by operating it while stooping down, extending a hand, twisting his/her body, etc.

4.2 New Design Process

We developed a design process that incorporates these two functions (Fig. 1). The flow is illustrated using a copy machine design example in Fig. 2.

Fig. 1. New design process

Fig. 2. Copy machine design example

The designer starts by considering the shape of the copy machine, asking him or herself, "What copy machine looks smart?" while drawing the idea life-size in mid-air.

The designer then considers the machine's operation by operating the sketch, thinking to him or herself, e.g., "This tray is difficult to pull out. It's too low. Pushing this button will eject the paper." He/She can then formulate the machine's operation rules by grasping and moving the sketch shown in 3D.

Next, the designer checks the machine's usability by operating the sketch while sitting down, stooping down, extending an arm, and so on. The designer may find, for example, that a button is hard to push because it is inconveniently located or that a tray is hard to pull out because the user has to get into an uncomfortable position. The designer can then simply erase the 3D sketch and start over.

4.3 Examples of Design Process

As shown in Fig. 3, this process can be used for various applications. It is particularly useful for control room design because it is very important to design a usable control room from the safety point of view, and it is prohibitively expensive to construct a complete mock-up. The designers would normally design it using a 3D-CAD system, which limits their ability to fully comprehend its size and operability.

In contrast, a designer using the latest version of our system would start by making a rough sketch of the control room (Fig. 3(a)). He/She would then define the operations of the levers, buttons, and warning lights (Fig. 3(b)). If any problems are found (Fig. 3(c)), they can be eliminated by redrawing the sketch (Fig. 3(d)).

Note that all this is done using hand-drawn sketches. The process can be completed in less than one hour.

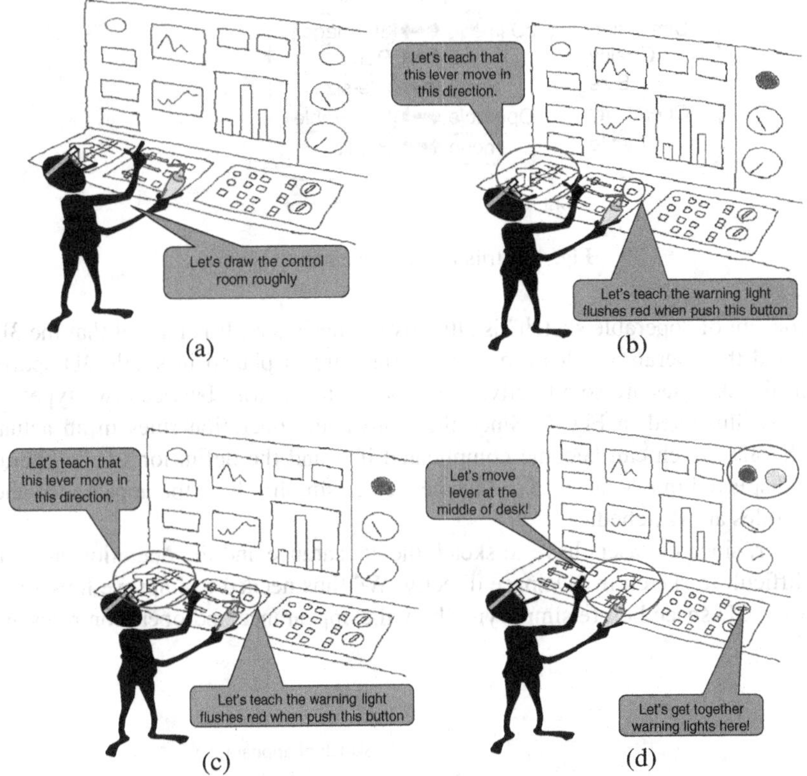

Fig. 3. Control room design example

4.4 Previous Prototype

We previously built a prototype system that includes life-size and operability functions and identified several problems.

First of all, designers complained that it was bothersome to always draw the image life size. Since the design process usually consists of several phases, they selected the design space that best matched the current design phase.

From our analysis of the design process, we had identified five attributes of the design space: dimension, quality, size, operability, and tactile. As shown in Fig. 4, "dimension" means that the designer works in a flat space, i.e., paper, or in 3D space. "Quality" means the level of design preciseness, such as rough sketch or detail. Our previous prototype supported only one combination of the attributes, the one shown by the red blocks in Fig. 4. That is why the designers complained. Although the total number of possible spaces is 32 (2^5), it is not necessary that the system support every one.

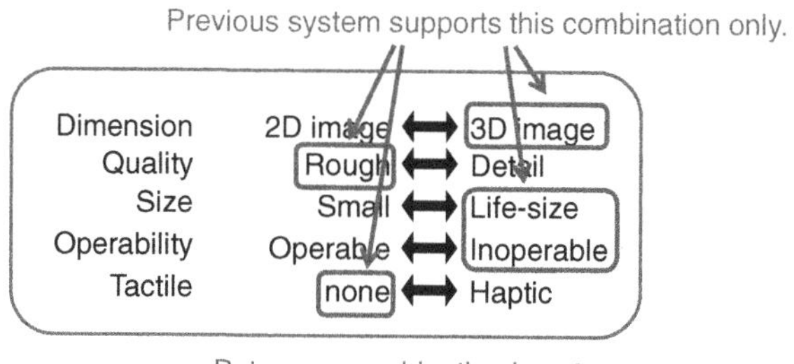

Fig. 4. Attributes of design space

The concept of "operable sketch" is attractive to designers. It is natural that the 3D sketches and the operation rules (i.e., trajectories) are displayed in single 3D space. However, the sketches are so attractive that confusion can arise between two types of sketches, as illustrated in Fig. 5. Since there are many operation rules in an actual design, the 3D sketch can become complicated if it and the definition of the operations are displayed in one space. We thus needed to simplify how the appearance and operation rules are sketched.

Moreover, since the users have to sketch the appearance and the operation rules, it is very difficult to sketch in 3D space directly. We thus needed to improve how lines are drawn in 3D space before simplifying how the appearance and operation rules are sketched.

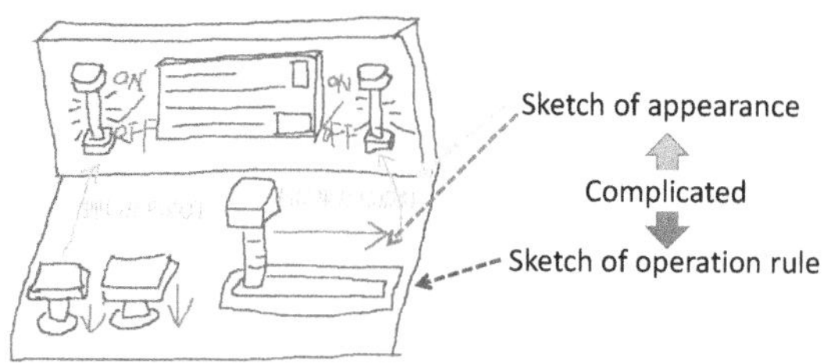

Fig. 5. Complicated sketch operation

5 Improved System

To address the designers' complaints, we developed an enhanced system that overcomes the problems we identified.

5.1 Extension of Life-Size Function

We identified the three most useful combinations of spaces and extended the design space on the basis of our findings.

(i) Design in 3D space should be both in life-size and sometimes in small size. Design in 2D should be in small size only.

(ii) Design in life-size 3D should support both operability and haptic nature. Design in small (miniature) 3D should support operability only.

(iii) Rough and detail design should be supported in all design spaces.

The first finding, that it should support 2D space and a miniature 3D space as well as a life-size 3D space, means that the system should support three spaces.

The second finding, concerning operability and tactile nature, means that the life-size 3D space needs both functions, that the miniature 3D space needs operability only, and that the 2D space needs neither of them.

The third finding means that the rough design and the detail design should be easy to traverse. The designer should be able to draw a handwritten sketch in any design space, and the sketch should be automatically converted into a detailed expression, such as font, straight line, circle, figure, and photo-realistic image , at any degree of detail and vice versa. The function should be supported in all three design spaces.

The structure of the three design spaces and the functions that each should have are illustrated in Fig. 6.

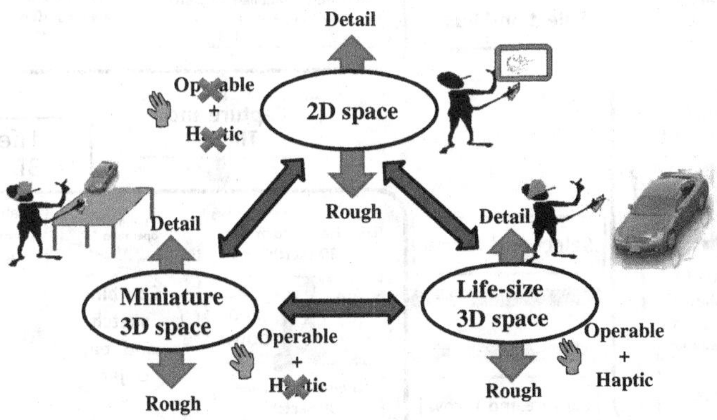

Fig. 6. Three design spaces and their supported functions

As illustrated in Fig. 7, we assigned three rough and detail design spaces: the desktop as the 2D space, the space above the desktop as the miniature 3D space, and the rest of the room as the 3D space. The corresponding experimental system is shown in Fig. 8.

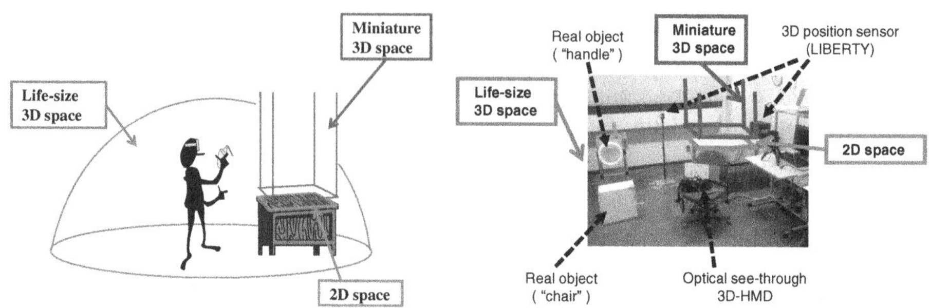

Fig. 7. Spatial assignment

Fig. 8. Experimental system

The new extended design flow containing a life-size 3D space is shown in Fig. 9. Note that the traverse between the rough design and the detail design is controlled by moving the pen "up and down." The degree of preciseness is controlled by adjusting the height of the pen. The designer can traverse to another design space by "throwing" the design to the target space. In the life-size 3D space, the sketch can be attached to the real object. The result is an operable and haptic object and sketch. For example, if the user turns the real object handle (shown in Fig. 8) the sketch attached to the handle rotates automatically.

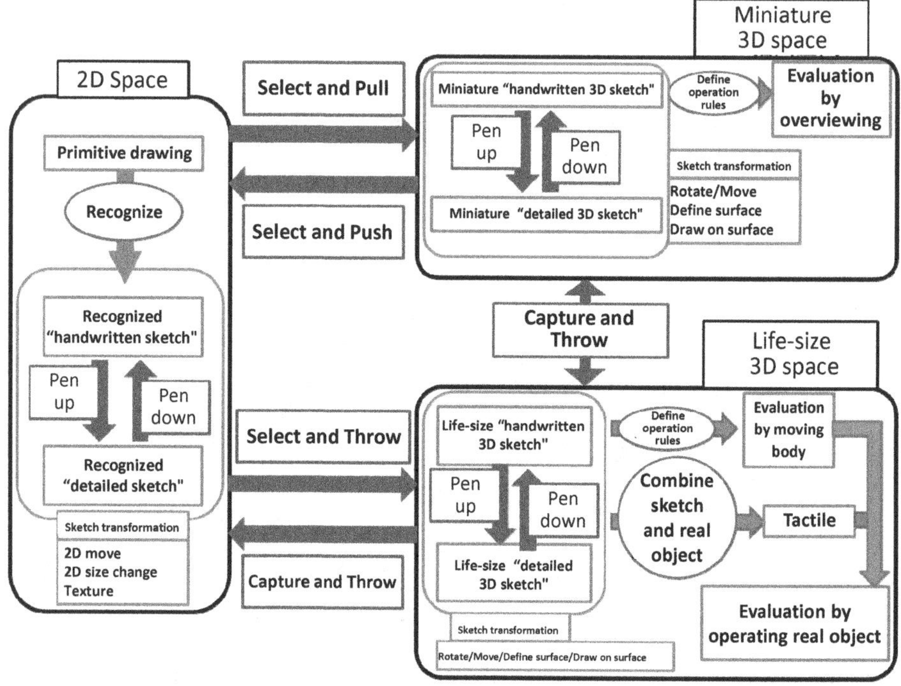

Fig. 9. New design process

5.2 Extension of Operability Function

(i) Improve how to draw lines in 3D space

There are two fundamental problems with 3D sketching: (1) it is difficult to perceive depth (distance) due to poor depth cues; (2) it is difficult to sketch on a flat plane in midair.

Our basic idea for overcoming these problems is to use a "virtual 2D plane" and an "auxiliary line." As illustrated in Fig. 10, the user freely controls the position and orientation of the virtual 2D plane by using his/her non-dominant hand. The virtual 2D plane can be seen as an extension of his/her palm. The user can easily perceive the depth of the target 3D sketch since the shadow of the target sketch is displayed on the virtual 2D plane, which continuously moves in synchronization with the hand.

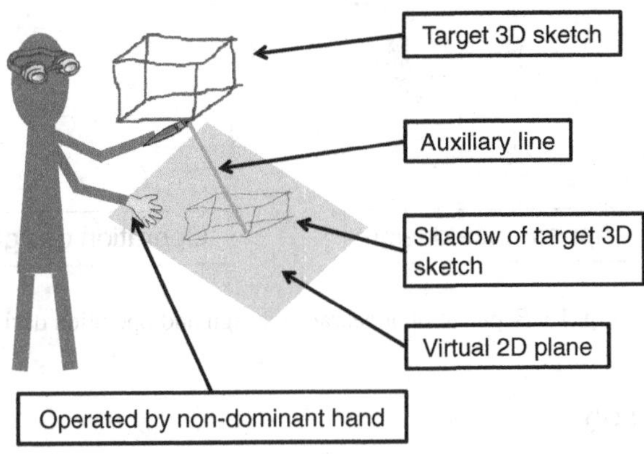

Fig. 10. "Virtual 2D plane" and "auxiliary line"

There are two types of auxiliary line. As shown in Fig. 11, a perpendicular one is used to draw a line in 3D space directly, and the shadow is displayed on the virtual 2D plane. This line connects the pen point and the shadow point. As shown in Fig. 12, an extended line enables the user to easily draw a line on a specific plane, i.e., the virtual 2D plane defined by the non-dominant hand. The virtual 2D plane improves the 3D drawing.

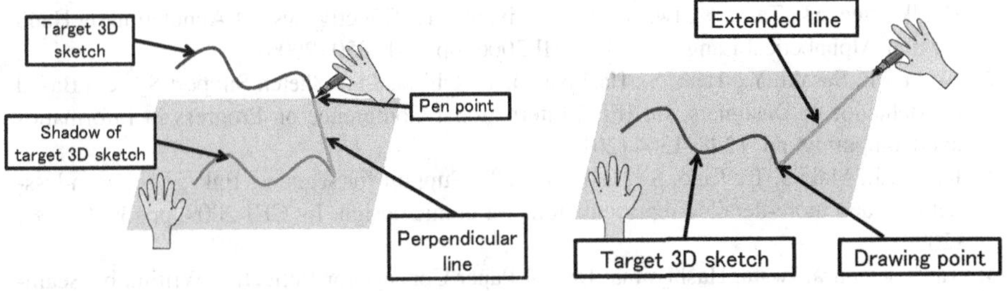

Fig. 11. Perpendicular line mode

Fig. 12. Extended line mode

(ii) Revise how to sketch appearance and operation
As shown in Fig. 13, we divided the design environment into two spaces, i.e., the appearance design space and the operation design space. In the appearance design space, the user concentrates on drawing the appearance. In the operation design space, the user can easily define the operation rules by drawing iconic symbols and trajectory lines.

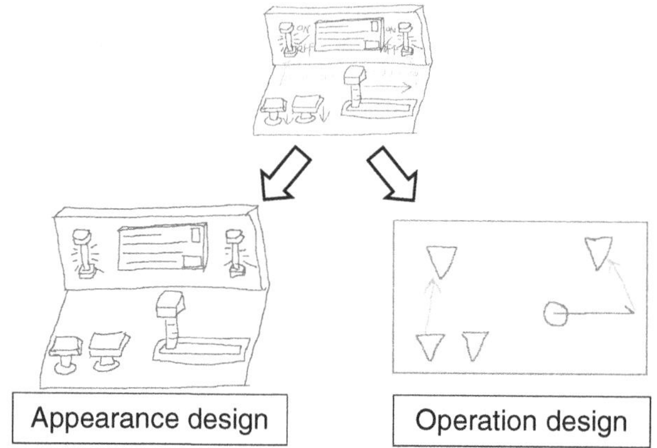

Fig. 13. Separate of appearance design and operation design

6 Summary

To address the problem of 3D sketch systems not being used by designers in the field, we implemented "life-size" and "operability" functions in a 3D sketch system. Prototype testing revealed several problems that were overcome by enhancing these two functions. The enhanced system should be a useful and effective tool for professional designers.

References

1. Dzulkhiflee, M., Tano, S., Iwata, M., Hashiyama, T.: Effectiveness of Annotating by Hand for non-Alphabetical Languages. In: CHI 2006, pp. 841–850 (2006)
2. Iwata, M., Sasaki, Y., Tano, S., Hashiyama, T., Ichino, J.: A Sketch Support System Based on Behavior of Designers. In: IEEE International Conference on Progress in Informatics and Computing, pp. 1298–1304 (2010)
3. Ichino, J., Makita, T., Tano, S., Hashiyama, T.: Support for seamless linkage between less-detailed and more-detailed representations for comic design. In: CHI 2009, pp. 3979–3984 (2009)
4. Tano, Kamura, Iwata, Hashiyama: Digital Paper Concept for Reflective Writing by Seamless Traverse between Handwritten and Coded Information. In: HCI International 2005, E-book (2005)

5. Tano, S.: Quantitative Study on the Effectiveness of Pen-based Computing on Experiential and Reflective Cognitive Modes. In: Mobile Computing in Education, pp. 46–49 (2009)
6. Tano, Kodera, Nakashima, Kawano, Nakanish, Hamagishi, Inoue, Watanabe, Okamoto, Kawagoe, Kaneko, Hotta, Tatsuoka: Godzilla: Seamless 2D and 3D Sketch Environment for Reflective and Creative Design Work. In: INTERACT 2003, pp. 131–138 (2003)
7. Tano, S., Komatsu, Y., Iwata, M.: Extended Godzilla: Free-form 3D-object Design by Sketching and Modifying Seven Primitives at Single 2D-3D Seamless Display. In: Masoodian, M., Jones, S., Rogers, B. (eds.) APCHI 2004. LNCS, vol. 3101, pp. 471–480. Springer, Heidelberg (2004)
8. Tano, Sugimoto: Natural Hand Writing in Unstable 3D space with Artificial Surface. In: CHI 2001, pp. 353–354 (2001)
9. Tano, S., Matsumoto, T., Iwata, M.: Quantitative Analysis of Human Behavior and Implied User Interface in 3D Sketching. In: Masoodian, M., Jones, S., Rogers, B. (eds.) APCHI 2004. LNCS, vol. 3101, pp. 481–490. Springer, Heidelberg (2004)
10. Tano, S., Yamamoto, M., Dzulkhiflee, M., Ichino, J., Hashiyama, T., Iwata, M.: Three Design Principles Learned through Developing a Series of 3D Sketch Systems: "Memory Capacity", "Cognitive Mode", and "Life-size and Operability". In: IEEE SMC 2012, pp. 880–887 (2012)
11. Wayne, et al.: Interactive Augmented Reality Techniques for Construction at a Distance of 3D Geometry. In: Eurographics 2003, pp. 19–28 (2003)
12. Steven, et al.: Surface Drawing: Creating Organic 3D Shapes with the Hand and Tangible Tools. In: CHI 2001, pp. 261–268 (2001)
13. Gerols, et al.: Free Drawer: A Free-Form Sketching System on the Responsive Workbench. In: VRST 2001, pp. 167–174 (2001)
14. Daniel, et al.: A Fully Immersive 3D Artistic Medium and Interactive Experience. In: Proceedings 2001 ACM Symposium on Interactive 3D Graphics, pp. 85–93 (2001)
15. Tovi, et al.: Creating Principal 3D Curves with Digital Tape Drawing. In: CHI 2002, pp. 121–128 (2002)
16. Shin, H., Igarashi, T.: Magic canvas: interactive design of a 3-D scene prototype from freehand sketches. In: GI 2007, pp. 63–70 (2007)
17. Olsen, L., Samavati, F.F.: Stroke extraction and classification for mesh inflation. In: Proc. of SBIM 2010, pp. 9–16 (2010)
18. Perkunder, K., Israel, J.H., Alexa, M.: Shape modeling with sketched feature lines in immersive 3D environments. In: Proc. of SBIM 2010, pp. 127–134 (2010)

An Interface Prototyper Supporting Free Design Components Specification

Pedro M. Teixeira-Faria[1] and Javier Rodeiro-Iglesias[2]

[1] School of Technology and Management - Polytechnic Institute of Viana do Castelo, Portugal
pfaria@estg.ipvc.pt
[2] School of Informatics Engineering, University of Vigo, Spain
jrodeiro@uvigo.es

Abstract. Complex components allow increasing the abstraction in a visual interface specification process, with independence of any platform or programming language to represent an user interface. In order to support this type of components a XML specification was created which allows specifying components visual appearance, composition and dialog. It provides a user interface abstraction to free design components (without any dependency of libraries of predesigned user interface components – toolkits). All information containing in the specification allows showing what will be the user interface final visual aspect, using a handmade or a computer technique (this is the objective of this paper). Using complex components, being incrementally more complex, simplifies the user interface designing and prototyping processes. In order to demonstrate the possibility to show the visual appearance of an interface and to validate the specification, a prototype to visualize any user interface specified using UIFD was created.

Keywords: User Interface Prototyper, Visual Appearance, User Interface Free Designer.

1 Introduction

In our days, direct manipulation interfaces [5] are virtually universal. Interfaces that use windows, icons and menus have become a standard in traditional computational systems. The process of building that final user interfaces can be represented by models. Usually, a model is supported in some user interface specification and according with [1][7][9] there are three elements that must be considered on a user interface specification:

- Interface graphic elements definition (visual presentation);
- Component composition;
- User interaction over the referred components (dialog).

In previous studies [10] the creation of a simple game for younger children was proposed, using DGAUI (*Abstract Definition of Graphical User Interface*) [9]. The interactive visual user interface prototype was created from an abstract representation

M. Kurosu (Ed.): Human-Computer Interaction, Part I, HCII 2013, LNCS 8004, pp. 490–499, 2013.

containing visual elements representing sport balls and sport fields that the user should connect with each other. After the interface has been implemented it was considered that certainly the implementation work could have been reduced if the DGAUI system embraced the *complex component* concept [13]. It was questioned if eventually could be possible to reduce the representation complexity in terms of number of states and visual transitions, through identification and grouping of visual elements which have a common logic. The *complex component* concept evolved from other abstract interaction objects concepts (*AIOs*) [2][3][11]. Basically, is a component composed of other components (*simple* or/and *complex*) which interact with each other through its *self* and *delegate events/actions* working toward a common goal (e.g. a *toolbar* allows a user to select a specific tool to perform some task at a given time).

The *complex components* creation process is based on a XML specification (*UIFD – User Interface Free Design*) developed to allow representing visual components freely designed. The specification has a structure divided in three fundamental parts: *repository*, *library* and *interface*. It allows increasing the abstraction level on the components representation process used to design the final user interface. Following, in order to verify and validate the XML specification, a prototyper was developed. An example of a game interface for younger children was used to verify loading components into a memory structure, to obtain the global visual states and to represent the visual components on the display, in order the user start interact with the interface.

1.1 Study Motivation

The term user interface is most of the times associated to what a user see and interact with. [6] for example, gives us an interesting interface definition: "*interface is where people and bits meet*". Thus, is imperative that an user interface defining process always take in consideration the indications of user needs in order to successfully accomplish the tasks that he needs/wants. Since a long time, a technique to achieve that is used and is called low-fidelity prototyping ("lo-fi" for short): the idea is building prototypes on paper (e.g. sketches) and testing them with real users. The value of prototyping is widely recognized [8] because it effectively educates developers to have a concern for usability and formative evaluation, and because it maximizes the number of times we get to refine the design before commit to code. Following, the next step will be the translation of those sketches to user interface components, usually called widgets (*wi*ndows ga*dgets*) because most of the visual interfaces are created for the user to interact with them, using those kinds of interactive visual components. However, usually those visual components are not sufficient to represent a complete user interface (regarding the visual appearance, the components composition and the dialog) in many cases by the dependency of libraries of predesigned user interface components (toolkits) that not allow user interface customization, as a user interface designer would like. Thus, we would like to focus this study on the importance for an interface designer, on having the possibility to design free visual components, to be used to represent complete interfaces prototypes.

1.2 Defined Problem

We developed a process which allows, from a XML representation, to test and to validate how a free component (*simple* or *complex*) would appear and could be used in a visual user interface. And, thereby, it is possible to refine the components (and consequently the user interface) according with user needs. However, we had the need to create a prototyper, in order to validate the specification previously created. The main question to be solved and presented in this study is the following: it is possible to obtain and to represent the global visual states of an user interface though grouping the visual states of individual components, designed with a XML specification and responding to user interaction through events over those components? The answer to this question must be considered under our concept in which we treat global visual user interface states as groups of visual components states. For example, a typical web form represents a single web state, but a form has several possible states, in result of user interaction with it. In result of this study we developed a prototyper to represent complete visual user interfaces obtained from the UIFD specification.

2 Free Design Components

Lately, to specify user interfaces using XML (XML-UIDL) is considered to be one solution for the standardization and interoperability between applications [4][12]. However, as previously referred, most of current approaches to interface complex components usage, refer using pre-defined widgets, which limits the designer ability to do components customization (at both visual appearance and dialog levels). Thus, a specification to support free design of user interface *complex components* was established (UIFD). It is a structure divided in three parts:

- *Repository*: contains components nominal definition (*simple* and *complex*) to be used on the *library*;
- *Library*: contains *complex components* complete description, ready to be used on the interface design. It is possible to use multiple instances of the same *repository* component to create a *library* component;
- *Interface*: this structure supports the interface (obtained from *library* components).

It is possible to verify below a XML structure (Fig. 1) of a library component. In this case is one of the sport fields' components (*CC_Field_1*).

Each one of the referred three specification parts is supported in a XML [14] file with the correspondent DTD validation. The XML files constructing process is triggered by the designer when he's constructing personalized *complex components* during the user interface design process.

From the referred previous study [10] we verify that knowing in advance the user interface functionality, it is possible to obtain a visual representation of it (in a form of a state diagram) having the states and the transitions between them, in result of user interaction.

```
<Complex_Component Name="CC_Field_1">
  <Composition>
    <SC>SC_Field_1_N</SC>
    <SC>SC_Field_1_C</SC>
  </Composition>
  <Visual_Appearance></Visual_Appearance>
  <CC_States>
    <CC_State ID="0" Visible="true" Active="true">
      <Status>
        <SC Name="SC_Field_1_N" Visible="true" Active="true" />
        <SC Name="SC_Field_1_C" Visible="false" Active="false" />
      </Status>
      <Dialog_State>
        <Self_Evt ID="1" Event="LeftClick" Component="SC_Field_1_N"
                                            Ini_State="0" End_State="1" >
          <Preconditions>
            <Pre_Cond Component="CC_Ball_3" State="1" />
          </Preconditions>
        </Self_Evt>
      </Dialog_State>
    </CC_State>
    <CC_State ID="1" Visible="true" Active="false">
      <Status>
        <SC Name="SC_Field_1_N" Visible="false" Active="false" />
        <SC Name="SC_Field_1_C" Visible="true" Active="false" />
      </Status>
    </CC_State>
  </CC_States>
  <External_Events>
    <Delegate_Actions>
      <Trigger_DA ID="1" SELF_STATE="1" TO="CC_Ball_3" Trigger_DE_ID="1" />
      <Trigger_DA ID="2" SELF_STATE="0" TO="CC_Ball_1" Trigger_DE_ID="2" />
      <Trigger_DA ID="3" SELF_STATE="0" TO="CC_Ball_2" Trigger_DE_ID="2" />
    </Delegate_Actions>
  </External_Events>
</Complex_Component>
```

Fig. 1. Example of a *complex component* designed using the UIFD specification (simplified)

We verify that the visual interface representation is simplified, although increasing the complexity of the components used to represent it. In order to measure the simplification obtained with our specification we must look at the decreasing number of components available as the abstraction level increases. This happens in virtue of encapsulation property available in *complex components*. We are using fewer components from lower to higher abstraction level, in result of the components being contained inside other components at a higher level. The use of this component type, being incrementally more complex and at the same time being at a more abstract level, simplifies the process of designing and prototyping the user interface.

Taking as an example the game interface for younger children previously mentioned, on (Fig. 2) is shown a simple schema of the process to increase the simplification on a user interface representation, while the abstraction level to represent visual components increases. At the top of the figure is possible to verify the existence of 15 simple components (on the left side) that will successively be grouped into *complex components* (6 in the first abstraction level, 2 in the second and 1 *complete complex component* that represents the final user interface). At the bottom of the figure two examples of *complex components* (*CC_Ball_1* and *CC_Field_1*) are shown. For each *complex component* it is possible to verify the visual states it contains, the restrictions, the internal visual transitions and the events it supports (user events, and *delegate events*). Thus, we verify the amount of information that is encapsulated in each *complex component*, and we also perceive that as complexity increases (as abstraction increases) at the same time the components are simplified to be used representing an user interface.

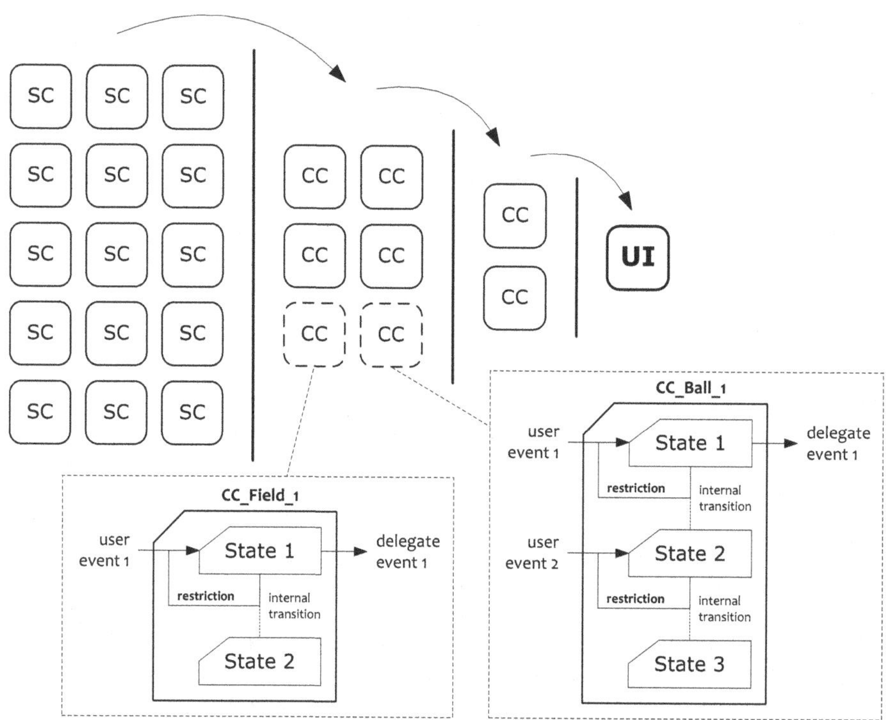

Fig. 2. Decreasing number of components as the abstraction level increases

Another important feature provided by *complex components* usage is their possibility of being reused (at semantic and functional levels). All components to be used are available in the common *repository* and the components personalization is done at the *library* level, promoting components reuse and also contributing to simplify the interface design and behavior, which can be freely established by the interface designer.

3 Interface Prototyper

In order to validate the XML specification previously indicated, an automatic interface prototyper was created. The developed tool allows reading an interface specification in XML and following, to represent the prototype of a concrete interface. The prototype obtained is a functional representation of a component visual appearance and behavior, which is also a complete user interface (*complete complex component*).

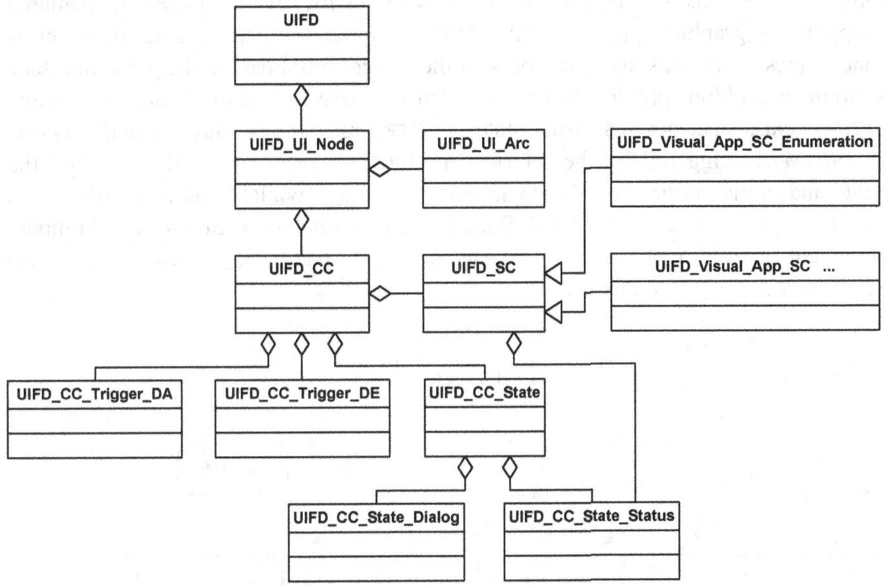

Fig. 3. Complex *component* core class architecture (simplified)

One of the major advantages of using *complex components* is the independence of any platform or programming language that can be used to represent an user interface. From several technologies available, it was decided to implement a first version of a prototype using Adobe Flash. Some advantages of this technology are:

- Currently, to be a technology widely distributed and able to be used by a large number of users;
- Supporting the visual design of graphical primitives and thereby to enable *complex components* visual representation, obtained from data structures (from the preloaded XML files). Despite being vector-based, allows bitmaps incorporation where needed;
- Its flexibility allows to export exactly the same content through web browsers and platforms, without any extra code;
- Supports video, audio, animation, and advanced interactivity, which provides flexibility for future evolution of *complex component* concept.

A simplified diagram of the class main architecture, respecting to the design and implementation of the interface prototyper is depicted in (Fig. 3). The diagram represents an overview of the application main classes that were used to achieve the experimental results here presented. The resulting framework architecture is rather flexible, enabling easy integration of new modules in the *complex components* context. The `UIFD_UI_Node` class supports all user interface global visual states and the connection between those states in result of user interaction is stored by `UIFD_UI_Arc` class. The `UIFD_CC` class is responsible for managing the *simple* and *complex components*. On the case of *simple components*, several classes are available to support any graphical primitives (the `UIFD_Visual_App_SC_Enumeration` class is one of these examples, used to represent the images employed in the game interface for younger children previously created). On the case of *complex components*, the `UIFD_CC` class manages his visual states in `UIFD_CC_State` class, which supports the *self events* triggered by the interface user (`UIFD_CC_State_Dialog`) and the *visible* and *active* properties of each *simple component* available on a *complex component* (`UIFD_CC_State_Status`). Finally, the *delegate events/actions* of a complex component are respectively managed by `UIFD_CC_Trigger_DE` and `UIFD_CC_Trigger_DA` classes.

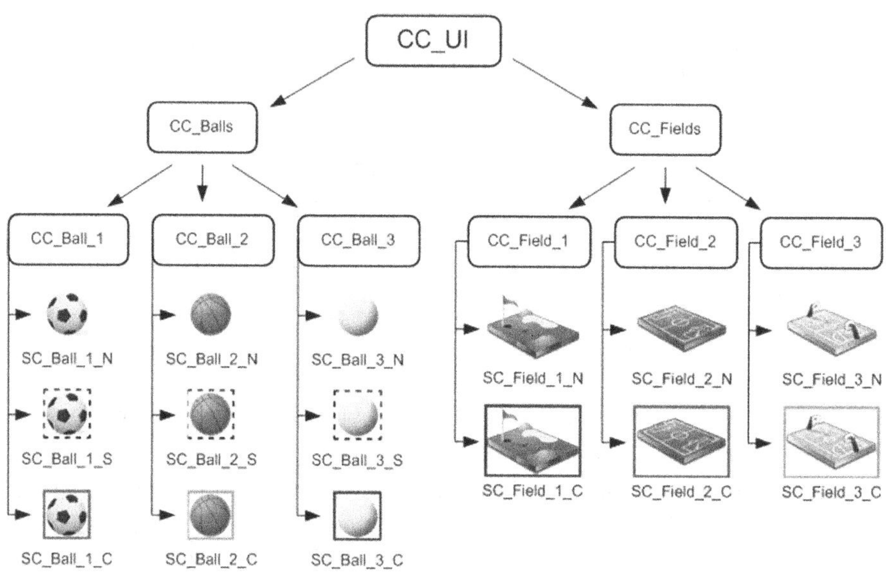

Fig. 4. User interface simple components arranged in a tree

Initially, the prototyper reads the .XML files, structured into a hierarchy of one components tree (Fig. 4). As we can verify on the figure the logical data structure of the game interface, which is composed of two *complex components* (*CC_Balls* and

CC_Fields) each one having three other *complex components*. Each ball (*CC_Ball_*) has three *simple components* and each sport field (*CC_Field_*) has two *simple components*. In order to simplify the global visual states generation, the following step of the algorithm is to convert the components tree into a data structure in memory, which is this case is a linked list (Fig. 5). Each list node (left side) represents all the *complex components* connected in sequence. And, each node has a list of connected arcs, representing the components (*simple* or *complex*) inside each one of the nodes.

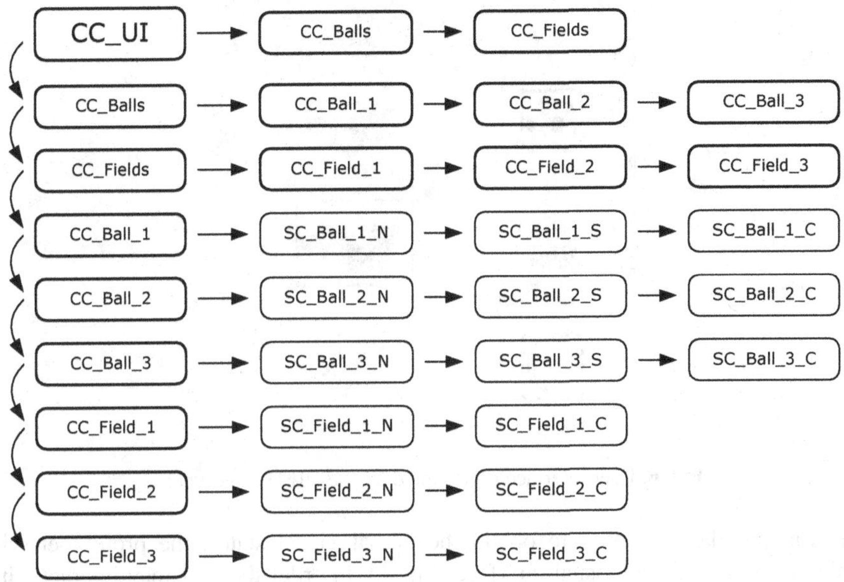

Fig. 5. Linked list obtained from components tree

After concluding the first step of uploading the components hierarchy into the memory structures, is necessary to calculate the user interface global visual states and relate each other according with the dialog events established to change from one visual state to the other. The objective is to obtain a state diagram representing the user interface functionality, with the global visual states (`UIFD_UI_Node`) and the existent transitions between them (`UIFD_UI_Arc`).

As previously indicated, we are at this step trying to obtain user interface states as groups of components states. Thus, an algorithm to traverse the memory structure and to obtain the global visual states was created. Basically, the algorithm follows the steps:

1. For each *self event* (*SE*) available in (`UIFD_CC_State_Dialog`) representing the dialog produced by user interaction over a *complex component* state, the algorithm will verify if any *delegate action* (*DA*) exists in (`UIFD_CC_Trigger_DA`), related to that state;

2. For each one of these (*DA*) found on the state dialog, which executes a *delegate event* (*DE*) the algorithm will look for what is necessary to change on the other affected *complex component*;
3. One global state will be the result of the changes caused by a (*SE*) on the *complex component* which it belongs plus the changes caused by (*DE*) triggered by other components.

Fig. 6. User interface represented by the UIFD prototyper

After running the algorithm to obtain the global visual states, the prototyper will graphically represent the visual interface (Fig. 6), in order the user may interact with it and test the interface prototype, which in this case is the game interface previously referred.

4 Conclusions

In previous studies a XML structure/specification to design user interfaces was created. That specification allows specifying *simple* and *complex components*. Based on these components, an user interface was created and then loaded by the developed prototyper in order to visually represent the user interface. Having a first version of a prototyper, which allows simulating all the global visual states and all the interaction with his components, the following study line will be to upgrade it, developing techniques and integrating a no-heuristic evaluation module, in order to obtain usability results from multiple interface users. Thus, will contribute to detect errors on interfaces under tests and consequently to improve user interfaces efficiency.

Acknowledgments. This work was supported by:

1. Grant SFRH/PROTEC/49496/2009 of MCTES – Ministério da Ciência, Tecnologia e Ensino Superior (Portugal).
2. Project TIN2009-14103-C03-03 of Ministerio de Ciencia e Innovación (Spain)
3. Project 10DPI305002PR of Xunta de Galicia (Spain).

References

1. Carr, D.: Specification of Interface Interaction Objects. In: CHI 1994 – ACM Conference on Human Factors in Computer Systems, pp. 372–378 (1994)
2. Cowan, D., Lucena, C.: Abstract Data Views: An Interface Specification Concept to Enhance Design for Reuse. IEEE Transactions on Software Engineering (1995)
3. Duke, D., Harrison, M.: Abstract interaction objects. Computer Graphics Forum 12(3), 25–36 (1993)
4. Guerrero-Garcia, J., González-Calleros, J., Vanderdonckt, J., Muñoz-Arteaga, J.: A Theoretical Survey of User Interface Description Languages: Preliminary Results. In: Latin American Web Congress, pp. 36–43 (2009), doi:10.1109/LA-WEB.2009.40
5. Hutchins, E., Hollan, J., Norman, D.: Direct Manipulation Interfaces, vol. 1, pp. 311–338. Lawrence Erlbaum Associates, Inc. (1985)
6. Negroponte, N.: Being Digital. Vintage Books, New York (1994)
7. Paterno', F., Santoro, C., Spano, L.D.: MARIA: A Universal, Declarative, Multiple Abstraction-Level Language for Service-Oriented Applications in Ubiquitous Environments. ACM Transactions on Computer-Human Interaction 16(4) (2009)
8. Rettig, M.: Prototyping for tiny fingers. Communications of the ACM 37(4), 21–27 (1994)
9. Rodeiro, J.: Representácion y Análisis de la Componente Visual de la Interfaz de Usuario. PhD Thesis, Universidad de Vigo (2001)
10. Rodeiro-Iglesias, J., Teixeira-Faria, P.M.: User Interface Representation Using Simple Components. In: Jacko, J.A. (ed.) Human-Computer Interaction, Part I, HCII 2011. LNCS, vol. 6761, pp. 278–287. Springer, Heidelberg (2011)
11. Savidis, A.: Supporting Virtual Interaction Objects with Polymorphic Platform Bindings in a User Interface Programming Language. In: Guelfi, N. (ed.) RISE 2004. LNCS, vol. 3475, pp. 11–22. Springer, Heidelberg (2005)
12. Souchon, N., Vanderdonckt, J.: A Review of XML-compliant User Interface Description Languages. In: Jorge, J.A., Jardim Nunes, N., Falcão e Cunha, J. (eds.) DSV-IS 2003. LNCS, vol. 2844, pp. 377–391. Springer, Heidelberg (2003)
13. Teixeira-Faria, P.M., Rodeiro-Iglesias, J.: Complex Components Abstraction in Graphical User Interfaces. In: Jacko, J.A. (ed.) Human-Computer Interaction, Part I, HCII 2011. LNCS, vol. 6761, pp. 309–318. Springer, Heidelberg (2011)
14. W3C Recommendation: XML, XML 1.0 (2008), `http://www.w3.org/TR/REC-xml/`

Structured Scenario-Based Design Method for Experience Vision

Yoshihiro Ueda[1], Kentaro Go[2], Katsumi Takahashi[3], Seiji Hayakawa[4], Kazuhiko Yamazaki[5], and Koji Yanagida[6]

[1] Fujitsu Design Ltd., Kawasaki, 211-8588, Japan
y.ueda@jp.fujitsu.com
[2] University of Yamanashi, Kofu, 400-8511, Japan
go@yamanashi.ac.jp
[3] Holon Create Inc., Yokohama, 222-0033, Japan
takahasi@hol-on.co.jp
[4] Ricoh Company, Ltd., Yokohama, 222-8530, Japan
hayakawa@rdc.ricoh.co.jp
[5] Chiba Institute of Technology, Narashino, 275-0016, Japan
designkaz@gmail.com
[6] Kurashiki University of Science and the Arts, Kurashiki, 712-8505, Japan
yanagida@arts.kusa.ac.jp

Abstract. *Experience Vision* is a comprehensive design method to innovative services, systems and products which reflect upon potential stakeholders' experiences and company mission and vision. It encompasses the entire human-centered design process and presents a new vision with experiential value for both the user and business sides. It then produces users' values, activities, and interactions in scenario format as part of design activities. It finally specifies requirements specifications for the innovative services, systems and products. In this paper, we introduce a Structured Scenario-Based Design Method (SSBDM) as part of *Experience Vision.* SSBDM employs personas and scenarios as human-centered representations for the innovative services, systems, and products. It contains three layers of scenarios: value scenario, activity scenario, and interaction scenario. Using an example of its application in a household account book, we demonstrate how the three layers of scenarios are specified and evaluated in SSBDM.

Keywords: experience vision, service design, scenario, scenario-based design.

1 Introduction

The social, economic environments and technological environments — centering on the information and communications technology (ICT) environments — around us today are rapidly changing. In addition, Japan has experienced the Great East Japan Earthquake and this has accelerated movements there that aim for a safe, secure and sustainable society. There are high expectations for ways to handle social issues that

M. Kurosu (Ed.): Human-Computer Interaction, Part I, HCII 2013, LNCS 8004, pp. 500–509, 2013.

are becoming increasingly complex, such as security measures, disaster measures and responses to problems with the global environment. To deal with environmental changes and new requirements such as these, it is thought that it will be important to not think of products, systems and services from the viewpoint of technology, but to anticipate future societies and human life and realize a vision-proposal type of design development that depicts services, systems and products for humans. To that end, we have proposed a Vision Centered Design method as a new approach to design [Fig. 1].

In the Vision Centered Design method, scenarios (which are described from the user's perspective) will be introduced as a tool to describe and convey a vision of the future. Using scenarios for the design of services, systems and products has been a commonly addressed issue in the field of Human-Centered Design (HCD).

In this paper, we introduce a Structured Scenario-Based Design Method (SSBDM). It contains three layers of scenarios: value scenario, activity scenario, and interaction scenario. Using an example of its application in a household account book, we demonstrate how the three layers of scenarios are specified and evaluated in SSBDM.

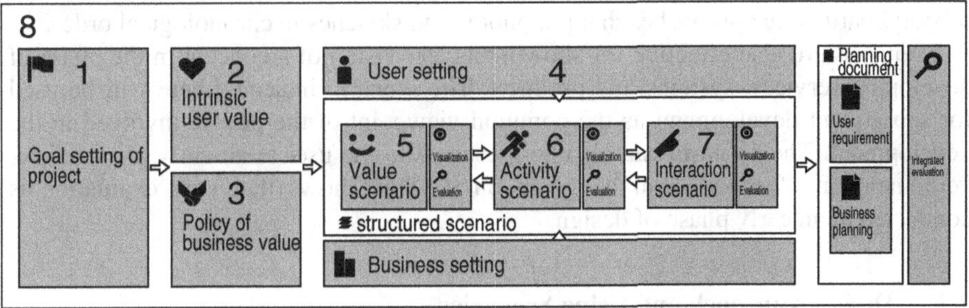

Fig. 1. Framework for Vision Centered Design Method and formats

2 Scenario for Design

A scenario is a story. When it is used for designing an artifact such as a service, system, or product (artifact), a scenario might contain a description of its use. For example, scenarios for designing a mobile phone might include information about who is the user, what is the mobile phone, in what situation it is used, what goal or expectation the user wishes to achieve, and how it is done. To summarize, a scenario is a description that includes actors, their background information, and assumptions about the environment, actors' goals, objectives or expectations, and sequences of actions and events. Some applications might omit one element or might express it implicitly.

2.1 Scenario Properties for Design Development

When conveying the general outline and features of services, systems and products, it is important to appropriately communicate the value which can be obtained by utilizing them. Explaining the practical procedures and relationships in due order will naturally compose a story. This is the scenario. It is used when creating ideas at an early stage of development, when explaining the idea to someone, and when keeping a written record of the idea. Thus, the scenario is first shared within the organization involved in the development. Then, when the services, systems and products are provided to the user, the scenario is utilized to explain how to use them. Promotional brochures and catalogues, for instance, explain concepts and features in a narrative form, and instruction manuals explain how to use a product step-by-step in an orderly sequence. In this way, scenarios are used in various situations that involve services, systems and products[1].

In the field of technical communication, it is conventionally said that using 5W1H (when, where, who, what, why, and how) is the most effective way to express an idea. The same applies to describing a scenario. For a product scenario, "When" and "Where" indicate the situation, "Who" indicates the user, "What" indicates the targeted services, systems and products, "Why" indicates the user's goals and expectations, and "How" indicates how to use the services, systems and products. Asking the question of "Who" leads to determining what is specifically described as a "persona," and therefore, scenarios and personas are closely related. Alternatives are comic style, or storyboard-style approaches that put photos and sketches in chronological order.

Scenarios are also effective for showing a clear vision of a concept in the phase of developing services, systems and products. The scenario indicated here will be used for subsequent development as the common viewpoint of the people involved in the development. The scenario can also be presented to the user at an early phase of development and feedback can be given on it. This shows that user evaluation is conducted at an early phase of design.

2.2 Design Approach and Using Scenarios

There are different ways of using scenarios in a problem-solving design approach and vision-centered design approach. In the problem-solving design approach, a scenario is used for describing the problems. If a system used by users does not meet their expectations due to an operation problem, a scenario (problem scenario) will be created to explain the problematic situation. If this situation is understood by the designer, the act of designing will be the problem-resolution tool. And if modifying the design of the system provides an immediate solution to the operation problem, a new design will be considered. In order to simply describe the new design in contrast to a problem scenario, a scenario (solution scenario) will be created to explain a situation where the users' expectations were met.

In the design action, the approach of using a scenario as a description of an intermediate product is called "scenario-based design"[2]. In some cases, scenarios are used in fragments of the design process but they can also be used as the main product.

3 Structured Scenario-Based Design Method

In the vision-theme design approach, however, a scenario is used to describe a vision. That is, a scenario is created to explain the future goal resulting from the development. In this case, the scenario will function as a development goal. Unlike the problem-solving design approach, the act of designing will not always begin based on a scenario which describes the problematic situation, and the action can begin according to the designer's free, original idea and technology seeds. As a result of the design, visualization is required to share and assess the effect on users.

3.1 Scenario Structure

With the vision-centered design method, the scenario will be classified according to the hierarchy and then structured. Classifying the function of a services, systems and products with the focus on its components will make it easier to understand. It can be classified into three hierarchies here: (1) value, (2) activity, and (3) interaction. This is because there are three hierarchies to actualize the overall function: (1) one that shapes value, (2) one that shapes the action to realize value, and (3) one that shapes the operation to realize action [Fig. 2]. Moreover, these hierarchies are not always structured in a top-down form — from value, to activity, and then to interaction — but are also repeatedly structured and re-structured in a top-down and bottom-up form, which leads to the actualization of the eventual overall function. Based on this viewpoint, each functional hierarchy of services, systems and products is clarified by writing the scenario according to the features. This is called a "structured scenario."

(1) Value scenario — Deals with value
(2) Activity scenario — Deals with activity
(3) Interaction scenario — Deals with operation

Fig. 2. Functional hierarchy of scenario

A structured scenario is a scenario classified into one of three types which correspond to the above hierarchy: (1) value scenario, (2) activity scenario, and (3) interaction scenario. Based on these scenarios, user requirements specifications, and project proposals including business plans can be obtained.

The value scenario corresponds to the description given for value hierarchy. This scenario describes an intrinsic value for users and business value as a provider. Here, a business goal and user's expectations are pictured. In this hierarchy, rather than minute technical requirements, categories with a relatively high level of abstraction will be determined; this can be the developmental goal. In this sense, the focused evaluation viewpoint is the business viewpoint. Attraction and novelty, which reflect user satisfaction in human centered design (HCD), are also the evaluation viewpoints discussed in this hierarchy.

The activity scenario corresponds to the description given for activity hierarchy. This scenario embodies scenes where the services, systems and products are used, which are the development objects, and visualizes the user's activity. The exclusive activity flow and the user's emotions are specifically visualized as a scenario. While a business viewpoint is also described, the main objects of description are the user's concrete image and its activity. The focused evaluation viewpoint is the effectiveness in HCD.

The interaction scenario corresponds to the description given for interaction with the hierarchy. In particular, a practical operation to make users head toward goals is pictured here, indicating the function of the services, systems and products. The focused assessing viewpoint provides efficiency in HCD.

3.2 Features of Structured Scenario-Based Design Method

Next, the features of each scenario in structured scenarios will be shown [Fig. 3]. With regard to the above scenarios, an image of realization from services, systems and products is described in the user requirements specifications and project proposals including business plans. The main object of description is the technology component, which is assessed from the viewpoint of feasibility. Alternatively, a structured scenario constitutionally fits the usability definition of ISO924-11. As previously stated, usability is defined as "effectiveness, efficiency, and satisfaction when a certain product is used by a designated user under a designated usage condition to achieve a designated goal."

The structured scenario clearly describes the user information in detail as a persona. The interactive scenario specifically and chronologically visualizes the users' goal and the activity process as they head towards the goal using the services, systems and products. Thus, efficiency can be evaluated here. The activity scenario describes the user experience to the abstract level which shows the overall activity flow, and effectiveness will be evaluated. The value scenario describes and assesses the users' satisfaction from the viewpoint of value provided to them. As stated above, the evaluation items in the usability definition are allocated to each hierarchy.

Type of scenarios	Business goal User expecta-tions	Users' concrete image activity	Object component	Technology	Major Evaluation viewpoint
Value Scenarios (User value, business value)	Good	Poor	Poor	Poor	・HCD ・Attraction ・Novelty
Activity Scenarios (User activity)	Average	Good	Poor	Poor	・HCD ・Usability
Interaction Scenarios (Concrete operation to head towards goal)	Average	Average	Good	Poor	・HCD ・Efficiency
Project proposal (Implemen-tation tool)	Average	Average	Average	Good	・Technology ・Feasibility

Fig. 3. Features of each scenario in structured scenarios

4 Features and Example of each Scenario

Here are the general outlines and features of the value scenario, activity scenario, and interaction scenario using a simple example. The example given here is a household account service for individual users, which will be used to differentiate between scenarios.

4.1 Value Scenarios

The value provided to the user is examined, generated, and described in the value scenario. As stated earlier, the necessary information is described in the value scenario focusing on the user's essential demands and the business provision policy. In particular, three items will be mainly described: 1) details of user information, 2) business information and 3) the scenario.

For details of the user, the participants involved in the services, systems and products will be listed. The user events obtained from interviews, observations, and inner comprehension will be recorded as user information. Also, the user's essential demands, which were abstracted by ranking the needs based on user information, will be described.

As for business information, the basic information on the business such as the business domain, business environment (opportunity/threat), management resources (strength/weakness), and business strategy is described. It is also effective to describe the results of SWOT (Strengths, Weaknesses, Opportunities, and Threats) analysis. In addition, there will be description of providing the policy of value based on business information, that is, providing business policy.

Lastly, the provided value will be described as a scenario. There is a particular focus on value here, and it is important not to describe the specific user image or services, systems and products. This is to keep from restricting implementation tools at the phase of examining the later services, systems and products. An example of a value scenario is shown below [Fig. 4].

Value Scenario
User Information Beginners in handling household accounts: would like to manage the payment balance, but do not want to make too much effort. **Business Information** Has advanced image analysis technology. Providing policy: Enable simple entry and data browsing with a high operability user interface (emphasize customer satisfaction). **Scenario** Beginners in handling household accounts accurately manage payment balance with fuss-free entry.

Fig. 4. Example of a value scenario

When evaluating the value scenario, confirmation is required to see whether the user's essential demand and the provision policy by the business are properly reflected. The specific evaluation viewpoints are as follows:

- Whether the project goal is achieved;
- Whether the user's essential demands are satisfied;
- Whether it corresponds with the provision policy of the business; and
- Whether it is consistent with the cast.

In the value scenario, effectiveness and satisfaction from the user's perspective is recognized, and efficiency is outside the scope for this hierarchy. Similarly, business strategy attribution, business attribution, and sociality are recognized from the business perspective, but feasibility is outside the scope in this hierarchy. These outside-the-scope viewpoints are the evaluation viewpoints that depend on the implementation of products, systems and services, which are addressed in the interaction scenario.

4.2 Activity Scenarios

In the activity scenario, one scene is set based on the value scenario, and the overall activity flow of that scene and the user's emotion is described so that the entire image can be visualized. A concrete persona is also introduced in the activity scenario.

In particular, the details of three items — user information, scene information, and scenario — will mainly be described.

As the user information, a candidate of a persona is chosen from the cast set in the value scenario and a specific persona will be pictured. If there are multiple casts, one activity scenario will be created for each one.

The scene assumed from the value scenario is described as the scene information. A number of scenes can be assumed to realize the value depicted in the value scenario; thus one activity scenario will be created for each scene. Multiple activity scenarios will, therefore, be created from one value scenario.

Based on the above information, the activity flow of the persona in the set scene and the emotion will be described in the scenario based on the goal of the persona. Be aware that in the activity scenario, the experience of the persona is focused on and the services, systems and products are not substantiated. Therefore, the activity scenario is not dependent on implementing the object and many possibilities for implementation remain. An example of an activity scenario is shown below [Fig. 5].

A concrete image of user information is introduced in this activity scenario. The expense record is assumed as a scene. Also, Takuya's activities are described at the abstract task level. You can see his attitude from his awkwardness.

In an activity scenario, the experience of a persona in the subject scene is valued, and the activities and the user's emotion are clearly described based on the person's goal. These must reflect the content of the premising value scenario. The viewpoint, therefore, is whether these are properly reflected when evaluating the activity scenario. Specifically, the points to examine are as follows:

- Whether the project goal is met;
- Whether (the scene written in) the value scenario is achievable; and
- Whether the persona is reflected.

In the activity scenario, the effectiveness and satisfaction from the user's perspective are recognized, and efficiency is outside the scope for this hierarchy. Similarly, the business strategy attribution, business attribution, and sociality of the business perspective are recognized, but feasibility is outside the scope in this hierarchy. These outside-the-scope viewpoints are the evaluation viewpoints that depend on the implementation of the services, systems and products, which are addressed in the interaction scenario.

Activity Scenario
User Information Takuya, a young second-year college student, lives in an apartment and studies in the faculty of engineering at a college in the suburbs. He works hard at his part-time jobs as he receives a small allowance from his parents and wants to socialize with his friends. He manages his income and expenses to avoid hassles at the end of the month. **Scene Information** Record expenses. **Scenario** Takuya uses this system to manage his balance. He sees the amount left in his monthly budget through this system. He also records his income and expenses. He wants to input the data discreetly and quickly as he feels awkward being seen recording such small amounts of money. During lunchtime, Takuya bought a boxed lunch at a convenience store near the college. He paid with cash and received a bag with the boxed lunch, change, and receipt. He had thrown away receipts in the past, but since he began keeping track of his household account, he has been recording the amount written on the receipt.

Fig. 5. Example of an activity scenario

4.3 Interaction Scenarios

Interaction scenarios describe a scenario of concrete interactions between persona and services, systems and products written in sequential order. At this point, the functional features of the services, systems and products and the activities of the target users must be clearly defined. In particular, three items will be described mainly — details of user information, business information, and scenario.

User information is written in the same way as activity scenarios. If an activity scenario is fully complete, the description of the persona can be transcribed from the activity scenario. If there is another description about the persona, information referencing the subject persona can be indicated.

As the next step, the tasks associated with the activity scenario are detailed. Multiple tasks are assumed in order to realize the activity depicted in the activity scenario;

thus, one interaction scenario will be created for each task. Therefore, multiple interaction scenarios can be generated from a single activity scenario.

Interaction scenarios are described based on these sets of information. Here, the relationships between the persona and services, systems and products are described in sequential order based on the task. When describing, it is especially important to express the ideas to realize the services, systems and products concretely and clearly. These realization ideas allocate functions and roles by properly factoring in the characteristic features of hardware, software, and humanware.

Interaction scenarios describe the relationships between persona and services, systems and products based on tasks in sequential order. These scenarios apparently need to contain the content of previously created activity scenarios. Therefore, an interaction scenario is evaluated from the perspective of whether these activity scenarios are properly reflected in it. Specifically, the points to examine are as follows:

- Whether the project goal is met;
- Whether (the tasks described in) the activity scenarios are realized; and
- Whether the persona is reflected.

All evaluation points are subject to evaluation in the interaction scenario. The efficiency of the user's perspective and the feasibility of the business perspective, neither of which are considered for value scenarios and activity scenarios, are assessed from the viewpoint of implementation. The following is an example of an interaction scenario [Fig. 6].

Interaction Scenario

User Information

Takuya, a young second-year college student, lives in an apartment and studies in the faculty of technology at a college located in the suburb. He works hard at his part-time jobs as he receives a small allowance from his parents and wants to socialize with his friends. He manages income and expenses to avoid hassles at the end of the month.

Task Information

Input information from receipts.

Scenario

Takuya took out his smartphone and started up an app by tapping the housekeeping book icon. A list of records was displayed in graphs and numbers by item and the current balance — 22,700 yen — was shown on the display. Takuya tapped the big "Payment" button.

The camera function was then started and a photo was taken. He took a photo by putting the camera on the receipt he had in his hands. The receipt was shown on the display and the amount paid — 480 yen — was highlighted with a thin frame line. Takuya tapped on the frame and selected "Lunch" from the menu displayed. The display changed to a *record list* view and he confirmed that the graph and numbers for food expenditure had increased.

Fig. 6. Example of an interaction scenario

Interaction scenarios are described with concrete actions. This example illustrates an individual action to achieve the subsidiary goal — to track expense amounts — which is derived from the main goal — to manage the balance of payments accurately. That is to say, it illustrates the action of inputting information from receipts. Efficiency can be evaluated because concrete actions are described in chronological order.

Project proposals containing user requirements specifications and business plans are created using the three types of scenarios above.

5 Conclusion

In this paper, we have described the role and characteristics of the structured scenario in the Vision Centered Design method. In addition, we have mentioned some cases and specifically given some descriptive content and shown the point of view used in evaluation for each of the three tiers in the structured scenario.

As a result of this study, we confirmed that it is possible to utilize the structured scenario method to state some ideas for vision-centered development. Moreover, we also confirmed that it is possible to elaborately expand ideas by describing the scenario in a hierarchical way. Further, we found that it is possible to describe multiple activity scenarios from one value scenario, that it is also possible to describe multiple interaction scenarios from one activity scenario, and that it is possible to generate multiple ideas and evaluate them.

We believe that a Structured Scenario-Based Design Method (SSBDM) as part of *Experience Vision* (Vision Centered Design method), is an effective way to efficiently produce sophisticated ideas.

References

1. Yamazaki, K., Ueda, Y., Go, K., Takahashi, K., Hayakawa, S., Yanagida, K.: Experience Vision. Maruzen Publishing Co., Ltd., Japan (2012) ISBN 978-4-621-08565-3 C 3050
2. Go, K.: What Properties Make Scenarios Useful in Design for Usability? In: Kurosu, M. (ed.) HCD 2009. LNCS, vol. 5619, pp. 193–201. Springer, Heidelberg (2009)
3. Edited by Japan Industrial Designers' Association: Product Design, Works Corporation, pp. 116–117 (2009)
4. Yanagida, K., Ueda, Y., Go, K., Takahashi, K., Hayakawa, S., Yamazaki, K.: Vision-proposal Design Method. In: Kurosu, M. (ed.) HCD 2011. LNCS, vol. 6776, pp. 166–174. Springer, Heidelberg (2011)
5. Yanagida, K., Ueda, Y., Go, K., Takahashi, K., Hayakawa, S., Yamazaki, K.: Structured Scenario-based Design Method. In: Kurosu, M. (ed.) HCD 2009. LNCS, vol. 5619, pp. 374–380. Springer, Heidelberg (2009)

Requirements for a Definition of Generative User Interface Patterns

Stefan Wendler and Ilka Philippow

Ilmenau University of Technology, Software Systems, Process Informatics Department
Helmholtzplatz 5, 98693 Ilmenau, Germany
{stefan.wendler,ilka.philippow}@tu-ilmenau.de

Abstract. Patterns for visual GUI design propagate the specification of user interfaces with proven usability and motivate model-based development processes with increased reuse of GUI component compositions. However, a common structure, that captures all the reusability and variability demands, neither has been established for the descriptive form nor the generative kind of user interface patterns. Dedicated GUI specification languages like UIML and UsiXML fail to express pattern definitions that can be instantiated in varying contexts. Thus, model-based processes are required to introduce own media to store those patterns. With our approach, we review the state of the art for generative user interface pattern definition and derive requirements which we refine by a Global Analysis. Finally, we developed a model that accommodates primary factors and their impacts towards the concept for a more sophisticated generative user interface pattern definition.

Keywords: HCI patterns, user interface patterns, GUI generation.

1 Introduction

For systems which are intended to provide a direct support for users in their operative tasks the user interface is of highest importance. The developers of the user interface have to be aware of three different basic requirements. Firstly, the user interface has to provide an effective and task-adequate access to the functional layer and data of a given system. Moreover, the user interface has to be visually designed and implemented in a way that enables the user to work with the system efficiently. Lastly, a business information system has to meet the before mentioned requirements after incremental adaptations to new demands imposed by the changed business processes and their environment.

Finally, these requirements for user interface systems lead to high efforts in initial development and the further lifecycle of the system. During the adaptation of a user interface to user requirements some aspects of the presentation layer essentials may see a potential for increased reuse. For these aspects, the basic layout of dialog types, their arrangement and navigation mechanism as well as reoccurring user interface controls (UI-controls) and their data type processing are considered to see more reuse in the future. System specific patterns seem to be helpful for the reuse as these aspects

M. Kurosu (Ed.): Human-Computer Interaction, Part I, HCII 2013, LNCS 8004, pp. 510–520, 2013.

feature a high variability, e.g. the content data of dialogs as well as the associated UI-controls and navigation options highly depend on the task to be supported. Finally, a need has emerged to both decrease the efforts for GUI development or individual customization and enable a homogenous assembly for of the architecture comprising the user interface components.

HCI-Patterns. The deployment of patterns for GUI development has been discussed for more than a decade now [1][2][3]. Besides architectural patterns that can be relied on for the definition of basic structures for GUI components, various definitions, approaches and modeling process have emerged from the application of patterns that provide solutions for the visual and interactive parts of the GUI, which are not addressed by the basic design patterns. However, no consistent definition for patterns dedicated to GUI development has been established yet.

In general, as increased reuse is propagated here and by other approaches applying model-driven processes [4], there is a need for a dedicated pattern definition. The pattern conception has to ensure that a GUI system will be developed homogenously along its hierarchy of visual and non-visual components, meaning that architecture and GUI patterns have to be comprehensive. If the pattern concept was not able to cover every context of application and thus in need for specialized solutions, the main problem of GUI development related efforts would persist. We claim that this is an issue for current research projects that may enable pattern-based solutions for GUI systems but at some point have to revert to manually refined structures not covered by mere pattern instantiation.

User Interface Patterns. To begin with, "user interface pattern" (UIP) [5] is used as a term for the further discussion of GUI specific patterns. UIPs are intended to aid in adaptation and creation of user interfaces with a similarity in task or data processing, visual and interaction design. Currently, UIPs are not considered as a strong asset as architectural or design patterns for enabling reuse of concepts and context aware instantiation. It is our goal to encourage a basic conceptual view on UIPs that may pave the way for their assured and unified integration as an artifact in development environments. Moreover, we strive for the elaboration of a requirement model for UIPs that should be able to capture all essential aspects and needs for context-specific application and instantiation of UIPs. GUIs created by generators tend to lack usability what could be improved by the involvement of established UIPs [6]. In sum, a process that enables the instantiation of UIPs and their composition to form a user interface of high usability and adaptability altogether would be of great value.

Objectives. As our objective, we see the review of the state of the art in the area of implementation related UIP approaches. After a problem analysis concerning the formalization of abstract UIPs, we formulate requirements that reflect the exploits of UIPs. During the analysis of requirements, we derive influence factors that are systematically presented via a Global Analysis.

Our aim is to raise the awareness of expert groups to focus on UIPs and their abstract pattern nature. The purpose behind UIPs was to act as patterns describing user interface commonalities and allowing instantiation. A first step for the formalization of UIPs required for automated processing is the identification of their characteristics and traits which embody the reusable aspects of a user interface.

2 State of the Art Review

2.1 UIP Definition and Collections

Stating a UIP definition is not easily done since a standardization of this term has yet to be reached [7]. What can be assumed is a separation of UIPs between their usage in specification or generation of software, hence the pattern idea for GUI systems found its roots in HCI [8] and now evolves towards automated or generative development [9]. As a result, UIPs have been separated into two types by Vanderdonckt:

Descriptive UIPs. Serving mainly as illustrative examples for GUI specification, descriptive UIPs are described and interpreted by human-beings and thus act as inspirations or best-practices for usability proven GUI design.

Generative UIPs. For our objective, the generative type of UIPs is of greater importance since these patterns have to store all relevant information for the automated processing by generators. For a set of given generative UIPs a defined set of design patterns or architectural structures have to be instantiated in source code. Each type of UIP determines a certain quality of architecture part. The final choice of UIP instances to be used for a part of GUI system merely determines the quantity of code structures to be instantiated by the generator. As reuse should be increased, the manual addition of linking code (glue code) must be omitted.

PLML. The descriptive specification of UIPs already poses an issue which is caused by the lack of a proper definition for this artifact. There have been attempts to create a unified description scheme with the introduction of PLML (pattern language markup language) in 2003 [10]. Engel, Herdin and Märtin conducted an investigation of common description schemes in [7]. Descriptive UIPs are established as specification elements and supported by the HCI community. Thus, one could be tempted to abstract the common structure of UIPs from the existing UIP collections. Following this course, Engel, Herdin and Märtin have discovered that a full compilation of necessary elements is difficult, since the patterns are still presented in a rather unstructured form [7] and missing attributes for technical considerations. In addition, PLML never was supported by a unified metamodel that satisfies all generative UIP needs. Several extensions have been proposed but there are still enhancements which have to be incorporated [7]. Furthermore, implementation aspects and relationships among UIPs are neither sufficiently nor clearly mentioned by PLML. With this status quo on the specification level, a proper formalization of UIPs as generative artifacts is hindered at an early stage.

UIP-Libraries. To some extent, descriptive UIPs have been filed in UIP-libraries like [11] and [12]. In contrast to the weaknesses of their content structure, UIP-libraries do motivate our approach towards a clearer definition of generative UIPs. They drive the pattern-based application of UIPs by depicting GUI example layouts, that do feature stereotype visuals and interactions which may be adapted to individual application contexts. Thus, UIP-libraries inspire the idea to compose individual GUI dialogs by choosing from the available pattern palette.

2.2 Modeling Processes Involving UIPs

A sophisticated development environment for generative UIPs was created by the University of Rostock [4]. Their example proves that UIPs can be instantiated to various application contexts and thus facilitate reuse in GUI development. However, the used presentation model implicitly defined the UIP to be applied. Consequently, a selection of a different UIP had to be done via a manual replacement by pre-defined GUI components (PICs) already resembling certain instances of UIPs. Thus, the variability was restricted to few applications. Besides, not all types of UIPs were supported or manual adjustments still were needed. Later on, a vote for the closer integration of model- and pattern-based processes was raised [13]. This goal implicitly demands for a mature definition of generative UIPs as there was still potential to increase reuse and lessen efforts for linking and integration models to be generated. In this context, UIPs were to be stored in an abstract form so that they could be instantiated. Finally, options for their formalization had to be considered.

Following this idea, modeling frameworks and processes for GUIs [14][15][16] are advancing and have already introduced their own notations for generative UIPs. However, these approaches are difficult to judge, since they are mostly presented as drafts and miss profound code examples. In fact, there exists no common requirement model for the common or similar goals they are striving to achieve. Their individual notations for UIPs are either based on customizations [14][16] of available GUI specification languages or even own XML language conceptions [15].

2.3 UIP Formalization

GUI Architecture Concerns. To assess the applicability of GUI specification languages for generative UIPs, feasible criteria have to be sourced. As the requirements and responsibilities for a component-based GUI system [17] alone are extensive, the patterns, which are intended to drive the creation of those components in a generative way, also have to be capable of supporting several concerns at once. Due to the fact that architectural patterns like MVC, PAC or the Quasar reference architecture for clients [18] are needed as additional mental models framing the rather elementary and universal structures of classes and components, the target architecture is of a complex basis, which rarely has been unified in its details. Without this unity of a common architectural basis and the dilemma concerning reference architectures [18], a formal UIP definition faces the problem to be acceptable for different architectural pattern interpretations and implementations.

Criteria. To avoid those architecture related issues, we first set up three fundamental criteria to be met by formal UIPs and came up with a generalized reflection of the variability concerns of UIPs by referring to a simplified MVC model covering basic responsibilities needed in most applications [19]. The interrelation of the criteria and variability demand for UIPs that can be combined freely and integrated in GUI entities without manual design modeling, as it would be needed for common architectural and design patterns. Formal UIPs have to enable at least the two criteria "reusability and variability of stored user interface patterns" and "ability of user interface patterns to be composed in order to form a hierarchy of GUI components" out of their pure pattern form. The latter is a main issue when UIP instances have to be created from their formal XML specifications.

Formal Languages for GUI Specification. In our previous work [5][19], we already went into the possibilities to express generative UIPs with the means of mature GUI specification languages UIML (User Interface Markup Language) [20] and UsiXML (USer Interface eXtensible Markup Language) [21]. Although these XML languages are focused on platform-independent GUI specification and intended to be machine processed, our assessment of UIML and UsiXML revealed that both languages failed in architecture and specification experiments to fully express UIPs with the two considered criteria. We assume that the languages are sophisticated tools for GUI specification and may be used as external domain specific languages for GUI generation, but they are not based on abstract patterns and do lack a conceptual definition of UIPs. However, developers have to revert to existing GUI specification languages, as there is still no dedicated language for UIP formalization.

UsiXML. The abstract user interface model (AUI) suggested by UsiXML sounds promising for storing UIPs. However, the facets and abstract interaction objects [9] used as elements therein create a model that is way too abstract to express the elements of specific UIPs, as their general types of UI-controls are mostly known and thus definable. In contrast, the concrete user interface model (CUI) of UsiXML can express platform specific instances of the AUI model contents, e.g., how an input or output facet is structured by certain UI-controls. In this respect, the CUI acts as a direct instantiation of the AUI and no longer resembles a pattern as the visual structure and behavior cannot be parameterized or reused for other contexts. Finally, both models are not suitable for storing UIPs as their abstraction level is not appropriate.

UIML. The UIML language also offers promising features for UIP formalization. With the <structure> section a "virtual tree" [20] of UI-controls is arranged. This tree can be sourced from more than one UIML file at once. In contrast, UsiXML models are stored in a single file. The UIML "virtual tree" can be modified by sub-sections or even other UIML files as they may restructure given parts (repeat, delete, replace and merge sub-trees) of the main tree [20]. Templates and their variables can be applied to adapt reoccurring UIML tree parts to various GUI descriptions. With those features, it is possible to assemble a GUI virtual tree by integration of several UIML files under utilizing most restructuring options. The style of UI-controls can also be governed by a global UIML definition to ensure a uniform presentation look. Nevertheless, the UIML mechanisms always need concrete inputs for the elements to be processed. For instance, template parameters of UIPs being sourced by other UIPs forming a composite pattern specification have to be specified with constant data like the number of elements to be included. As the UIML file is being specified, the developer has to provide certain input to govern the occurrences of UIML elements or templates. Therefore, the effect of a pattern featuring structural variability is neglected for UIP compositions. In addition, UIML provides no facilities to describe behavior for elements that are abstract and yet to appear when the UIP is instantiated. In the end, UIML specifications will tend to be too concrete to store the abstract UIPs.

To conclude, the main disadvantage of both languages lies in the incapability to provide a separation of UIP definition and instantiation. UIPs need to be specified in a concrete manner in order to be compatible with the schema definitions of the languages. Invariant UIPs like "Date Selector" [11] or "Input Prompt" [12] can be specified by the languages as there is no need for variability. Concerning UIML, elementary UIPs may be expressed by using templates along with parameters, but nested UIPs pose a problem as included UIPs have to resemble a specific instance.

3 Our Approach

Requirements. A first step towards a more sophisticated UIP model definition was the elicitation of requirements. To source the appropriate information, we relied on our previous work [5][19], an industry project in the E-Commerce domain and the presented state of the art. Since the requirements were scattered across concerns and could not be mapped easily to artifacts or rationale, we decided to apply the Global Analysis [22] as a method to create another view on the requirements so that they could be analyzed concerning their impact, relations and strategies.

Global Analysis. The Global Analysis originally serves as a method to systematically derive and describe the leading factors for architecture design. With this analysis, the given set of requirements is assessed concerning the impact of individual requirements on the system design. Requirements with significant impact are marked as factors, which are classified to one of three factor types. For a set of factor impacts, design strategies are elaborated to realize the specific requirements or overcome their restrictions. The method provides steps to relate requirements to certain decisions and high level system artifacts that drive the design of multiple system components. Following this consideration, it is attempted to limit the impact of factors to artifacts or system structures which can be handled more easily.

In our application of the method, we incorporated some adjustments differing from the original source. In short, factors may be detailed as they are composed of nested factors, they may be operationalized by other factors when they cannot be associated to impacts clearly, and finally, the design rationale is incorporated as an additional artifact influenced by the design strategies. An overview of the method we applied for requirement elicitation is provided in Fig. 1, which also serves as a legend.

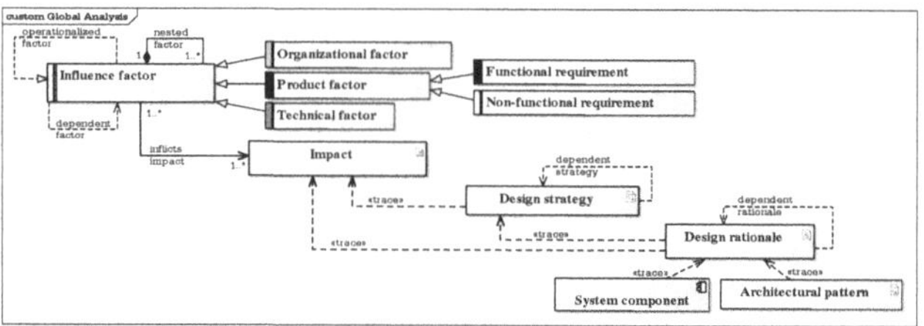

Fig. 1. Metamodel of our customized Global Analysis method

4 Global Analysis Results

The Global Analysis we conducted resulted in the factors presented in Fig. 2. Most factors were derived from the industry project. Consequently, the essential model [23] of the E-Commerce software was to be included as an important factor, since the UIPs should be reused to support existing tasks, functions and objects of that domain. As the user interface needs to be related to a user model [23] and thereby to the essential model, UIPs may be promising, as they may replace the need for a dedicated user model [5]. Hence, UIPs have to be mapped to the essential model. Concerning this matter, extensive work has been conducted by the University of Rostock [4].

The technical factors are based on our consideration to apply XML languages for UIPs already instantiated and thus the description of a concrete GUI [19]. Therefore, the generation of XML code was chosen as an approach which requires a detailed definition of UIPs as shown in Fig 2.

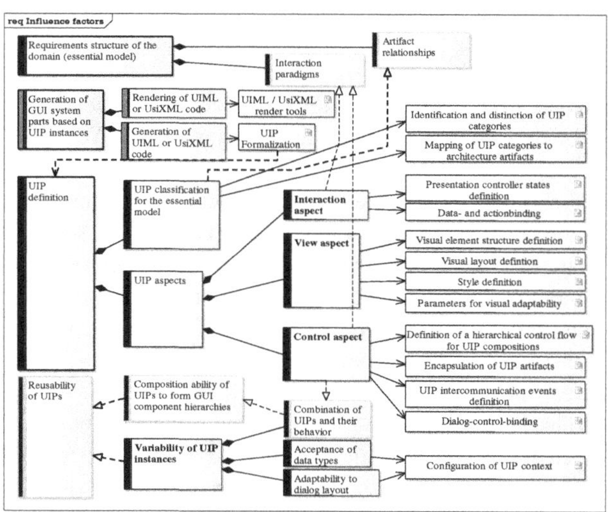

Fig. 2. Influence factors elaborated for the UIP analysis

The UIP definition factor was based on our previous work, as we enriched the three UIP aspects described in [19] with impacts, which provide a more detailed description of their influence on UIP specification models. Concerning the view factor, the impacts are mostly apparent. A view structure has to be defined, along with the layout and style information as the foundation of each UIP. Additionally, parameters have to be considered for the former to enable the adaptation to various contexts.

Being determined by user input the interaction aspect demands for the binding of view structure elements to certain data and presentation actions. The latter may trigger a change of view structure states, e.g., manipulating single UI-controls or interfering with multiple UIPs within hierarchical view structures and their lifecycle.

The control aspect poses the most demanding impacts. For each UIP of a certain class, a corresponding control flow on the same abstraction level has to be defined. In order to allow both the collaboration of composite UIPs and their versatile combination, the encapsulation of UIPs is necessary as well as the communication via defined events. Embedded UIPs are supposed to send events to their controlling UIPs and the latter require to communicate with the dialog controller, which governs the application related states and data.

The reusability factor was derived from the two criteria in Section 2.3. Two other factors, composition ability and variability, were nested in this factor. The former was mainly operationalized by the control factor which already detailed most of the necessary impacts. Initially, the primary requirements of the project were of non-functional kind and have been used to underline the benefits of UIPs. In Fig. 3 the operationalization of these factors is shown.

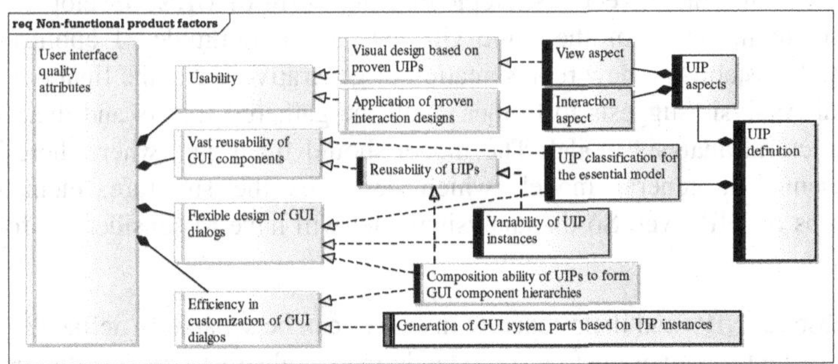

Fig. 3. Operationalized non-functional requirements

Actually, the UIPs were introduced to realize the main projects needs. As considerable HCI specification units, UIPs were supposed to ensure a high degree of usability. Important and at the same time difficult to master requirements on the left hand side in Fig. 3 should be realized by the composition of reusable and generative UIPs.

Design Strategy. The result of the Global Analysis emerged as a solution strategy which demands for the design of a basic UIP description model. As another requirement model closer to a formalization artifact, it should be able to capture all mandatory characteristics of generative UIPs within a structure. For our objective, we need a general model that represents the requirements more clearly and structured in model whose elements and relationships can be transferred to a formal UIP modeling approach. In this regard, the model has to be independent from GUI specification language definitions of UIML or UsiXML, hence it should be used to overcome the limitations of the former concerning UIP expression. Consequently, the primary concern is to capture the requirements for formal UIPs in a model that may share structural analogies with future formalizations. Furthermore, generative solutions for UIPs are rather seldom and cannot be sourced for our objective. Therefore, the description model should serve as a further enhancement in the assessment of formalization options for generative UIPs and their properties. Finally, it should prove to be applicable in different domains rather than just for one specific application infrastructure.

5 Conclusion and Future Work

With our contribution, a model consisting of influence factors and their impacts related to UIP instantiation, reuse and variability is presented. In the first place, this model can be used to judge to capabilities of available formal languages to express the defined characteristics of a UIP. Besides the judgment, the model can propose applicable enhancements to used languages and models in an environment based on UIPs. In this context, the model also may serve for verification.

The remaining problem is embodied by the need to find an abstract formal representation of generative UIPs. Deploying this form of UIPs, developers will be able to create instances of the same UIP but for a multitude of applications or variations. To establish a new representation of generative UIPs, the final outcome of our Global Analysis suggests to further detail the gathered factors and their impacts with a structural analysis model. The model should fill a gap, where there has not been presented a general model, which describes the structure, elements and relationships of UIPs, yet. So the analysis model will have to consider the following questions:

- How abstract UIPs and their concrete instances can be separately defined?
- Which instantiation parameters are to be defined in abstract UIP specifications?
- How UIP compositions are to be compiled and interaction events are defined in the resulting GUI element cascade?

In any case, a new language or extensions for the XML languages are to be sought after. The new media must facilitate the expression of the generative UIPs, their variability and composition options. For that purpose, a unified UIP model has to be established, which holds all information for the definition of generative UIPs in an abstract form, augmented with parameters allowing for their transformation to single instances or compositions forming a concrete GUI model. To progress towards this goal, existing approaches like [14][15][16] have to be analyzed in detail in order to enhance the presented factor model and discover limitations yet to overcome.

References

1. Mahemoff, M., Johnston, L.: Principles for a usability-oriented pattern language. In: OZCHI 1998, Adelaide, Australia, pp. 132–139 (1998)
2. Todd, E., Kemp, E., Phillips, C.: What makes a good User Interface pattern language? In: AUIC 2004, Dunedin, New Zealand, pp. 91–100 (2004)
3. Dearden, A., Finlay, J.: Pattern Languages in HCI: A critical Review. In: Human-Computer Interaction, vol. 21(1), pp. 49–102 (2006)
4. Wolff, A., Forbrig, P., Dittmar, A., Reichart, D.: Tool Support for an Evolutionary Design Process using Patterns. In: Workshop: Multi-Channel Adaptive Context-sensitive Systems: Building Links Between Research Communities, Glasgow, Scotland, pp. 71–80 (2006)
5. Wendler, S., Ammon, D., Kikova, T., Philippow, I.: Development of Graphical User Interfaces based on User Interface Patterns. In: Proceedings of the 4th International Conferences on Pervasive Patterns and Applications, Nice, France. IARIA Proceedings, pp. 57–66 (2012)
6. Meixner, G., Paterno, F., Vanderdonckt, J.: Past, Present, and Future of Model-Based User Interface Development. i-com 10(3), 2–11 (2011)
7. Engel, J., Herdin, C., Maertin, C.: Exploiting HCI Pattern Collections for User Interface Generation. In: Proceedings of the 4th International Conferences on Pervasive Patterns and Applications, Nice, France. IARIA Proceedings, pp. 36–44 (2012)
8. van Welie, M., van der Veer, G., Eliëns, A.: Patterns as Tools for User Interface Design. In: Farenc, C., Vanderdonckt, J. (eds.) Tools for Working with Guidelines, pp. 313–324. Springer, London (2000)
9. Vanderdonckt, J., Simarro, F.M.: Generative pattern-based Design of User Interfaces. In: Proceedings of the 1st International Workshop on Pattern-Driven Engineering of Interactive Computing Systems, Berlin, Germany, pp. 12–19 (2010)
10. Fincher, S.: PLML: Pattern Language Markup Language, `http://www.cs.kent.ac.uk/people/staff/saf/patterns/plml.html`
11. van Welie, M.: A pattern library for interaction design, `http://www.welie.com`
12. Open UI Pattern Library, `http://www.patternry.com`
13. Radeke, F., Forbrig, P., Seffah, A., Sinnig, D.: PIM Tool: Support for Pattern-driven and Model-based UI development. In: Coninx, K., Luyten, K., Schneider, K.A. (eds.) TAMODIA 2006. LNCS, vol. 4385, pp. 82–96. Springer, Heidelberg (2007)
14. Radeke, F., Forbrig, P.: Patterns in Task-based Modeling of User Interfaces. In: Winckler, M., Johnson, H. (eds.) TAMODIA 2007. LNCS, vol. 4849, pp. 184–197. Springer, Heidelberg (2007)
15. Engel, J., Märtin, C.: PaMGIS: A Framework for Pattern-Based Modeling and Generation of Interactive Systems. In: Jacko, J.A. (ed.) Human-Computer Interaction, Part I, HCII 2009. LNCS, vol. 5610, pp. 826–835. Springer, Heidelberg (2009)
16. Seissler, M., Breiner, K., Meixner, G.: Towards Pattern-Driven Engineering of Run-Time Adaptive User Interfaces for Smart Production Environments. In: Jacko, J.A. (ed.) Human-Computer Interaction, Part I, HCII 2011. LNCS, vol. 6761, pp. 299–308. Springer, Heidelberg (2011)
17. Haft, M., Olleck, B.: Komponentenbasierte Client-Architektur. Informatik Spektrum 30(3), 143–158 (2007)
18. Haft, M., Humm, B., Siedersleben, J.: The Architect's Dilemma – Will Reference Architectures Help? In: Reussner, R., Mayer, J., Stafford, J.A., Overhage, S., Becker, S., Schroeder, P.J. (eds.) QoSA 2005 and SOQUA 2005. LNCS, vol. 3712, pp. 106–122. Springer, Heidelberg (2005)

19. Ammon, D., Wendler, S., Kikova, T., Philippow, I.: Specification of Formalized Software Patterns for the Development of User Interfaces. In: The 7th International Conference on Software Engineering Advances, Lisbon, Portugal. IARIA Proceedings, pp. 296–303 (2012)
20. UIML 4.0 specification, `http://docs.oasis-open.org/uiml/v4.0/uiml-4.0.html`
21. Vanderdonckt, J., Limbourg, Q., Michotte, B., Bouillon, L., Trevisan, D., Florins, M.: UsiXML: a User Interface Description Language for Specifying multimodal User Interfaces. In: WMI 2004, Sophia Antipolis, France, pp. 35–42 (2004)
22. Hofmeister, C., Nord, R., Soni, D.: Applied Software Architecture. Addison-Wesley, Boston (2000)
23. Ludolph, M.: Model-based User Interface Design: Successive Transformations of a Task/Object Model. In: Wood, L.E. (ed.) User Interface Design: Bridging the Gap from User Requirements to Design, pp. 81–108. CRC Press, Boca Raton (1998)

Characterizing Incidents Reporting Systems across Applications Domains

Marco Winckler, Cédric Bach and Regina Bernhaupt

University of Toulouse (UPS), Institute of Research in Informatics of Toulouse (IRIT)
118 route de Narbonne, 31062 Cedex 9, Toulouse, France
{Winckler,cedric.bach,regina.bernhaupt}@irit.fr

Abstract. Incident reporting is a very well-known technique in application domains such as air traffic management and health, where specialized users are trained to provide detailed information about problems. Incident reporting systems are indeed complex systems that include many actors including the users reporting incidents, user's colleagues and neighbors, stakeholders, policymakers, systems integrations. Incident report systems might change (positively or negatively) the users' environment in many ways. In recent years, this kind of technique has been also been used in crisis management such as the hurricane Katrina. However, despite the fact that incident reporting systems using mobile technology are becoming more common, little is known about its actual use by the general population and which factors affect the user experience when using such system. In this paper we discuss the use of incident reporting system in critical context of use. In this paper we discuss the use of incident reporting system in several application domains. In particular we report findings in terms of dimensions that are aimed to identify social and technical aspects that can affect the design, development and use of incident reporting systems.

Keywords: Incident reporting, mobility, geo-localization, user interface patterns, m-government, e-government.

1 Introduction

Incident reporting is a very well-known technique in application domains such as air traffic management [6] and health [7], where specialized users are trained to provide detailed information about problems. What has been found in these areas is that incident reporting is an important means to improve safety by enabling authorities to improve technical systems, design or (work) procedures based on the incident reports. Incident reporting in these safety-critical domains is characterized by being part of the work routine, enabling special benefits for users reporting incidents.

However, in more recent year, incident reporting system has been extended to be used for ordinary people outside of their working settings. In recent years, this kind of technique has been also been used in crisis management such as the hurricane Katrina [11]. Many governments have also started to make use of mobile technology for

M. Kurosu (Ed.): Human-Computer Interaction, Part I, HCII 2013, LNCS 8004, pp. 521–530, 2013.

allowing citizens to report incidents in their neighborhood (e.g. broken street lamps, street water leak) to the local administration [13]. These applications (featuring crowdsourcing systems [3]) are part of a variety of initiatives for promoting active participation of citizens in the actions of the government through the use of information and communication technology (e/m-government) [4][9]. The latest generation of mobiles device include touch interaction, GPS and camera, so that mobile phones (smartphones) provide users/citizens with means to report incidents by specifying location (e.g. typing on a map), sending a precise location (e.g. using GPS) and providing photos or videos of incidents. Such as information enhance the quality of incident descriptions and can be used as proof/evidence such as demonstrated by the applications ispot [5] which illustrates how ordinary people can contribute to conservation initiatives by reporting bird's migration. Thus, despite the fact that incident reporting systems are often associated to safety-critical domains, there is no reason they could not be used to report less critical incidents in users' life.

Nonetheless, reporting incidents in a mobile setting seems to be a quite complex activity as it requires a certain amount of knowledge to describe successfully the observed problem (attributes enabling the identification of the incident itself), time and spatial constraints (ex. incident reporting might not occur by the time/space of the incident itself), privacy issues. Moreover, the importance of these dimensions might vary accordingly to user needs and the application domain. For example, contrary to the work-oriented incident reporting in the safety-critical domain, any mobile phone application for the general public must support the privacy of the citizens/users. In order to analyze the similarities and idiosyncrasies of different implementations of incident reporting system, we propose in this paper a domain space for characterizing incident reporting systems. Such domain space is based on a review of the literature and it provides a synthesis of our previous work on the field [1][14]. In section 2, we start presenting a model-based task analysis of incident reporting systems using mobile phones; this section is aimed to show how generic user tasks can be used to extract a large set of scenarios that can accommodate a large set of scenarios for reporting an incident. In section 3, we discuss a set of dimensions that can influence the decision to implement a particular scenario. Lately in section 4 we present conclusions and future work.

2 Report Incident with Smartphones: Task Model

Task analysis is widely recognized as one fundamental way to focus on the specific users' needs and to improve the general understanding of how users may interact with a user interface to accomplish a given interactive goal [2]. In this section we present a generic task model for incident reporting systems. The main goal of this model-based task analysis is to describe all possible scenarios leading users to successfully report an incident. The current task model assumes the use of mobile phones as a possible target platform for the system.

2.1 Characterization of User Tasks when Reporting Incidents

Despite that incident reports might be virtually used in different situations, let us assume a simple case of incident reporting system allowing a citizen (i.e. a user) to digitally declare, in a mobile context, an urban incident. This activity involves several preconditions: First, a citizen must identify something that matches his mental representation of what is an incident. Mental representations are strongly depended on background, education, cultural values, demographics, involvement, and many other factors. Classical approaches to solve these difficulties should be (a) the clinical approach allowing people to explain their own point of view of an incident, (b) the classification approach providing citizens with a taxonomy from which the users can infer the possible occurrence of an incident (e.g. beach incident category will fit Rio de Janeiro, Cannes, etc. but will not fit Madrid or Washington DC). Second, the citizen must be aware of the existence of the incident reporting service, and then estimate that that service can solve the incident better than any other effort from the citizen him/herself. Third, the citizen must dispose of a device and a service to report the incident.

For the declaration there are three subsequent questions to take into account: What *is an incident?* Several attributes can be used to characterize an incident. It is often mandatory to know where the incident occurred and what its nature is. The localization of the incident is a mandatory attribute to report an incident, even if the location is approximated. If this information is not provided, it will be difficult to solve the incident. Knowing the nature of the incident also helps to solve it more efficiently, so an incident report needs a description (either informal or derived from taxonomy of known types of incidents). *When the incident occurred?* The accuracy of time might differ accordingly to the type of incidents. Whilst some incident reporting will contain exact data and time (e.g. witnessing car crashing) other might be unknown (e.g. when a pothole appears in the lane). The frequency of incidents might also be requested as a mean to better characterize the incident. *Who reports the incident?* Declaration might be anonymous but identification of users reporting incidents might be necessary to prevent spam or trust on the information provided. *How the incident is reported?* Users can describe the incident by writing a note in a paper, sending an email or using a dedicated mobile application featuring a structured form. Devices and technological means will heavily affect the user activity. Technology that supports human memory, provide sense of orientation and the categorization tasks will be useful in this activity. Furthermore, technology is aimed at conciliating space and time between the incident observation and the incident report. At this point, the users have all they need to digitally report an urban incident. To complete the task there would be still the post-condition to this activity. It concerns the feedbacks about the report and refers to the resolution of the incident. This point mainly depends on the back-office activity (e.g. authorities that collect the reports).

2.2 Model-Based Task Analysis

In order to describe the tasks we employ a task model notation called HAMSTERS (Human-centred Assessment and Modelling to Support Task Engineering for Resilient Systems) [8]. Task models described in HAMSTERS feature a hierarchical graph decomposing complex tasks into more simple ones. Tasks are depicted accordingly to the actors involved in the task execution (i.e. the user, the system or both at a time). Complex tasks are called abstract tasks. In additional to hierarchical decomposition of tasks, it is possible to connect two tasks using logical and temporal operators for expressing dependence between task execution (ex. sequence, choice, order independence). Hereafter we only provide the basic constructs of the notation that are necessary for understanding our models. For further information about the HAMSTERS notation please refer to [8]. When reporting an incident the following three main tasks have to be performed: (1) *to detect the incident*, (2) *to submit an incident report* and (3) *to follow up on an incident report.* Figure 1 illustrates the hierarchical organization of these tasks using the HAMSTER notation. The operator >> indicates that these tasks should be performed in a sequence. The execution of the task detect incident is the first step towards incident reporting. Once an incident is detected, users can submit an incident report. As users might edit a report several times before effectively submitting it, this task is set to be iterative (see the left-hand side symbol). Once it has been sent, the user can follow up an incident report; this task is represented as optional (see right-hand side symbol) as not all citizens will be interested in the outcomes of an incident report.

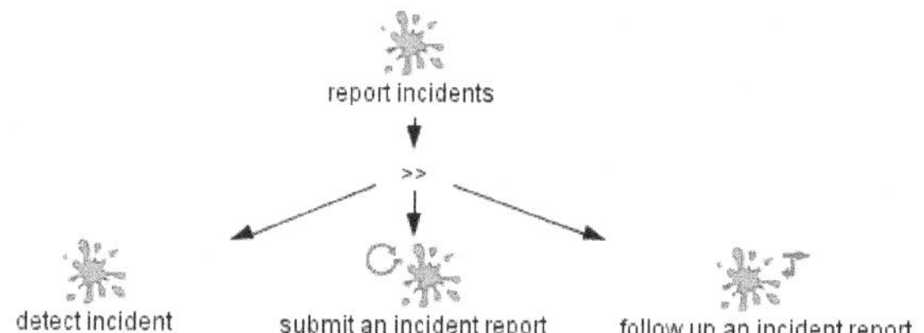

Fig. 1. Main tasks for reporting an incident

Figure 2 provides a more detailed view of user activity by decomposing all complex tasks into more simple ones. Thus the task detect incident is decomposed in several cognitive sub-tasks including the perceptive sub-task recognize an incident and the cognitive sub-tasks identify who should solve an incident and decide to report the incident. These tasks aim at capturing the main issues that occur on the users' side before reporting an incident. For example, to identify who should solve an incident is necessary for determining a system or at least destination for the incident report. Moreover, users should decide [if it is worthy or not] to report an incident. If the user is able to solve these questions he can proceed with the description of the incident.

Generally speaking, the information requested in the identification of the incident includes a description, a location, the time associated to the occurrence of the incident and the identification of the person reporting the incident. Not all this information is mandatory; however at least the description and the location of the incident should be provided. The task "submit an incident" is set as iterative, which means it can be revised until users send the report. It is noteworthy that a user might decide to cancel the submission at any time; this feature is supported by the operator disabling ([>).

Users describe an incident by informing the incident category rating the perceived severity or providing a description for it. For the description, users can perform a textual description, provide a picture/video that shows the problem or incident or call a hot line. The operator |=| indicates these activities can be done in any order. The location of an incident is mandatory; otherwise it would be very difficult to put the means in place to fix it. However, accordingly to the context, users can provide diverse information about the position of the incident: for example by performing the task to provide an address, pinpoint it on a map, use landmarks (ex. in front of the Eiffel tower) or solve GPS coordinates. A report can be completed by adding optional information about the time and the user. In some situations, users are able to report the time for the incident, which implies the user task tell when the incident occurred and the system task record when the incident is reported. The sub-task report time for the incident is optional because it is very likely that incidents occur without any witness so that the exact time for an incident is unknown.

Users might be requested to provide personal identification either by identifying themselves or allowing the system to use personal coordinates already known by the system (ex. cellphone number). Identification of users can vary considerably from a system to another. Precise user identification might help to prevent spam and false reporting, or to contact users if needed. However, we shall notice this is a requirement for the authorities, not for the users. Indeed, incidents description might remain accurate and valid even if reported anonymously. After submitting a report, some users might want to follow up an incident report. It is worth noting that the subscription for a notification might also engage users in a communication with the back-office. Some users might also want to share reports using a social network or just be interest in to see reports sent by others users. Of course not all users will follow up an incident report so closely, so this and all subsequent sub-tasks are described as optional. The task model presented in Figure 2 provides a comprehensive view of tasks related to incident reporting; however it does not impose any particular design for the system. Using the simulator embedded into the HAMSTER editor it is possible to extract 122 alternative sequences of tasks leading to the same goal. For example, from our task model we could extract a simple scenario that requires very few information through basic text fields to report an incident. Another scenario extracted from the model integrates tasks allowing users to provide pictures for the incident and allowing the system to solve GPS coordinates that will be automatically added as part of the incident report. We assume that by extracting the appropriate scenarios from this task model we are able to describe a large set incident reporting in various applications domains such as health, ATM, e/m-government.

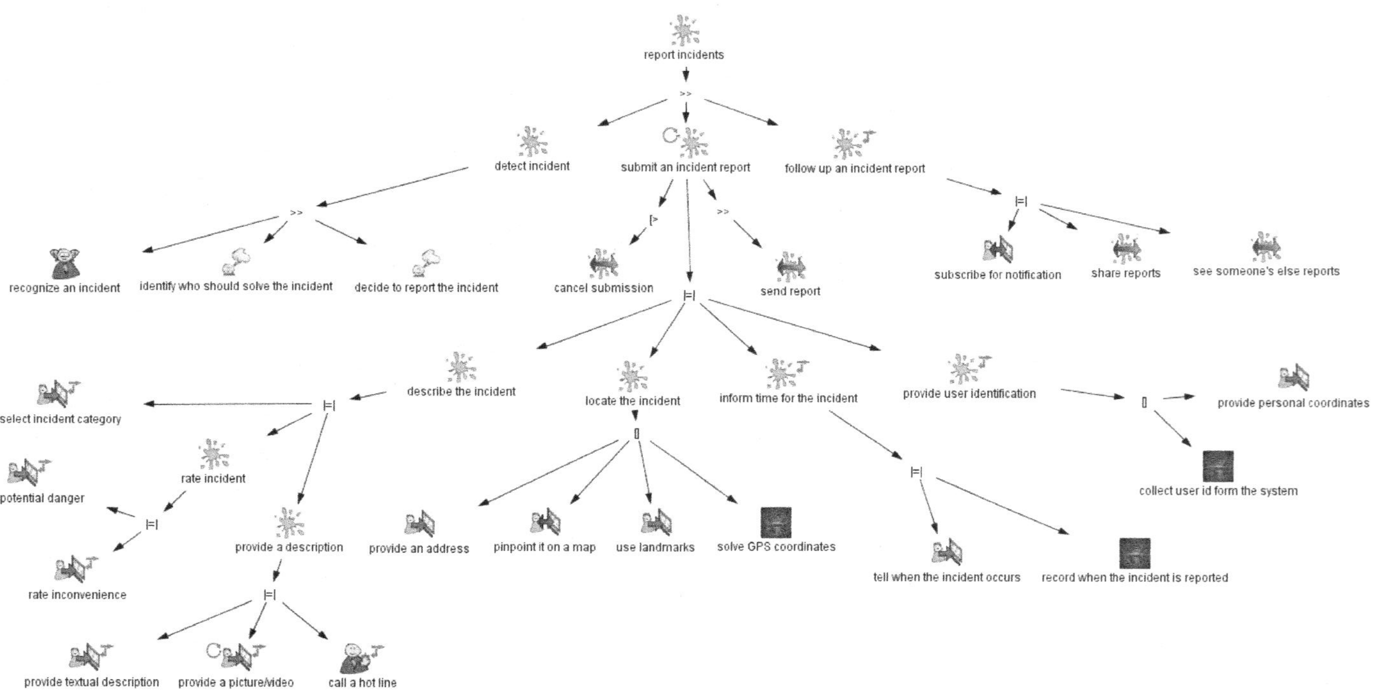

Fig. 2. Generic task model for reporting an incident

3 Dimensions Characterizing Incident Information Systems

This section presents a set of dimensions for characterizing incident reporting systems. These dimensions are heavily inspired from the task analyzed presented in previous sections but also from our previous work [1][14] and review of the literature, in particular [10][12]. Table 1 provides a view at glance of the dimensions including possible values for each category.

Table 1. Domain space for incident reporting systems

Incidents characteristics	**Type**	uncategorized	user's categorization	Taxonomy	
	Severity	minor incident	important	dangerous	safety-critical
	Inconvenience	none	low	medium	high
	Location	address	GPS coordinates	contextual location	moving incident
	Frequency	one shoot	recurrent	event based	unpredictable
	Duration	undefined	punctual	fixed duration	evolving
	Level of accuracy	informal description	structured description	evidence (photo)	certified report
Users characteristics	**Identification**	Anonymous	profile	role	person
	User's involvement	none	observer	witness	responsible for
	User's motivation	none	low	medium	high
Technology	**Technologies**	paper	desktop application	Website	smartphone application
	Outcomes	no feedback	system acknowledgment	personalized feedback	follow up incident
	Proactivity	no prompt	help	safeguarding	prompting

3.1 Incident Characteristics

The following dimensions are used to define the characteristics of an incident:

- The *type* of an incident concerns a graduation of incidents categorizations that would be used to classify incidents. This follows a scale that ranges from less accurate to more accurate categorizations: *Uncategorized incident*, *Incident categorized directly by users* and finally using *taxonomy of incident* types.
- *Location* refers to the different means and characteristics of incident location. The localization of the incident is a mandatory issue to report an incident. If this issue is not completed, it will almost be impossible to solve the incident. This dimension also follows a graduation: address, GPS, contextual location and finally a moving incident (e.g. a stray dog).

- *Severity*. We assume that users differentiate incidents with different degrees of severity ranging from a minor incident to dangerous incidents. The report of a minor incident will generally be driven by the perception that it is a users' duty.
- *Inconvenience*. The level of inconvenience is characterized by the troubling nature of the incident either from an organizational point of view or in terms of moral or material values. Inconvenient incident may damage equipment or disturb the peace. It would be range from *none* inconvenience to variable scale that is illustrated here as *high inconvenience*.
- *Frequency* is a temporal dimension aiming at defining the repetition of an incident. Possible values include *one shoot* (single occurrence), *recurrent* id users said that this is not the first time it occurs, *event based* when users are able to identify the event that triggers the incident, and or *unpredictable*.
- *When the incident occurs*. This is another temporal dimension. Possible values for duration might include: *undefined* when users cannot tell it, *punctual* when the date/time can be determined as a unit of time, *fixed duration* when users can inform the beginning and the end of an incident, and *evolving* when the incident is a continuous event that users cannot inform either the start and/or the end.
- *Accuracy* refers to the quality of the information in an incident report. Possible values are *informal description* of an incident, clear and *structured description* (possibly characterizing all attributes of an incident), *and evidence* such as photos or factual data provided by the users, and *certified report* when users can provide a proof of the occurrence of the incident or when the user is a certified expert whose reports are legally trusted by authorities.

3.2 Users Characteristics

The following dimensions characterize the users that report an incident:

- *Identification* refers to which extension a person can be associated to an incident report. For example, the report can be *anonymous*, identified by a *user profile* such as a young/elder user, a *role*, the attributes such as name, sex, addresses that provides a clear identification of a *person*.
- *User's involvement in the incident* describes the particular role of a user in the incident such as *observer, witness* or *responsible for* the incident.
- *User's motivation* might encompass one of the following: (a) identification of an event that could be perceived as a nuisance/problem, (b) detection of an event that could prevent the occurrence of an likely nuisance/problem, and (c) identification of something worthy reporting that could improve the quality of the environment and/or its management. The detection of an incident is based on tangible characteristics identified in the environment and how an individual interprets them in the respective location. The perception of an individual of the nature of an incident appears to have an impact on its level of involvement in the reporting process, it also influencing the time and the number of operations a user is willing to spend and to perform an incident report.

3.3 Technology

Technology covers three main dimensions that characterize the technological means used with incident reporting systems.

- *Technologies.* This dimensions includes the diversity of platforms (e.g. Android, iPhone, Windows Phone,...) and the types of communication means (i.e. direct interaction as on desk in a city hall, use of paper forms, synchronous communication such as in phone call or asynchronous as in text message) seems to affect the effective use of incident report systems. This dimension follows a graduation of different technical means as desk, paper forms, website, and smartphone application.
- *Outcomes* refers to the type of feedback users can get after reporting an incident. It might include: *no feedback, system acknowledgment, personalized feedback* and the possibility for a user to *follow up incident.*
- *Proactivity* refers to the level on which the system implements features for prompting users to report incidents. Possible values are: *no prompt, help* is provided when users ask for it, *safeguarding* users from performing dangerous tasks, or *prompting* when the systems explicitly request users to provide information.

4 Discussions and Future Work

Incident reporting systems can be used in different context such as reporting problems in working setting, promote citizens involvement with governmental initiatives, monitoring the environment, etc. In this paper we have discussed dimensions involved in incident reporting activity. We have presented a task model from which we can extract a large set of scenarios that can accommodate many types of incident reporting systems. Moreover, we have provided a preliminary domain space model with the main dimensions that can be used to tune the profile of scenarios supported by incident reporting systems. By extracting the appropriate scenarios and using the values associated to which dimension of the domain space we are able to characterize a large set of incident reporting systems. This is first step leading to the comparison between different incident reporting systems across application domains.

We also have discussed several concerns that should be taken into account when designing the user interface. Our results are very preliminary but they raise several questions of both scientific and practical significance: what are the user needs for reporting incidents? What are the dimensions and how do they affect the user experience when reporting incidents? How to reduce training with the user interface for reporting incidents and still provide accurate description of problems? How to handle localization issues on urban context of issues? How to cope with temporal constraints related to the occurrence of the incident and the time of reporting it? What is the minimal information for identifying incidents? What is the role of social networking activities in policing incident reports? How to compare incident reporting systems used for different purposes and in different application domains? Can design solutions for reporting incidents in a domain be transferred to another application domain? How mobile technology might affect users' tasks for reporting incidents?

The present work is a first step forwards the identification of best (and bad) practices for the design of user interface of critical incidents. Most of the analysis held in the current paper is based on user requirements and analysis of user tasks. Our future work will include the validation of the dimensions of the information space with more real case studies. The goal is to make sure that none dimension necessary to characterize the information space was let out.

Acknowledgments. This work is part of the Ubiloop project partly funded by the European Union. Europe is moving in France Midi-Pyrenees with the European Regional Development Fund (ERDF). Genigraph and e-Citiz are partner of this work.

References

1. Bach, C., Bernhaupt, R., Winckler, M.: Mobile Incident Reporting in Urban Contexts: Towards the Identification of Emerging User Interface Patterns. In: 5th IFIP's WG 13.2 Workshop PUX, Lisbon, Portugal, September 5 (2011)
2. Diaper, D., Stanton, N.A. (eds.): The Handbook of Task Analysis for Human-Computer Interaction, 650 pages. Lawrence Erlbaum Associates (2004)
3. Doan, A., Ramakrishnan, R., Halevy, A.Y.: Crowdsourcing systems on the World-Wide Web. Commun. ACM 54(4), 86–96 (2011)
4. El Kiki, T., Lawrence, E.: Mobile User Satisfaction and Usage Analysis Model of mGovernment Services. In: Proc. of Euro mGov 2006: Second European Conference on Mobile Government, Brighton, UK (2006)
5. ispot (2012), http://www.ispot.org.uk/
6. Johnson, C.W.: Failure in Safety-Critical Systems: A Handbook of Accident and Incident Reporting. University of Glasgow Press, Glasgow (2003)
7. Kaufmann, M., Staender, S., von Below, G., Brunnerc, H., Portenier, L., Scheidegger, D.: Déclaration anonyme informatisée d'incidents critiques: une contribution à la sécurité des patients. Bulletin des Médecins Suisses 84 (2003)
8. Martinie, C., Palanque, P., Winckler, M.: Structuring and Composition Mechanisms to Address Scalability Issues in Task Models. In: Campos, P., Graham, N., Jorge, J., Nunes, N., Palanque, P., Winckler, M. (eds.) INTERACT 2011, Part III. LNCS, vol. 6948, pp. 589–609. Springer, Heidelberg (2011)
9. Misuraca, G.: Futuring e-Government: governance and policy implications for designing ICT-enabled Knowledge Society. In: Proc. ICEGOV 2009, Bogota, Colombia (2009)
10. Moon, J.: From e-Government? Emerging practices in the use of m-technology by state governments. IBM Center for the Business of Governement (2004)
11. Moynihan, D.P.: From Forest Fires to Hurricane Katrina: Case Studies of Incident Command Systems. IBM Center for the Business of Government (2007)
12. Reason, J.T.: Human Error: models and management. Br. Med. J. (2000)
13. Song, G.: Transcending e-Government: a Case of Mobile Government in Beijing. In: Proc. of The First European Conference on Mobile Government, Sussex (July 2005)
14. Winckler, M., Bach, C., Bernaupt, R.: Identifying User experiencing factors along the development process: a case study. In: Proc. of Int. Workshop on the Interplay between User Experience Evaluation and System Development, I-UxSED 2012, Copenhagen, Denmark, October 15 (2012)

Method Format for Experience Vision

Koji Yanagida[1], Yoshihiro Ueda[2], Kentaro Go[3], Katsumi Takahashi[4], Seiji Hayakawa[5], and Kazuhiko Yamazaki[6]

[1] Kurashiki University of Science and the Arts, Kurashiki, 712-8505, Japan
yanagida@arts.kusa.ac.jp
[2] Fujitsu Design, Ltd., Kawasaki, 211-8588, Japan
y.ueda@jp.fujitsu.com
[3] University of Yamanashi, Kofu, 400-8511, Japan
go@yamanashi.ac.jp
[4] Holon Create Inc., Yokohama, 222-0033, Japan
takahasi@hol-on.co.jp
[5] Ricoh Company, Ltd., Yokohama, 222-8530, Japan
seiji.hayakawa@nts.ricoh.co.jp
[6] Chiba Institute of Technology, Narashino, 275-0016, Japan
designkaz@gmail.com

Abstract. The "Experience Vision: Vision Centered Design Method" is a comprehensive method which makes it possible to propose new and innovative products, systems and services that are currently unavailable, as well as proposing advances for those that currently exist. It encompasses the entire HCD (Human Centered Design) process, and presents a new vision with experiential value for both user and business from an HCD viewpoint.

This paper discusses a set of eight formats developed as a practical design tool for implementing this method. They include Goal setting of the project, Intrinsic user value, Policy of business value, Persona, Value scenario, Activity scenario, Interaction scenario and Experience vision (summary). Case studies showed effectiveness and usefulness of the formats as a design tool for this method.

Keywords: experience vision, vision centered design method, structured scenario.

1 Introduction

In the present day, product development for matured markets requires a research method of user needs that even users do not yet anticipate. In order to create attractive experiential value, it is necessary to develop products, systems and services not from the viewpoint of technology, but from the viewpoint of value to be provided.

Under such circumstances, it often happens that the problem solving design approach for existing products, systems and services no longer works sufficiently, and therefore a new design approach is expected as a complement. This is a vision

M. Kurosu (Ed.): Human-Computer Interaction, Part I, HCII 2013, LNCS 8004, pp. 531–539, 2013.

centered design approach that can create new products, systems and services which propose new visions from the viewpoint of HCD (Human Centered Design) and are sure to be introduced and attractive to people and society in general. Since 2007, the authors organized a working group within the Ergonomic Design Research Group of the Japan Ergonomics Society. In 2012, we completed development of the "Experience Vision: Vision Centered Design Method", a comprehensive design method which consistently allowed for the introduction of HCD into the design process [1][2][3].

In this paper, the formats prepared for this method are first explained, and then the effectiveness of the formats are confirmed by showing examples in which the formats have been used.

2 Framework for Vision Centered Design Method and Formats

The following eight formats are available within the vision centered design method and can be utilized in the design processes.

1. Goal setting of the project
2. Intrinsic user value
3. Policy of business value
4. Persona
5. Value scenario
6. Activity scenario
7. Interaction scenario
8. Experience vision (summary)

By superimposing each format on the relevant component of the framework for the vision centered design method, the location of each format can be illustrated (Fig. 1). Proceed with processes from the left side of the framework to the right side using the formats, and the information to be used in the investigation of user requirement documents and business planning documents can finally be output. Each format will be explained in detail hereinafter.

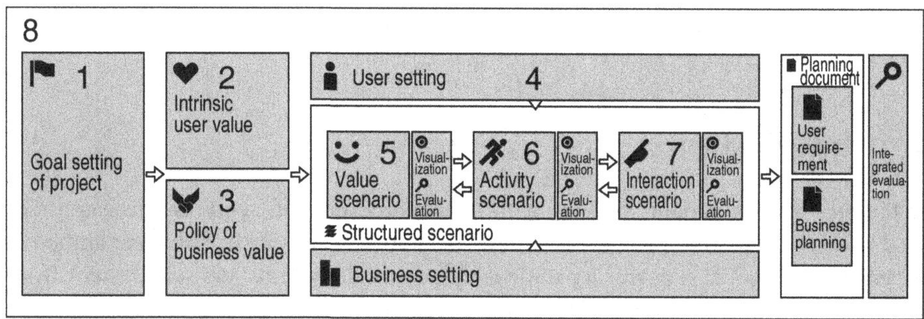

Fig. 1. Framework for Vision Centered Design Method and formats

2.1 Goal Setting of the Project

At the beginning of the process, set the goal of the project. Summarize the outline of the project, basic information, goal, contents of activities and schedule, members, and budget plan from the viewpoint of users and business (Fig. 2).

2.2 Intrinsic User Value

Identify the intrinsic user value by reading out the users' needs from the user information and analyzing them hierarchically. First, position the user facts obtained through interviews, observation and introspective research in the lowest fields of the format as the lowest base needs. Subsequently, utilize the Superior-Subordinate Relationship Analysis Method [4] to search for the needs of the upper hierarchy. The users' activity goal is located in the upper field of the user facts as medium needs and the intrinsic user value is extracted above that. It is not always necessary to have three hierarchies. The number of hierarchies differs depending on the result of the analysis (Fig. 3).

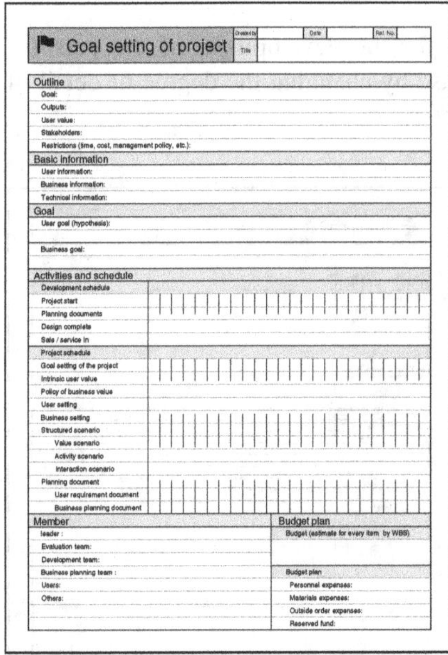
Goal setting of project
Created by | Date | Ref. No.
Title

Outline
Goal:
Outputs:
User value:
Stakeholders:
Restrictions (time, cost, management policy, etc.):

Basic information
User information:
Business information:
Technical information:

Goal
User goal (hypothesis):
Business goal:

Activities and schedule
Development schedule
Project start
Planning documents
Design complete
Sale / service in
Project schedule
Goal setting of the project
Intrinsic user value
Policy of business value
User setting
Business setting
Structured scenario
Value scenario
Activity scenario
Interaction scenario
Planning document
User requirement document
Business planning document

Member
leader :
Evaluation team:
Development team:
Business planning team :
Users:
Others:

Budget plan
Budget (estimate for every item by WBS)
Budget plan
Personnel expenses:
Materials expenses:
Outside order expenses:
Reserved fund:

Fig. 2. Goal setting of the project format

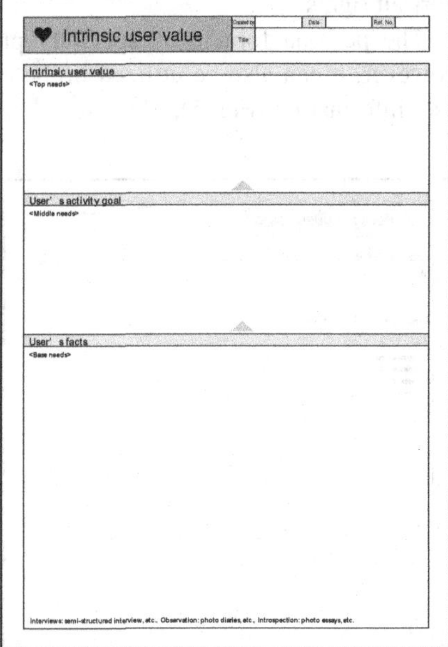
Intrinsic user value
Created by | Date | Ref. No.
Title

Intrinsic user value
<Top needs>

User' s activity goal
<Middle needs>

User' s facts
<Base needs>

Interviews: semi-structured interview, etc., Observation: photo diaries, etc., Introspection: photo essays, etc.

Fig. 3. Intrinsic user value format

2.3 Policy of Business Value

The policy of the business value demonstrates the strategy for the project theme, and thus the policy is to be identified based on the business information including the business domain, business environment (opportunity and threat), management resources (strength and weakness) and business strategy. In the format there is a list of items for each piece of information. These items are to provide general viewpoints for investigation, and therefore it is acceptable to make a choice or study other items depending on each project. The policy of business value is described in the lowest field of the format (Fig. 4).

2.4 Persona

Set up the persona from the user information. The persona should finally be developed by elaborating the image of the intended users step-by-step from the list of users and stakeholders, the cast and then to persona.

In addition to the goal of the persona, basic information, characteristics, roles and preferences should be described in the format while considering the relationship with the project theme. To promote understanding of persona by members of the development team, enter a key phrase which simply illustrates characteristics and the goal of the persona in the upper field of the format. Furthermore, to imagine a visual understanding of the persona, a photograph or an illustration should be inserted. When using images and graphic content, it is important not to infringe on any copyrights and portrait rights.

The persona format is especially prepared for the development of the persona, however, it can also be utilized in the cast phase by changing the degree of detail of user information (Fig. 5).

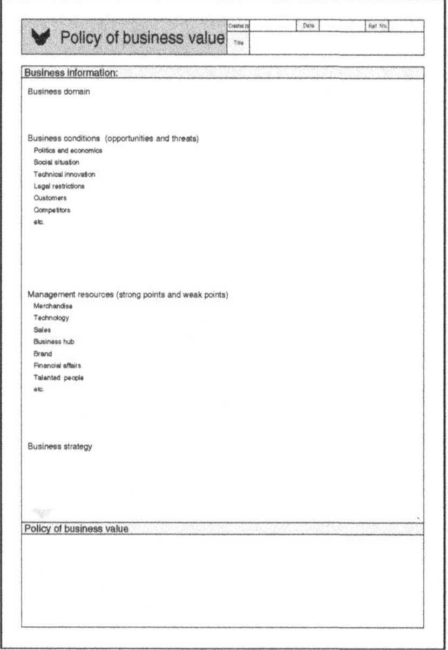

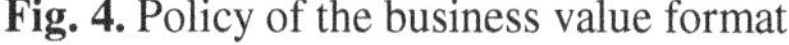

Fig. 4. Policy of the business value format

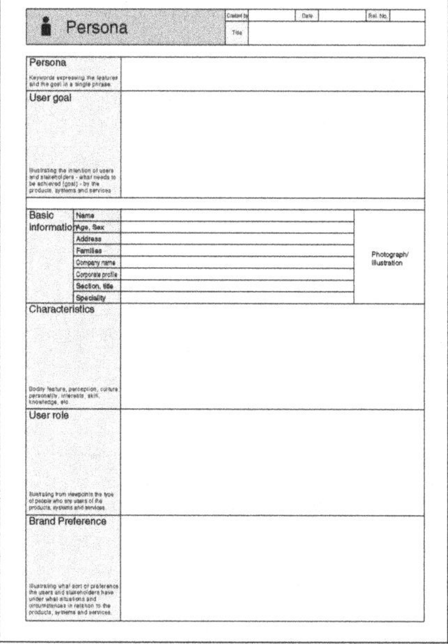

Fig. 5. Persona format

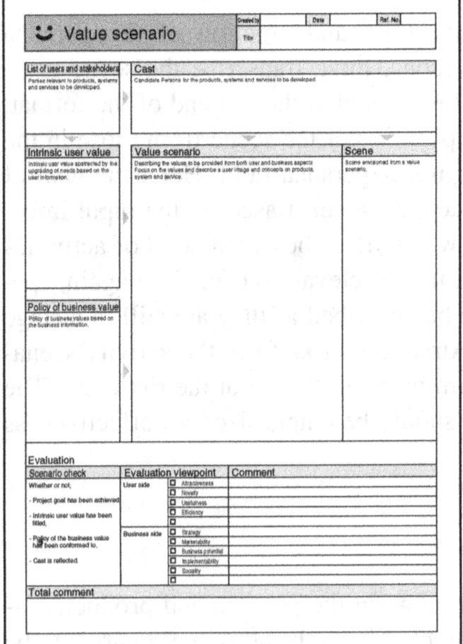

Fig. 6. Value scenario format

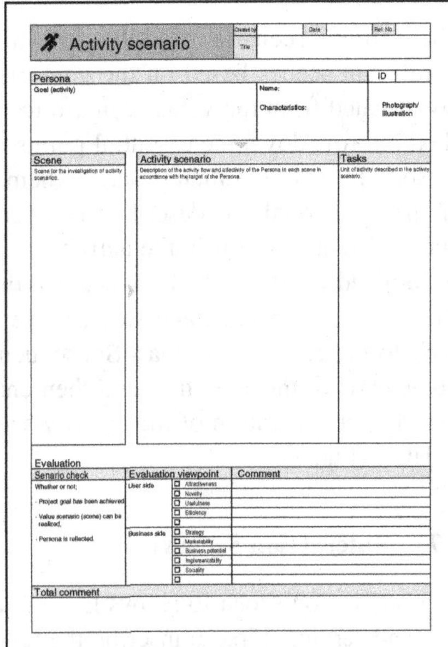

Fig. 7. Activity scenario format

2.5 Value Scenario

The value scenario illustrates the images of users and concepts on products, systems and services by focusing on the values. In the upper field of the format there is the area to be used for investigation on intended users. Enter elaborated content along with the project theme in the sequence of the list of users and stakeholders and cast from the left. On the middle left side of the format there is the field for the intrinsic user value of the user aspect and the policy of business value of the business aspect. The respective content studied in the previous processes should be transcribed and checked. Based on this input information, derive a value scenario for both user and business viewpoints. Specific user images and ideas for products, systems and services should not be described here as they have yet to be materialized in this phase. This is in order to prevent any restrictions which could happen in the subsequent idea generation phase. Once the value scenario has been fixed and described in the center field, study for envisioned scenes and describe them in the field at the right end.

Evaluate the value scenario from both user and business aspects using the evaluation field at the bottom of the format. The user aspect evaluation puts an emphasis on satisfaction for the HCD, and thus attractiveness and novelty become important viewpoints (Fig. 6).

2.6 Activity Scenario

The activity scenario describes the affectivity flow and emotion of the persona in relevant scenes based on the goal of the persona. First, transcribe the scene to be investigated from the value scenario format into the field at the left end of the format. Next, narrow down the essential points of the persona for the scene from those in the persona format, and then describe them in the upper persona field. Here, the goal of the persona should be described in a form of activity level. Based on the input information, create and fill in the activity scenario which describes what sorts of activities are utilized for the persona to achieve the goal in the relevant scene. Here again, specific products, systems and services are not to be described as they are still in a stage prior to the creation of ideas. Subsequently, extract the tasks from the activity scenario as parts of the activities, and then enter them in the task field at the right end. The user aspect evaluation of the activity scenario should be emphasized on effectiveness of HCD (Fig. 7).

2.7 Interaction Scenario

The interaction scenario shows the interaction between the persona and product, system and service. First, transcribe the tasks abstracted from the activity scenarios to be investigated in the right end field of the format. In the upper part of the persona field, a persona which is the same as the activity scenario format is normally described. Here, the goal of the interaction should be specified. Describe the interaction scenarios chronologically in detail by considering the interaction which occurs in the course of the utilization of products, systems and services by the persona in accordance with tasks. Within this, specific products, systems and services, as well as ideas of the interaction, are expressed, therefore, technical factors required for the specifications is also identified. For a more detailed investigation without missing descriptions, investigate using features of hardware, software and human-ware. Abstract requirements for tangible specifications from the described interaction scenarios, and then enter them in the field of comments for specifications at the right end. The user aspect evaluation of the interaction scenario should be emphasized on efficiency of HCD (Fig. 8).

2.8 Experience Vision (Summary)

The contents studied using the seven formats so far are summarized in the experience vision format. Transcribe each item of the format by phase or after the completion of all phases. For the last, fill in the user requirements and the business plans in the planning document field at the right end of the format. The experience vision format is used to overview the entire field and to confirm and investigate the proposed experience vision. This is also effective not only to study one proposal but to study and compare multiple numbers of proposals (Fig. 9).

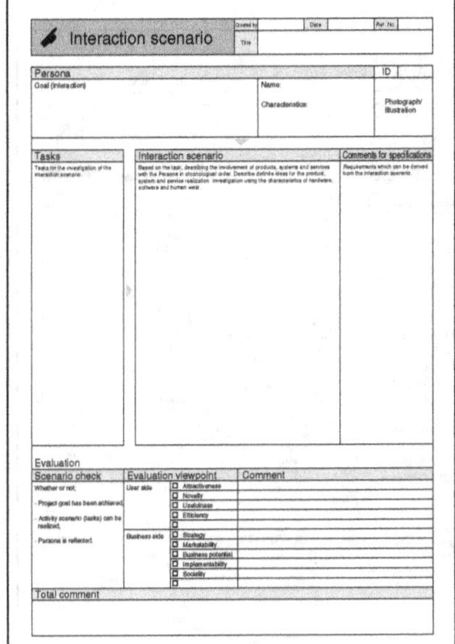

Fig. 8. Interaction scenario format

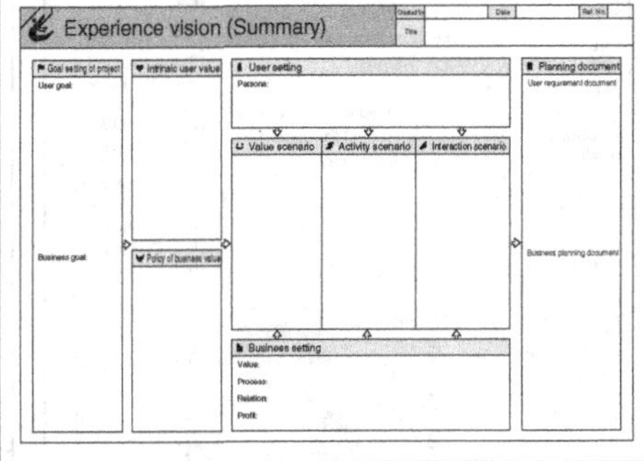

Fig. 9. Experience vision format

3 Three Scenario Formats

The three scenario formats have the same item layout as the framework for the Vision Centered Design Method so the interrelationship of the scenarios can easily be understood. The entire structure can be tracked simply by placing the three formats side-by-side (Fig. 10). At the upper part of each scenario format there is a field for objective users. These are elaborated upon step-by-step as they move from the left side to the right side and become persona in the end. In the middle there is the field in which scenarios are described. At the beginning, enter two items of information; the intrinsic user value and policy of business value in the left end. While continuing to work from the left to the right by inputting entries of user settings from the top, three scenarios can be derived in three layers over the three formats. At this time, the business setting can be input from the bottom, as shown in the framework of this method, although there are no business fields within the format.

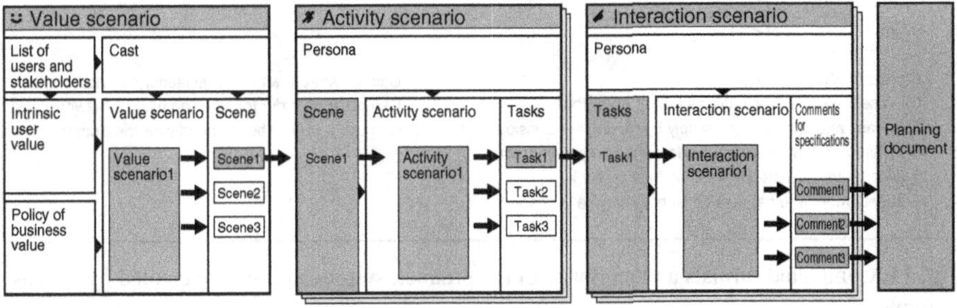

Fig. 10. Correlation between three scenario formats

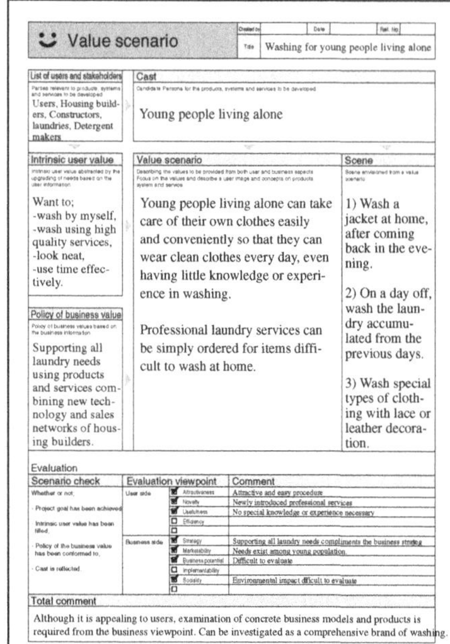

Value scenario

Created by | Date | Ref. No.

Title: Washing for young people living alone

List of users and stakeholders
Parties relevant to products, systems and services to be developed
Users, Housing builders, Constructors, laundries, Detergent makers

Cast
Candidate Persona for the products, systems and services to be developed
Young people living alone

Intrinsic user value
Intrinsic user value abstracted by the upgrading of needs based on the user information
Want to;
-wash by myself,
-wash using high quality services,
-look neat,
-use time effectively.

Policy of business value
Policy of business values based on the business information
Supporting all laundry needs using products and services combining new technology and sales networks of housing builders.

Value scenario
Describing the values to be provided from both user and business aspects. Focus on the values and describe a user image and concepts on products, system and service
Young people living alone can take care of their own clothes easily and conveniently so that they can wear clean clothes every day, even having little knowledge or experience in washing.

Professional laundry services can be simply ordered for items difficult to wash at home.

Scene
Scene envisioned from a value scenario
1) Wash a jacket at home, after coming back in the evening.
2) On a day off, wash the laundry accumulated from the previous days.
3) Wash special types of clothing with lace or leather decoration.

Evaluation

Scenario check	Evaluation viewpoint		Comment
Whether or not;	User side	☑ Attractiveness	Attractive and easy procedure
· Project goal has been achieved		☑ Novelty	Newly introduced professional services
· Intrinsic user value has been filled,		☑ Usefulness	No special knowledge or experience necessary
· Policy of the business value has been conformed to,		☐ Efficiency	
· Cast is reflected.		☐	
	Business side	☑ Strategy	Supporting all laundry needs compliments the business strateg
		☑ Marketability	Needs exist among young population.
		☑ Business potential	Difficult to evaluate
		☐ Implementability	
		☑ Sociality	Environmental impact dficult to evaluate
		☐	

Total comment
Although it is appealing to users, examination of concrete business models and products is required from the business viewpoint. Can be investigated as a comprehensive brand of washing.

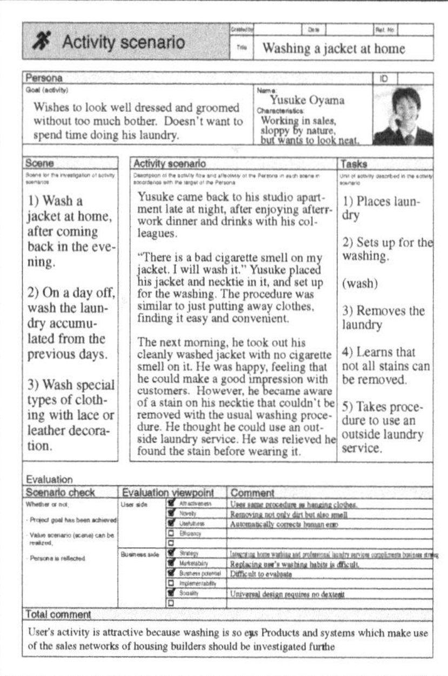

Activity scenario

Created by | Date | Ref. No.

Title: Washing a jacket at home

Persona ID

Goal (activity): Wishes to look well dressed and groomed without too much bother. Doesn't want to spend time doing his laundry.

Name: Yusuke Oyama
Characteristics: Working in sales, sloppy by nature, but wants to look neat.

Scene
Scene for the investigation of activity scenarios
1) Wash a jacket at home, after coming back in the evening.
2) On a day off, wash the laundry accumulated from the previous days.
3) Wash special types of clothing with lace or leather decoration.

Activity scenario
Description of the activity flow and affectivity of the Persona in each scene in accordance with the target of the Persona
Yusuke came back to his studio apartment late at night, after enjoying afterr-work dinner and drinks with his colleagues.

"There is a bad cigarette smell on my jacket. I will wash it." Yusuke placed his jacket and necktie in it, and set up for the washing. The procedure was similar to just putting away clothes, finding it easy and convenient.

The next morning, he took out his cleanly washed jacket with no cigarette smell on it. He was happy, feeling that he could make a good impression with customers. However, he became aware of a stain on his necktie that couldn't be removed with the usual washing procedure. He thought he could use an outside laundry service. He was relieved he found the stain before wearing it.

Tasks
Unit of activity described in the activity scenario
1) Places laundry
2) Sets up for the washing.
(wash)
3) Removes the laundry
4) Learns that not all stains can be removed.
5) Takes procedure to use an outside laundry service.

Evaluation

Scenario check	Evaluation viewpoint		Comment
Whether or not;	User side	☑ Attractiveness	Uses same procedure as hanging clothes.
· Project goal has been achieved		☑ Novelty	Removing not only dirt but also smell
· Value scenario (scene) can be realized,		☑ Usefulness	Automatically corrects human erro
· Persona is reflected		☐ Efficiency	
		☐	
	Business side	☑ Strategy	Integrating home washing and professional laundry services compliments business strateg
		☑ Marketability	Replacing user's washing habits is dficult.
		☑ Business potential	Difficult to evaluate
		☐ Implementability	
		☑ Sociality	Universal design requires no dexterit
		☐	

Total comment
User's activity is attractive because washing is so eys Products and systems which make use of the sales networks of housing builders should be investigated furthe

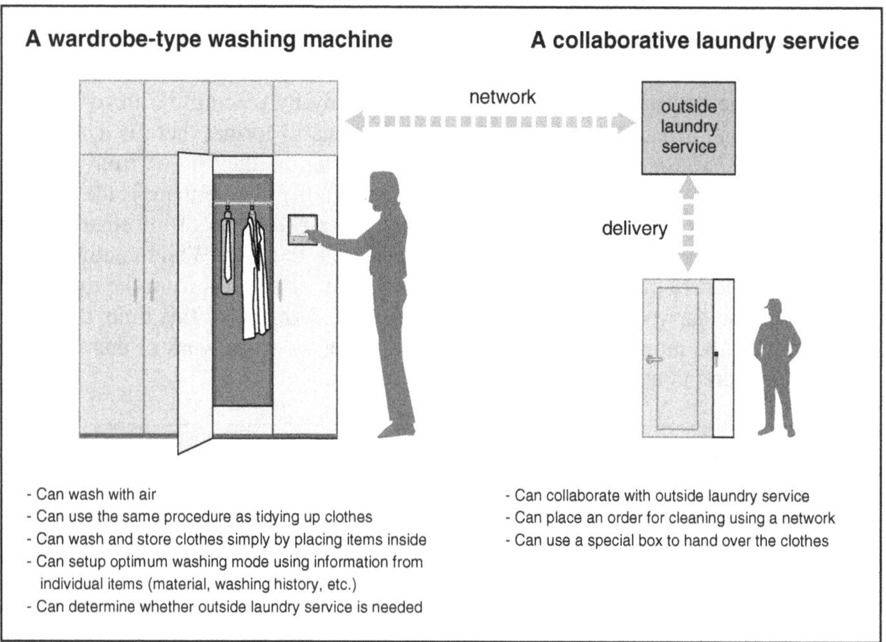

A wardrobe-type washing machine
A collaborative laundry service
network
outside laundry service
delivery
- Can wash with air
- Can use the same procedure as tidying up clothes
- Can wash and store clothes simply by placing items inside
- Can setup optimum washing mode using information from individual items (material, washing history, etc.)
- Can determine whether outside laundry service is needed
- Can collaborate with outside laundry service
- Can place an order for cleaning using a network
- Can use a special box to hand over the clothes

Fig. 11. Completed formats and an image of the product, system and service created by the case example

The interfaces for these three scenarios are scenes and tasks. The specification comments which are output at the end are the link between the structured scenario and the next planning document.

There is a field for the evaluation of derived scenarios below each scenario format. The Vision Centered Design Method emphasizes evaluation from both user and business aspects including four viewpoints of the user aspect and five viewpoints of the business aspect as general evaluation viewpoints. Utilize these viewpoints by marking their boxes considering the theme and goal for the project. It is also possible to add new viewpoints along with each project theme and goal. The evaluation viewpoints can be weighted and scored. Enter comments for each evaluation viewpoint in the comment field, fill in the total comment and then move to the next phase.

4 Application of the Method and the Formats

The case example shown here is created to verify usefulness and effectiveness of the formats. In this case example, the new experience values are created from the intrinsic user value and the policy of business value relevant to the theme "Washing," and then "A wardrobe-type washing machine using an air washing function and a collaborative laundry service" are proposed as an idea for a definite product, system and service in accordance with user activities and interactions (Fig.11).

5 Summary and Future Work

In this paper, eight different types of formats developed as practical tools for the vision centered design method have been illustrated. In addition to this, a case example using these formats showed usefulness and effectiveness of the formats. We continue our activities to advance this method and its formats through a wide range of practices including practical workshops intended for business and academic parties and information exchanges.

References

1. Yamazaki, K., Ueda, Y., Go, K., Takahashi, K., Hayakawa, S., Yanagida, K.: Experience Vision. Maruzen Publishing Co., Ltd., Tokyo (2012) (in Japanese)
2. Yanagida, K., Ueda, Y., Go, K., Takahashi, K., Hayakawa, S., Yamazaki, K.: Vision-proposal Design Method. In: Kurosu, M. (ed.) HCD 2011. LNCS, vol. 6776, pp. 166–174. Springer, Heidelberg (2011)
3. Yanagida, K., Ueda, Y., Go, K., Takahashi, K., Hayakawa, S., Yamazaki, K.: Structured Scenario-based Design Method. In: Kurosu, M. (ed.) HCD 2009. LNCS, vol. 5619, pp. 374–380. Springer, Heidelberg (2009)
4. Marketing Concept House: Group Dynamic Interview. Dobunkan Shuppan, Tokyo (2005) (in Japanese)

Case Study for Experience Vision Designing Notebook PC

Der-Jang Yu, Ming-Chuen Chuang, and Steven Tseng

Institute of Applied Arts, National Chiao Tung University, 1001 University Road, Hsing-chu, 300, Taiwan, R.O.C.
ASUSTeK Computer Inc, 15, Li-Te Road, Peitou, Taipei, 112, Taiwan, R.O.C.
djyu@scenariolab.com.tw

Abstract. It is challenging to do a thorough user-centered innovation process in the PC industry due to the very fast paced product development cycle and the nature of how innovations are usually technology driven. User-centered innovation activities can be held before the start of each project to overcome these challenges. And in the end, applications of technology must be able to be traced back to user insights. User Experience Innovation Process (UXIP), a three-phase innovation process is proposed in this paper. UXIP can help incorporating the Experience Vision approach into the PC industry. This process is consisted of three phases: research, create, and strategy. During the process, sets of flashcard that captures user insights and concept scenarios are used. Through the innovation tools, new user experience-based and technology-related concepts can be captured early on. UXIP was able to help companies save time and make better decisions. The results were remarkable. The company was able to lunch incredibly innovative PC products in a very short period of time since the concepts behind the product were already produced a year before hands.

Keywords: User experience, scenario-based design, product innovation.

1 Background

The personal computer industry is a highly competitive industry with very fast paced product development cycles. However, when doing user-centric innovations, the design process could be time consuming due to all the research, creativity, and prototyping involved. Designers in a PC company are often asked to come up with a solution quick because of the competitive nature of the personal computer industry. Therefore all the front-end work that focuses on user-centric innovations are often sacrificed.

In addition, the PC industry innovation is majorly driven by the development of PC components technologies instead of user experiences. When designers are asked to do design making use of the latest technology, it could be difficult to incorporate the perspective of user-centric design.

For integrating the Experience Vision approach into the PC development process, the key challenges are how to provide a way to make use of user experience innovation in the fast paced product development cycle, and how to provide technology-oriented ideas that also provides valuable user experience perspective.

M. Kurosu (Ed.): Human-Computer Interaction, Part I, HCII 2013, LNCS 8004, pp. 540–546, 2013.

2 The User Experience Innovation Process

The User Experience Innovation Process (UXIP) is an innovative development process developed by Scenario Lab and Asus. The goal is to capture user's insight and give big organizations, such as a company, that during the long process of decision-making, they can always make sure that all decisions can be tied back to user's insights.

The framework of the UXIP consists of three different phases of: research, create, and strategy (Figure 1). While each phase offers unique contributions to the process, two different tools are used to make connections between the different contributions each phases provide. The two different tools are the "User Experience Knowledge Module" and the "Corporate Idea Knowledge Module". These are both organized through the form of flashcards. The former focuses on capturing and organizing user insights while the latter focuses on gathering concepts that were generated from user insights. By using these two tools, it is possible to make sure that all the findings and concepts from the earlier phases can be translated into the later phrases during the whole process. So at the end of the day, any end result can be linked back to the users. With the three phases and two tools, the UXIP provides an innovative process that translates user insights into company's decision-making.

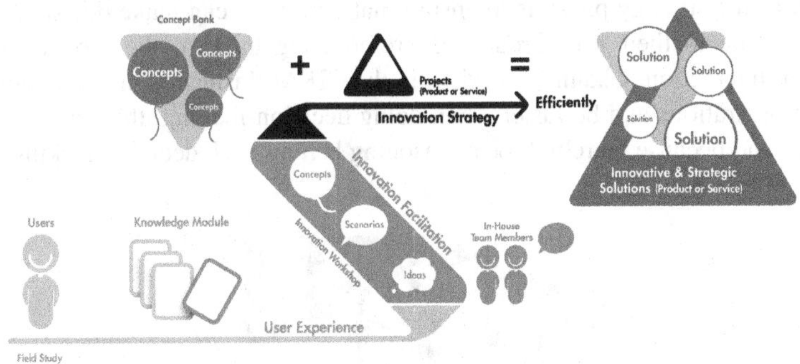

Fig. 1. User Experience Innovation Process

Research Phase

The goal of the research phase is to select a specific user group and understand them thoroughly. This step can be done through research methods such as User Diary, Guided Tour, Depth Interview, etc. No matter how the information is gathered, in the end all these information can be analyzed and synthesized into user insights. The user insights can then be made into User Experience Knowledge Module flashcards.

User Experience Knowledge Module (UXKM)

User insights that were gathered through the research phase can be organized and made into flashcards, one insight per flashcard. These flashcards can later be used to teach people about the user groups and help people generate creative ideas.

Create Phase

The goal of the create phase is to help companies generate new ideas from user insights. To achieve this goal, corporate can do workshops by using the UXKM flashcards. By using the UXKM flashcards, not only can people have a better understanding of their user groups, most important of all, they can be inspired and create new innovative concepts. Each concept that people come up with can be categorized as either Function, Interaction, Channel, or Service. Then each concept can be captured by being turned into scenarios. In each scenario, concepts will be described in terms of users, occasions, locations, objects, and activities. Each scenario can then be made into Corporate Idea Knowledge Module flashcards.

Corporate Idea Knowledge Module (CIKM)

Scenarios that depict the concepts can be organized and made into flashcards, one scenario per flashcard. These flashcards can later help companies make more precise, faster, and better decisions (Figure 2).

Strategy Phase

The goal of the strategy phase is to ensure that corporate can make decisions that are faster and true to their user groups. By referencing back to the proper categories (Function, Interaction, Channel, Service) in the CIKM flashcards, not only companies can find inspirations and be faster when doing decision-making, they can also have a peace of mind because there will be a reasoning behind each decision-making.

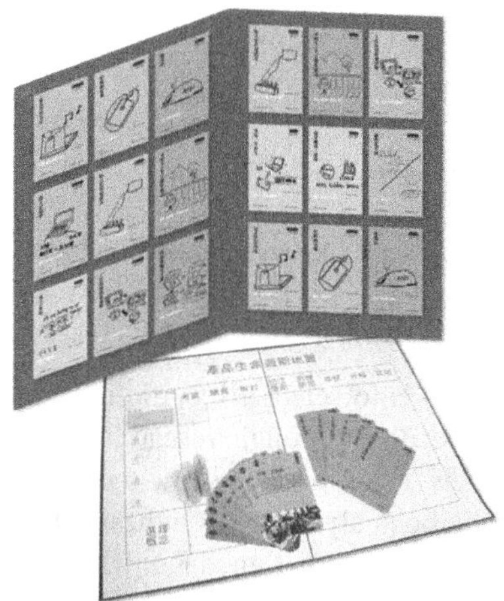

Fig. 2. UXKM flashcards and CIKM flashcards

3 SSBD and UXIP

Structural Scenario Based Design (SSBD) is a process that helps transforming a user-experience design concept into a thorough written document. Through the process of SSBD, the results from the UXIP can be captured in terms of Business Data, User Data, Persona, Value Scenarios, Activity Scenarios, Interaction Scenarios and Product/Service, Specification.

Since the scenario has been already further developed by SSBD, we are able to apply even higher level of methods, such as Scenario Planning Workshop or Scenario Walk-through Workshop, to develop an ever more detailed and mature concept (Figure 3).

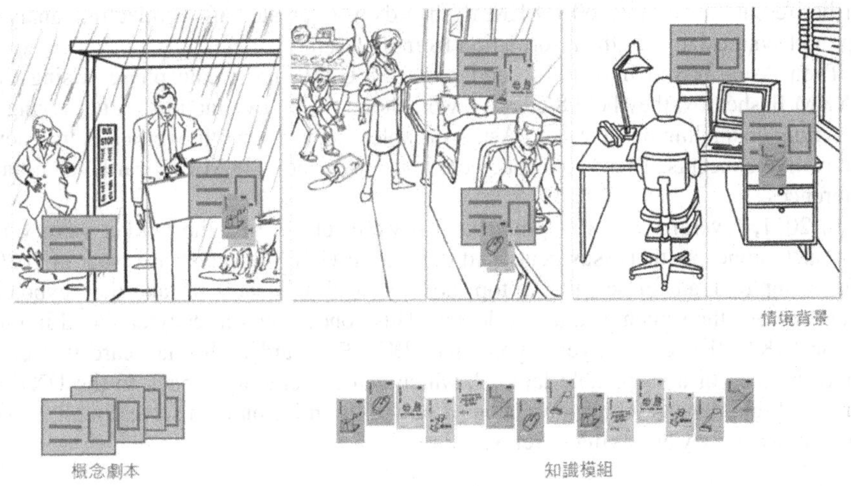

Fig. 3. CIKM in use

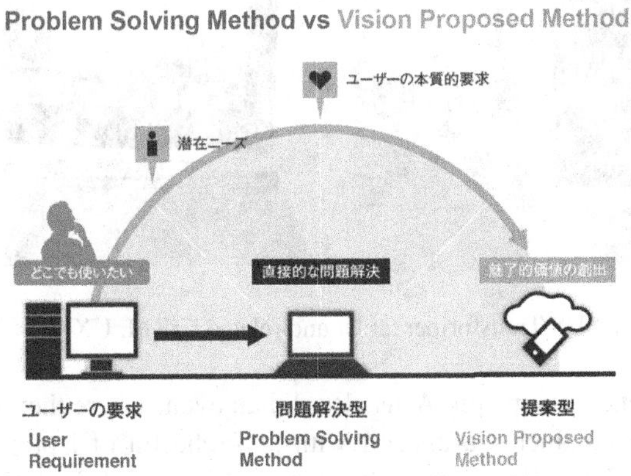

Problem Solving Method vs Vision Proposed Method

ユーザーの本質的要求

潜在ニーズ

どこでも使いたい

直接的な問題解決

ユーザーの要求
User Requirement

問題解決型
Problem Solving Method

提案型
Vision Proposed Method

Fig. 4. Vision Proposed Method

By combining the process of UXIP and SSBD, companies can form and design new experiences with examples of existed experiences. The flexibility of the UXIP can also provide creativity inspirations for the development of concept. Then, through doing UX prototyping several times around, companies would be able to realize a higher level of value when designing and see a wider perspective with the addition of user insights (Figure 4).

4 The ASUS Cases

May 2010, Asus performed the UXIP process to investigate on new concepts for PC laptops. During the first phase, the research phase, a focus group session was held. 14 users participated. Out of the 14 participants, 6 participants were selected to perform further research activities. 60 UXKM flashcards were created after collecting, analyzing, and synthesizing all the information from the users.

Then Asus moved into the second phase of UXIP, the create phase. Using the UXKM flashcards, they held 8 creative workshops within two months. After having a better understanding of their user, Asus was able to come up with over a hundred new innovative concepts. These concepts were later made into CIKM flashcards for future references.

In 2011, several successful products that were released on the market were very similar to concepts that Asus generated during the UXIP Create Phase back in 2020. For example, Transformer, the laptop model that allows users to take the keyboard apart and use the screen as a tablet device. This concept was already captured in one of the CIKM flashcards a year ago. This CIKM flashcard is the flashcard that captured the idea of a "separable laptop", which can be referenced back to the UXKM flashcard that depicts the phenomenon of how users position themselves in all possible way when they are trying to relax.

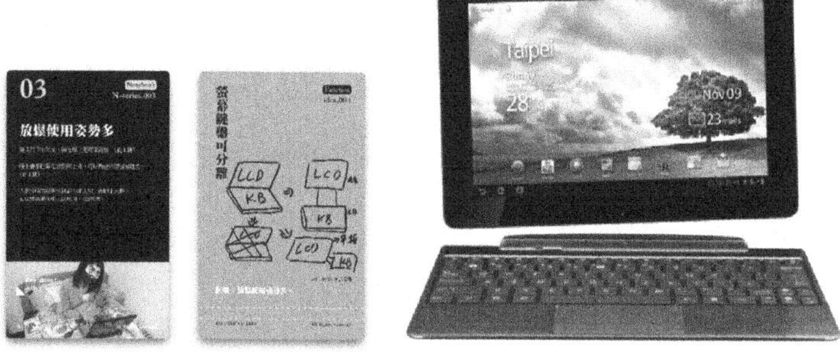

Fig. 5. ASUS Transformer tablet and related CIKM, UXKM flashcards

In their marketing campaign, Asus also did an event where they had their chairman Mr. Jonney Shih conducted a concert with an orchestra of laptops with the famous singer Jay Chou. This concept was also captured in one of the CIKM flashcards that were generated during one of the creative workshops Asus held. The CIKM flashcard is called the "N-concert", which can also be traced back to one of the UXKM flashcard. The corresponding UXKM flashcard is a flashcard that depicts the idea of how things seem to go well when there's fitting music. Just like how the Asus concert was held to build the image of how their laptop would produce high quality media output, which would help make things go well for their users.

Fig. 6. The marketing campaign and related CIKM, UXKM flashcards

In 2011, Asus preformed a process of innovation for UX prototyping and evaluation. They first combined the method of scenario planning with the outcome of CIKM that was generated when they first preformed UXIP. Then sets of strategy plans were developed and tested out with paper mockup and SSBD's scenario methods. That time, core members of the company and some end users were invited to evaluate the results. It is proven that the UXIP workshops were able to produce a lot of value and insights, and the results could influence future product and innovative concepts. For example, the PADFONE concept was actually an outcome of the workshops.

5 Conclusions

Because of the emphasis that is put on fast production in the PC laptop industry, it would be effective to have a pool of innovative concepts available for the company. That's one of the benefits UXIP can bring to a company. UXIP can also provide company members with bigger visions. Visions that can help the company realize user needs and produce more innovative concepts. Being able to put company members in the innovative mode is another benefit that UXIP can bring to a company.

As a saying goes, opportunities are only for the people who are prepared. The UXIP process is a way to prepare companies, so that when opportunity comes, they have the ability to react quickly with effective user experience proposals.

References

1. Yanagida, K., Ueda, Y., Go, K., Takahashi, K., Hayakawa, S., Yamazaki, K.: Structured Scenario-Based Design Method. In: Kurosu, M. (ed.) HCD 2009. LNCS, vol. 5619, pp. 374–380. Springer, Heidelberg (2009)
2. Yu, D.-J., Lin, W.-C.: Facilitating Idea Generation Using Personas. In: Kurosu, M. (ed.) HCD 2009. LNCS, vol. 5619, pp. 381–388. Springer, Heidelberg (2009)
3. Carroll, J.M.: HCI Models, Theories, and Frameworks. Morgan Kaufmann Publishers, San Francisco (2003)
4. Carroll, J.M.: Scenarios and Design Cognition. In: Proceedings of the IEEE Joint International Conference on Requirement Engineering (2002)
5. Schank, R.: Tell Me a Story: Narrative and Intelligence. Northwestern University Press, Evanston (1995, 2001)
6. Rosson, M.B., Carroll, J.M.: Usability Engineering. Morgan Kaufmann Publishers, San Francisco (2002)
7. Yu, D.J., Lin, W.C., Wang, J.C.: Scenario-Oriented Design, Garden City, Taipei (2000)

Part IV
Aesthetics and Kansei in HCI

Investigating the Effects of Font Styles on Perceived Visual Aesthetics of Website Interface Design

Ahamed Altaboli

Industrial and Manufacturing Systems Engineering Department,
University of Benghazi,
Benghazi, Libya
altaboli@gmail.com

Abstract. The purpose of this study is to compare the effects of the two font styles (serif and sans-serif) on the users' perception of visual aesthetics of website interface design. Two font types were tests in this study, namely: "Time News Roman" representing the "serif" style and "Calibri" representing the "sans-serif" style. They were chosen because they are two of the widely used font types on the web and because they are the default font types of many of the most popular word processing and web developing software. Analysis of results showed that font type has a statistically significant effect on perceived visual aesthetics. The designs with the Time New Roman font was perceived as having better visual aesthetics. However, this effect was only significant on the overall perception of visual aesthetics; it wasn't significant in each of the four facets of visual aesthetics tested in this study.

Keywords: font style, font type, perceived visual aesthetics, website interface design.

1 Introduction

Most of font types used in printing and on screen belong to two font styles: serif and sans-serif. A "serif" is a French term for a short decorative line (edge) at the start or finish of a stroke in a letter, and "sans-serif" is a French term meaning "without-serif". i.e. the serif style has edges that project from the main letter block, while the sans-serif style doesn't have these edges.

The effect of each style on readability and legibility is one concern of the field of document, screen and interface design, finding of related studies mostly agree that on printed papers the serif style gives better readability and legibility than the sans-serif style [1], while; on a computer screen this advantage of the serif types is reduced, and findings of several studies indicated that the sans-serif types have more readability and legibility [1, 3, 4 and 7]. This is due to the fact that on computer screens each character is displayed as dot-matrix (or pixels), which results on the character with the edges "serif" appears jagged. This effect increases with low resolution of the screen

M. Kurosu (Ed.): Human-Computer Interaction, Part I, HCII 2013, LNCS 8004, pp. 549–554, 2013.

and should be reduced with higher screen resolutions. As screen resolution increases this jagged effect should be eventually eliminated [1].

Other than the issues of readability and legibility, there is the issue of which font style would be more aesthetically appealing for the users and how it would affect the overall visual appeal and aesthetics of the interface. This issue is the concern of this study. The purpose of this study is to compare the effects of the two font styles (serif and sans-serif) on the overall perception of visual aesthetics of website interface design.

Two font types were tests in this study, namely: "Time News Roman" representing the "serif" style and "Calibri" representing the "sans-serif" style. They were chosen because they are two of the widely used font types on the web and because they are the default font types of many of the most popular word processing and web developing software.

2 Method

2.1 Design of the Experiment

An experiment was designed and conducted to test the effects of font type on participants' perceived visual aesthetics of website design.

A one- factor (font type) within subject design was utilized with two levels associated with the two font types to be tested (Times New Roman and Calibri). Two designs of a webpage were prepared to represent the two levels. Both designs have identical formats (colors, menus ...etc); the only difference is the font type used in each design; in one design the Times New Roman font type was used in all text in the webpage, in the other design the Calibri font type was used.

User perception of visual aesthetics was measured using the VisAWI (Visual Aesthetics of Website Inventory) questionnaire [6]. The instrument is based on four interrelated facets of perceived visual aesthetics of websites: simplicity, diversity, colorfulness, and craftsmanship. Simplicity comprises visual aesthetics aspects such as balance, unity, and clarity. The Diversity facet comprises visual complexity, dynamics, novelty, and creativity. The colorfulness facet represents aesthetic impressions perceived from the selection, placement, and combination of colors. Craftsmanship comprises the skilful and coherent integration of all relevant design dimensions. Each of the first two facets is presented by five items in the questionnaire, while each of the last two facets has four items.

The font type with its two levels (Times New Roman and Calibri) is the independent variable. Questionnaire scores represent the dependent variable. Fig. 1 shows screen shots of the two designs of the webpage. The webpage represents a homepage of a hypothetical website that talks about the ancient history of a certain region of North Africa.

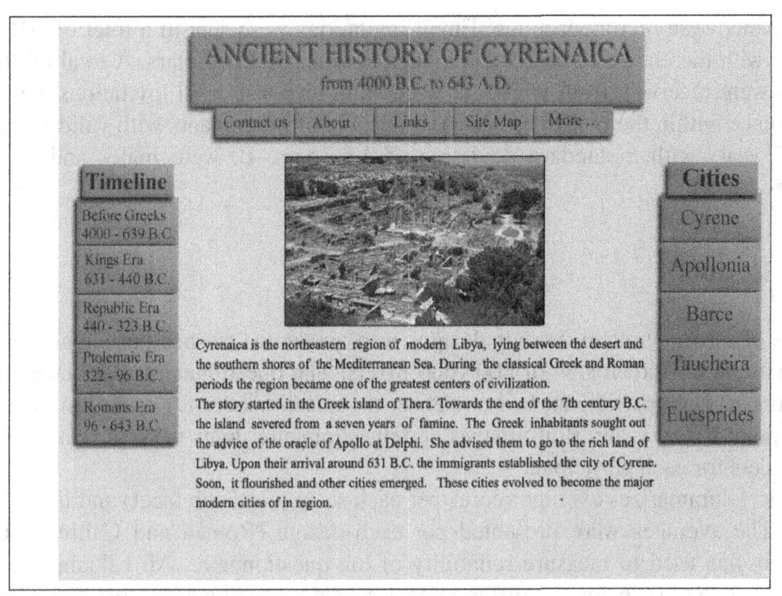

The Times New Roman design

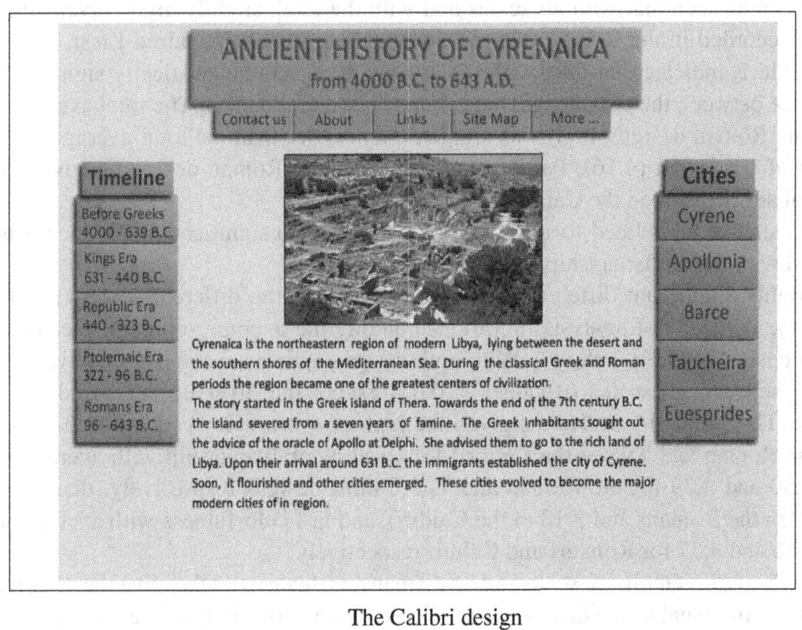

The Calibri design

Fig. 1. Screen shot images of the two designs of the webpage

2.2 Participants

Participants were recruited online. Email invitations were sent to a total of 201 individuals with the choice of entering a lottery to win 100 US dollars. A total of 30 responses were received, from which 22 were valid responses. All invitations were sent to audience within the United States. Average age of participants with valid responses is 49.7 years with a standard deviation of 4.8 years. 10 were males and 12 were females.

3 Results

Images of screen shots of the two designs were presented to each participant one at a time with an on screen size of 800X600 pixels. The questionnaire was placed under each image. Each participant had to answer the questionnaire for each design using a seven-point Likert scale. Both images and questionnaire items were presented in random orders for each participant.

Table 1 summarizes average scores per each scale (aesthetic facet) and for the total score. The averages were presented per each design (Roman and Calibri). Cronbach's α was used to measure reliability of the questionnaire. All calculated values were larger than 0.86 for the different scales of the questionnaire, indicating an acceptable level of reliability.

It can be seen that with all scales and with the total, slightly higher average scores were recorded in the Roman design. However; results of the paired-t test, also given in Table 1, indicate that only with the average total score, statistically significant difference between the two designs was found (p-value = 0.038). The total average score for the Roman design (4.33) was significantly higher than the total average score for the Calibri design (4.16), Participants perceived the Roman design as having better visual aesthetics than the Calibri design.

It can also be noticed form the table that a close to significant difference was recorded with the craftsmanship scale (p-value = 0.055).

Highly significant differences were found among the different scales (p-values < 0.001), as results of analysis of variance among the average scores of the scales for each design in Table 2 show. With both designs, pair-wise comparisons were significant between all scales (p-values < 0.05) except the diversity scale and the color scale. The simplicity scale was given the highest average score in both designs (5.18 in the Roman and 4.98 in the Calibri) followed by craftsmanship with average scores of 4.59 and 4.29 for the Roman and The Calibri designs respectively, than diversity (3.89 in the Romans and 3.18 in the Calibri), and last colorfulness with average scores of 3.66 and 3.57 for Romans and Calibri respectively.

Both of the simplicity scale and craftsmanship scale are related to the classical dimension of visual aesthetics, while the diversity and colorfulness are considered to be representatives of the expressive dimension of visual aesthetics [5]. The higher average scores given to the simplicity scale and the craftsmanship scale indicate that participants perceived the two deigns of the webpage as more classical than expressive.

Table 1. Average questionnaire scores and results of the paired-t test

Scale	Font Style	Average	Standard Deviation	T	P-value
Simplicity	Roman	5.18	1.21	1.50	0.147
	Calibri	4.98	1.16		
Diversity	Roman	3.89	1.21	0.63	0.267
	Calibri	3.18	1.37		
Colorfulness	Roman	3.66	1.57	0.66	0.259
	Calibri	3.57	1.55		
Craftsmanship	Roman	4.59	1.44	2.02	0.055
	Calibri	4.29	1.49		
Total	Roman	4.33	1.17	2.20	0.038
	Calibri	4.16	1.20		

Table 2. Results of analysis of variance for scales

Case	F	P-value
Roman	16.20	< 0.001
Calibri	12.27	< 0.001

4 Conclusions

The purpose of this study was to study the effects of the two font styles (serif and sans-serif) on the perception of visual aesthetics of website interface design. Two font types were tests in this study, namely: "Time News Roman" representing the "serif" style and "Calibri" representing the "sans-serif" style.

Analysis of results showed that font type has a statistically significant effect on perceived visual aesthetics. The designs with the Time New Roman font was perceived as having better visual aesthetics. However, this effect was only significant on the overall perception of visual aesthetics (the overall questionnaire score); it wasn't significant in each of the four parts of the questionnaire (representing the facets of visual aesthetics).

Regarding the visual aesthetics design of the webpage used in this study, results showed that participants perceived the design as more classical than expressive. It would be interesting to see if the above results (regarding font styles) would hold in cases of more aesthetically expressive designs.

Several previous studies have found evidences of possible effects of context of use (serious context vs. funny and pleasurable context) on perception of visual aesthetics of webpage design [2 and 8]. The context of use in the current study can be considered as a more serious one; would the outcomes of the test change in case of a more pleasurable context? This needs further experimental investigation.

Finally, it would be also interesting to see how using a mixture of different font styles and font types in the same webpage (compared to the single styles and types used in the current study) would affect perception of visual aesthetics of the page design.

References

1. Bernard, M., Chaparro, B., Mills, M., Halcomb, C.: Comparing the effects of text size and format on the readability of computer-displayed Times New Roman and Arial text. Int. J. Human-Computer Studies 59, 823–835 (2003)
2. De Angeli, A., Sutcliffe, A., Hartmann, J.: Interaction, usability and aesthetics: what influences users' preferences? In: Proceedings of the Sixth ACM Conference on Designing Interactive Systems, PA (June 2006)
3. Dix, A., Finlay, D., Abowd, G., Beale, R.: Human-Computer Interaction, 3rd edn. Pearson Education (2004)
4. Ling, J., Van Schaik, P.: The influence of font type and line length on visual search and information retrieval in web pages. Int. J. Human-Computer Studies 64, 395–404 (2006)
5. Laviea, T., Tractinsky, N.: Assessing dimensions of perceived visual aesthetics of web sites. Int. J. Human-Computer Studies 60, 269–298 (2004)
6. Moshagen, M., Thielsch, M.T.: Facets of visual aesthetics. Int. J. Hum.-Comput. Stud. 68(10), 689–709 (2010)
7. Sheedy, J., Subbaram, M., Zimmerman, A., Hayes, J.: Text Legibility and the Letter Superiority Effect. Human Factors 47(4), 797–815 (2005)
8. Van Schaik, P., Ling, J.: The role of context in perceptions of the aesthetics of web pages over time. Int. J. Human-Computer Studies 67, 79–89 (2009)

A Color Schemer for Webpage Design Using Interactive Mood Board

Zhenyu Gu, Zhanwei Wu, Jiamin Yu, and Jian Lou

Shanghai Jiao Tong University,
Dong Chuan RD, 800, Shanghai, China
{zygu,zhanwei_wu}@sjtu.edu.cn

Abstract. In this paper, we present a web tool called Webpage Color Schemer (WCS), which enables people to easily redefine an existing webpage's color scheme. WCS can adapt the webpage's color scheme towards a new visual effect expressed nonverbally with an interactive mood board, which is actually a collage of sample images or design examples reflecting designer's preference.

WCS is simple and fun to use. It has two major functionalities: an interactive mood board with a color quantization algorithm for extracting color themes; A genetic algorithm for generating best assignment of the theme colors from the mood board to the web page, with respect to necessary design objectives. The objectives are formulated as fitness functions for the evolutionary optimization. Our initial experiments show that three fitness functions are essential for the color scheme optimization: histogram evaluator, contrast evaluator and harmony evaluator, to make sure the scheme has a preferable color tone, legible contrast ratio and harmonious color matching, respectively. The evaluators are generally devised in the light of some well-established color design theories. Some efforts of this research, however, has moved towards using computational model to uncover design knowledge depositing in large set of design cases. WCS uses a kind of RBF network predicting proper contrast ratio of certain class of page elements, regarding its measurable features and context. The performance of the model is encouraging.

Keywords: Website color, Adaptive webpage scheme, CSS.

1 Introduction

Color is undoubtedly the essential means to touch the emotions of website viewers[1]. Our visual and cognitive systems have adapted to perceive and process color information, which is contained in every visual stimulus we encounter, calm or excite, arouse plenty of feelings and stimulate to actions [2]. Color scheme is an important aspect of designing a visually pleasing website. Quite a lot empirical methods and theories of color have been presented in design literatures [3, 4].

Choosing the right color combinations for a website can be difficult even for professional designers. Some efforts have been made to use computational models to support color designs of graphics and websites [5-8] . In this paper we present a tool

M. Kurosu (Ed.): Human-Computer Interaction, Part I, HCII 2013, LNCS 8004, pp. 555–564, 2013.

called Webpage Color Schemer (WCS), which enables people to intuitively redefine a webpage's color scheme online. The tool we developed has two major functionalities:

The first is an interactive mood board that allows people interactively to create a color palette (color theme). Mood boards are often used by graphic designers to illustrate the direction of visual style, which they are pursuing[9]. A mood board is usually a rough collage of colors, textures and pictures to evoke specific feelings. It is extremely useful for establishing the aesthetic feel of a web site. Things that can be explored in the mood board include photography style, color palettes, typography, and the overall look and feel of the site. In WCS, a digital mood board is firstly devised to enable a user interactively produce and refine a color theme. The second, more importantly, WCS recolors a targeting webpage by transferring the color theme to the web page. That means to generate a color scheme based on the wireframe of the page by intelligently assigning the colors from the palette to certain figural or background areas of the page. The process is a multi-objective combinational optimization led by some aesthetic and accessibility criteria, such as rules of color harmony and contrast. And the recolored webpage must also approximate the color tone of the mood board as closely as possible. The mood board and its resulting color palette are interactively editable. It enables the user to seek intuitively for a desirable color theme and then a satisfactory color composition of the webpage. For those web pages with pre-specified color contents, such as pictures and logos, WCS is especially useful approach to find harmonic colors compatible with them.

1.1 Related Work

Modern color theory, which was developed at the beginning of the 20th century, deals mainly with visual design in which color is relevant. Itten inductively elaborated the principles of color contrast and harmony using musical chord metaphors to explain harmonious principles of chroma [10]. Munsell's color space based on pigment and dye color [11]. Colors in isolation or unrelated to a layout composition will fail to provide all the necessary information to make a color choice[5]. People rarely deal with a single color in isolation. Most of the time, they deal with a composition of colors, also called color scheme. The colors in the scheme are seldom haphazard, usually they have to fulfill some constraints like being in harmony or contrasting[12]. Kagawa et al. proposed a color design supporting method that help users to obtain various color patterns from pictures[6]. The method implements an interactive evolutionary algorithm. The users can easily find a new color pattern by selecting a picture with most pleasant color design in a database or from web. Hu et al. presented an interactive visualization tool for generating color schemes for novice designers based on two color harmony principles from conventional color theories[8]. The interactive tool enables users to efficiently generate color palettes containing harmonic color combinations in the HSL (hue, saturation, and lightness) space.

There are a number of online tools that can help people to create or share their color themes, such as the websites: Adobe Kuler, COLOURlover, ColorSchemer, ColorExplorer and so on. Most of them provide tools that can abstract color themes from images or graphics. All the researches so far are mainly focusing on the problem of color harmony, which is undoubtedly one of key issues of generating a color scheme. Most of them adopt the idea of color quantization[13], a simple approach using images to generate color sets, in the belief that main colors extracted from a beautiful image must be harmonious anywhere else. This is actually not always true. A color palette from a harmonious image does not always assure a harmony when it is applied to different situations. One problem existing in present researches and tools is that the color scheme creation isolated from its context of use, therefore may be difficult for designers to make right decisions and fine tunings.

2 The Framework of WCS

To solve this problem, we developed a new tool WCS, which supports the evaluation of a color scheme in a real composition of webpage. The tool enables designers to create and edit color theme in a mood board and meanwhile to view the feedback of the consequent visual effect on the web page. The system is illustrated in Fig. 1. It consists of client zone (the upper block) and a server zone (the lower block). The communication between client and server is xmlrpc. The client zone has an interactive Mood Board and a browser for a webpage waiting for recolor. The server zone has three major modular: the evolutionary design module GA, which reproduces better color combinations (schemes) for the webpage; the color quantizer, which extracts a color theme from the Mood Board, therefore defines an available color set (palette) for the webpage; the Style Analyzer, which parses the webpage's CSS file to get all existing variables of colors for change.

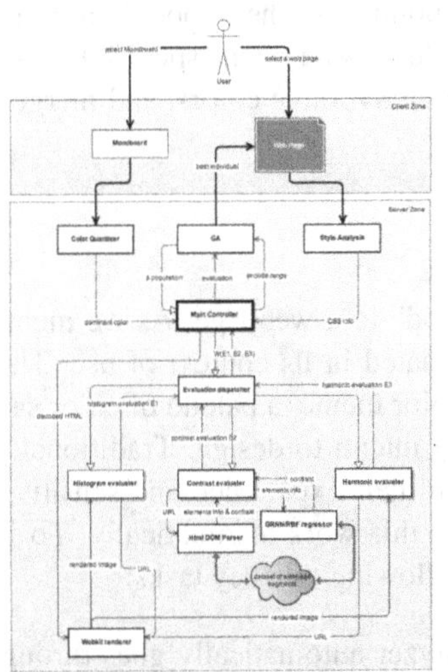

Fig. 1. WCS system framework

The user creates a desirable mood on the Mood Board by interactively pasting certain effects of images on the board (see Figure 2). Quantizing representative colors from the mood board, the system generates a palette of colors using the K-means algorithm in the HSV color space. More details of the Mood Board are given in Section 3. The Main Controller encodes all solutions to assign some of the colors on the palette to the color variables in the CSS. With the encoded solution set, the Genetic Algorithm keeps regenerating new color style definitions of the web page, and sends them to the Main Controller. The Main Controller uses JavaScript simulator to rewrite the web page with new color styles, and saves the page into MEMCACHE. Evaluation Dispatcher fetches every new page in MEMCACHE and sends it to three fitness evaluators: Histogram Evaluator, Contrast Evaluator and Harmony Evaluator.

The detailed explanations of the evaluators are given in Section 4. The fitness evaluations will be fed back to GA for further selection and reproduction. After a number of iterations, The GA will converge to an optimum solution of color scheme. And the best solution of the recolored webpage will be presented to the user.

2.1 The Interactive Mood Board

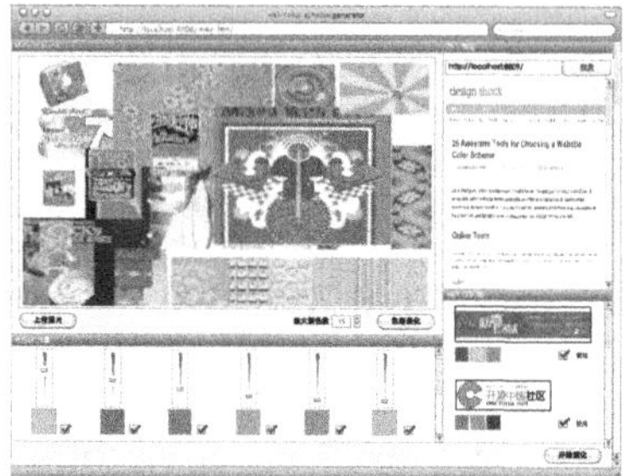

Fig. 2. The interactive Mood Board

The mood board (fig. 2) provides an intuitive way for designers to visualize and refine the "mood" of color. The board also provides an interface for users to interactively abstract the mood board to be a color theme, a row of color patches. The color theme are extracted using k-means color quantization algorithm [13]. Designers can interactively sample the color points on the mood board to pick color clusters he want, specify the number of total clusters in a quantization process, delete unfavorable colors, and merge some color patches to be a blended one.

2.2 Transfer the "Mood" to a Webpage

The ultimate goal of WCS is to transfer the "mood" to a webpage. As we mentioned in last section, the color theme can only be evaluated in its context of use. Thus we need an efficient approach to quickly apply the color theme, a palette of color samples from the Mood Board onto the webpage that we intend to design. Traditionally, designers do the process in trial and error based on their experience and sensitivity. In WCS, a genetic algorithm is devised to complete this work automatically. To implement the algorithm, the WCS need to complete following two key tasks:

Encode All Possible Solutions. WCS style analyzer automatically goes through the html DOM tree to sort out all existing the tags of color values that are editable. Colors on the color palette of the mood board are indexed with a series of binary numbers. Suppose the palette has n colors on it, and the webpage has m tags of color value, then the size of solution set is n^m. The chromosome of the genetic algorithm is constructed with a binary string, which consists of m serial numbers (genes). Every time a legal gene randomly generated at a certain position in the chromosome, the value of a corresponding color tag on the DOM tree will be defined. The n colors are encoded respecting to their relative positions in HSV color space.

Evolve under a Number of Fitness Functions. In real design activities, adjusting of a website color scheme usually follows designers' intents, obeys some design rules and constraints. In WCS, to find an optimum solution, the evolution should also follow some objectives, which are concluded from interviews and discussions with some professional graphic designers:

- The recolored webpage must have an overall color tone as close as possible to the original mood board. That means the componential colors of both are roughly in same proportion
- The recolored webpage must follow some harmony rules of color matching.
- To be accessible, the webpage must have proper color contrast ratio between background and foreground items, such as texts, buttons, images, etc.

To fulfill those objectives, several fitness functions are formulated for the genetic algorithm.

3 Fitness Functions

There are three fitness functions in respect to three objectives mentioned above.

3.1 Histogram Evaluator

The Main controller calculates both the color histograms of the webpage and the Mood board. The two histograms are discrete bins indexed with the color palette. By comparing the two histograms, we can evaluate how similar the two color tones are. The difference between two histograms can be calculated using Earth Mover's Distance [14] or Histogram Intersection Distance. Here we simply use intersection of two normalized color histograms

$$E1 = \sum_i \sum_j \min(\frac{Hcmb_i}{|Hcmb|}, \frac{H_j}{|H|})/D_{i,j}^3 \quad ,i,j \in (1, \dots k) \tag{1}$$

Suppose there are k colors on the palette. $Hcmb_i$ and H_j are heights of ith and jth bin in the color histograms of the mood board and the web page correspondingly. |Hcmb| and |H| gives the magnitude of each histogram, which is equal to the number of samples.

3.2 Contrast Evaluator

Contrast ratios of colors on a web page are relevant to visual saliences distribution. To set proper contrast ratios for different elements on a web page is important for both visual pleasure and accessibility. Strong Contrast Insures Legibility and proper contrast is important for harmony [15]. Graphical elements such as menus and page headers usually use more notable color, which can either be a stronger tint or a contrasting color on a neutral background. High contrast ratio is used for elements that require more attention. Text has high contrast ratio leads to greater readability. For the main body of the content frame, it should be clear but calm, rather than with an active tint. Designers believe that contrast ratios for different kinds of elements on a webpage have some regular patterns. And the contrast as one property of the elements has relation with their other properties like: type, location, occupied area, content and on.

Therefore, in this research, we try to formulate a model of contrast ratio, so that WCS can predict proper contrast ratios for different kinds of elements on the page. A large set of design cases are collected. (So far we have collected and analyzed the pages of Fortune 500 companies.)

To distinguish different elements on a web page, we first need to segment a web page into a set of blocks. Our method for web page segmentation is a DOM tree based segmentation[16]. By parsing the DOM tree, the method divides the webpage into a number of visible blocks. From calculated styles of every block, we extract the properties like: ID, tag, class, position, scrollWidth, scrollHeight, parent node, number of siblings, and some color properties: background-color, background-image, color etc. the contrast ratio of each element is defined as a vector, which is calculated from four consecutive color pairs: P1: color/background-color; P2: color/parent node's color; P3: background-color/1px border color; P4: background-color/parent node's color.

Contrast ratio C = (L1+ 0.05) / (L2 +0.05) , where L1 is brighter color of the pair, while L2 is dark one. L = 0.2126 * R + 0.7152 * G + 0.0722 * B. it is brightness value calculated from weighted linear combination of RGB channels.

A data set of samples of webpage elements is established. All samples can be represented with data pairs (X, C) where X is the normalized feature vector represents measurable properties and C is the corresponding color contrast ratio.

A kind of neural network is adopted to learn the general contrast ratio models. The model, once be trained, must has an desired output Ce that approximates the conditional mean of the response C, that is, the regression of C conditioned on X.

$$Ce = E [C \mid X] \quad (2)$$

Ce is expected C conditioned on X.

With this model, WCS can evolve a webpage's color following some expected local contrast ratios. Here is a fitness function of contrast ratio

$$E2 = \sum_{i=1}^{n} \frac{\|Ce_i - Cr_i\|}{n} \quad (3)$$

where, Cr is current real contrast ratio of ith element on the webpage. Ce is expected contrast ratio predicted with the regression model. The n is total number of elements on the webpage.

The regressor is Radial basis function (RBF) network. RBF network places Gaussian kernels centered at some clusters of the samples. The number of kernels, center of the kernels, and weights of connections to output layer must been optimized in offline learning process. As a special type of RBF network, General Regression Neural Network (GRNN) simplifies the learning by placing a Gaussian at every sample point x and with connection weight equal to corresponding output C

$$\mathrm{Ce(x)} = \frac{\sum_i C^i \exp\left(-\left\|x - x^i\right\|^2 / 2\sigma^2\right.}{\sum_i \exp\left(-\left\|x - x^i\right\|^2 / 2\sigma^2\right.} \quad (4)$$

where x is a new case, x^i is ith sample in training dataset X, C^i is ith sample's C. Both networks are testified in our experiments. The RBF network has much more fast response speed while GRNN is more safe and reliable to predict.

3.3 Harmony Evaluator

Besides the contrast, harmony is also important for pairwise matching on a webpage. To sort out harmonic colors from the color palette, a harmony evaluator would be necessary. Harmonious colors are sets of colors that provide a pleasant visual perception. Harmony among colors is not determined by specific colors, but rather by their relative position in color space[17].

The notion of color harmonization in this work compromises the Moon-Spencer model and the schemes developed by Matsuda [18]. Color harmony is mainly affected by the hue channel. Matsuda's model presents nine templates of color distributions on the hue wheel. The harmonic templates may consist of shades of the same colors (types i, V and T), possibly with complementary colors (templates I, Y, X) or more complex combinations (template L and its mirror image). Among those templates, O'Donovan's research further shows that monochromatic, analogous, and complementary templates are the most popular[19]. This statement are coincident to the Moon-Spencer model which induces three types of color harmonic relations of any color pair: 'Contrast,' a state the two color are significantly different from each other, 'Similarity,' a resembling state, and 'Identity,' a state with an identical hue.

Based on the notions of the three basic types of color harmony, we formulated a color compatibility measurement for a color pair. Suppose we have a color pair P, then the compatibility measurement

$$H(P) = \text{argmin}_{\alpha}\left(\left|\|h(P)\| - \alpha\right| \cdot S(P)\right), \alpha \in \left\{0, \frac{\pi}{4}, \pi\right\} \tag{5}$$

where H denotes the hue channel. $\|h(P)\|$ denotes the arc-length of the color pair P on the hue wheel. The angle α represents three harmonious templates: monochromatic α =0; analogous $\alpha = \frac{\pi}{4}$; and complementary $\alpha = \pi$. The argmin determines the template that best fits the color pair, and the difference is regarded as the deviation from the harmonic state. The less the deviation is measured, the more harmony the pair has.

Note that the above formula also take into account the channel of saturation denoted with S, since the hue distances between colors with low saturation are perceptually less noticeable than the distances between those of high saturation. The S(P) represent the sum of two colors' saturations in [0 ,1.0]. Also note that the formula implies that two colors with same hue value are absolutely harmony. And two colors along the gray pole (with S=0) are absolutely harmony. That is reasonable from designer's point of view.

Then, by summing up all local color pairs' harmony values of a webpage, the overall color harmony of the page can be roughly assessed.

$$E3 = \sum_{j=1}^{n} \sum_{i=1}^{4} H_j\ (P_i) \tag{6}$$

Suppose there are n visual segments on the webpage. And each segment has four layered fore-background color pairs as we mentioned in contrast evaluator. Probably some of the pairs have identical colors and therefore score zero.

M. Nishiyama et al [20] demonstrated that the sum of the color harmony scores computed from local regions of an image is positively correlated with the overall aesthetic quality of the image. An image with high (low) aesthetic quality often contains a large number of local color patterns with high (low) color harmony scores. The harmony model they adopted is the Moon-Spencer model.

3.4 Multi Objective Optimization

With three fitness functions: E1, E2 and E3 and a well-encoded solution set, we cast web color scheme creation as a constrained multi objective optimization problem, which tries to strike a balance among the desirable color "mood", the spatial harmonious pairwise color combination as well as necessary figural-background color contrast for legibility and saliency. The energy function is defined as

$$E = \alpha E1 + \beta E2 + \gamma E3 \tag{7}$$

where α, β and γ are the weighting coefficients of E1, E2 and E3 respectively. The changes of the coefficients shift the minimum of the energy function. To determine the proper values of them, we fix one of them and manually adjust the other two, meanwhile, to observe the resulting outcomes of the evolutionary algorithm. In our experiments, we set α to -1, γ and β are varies in between 5~10. These three terms altogether make the system converge to an expected state, fulfilling all the three objectives.

4 Results and Application

We conducted an informal experiment to test the usefulness of the WCS in the context of a webpage design. We found that most color schemes generated by the tool are aesthetically preferable. Sometimes the evolution may be stuck in a local optimum, with one or two parts of the webpage not so well settled. With the proper weights of the energy function and a well-encoded solution set, the optimal color schemes produced by evolutions in different sessions are pretty consistent.

Initial experiments show that the three fitness functions are all essential for the optimization of the color scheme. Removing any one of them, the results of the evolution are not so acceptable, especially the E1 and E2. Changing the weights of the functions, the resulting schemes could be slightly different. The interactive Mood Board is easy and intuitive to use. WCS demonstrates that novice users can compose desirable color schemes for webpages as easily as professional designers do.

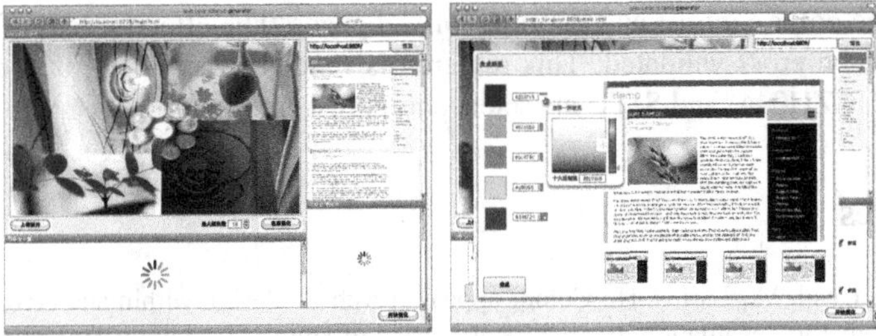

Fig. 3. The upper is a new mood board created by a user. The lower is the consequent new webpage color scheme generated by WCS.

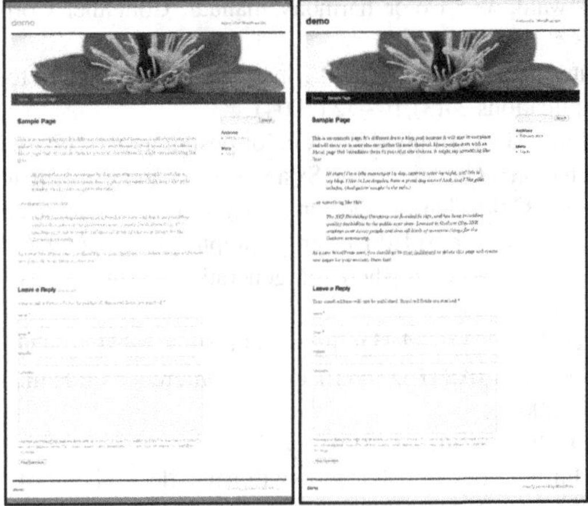

Fig. 4. The left is original webpage. The right is a new color scheme generated by WCS, using the flower picture on the page as a mood board.

5 Conclusion

This WCS we are developing demonstrates a general framework of a computational approach to web color scheme design. The framework generally performs well. The application is developed for both professional designers and amateurs. It can be used right after the wireframe design stage, or to redesign an existing webpage's color scheme. It is especially helpful when parts of the webpage are composed with pictures that have distinct color tones: the system is capable of harmonizing the colors of the webpage. The algorithms and models in the framework, however, still need more convincing validations and refinements. Some alternative algorithms and models may be compared in future experiments. K means clustering is rough for color theme extraction. We shall devise some new clustering algorithms, which are more faithfully reflecting people's color perception. Some unsupervised feature learning and knowledge-discovering techniques may be added into the computational models for assessing the color contrast and harmony of webpages. The effectiveness of the models needs to be cross-validated. This research is funded by ministry of education of China (11YJCZH044) and SJTU art-science joint research fund.

References

1. Cyr, D., Head, M., Larios, H.: Colour appeal in website design within and across cultures: A multi-method evaluation. International Journal of Human-Computer Studies 68(1), 1–21 (2010)
2. Elliot, A.J., Maier, M.A.: Color and psychological functioning. Current Directions in Psychological Science 16(5), 250–254 (2007)
3. Zelanski, P., Fisher, M.P.: Colour: for designers and artists. Herbert Press (1989)
4. Jacobson, E., Ostwald, W.: Color harmony manual. Container Corporation of America (1948)
5. Meier, B.J., Spalter, A.M., Karelitz, D.B.: Interactive color palette tools. IEEE Computer Graphics and Applications 24(3), 64–72 (2004)
6. Kagawa, T., Nishino, H., Utsumiya, K.: A color design assistant based on user's sensitivity. In: IEEE International Conference on Systems, Man and Cybernetics. IEEE (2003)
7. Liu, J., Li, J., Lu, G.: Color Scheme Design through Color Semantic and Interactive Genetic Algorithm. J. of Computer-Aided Design & Graphics 24(5), 669–676 (2012)
8. Hu, G., et al.: An interactive method for generating harmonious color schemes. Color Research & Application (2012)
9. Lucero, A., Vaajakallio, K.: Co-designing mood boards: creating dialogue with people. In: Proceedings of the Third IASTED International Conference on Human-Computer Interaction, pp. 254–260 (2008)
10. Itten, J.: The elements of color, vol. 4. Wiley (1970)
11. Munsell, A.H.: Munsell book of color: glossy finish collection (1966)
12. Beretta, G.B., Moroney, N.M.: Harmonious colors: from alchemy to science. Society of Photo-Optical Instrumentation Engineers (SPIE) Conference Series (2012)
13. Morse, B.S., et al.: Image-Based Color Schemes. In: IEEE International Conference on Image Processing. IEEE (2007)
14. Rubner, Y., Tomasi, C., Guibas, L.J.: A metric for distributions with applications to image databases. In: Sixth International Conference on Computer Vision. IEEE (1998)
15. Schloss, K.B., Palmer, S.E.: Aesthetic response to color combinations: preference, harmony, and similarity. Attention, Perception, & Psychophysics 73(2), 551–571 (2011)
16. Cao, J., Mao, B., Luo, J.: A segmentation method for web page analysis using shrinking and dividing. International Journal of Parallel, Emergent and Distributed Systems 25(2), 93–104 (2010)
17. Cohen-Or, D., et al.: Color harmonization. ACM Transactions on Graphics, TOG (2006)
18. Matsuda, Y.: Color design. Asakura Shoten 2(4) (1995)
19. O'Donovan, P., Agarwala, A., Hertzmann, A.: Color Compatibility From Large Datasets. ACM Transactions on Graphics 30(4) (2011)
20. Nishiyama, M., et al.: Aesthetic quality classification of photographs based on color harmony. In: 2011 IEEE Conference on Computer Vision and Pattern Recognition (CVPR). IEEE (2011)

Study on Effects of Text Decoration for a Text Based Communication Tool in Education

Masateru Hishina[1,2], Katsuaki Miike[3], Nobutake Asaba[4], Satoru Murakami[2], Yuichi Ohkawa[2], and Takashi Mitsuishi[5]

[1] School of Business and Commerce, Tokyo International University, Saitama, Japan
hishina@tiu.ac.jp

[2] Graduate School of Educational Informatics, Tohoku University, Sendai, Japan
{hishina,b0fm1009,kuri}@ei.tohoku.ac.jp

[3] Department of Shinshu Junior College, Saku University, Nagano, Japan
k-miike@shintan.ac.jp

[4] Center for Fundamental Education, The University of Kitakyushu, Fukuoka, Japan
n-asaba@kitakyu-u.ac.jp

[5] Center for Information Technology in Education, Tohoku University, Sendai, Japan
takashi.mitsuishi@cite.tohoku.ac.jp

Abstract. In this paper, the authors have focused on effects of text decoration function on text based communication system in education. In recent years, chance of the text based communications between a teacher and students in face-to-face lessons has increased. However, there are few investigations of the effects mounting text decoration function in education. Therefore, the authors performed the experiment to investigate effects of text decoration function using text based communication system in face-to-face lessons. As a result of the experiment, it was clarified that there are a wide variety of the expressions in text messages, which made by students using text decoration function. And most of them have felt strongly the necessity of text decoration function. Furthermore, it was clarified that several in them felt "Interest for the text decoration" and "Affinity with the teacher".

Keywords: decoration, text, message, expression, necessity, interest, affinity.

1 Introduction

In recent years, chance of the text based communications using information communication technology between a teacher and students in face-to-face lessons has increased. Most of the text messages are plain text. The text decoration function (e.g., font settings of emphasis, size and color, or insertion of pictorial symbols) is standard mounted in smart phone, which have installed a text based communication application program. However, there are few investigations of the effects mounting text decoration function on text based communication system in education. Therefore, the purpose of this study is to investigate effects of text decoration function. The authors performed the experiment to compare effects of text decoration function using text

M. Kurosu (Ed.): Human-Computer Interaction, Part I, HCII 2013, LNCS 8004, pp. 565–574, 2013.

based communication system in face-to-face lessons. In this paper, the authors reported on result of the experiment and the effects of text decoration function in face-to-face lessons.

2 Interactive Communications in Education

Messages such as question and impression about a lesson from students become key indicators for teacher as the formative evaluation of instruction [1]. On the other hand, messages such as answer and encouragement from teacher become key factors for students to improve the level of understanding and the willingness to learn [2]. Interactive communications are very important in education.

However, the interactive communications between a teacher and students are limited compared with the one direction communication such as presentations concerning course content from a teacher to students in face-to-face lesson in Japan. The reasons are much of lesson time that is spent on presentations concerning course content. And many students behave shyly in face-to-face class.

2.1 One-to-One Text Based Communications Process

To overcome such problems, in Japan, the one-to-one text based communication methods with the paper card and the questionnaire is proposed [3-4]. The methods are as follows. First, a student writes and hands the text messages to a teacher just before the end of a lesson. Secondly, the teacher receives and reads the text messages from the students after the lesson ends. Thirdly, the teacher writes the answer to the student's text messages until upcoming a lesson. Finally, the teacher hands the answer to the students, and the student reads the answer from the teacher in the beginning of upcoming a lesson. In one semester, these are repeated for usual lessons. Recently, the cases that replaced from the paper card and the questionnaire to the text based communication system on the computer is increasing [5].

2.2 Plain Text Messages and Text Decoration Function

Most of the text messages in text based communications are plain text. Nonverbal messages (e.g., voice and countenance, and gesture, etc.) in face-to-face communications are limited in text based communications. To overcome such problems, we contrive arrangements by a combination of some characters in the text message instead of the nonverbal message. For examples, as a result of the experiment in the discussion board, it is clarified that the user puts space between characters, and makes emoticon that combines characters [6]. Recently, the text decoration function is standard mounted in smart phone, which have installed the text based communication application program.

2.3 Effects of Text Decoration Function in Education

There are few investigations of effects mounting text decoration function on text based communication system in education. Then, the authors have tried to perform the experiment to investigate effects of text decoration function in face-to-face lessons. The authors pay attention in effects of the students' side. The authors have made the following four hypotheses about effects mounting text decoration function on the students' side.

The hypotheses shown in (i) and (ii) are expected to become materials for a teacher who guesses a student's understanding level, willingness to learn, and feelings, etc. And (iii) is expected to activate communications with a teacher. And (iv) is expected to become an additional resource that improves a student's willingness to learn [6-9].

(i) A student will use a wide variety of expressions such as emphasis and feelings in text messages.
(ii) Amount of a student's text message will increase, and the topic will be diversified.
(iii) Text base communications with a teacher will become interesting and happy impressions for a student.
(iv) A student's affinity with the teacher will rise.

3 Experiment to Investigate Effects of Text Decoration

The authors performed the experiment to investigate effects of text decoration function using text based communication system in face-to-face lessons. In the experiment, the authors used text based communication system that developed originally. The system was named "iConversation" (*interpersonal*-Conversation *system for teacher-learner human relations*) (the following describes it as "iCon"). The authors developed the iCon for one-to-one text communications between a teacher and a student in face-to-face lessons. The iCon has been used in 11 classes at four universities in Japan since fiscal year 2012.

3.1 A Text Based Communication System : iConversation

The authors modified two kinds of the iCon with a different feature for the experiment in this study. It is "iCon-plain" and "iCon-decoratable".

The iCon-plain hasn't mounted text decoration function to change font settings and to insert pictorial symbols. Figure 1 shows an interface of the iCon-plain for a student. An interface of the iCon for a teacher is basically same for a student. A student can input text messages to area of "Message to the teacher", and can input 18 Japanese characters in one line to the area (Case of the alphanumeric characters; 36 characters). The text of 12 lines can be input to the displayed the area. And more characters can be input when scrolling. In area of "Conversation log", a student can read his/her last messages and answer from a teacher. The messages exchanged between a teacher and a student in past is displayed like "discussion board" in the area.

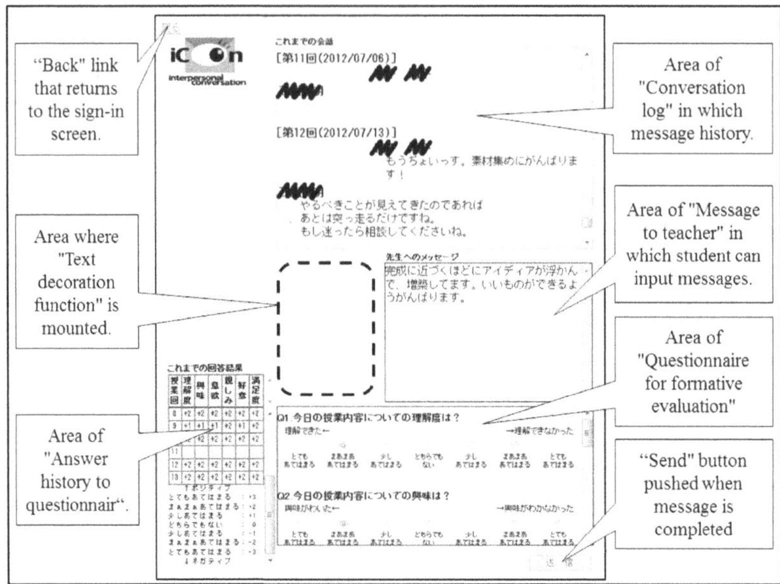

Fig. 1. An interface of the iCon-plain for a student

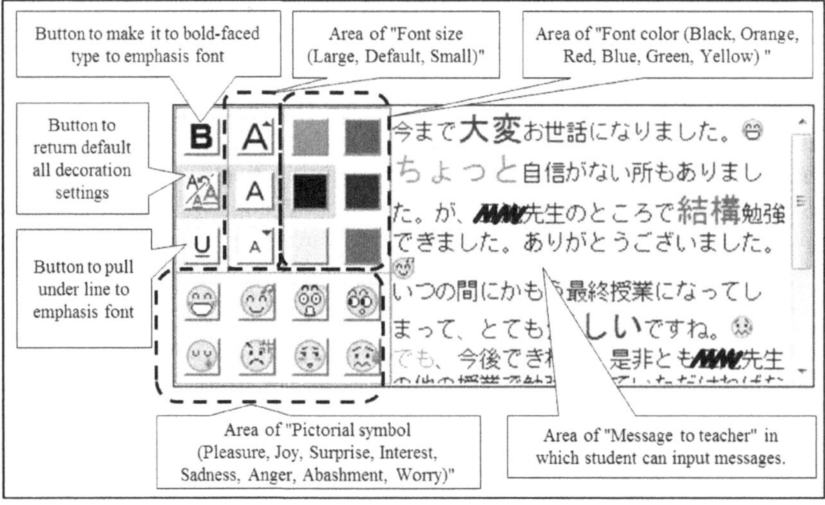

Fig. 2. The iCon-decoratable : The iCon with Additional Component for Text Decoration

On the other hand, the iCon-decoratable has mounted text decoration function to change font settings (e.g., emphasis, size and color) and to insert the pictorial symbols. The iCon-decoratable and the iCon-plain are same interfaces basically. The iCon-decoratable has an addition of text decoration function to the iCon-plain. An interface of the added text decoration function is shown in Figure 2. When the user clicks button of decoration function, the characters is decorated with font settings, or pictorial symbols are inserted. These message areas of the iCon-decoratable are achieved with various tags conforming to HTML 4.01 in order to obtain font settings and pictorial symbols. Therefore, various tags are recorded in text messages. Of course, the users can use decoration function without thinking about various tags, and the users cannot see various tags.

3.2 Outline of the Experiment

The experiment that used the iCon was performed by two classes of face-to-face lessons in which 1 teacher and about 20 students participated. These are same course; it is conduct a lesson respectively at first term and latter term. This course is a practice to learn the base of server-client system for students of third grader or more. The teacher of this course was one person in authors. In the classroom, each one has one desk-top PC for a teacher and students, and all PC is connected with Internet. When a usual lesson was begun and ended, a teacher and students used the iCon with a browser installed in desk-top PC.

In the experimental group, a teacher and students used the iCon-plain for six times of first half, and used the iCon-decoratable for six times of latter half (The students kept free whether to use the text decoration function, though the teacher had the text decoration function used without fail). On the other hand, in the control group, a teacher and students used the iCon-plain for 12 times in total. Just before the end of a lesson, it was demanded that students make text messages concerning free topics (questions on the lesson, consultation of worry, and topics concerning hobby each other, etc.) at the time of about ten minutes.

In this paper, the authors reported on the result that is analyzed with three points shown as follows.

(a) Analysis concerning signs of decoration recorded in text messages
The HTML tags as signs using text decoration function are extracted from text messages and the authors analyzed the tags to investigate the hypothesis "(i) A student will use a wide variety of expressions such as emphasis and feelings in text messages" described in paragraph 2.3.

(b) Analysis concerning quantity and content in text messages
The authors analyzed the number of characters and the topics of text messages to investigate the hypothesis "(ii) Amount of a student's text message will increase, and the topic will be diversified" described in paragraph 2.3.

(c) Consciousness survey by questionnaire
The questionnaire is performed for students and the authors analyzed the answer to investigate the hypothesis "(iii) Text base communications with a teacher will become interesting and happy impressions for a student" and "(iv) A student's affinity with the teacher will rise" described in paragraph 2.3.

Table 1. Result of utilization the text decoration function in the experimental group

	15-Jun-12	*22-Jun-12*	*29-Jun-12*	*6-Jul-12*	*13-Jul-12*	*20-Jul-12*	*Total*
Student who sent message	18	20	18	19	17	17	109
Student who used decoration function	17	16	15	16	17	11	92
Ratio of student who used decoration function	94.4%	80.0%	83.3%	84.2%	100%	64.7%	84.4%
Total of used decoration function	103	75	52	60	79	67	436
Average of used decoration function / a person	6.06	4.69	3.47	3.75	4.65	6.09	4.74

Table 2. Summary of the quantity consumed of each kind of the decorations

Emphases		*Size settings*		*Color settings*				
Bold	Underline	Large	Small	Orange	Red	Blue	Green	Yellow
30	5	35	9	30	34	33	23	6
Pictorial symbols								*Total*
pleasure	joy	surprise	interest	sadness	anger	abashment	worry	
88	55	6	8	17	2	14	41	436

3.3 Result of the Experiment

The lessons of the experimental group were conducted between April and July, 2012, and 22 students participated. The lessons of the control group were conducted between September, 2012 and January, 2013, and 24 students participated. (It omitted students who were participating in both classes from the analysis object.)

(a) Analysis concerning signs of decoration recorded in text messages

The result of utilization the text decoration function (The HTML tags in messages are counted.) in the experimental group is shown in Table 1. The students of 84.4% in average were using text decoration function in usual lessons. And the students were using 4.74 kinds of text decorations in average per person by usual lessons.

The summary of the amount used of each kind of text decorations is shown in Table 2. Most decorations used by the students were a pictorial symbol of meaning of "pleasure". Moreover, there was a lot of font settings in which the emphases was set to Bold, the size was set to Large, and the color was set to Red.

On the other hand, in the both groups, there were emoticons and the gestures which expressed by composing of a combination of characters in text messages instead of nonverbal messages. Many of cases were about 1-2 kinds of a combination of characters per one direction communication from a student to a teacher in a lesson. The total of communications in the experimental group were only about 31 (The first half is 22, and the latter half is 9.). And the total of communications in the control group were only about 25 (The first half is 9, and the latter half is 16.). These are littler than scales using 436 text decoration function.

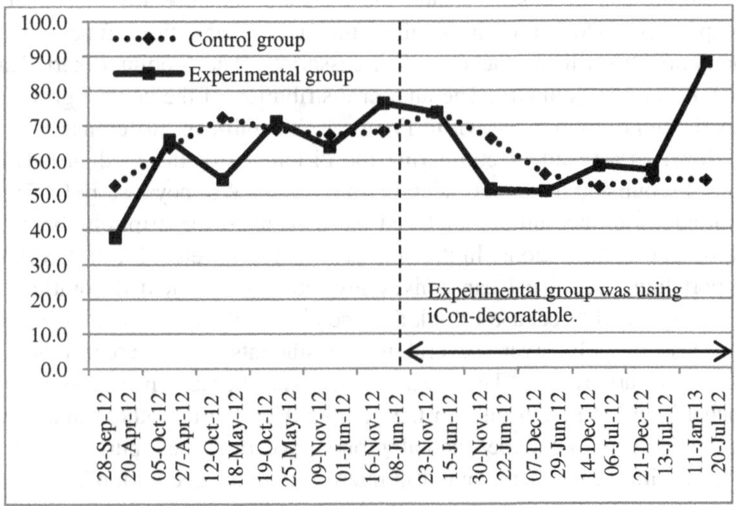

Fig. 3. The average transition of number of the character

(b) Analysis concerning quantity and content in text messages

The average transition of number of the characters that the student input to text messages in usual lessons is shown in Figure 3. A big difference was not seen between the average value at the first term and latter term in the experimental group, and a big difference was not seen it in the control group, too (t-test and Wilcoxon test). When the experimental group was compared with the control group, an especially big difference was not seen it excluding the final day (t-test and Mann-Whitney test).

On the other hand, a significant difference was seen in 5% level as a result of comparing the average value between the control group and the experimental group only at the final day (t-test, $p<0.05$).

To clarify reasons for the difference, contents of the text messages on the final day were analyzed. As a result, most of the students in the experimental group were almost inputting about the impression for the lesson and the word of thanks to the teacher. Half of the students in the control group were inputting about the impression for the lessons and the word of thanks to the teacher.

On the other hand, the more than half of the students in the control group were inputting about the topic concerning the examination and the academic achievement. Only the students of 20% in the experimental group were inputting about the topic concerning the examination and the academic achievement.

(c) Consciousness survey by questionnaire

The authors surveyed concerning the necessity of text decoration function by the questionnaire at final day. The question sentence for the control group was "Do you think that the text decoration function in text communications to a teacher is necessary?", and the question sentence for the experimental group was "Do you think that the text decoration function in text communications to a teacher was necessary?". The 5-point Likert Scale was used at the questionnaire. The answer distribution of the control group and the experimental group is shown in Figure 4. A significant difference was seen in 5% level as a result of comparing the difference of the median between the control group and the experimental group (Mann-Whitney test, $p<0.05$).

In addition, the authors analyzed the contents of description about selected reason in these questions. In the both groups, there were a lot of descriptions of purport like "Because I can convey my feelings with text decorations, it was necessary", and "Because I think that the kind of the expression became rich, it is necessary". However, several in the students of the control group have described purport like "There was no necessity because it was impolite to the teacher", and "Enough only in the plain-text". On the other hand, several in the students of the experimental group have described purport like "I feel affinity with the teacher", and "I'm interesting in the decoration".

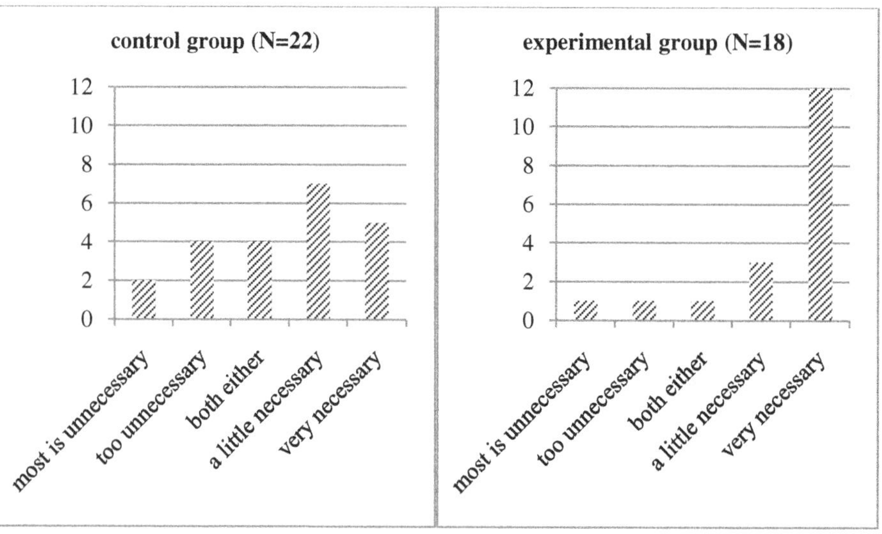

Fig. 4. Distribution of the questionnaire concerning the necessity

3.4 Discussion

The hypotheses described in paragraph 2.3. were considered based on the results of the experiment.

(a) **Analysis concerning signs of decoration recorded in text messages**
In the both groups, the number of nonverbal messages which expressed by composing of a combination of characters was little amounts. On the other hand, the students in the experimental group of 80% or more were using text decoration function in usual lessons. And the students were using 4.74 kinds of text decorations in average per one person in usual lessons. It is guessed that the students in the experiment group tried to express the emphasis and feelings in variegation by using text decoration function. In addition, it is necessary to survey the intention of these expressions.

(b) **Analysis concerning quantity and content in text messages**
When the average value of number of characters that the students in the experimental group input was compared with it that the students in the control group input, an especially big difference was not seen it excluding at the final day. On the other hand, a significant difference was seen in 5% level as a result of comparing the average value between the control groups and the experimental group only at the final day. The content of topics was some different tendency in the comparison between the experimental group and the control group. In addition, it is necessary to perform the subsequent analysis of the content of topics.

(c) **Consciousness survey by questionnaire**
As a result of the survey, it was clarified that the students of the control group did not strongly feel the necessity of text decoration function. On the other hand, it was clarified that most students of the experimental group strongly feel the necessity of it. In addition, there were some students in the experimental group have felt "Interest" for the use of the text decoration function, and have felt "Affinity" with a teacher. In the experimental group, it was confirmed that impression of interest to text decoration and sense of affinity with a teacher improved.

4 Conclusion

The authors performed the experiment to compare effects of text decoration function using the text based communication system in face-to-face lessons. As a result, it was clarified that the students of 80% or more was using the text decoration function, and the students tried to express the emphasis and feelings in variegation by using text decoration function. And they strongly felt the necessity of text decoration function. Furthermore, it was clarified that several in them felt "Interest for text decoration" and "Affinity with the teacher".

The experiment reported with this paper was small-scale. The authors think that the result of the reported this paper should confirm whether to be reproduced in other classes in the future.

References

1. Gagne, R.M., Wager, W.W., Golas, K., Keller, J.M.: Principles of Instructional Design, 5th edn. Wadsworth Publishing, Kentucky (2005)
2. Yano, Y.: Knowledge of Results, Encyclopedia of Educational Technology, pp. 16–17. Jikkyou Shuppan, Tokyo (2000) (in Japanese)
3. Suzuki, K.: Interactive Communications in Lecture in which a lot of Students Participate, Technique of Lesson in University, pp. 240–243. Yuhikaku Publishing, Tokyo (1997) (in Japanese)
4. Oda, K.: Attempt of " Daifuku-cho (Shuttle Card) "- Formative Evaluation Used in Course of Educational Psychology, Improvement of Lesson in University, pp. 186–191. Yuhikaku Publishing, Tokyo (1999) (in Japanese)
5. Susono, H., Shimomura, T., Oda, K., Koyama, H.: Development of Electronic Daifuku-cho and Using it for The Students and The Teacher. Bulletin of the Faculty of Education 26, 67–72 (2006) (in Japanese)
6. Richmond, V.P., McCroskey, J.C.: Nonverbal Behavior in Interpersonal Relations, 5th edn. Pearson Education Inc., New Jersey (2003)
7. Maslow, A.H.: Motivation and Personality, 2nd edn. Harper & Row Publishers, New York (1970)
8. Heider, F.: The Psychology of Interpersonal Relations. John Wiley & Sons, New York (1958)
9. Hishina, M., Okada, R., Suzuki, K.: Measuring the Effects of Human Relations on Willingness-to-Learn for CMC-based One-to-One Instruction. Transactions of Japanese Society of Information and Systems in Education 24(4), 395–402 (2007) (in Japanese)

Ease of Icon Processing Can Predict Icon Appeal

Siné McDougall[1] and Irene Reppa[2]

[1] Bournemouth University, UK
[2] Swansea University, UK
smcdougall@bournemouth.ac.uk, i.reppa@swansea.ac.uk

Abstract. Correlations between subjective ratings of interface usability and appeal have been frequently reported. This study examined the possibility that the relationship between usability and appeal are underpinned by implicit perceptions of ease of processing which act as a heuristic in making judgments of appeal. Ease of processing was manipulated by varying the amount of experience participants gained with icons in a search task prior to judging appeal, as well as varying the familiarity and visual complexity of the icons presented. These manipulations systematically affected response times in the search task (an *objective* measure of usability). The effects observed in appeal judgments followed the *same* pattern as for search times, demonstrating that ease of processing predicts judgments of appeal. This suggests that our understanding of interface appeal needs to be predicated on an appreciation of the factors affecting the ease with which information on an interface is processed.

Keywords: Interface appeal; usability; processing fluency; icons.

1 Introduction

1.1 The Relationship between Usability and Appeal

Interface usability typically refers to the ease with which an interface can be learned and how swiftly and accurately it can be used [1,2]. It is now recognized that enhancing the aesthetic appeal of an interface may be just as important as improving its usability [3]. Recent research has therefore often focused on how interface appeal can be enhanced [4-8].

A number of studies have observed a relationship between ratings of perceived usability and ratings of aesthetic appeal. These studies have typically obtained ratings of usability and ratings of appeal for interfaces such as websites, MP3 players, or mobile phones and analyzed the correlation between ratings [9-11]. In a recent review Hassenzahl & Monk [12] found that correlations between ratings of usability and appeal are commonly reported and that the strength of the correlation varied in accordance with the context, the nature of the interface, and the task demands.

1.2 Using Ease of Processing as a Heuristic to Judge Appeal

The relationship between usability and appeal may be explained by *ease of processing* accounts of aesthetic appeal. The ease of processing of a stimulus has been suggested

M. Kurosu (Ed.): Human-Computer Interaction, Part I, HCII 2013, LNCS 8004, pp. 575–584, 2013.

as a potential general heuristic which may influence judgments of appeal [13, 14]. Alter & Oppenheimer [13] argued that the ease with which stimuli can be processed generates a corresponding *fluency experience.* It is this fluency experience which then acts as a heuristic in determining judgments of appeal.

This rationale can be used to explain the observed correlation between interface usability and appeal. If interfaces are easy to use (i.e. facilitate ease of processing and generate a corresponding fluency experience) then they will be judged as more appealing. Conversely, if interfaces are difficult to use (i.e. are difficult to process, generating a poor fluency experience) then they will be judged as less appealing.

1.3 Factors Influencing Ease of Processing

The aim of the current study was to examine the hypothesis that ease of processing can indeed influence judgments of appeal, using icons as stimuli. Ease of processing was measured objectively - rather than subjectively - by measuring performance during a search task. The search task, in which participants were asked to search for icons in an array, was designed to be analogous to the everyday task of searching for icons on an interface. Ease of processing was manipulated experimentally by varying (a) the amount of experience users gained with icons before rating appeal and (b) the nature of the icons presented in the search task (i.e. their familiarity and visual complexity).

Experience with the Icons. Icons were presented to participants over 9 blocks of search trials. Ratings of appeal were obtained after the first and ninth blocks of trials. It was expected that ease of processing, and hence ratings of appeal, would improve as they gained experience with the icons over blocks of trials.

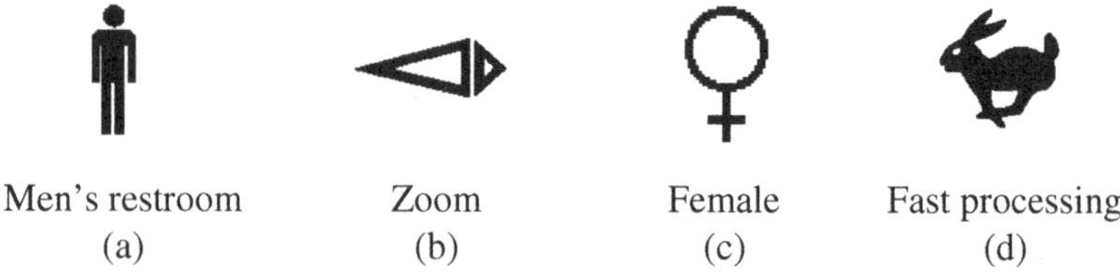

Men's restroom	Zoom	Female	Fast processing
(a)	(b)	(c)	(d)

Fig. 1. Examples of icons

Familiarity with the Icon. Familiarity is one of the most important predictors of speed and accuracy of icon processing [15, 16]. For example, our familiarity with the icon for men's restroom allows us to search for it more quickly in an array in comparison to an icon representing the 'zoom' function on cameras (c.f. Fig. 1a and b). This cannot be accounted for simply because one icon is pictorial and the other is not: our familiarity with the abstract icon representing 'female' (Fig. 1c) allows us to identify it more quickly and effectively compared with the pictorial icon representing 'fast processing' which is not familiar (Fig.1d; see [15]).

On the basis of previous research it was therefore expected that familiar icons would be found faster in the search arrays in comparison to unfamiliar icons. As a result, participants' fluency experiences between these types of icons would differ resulting in familiar icons being rated more positively for appeal than unfamiliar icons.

Visual Complexity of the Icon. The visual complexity of an icon or picture can be measured in a number of ways but generally can be taken to refer to the level of intricacy or detail in a stimulus [c.f., 17-19]. Simple icons can enhance performance because they can be discriminated more easily in arrays [20] and are located more easily, or pop-out, in visual search [20-23]. It was expected that simple icons would be regarded as more appealing than complex icons because of the relative ease with which they may be processed.

Prior familiarity and visual complexity of the icons were varied orthogonally (see Figure 2). Icons were either simple or complex, familiar or unfamiliar.

	Visual Complexity	
Familiarity	Simple	Complex
Familiar	 Picnic Area	 Risk of explosion
Unfamiliar	 Balance	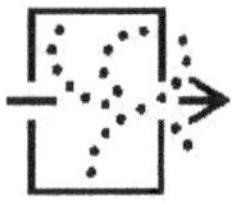 Rinse

Fig. 2. Types of icons presented in the visual search task which varied orthogonally on familiarity and visual complexity

1.4 Controlling Icon Appeal

Importantly, the appeal of icons *prior* to the experiments was held constant across all 4 types of icon presented to participants. This is because both the visual complexity and our familiarity with a stimulus are known to affect judgments of appeal.

Familiarity with the Icon. Stimulus familiarity is an important predictor of appeal judgments with familiar stimuli rated more highly than unfamiliar ones and correlates significantly with ratings of appeal [24-30].

Visual Complexity of the Icon. Similarly, visually simple stimuli tend to be preferred or rated more highly on appeal than visually complex ones [26, 31, 32].

Mean ratings of appeal obtained previously from an icon corpus were therefore used to ensure that icons in all four experimental conditions shown in Fig. 2 did not differ in appeal (see Materials for details). This meant that differences in appeal which emerged during the study could be attributed to differences in ease of processing rather than merely being the result of prior differences between experimental materials.

To summarize, if ease of processing during the search task determines perceptions of appeal we should expect the following:-

(a) If response times are lower for simple and familiar icons then ratings of appeal will be higher
(b) Ratings of appeal will increase as we gain experience with icons.

2 Method

2.1 Participants

Forty-two undergraduate and postgraduate students from Bournemouth University took part in this experiment. Twenty-one participants provided ratings of appeal after completing 1 block of experimental trials. Their mean age was 20.83 years (12 females, 9 males). Twenty-one participants provided ratings of appeal after completing 9 blocks of experimental trials. There mean age was 22.33 years (13 females, 8 males). Each participant received £12 or course credits for taking part in the study.

2.2 Procedure

Participants carried out a search task designed to be analogous to searching for icons on an interface. They searched for a pre-determined target icon among an array of nine icons. Participants were initially shown the target for 2 seconds and, once it disappeared from the screen, an OK button appeared. Participants then pressed the OK button to display the search array and used the mouse to click as quickly as possible on the icon they had seen where it was displayed in the array. Once participants had clicked on an icon in the array, the array disappeared and the next experimental trial began.

There were 9 blocks of trials, with 40 trials per block. In each block, 40 icons were search targets, 10 icons of each icon type shown in Figure 2. Appeal judgments were obtained from two separate experimental groups, one providing ratings at block 1, the other at block 9.

Ease of processing was measured as the time taken by participants to search for an icon in an array (a task similar to searching for icons on an interface). Participants were asked to rate icons on a 1-5 scale (from really dislike to really like) *either* after completing 1 block of experimental trials *or* after completing 9 blocks of experimental trials.

2.3 Design

Participants completed two tasks, a search task and a rating task. The search task was based on a repeated-measures design manipulating three within-participants independent variables. These were icon familiarity with 2 levels (familiar and unfamiliar), icon complexity with 2 levels (simple and complex), and blocks of trials with 9 levels (Blocks 1-9). The combination of icon familiarity and icon complexity gave rise to four icon types which were presented in each of 9 blocks of trials. The dependent measure for the search task was the response time taken to find the target icon in an array of icons.

In the rating task there were also three independent variables: icon familiarity (familiar and unfamiliar) and icon complexity (simple and complex) were within-participant variables (as in the search task), but blocks of trials was manipulated between-participants and it had only two levels (block 1 and block 9). The dependent measure for the ratings task was mean appeal rating per condition per block.

2.4 Materials

Icons were selected from a corpus of 239 icons rated for familiarity, complexity and appeal [26, 33]. As shown in Fig. 2, 40 icons were presented in the visual search trials which varied orthogonally in their familiarity and visual complexity: they were (a) 10 familiar and complex icons, (b) 10 familiar and simple icons, (c) 10 unfamiliar and complex, and (d) 10 unfamiliar and simple icons. A further 60 icons were used in the ratings booklet which participants were asked to complete after blocks 1 and 9. These included a matching set of 40 icons of the same 4 types which participants had not seen before, as well as a set of 20 previously unseen 'neutral' stimuli whose familiarity and complexity fell in the mid-range. Data analyses reported here refer only to the 40 icons shown to participants.

A series of one-way analyses of variance followed by Newman-Keuls comparisons was conducted to ensure that ratings differed in accordance with the requirements of each experimental condition. Ratings of familiarity differed significantly, $F(3,36) = 25.20$, $p < .001$. Newman-Keuls comparisons revealed that familiar simple and complex icons had significantly higher familiarity ratings than unfamiliar icons; M(complex/familiar)=3.41, M(simple/familiar)=3.61, M(complex/unfamiliar)=2.01, M(simple/unfamiliar)=2.04. Ratings of visual complexity also differed significantly, $F(3,36) = 63.88$, $p < .001$. Newman-Keuls comparisons revealed that complex familiar and unfamiliar icons had significantly higher complexity ratings than simple icons; M(complex/familiar)=3.44, M(complex/unfamiliar)=3.47, M(simple/familiar)=2.00, M(simple/unfamiliar)=2.02. Ratings of icon appeal did not differ significantly, $F(3,36) = 2.69$, $p > .05$; M(complex/familiar)=2.96, M(complex/unfamiliar)=2.68, M(simple/familiar)=3.29, M(simple/unfamiliar)=2.90.

3 Results

3.1 Response Times

An analysis of variance was conducted to examine the effects of experience (blocks of trials 1-9), icon familiarity (familiar vs. unfamiliar) and icon complexity (simple vs. complex) on participants' response times.

As expected, response times reduced as participants gained experience with icons in the search task, $F(8,320) = 13.05$, $p < .001$, M(block 1)=1239 ms, M(block9)=1101 ms. Response times were faster for familiar in comparison to unfamiliar icons, $F(1,40) = 79.69$, $p < .001$, and faster for simple in comparison to complex icons, $F(1,40) = 91.40$, $p < .001$. An interaction between familiarity and complexity was observed, $F(1,40) = 10.47$, $p = .002$. This interaction is shown in Figure 3a. Further analyses revealed that the difference in response times between familiar and unfamiliar icons was greater for simple icons than for complex icons, $t(41) = 3.27$, $p = .002$. No other interactions were significant.

3.2 Ratings of Appeal

A similar analysis of variance was conducted to examine the effects of experience (block 1 vs. block 9), icon familiarity (familiar vs. unfamiliar) and icon complexity (simple vs. complex) on participants' ratings of appeal.

There was a significant main effect of blocks of trials, $F(1,40) = 5.46$, $p < .001$. Participants who had gained more experience with the icons gave them higher ratings of appeal, M(block 9)=3.06, than those with less experience of the icons, M(block 1)=2.81. Ratings were higher for familiar than for unfamiliar icons, $F(1,40) = 17.55$, $p < .001$, and for simple as opposed to complex icons, $F(1,40) = 8.87$, $p < .001$. Furthermore, there was a significant interaction between familiarity and complexity, $F(1,40) = 4.77$, $p = .035$ (see Figure 3b). A paired t-test was carried out to examine the interaction further and showed that the difference in ratings between familiar and unfamiliar icons was greater for simple icons than for complex icons, $t(41) = 2.17$, $p = .035$. No other interactions were significant.

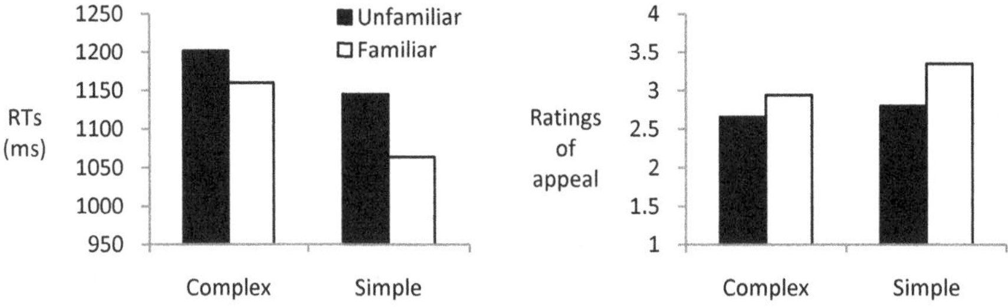

Fig. 3. Interactions between icon familiarity and complexity for (a) response times in the search task and (b) ratings of appeal

The findings for ratings of appeal mirror those found for response times. Because participants were not given any information about the visual complexity or familiarity of icons, it is difficult to explain these findings in terms of explicit awareness. This is particularly true of the interaction observed between familiarity and complexity. Participants' judgments of appeal appeared to be determined by an implicit awareness of the ease with which items had been processed as measured the time they took to respond in the search task. Furthermore, despite the fact that ratings were obtained from two participant groups *either* after 1 *or* 9 blocks of experimental trials, ratings of appeal were higher at block 9 than block 1.

4 Discussion

In their recent review of the literature examining the role of processing fluency on our judgments, Alter & Oppenheimer [13] stated the following:

> Processing fluency, or the subjective experience of ease with which people process information, reliably influences people's judgments across a broad range of social dimensions. Experimenters have manipulated processing fluency using a vast array of techniques, which, despite their diversity, produce remarkably similar judgmental consequences. For example, people similarly judge stimuli that are semantically primed (conceptual fluency), visually clear (perceptual fluency), and phonologically simple (linguistic fluency) as more true than their less fluent counterparts. ... Because every cognition falls along a continuum from effortless to demanding and generates a corresponding fluency experience, [the authors argue that] fluency is a ubiquitous metacognitive cue in reasoning and social judgment. p. 219

Given the diversity and extent of research examining how fluency affects cognition, it is perhaps surprising that it has not informed our understanding of individuals' judgments about interfaces, particularly given the current focus on interface appeal.

4.1 Usability, Processing Fluency, and Appeal

The aim of the current research was to explore the possibility that processing fluency could be used as a way of explaining the relationship between perceived usability and appeal that has been observed in a number of studies. Rather than relying on subjective measures of usability (i.e. ratings of perceived ease of use), response time in a search task was used as the index of ease of processing. The search task was designed to be analogous to our everyday search for icons on interfaces.

The results showed that the factors affecting ease of processing – experience and the familiarity and complexity of the icons – can predict judgments of appeal. Specifically, icon familiarity and complexity influenced both response times and appeal ratings. Most surprisingly, familiarity interacted with complexity in the same manner for both response times and appeal ratings (Fig. 3). In other words, appeal ratings for icons that were *pre-experimentally equated in terms of appeal*, followed the exact same pattern as the pattern of performance. This demonstrated that implicit awareness of ease of processing was driving judgments of appeal.

At a practical level, we therefore suggest that in order to optimize interface design, the current focus on interface appeal needs to be closely tied to a sound understanding of the factors influencing speed and efficacy of responding to interfaces, i.e. ease of processing.

4.2 Fluency Discounting in Judgments of Appeal – Future Research

While the current findings suggest that processing fluency can be a strong driver of appeal judgments, evidence to date suggests that fluency may be discounted in favor of other, more salient, cues for decision making [e.g. 34, 35]. Current research in our laboratory is focussing on what cues might be used to *decouple* ease of processing information from appeal judgments. It seems likely that this will be relatively nuanced and situation specific and may well be in accordance with the pattern of correlations found by Hassenzahl and Monk [12] in their recent review of correlations between ratings of usability and appeal.

Acknowledgements. We gratefully acknowledge the help in gathering data for this study which we had from Josh Denness, Jessica Emmett and Henrik Waerland.

References

1. Butler, K.A.: Usability engineering turns 10. Interactions 3, 59–75 (1996)
2. Neilsen, J.: Usability Engineering. Morgan Kaufmann, San Francisco (1993)
3. Hassenzahl, M., Tractinsky, N.: User experience: A research agenda. Behavior & Information Technology 25, 91–97 (2006)
4. Bauerly, M., Liu, Y.: Effects of symmetry and number of compositional elements on interface and design aesthetics. International Journal of Human–Computer Interaction 24, 275–287 (2008)
5. Lavie, T., Tractinsky, N.: Assessing dimensions of perceived visual aesthetics of websites. International Journal of Human–Computer Studies 60, 269–298 (2004)
6. Schenkman, B.N., Jönsson, F.U.: Aesthetics and preferences of web pages. Behaviour & Information Technology 19, 367–377 (2000)
7. Hartmann, J., Sutcliffe, A., De Angeli, A.: Towards a theory of user judgment of aesthetics and user interface quality. ACM Transactions on Computer–Human Interaction 15, 15–30 (2008)
8. Thuring, M., Mahlke, S.: Usability, aesthetics and emotions in human technology interaction. International Journal of Psychology 42, 253–264 (2007)
9. Cyr, D., Head, M., Larios, H.: Color appeal in website design within and across cultures: a multi-method evaluation. International Journal of Human–Computer Studies 68, 1–21 (2010)
10. Hassenzahl, M.: The interplay of beauty, goodness, and usability in interactive products. Human–Computer Interaction 19, 319–349 (2004)
11. van Schaik, P., Ling, J.: An integrated model of interaction experience for information retrieval in a Web-based encyclopaedia. Interacting with Computers 23, 18–32 (2011)

12. Hassenzahl, M., Monk, A.: The inference of perceived usability from beauty. Human-Computer Interaction 25, 235–260 (2010)
13. Alter, A.L., Oppenheimer, D.M.: Uniting the tribes of fluency to form a metacognitive nation. Personality & Social Psychology Review 13, 219–235 (2009)
14. Hertwig, R., Herzog, S.M., Schooler, L.J., Reimer, T.: Fluency heuristic: A model of how the mind exploits a by-product of information retrieval. Journal of Experimental Psychology: Learning, Memory & Cognition 34, 1191–1206 (2008)
15. Isherwood, S.J., McDougall, S.J.P., Curry, M.B.: Icon identification in context: The changing role of icon characteristics with user experience. Human Factors 49, 465–476 (2007)
16. McDougall, S., Isherwood, S.: What's in a name? The role of graphics, functions and their interrelationship in icon identification. Behavior Research Methods 41, 325–336 (2009)
17. Forsythe, A., Sheehy, N., Sawey, M.: Measuring icon complexity: An automated analysis. Behavior Research Methods, Instruments & Computers 35, 334–342 (2003)
18. García, M., Badre, A.N., Stasko, J.T.: Development and validation of icons varying in their abstractness. Interacting With Computers 6, 191–211 (1994)
19. Snodgrass, J.G., Vanderwart, M.: A standardized set of 260 pictures: Norms for name agreement, image agreement, familiarity, and visual complexity. Journal of Experimental Psychology: Human Learning & Memory 6, 174–215 (1980)
20. Byrne, M.D.: Using icons to find documents: Simplicity is critical. In: Proceedings of INTERCHI 1993, pp. 446–453 (1993)
21. Scott, D.: Visual search in modern human-computer interfaces. Behaviour and Information Technology 12, 174–189 (1993)
22. McDougall, S., Tyrer, V., Folkard, S.: Searching for signs, symbols, and icons: Effects of time of day, visual complexity, and grouping. Journal of Experimental Psychology: Applied 12, 118–128 (2006)
23. McDougall, S., de Bruijn, O., Curry, M.: Exploring the effects of icon characteristics on user performance: The role of concreteness, complexity and distinctiveness. Journal of Experimental Psychology: Applied 6, 291–306 (2000)
24. Bornstein, R.F.: Exposure and affect: Overview and meta-analysis of research. Psychological Bulletin 106(2), 265–289 (1989)
25. Lindgaard, G., Fernandes, G., Dudek, C., Brown, J.: Attention web designers: You have 50 milliseconds to make a good first impression! Behaviour & Information Technology 25, 115–126 (2006)
26. McDougall, S.J.P., Reppa, I.: Why do I like it? The relationships between icon characteristics, user performance and aesthetic appeal. In: Proceedings of the Human Factors and Ergonomics Society 52nd Annual Meeting, pp. 1257–1261. Human Factors Society, Chicago (2008)
27. Reber, R., Winkielman, P., Schwarz, N.: Effects of perceptual fluency on affective judgments. Psychological Science 9, 45–48 (1998)
28. Zajonc, R.B.: Attitudinal effects of mere exposure. Journal of Personality & Social Psychology Monographs 9, 1 (1968)
29. Zajonc, R.B.: Emotions. In: Gilbert, D.T., Fiske, S.T., Lindzey, G. (eds.) The Handbook of Social Psychology, pp. 591–632. McGraw-Hill, New York (1998)
30. Zajonc, R.B.: Mere exposure: A gateway to the subliminal. Current Directions in Psychological Science 10, 224–228 (2000)
31. Berlyne, D.E.: Studies in the new experimental aesthetics. Hemisphere, Washington, DC (1974)

32. Eisenman, R.: Birth-order and sex differences in aesthetic preference for complexity-simplicity. Journal of General Psychology 77, 121–126 (1967)
33. McDougall, S.J.P., Curry, M.B., de Bruijn, O.: Measuring symbol and icon characteristics: Norms for concreteness, complexity, meaningfulness, familiarity, and semantic distance for 239 symbols. Behavior Research Methods, Instruments, & Computers 31, 487–519 (1999)
34. Oppenheimer, D.M.: Spontaneous discounting of availability in frequency judgment tasks. Psychological Science 15, 100–105 (2004)
35. Oppenheimer, D.M.: Consequences of erudite vernacular utilized irrespective of necessity: Problems with using long words needlessly. Applied Cognitive Psychology 20, 139–156 (2006)

Basic Study on Kawaii Feeling of Material Perception

Michiko Ohkura and Tsuyoshi Komatsu

Shibaura Institute of Technology,
3-7-5, Toyosu, Koto-ku, Tokyo, 135-8548, Japan
{ohkura,ma11068}@shibaura-it.ac.jp

Abstract. In the 21st century, the importance of kansei (affective) values has been recognized. However, since few studies have focused on kawaii as a kansei value, we are researching its physical attributes of artificial products. We previously performed experiments on kawaii shapes, colors, and sizes. This article describes our experimental results on kawaii feelings in material perception using virtual objects with various visual textures and actual materials with various tactile textures.

Keywords: kansei (Affective) value, kawaii, texture, visual sensation, tactile sensation.

1 Introduction

Recently, the kansei (affective) value has become crucial in industrials in Japan. The Japanese Ministry of Economy, Trade and Industry (METI) determined that it is the fourth most important characteristic of industrial products after function, reliability, and cost [1]. According to METI, it is important not only to offer new functions and competitive prices but also to create a new value to strengthen Japan's industrial competitiveness. Focusing on kansei as a new value axis, METI launched the "Kansei Value Creation Initiative" in 2007 [1][2] and held a kansei value creation fair called the "Kansei-Japan Design Exhibition" at Les Arts Decoratifs (Museum of Decorative Arts) at the Palais du Louvre in Paris in December 2008. Launched as an event of the "Kansei Value Creation Years," the exhibition had more than 10,000 visitors during its ten-day run and was received favorably [3].

In Japan, the cute aesthetic is widely used by many organizations and for many purposes, including police mascots [4] and warnings for dangerous areas [5]. Although using cute to motivate and inform might seem strange, cute offers potential. Dr. Cheok et al. at the National University of Singapore argued that Japanese kawaii embodies a special kind of cute design that reduces fear and increases the appeal of dreary information [6]. Various Japanese kawaii characters such as Hello Kitty and Pokemon have become popular all over the world. In this article, the cuteness of those

M. Kurosu (Ed.): Human-Computer Interaction, Part I, HCII 2013, LNCS 8004, pp. 585–592, 2013.

characters is called kawaii, which is a Japanese word that represents an affective value; it has such positive meanings as cute, lovable, and small.

For the past several years, we have been focusing on the kawaii attributes of industrial products or the interfaces of interactive systems, because we consider kawaii a kansei value. However, since few studies have focused on kawaii attributes, we systematically analyze the kawaii interfaces themselves: the kawaii feelings caused by such attributes as shapes, colors, and materials. Our aim is to clarify a method for constructing a kawaii interface from our research results. We believe that kawaii has the potential to become an important kansei value for future interactive systems and industrial products.

We previously performed experiments and obtained interesting tendencies about kawaii attributes [7][8][9][10][11]. For example, such curved shapes as tori and spheres tend to be evaluated as more kawaii than straight-lined shapes [8][9].

This paper describes our basic study about the kawaii feelings of material perception. The former part describes our experimental results on kawaii feelings for various visual textures of virtual objects, and the latter part describes our experimental results on kawaii feelings for various tactile textures of actual materials.

2 Background Survey

One of the authors lectured on kawaii research and asked the undergraduate students to list five kawaii products or living creatures and to explain their reasons. The listed goods were classified into three categories: living creatures, artificial products, and cartoon characters (Table 1). We morphologically analyzed their explanations for the kawaii feelings and made histograms of the morphemes. Fig. 1 shows histograms of the physical attributes for the three categories. We confirmed that shape, color, and size were important attributes for feeling kawaii. Our next target is material perception.

Table 1. Classification of Kawaii Goods

Class	Examples
Living ceatures (LC)	ant, dog, cat, penguin, bird, sparrow, frog, child, girl, baby, hamster, panda, chick
Artificial products (AP)	iPod, mobile phone, strap, round button, cake, necklace, stuffed animal
Cartoon characters	Doraemon, Pikachu, Winnie the Pooh, Donald Duck, Stitch, Moomin

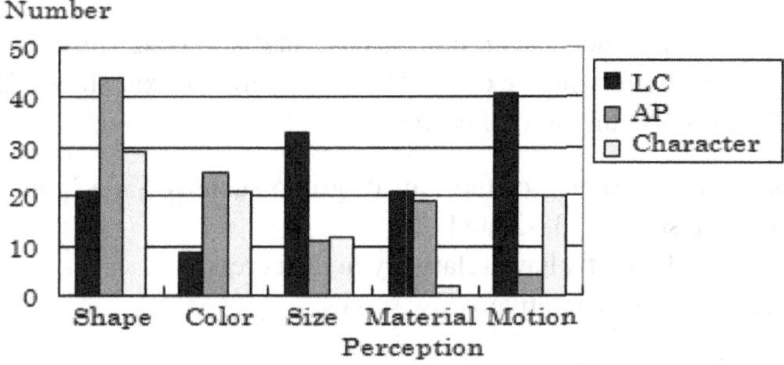

Fig. 1. Histogram of physical attributes

3 Kawaii Feeling in Material Perception for Virtual Objects

3.1 Method

We employed a 46-inch-LCD monitor and polarized glasses to stereoscopically show virtual objects for the experimental setup. Based on th results of our previous experiments, we employed a cylinder for the shape of the objects, and pink for their color. We employed nine textures (Fig. 2). Participants were randomly presented nine objects one by one for 20 seconds to evaluate their kawaii degree on a 7-point Likert Scale, where -3 is extremely non-kawaii, 0 is neutral, and +3 is extremely kawaii. Participants also justified their evaluations.

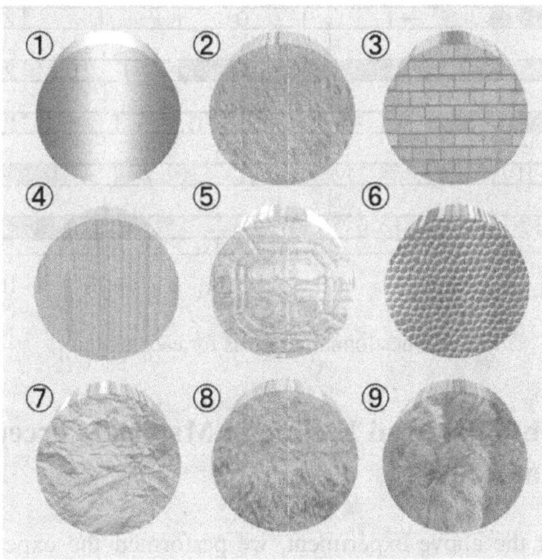

Fig. 2. Nine displayed objects

3.2 Results and Discussion

We performed our experiments with nine female and nine male students in their 20s. Fig. 3 shows the results for each texture, where the vertical axis shows the kind and the horizontal axis shows the ratio of each scale.

- Each texture got both scores of the kawaii group such as +3, +2, and +1 and the non-kawaii group such as -3, -2, and -1.
- Textures #9, #8, #3, and #4 have relatively high scores.
- Textures #2, and #5 have relatively low scores.

We obtained the following results:

- Although each texture has both positive and negative scores, a large difference exists among the averages of the textures; a product's texture affects its kawaii degree.
- Textures evoking words related to such tactile sensation as soft, furry, and tangible are generally kawaii.
- Textures #2, and #5 have relatively low scores.

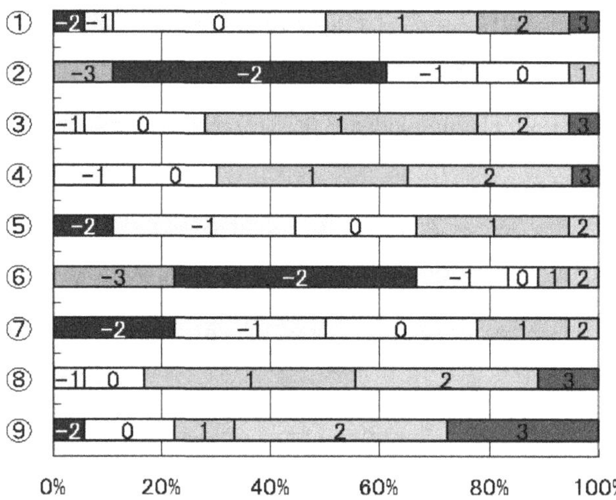

Fig. 3. Questionnaire results for each texture

4 Experiment of Kawaii Feeling in Material Perception for Real Tactile Materials

From the results of the above experiment, we performed the experiment using real tactile materials.

4.1 Method

We employed 109 materials with different tactile sensations [12]. The features of those materials were that they were linked to Japanese onomatopoeias such as "mokomoko" and "zarazara" [12]. Examples of tactile materials are shown in Fig.4. Blindfolded participants were shown paired materials one by one and asked to determine which is more kawaii. The answer of participant was "Right," "Left," or "Same." All materials were ranked by a quick sort algorithm (Fig. 5).

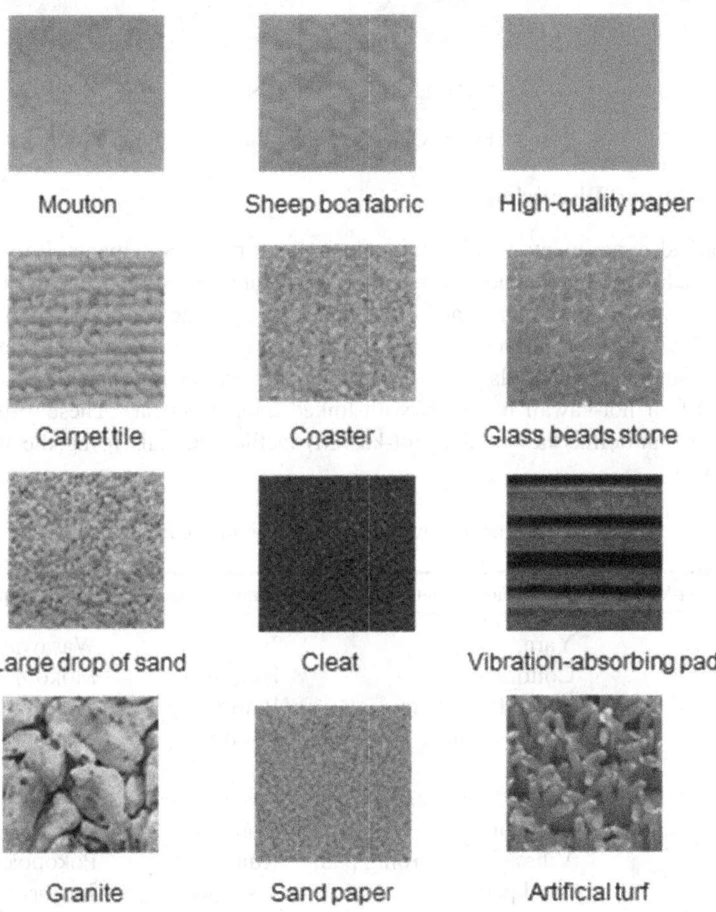

Fig. 4. Examples of tactile materials

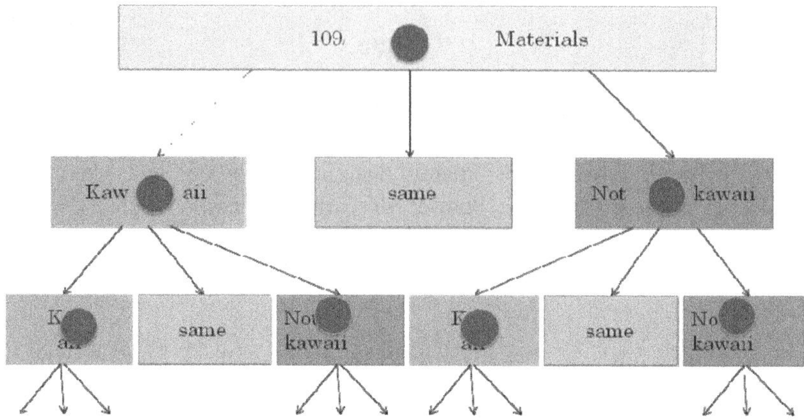

Fig. 5. Quick sort algorithm

4.2 Results and Discussion

We performed experiments with two female and two male participants. It took 2 to 3 hours for each experiment and learned that four materials were deemed kawaii the first two times by all participants and eight materials by three out of four participants. On the other hand, no materials were deemed not-kawaii the first two times by all participants and four materials by three out of four participants. Table 2 shows four kawaii and four not-kawaii materials with linked onomatopoeias. These results indicate that we can define kawaii (and not-kawaii) tactile materials using the materials we employed.

Table 2. Outline of kawaii and not-kawaii tactile materials

Kawaii/not-kawaii	Tactile materials	Onomatopoeia 1	Onomatopoeia 2
Kawaii	Yarn, Cotton, Sheep boa fabric, Cotton cloth	Jashijashi Fukafuka Pofupofu Fusafusa	Wasawasa Mokomoko Mofumofu Mosamosa
Not-kawaii	Large drop of sand, Granite stone, Vibration-absorbing pad, Sand paper	Jarijari Gorogoro Kunikuni Jusajusa	Zaguzagu Pokopoko Jorijori

From the comparison results for each participant, we ranked the kawaii degree of each material, where the ranks were identical when the materials were judged the same by the participants. Then we averaged the kawaii ranks of all the participants. We defined the materials from the top and the 20th as the kawaii group, and materials from 90th to the bottom as the non-kawaii group. By comparing these two groups, we obtained the following:

- Kawaii group has such features as bushy, fluffy, soft, smooth, and elastic. On the other hand, non-kawaii group has such features as crumbly, hard, and rough.
- The onomatopoeias of the kawaii group have such consonants as /f/, /m/, and /p/. On the other hand, those of the non-kawaii group have /z/, /j/, and /g/.

These results resemble those of the experiment for virtual visual objects and suggest that common features of kawaii feeling exist in material perception.

5 Conclusions

We performed two experiments about the kawaii feelings of material perception. The first experiment was on kawaii feelings for various visual textures of virtual objects, and the second experiment was on kawaii feelings for various tactile textures for actual materials. We can confirm that common features of kawaii feelings exist in material perception.

Future work includes more detailed experiment and analysis.

Acknowledgments. We thank Prof. Sakamoto of The University of Electro-Communications for supplying tactile materials with related onomatopoeia as well as the students of Shibaura Institute of Technology for their taking parts as experimenters and participants of our experiments.

References

1. Kansei Value Creation Initiative, `http://www.meti.go.jp/english/information/downloadfiles/PressRelease/080620KANSEI.pdf`
2. Araki, J.: Kansei and value creation initiative. Journal of Japan Society of Kansei Engineering 7(3), 417–419 (2007) (in Japanese)
3. Announcement of the "Kansei Value Creation Museum", `http://www.meti.go.jp/english/press/data/20090119_02.html`
4. Metropolitan Police Department, "Pipo town" (in Japanese), `http://www.keishicho.metro.tokyo.jp/sikumi/pipo/pipo.htm`
5. Doanigochuui (in Japanese), `http://mito.cool.ne.jp/busbybus/doanigochuui.html`
6. Cheok, D.A., Ohkura, M., Fernando, O.N., Merritt, T.: Designing cute interactive media. Innovation 8(3), 8–9 (2008)
7. Ohkura, M., Aoto, T.: Systematic study for "kawaii" products. In: Proceedings of the 1st International Conference on Kansei Engineering and Emotion Research 2007 (KEER 2007), Sapporo. Japan Society of Kansei Engineering, Tokyo (2007)
8. Ohkura, M., Konuma, A., Murai, S., Aoto, T.: Systematic study for "kawaii" products (The Second Report) -comparison of "kawaii" colors and shapes-. In: Proceedings of SICE Annual Conference 2008, Chofu, pp. 481–484. SICE, Tokyo (2008)

9. Murai, S., Goto, S., Aoto, T., Ohkura, M.: Systematic study on kawaii products (The Third Report) –comparison of kawaii between 2D and 3D-. In: Proceedings of Annual Conference of the Virtual Reality Society in Japan 2008, Nara, pp. 544–547. The Virtual Reality Society in Japan, Tokyo (2008) (in Japanese)
10. Ohkura, M., Goto, S., Aoto, T.: Systematic study for 'kawaii' products: study on kawaii colors using virtual objects. In: Proceedings of the 13th International Conference on Human-Computer Interaction, San Diego, pp. 633–637. Springer, Heidelberg (2009)
11. Komatsu, T., Ohkura, M.: Study on evaluation of kawaii colors using visual analog scale. In: Smith, M.J., Salvendy, G. (eds.) HCII 2011, Part I. LNCS, vol. 6771, pp. 103–108. Springer, Heidelberg (2011)
12. Watanabe, J., Kano, A., Shimizu, Y., Sakamoto, M.: Relationship between judgments of comfort and phonemes of onomatopoeias in touch. Transactions of the Virtual Reality Society of Japan 16(3), 367–370 (2011) (in Japanese)

Centrality of Visual Aesthetics in the Online Context: An Assessment and Empirical Evidence

Supavich Pengnate, Rathindra Sarathy, and Todd Arnold

Spears School of Business, Oklahoma State University, Oklahoma, U.S.A.
{fone.pengnate,rathin.sarathy,todd.arnold}@okstate.edu

Abstract. This research investigates individual differences in the centrality of visual aesthetics (CVA) in the online context. The study examines the influence of CVA on online user responses, namely perception of website visual appeal, trust, and intention to use websites. A series of three experiments provide evidence that CVA influence user responses, especially when users' CVA is assessed by the indirect measure developed in this study. The results indicate that the impact of CVA on user responses is stronger among users with high CVA than those with low CVA, and especially when the users are exposed to website with relatively low visual appeal.

Keywords: Centrality of Visual Aesthetics, Website Design, Visual Appeal, Trust, Intention to Use.

1 Introduction

Several studies in Information Systems (IS) and human-computer interaction (HCI) domains have attested the significance of website visual appeal such that it produces significant effects on user responses and behavioral intentions [1, 2]. In an analysis of website credibility, Fogg et al. [3] found the quality of website visual design to be the most important determinant of e-retailers' credibility. Researchers have found that website visual design influences user evaluations of e-retailers because it impacts the users' emotional responses [4] which consequently shape the users' perceptions of website and e-retailer quality [5].

In the marketing literature, product visual appeal has been found to influence consumers' perceptions in several ways. Studies have suggested that products with superior visual designs distinguish themselves from those of competitors and help gain recognition in a crowded marketplace [6, 7]. Visual appeal influences the formation of consumer/product relationships since it is the first attribute of a product that connects with potential buyers through a sensory experience, which further shapes their judgments of the product regardless of product class [8]. In addition, successfully implementing an visual design strategy can create identity for the organization and its brands, as well as providing value by satisfying customers' aesthetic needs [7]. This notion of visual appeal from the marketing literature has been embraced by the IS and HCI communities in the development of products (interactive systems) such that the

M. Kurosu (Ed.): Human-Computer Interaction, Part I, HCII 2013, LNCS 8004, pp. 593–600, 2013.

systems should no longer be seen as simply providing functional features, but should also dazzle users' senses, touch their hearts, and stimulate their minds [9].

In the online context, although website visual design features have been explored extensively in the past decade, most studies focus on the impact of website design from the perspective of the designer, for example, color [10], layout [11], and the use of images [12]. However, an empirical study on user perspectives which can provide a better understanding of how website visual design features influence users' perceptions has received much less attention from researchers in the IS and HCI domains. Previous studies investigating website visual design features from the user aspects include cultural differences [1, 10], gender [13], and disposition [14].

Consequently, it is important to take into account individual differences when studying user perspectives on website visual design. In particular, this study has two objectives. The first objective is to empirically investigate the role played by individual differences in the centrality of visual aesthetics in the online context. In addition, based on literature in the marketing domain, the second objective of this study is to develop a scale to indirectly measure differences in this centrality across users in the online context.

2 Theortical Background and Hypotheses

2.1 Online User Characteristics and Aesthetic Perceptions

According to Tractinsky and Lowngart [15], user perception of website visual aesthetics is considered as a function of website design characteristics and user characteristics. The website design characteristics are objective properties of the visual design (e.g., shape, color, or layout) and may be used to intentionally affect user percpetions by the designer. However, users may not have the same interpretation or aesthetic perception as intended by the designer since the users' peceptions may be influenced by dispositions of the users (e.g., individual differences, nationality, or prior experience). Empirical evidence of the effect of user characteristics has been reported in the HCI literature [16, 17], such that ratings of website visual appeal are not consistent across different user groups. Accordingly, it is suggested that the differences in the ratings of visual aesthetics found in their study should be further investigated.

Alhough several studies in the IS and HCI areas have exlored the impact of website aesthetics on user responses, those studies focused largly on website design characteristics (e.g., [1, 11, 18]); however, there are relatively few studis examining the relationships between customers' characteristics and their aesthetic percpetions [19]. Therefore, the current study aims to empirically investigate such effects.

2.2 Individual Differences in the Centrality of Visual Aesthetics (CVA)

We account for individual differences in users, as they relate to visual aesthetics, by drawing on the concept of the centrality of visual product aesthetics (CVPA) from the marketing literature [20]. According to Bloch et al. [20], CVPA is defined as "the level of significance that visual aesthetics holds for a particular consumer in his/her relationship with products" (p. 552). They suggest that CVPA encompasses three related dimensions: (1) acumen, or the ability to recognize, categorize, or evaluate product designs, (2) the value a consumer assigns to product appearances in enhancing personal and even societal well-being, and (3) the level of response to visual design aspects of products. Table 1 represents CVPA items from Bloch et al.'s [20] study.

2.3 Perceived Website Visual Appeal and User Responses

In this study, we aim to investigate the effect of CVA on the relationship between website visual appeal and user responses, namely trust and intention to use websites. In the IS domain, trust and intention to use websites have been considered as key factors in the success of online vendors [21, 22]. The influence of website visual appeal on user responses can be explained by the affect-as-information model [23]. According to the affect-as-information model, a person's emotional state alters the assessment of new stimuli by pushing them into the direction of the valance of the emotion (positive or negative) that is already being experienced. As a result, emotional states can bias individuals' cognitive process in the evaluation of new stimuli. With respect to website visual appeal, visually-pleasing websites can invoke users' positive emotional states [4], which subsequently positively influence the users' evaluation of website trust as well as intention to use websites.

2.4 Hypotheses

According to the of affect-as-information model and users' differences in the centrality of visual aesthetics as mentioned in the previous section, we hypothesize that individual differences in the centrality of visual aesthetics (CVA) moderates the relationship between website visual appeal, perceived visual appeal, trust, and intention to use websites as follows:

Hypothesis 1: CVA moderates the influence of website visual appeal on users' perceptions of visual appeal; that is, website visual appeal will have a greater effect on the users' perception of visual appeal for users with higher CVA as compared to users with lower CVA.

Hypothesis 2: CVA moderates the influence of website visual appeal on trust; that is, website visual appeal will have a greater effect on the users' trust in website providers for users with higher CVA as compared to users with lower CVA.

Hypothesis 3: CVA moderates the influence of website visual appeal on intention to use websites; that is, website visual appeal will have a greater effect on the users' intention to use websites for users with higher CVA as compared to users with lower CVA.

3 Methodology

Overall, three experiments were conducted to examine the impact of CVA on users' perceptions of websites by using different CVA measurement approaches. Participants in all experiments were asked to perform the same hypothetical task, which was to consider making an online donation to Japan's tsunami victims in 2011. According to the theoretical frameworks of website visual appeal, trust, and behavior, an identical set of independent variables and dependent variables were used across the three experiments. The independent variable included website visual appeal, while the dependent variables included users' perception of visual appeal, trust, and intention to use the website.

An experimental website unfamiliar to participants was created to avoid the effects of content and branding. However, we retained the realism of the website by mimicking an existing website. Three versions of the charity website were created. They vary only in terms of visual appeal, all three providing the same information, content, and features to avoid the effects from other variables that may impact the observed variables.

In Experiment 1, we tested the effect of CVA on Web users' perceptions of the experimental website using a direct self-reported CVA measure adapted from Bloch et al. [20]. The effect of CVA was in the expected direction, but it was not strong enough to elicit a statistically significant impact of CVA in shaping user evaluations of websites. Even though many studies in behavioral science typically use traditional self-reported measures to assess individual differences, naturally, the results obtained by such direct measures can be susceptible to measurement bias and error [24, 25]. Therefore, in Experiment 2, in addition to the direct self-reported measure of CVA used in Experiment 1, we developed an alternative measurement approach to indirectly measure CVA. The indirect measure of CVA was developed based on the original CVA measure adapted from Bloch et al. [20] used in the previous experiment.

In Experiment 2, CVA was indirectly measured by involving a task that requires participants to rate visual appeal of 18 websites (9 high-visual-appeal websites and 9 low-visual-appeal websites). The 18 websites were selected by website design experts. Each of the 18 websites was displayed for 7 seconds with a semantic differential question. The semantic differential questions were developed based on the three dimensions of CVA (acumen, value, and response) used in Experiment 1. The terms for the semantic differential questions included Ugly-Beautiful, Terrible-Wonderful, Worst-Excellent, Fear-Joy, Pain-Pleasure, Dislike-Like, Avoid-Approach, Abandon-Adopt, and Leave-use. These terms were tested by graduate students in the English major to assure that the semantic terms match the CVA items. Two conditions (high vs. low visual appeal) of the charity website used in Experiment 1 were used as the stimuli in this experiment. The experimental task remained the same as in Experiment 1. Convergence of the results from the indirect CVA measure substantially increased the findings' validity of the experiment. The results were then compared to the direct CVA measure used in Experiment 1.

In general, the results of Experiment 2 suggest that the indirect CVA measure tends to perform better in assessing users' CVA. More specifically, the results indicate that

CVA produces a stronger impact on users' perceptions and responses when website visual appeal is relatively low. Therefore, Experiment 3 was designed to investigate the following questions such influences of CVA in the low visual appeal website setting. The only website condition with low visual appeal was used in the experiment. The indirect CVA measure developed in Experiment 2 was used in Experiment 3.

4 Results

4.1 Experiment 1

A total of 99 undergraduate students enrolled in a major Midwestern university participated in the experiment (25 females and 74 males). The CVA measure was assessed for construct quality by testing reliability and convergent validity by a confirmatory factor analysis (CFA). The results demonstrate relatively high correlations between items of the same construct. Construct reliability of the CVA items was assessed by Cronbach's Alpha (0.811), suggesting that the items have relatively high internal consistency.

In order to test the proposed hypothesis, a 3 × 3 factorial design was used. An overall CVA score was computed for each subject from the items highly loaded on the three sub-dimensions of the CVA measure. The mean CVA score for this sample is 6.42 (SD = 1.21). The sample was divided into three groups by CVA scores, and a series of two-way ANOVA was conducted using 3 × 3 design (3 levels of website visual appeal vs. 3 levels of CVA). The mean scores for the high CVA subject group (n = 30), moderate CVA subject group (n = 30), and low CVA subject group (n = 31) were 7.69 (SD = 0.48), 6.57 (SD = 0.23), and 5.06 (SD = 0.78), respectively.

The results of a series of ANOVA on perceived visual appeal, trust, and intention to use indicate that the three conditions of website visual appeal are significantly different on perceived visual appeal ($F=80.04$, $p < 0.000$), trust ($F=16.50$, $p < 0.000$), and intention to use ($F=28.06$, $p < 0.000$). With regard to the interaction effects of CVA and website visual appeal, even though some of the effects are in the predicted direction, the interaction effects are not statistically significant on perceived visual appeal, trust, and intention to use.

4.2 Experiment 2

The dataset contained 77 usable responses. The sample consisted of 29 females and 48 males. In order to test the proposed hypothesis, a 2 × 2 factorial design was used (2 levels of visual appeal × 2 levels of CVA). Two types of overall CVA scores were computed for each subject from the indirect CVA measure and the direct CVA measure. The sample was then divided into terciles by CVA score and only the high CVA group and the low CVA group were used in the analysis. According to the results of a series of ANOVA on perceived visual appeal, trust, and intention, the indirect CVA measure tends to perform better in discriminating participants' CVA than the direct CVA measure, especially in the low visual appeal website condition. In the indirect CVA measure, the interaction effects of CVA on trust ($F=6.082$, $p=0.017$) and intention to use (F=7.309, p=0.010) are statistically significant at the level of 0.05. However, none of the interaction effects of CVA assessed by the direct measure are statistically significant.

4.3 Experiment 3

The dataset contains a total of 87 usable responses. The CVA scores for both indirect and direct measures were calculated according to the procedure used in Experiment 2. The sample was then divided into terciles by CVA score for both the indirect and direct CVA measures. A series of one-way ANOVA was conducted on perceived visual appeal, trust, and intention to use across three CVA groups. As expected, univariate tests show significant differences of perceived visual appeal, trust, and intention for the high and low CVA groups assessed by the indirect CVA measure. However, such effects are not found in the CVA groups assessed by the direct self-reported CVA measure. Overall, according to the indirect CVA measure, the results suggest that high CVA subjects discriminate more strongly than low CVA subjects across all the dependent variables (F=4.005, p=0.22 for perceived visual appeal; F=7.305, p=0.001 for trust; and F=6.764, p=0.002 for intention to use).

5 Contributions and Conclusions

Based on this study, CVA appears to be both a theoretically and managerially relevant variable. This result is in line with the original CVA study in the marketing literature [20]. The major theoretical contribution of this study is establishing the CVA construct in the IS and HCI domains, such that CVA influences online users' perceived visual appeal, trust, and intention to use websites. The results suggest that future studies on website visual appeal should take CVA into account as a moderating variable. In addition, the results of this research also reveal that the effects of CVA may be more salient when using indirect measurement.

As for practical contributions, the outcome of this research will be of interest to managers and web designers. The present study has direct application to the managerial question of how to effectively design websites targeted to a specific user segment, which can help managers create websites that improve user experience and, consequently, elicit desired behaviors. As indicated by the results of this study, CVA produces a stronger impact on user responses when website visual appeal is relatively low. Therefore, managers need to be more careful when making any changes to the design of their website, since they may unintentionally attenuate visual appeal and, in turn, affect their users, especially the users with high CVA.

In summary, in order to develop truly effective and efficient websites, it will be essential for online vendors to understand their users' characteristics and preferences since the users rely on different website attributes as signals in making decisions or website and vendor evaluations, which subsequently, are critical factors of online commerce success.

References

1. Cyr, D.: Modeling Web Site Design across Cultures: Relationships to Trust, Satisfaction, and E-Loyalty. Journal of Management Information Systems 24(4), 47–72 (2008)
2. Hassenzahl, M.: The Interplay of Beauty, Goodness, and Usability in Interactive Products. Human-Computer Interaction 19(4), 319–349 (2004)
3. Fogg, B.J., Soohoo, C., Danielson, D.R., Marable, L., Stanford, J., Tauber, E.R.: How Do Users Evaluate the Credibility of Web Sites?: A Study with Over 2,500 Participants. In: Proceedings of the 2003 Conference on Designing for User Experiences, pp. 1–15 (2003)
4. Éthier, J., Hadaya, P., Talbot, J., Cadieux, J.: B2C Website Quality and Emotions During Online Shopping Episodes: An Empirical Study. Information & Management 43, 627–639 (2006)
5. Loiacono, E.T., Watson, R.T., Goodhue, D.L.: WebQual: An Instrument for Consumer Evaluation of Web Sites. International Journal of Electronic Commerce 11(3), 51–87 (2007)
6. Bloch, P.H.: Seeking the Ideal Form: Product Design and Consumer Response. The Journal of Marketing 59(3), 16–29 (1995)
7. Schmitt, B., Simonson, A.: Marketing Aesthetics: The Strategic Management of Brands, Identity and Image. Free Press, New York (1997)
8. Hollins, B., Stuart, P.: Successful Product Design. Butterworths, London (1990)
9. Schmitt, B.: Experiential Marketing. Free Press, New York (1999)
10. Cyr, D., Head, M., Larios, H.: Colour Appeal in Website Design within and Across Cultures: A Multi-Method Evaluation. International Journal of Human-Computer Studies 68(1-2), 1–21 (2010)
11. Deng, L., Poole, M.S.: Affect in Web Interfaces: A Study of the Impacts of Web Page Visual Complexity and Order. MIS Quarterly 34(4), 711–730 (2010)
12. Cyr, D., Head, M., Larios, H., Pan, B.: Exploring Human Images in Website Design: A Multi-Method Approach. MIS Quarterly 33(3), 539–566 (2009)
13. Cyr, D., Bonanni, C.: Gender and Website Design in E-business. International Journal of Electronic Business 3(6), 565–582 (2005)
14. McKnight, D.H., Chervany, N.L.: What Trust Means in E-Commerce Customer Relationships: An Interdisciplinary Conceptual Typology. International Journal of Electronic Commerce 6(2), 35–59 (2001)
15. Tractinsky, N., Lowengart, O.: Web-Store Aesthetics in E-Retailing: A Conceptual Framework and Some Theoretical Implications. Academy of Marketing Science Review 11(1) (2007)
16. Tractinsky, N., Cokhavi, A., Kirschenbaum, M., Sharfi, T.: Evaluating the Consistency of Immediate Aesthetic Perceptions of Web Pages. International Journal of Human-Computer Studies 64(11), 1071–1083 (2006)
17. Papachristos, E., Avouris, N.: Are First Impressions about Websites Only Related to Visual Appeal? In: Campos, P., Graham, N., Jorge, J., Nunes, N., Palanque, P., Winckler, M. (eds.) INTERACT 2011, Part I. LNCS, vol. 6946, pp. 489–496. Springer, Heidelberg (2011)
18. Agarwal, R., Venkatesh, V.: Assessing a Firm's Web Presence: A Heuristic Evaluation Procedure for the Measurement of Usability. Information Systems Research 13(2), 168–186 (2002)
19. Hassanein, K.S., Milena, H.M.: Building Online Trust Through Socially Rich Web Interfaces. In: Proceedings of the 2nd Annual Conference on Privacy, Security and Trust. Fredericton, New Brunswick, Canada (2004)

20. Bloch, P.H., Brunel, F.F., Arnold, T.J.: Individual Differences in the Centrality of Visual Product Aesthetics: Concept and Measurement. The Journal of Consumer Research 29(4), 551–565 (2003)
21. Hong, W., Thong, J.Y.L., Tam, K.Y.: Does Animation Attract Online Users' Attention? The Effects of Flash on Information Search Performance and Perceptions. Information Systems Research 15(1), 60–86 (2004)
22. Ratnasingham, P.: The Importance of Trust in Electronic Commerce. Internet Research: Electronic Networking Applications and Policy 8(4), 313–321 (1998)
23. Schwarz, N.: Feelings as Information: Informational and Motivational Functions of Affective States. In: Higgins, T., Sorrentino, R.M. (eds.) Handbook of Motivation and Cognition. The Guilford Press, New York (1986)
24. Arnold, H.J., Feldman, D.C.: Social Desirability Response Bias in Self-Report Choice Situations. The Academy of Management Journal 24(2), 377–385 (1981)
25. Lewicki, P.: Self-image Bias in Person Perception. Journal of Personality and Social Psychology 45(2), 384–393 (1983)

The Feeling of Kawaii Is a Function of Interaction

Hisao Shiizuka

Department of Information Design
Kogakuin University
Nishishinjuku 1-24-2, Shinjuku, Tokyo 163-8677, Japan
shiizuka@cc.kogakuin.ac.jp

Abstract. The author discusses the structure of the feeling of kawaii to clarify that it is a function of interaction. Interaction in this paper has a broader meaning, which is communication between a character and a person, while its general definition is mutual communication between a person and a person, or a person and a machine (computer). Clarification of the structure of the kawaii system is also useful in specific system structures in terms of engineering. The main outcome of this paper is a conclusion, based on a discussion of interaction and sensitivity, that interaction occurs where the recipient's sensitivity resonates with the sender's sensitivity, and consequently, its inclusive relation with the factors around kawaii is elucidated.

Keywords: Kawaii, interaction, sensitivity, visual communication.

1 Introduction

The Japanese adjective, kawaii, is characterized by its uniqueness to Japanese culture. The word kawaii was exported to English and French-speaking cultures and has found a place as is, without recourse to translation. The word "cute" may be regarded as an English counterpart of the Japanese kawaii, but this adjective implies quick-witted prettiness or vivaciousness on the part of girls, and does not contain the nuance of "infantile prettiness" that characterizes many Japanese anime characters. Thus, kawaii, written in the Roman alphabet, has gained currency outside Japan. Kawaii is often used in the titles of English-language websites describing anime works.

Whether or not you feel kawaii or how much you feel it varies from person to person. In this sense, it is a matter of sensitivity or sensibility and is subtly related to certain specific concepts.

The author proposes that omoshirosa, or "amusingness," occurs as a result of interactivity, and that kawaisa, which is the noun form of kawaii (hereinafter "kawaiiness,") similarly occurs as a function of interactivity [1-2]. I propose that, to be able to clarify its essence, it is essential to discuss the concept of kawaii from the cultural or semantic viewpoints hidden in its background. I believe that discussion of this question centering on the concept of "interaction" will produce the most useful results, centered on the notion of the Shannon-Weaver communication model, by which a message is transmitted through a medium between the designer and the recipient as a mechanism of our feeling kawaii from a character or artifact [1].

M. Kurosu (Ed.): Human-Computer Interaction, Part I, HCII 2013, LNCS 8004, pp. 601–610, 2013.

In this paper, I discuss the structure of the feeling of kawaii to clarify that it is a function of interaction. Interaction in this paper has a broader meaning, which is communication between a character and a person, while its general definition is mutual communication between a person and a person, or a person and a machine (computer). In discussing the relationship between interactivity and kawaii-ness, I focus on following subjects: (a) interactive loop, (b) amount of information and narrativity.

Conventionally, the constituting factors of kawaii-ness are discussed from the psychoanalytical viewpoint. This feeling is composed of several terms, all of which are inextricably linked. As mentioned earlier, clarification of the relationship between kawaii-ness and "interaction" will be useful for future research on kawaii and may promote new developments in kawaii theory. Clarification of the structure of the kawaii system is also useful in specific system structures in terms of engineering.

The main outcome of this paper is a conclusion, based on a discussion of interaction and sensitivity, that interaction occurs where the recipient's sensitivity resonates with the sender's sensitivity, and consequently, its inclusive relation with the factors around kawaii is elucidated.

2 The Character Transmission Model

According to Kojien, one of the major dictionaries of the Japanese language, published by Iwanami Shoten, character as a Japanese word has the following meanings: (1) character or personality, (2) character in a novel, movie, theatrical play or manga, and its role, and (3) character, letter, or sign. In analyzing the word "character" in this paper, the generic definition that contains all of these is used. Today, we have quite a large number of characters, including what are called "local characters" [3].

There are no end of questions to be answered about characters, such as "What are the factors common to popular characters?", "What has made a specific character so popular?," and "What are the differences between popular characters and other characters?." Communication between people and characters may be regarded as visual communication [4].

There are no generally known methods of identifying specific characteristics from these characters. In general, characters are often created based on the experience and hunches of their designers. It is important to think about how those characteristics are transmitted to the audience.

Now let's use the concept of Shannon-Weaver's transmission model of communication, as shown in Fig. 1(a), as the transmission model of information [5]. Applying this model to the design process, we get (b) of Fig. 1. The messages and ideas of a client are converted by the designer. There are three levels around the designer: technical, effective, and semantic, as shown in Fig. 1 (c). These levels are subject to correction or modification in response to feedback from the audience. Considering this condition, it suggests a greater reduction in the importance of the role of the designer. In other words, the expectations of the audience are fed back into the design to eventually determine its final form. This feedback loop promotes the evolution of the character.

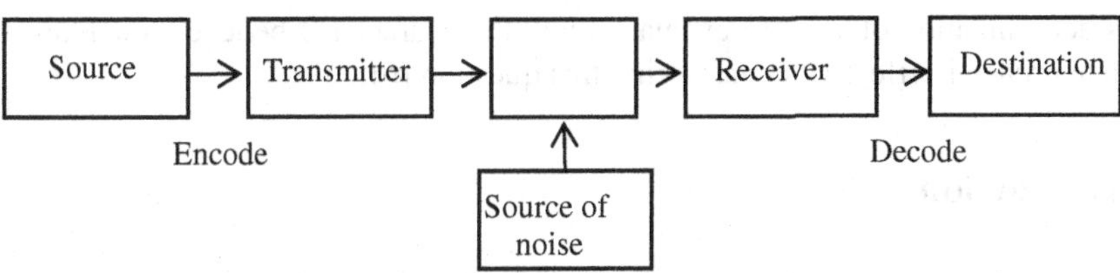

(a) Shannon-Weaver's transmission model of communication

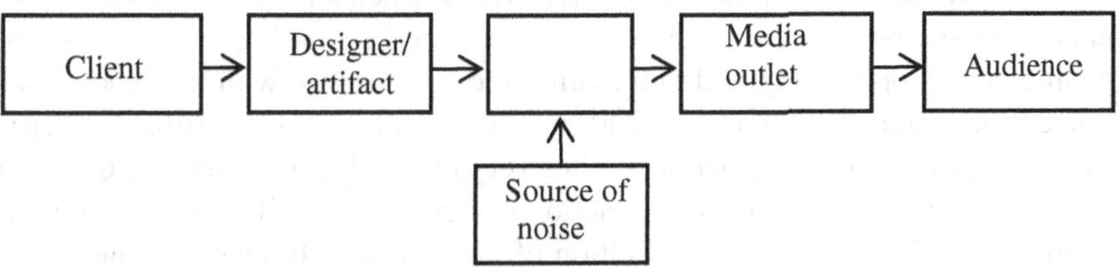

(b) Visual communication process

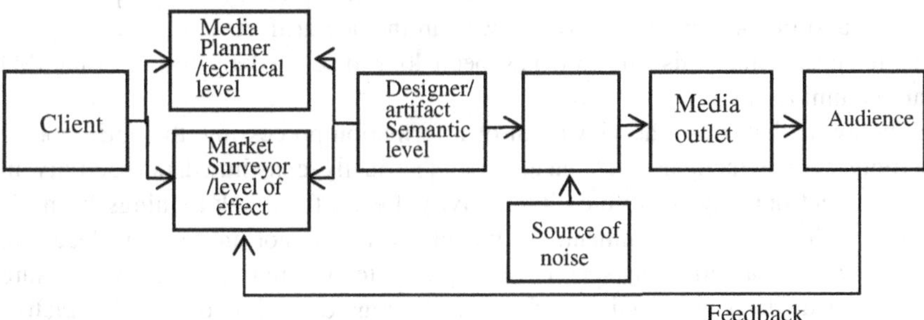

(c) Addition of three levels (technical, effective, and semantic) that makes the designer's role look smaller

Fig. 1. Change from the original Shannon-Weaver version to the modern post-Shannon version

When this concept is applied to a character, the source of transmission in the left half in Fig. 1 is the core idea of the character. It is manifested as a character in one way or another (encoding) and transmitted by the sender (transmitter) to the general public. Some noise is contained in the transmission process (transmission route) that is interpreted (decoded) when received by the audience. It is logical to assume that redundancy and entropy influence this noise.

The problem here is how the audience interprets the character when the character is shown to them (sensitive evaluation). That is, the key question is how to create a character with less noise. The question here is how to connect the character's interactivity to the audience's interpretation.

When designers create designs, they tend to create simple versions that contain as little noise as possible. This is because the simpler the design, the better it is transmitted to the receiver. In other words, noise (N) has to be low to increase the strength of the signal to be sent (S).

Is the S/N ratio of a hit character small? Quantitative verification of this question requires determination of what to evaluate about the character. I believe a qualitative research approach is effective in answering this question [6].

3 Interaction

When a person carries out an action (operation or movements), their counterpart (equipment or system) reacts to that action. This is the basis of the concept of interaction. In the field of human-computer interaction (HCI), when a person inputs data into a computer or its peripheral equipment, the purpose of HCI is to improve ease of use of the equipment by optimizing and automating the relationship with the reaction of the equipment or system. Since in this field, interaction addresses an artifact, specifically a computer, the idea of interaction applies very elegantly. However, the question naturally arises about whether or not interaction is a concept specific to computers or their peripherals. In ISO 13407, the definition of interaction is limited to "interactive computer-based systems." However, the understanding that this concept of interaction can be applied more broadly has become generally accepted by the people in this field. The question is, then, as to how far we can include artifacts as subjects of interaction. It appears that this question has been long discussed by the relevant ISO standard committee [7].

One notion is that, from the viewpoint of information processing, the definition of interactivity should include mechanically or electrically constituted interactivity in addition to electronically constituted interactivity. Let us then look at things from the viewpoint of "interactive equipment." A bicycle, which is not an item of electronic equipment, travels at different speeds in response to different degrees of pressure being applied to its pedals, and therefore can be regarded as a form of interactive equipment. By the same token, wheelchairs, cigarette lighters, ballpoint pens, scissors, umbrellas, and even zippers and buttons on clothes also fall into the category of interactive equipment. This concept appears to be more or less accepted by interface field people as a broad definition of interactive equipment.

The question of whether or not a character is interactive naturally falls within this discussion. To be specific, a character is just a doll if it is simply placed in a location, as it contains no interactivity. However, if one reaches out for the character, the character can create the effect of soothing or curing one's personal feelings according to how one holds it or talks to it. A specific operation, then, generates a specific effect. In this sense, this set of conditions may be also regarded as interactive.

Seen from a different angle, if you do not properly connect to the character or you do not talk to it, you will not be able to achieve the expected result. In other words, these "visible objects" in a sense exert effects that are specific to how they are treated, and in this sense, they can be regarded as "interactive equipment" or "interactive tools."

Based on the above concept, a broader sense of interaction is therefore used in this paper.

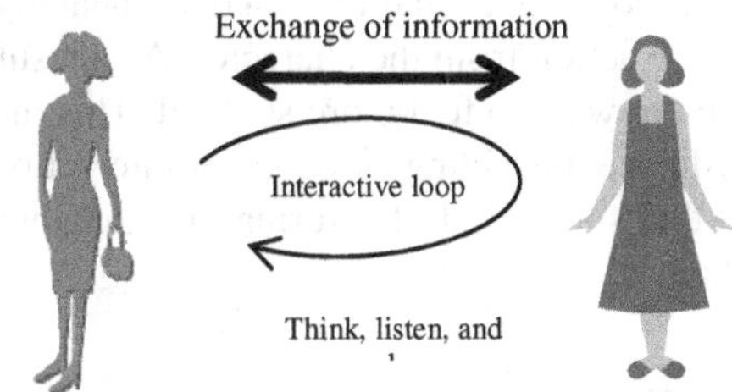

(a) Interactive loop (person to per-

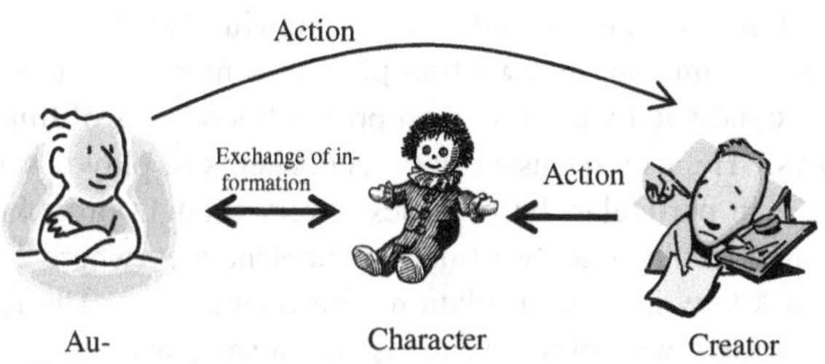

(b) Using a character as a medium

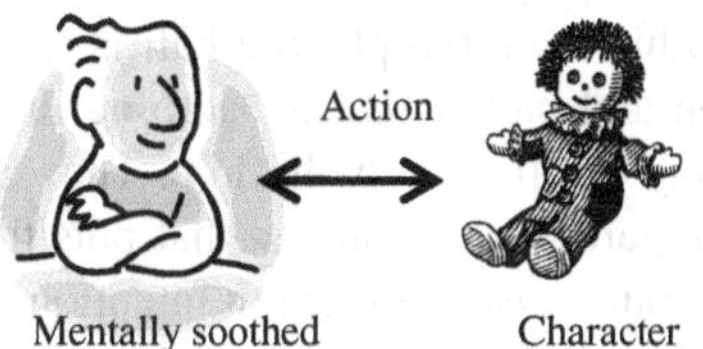

(c) Action occurs, so change also takes

Fig. 2. Concept of interactive loop

4 *Kawaii*-ness and Interactivity

When information is cyclically exchanged between two people, as shown in Fig. 2(a), it is interactive. An interactive loop is formed when two people individually think or listen to and speak to each other. Information is exchanged via this interactive loop, so it is also an information flow loop.

It is logical to assume that this kind of interactive loop is also formed when the counterpart is a character, as shown in Fig. 2(b).

In this situation, there is the creator who created the character present behind the character. The character may thus be understood to play the role of "medium." Since it is necessary to dynamically change the character to make it more attractive in the prevailing environment, actions on the part of the two players are necessary. That is, interaction is necessary, and so it does, in fact, take place. In addition, as shown in

Fig. 2(c), when the audience contacts a character and is mentally soothed by it, it means they are subject to some action from the character. As a result, a change occurs in the audience that makes them want to feel more soothed. This indicates an ongoing change on the part of the audience, providing evidence of interaction between the two. It is then natural to believe that some kind of information exchange has occurred between the person and the character.

5 Interactivity and *Kawai*-ness

What is the relationship between interactivity and kawaii-ness? I'd like to discuss this question using "Homo Ludens," a book written by Johan Huizinga [8].

In his work, Huizinga points out that we find play present everywhere. He defines play as "a free activity conducted within its own proper boundaries of time and space according to fixed rules." He also discusses various concepts of play observed in different human activities. In particular, he provides a very thought-provoking suggestion about the universality of play that "we find play present everywhere."

In fact, this play has a very important relation with interactivity. The relation with kawaii-ness" will be clarified, with play serving as an intermediary.

Huizinga notes that the ancient Greeks differentiated play into two forms: agon and paidia. Agon is play as a competitive activity, a deadly serious pursuit within certain constraining rules, whereas paidia is play as a joyful activity. A track and field event at the Olympic Games is agon, while children playing ball is paidia. There is nothing in common between them. Agon and paidia sharing nothing in common means that track and field athletes cannot play together with children. They cannot coexist simultaneously. Interactivity may be regarded as a catalyst that puts these two very different things together. Let's think about a disagreement in intentions among adults. If the adults fully share the same opinion, their intentions run in parallel. If their opinions are far apart, their intentions collide head-on. There is an intermediate situation somewhere between them. When the intentions of the two parties are the same and run in parallel, there is no wonder, and nothing to learn. They just nod and agree with each other. In other words, nothing is created from a shared identical status. The ground for interaction is produced in a situation where people feel some disagreement in intentions. That is, no interaction will be created if everything is already known [9]. It is also reasonable to assume that interaction occurs where there is high entropy.

Here is one familiar example of interaction. A child deliberately fakes a disagreement in intentions to start an interaction with his parents. That is, the child sometimes plays a little trick to draw their attention. This is a typical example of interaction that occurs when there is a disagreement of intentions between two people.

The origin of the feeling of kawaii crucially needs an element of discommunication. The feeling of kawaii holds a fragile balance between the feeling of childishness that is totally devoid of the property of being empathized with, and a sense of eeriness. To engage in interaction with a character, a disagreement in intentions is necessary that can correspond to discommunication. I mentioned earlier that Sanrio characters are metonymic (animal-like) because of their inability to be emphasized with.

Japanese characters are established as extremely distinct signs. They are overwhelmingly emotionless, as you can see from the faces of Rilakkuma, Banao, or Capybara-san. What you sense from them is a childish feeling, devoid of the property of being empathized with, which is considered to create the kawaii property. Based on the relational chains of kawaii, "lack of sympathism," "disagreement in intentions," and "interaction," the kawaii property may be taken as a function of interaction. Hence,

$$\text{Degree of } \textit{kawaii} \text{ property} = f\,(\text{interaction}) \tag{1}$$

This leads to the structure shown in Fig. 13.

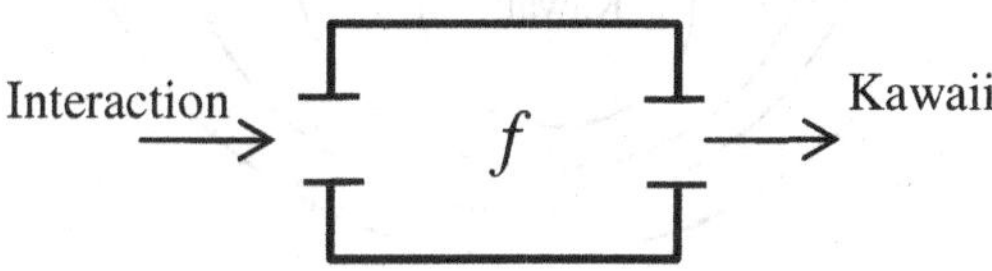

Fig. 3. Structure of the *kawaii* system

It is speculated that when people find a subject kawaii, they want interact with it and reinforce that interaction. What is called the "creation of kawaii-ness" or constituting the "function of kawaii-ness (function f)" needs to be analyzed from the viewpoint of the kawaii system." An approach from the engineering aspect should be useful for specific system configuration. For instance, if you find bread that is shaped like a certain character kawaii, you may feel an unavoidable urge to pick it up and eat it. On the other hand, you may want to keep it without eating it. This is an example of the urge to engage in interaction.

6 Interaction and Sensitivity

There are two kinds of sensitivity: the sensitivity of the recipient and that of the sender. Interaction occurs where the sensitivity of those two parties resonates. Sensitive deviation from this expectation causes a disagreement in intentions. Unless either the sender or the recipient has a degree of sensitivity, no interaction will occur. If the measure of the sender's sensitivity and the measure of the recipient's sensitivity deviate from the expected value (the criterion for our finding something kawaii in general), two conditions occur: the subject is "not kawaii" or the subject is "very kawaii." As indicated in Fig. 14, "the lack of the property of being empathized with" is a sufficient condition of kawaii," "a disagreement in intentions" is a sufficient condition of "the lack of sympathism," and "a disagreement in intentions" is a sufficient condition for "interaction." In other words, it reveals the condition to be in the following inclusive relation: kawaii ⊂ lack of the property of being empathized with ⊂ disagreement in intentions ⊂ interaction. However, a detailed discussion of "necessary condition" and "sufficient conditions" related to those items is clearly needed.

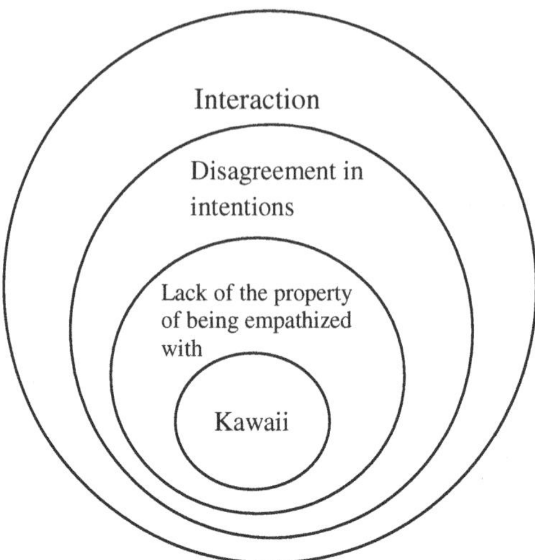

Fig. 4. Inclusive relation for *kawaii*

Fig. 5. There is a disagreement in intentions between the boy and the ball, since the ball bounces back in unexpected directions. Hence, there is interaction.

Interaction occurs in various situations. Take the case in Fig. 15, for instance. When a child throws a ball toward the wall, he throws it over and over because he finds it very interesting, since ball does not bounce back to where he would expect, but bounces back in unforeseen directions. This means there is a disagreement in intentions between the child and the ball. Hence, there is interaction. But if the child eventually realizes that the ball bounces back according to a physical rule, the instant he realizes this, he stops throwing the ball. The child has understood the reason why the ball comes back in different directions (which means there is no disagreement in intentions), and so that particular interaction has disappeared.

7 Conclusion

The author studied, from several viewpoints, the conceptual structure of the feeling of kawaii, which may be able to provide underlying basic knowledge related to the discussion of products and affective engineering. To begin with, a study from the viewpoint of interaction with characters (products) successfully clarified the relationship between kawaii-ness and interactivity.

Shannon-Weaver's model of communication was then applied to the transmission model between the sender (designer) and the recipient, and the author successfully proved that the model can be further evolved to a more general model that includes a feedback loop.

It is still necessary to develop an algorithm that conducts actual calculations using a definitional equation of the degree of interactivity. Application of an algorithmic approach to subjects that cannot readily undergo visualization by the name of interaction is an interesting task that remains to be tackled.

Since interaction occurs between the creator and the recipient, with a character serving as an intermediary, it is now clear that extending the definition of interaction to include visible objects is a natural process. Reinforcement of interaction means increase in entropy; otherwise, the kawaii property diminishes. Characters are evolved to create such a dynamic situation. Simply creating them without any follow-up will not do. In other words, the key point is that there must be interaction between the creator and the recipient, since the characters (products) must constantly evolve.

Analysis of kawaii from the viewpoint of Peirce's semiotics allows us to experience the sense of kawaii as a process of awareness in brand recognition within the concept of brand awareness. It therefore successfully provides a new aspect of kawaii research.

One of the major outcomes of this paper is the clarification of the inclusive relation of "kawaii lack of sympathism disagreement in intentions interaction." This result will has great potential usefulness for future research on kawaii. The most important task is to elucidate what kind of interaction creates kawaii.

References

1. Shiizuka, H.: Where does the *kawaii* feeling come from? - From Shannon's Model of Communication to the *Kawaii* System Theory, Japan Society of Kansei Engineering *kawaii* Artifacts, Research Group 2nd Anniversary Symposium Compendium of Lecture Papers (2012)
2. Shiizuka, H., Hashizume, A.: Interactivity and Fun of Characters. In: König, A., Dengel, A., Hinkelmann, K., Kise, K., Howlett, R.J., Jain, L.C. (eds.) KES 2011, Part III. LNCS, vol. 6883, pp. 197–206. Springer, Heidelberg (2011)
3. Recca Sha Corp.: A Perfect Guide to "Local Characters" in Japan. PHP Bunko (2009)
4. Baldwin, J., Roberts, L.: Visual Communication: From Theory to Practice. Academia (2006)
5. Weaver, W., Shannon, C.E.: The Mathematical Theory of Communication. University of Illinois Press (1949)

6. Shiizuka, H.: How Should Kansei Loss be Compensated? A Consideration of Qualitative Research in Evaluations of Kansei. Kansei Engineering 10(4), 155–163 (2011)
7. Kurosu, M.: What is Interaction? http://www.usability.gr.jp/lecture/20010910.html
8. Huizinga, J.: Homo Ludens, Chuko Bunko (1973) (translated by Takahashi, H.)
9. Crawford, C.: The Art of Interactive Design. Ohmsha Ltd. (2004) (translated by Yasumura, M.)

Comparison of Kansei Information between Joyful and Happy Expressions in Dance

Nao Shikanai[1] and Kozaburo Hachimura[2]

[1] Graduate School of Science and Engineering,
Ritsumeikan University
1-1-1, Noji-Higashi, Kusatsu, Shiga, 525-8577, Japan
gr0053hp@ed.ritsumei.ac.jp
[2] College of Information Science and Engineering,
Ritsumeikan University
1-1-1, Noji-Higashi, Kusatsu, Shiga, 525-8577, Japan
hachimura@media.ritsumei.ac.jp

Abstract. This research was designed to investigate the relationships between Kansei information and movement characteristics in dance. The purpose is to specify the parameters contributing to the perception and identification of joy and happiness from dance movements. Professional and expert dancers expressed joy and happiness without using facial expressions. For capturing and recording expressions, we used a 3D motion capture system and digital video cameras. There were 54 observers who rated 50 items of Kansei information in both expressions. The results showed the scores of Kansei information for joyful expressions—happy, dynamic, energetic, strong, accelerated, decelerated, extended, high, asymmetrical, fast, accented, big, down, and sudden—were higher than those for happy expressions. We calculated acceleration for kinematic features, and the results showed that acceleration in joyful expressions was higher than in happy expressions. Our findings demonstrated the differences in strength of movements and emotions between joyful and happy expressions in dance.

1 Introduction

Previous studies of nonverbal expressions of feelings and emotions have examined various aspects of body movements. Observers have been found to be able to identify joy from gestures [1]. High levels of activity and large movements were perceived to express joy and anger in the performances of actors [2]. Previous studies tried to identify some emotions from valence and action level [3]. Moreover, for positive emotions, it is not clear which bodily movements should be associated with an emotion [4], and errors occurred more for the positive than for the negative emotions when observers identified actors' emotions [3].

Some dance studies focus on the relationship between audience perception and the movement characteristics of dance. A previous study [5] investigated the relationship between feelings and movement characteristics using three elements: time, energy,

M. Kurosu (Ed.): Human-Computer Interaction, Part I, HCII 2013, LNCS 8004, pp. 611–619, 2013.

and design. Observers evaluated dance movements that expressed seven feelings and classified their interpretations based on the elements. Their results showed that expressions of happiness involve high speed, high energy, skipping, jumping, and turning, with many changes. In contrast, other studies [6] reported on emotionally expressive movements. The expression of joy was associated with many changes in the tempo of movements or extended movements from the center of the body. A study using kinematic data [7], [8] showed an association between three emotional expressions (joy, sadness, anger) and arm movement characteristics. This study found that three parameters of movement characteristics—speed, force, and directness—were useful for discriminating emotional expressions. Another study also showed a relationship between Kansei information and movement characteristics of the whole body by using motion capture [9], [10].

Although these previous studies have reported that body movements in dance have characteristics related to clear emotions which are not difficult to identify, it remains difficult to specify the distinctive parameters when using the whole body to convey similar expressions of feelings and ambiguous emotional expressions, particularly positive emotions. The purpose of this study is to specify the information and parameters that contribute to the perception and identification of joy and happiness from dance movements.

2 Methods

2.1 Dancers

Three dancers were asked to express joy and happiness through dance. One was a professional dancer, and the others were expert dancers, (a) and (b), with an average of six years of experience in varying forms of dance.

2.2 Procedure for Recordings to Joy and Happiness

Each dancer performed 3 different short dances to express joy and happiness. They were instructed to use their entire bodies. A total of 18 trials (2 expressions × 3 varieties × 3 dancers) were recorded. Each trial was performed twice and lasted for about 15 seconds. Before recording, they were allowed to practice for as long as they wished.

2.3 Apparatus

A video camera and 3D motion capture systems (Motion Analysis Corp., California) with 15 cameras were used to capture and record the dances. The sampling rate was 60 Hz. The acquired data were obtained as a time series of coordinate values (x, y, z) of each marker position in each frame. There were 32 reflective markers attached to the bodies of each dancer (Fig. 1).

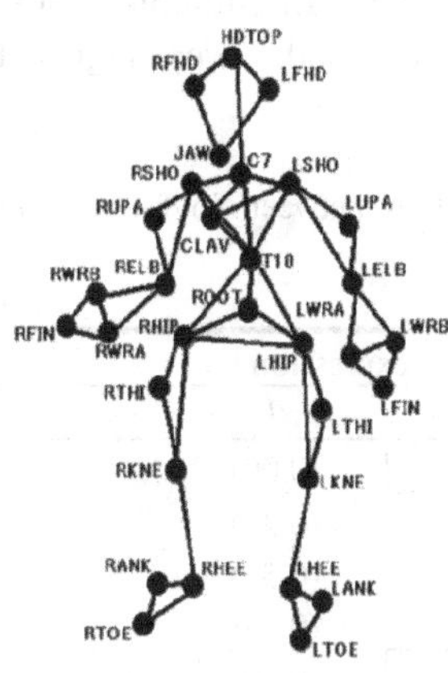

Fig. 1. Positions of markers

2.4 Displays for Evaluation

We used EvaRT software for motion capture data and created stick-figure displays from these data with 3D animation software Motion Builder 2012 (Autodesk Inc., California) for evaluation of the experiments.

2.5 Observers

A total of 54 observers who were university students (30 males and 24 females) participated in the evaluation. They were novices in dance, and their experience in this area consisted of viewing dance on television or dance training in physical education.

2.6 Evaluation

The 18 dance movements of the stick figures were presented in random order to the observers, and they completed a response sheet immediately after viewing a movement. The questionnaires for surveying expression and Kansei information are described in Table 1.

2.7 Items of Kansei Information

Observers were requested to watch the dances, and to rate words related to Kansei on a 5-point scale (*not expressive* (1) to *expressive* (5)). The words related to Kansei of dance included 36 items [11], and 14 items [12] were constructed based on the advice of the dancers.

3 Results

3.1 Comparison of Kansei Information between Joyful and Happy Expressions

To examine the differences in Kansei information between joyful and happy expressions, we conducted *t*-tests and compared means among joy and happiness responses for each Kansei information item.

The result is shown in Table 1. The squares in the table show that scores are more than 4.00, and there are significant differences between joy and happiness in the scores.

Scores of Kansei information for joyful expressions—happy, dynamic, energetic, strong, accelerated, decelerated, extend, high, asymmetrical, fast, accented, big, down, and sudden—were higher than those for happy expressions. In addition, scores of Kansei information for happy expressions—flowing and smooth—were higher than those for joyful expressions.

Table 1. Comparison of mean scores of Kansei information between joyful and happy expressions

	Joyful expression		Happy expression		
Items	*mean*	(*SD*)	*mean*	(*SD*)	*p*
happy	4.51	(0.56)	4.00	(0.00)	*
lonely	2.00	(0.58)	1.14	(0.38)	**
sharp	2.57	(0.98)	1.57	(0.53)	*
solemn	3.00	(1.00)	3.43	(0.53)	
dynamic	4.57	(0.53)	4.00	(0.00)	*
flowing	4.00	(0.00)	4.57	(0.53)	*
usual	1.86	(0.90)	1.00	(1.00)	
pointed	2.00	(0.58)	1.43	(0.53)	
rounded	3.14	(1.21)	4.00	(0.00)	
dull	1.00	(0.00)	1.00	(0.00)	
energetic	4.57	(0.53)	4.00	(0.00)	*
depleted	1.00	(0.00)	1.29	(0.76)	*
strong	4.57	(0.53)	3.57	(0.53)	**
weak	1.86	(0.38)	2.00	(0.82)	
liner	4.00	(0.00)	3.43	(0.98)	
flat	1.29	(0.49)	1.29	(0.49)	
tense	1.57	(0.98)	1.86	(1.07)	
relaxed	1.57	(0.98)	1.57	(0.98)	
accelerated	4.83	(0.38)	4.14	(0.38)	**
decelerated	4.00	(0.82)	2.14	(1.21)	**
large	4.29	(0.49)	4.00	(0.00)	
narrow	1.43	(0.53)	1.43	(0.79)	
extended	4.29	(0.49)	4.00	(0.00)	*
flexed	2.86	(1.07)	1.43	(0.79)	
lateral	4.29	(0.49)	4.00	(0.00)	
vertical	4.29	(0.49)	4.00	(0.00)	
high	4.43	(0.53)	2.50	(0.84)	**
low	2.00	(1.29)	2.71	(1.38)	
regular	1.57	(0.79)	2.86	(0.38)	**
irregular	4.00	(0.00)	3.71	(0.49)	
equal	3.14	(0.38)	3.14	(0.38)	
unequal	2.71	(0.49)	3.00	(0.58)	
complex	3.86	(0.38)	3.71	(1.25)	
simple	1.43	(0.53)	1.29	(0.76)	
symmetrical	1.29	(0.82)	3.00	(1.00)	**

Table 1. *(continued)*

asymmetrical	4.00	(0.58)	2.00	(1.00)	**
fast	4.77	(0.53)	4.00	(0.00)	**
slow	2.00	(0.82)	2.41	(1.21)	
accented	4.14	(0.53)	2.00	(0.00)	**
smooth	3.58	(0.90)	4.43	(0.49)	*
big	4.29	(0.49)	3.14	(0.38)	**
small	1.43	(0.53)	1.43	(0.79)	
open	4.29	(0.49)	4.14	(0.38)	
closed	2.86	(1.07)	1.43	(0.79)	
up	4.29	(0.49)	4.00	(0.00)	
down	4.29	(0.49)	3.00	(0.00)	**
sudden	4.57	(0.53)	3.71	(0.49)	*
constant	1.57	(0.79)	2.86	(0.38)	*
steady	1.57	(0.53)	3.14	(0.38)	**
balanced	3.43	(0.53)	3.29	(0.76)	

* $p < 0.05$, ** $p < 0.01$

3.2 Comparison of Acceleration between Joyful and Happy Expressions

The results of 3.1 showed there are differences in Kansei information between joyful expressions and happy expressions. Because scores of Kansei information to joyful expressions—happy, dynamic, energetic, strong, accelerated, decelerated, extend, high, asymmetrical, fast, accented, big, down, sudden—were higher than those for happy expressions, we focused particularly on energetic, strong, accelerated, decelerated, fast, accented, and sudden. The information of energetic, strong, accelerated, and decelerated are related to dynamism [5], [12]. In addition, previous studies [7], [10], [13] have indicated that the relationship between the physical features of dance movements and their dynamism is driven by the velocity and acceleration of the bodies. We tried to find a relation between the dynamic elements of Kansei information for joyful expressions and happy expressions in these results and the acceleration as kinematic features. We compared the accelerations between joyful and happy expressions.

The acceleration was calculated from motion capture data. Because dance movements of 16 counts (8 counts × 2 times) take about 15 seconds, we determined the mean acceleration in 48 counts (16 counts × 3trials). The body parts used to calculate acceleration were the hip, right shoulder, and left shoulder (ROOT, RSHO, LSHO in Fig. 1). These parts are consisted as the body trunk which is important for moving in all kinds of dances. We compared the mean of each acceleration by the professional dancer and the expert dancers. We compared the acceleration between joyful and happy expressions using a *t*-test for each dancer. Table 2 shows the results for the professional dancer's acceleration, and Tables 3 and 4 show the results for the expert dancers' acceleration.

As shown by Table 2, there are no differences in acceleration between joyful and happy expressions in expert dancers' hip and both shoulders (hip: t (94) = 1.48, *n.s.*, right shoulder: t (94) = 1.56, *n.s.*, left shoulder: t (94) = 1.12 = *n.s.*).

However in the expert dancers, there are significant differences between joyful and happy expressions (Tables 3 and 4). For expert (a), the mean scores for acceleration in joyful expressions were significantly higher than those in happy expressions for the hip, right shoulder, and left shoulder (hip: t (94) = 3.76, $p < 0.01$, right shoulder: t (94) = 3.40, $p < 0.01$, left shoulder: t (94) = 4.37, $p < 0.01$) Also, for expert (b), the mean scores for acceleration in joyful expressions were significantly higher than those in happy expressions for the hip and left shoulder (hip: t (94) = 2.39, $p < 0.05$, right shoulder: t (94) = 1.14, *n.s.*, left shoulder: t (94) = 2.12, $p < 0.05$). The expert dancers' results showed that scores for acceleration in joyful expressions was higher than in happy expressions, which indicated that joyful expressions have dynamic movement characteristics compared to happy expressions regardless of focusing on the body trunk not the limbs.

Table 2. Comparison of mean scores for acceleration between joyful and happy expressions by the professional dancer

	Professional dancer				
Acceleration (cm/s^2)	Joyful expression		Happy expression		
	Mean	(*SD*)	*mean*	(*SD*)	*p*
Hip (Root marker)	3.33	(2.32)	2.67	(2.13)	*n.s.*
Right shoulder	3.54	(3.67)	2.78	(2.10)	*n.s.*
Left shoulder	3.44	(3.76)	2.85	(2.22)	*n.s.*

Table 3. Comparison of mean scores for acceleration between joyful and happy expressions by expert dancer (a)

	Expert dancer (a)				
Acceleration (cm/s^2)	Joyful expression		Happy expression		
	Mean	(*SD*)	*mean*	(*SD*)	*p*
Hip (Root marker)	2.33	(1.67)	1.33	(0.91)	**
Right shoulder	2.44	(1.76)	1.43	(1.14)	**
Left shoulder	2.45	(1.67)	1.27	(0.90)	**

** $p < 0.01$

Table 4. Comparison of mean scores for acceleration between joyful and happy expressions by expert dancer (b)

	Expert dancer (b)				
Acceleration (cm/s^2)	Joyful expression		Happy expression		
	Mean	(*SD*)	*mean*	(*SD*)	*p*
Hip (Root marker)	2.41	(1.90)	1.66	(1.09)	*
Right shoulder	2.26	(1.55)	1.92	(1.25)	*n.s.*
Left shoulder	2.46	(1.82)	1.81	(1.12)	*

* $p < 0.05$

4 Discussion

This experiment sought to determine the parameters that contribute to perception and distinction of Kansei information between joy and happiness in dance expressions. We used a multivariate dataset of dance expressions and analyzed Kansei information and kinematic features. The results of t-tests for acceleration of the hip (root of body) and shoulders indicated that expressions of joy and happiness in dance each have a particular parameter.

Joyful expressions and happy expressions are both positive emotions, but we found that there are differences in the Kansei information. Kansei information for joyful expressions—happy, dynamic, energetic, strong, accelerated, decelerated, extended, high, asymmetrical, fast, accented, big, down, and sudden—were higher than those for happy expressions. Kansei information for happy expressions—flowing and smooth—were higher than those for joyful expressions. This indicated that joyful expressions have more strength, stimulus, or intensity than happy expressions. Because the degree of the happy item was stronger for joyful expressions, the score for the happy item may be higher for joyful expression. However, happy expressions do not instantaneously stimulate positive emotional expressions, but they may continuously stimulate constant positive emotional expressions.

We found that the difference of acceleration between expressions, and the acceleration for joyful expressions was higher than that for happy expressions. The acceleration is a kinematic feature indicating a movement's strength [7], [10], [13]. It was demonstrated that leg movements expressing anger were characterized by acceleration [8]. These previous studies convey information about strength and speed. In addition, we showed that joyful expressions have more strength than happy expressions.

We can express delicate differences when we show positive emotions. We can express emotions bodily and not just with facial expressions. Facial emotional expressions are identified basically as six emotions: happy, sad, angry, surprised, afraid, and disgusted [14]. Researchers have also tried to identify six bodily expressions of emotions: joy, sadness, anger, anxiety, pride, and contentment [3], and to discover how positive and negative emotions might change due to their range in valence and action level. Of course, it is difficult to identify emotions only from bodily information (without facial expressions). It is not clear how to discriminate positive emotions from a specific action [3], [4]. However, we found a difference between joyful expression and happy expression from the point of view of Kansei information through observer evaluations, although the expressions were focused on positive emotions and dance movements. In addition, we used motion data and observed differences in acceleration as kinematic features. The relation of Kansei information to kinematic features contributes to confusion in emotional perception and recognition of vague expressions. Moreover, our results encourage further research into addressing emotional expressions in dance, and in the creation and reproduction of vague emotional expressions using computer-generated (CG) animation, game characters, and humanoid robots.

Nevertheless, in the results for acceleration, there were no differences between joyful expressions and happy expressions in the data from the professional dancer. This reason may be that we were averaging the kinematic data. Because the standard deviation of the acceleration of the professional dancer for all body parts was very large, this indicated that the professional dancer freely accelerated and decelerated his own body with breaks in his movements. Expressions by the professional dancer were specialized, meaning they were difficult to generalize. From an artistic point of view, it is necessary for professional dancers to show expressions which are different from those of other dancers. When investigating the expressions of professional dancers and artistic movements, we have to focus on different movements in each case and then analyze them. However, the expert dancers had the basics of movements and could do formulary expressions rather than free expressions. Particularly, novice dancers and dance students can use this expert dancer's results as an example of moving well and recognizing well. This research demonstrated that it is also important to move the body trunk, hips, and shoulders as a way to express differences between joy and happiness.

References

1. Montepare, J.M., Koff, E., Zaitchik, D., Albert, M.: The use of body movements and gestures as cues to emotions in younger and older adults. Journal of Nonverbal Behavior 23, 133–152 (1999)
2. Wallbott, J.G.: Bodily expression of emotion. European Journal of Social Psychology 28, 879–896 (1998)
3. Gross, M.M., Grane, E.A., Fredrickson, B.L.: Methodology for Assessing Bodily Expression of Emotion. Journal of Nonverbal Behavior 34, 223–248 (2010)
4. Fredrickson, B.L.: What good are positive emotions? Review of General Psychology 2, 300–319 (1998)
5. Matsumoto, C.: Dance research: Problem situation and learning of problem solving qualities of movements and feeling values. In: Proceedings of Lecture at the Tenth Congress of the International Association of Physical Education and Sport for Girls and Women, pp. 53–89 (1987)
6. Camurri, A., Lagerlöf, I., Volpe, G.: Recognizing emotion from dance movement: Comparison of spectator recognition and automated techniques. International Journal of Human Computer Studies 59, 213–225 (2003)
7. Sawada, M., Suda, K., Ishii, M.: Expression of emotions in dance: Relation between arm movement characteristics and emotion. Perceptual and Motor Skills 97, 697–708 (2003)
8. Sawada, M., Suda, K., Ishii, M.: Relationship between leg movement quality and emotional expression in dance. Poster session presented at the Annual Meeting of the International Association for Dance Medicine & Science, London, England (2003)
9. Sakata, M., Hachimura, K.: Relational models for KANSEI Information of Human Body Movement. Journal of Cultural Studies in Body Design, Media, Music and Text 6, 191–202 (2006)
10. Sakata, M., Hachimura, K.: KANSEI Information processing of human body movement. In: Smith, M.J., Salvendy, G. (eds.) HCII 2007. LNCS, vol. 4557, pp. 930–939. Springer, Heidelberg (2007)
11. Shikanai, N., Hachimura, K., Sawada, M.: Investigation of Kansei information related to emotional expressions in dance – by using video and point-light displays –. IPSJ SIG Technical Report, 2011-CH-92(2), 1–8 (2011)

12. Shikanai, N., Sawada, M., Ishii, M.: Development of the Movements Impressions Emotions Model, Evaluation and movements and impressions related to the perception of emotions in dance. Journal of Nonverbal Behavior (in press)
13. Iwadate, Y., Inoue, M., Suzuki, R.: Study on Emotional Feature Extraction from Human Motion, An Application for Interactive Dance System. ITE Technical Report 24, 7–12 (2000)
14. Ekman, P., Friesen, W.V.: Unmasking the Human Face, A guide to Recognizing Emotions from Facial Expressions. Malor Books, Cambridge (2003)

Study of Kawaii-ness in Motion – Physical Properties of Kawaii Motion of Roomba

Shohei Sugano[1], Yutaka Miyaji[2], and Ken Tomiyama[1]

[1] Chiba Institute of Technology, 2-17-1 Tsudanuma, Narashino-shi, Chiba 275-0016, Japan
[2] Aoyama Gakuin University, 5-10-1 Fuchinobe, Sagamihara-shi, Kanagawa 252-5258, Japan
mad.hatter.teaparty3173@gmail.com, uta@si.aoyama.ac.jp

Abstract. In this paper, as the second report of the study on Kawaii-ness in motion, we investigate the relationship between physical properties of motion and Kawaii-ness using Roomba. Kawaii is one of the representative concepts of Japan-original Kansei. First, we computed parameters of seven physical properties (position, velocity, acceleration, angle, angular velocity, angular acceleration, and time) from three types of motions of Roomba used in the first study. Second, we composed 24 types of robot motions and asked the subjects to evaluate their impressions. We asked the subjects to answer the questionnaire consisting of the 20 pairing adjectives prepared according to the SD method. The extracted physical features in seven physical parameters in composed motions are correlated with the Kawaii-ness based on the result of the questionnaire. We report our findings in detail in this paper.

Keywords: Kawaii, Kansei values, Robot motion, Physical Property.

1 Introduction

In this study, we investigate Kawaii-ness in motion. Kawaii, a Japanese original concept, is spreading around the world and became known to people in many countries. Kawaii is one of the Kansei categories that describe favorable characters such as pretty, adorable, fairy-like, and cute. Kansei is a Japanese word for expressing sensibility, sensitivity, feeling, emotion, and so on. Kawaii is among the Kansei values that have become important in manufacturing in Japan. The Japanese Ministry of Economy, Trade and Industry (METI) has been conducting a project called the "Kansei Value Creation Initiative" from 2007 [1] [2]. The main objective of the project is to introduce a new value axis in addition to the conventional value axes of reliability, performance, price and so on, which have been recognized in the manufacturing sector. METI held a Kansei value creation fair, called the "Kansei-Japan Design Exhibition," at Les Arts Decoratifs (museum of decorative arts) in Musée du Louvre, Paris in December 2008. Launched as an event of the "Kansei Value Creation Years," the exhibition had more than 10,000 visitors during the ten-day period and was received quite favorably [3]. Thus, "Kansei" is an important factor that increases the attractiveness of the products in Japanese manufacturing.

M. Kurosu (Ed.): Human-Computer Interaction, Part I, HCII 2013, LNCS 8004, pp. 620–629, 2013.

Japan also enjoys large attention from the world in robotics technologies. Robotics technologies have advanced to allow robots to work more closely with people. Even if the robots, however, have acquired useful features and human-friendly designs, that is not enough for them to commence smooth communication with humans and to become true coworkers of humans. To achieve this goal, we believe that the robots must be able to communicate with humans at metaphysical level and must have software backbone to support such communication.

Therefore, we have started studying Virtual Kansei for robots where robots can understand human emotions, can generate own (virtual) emotion and can express own emotion while performing given tasks [4] [5]. In the past, we had studied the estimation, the generation and the expression of (virtual) emotion, a part of the virtual Kansei, based on Ekman's six basic emotions [6] [7]. We, however, are aware of that the emotion is not sufficient and that study on mood and Kansei itself are necessary. Our study on mood will be reported elsewhere. We present our study on Kawaii-ness here.

Researchers have started studying Kawaii-ness features from various directions. For example, colors and shapes have been studied by Ohkura and Murai [8] [9]. Their results showed that curved shapes such as a torus and a sphere are generally evaluated as more Kawaii than straight-lined shapes. Ohkura also studied Kawaii tactile sensation using tactile materials [10]. On the other hand, we focus on studying Kawaii-ness in motion because we are interested in applying the findings to robotics.

In our first report [11], we segmented continuous motion of Roomba into identifiable motion parts and classified those motions to ten types. We, then, asked the subject to choose Kawaii motions out of ten types and to answer a questionnaire consisting of pairs of adjectives with five notch scale prepared according to the SD method on the chosen motions. The answers to the questionnaire were analyzed for common features of Kawaii motions and we found three factors that may influence Kawaii-ness. They are "simple," "regular," and "smooth."

This paper investigates the relationship between physical properties of those motions of Roomba and impression of Kawaii-ness.

2 Overview of Autonomous Mobile Robot – Create

We adopted a robot called Create by iRobot, shown in Figure 1, as the robot for main experiment. Create is a programmable counterpart of Roomba, where programmability and space for more sensors are added in lieu of the cleaning function of Roomba. This is a robot for education and research and sold by iRobot Corporation from 2007. This robot can run at the maximum 500 mm/s and can detect objects and steps using infrared sensors. Touch sensors on the front bumper and the wheel drop sensors are also equipped. This robot has a two-wheel steering system. It can rotate on a spot and can revolve around any point at the maximum 2000 mm away. In addition, it is also possible to use remote control, Home Base for charging and Virtual Wall (the invisible artificial electromagnetic wall). We fitted

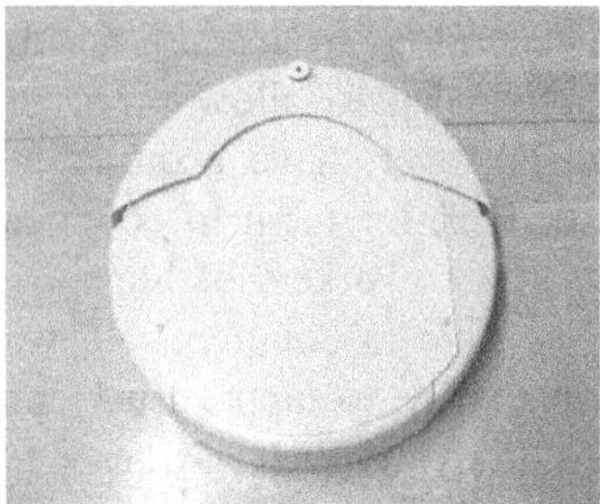

Fig. 1. Picture of Create for composing test motions

Create with a plastic cover to hide internal parts such as the power button. Thus, we have eliminated mechanical impression induced from the internal structure of the robot.

3 Extraction of Physical Properties

We extracted physical properties from Kawaii motions of Roomba used in our first report.

3.1 Data Extraction

We have analyzed three motions (Bounce, Spiral, Dizzy) chosen as the most Kawaii by male and female subjects. Each motion is as follows:

- Bounce: Roomba changes the direction of travel after colliding with an object.
- Spiral: Roomba moves along an outward spiral.
- Dizzy: Roomba wonders about at a nearly constant speed.

This time, we decided to extract seven parameters (position, velocity, acceleration, angle, angular velocity, angular acceleration, and time) as the physical properties related to three elements (simple, regular, and smooth). Here, the time parameter indicates the total length of the motion video. The reference coordinate system is discussed in the next section.

3.2 Extraction Method

We defined two coordinate systems; the world coordinate system fixed on the floor and the local coordinate system fixed on Roomba to extract the position and the angle from the recorded Roomba motions (Figure 2). First, we computed the coordinate of the center of Roomba as the position of Roomba and of the infrared sensor on the surface of the front of Roomba. Then the position and the relative angle of the local coordinate on Roomba can be computed from those two positions. The positions

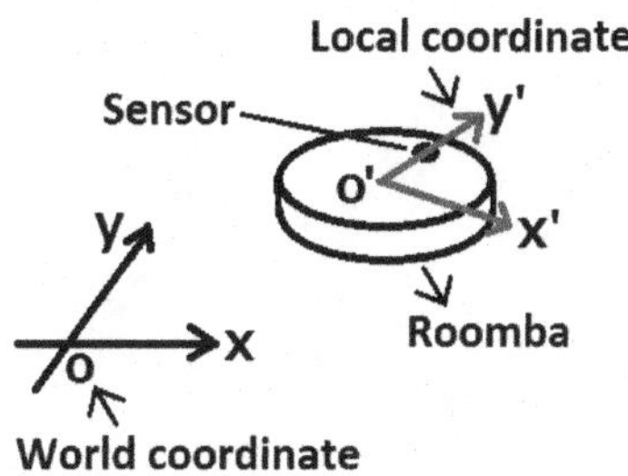

Fig. 2. The world coordinate and the local coordinate

were sampled every one tenth of a second. The velocity was computed by the back difference of positions, namely, the difference of the current and the last positions. Similarly, the acceleration was computed by the back difference from the speed. The angular velocity and the angular acceleration were computed similarly.

3.3 Properties of Extracted Data

We first extracted characteristic portions of motions and then computed physical properties of those portions. For example, the motion of "Bounce" is a rebounding motion after hitting the wall. This motion has a rapid change in acceleration that called jerk. Figure 3 shows the trajectory of Bounce and Fig. 4 shows the time history of the jerk of the center of Roomba. Roomba collides with the wall and the obstacle in this motion and the sharp increases in jerk about four and seven seconds indicates those collisions. Two large increases in the jerk near four seconds are caused by the collision itself and the sudden reversal of motion.

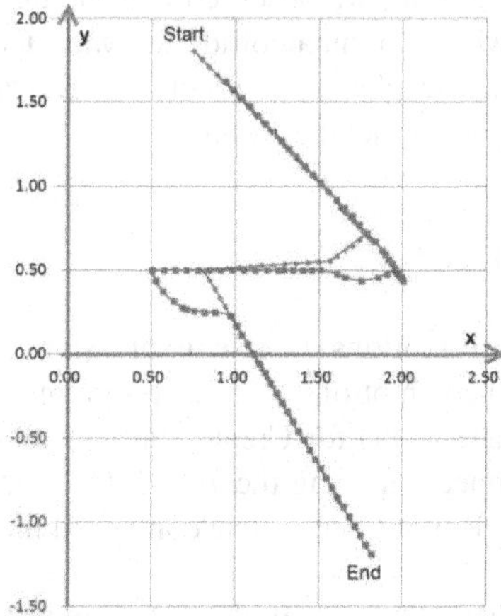

Fig. 3. The trajectory of Bounce motion. The red and blue lines indicate the positions of the tip and the center of Roomba, respectively.

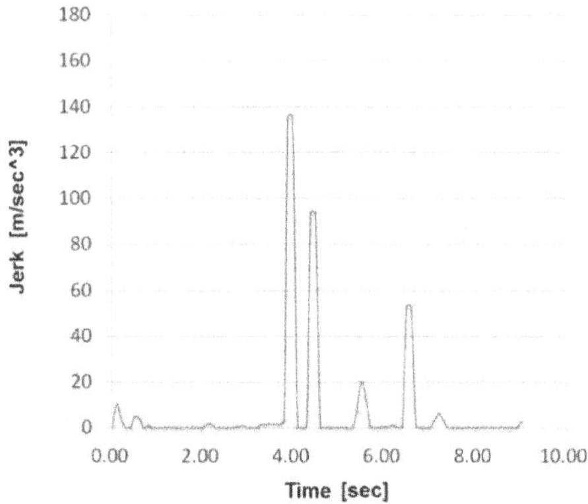

Fig. 4. Time history of the jerk of motion of the origin of the center coordinate system

As a result, we obtained some properties of physical based on extracted data.

- Almost constant velocity except at the start and end of the motion
- Periodic variation of the angle
- Changes of the jerk at collisions
- Nominal speed of Roomba is approximately 300mm/s

We, then, composed motions using extracted properties.

3.4 Hypothesis Formulation

According to our first report, many subjects commented that "the motion when Roomba collide the wall is Kawaii" against a question that "why did you feel the motion Kawaii?" On other hand, we observed that the instantaneous changes of the acceleration are occurred when Roomba collide the wall. Consequently, we formed a hypothesis that changes in acceleration affect the Kawaii-ness. We tested the validness of the hypothesis using the questionnaire.

4 Composing Motions

We composed 24 types of motions to use expression experiment based on the trajectories of the extracted motions. We programmed these motions using application program interface (API) for Create, called iRobot Create Open Interface. We also used the serial connection using the 7pin MINI-DIN connector and Realterm software recommended by iRobot Corp. The composed motions are as follows:

- Attack: Create repeats the collision with the object at 300mm/s.
- Straight_A: Create travels from left to right without stopping.
- Straight_B: Create travels from left to right with deceleration, stop and acceleration phase in the middle.

- Straight_C: Create travels from left to right with a sudden stop in the middle.
- Bounce_A: Create collides obliquely against the wall and travels again after rotating 90 degrees.
- Bounce_B: Create stops 1.5 seconds after colliding obliquely against the wall and travels again after rotating 90 degrees.
- Spin_A: Create spins around at a constant speed like a top spinning at a spot.
- Spin_B: Create spins with gradually increasing speed from 0 to 500mm/s (LH) or gradually decreasing speed from 500 to 0mm/s (HL).
- Spiral: Create moves along an outward spiral.

All motions except Attack and Spin_B are composed with three speeds; 100mm/s, 300mm/s, and 500mm/s. Thus, we composed the total of 24 types of motions

5 Main Experiment

We produced video footages of the 24 types of motions using Create. We conducted a survey to evaluate Kawaii-ness using the composed motions. The experiment was carried out with one subject at a time, and was carried out using a PC with a touch panel display. The touch panel display was used to simplify the I/O for the survey. The experimental procedure is as follows:

1. The experimenter describes the experiment.
2. The subject answers three questions relevant to Kawaii-ness.
3. The experimenter shows a photo of Create.
4. The subject answers the question "Do you think this robot is Kawaii?" by choosing one among (yes), (so so) (not really) and (no), then the second question "Why do you think so?"
5. The experimenter describes how to use of the interface.
6. The subject chooses one button from the four buttons on the display to choose the motion to watch.
7. The subject answers a questionnaire about the presented motion video.

Three questions in Step 2 are as follows:

A) How many times do you use the word Kawaii on a daily basis?
Choose from (often), (sometimes), (rarely) and (never).
B) What do you use Kawaii for?
Please describe the object that you use the word Kawaii.
C) If you feel something moving is Kawaii, what motion could it be?

In Step 2, we used the first question to investigate whether or not the subject is familiar with the concept of Kawaii. The role of the second question in Step 2 was to find the types of Kawaii-ness used by the subjects. The third question is the question to encourage the subjects to become more aware of Kawaii-ness of the motions. Figure 1 in Chapter 2 is the photo image presented to the subjects at Step 3. Step 6 is inserted to let the subjects to choose the motion to watch by themselves in order to let them feel like performing the experiment voluntarily. Steps 6 and 7 were repeated twelve times. The subject answered either "Kawaii" or "Not Kawaii" against the presented motion video one by one. Similar to the methods used in the first report, we asked subjects to describe any part of motions that they felt Kawaii. We asked to identify those Kawaii motions using arrows of various shapes, such as a circular arrow for circling motion. Answers in the questionnaire were analyzed by the Semantic Differential method. Table 1 shows the 20 pairing adjectives in the questionnaire. They were listed with 5 point scale. The markings were converted to numbers of -2 to 2 from the left adjective to the right one.

Table 1. The pairing adjectives used in the questionnaire

No	Adjective pairs	No	Adjective pairs
1	Young – Elder	**11**	Fancy – Sober
2	Speedy – Tardy	**12**	Free – Bound
3	Serious – Sloth	**13**	Sensitive – Obtuse
4	Smart – Stupid	**14**	Steady – Unstable
5	Natural – Artificial	**15**	Hasty – Gradual
6	Quick – Slow	**16**	Humanly – Mechanical
7	Familiar – Unknown	**17**	Idle – Busy
8	Obedient – Rebellious	**18**	Regular – Irregular
9	Simple – Complicated	**19**	Yielding – Stubborn
10	Smooth – Ragged	**20**	Dynamic – Static

6 Result of Main Experiment

There were 3 female and 17 male participants of twenties for the evaluation experiment. The answer on frequency of use of "Kawaii" is summarized in Figure 5(a). It is noted that 3/4 of all the subjects use frequently or sometimes. In other words, it may be said that most people use Kawaii on a daily basis. Table 2 lists top three objects for which subjects use Kawaii. 80% of all the subjects responded animals, and many answered dogs and cats. Small objects were also answered by half the subjects. Figure 5(b) shows the aggregate results of the answer to Kawaii-ness of Create. 80% of all the subjects responded No or Not really. There was no Yes answer for this question. Most of the subjects commented that Create does not have any standing features and that would be the reason why there was no Yes answer.

Table 3 shows top three motions that are classified Kawaii. An interesting observation here is that although 80% of all the subjects answered Create not Kawaii but 80% of them found Spiral (300mm/s) motion Kawaii. Consequently, it means that Kawaii-ness is present in the composed motion rather than the robot itself. Figure 6 lists the degrees of Kawaii-ness of the composed motions. The degrees of Kawaii-ness are defined as the ratio of the number of people who felt the motion Kawaii over the number of people who saw the motion. It is noted that rotational motions were found more Kawaii than linear motions. When focusing on the rotational motion, slow motions (100mm/s) were evaluated more Kawaii than fast motions (500mm/s). On the other hand, linear motions with sudden changes in acceleration are generally found more Kawaii, but not always. Subjects evaluated the motion more Kawaii when the sudden changes in acceleration were caused by collisions. This indicates that subjects found the motion more Kawaii when they felt those motions were of living creatures. Medium (300mm/s) and high speed (500mm/s) linear motions were relatively evaluated Kawaii among the linear motions. However, the degrees of Kawaii-ness fluctuated. This indicates the fact that each subject has own Kawaii speed of motion.

In the free answer item, nearly everyone regarded Create an animal. They also found motions Kawaii when they felt the motion biological and intentional. This fact suggests that Kawaii-ness may be associated with animacy perception.

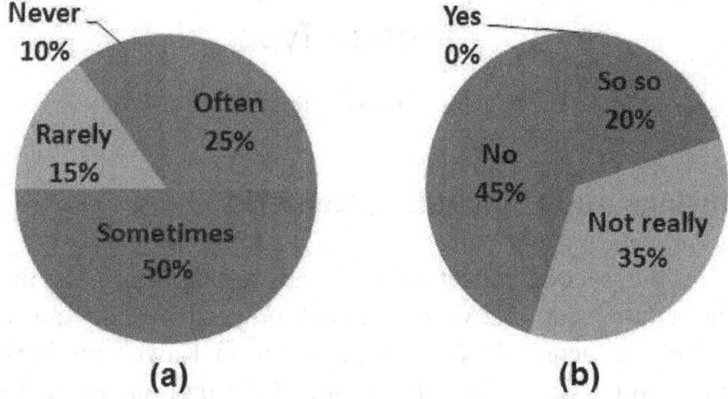

Fig. 5. Response of the questions; (a) "How many times do you use the word Kawaii on a daily basis?" and (b) "Do you think this robot is Kawaii?"

Table 2. Top three objects to use the work Kawaii

Rank	Score (%)	Kawaii Target
1st	80 %	Animals
2nd	50 %	Small objects
3rd	33 %	Baby

Table 3. Top three Kawaii motions

Rank	Score (%)	Motion Type (Speed)
1st	80 %	Spiral (300)
2nd	71 %	Bounce_B (500)
3rd	70 %	Spiral (100)

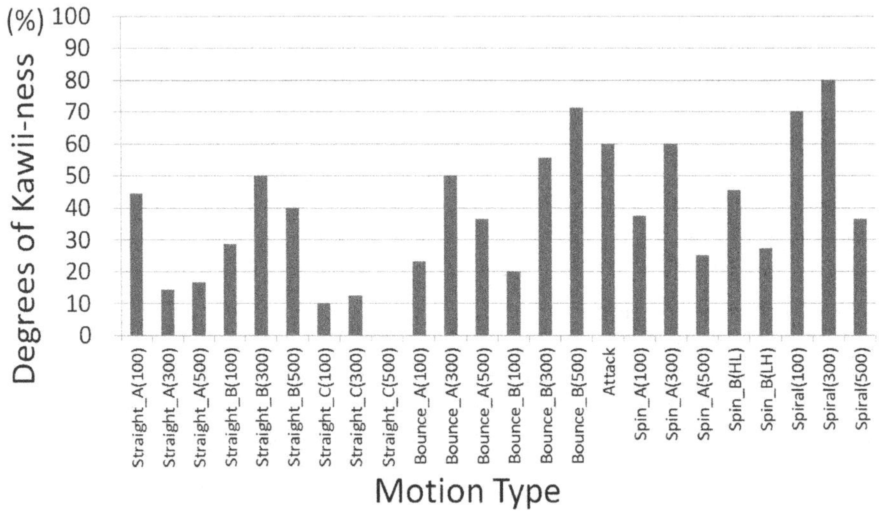

Fig. 6. The degrees of Kawaii-ness of each motion

7 Conclusions and Concluding Remarks

In this study, as the second report of the study on Kawaii-ness in motion, we investigated the relationship between physical properties and Kawaii-ness using Roomba. We first extracted physical properties from Kawaii motions of Roomba used in our first report. Since the subjects found the motion with collision Kawaii where the instantaneous changes of the acceleration occurred, we formed a hypothesis that changes in acceleration will affect the Kawaii-ness. We composed 24 types of motions to use in impression experiment to check this hypothesis. We showed those motions to subjects and asked them to evaluate those motions they found Kawaii by marking between pairs of adjectives.

It was observed that, although 80% of all the subjects answered Create (a programmable counterpart of Roomba) not Kawaii but 80% of them found Spiral (300mm/s) motion Kawaii. When focusing on the rotational motions, we found that slow motions (100mm/s) were rated more Kawaii than fast motions (500mm/s). With linear motions, many motions where the acceleration changes instantaneously were found Kawaii. The motions with instantaneous change in acceleration caused by collisions were evaluated more Kawaii than the motions without collisions. The motions that gave biological and intentional impression were also evaluated Kawaii. In other words, Kawaii-ness may be associated with animacy perception. Thus, our hypothesis was shown to be valid.

It is our immediate task to increase the number of subjects and to investigate if the findings here are generalizable. A more important and interesting task is to investigate the effects of other physical properties on Kawaii-ness.

Acknowledgements. We thank to the students and their families of Chiba Institute of Technology who contributed to this research and served as volunteers.

References

1. The Japanese Ministry of Economy, Trade and Industry (METI): Kansei Value Creation Initiative (2008), http://www.meti.go.jp/english/information/downloadfiles/PressRelease/080620KANSEI.pdf
2. Araki, J.: Kansei and Value Creation Initiative. Journal of Japan Society of Kansei Engineering 7(3), 417–419 (2007)
3. The Japanese Ministry of Economy, Trade and Industry (METI): Announcement of the "Kansei Value Creation Museum" (2009), http://www.meti.go.jp/english/press/data/20090119_02.html
4. Miyaji, Y., Tomiyama, K.: Virtual KANSEI for Robots in Welfare. In: International Conference on Complex Medical Engineering Proceedings (2007)
5. Kogami, J., Miyaji, Y., Tomiyama, K.: Kansei Generator using HMM for Virtual KANSEI in Caretaker Support Robot. KANSEI Engineering International, 83–90 (2009)
6. Zenkoyoh, M., Tomiyama, K.: Surprise Generator for Virtual KANSEI Based on Human Surprise Characteristics. In: Smith, M.J., Salvendy, G. (eds.) HCII 2011, Part I. LNCS, vol. 6771, pp. 190–198. Springer, Heidelberg (2011)
7. Miyaji, Y., Tomiyama, K.: Construction of Virtual KANSEI by Petri-net with GA and Method of Constructing Personality. In: Proceedings ROMAN 2003, 12th IEEE Workshop Robot and Human Interactive Communication, pp. 6B4(CD–ROM) (November 2003)
8. Ohkura, M., Konuma, A., Murai, S., Aoto, T.: Systematic Study for "Kawaii" Products (The Second Report) -Comparison of "Kawaii" colors and shapes-. In: Proceedings of SICE 2008, Chofu, Japan (2008)
9. Murai, S., Goto, S., Aoto, T., Ohkura, M.: Systematic Study for "Kawaii" Products (The Third Report) -Comparison of "Kawaii" between 2D and 3D-. In: Proceedings of VRSJ 2008 (2008) (in Japanese)
10. Ohkura, M., Komatsu, T., Osawa, S., Sakamoto, M.: Systematic Study on Kawaii Products (The Fourteenth Report) -Basic Study of Kawaii Tactile Sensation using Tactile Materials-. In: Proceedings of the Institute of Electronics, Information and Communication Engineers, IEICE (2012)
11. Sugano, S., Morita, H., Tomiyama, K.: Study on Kawaii-ness in Motion -Classifying Kawaii Motion using Roomba-. In: International Conference on Applied Human Factors and Ergonomics 2012, San Francisco, California, USA (2012)

Author Index